CompTIA Server+ Certification

Complete coverage of all CompTIA Server+ certification objectives

Ron Gilster

www.bpbonline.com

First Edtion 2024

ISBN: 978-93-55513-861

LIMITS OF LIABILITY AND DISCLAIMER OF WARRANTY

Distributors:

BPB PUBLICATIONS
20, Ansari Road, Darya Ganj
New Delhi-110002
Ph: 23254990/23254991

DECCAN AGENCIES
4-3-329, Bank Street,
Hyderabad-500195
Ph: 24756967/24756400

MICRO MEDIA
Shop No. 5, Mahendra Chambers,
150 DN Rd. Next to Capital Cinema,
V.T. (C.S.T.) Station, MUMBAI-400 001
Ph: 22078296/22078297

To View Complete BPB Publications Catalogue Scan the QR Code:

Published by Manish Jain for BPB Publications, 20 Ansari Road, Darya Ganj, New Delhi-110002 and Printed by him at Manipal Technologies, Manipal

www.bpbonline.com

Dedicated to

My wife **Connie**
whose prayers, love and
support have been constant

About the Author

Ron Gilster has written over 50 books on a variety of topics in the areas of IT career certifications, programming, computer technology, and a few in finance, real estate, and business. His commitment to his readers has always been a desire for their success.

Ron's career has included a range of IT-related positions that range from machine operator to programmer, to instructor, and to senior executive. He has worked in higher education, consulting, manufacturing, software development, and telecommunications.

About the Reviewer

Simone Bertulli is a cyber-security professional, currently holding a senior position at the Cyber Defense Center of an important Italian company.

He has more than 15 years of experience in the IT field and with expertise in Enterprise-class infrastructure technologies, where he obtained the CompTIA Server+, CompTIA Cloud Essentials, CompTIA Cloud+, CompTIA Storage+, CompTIA Linux+ and the LPIC-3 Virtualization & High Availability certifications.

He is a passionate supporter of Open Source, he actively contributes to the Community, writing on the Linux Professional Institute blog and holding tech talks always on FOSS themes, both on technical fields and on professional training.

Acknowledgement

I want to express my deepest gratitude to my wife Connie for her unwavering support and encouragement throughout the creation of this book.

I am very grateful to BPB Publications for this opportunity and for their guidance and expertise in bringing this book to fruition. I would especially like to express my appreciation for the hard work of Bertulli Simone Davide, the technical reviewer, and the BPB editors, whose assistance and guidance were valuable to produce this book's overall quality.

Preface

Although the CompTIA Server+ Certification may not be as well-known as other CompTIA certifications, such as A+, Network+, and Security+, and a few others, it does verify that its holder has the knowledge and understanding of the configurations, operations, and security of network servers and their components. The Server+ certification is intended for IT professionals with two- to four-years of experience working with network servers and computer networks.

CompTIA Server+ is a vendor-neutral certification that is at the same level as vendor-specific certifications, such as the Microsoft MCSA Server Administrator and Cisco Systems'CCNA Data Center. Unlike the Microsoft and Cisco certifications, CompTIA Server+ covers a broader base of server and networking fundamental principles, rather than a specific product line.

The Server+ exam verifies knowledge and understanding in four specific areas: server hardware installation and management, server administration, security and disaster recovery, and troubleshooting.

This book provides informaiton and detail for each of the specific areas identified in the Server+ certification examination's objectives. The material presented is specific to each of the objective items areas to provide the reader with the knowledge and understanding it requires. This book provides in-depth explanations and discussions for all the concepts measured by the exam. It is written at a level that prepares both the well-experienced and the less-experienced IT professionals to prepare for the successul completion of the Server+ certification exam with a qualifying score.

The material presented in each of the chapters is outlined in the following summaries:

Chapter 1: Physical Hardware – This chapter focuses on the server's internal and external components, racking, cabling, and support hardware. The hardware generally discussed is most commonly associated with larger networks and data centers, but the systems found in smaller networks is also addressed. The specific areas covered in this chapter are: racking systems, power cabling, network cabling, server chassis types, and server components.

Chapter 2: Data Storage – This chapter focuses on various technologies used in data storage devices, including hard disk drives, RAID levels and types, capacity planning, hard drive media types, interface types, and shared storage.

Chapter 3: Server Hardware Maintenance – This chapter reviews the administration, management, and preventive maintenance of local and remote server hardware processes and procedures, including out-of-band management, local hardware administration, drive maintenance, hot-swappable hardware, firmware upgrades, and BIOS/UEFI.

Chapter 4: Server Operating Systems – This chapter reviews the administration, management, and preventive maintenance of local and remote server hardware processes and procedures, including minimum hardware requirements, operating system installations, installation types, partition and volume types, and file system types

Chapter 5: Network Infrastructure Services – This chapter reviews the administration, management, and preventive maintenance of local and remote server hardware processes and procedures, including IP configuration, addressing protocols, firewalls, static vs. dynamic routing, and MAC addressing.

Chapter 6: Configure Network Servers – This chapter reviews the administration, management, and preventive maintenance of local and remote server hardware processes and procedures, including server roles and requirements, storage management, server monitoring, data migration and transfer, and administrative interfaces.

Chapter 7: High Availability – This chapter discusses the technologies and methods associated with high availability, fault tolerance, clustering, load balancing, and redundant server network infrastructures.

Chapter 8: Virtualization – This chapter discusses the fundamentals of virtualization and its use in a networking environment, including virtualization, host vs. guest virtualization, resource allocation and provisioning, VM testing, and cloud models.

Chapter 9: Scripting – This chapter looks at how scripts are used in system and network administration. Its specific topics include scripting in server administration, script types, basic scripting constructs, scripting terminology, basic data types, Windows and Linux environmental variables, and script commenting.

Chapter 10: Asset Management – This chapter looks at the process of asset management, including documentation management, document availability, and the policies and procedures of asset management.

Chapter 11: Licensing – This chapter looks at the various types of software versions along with the conditions and rights a software provider grants its users, including software licensing, licensing agreements, licensing models, and version compatibility.

Chapter 12: Data Security – This chapter looks at the methods, processes, and concepts of data security, including encryption, data retention policies, data storage, data protection, and business impacts.

Chapter 13: Physical Security – This chapter looks at the physical security approaches, devices, and environmental controls that an organization can install to protect its systems, including access controls, architectural security reinforcements, authentication factors, and environment controls.

Chapter 14: Access Management – Access management is primarily an information security, IT and data governance process used to grant access to valid users and prohibit invalid users. This chapter covers user accounts, access controls, permissions, auditing, and single sign-on.

Chapter 15: Risk and Mitigation – This chapter discusses the risks to which servers are exposed, how those risks may be mitigated, and the regulatory and legal constraints that must be incorporated into an organization's security program, including security information and event management (SIEM).

Chapter 16: Server Hardening and Decommissioning – This chapter deals with keeping the operating system and applications up-to-date with fixes, updates, patches and the processes required to secure a network server, including hardening, patch management, change management, server decommissioning, media destruction, media retention requirements, and electronics recycling.

Chapter 17: Backup and Restore – This chapter looks at various aspects and practices of a backup and restore policy, including backup and recovery methods, restore methods, and backup validation.

Chapter 18: Disaster Recovery – This chapter discusses the elements and actions that may be a part of a disaster recovery plan, including disaster recovery planning, recovery sites, replication, testing, failovers and failbacks, and testing.

Chapter 19: Troubleshooting Methods – This chapter reviews the methods recommended for use when troubleshooting a failure or fault in any general hardware, software, network, storage device, and security policies or devices. This chapter covers the standard troubleshooting steps and the documentation of findings, actions, and outcomes.

Chapter 20: Hardware Issues – This chapter looks at the problems that can occur on server hardware, including memory issues, causes of common problems, and tools and techniques.

Chapter 21: Storage Issues – This chapter looks at data storage devices, their issues and causes, and the processes used to detect them, including common storage device problems, and the causes of common storage problems.

Chapter 22: Operating System and Software Issues – This chapter reviews common software problems, their causes, and some of the tools and utilities used to troubleshoot them.

Chapter 23: Software Tools and Techniques – This chapter looks at the tools and techniques available to resolve and fix problems and issues associated with a network server.

Chapter 24: Network Connectivity Issues – This chapter identifies the common problems, issues and their causes that occur on a computer network.

Chapter 25: Network Tools and Techniques – This chapter identifies the network operating system utilities and tools that are commonly a part of the troubleshooting process.

Chapter 26: Troubleshooting Security Issues – This chapter discusses the common data security concerns associated with network servers and the security tools used to diagnose and remedy any issues found.

Appendix A: CompTIA Server+ Certification Exam: Practice Test 1

Appendix B: CompTIA Server+ Certification Exam: Practice Test 2

Appendix C: CompTIA Server+® Acronyms

Appendix D: Key Terms/Concepts

Appendix E: Answers to Practice Test 1

Appendix F: Answers to Practice Test 2

Coloured Images

Please follow the link to download the
Coloured Images of the book:

https://rebrand.ly/xtukgt4

We have code bundles from our rich catalogue of books and videos available at **https://github.com/bpbpublications**. Check them out!

Errata

We take immense pride in our work at BPB Publications and follow best practices to ensure the accuracy of our content to provide with an indulging reading experience to our subscribers. Our readers are our mirrors, and we use their inputs to reflect and improve upon human errors, if any, that may have occurred during the publishing processes involved. To let us maintain the quality and help us reach out to any readers who might be having difficulties due to any unforeseen errors, please write to us at :

errata@bpbonline.com

Your support, suggestions and feedbacks are highly appreciated by the BPB Publications' Family.

Piracy

If you come across any illegal copies of our works in any form on the internet, we would be grateful if you would provide us with the location address or website name. Please contact us at **business@bpbonline.com** with a link to the material.

If you are interested in becoming an author

If there is a topic that you have expertise in, and you are interested in either writing or contributing to a book, please visit **www.bpbonline.com**. We have worked with thousands of developers and tech professionals, just like you, to help them share their insights with the global tech community. You can make a general application, apply for a specific hot topic that we are recruiting an author for, or submit your own idea.

Reviews

Please leave a review. Once you have read and used this book, why not leave a review on the site that you purchased it from? Potential readers can then see and use your unbiased opinion to make purchase decisions. We at BPB can understand what you think about our products, and our authors can see your feedback on their book. Thank you!

For more information about BPB, please visit **www.bpbonline.com**.

Join our book's Discord space

Join the book's Discord Workspace for Latest updates, Offers, Tech happenings around the world, New Release and Sessions with the Authors:

https://discord.bpbonline.com

Table of Contents

Part - 1
Server Hardware Installation and Management

Regardless of its purpose or role in a network, a server has two primary components: hardware and software. In this part, you review the system and data storage hardware, their installation, function, and maintenance.

Part 1 includes the following chapters:

- Chapter 1: Physical Hardware
- Chapter 2: Storage Devices
- Chapter 3: Server Hardware Maintenance

CHAPTER 1
Physical Hardware

Introduction

When we think about a network server, we lump the hardware and software into one system. For the most part, this is not entirely wrong, but technically, a server is a software and its support services. We commonly refer to the physical hardware as a server, even though it could have multiple server software running on it. In this chapter and the whole book, the term server is used interchangeably to indicate both. Keep in mind that there is some difference between server hardware and server software. So, it is okay to see a server as the combination of the hardware and the software in the context of the service it provides to a network. Regardless, without its hardware or its software, there would be no server.

This chapter focuses on the server's internal and external components, racking, cabling, and support hardware. The hardware discussed in this chapter (and most of this book), is generally associated with larger networks and data centers. However, all servers, even the **small offices or home offices (SOHO)**, require the same support systems, in one form or another. With that understanding, let us look at the various types of hardware and support systems that provide for the operations of a server.

Structure

The chapter covers the following topics:

- Racking systems
- Power cabling
- Network cabling
- Server chassis types
- Server components

Objective

By the end of this chapter, you will be able to identify and describe the sub-objectives of the following Server+ examination objective: *Given a scenario, install physical hardware.*

Racking systems

The hardware on which server software runs can be a standalone computer or a computer system specifically designed for that purpose. The computers/servers in large networks are commonly contained in specially designed computer rooms, data centers, or server farms. In these environments, the server hardware is typically mounted on open racks or in cabinets. *Figure 1.1* shows examples of an open rack and a rackmount cabinet like those commonly found in data centers:

Figure 1.1: *Server hardware is commonly mounted on an open rack (left) or a server cabinet (right) in large data centers* [1]

1. Images courtesy of Datarack Co.

Rack dimensions

The dimensions of a mountable rack device have a standard width and height sizing. The majority of rackmount devices have a width of 19-inches, but their heights can vary with the type and purpose of each device. Racking systems, like those shown in *Figure 1.1*, have either two or four vertical rails. Server hardware and other devices are attached to the rails using a rail kit. A rail kit is typically specific to the device with horizontally mounted rails on which the device sits, and fasteners to secure the device to the vertical rails. A two-rail rack has no depth limitations, but a four-rail rack is typically either 24 or 48-inches in-depth and is designed to enclose devices.

Rackmount systems are designed to accommodate varying device heights. The height of a device is measured using the rack unit or "U." One U, or "1U," is standardized at 1.75 inches. *Figure 1.2* illustrates the size of 1U. Most racks or cabinet systems are 42U in height. Rack-mountable server hardware is 2U or 3.5-inches tall. Theoretically, twenty-one 2U devices could be mounted in a 42U rack:

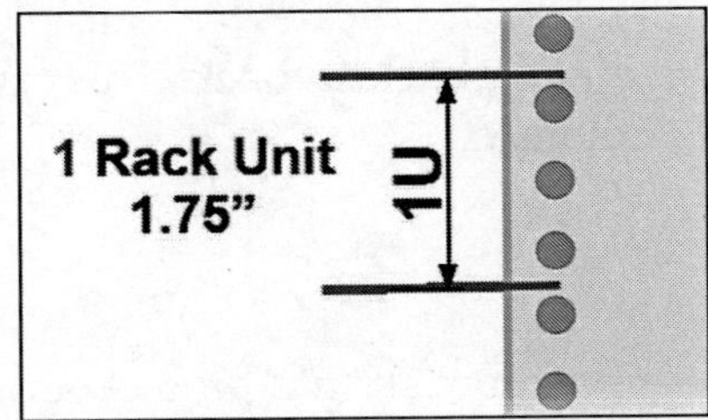

***Figure 1.2**: One rack unit (1U) is 1.75 inches in height*

Rack layout

Racking systems are designed to hold all standard rack-mountable devices, including server hardware, **uninterruptible power supplies** (**UPS**), **power distribution units** (**PDUs**), cable management devices, **keyboard-video-mouse** (**KVM**) switches, patch panels, and more. However, the placement of certain devices can affect the effectiveness of the cooling system and its airflow.

Before inserting devices into a rack, you should plan where each device should be in relationship to the other devices. If there are multiple racks, consider the power and cooling systems of the facility. Heavier devices, such as a UPS, should be placed at the bottom of the rack, and the lightest devices should tend toward the top. Devices common to a rack installation, such as patch panels, routers, switches, firewalls, etc., are typically placed in the upper part of the rack. This is for the ease of installation, access, and cable management.

Cooling management

Generally, a building's **heating, ventilation, and air conditioning** (HVAC) system is insufficient to cool a well-populated server room or data center. This is because the heat levels of the space will fluctuate. A server room requires temperature and humidity regulation. A server room's recommended temperature and humidity levels are 68 to 72 degrees Fahrenheit and 40 to 55 percent humidity.

Humidity can be a particular problem for a server room. Humidity levels higher than 40 to 55 percent can result in condensation, which can damage electrical or electronic components. Lower humidity can result in an increased chance of electromagnetic discharge (static electricity), which can also damage the electronics of the systems. The temperature and humidity typically require the server room to have a dedicated HVAC system to control both. An important element of a server room's cooling system is *airflow*, which has two primary tasks: pulling out hot air and pushing in cool air. The hot air from the devices in a rack should exhaust in the same direction and be handled by the cooling system. The cool air should be directed into the device's air intake. A common server room layout creates *hot* and *cold aisles* that sit back-to-back. This layout pulls air from the cool aisle and exhausts hot air into a hot aisle.

Safety

The safety considerations for a server room should protect both the equipment and people. The following includes some considerations for a server room safety policy and plan:

- **Securing access**: Unauthorized visitors in a server room pose a danger to the equipment, themselves, and others. They are likely unfamiliar with the equipment, its operations, and the environment. Any key presses, button pushes, or inadvertent cable disconnects could cause serious problems or injuries. Authorized data center employees should always accompany all visitors in the server room.
- **High voltage**: A server room, especially a larger one, consumes high-voltage electricity. Typically, the equipment includes UPS and PDU devices that deal with high-voltage power and myriad power cables supplying electricity to servers and other devices. This is a dangerous situation for any unauthorized visitors and inattentive employees. High-voltage equipment should be marked and restricted to only qualified technicians.
- **Disorganized cables and wiring**: Too often, expanding a server room or a network involves adding new devices, cables, and wiring as quickly as possible with the mindset that it can be cleaned up later, which may never happen. The result is a tangled mess of wires and cables that could cause accidental tripping, disconnections, and other possible hazards. Cable management, discussed in the following section, should always be a priority to maintain a safe work and operating environment.

- **Personal injuries**: Besides the possible tripping, electrocution, and dangerous visitor threats, technicians working in a server room (or elsewhere) should use proper lifting techniques to avoid back, leg, or arm injuries. The recommended techniques to employ when lifting heavy objects include the following:
    - Stand close to the object
    - Bend your knee
    - Grip the object securely
    - Use your legs to lift
- **Floor load limitations**: Nearly all server rooms or data centers have a raised floor, which means floor tiles are set on a framework of metal supports. The space under the floor allows for cabling and power cords to be hidden and kept out of the way. However, because the floor is suspended, it has a weight or load limitation. When laying out the server room, the weight of the rackmounts and equipment must be considered to avoid flooring failures. In general, depending on the material of the floor tiles, the load limitation for raised flooring is 1,000 to 2,000 pounds per square meter.

Power Distribution Unit

A **power distribution unit** (**PDU**) is a rack-mounted device that provides multiple electrical outlets. A PDU, like the one shown in *Figure 1.3*, controls and distributes electrical power to devices in a rack that are connected to it. A PDU can be mounted to a rack, placed vertically on a rack rail as a 0U device, or horizontally in a 1U slot.

Figure 1.3*: A 20-outlet 0U power distribution unit (PDU)* [2]

A PDU can be unmanaged or managed. An unmanaged PDU is simply a multiple outlet extension cord. A managed PDU will usually have one or more Ethernet ports, perhaps a USB port or two, with integrated sensors, LEDs, and LCD displays that are used to signal any power issues in real-time. Most managed PDUs can be administered locally or remotely through a web/console interface.

Keyboard-Video-Mouse

A **keyboard-video-mouse** (KVM) switch (see *Figure 1.4*), is a device that allows one set of control devices to be switched to interface with multiple devices. In a server room with several server hardware units and support devices, a single set of **input/output (I/O)**

2. Image courtesy of Cyber Power Systems (USA), Inc

devices can be switched to any connected device for interaction and control. KVM switches typically support a variety of video, peripheral, or network interface connections, including VGA and HDMI for video, USB and PS/2 for peripheral devices, and Ethernet connections for networking. A KVM switch eliminates the need for each device to have a dedicated keyboard, video, and mouse.

Figure 1.4: *An 8-port KVM switch* [3]

Power cabling

The title of this section is specified in the Server+ exam objectives. At first glance, you might think *power cabling* is about the power cords that connect devices to electrical power. However, while it does include those, the power distribution and management of a server room involve much more than just power cables. This section looks at ways to provide redundant power, the different types of power connectors, and how to manage power and network cables to avoid problems and safety issues.

Redundant Power

Regardless of its size or how critical it may be, a server room must have a reliable electrical power source. Whether it is required 8 hours a day or 24/7, electrical power must be available without interruption during its mission-critical operations. The goal in any server room is high availability, meaning the server and other systems are powered and available as much as possible. **Redundancy** is a primary element in a highly available system.

Power supply redundancy can be achieved in two ways:

- One way is through an active PSU backed up by one or more PSUs in standby mode.
- The second method uses a low voltage loss **metal-oxide-semiconductor field-effect transistor** (**MOSFET**) controller to automatically switch from a failing PSU to a redundant standby unit, a process called **hot swapping**.

---

3. Image courtesy of IOGEAR

Uninterrupted Power Supply

Another vital component of a redundant power system is an **uninterrupted power supply** (**UPS**). A UPS is a separate device that independently provides continuous electrical power in the event that the main power supply is interrupted. During normal operation, a UPS stores power in an on-board battery while passing the live power stream onto the connected devices. However, should the power source be interrupted, a UPS can only supply the power stored in its battery. Should a power outage extend beyond the stored power of the UPS, this may not be the long-term solution. Generators, small or large, can be used to provide a failover electrical power supply in the event of a lengthy power outage.

When a UPS senses the loss of its primary power source, it sounds an alarm, and can be or is automatically switched over to provide battery power to the devices connected to it. A UPS can be unmanaged, which means it may require manual switchover in the event of a power interruption. Other UPS devices are considered "smart." These types of UPS devices can be interfaced with servers and management systems as a part of an automated power management system.

Separate circuits

In data centers with a large number of servers and supporting devices, a common approach to redundancy is using two separate dedicated electrical circuits, each extended with a UPS. Server room equipment is divided into two parallel circuits.

Separate providers

If the same provider is the source for two parallel electrical circuits, should a general power failure affect its distribution system, the UPS units and possibly a generator are still the backup. To have a separate and independent source for each, a two-circuit system may be more reliable in extreme cases. One circuit might come from the local electrical utility and the other from a large generator, either private or commercial.

Power connection types

The power cord most common to rackmount servers and equipment are cables with **International Electrotechnical Commission** (**IEC**) C13 and C14 connectors. These cables (also called *jumper cords*) connect server and network equipment power sources to PDUs and other power sources. Jumper cords have three parts: a *male connector* for **alternating circuit** (**AC**) source, a *female connector* for attaching to a device, and an electrical cord connecting the two connectors.

Server room power cables conform to a number of standards that define the number of wires, connector blade material, wire jacket colors, wire gauge, connector size, cable insulation, cable shielding, the shape of the plug housing, and layout of the connection tines or receptacles. The two primary standards are the *IEC 60320* and the **National Electrical Manufacturers Association (NEMA)** power cord standards. The most popular power cables in the United States have an IEC connector that connects to the server (female) and a NEMA connector (male) that connects to the power supply. *Figure 1.5* shows an example of an IEC C13 to NEMA cable:

Figure 1.5: *An IEC C13 to NEMA server power cable* [4]

Cable management

A cable routing plan should be completed before cables are installed in a server room. This plan should detail the pathway of cable runs and where cables begin and end. In most server rooms, the cables connecting a server rack with communication services and other devices outside the server room are installed under the raised flooring or above a lowered ceiling.

The cabling from the devices in a rack system should be organized through a *cable management device*. The connecting cables between devices within a rack can be organized into a vertical cable management bar. The cables running between racks can be bundled using cable ties and routed through horizontal cable management devices, like the one shown in *Figure 1.6*:

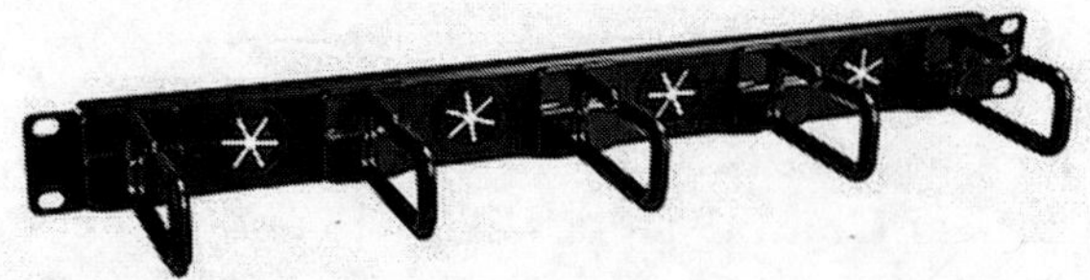

Figure 1.6: *An example of a horizontal cable management bar* [5]

4. Image courtesy of Tripp Lite, a division of the Eaton Corporation
5. Image courtesy of StarTech.com Ltd.

Network cabling

Server rooms and data centers are hard-wired with physical cabling, either copper or fiber optic core. These cables interconnect the server hardware devices for communication. The cabling used depends on several factors, including the network layout, the protocols in use, the standards applied, and the overall size of the network or server room.

Note: Copper Ethernet cables (twisted-pair or coaxial) and electrical power cords should not be bundled or routed together. The electrical cords most likely emit electromagnetic interference (EMI) that can result in data transmission problems. A best practice is that even though Ethernet cables may include shielding, cabling should be separated by type and purpose.

Redundant networking

A key element in redundant networking is *cable redundancy*. A redundant cable is installed between network nodes to provide two or more active paths for data transmission. Each redundant cable has a separate physical pathway so that damage to a pathway does not damage both cables.

Copper cabling

Copper cabling is the most common cable type used in networks of all sizes. There are two categories of copper cables: **twisted pair** (**TP**) and coaxial. TP cabling is made up of multiple pairs of wires that are twisted around each other. TP cables can be either **unshielded** (**UTP**), the most common, or **shielded** (**STP**), used in specific applications.

A coaxial cable has a solid core center conductor that is encased in a conductive shield, which is then encased by insulation, and a protective outer jacket. Coaxial cable is most commonly used to transmit high-frequency signals in telephone, internet, high-speed transmissions, cable television, and receiver to antenna connections. Both coaxial and TP cabling are primarily used for shorter cable runs.

Fiber optic cabling

Fiber optic cables are used for longer and generally more secure network and server room cabling. A fiber optic cable comprises one or more glass or high-grade plastic filaments, usually less than a human hair's diameter. The filament carries a transmitted visible light data stream. The filament is encased in *cladding*, which keeps the light inside the filament. Surrounding the cladding are layers of acrylic plastic, Kevlar fibers for added protection, and a **polyvinyl chloride** (**PVC**) outer cover.

There are two general types of fiber optic cables:

- **Single-mode**: This cable type has just one filament over which a single signal can be transmitted. Single-mode fiber has a range of 30 miles.
- **Multimode**: This cable type has thicker filaments that carry multiple signals simultaneously, each on a different mode or path. Multimode fiber has a range of about 3,000 feet. While multimode fiber cable has a shorter transmission distance than single-mode, it transmits data at much higher speeds. This is why fiber optic is the cable of choice in most data centers.

Fiber optic cable connectors

The two most common connectors used for fiber optic cabling are:

- **Subscriber connector (SC) connectors**: A standard-duplex fiber-optic connector with a square body with push-pull locking (see *Figure 1.7*). SC connectors are standard in data and voice communication and cable television.
- **Lucent or Local connector (LC)**: This type of connector also uses a push-pull locking mechanism about half the size of an SC connector (as shown in *Figure 1.7*). LC connectors are common where there is a high density of cables and connectors in smaller spaces.

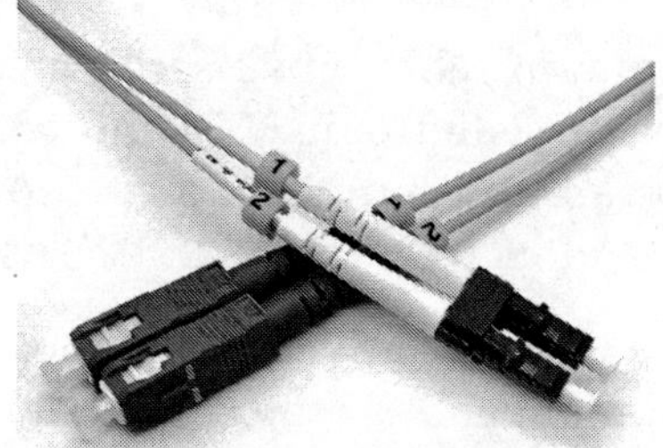

***Figure 1.7**: Examples of SC (left) and LC (right) fiber optic connectors* [6]

Gigabit networks

At one time, only fiber optic cabling supported *gigabit* (one billion bits) transmission speeds. For long-distance transmission, this is still true. However, for SOHO, enterprise, and server room applications, *1000BaseT* copper cabling (CAT 5e and CAT6) and coaxial cabling (DOCSIS 3.1) now support gigabit speeds.

A newer and much faster network technology is **10 gigabit Ethernet (*10GigE*)**. 10GigE operates in full-duplex mode, meaning it supports simultaneous transmissions in two directions with a need for collision detection. 10GigE technology runs on CAT6, CAT6a, or CAT7 copper cabling.

6. Image courtesy of Pier Telecom

Small form-factor pluggable

A **Small Form-factor Pluggable (SFP)** is a compact, hot-swappable, input/output **transceiver (transmitter/receiver)**. SFP provides an interface between network devices, such as routers and switches, with transmission speeds up to 4.25 Gbps. SFP can also convert optical signals (fiber optic) to electrical signals (copper). SFP supports several communication standards, including the **synchronous optical network (SONET), synchronous digital hierarchy (SDH), gigabit Ethernet, and Fiber Channel (FC).**

SFP+ is an enhanced version of SFP with transmission speeds up to 16 Gbps. Another version is **Quad SFP+** *(QSFP+)*, with a transmission speed of up to 40 Gbps. However, as the rate goes up, the *attenuation* distance (the point at which the signal begins to degrade) reduces. *Table 1.1* shows the attenuation points for SFP specifications:

Specification	Medium	Data Speed	Attenuation
SFP	Single-mode Fiber	1 Gbps	120 kilometers (km)
SFP	Multimode Fiber	1 Gbps	500 meters (m)
1000BASE-T SFP	Copper Cable	1 Gbps	100 m
SFP+	Single-mode Fiber	16 Gbps	400 m
QSFP+	4 x Single-mode Fiber	40 Gbps	150 m

***Table 1.1**: Comparison of SFP Specifications*

Server chassis types

Network server chassis has three basic form factors (size, shape, and mounting): tower, rackmount, and blade. Each is designed for a particular situation and use.

Tower chassis

A *tower chassis* form factor is a standalone computer contained in a rectangular or square system case. This chassis type stands on footing integrated into its case. Its primary components are inside the case and include at least one **power supply unit (PSU)**. Towers explicitly designed for use as server hardware may also include redundant power supplies and *hot-swappable* (replaceable without powering down the computer) fans and disk drives. Tower computers have dedicated keyboards, video displays, and mouse units.

Rack mount chassis

Mounting servers in a rack can be much more space efficient than multiple tower systems. *Rack mount chassis* servers have a standard width of 19-inches and a height of 1U to 4U.

Since a server rack is configured to share electrical power, network connections, storage devices, and typically a KVM switch, multiple rack mount servers can be mounted in a rack or cabinet.

Blade chassis

A *blade chassis* is an enclosure into which blade computers, scaled-down computers on a single circuit board, are inserted. Each blade computer has the components required to perform its internal processing. The blade design reduces the size, the number of interfaces, and the power usage of a server. Cooling, power, networking, cabling, and management systems are provided by the blade enclosure or support devices, such as disk storage and internetworking. *Figure 1.8* shows multiple server blades can be mounted in the blade enclosure. In most applications, it is common for one server blade to support only one application or service. However, each blade can support multiple virtual machines in a virtualized environment.

***Figure 1.8**: Multiple server blades in the rack-mount chassis of a blade server* [7]

Server components

The computer hardware on which server software is installed must have a minimum level of configuration to provide the capabilities and resources required by network users. In this section, we look at the server components you can expect to encounter on the Server+ exam.

Hardware compatibility list

Software, whether it is system software (operating system, device drivers, etc.) or application software, may require a certain set of hardware and processing capabilities to operate as it should. If there is a specific set of requirements, they are specified in a **hardware compatibility list** (HCL). An HCL specifies the internal and peripheral hardware and system software compatible with the system to be installed.

7. Photo courtesy of Super Micro Computers, Inc.

For example, Microsoft states that to install Windows 11 on a PC, the PC must meet the following two minimum hardware requirements:

- **Processor**: 1 gigahertz (GHz) or faster with two or more cores on a 64-bit processor or **system on a chip** (**SoC**).
- **Memory**: A minimum of 4 **gigabytes** (**GB**) of RAM.

However, the HCL for Windows and other OSs are generally more specific in other areas of the hardware, processors, chipsets, peripherals, and system capabilities. Some may go so far as requiring a minimum standard for RAID controls, network adapters, hard disk or solid-state drives, and more. Meeting the minimum requirements of an HCL doesn't guarantee that the system will operate at its full capabilities; only that it will run at all.

Central Processing Unit

Server hardware typically requires capabilities beyond those of a desktop computer. This is especially true with microprocessors and **central processing units** (**CPU**s). In fact, most server-specific CPUs are not interchangeable with those designed for desktops.

Instruction sets

A CPU is categorized by its instruction set, which can be a **complex instruction set computer** (**CISC**), **reduced instruction set computer** (**RISC**), and the 64-bit very **long instruction word** (**ILIW**). The CISC architecture is structured so that a single instruction can execute several low-level operations. A RISC CPU needs more instructions to accomplish a task because its instructions are in simpler code. The CISC and the RISC architectures require instructions to be executed in sequence. However, the ILIW architecture allows programs to explicitly specify instructions to execute in parallel and not necessarily in any particular sequence.

Most home and office computers have CISC CPUs, which have slower operating speeds than the RISC CPUs of most server systems. RISC CPUs are more specific to processing needs and are more energy efficient than CISC processors.

CPU vs. cores

In a server environment, it is common for each network host to be supported by one or more physical CPUs to provide processing power and response. Modern CPUs house separate computing units (cores) that divide the workload for processing efficiency.

Some CPUs also include hyperthreading technology that, when needed, creates virtualized duplicates of the physical processor cores. This technology provides additional processing power for performing certain operations simultaneously (a.k.a. multithreading). For example, if a CPU has 4 physical cores, it provides 8 cores (4 physical and 4 virtual) to the operating system.

Graphics Processing Unit

Once upon a time, the graphics (such as they were) displayed by a computer were processed solely by the CPU, the same CPU that processed everything else. These days, the rendering of graphics on a computer's video display is performed by a **graphics processing unit** (GPU).

The two basic types of GPUs are, integrated and discrete/dedicated:

- Integrated GPUs are built into the CPU. An integrated GPU, also called an onboard GPU, is included in the same processor package as the CPU, which means that the GPU shares its resources with the CPU.
- Discrete GPUs, also called dedicated GPUs, are contained on graphics expansion cards that remove graphics processing from the CPU. A graphics card is independent and has its processing capabilities, including memory and power management. A discrete graphics card holds the GPU and the dedicated memory, cooling system, and power unit it needs.

A graphics expansion card is typically either an **Accelerated Graphics Port** (**AGP**) or a sixteen-lane **Peripheral Component Interconnect Express** (**PCIe**) x16 slot. *Figure 1.9* compares AGP and PCIe expansion slots:

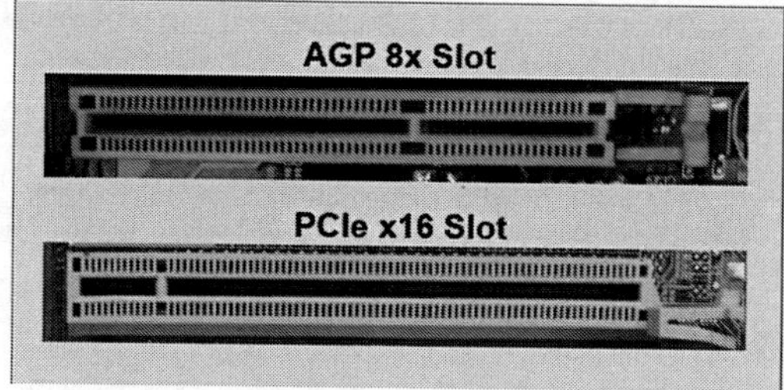

***Figure 1.9**: An AGP 8x slot (top) and a PCIe 16x slot (bottom) are the most common expansion slots for graphics cards*

Memory

Server memory is specified by its **data transfer rate** (**DTR**), measured in **millions of transfers per second** (**MT/s**). MT/s is the number of transfer cycles or operations a device can perform in one second. However, the MT/s rating does not specify DTR, the amount of data (in bytes) moved from one location to another in a second. MT/s can be converted to DTR, measured in bytes per second, by multiplying the MT/s transfer rate by 8 (bits per byte). For example, a **dual inline memory module** (**DIMM**) with a 2,133 MT/s transfer rate provides a DTR of about 17 GBps.

There are three types of **dual inline memory modules (DIMMs)** for servers:

- **Registered DIMM (RDIMM)**: RDIMMs insert a register between the CPU and the memory chips to buffer data transmission. Buffering shortens the transmission distance and improves efficiency. A 16 GB RDIMM supports throughout as high as 1,600 MT/s. RDIMMs are common when a server has large amounts of memory.
- **Unbuffered DIMM (UDIMM)**: UDIMMs do not buffer data transmissions. This can increase its overall performance by eliminating the latency caused by the buffering process. UDIMMs also have a maximum transfer rate of 1,600 MT/s due to their higher electrical requirements. UDIMMs are limited to 4 GB and only two DIMMs per channel. These modules are common on secondary servers with lower memory capacity.
- **Load-reduced DIMM (LRDIMM)**: Like RDIMMs, LRDIMMs use buffering, but its buffering is used to reduce its electrical load significantly. The LRDIMM buffering scheme provides for the highest memory capacity on a server. However, not all server hardware supports LRDIMMs.

Note: These memory types cannot be mixed; only one type can be installed in a server.

Server interfaces

An **interface** is a communication portal between two devices, programs, or users. The interfaces commonly found on a server are hardware, software, and user interfaces.

Hardware interfaces

A hardware interface facilitates connections and communications between internal or peripheral devices. Some common hardware interfaces are:

- **Universal serial bus (USB)** interfaces: USB interfaces (ports) connect a wide variety of devices, such as scanners, printers, digital cameras, external storage devices, mouse units, keyboards, and other input and output devices.
- **Serial interfaces**: Data transmitted over a serial interface is a single stream of bits from one digital system to another. Serial interfaces are used for small-scale points of connection, for example, a mouse or a modem to a computer.
- **Parallel interfaces**: A parallel transmission sends bits across multiple wires or channels simultaneously. A parallel interface is much faster than a serial interface and is more efficient for large-scale connections, such as a scanner or a printer.

Software interfaces

Software interfaces are used by system and application software to communicate on a computer's internal system. Internal communication may be commands to control system resources, data, or instructions passed from one process to another. Some examples of software interfaces are:

- **Operating system (OS)**: An OS communicates with hardware controllers, application software, the processor, and peripheral devices through a variety of system resources, which include main memory, cache memory, storage space, IRQs, I/O addressing, and DMA channels. These resources provide a mechanism through which the operating system manages and coordinates hardware resources and their use by the applications and services running on the computer.
- **IP network protocols**: They enable encapsulated data to move over the global network to their intended destinations.
- **Device drivers**: A device driver provides a translation point that enables a device to communicate with the operating system.

User interfaces

A **user interface** (UI) allows a human to interact with a computer, enabling the human to issue commands and make selections and for the computer to provide feedback and information to the user. Some types of user interfaces are:

- **Command-line interface (CLI)**: This interface allows users to enter basic commands to the operating system.
- **Graphical user interface (GUI)**: This interface enables users to select and control application software and hardware devices by interacting physically with graphical icons.
- **Menu-driven interface**: This interface displays a series of options, called menus, from which a user can select the action they wish to take.
- **Conversational user interface**: This interface allows a user to speak vocal commands that the system identifies through voice recognition capabilities.

Conclusion

In this chapter, we reviewed the hardware components of a server computer and the methods and practices involved in their installation and management. The major areas we reviewed were racking systems, power cabling, network cabling, the different server chassis types, and the key server components.

In the next chapter, we will look at data storage systems and their interactions with servers.

Points to remember

- The height of a rack mountable device is measured in Us.
- A server room should be kept at temperature and humidity levels of 68 to 72 degrees Fahrenheit and 40 to 55 percent humidity.
- A PDU is a rack-mounted device that provides multiple electrical outlets.
- A KVM switch allows one set of control devices to be switched to interface with multiple devices.
- A UPS provides continuous electrical power when the main power supply is interrupted.
- There are two types of copper cables: **twisted pair** (**TP**) and coaxial. TP cables are UTP or STP.
- There are two types of fiber optic cables: single-mode and multimode.
- Common connectors for fiber optic cables are SC and LC.
- 10GigE operates in full-duplex mode.
- The form factors for server computers are tower, rack mount, and blade.
- An HCL specifies the requirements for a system to be installed.
- CPU instruction sets are CISC, RISC, or ILIW.
- GPUs are integrated or discrete. A graphics card is an AGP or PCIe.
- Computer memory is specified by DTR, which is measured in MT/s.
- Server memory is RDIMM, UDIMM, or LRDIMM.
- Common hardware interfaces are USB, serial, and parallel.
- Software interfaces are OS, IP protocols, and device drivers.
- UI interfaces are CLI, GUI, menu-driven, and conversational.

Join our book's Discord space

Join the book's Discord Workspace for Latest updates, Offers, Tech happenings around the world, New Release and Sessions with the Authors:

https://discord.bpbonline.com

CHAPTER 2
Data Storage

Introduction

Among the more critical components of server hardware are the data storage devices. Data storage devices in or attached to a server system are essentially the same as those found on a desktop computer. However, because of the large volume of data, the number of reads and writes to and from the data storage devices associated with servers, enhanced security is much more complicated and requires more attention. This chapter focuses on the various technologies of data storage devices, including RAID, interfacing, networking, and the devices and media.

Structure

The chapter covers the following topics:

- Hard disk drives
- Hard drive interfaces
- RAID levels and types
- Disk drive media
- Shared storage

Objective

By the end of this chapter, you will be able to identify and describe the sub-objectives of the following Server+ examination objective: *Given a scenario, deploy and manage storage.*

Hard disk drives

A **hard disk drive** (**HDD**) is an electro-mechanical device where the data is stored on a non-volatile medium. An HDD consists of one or more platters that hold the data written to them. This data includes the operating system, application programs, and data files. The platter spins to move data under a read-write head positioned by an actuator arm. The following figure shows A hard disk drive unit with its outer case removed:

***Figure 2.1**: A hard disk drive unit with its outer case removed*

Hard disk drive specifications

An HDD's specifications detail its technology, interface, capacity, and speeds. HDDs have two specification sets: device specifications and logical specifications. Device specifications are measurements of components and operations. The logical configurations reflect the net effect of formatting or partitioning the drive's media.

The device specifications that are important for all HDDs are:

- **Revolutions per minute** (**RPM**): The RPM rates (most commonly used), if SSDs are not installed, are HDDs with RPMs of 10,000 to 15,000. These numbers represent the rotation speeds of the disk platters of an HDD. The higher the RPM value, the faster the disks rotate. This means the bits stored on the disk platter move under the read/write head faster, which, in turn, speeds up the data transfer process.
- **Interface**: The communication interface can determine the capacity of a drive, the width of its bus (used to transfer data to or from the HDD), and its maximum storage capacity (see *Hard Disk Interfaces*, later in this chapter for more information).

- **Access time**: This is an accumulation of the time between the disk controller initiating an I/O action and just before data is read or written to or from the disk. The actions included in access time are:
    - o **Seek time**: The time for the actuator arm to move the read/write head over the disk track that contains the targeted data sector.
    - o **Rotational latency**: The time required for the disk platter to rotate the targeted data sector under the read/write head.
- **Data transfer rate (DTR)**: The time required to move data from the read/write head to memory or from memory to a read/write head.
- **I/O operations per second (IOps [pronounced "eye-ops,"])**: The number of read and/or write operations from/or to random addresses in one second.

The rotational speed of an HDD's disk platters is the basis of its overall speed. A primary speed and efficiency indicator is **input output per second** (**IOps**). IOps measures the number of reads or writes that can occur in one second. Faster rotational speeds result in higher IOps ratings. An HDD can have a rotational speed of 5,400 RPM, 7,200 RPM, 10,000 RPM, or 15,000 RPM. A 5,400 RPM drive supports 60 IOps, and a 15,000 RPM disk drive provides 110 IOps. Comparatively, a slow SSD drive provides 20,000 IOps.

Hard drive interfaces

A hard disk drive interface is a bus structure that is used to pass data requests and the data requested between a device driver, the hard disk device, RAM, and disk drive controllers. HDD interfaces are word-serial or bit-serial. **Word-serial interfaces** transfer data in a 8-bit, 16-bit, or 32-bit words. The **Small Computer Serial Interface** (**SCSI**) and the **Parallel Advanced Technology Attachment** (**PATA**) are word-serial interfaces. Bit-serial interfaces include **Serial Advanced Technology Attachment** (**SATA**), and **Serial-attached SCSI** (**SAS**). External storage devices require a **host-bus adapter** (**HBA**) that connects a storage device on a network to a server, such as. **Fibre Channel** (**FC**). Each of the interfaces named in this paragraph are detailed later in this chapter.

Interface types

A hard disk interface provides a communication connection between the HDD and the host computer, specifically between the hard disk's cache and primary memory. Each hard disk interface provides different data transfer speeds and characteristics.

Most of the recently available computers, desktops, laptops, or servers have disk drives using either SATA or a **Serial attached SCSI** (**SAS**) interface. Some systems may have both, and some may even include other interface types.

Serial ATA

Serial ATA (SATA) hard drives are the most popular disk drives in the SOHO market and are commonly used in low- to mid-range servers. SATA, as its name implies, communicates over a serial connection, and is limited to one disk drive on a connection. Two important features of SATA drives are they are hot swappable and have a capacity of up to 20 **terabytes (TB)**.

The SATA standard was introduced in 2003 to replace the parallel SATA (PATA) interface. The SATA II revision improved SATA 1's data transfer rate, bandwidth, and throughput. SATA II, the current standard (see *Figure 2.2*), increased the data transfer rate and added a locking mechanism to secure the connection.

Figure 2.2: *Top (left) and bottom (right) views of a SATA III connector* [1]

A SATA hard disk drive has two primary connections: data and power.

- The SATA data connector (shown in *Figure 2.2*) has seven horizontal pins and connects to the SATA port on the motherboard.
- The SATA power cable has fifteen horizontal pins to connect to the disk drive. The cable connects the drive to the motherboard and may need a Molex power connector at that end of the cable to do so.

A variation of the SATA interface is the **external SATA (eSATA)** interface. eSATA is used to connect external peripheral devices to a computer. It uses the same protocols as the SATA interface and provides the same data transfer rates. Another SATA variation is the *eSATA* **USB Hybrid Port (EUHP)**, also called **eSATAp**. The eSATAp interface merges four USB pins with two 12-volt power pins to eliminate the need for an external power cable.

Serial Attached SCSI (SAS)

The SAS interface replaced the parallel SCSI standard with serial communication between hard disk storage and the **host bus adapter (HBA)** of a computer. You will find references

1. Image courtesy of Sabrent

to the SAS interface as a software suite or a protocol because it supports the legacy SCSI command set. An SAS interface has four primary components:

- **Targets**: The disk drives are connected to the SAS interface.
- **Initiators**: Send requests and receive responses from targets.
- **Service delivery**: A dedicated cable pin or expansion hardware that links the targets to the initiator.
- **Expanders**: Optional components that provide additional ports to add more devices to the SAS subsystem. SAS supports 255 direct connections but could be expanded, theoretically, to 65,535 devices.

The SAS interface is more reliable than the SATA interface. Because SAS has twice as much bandwidth as SATA, its transfer speed, and the average IOps rate is higher (SATA at 80 IOps; SAS at 180 IOps). However, an SAS drive has a storage capacity of only 2 TB.

The SAS connector (see *Figure 2.3*) uses the same connector pinning as the SATA connector. However, the SAS connector combines the data and power connections side-by-side into a single plug.

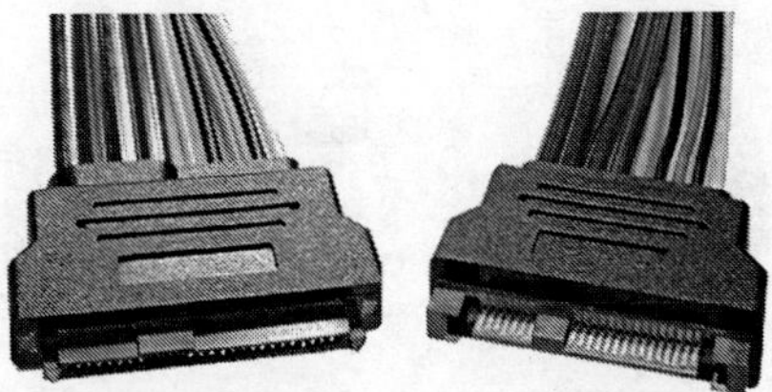

***Figure 2.3**: Top (left) and bottom (right) views of a SAS connector.*
Image courtesy of CS Electronics

Peripheral Component Interconnect

The **Peripheral Component Interconnect** (**PCI**) interface, which has largely been replaced by the **PCI Express** (**PCIe**) interface is both, a connection interface and a system bus. As its name suggests, PCI was commonly used to attach peripheral devices, such as network adapters and video and sound cards, to a computer's motherboard. Most recent computers now feature **universal serial bus** (**USB**) or PCIe interfaces, or both. However, many motherboards also include a PCI slot for backward compatibility. A PCI expansion card connector on a motherboard can be either 32-bit or 64-bit that runs at 33 **megahertz** (**MHz**) or 66 MHz, respectively.

Universal Serial Bus

USB has become one of the most popular external device interfaces and connectors. The USB standards have gone through seven revisions since their introduction in 1996. *Table 2.1* lists the versions of the USB standard with the data transfer rates connector standards:

USB Standard	Data Transfer Rate (DTR)	Connector Standards
USB 1.0	12 Mbps	Type A, Type B, Mini-A, Mini-B, Micro-A, Micro-B
USB 2.0	480 Mbps	Type A, Type B, Mini-A, Mini-B, Micro-A, Micro-B
USB 3.1 Gen 1	5 Gbps	Type A, Type B, Mini-B, Micro-B
USB 3.1 Gen 2	10 Gbps	Type A, Type C
USB 3.2	20 Gbps	Type C

Table 2.1: USB Standards

The USB standards specify cables, connectors, connection, communication, and power supply protocols for interfaces between computers and peripherals. There have been many different USB standard connectors, most of which have been deprecated since USB 3.2 was released. USB Type C is the current standard. *Figure 2.4* illustrates the different types of USB connectors:

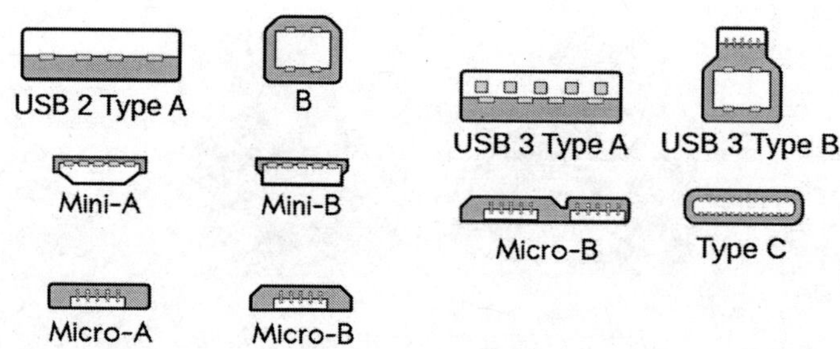

Figure 2.4: USB Male Connector Types

Secure Digital Card

A **secure digital** (**SD**) card is a small memory card with a large storage capacity, higher data transfer rates on most cards, and low-battery or power consumption. An SD card stores data in non-volatile flash memory. *Figure 2.5* shows an example of an SD card:

Figure 2.5: An SD card [2]

2. Image courtesy of Kingston Technology Corporation

RAID levels and types

Redundant Array of Independent Disks (RAID) is a high availability technology that can improve the integrity, reliability, and performance of data storage systems. RAID systems are common in larger data centers and cloud computing systems, among other high-volume processing systems. While there are no RAID standards, resulting in a variety of approaches and solutions, there are some common practices and configurations implemented.

Striping and mirroring

Striping and mirroring are used in a RAID system to create data redundancy.

Striping divides data into blocks (stripes) that are stored across two or more disk drives. The size of the stripes varies by provider, but can range from a single byte, to fixed-length blocks, or an entire partition. For instance, a 3 HDD RAID system could stripe 128 KB data blocks on each of the three drives. A 10 HDD RAID system might stripe a 10 MB file by storing 1 MB stripes on each disk.

Mirroring duplicates data to two or more disk drives. Mirroring makes an exact copy of data as a backup in case the original file or the disk on which it is stored is damaged. A mirrored data block is essentially an online backup and immediately available. Mirrored data are synchronized. Updates to the original data are also made to the mirrored data.

RAID levels

The methodology of a particular RAID approach, called a **RAID level**, applies system striping, mirroring, or parity in different combinations. While more than 10 RAID levels have been introduced by storage device providers and manufacturers, only five have been commonly used to become quasi-standards. *Table* 2.2 lists the more commonly used RAID levels, which are also the ones you will encounter on the Server+ exam:

RAID Level	Description	Minimum # of Disks
0	Block striping; no parity	2
1	Mirroring; no parity	2
5	Block striping; with parity	3
6	Block striping; double parity	4
1+0 (10)	Block striping with mirroring; no parity	4

Table 2.2: *RAID levels*

The RAIL levels include:

- **RAID 0**: RAID 0 does not provide redundancy or data recovery; if one disk fails, all the data is lost. It is used more for performance enhancement. By striping data to two or more disk drives, I/O processes are more efficient. *Figure 2.6* illustrates striping on two disks:

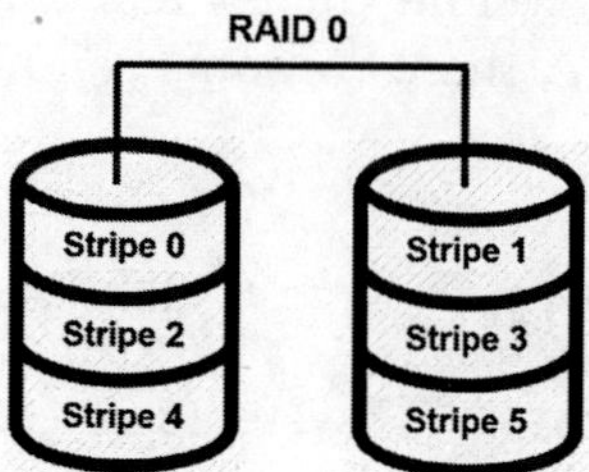

***Figure 2.6**: RAID 0 with data blocks striped across two disks*

- **RAID 1**: RAID 1 copies a mirror image of a data block to another disk drive. The mirror block is then available should the original block become corrupted or unavailable. *Figure 2.7* illustrates RAID 1 mirroring:

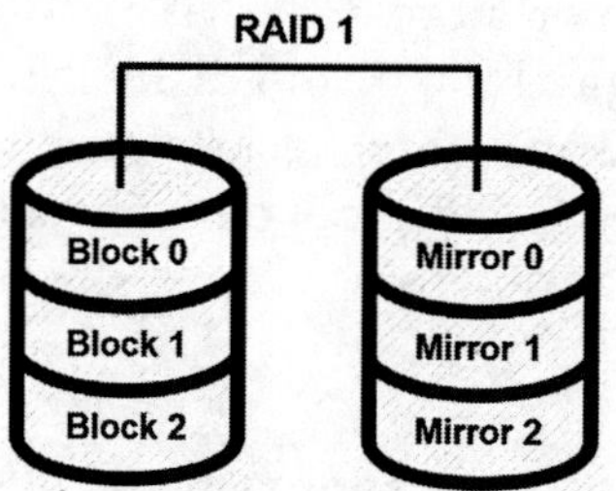

***Figure 2.7**: RAID 1 with data mirrors saved to another disk*

- **RAID 5**: RAID 5 is RAID 0 with parity added (see *Figure 2.8*). Parity checks if data may be lost, corrupted, or written when it is being moved from one storage location to another. RAID 5 uses the striped data and parity of a data block on a failing storage device to reproduce the block on an active drive to avoid an interruption in processing. A drawback to RAID 5 is latency due to the parity calculations on a system with many I/O operations.

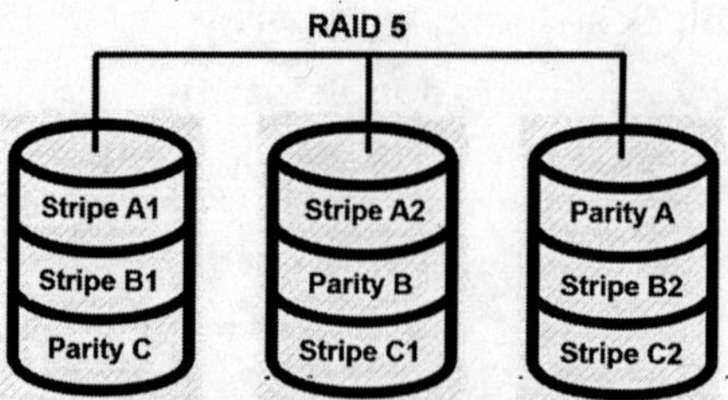

***Figure 2.8**: RAID 5 with data and parity striped to multiple drives*

- **RAID 6**: RAID 6 is RAID 5 with its parity data information duplicated. The idea is that if two or more disk drives fail, processing could continue. However, the number of disks required is N+2, which means that two or more physical disk drives plus two more must be in the RAID array. RAID 6 is commonly implemented in enterprise network data centers by **cloud service providers (CSPs)**.
- **RAID 10**: RAID 10 or 1+0 is a combination of RAID 1 mirroring and RAID 0 striping without parity. RAID 10 is implemented primarily on small and SOHO networks and servers through software RAID applications.

Just a bunch of disks

There are also disk architectures that are grouped as "non-RAID." One of the more commonly used has the very descriptive name of **Just a Bunch of Disks**, or **JBOD** for short. JBOD combines multiple HDDs or SSDs into logical units. JBOD is used by enterprises with the need for expanding local storage capacity without adding multiple servers.

Hardware RAID versus software RAID

RAID implementations, regardless of the RAID level in use, are managed by a RAID controller that manages the disk array. The controller, a hardware RAID implementation, provides the interface between the disk array and the user. However, RAID can also be implemented through software in which the disk controller is added to or is a part of a server's operating system.

Functionally, the two RAID implementations are about the same. The differences between the hardware and software RAID implementations appear where the RAID processing occurs. In software RAID, the server's (typically a RAID host server) CPU performs the processing. Hardware RAID is typically implemented with a RAID controller expansion card (see *Figure 2.9*), but it can also be implemented with a standalone RAID controller appliance, or with HDDs that have embedded RAID controllers. Hardware RAID is generally preferred because of its better performance, but this depends on the number of drives and the RAID level applied.

***Figure 2.9**: A hardware RAID controller expansion card*[3]

3. Image courtesy of Microchip Technology Inc...

A RAID controller has three main components: a processor, RAM, and I/O interfaces.

- The processor manages incoming data requests or data to be stored.
- The instructions and addressing information to fulfill requests are stored in RAM.
- The I/O component has at least one front-end port to communicate with the host computer and a back-end port for communicating with the disk drives.

In larger RAID implementations, a **redundant disk array controller** (**RDAC**) shares a dual-port connection with the primary controller and serves as a backup controller if the primary controller fails. Without an RBAC, should the primary controller fail, the RAID array is unreachable.

Capacity planning

Determining the amount of data storage space needed in the near- or long-term can be difficult. You do not want to spend money on unneeded storage capacity, but running out of storage space could also cause problems. The task is to forecast just the right amount of disk space for the right time. HDD manufacturers provide disk capacity planning calculators or software you can use to forecast storage capacity, and many system management software packages have a capacity planning function included.

The two most common ways to forecast data storage capacity requirements are:

- **Spreadsheets**: Using the metrics of the current data storage utilization, perform an analysis of past and current usage to develop possible trends.
- **Chargeback**: Whether you charge a fee for storage usage to other departments or groups, you can track the storage space utilization for each. This will indicate past usage and possible trends.

Before you start forecasting future storage capacity needs, identify where the need for additional disk storage capacity will come from and what other technologies or approaches may address the capacity requirements. Disk storage technologies and methods like tiered storage, data compression, virtualization, SAN, and NAS, may be a better and more economical way to go if you wish to keep it in-house. However, you may also wish to consider a cloud data storage option, which may eliminate the need for capacity planning altogether.

Disk drive media

On a data storage disk drive, or any type of data storage device, **storage media** can refer to an entire device or the material used to store data bits. HDDs and SSDs are storage media, but so are ferrous oxide, microchips, and MOSFETs. For the Server+ exam, storage media refers to the different types of storage devices. Also, the disk drive is an HDD or SSD.

Solid-State devices

The biggest difference between an SSD and an HDD is the SSD's lack of moving parts. This removes several characteristics of an HDD from the comparison, such as RPM, rotational delay, seek time, and settle time. An SSD operates with less electrical power, generates less heat and does not have the balancing and vibration issues of an HDD. Another difference is speed; the SDD is faster. An SSD drive is a random-access device, and the data can be accessed directly without the latency issues of an HDD. *Figure 2.10* shows an illustration of an SSD internal drive:

***Figure 2.10**: An internal SSD drive* [4]

There are several types of SSDs available, each based on its connection interface to the server hardware. The more common SSD devices available have the following interfaces:

- **SATA**: SATA is perhaps the most common connection interface used for storage devices, including many SSD models. SATA has data transfer speeds of up to 600 **megabytes per second** (**MBps**), which is the slowest of the SSD types.
- **Non-Volatile Memory Express** (**NVMe**): NVMe is a protocol for SSDs and flash drives with data transfer speeds of up to 2,600 MBps using the PCIe connection interface. NVMe, because of its higher cost and power requirements, are most common in server and enterprise systems.
- **M.2 (m-dot-two)**: M.2 is a form factor and not an interface technology that supports smaller SSDs for ultralight and smaller PCs using either SATA or NMVe interfaces.

Wear factors

While SSDs have a long lifespan, it is limited by various factors. Writing to an SSD is more wearing to its flash memory than reading from it. Each flash memory cell has an oxide component, which is two layers of a chemical mixed with oxygen. As data is written to the cell, electrons can be caught between the oxide layers. The trapped electrons weaken

4. Image courtesy of Micron Technology, Inc.

the oxide layers, and eventually, they can no longer store electrons and cannot be read correctly. Writing data to an SSD cell too much will eventually degrade the drive.

Use factors

SSD drives are manufactured in three primary types, each of which is best suited for a particular type of use:

- **Read intensive**: This type of SSD is designed for systems that read data more frequently than they write. The storage technology and interfaces in a read intensive device have a much lower lifespan than are used in write or mixed intensive SSDs. Read intensive SSDs are used in retail websites, video-on-demand, social media, data warehousing, and business intelligence.
- **Write intensive**: SSDs have a limited storage life that is affected far more by write operations than read operations. Write intensive SSDs have a more robust storage technology that ranges from single-level cells (1 bit and 2 charge states) to multi-level cells (2 bits and 4 charge states), to triple-level cells (3 bits and 8 charge states), and even quad-level cells (4 bits and 16 charge states). However, as the number of bits a cell can hold increases, the lifespan of the device decreases. Write intensive SSD applications are call centers, online retail, high-volume order desks, and data capture.
- **Mixed intensive**: This type of SSD device is better in situations where the workload is relatively balanced between reading and writing to the drive.

Shared storage

Shared storage, as its name says, is a central data storage resource that authorized network users and systems can access virtually, simultaneously. Shared storage simplifies data management by providing a single data security point and backup and restore location. The sections that follow describe **Network Attached Storage** (NAS), **Network File System** (NFS), **Common Internet File System** (CIFS), and **Storage Area Network** (SAN), all of which are shared storage systems.

Network attached storage

NAS is a centralized system that provides network users and devices with data retrieval and storage services. A NAS is an independent node on a network with a **media access control** (MAC) address and, where necessary, an **Internet Protocol** (IP) address. A NAS stores unstructured data, including audio, video, website content, text, and productivity suite documents (such as spreadsheets, letters, etc.).

A NAS system is made up of the following components:

- **CPU**: A CPU processes data requests and manages the file systems on the NAS system.
- **Hard disk drives**: A NAS system typically has from two to five hard disk drives, depending on the needs of the organization and its network users. The hard drives, which are hot swappable, are configured as RAID to provide fault tolerance.
- **Network interface**: NAS systems connect to a network through an Ethernet connection, either wired or wireless. Most NAS units provide two or more Ethernet interfaces, each with the bandwidth of 1 Gbps or higher. Some NAS OSs support network interface bonding and interface teaming. NAS systems may also have USB ports for user interactions.
- **Operating system**: High-volume NAS systems use an OS as an interface between the hardware and the user.

A NAS system uses communication and file formatting protocols to provide file sharing services. The communication protocols are commonly IP and TCP. Network client requests for data are issued by a host operating system, such as Windows or Linux, A NAS file formatting protocol is used to format the data before responding. The common file formatting protocols are:

- **Network File System (NFS)**: NFS is platform-neutral and is implemented on Windows, Linux, and several other operating systems.
- **Server Message Blocks (SMB)**: SMB is a Windows system file formatting protocol.
- **Apple Filing Protocol (AFP)**: AFP is a macOS file formatting protocol for Apple PCs.

Storage area network

A **storage area network (SAN)** system provides network services and host devices with data storage services on multiple storage devices on the network. Network clients see SAN as a single entity that provides centralized data access and security. A SAN differs from a NAS, where the NAS unstructured data, and a SAN stores *structured data* in block form.

A SAN organizes data blocks into **logical disk units (LUNs)**, which network clients see as a logical disk volume. These blocks are partitioned and formatted by the server and a shared-disk file system. A shared-disk file system, also called a clustered file system, provides direct access to the data blocks for multiple network clients. The data retrieved from a SAN must be translated into the necessary file format on the requesting host system. Examples of shared-disk file systems are Microsoft **Cluster Shared Volumes (CSV)**, **Oracle Cluster File System (OCFS)**, Red Hat **Global File System (GFS2)**, VMware VMFS, and Apple Xsan.

A SAN implements block-level or storage network protocols that define how data blocks are transmitted over a network. There are several block-level protocols used with SAN systems, but for the Server+ exam, the ones you should know are:

- **Fibre Channel Protocol (FCP)**: FCP is a fast, low latency storage network protocol with bandwidth ranging from 2 to 25 Gbps. An FC fabric (network) connects host bus adapters (server storage device adapters) with the storage system controllers and disks, and FC switches. FCP implements SCSI on an FC network.
- **Fibre Channel over Ethernet (FCoE)**: FCoE allows FC communication to be transmitted on an Ethernet network by merging data storage and communication protocols into a single interface.
- **Internet SCSI (iSCSI)**: iSCSI defines how SCSI packets are transmitted over a TCP/IP network. iSCSI transports block-level data between an initiator on a server and a target (storage device).

Conclusion

This chapter reviewed storage devices and technologies commonly implemented on networks and network servers, including HDDs and **solid-state drives (SSDs)**, other storage devices and form factors. It also described the different disk interface technologies and the data storage methods used in a RAID system. NAS and SAN shared-storage systems were also discussed. These are the areas of focus for data storage on the Server+ exam.

The next chapter looks at server hardware maintenance to complete *Part 1*.

Points to remember

- HDD device specifications are measurements of components and operations. HDD logical configurations are the result of formatting and partitioning a drive's media.
- An HDD interface is a bus that passes requests and data to and from device drivers, the HDD, RAM, and drive controllers. HDD interfaces are word-serial or bit-serial.
- SATA communicates over a serial connection, are hot swappable and a capacity of up to 18 TB. A SATA drive has two connections: data and power.
- eSATA connects external devices to a computer. EUHP eliminates the need for an external power cable.
- The SAS interface uses serial communication between an HDD and the HBA. SAS interfaces have four primary components: targets, initiators, service delivery, and expanders. The SAS drive has a storage capacity of 2 TB.
- The PCI and PCIe are both connection interfaces and system buses that are 32-bit or 64-bit and run at 33 MHz and 66 MHz, respectively.

- The USB Type C is the current standard.
- An SD card is a large storage capacity memory card with a high data transfer rate, and low power consumption.
- RAID is a high availability technology. Striping and mirroring create data redundancy.
- Five RAID levels are commonly used: RAID 0, RAID 1, RAID 5, RAID 6, and RAID 10.
- JBOD expands local storage capacity without adding multiple servers.
- A RAID controller has three components: a processor, RAM, and I/O interfaces.
- An SSD drive is a random-access device without moving parts from which data can be accessed directly without the latency issues of an HDD. SSD interfaces are SATA, NVMe, and M.2.
- Shared storage is a central storage resource that provides a single data security point and backup and restore location. Shared storage systems include NAS, NFS, CIFS, and SAN.
- A SAN system is a single entity providing centralized data access and security that stores structured data in block form. A SAN implements FCP, FCoE, and iSCSI.

CHAPTER 3
Server Hardware Maintenance

Introduction

A computer network becomes an integral part of an organization's culture almost immediately after it is deployed. It is an essential work tool and communication device and system; without it, the pace of work slows down. The servers are one of the most critical parts of a computer network, if not the most important. And what may be the most essential part of a server is the server hardware.

This chapter reviews the administration, management, and preventive maintenance of local and remote server hardware processes and procedures you need to know for the CompTIA Server+ exam.

Structure

The chapter covers the following topics:

- Out-of-band management
- Local hardware administration
- Drive maintenance
- Hot-swappable hardware

- Firmware upgrades
- BIOS/UEFI maintenance

Objective

By the end of this chapter, you will be able to identify and describe the maintenance processes and procedures for network servers. The Server+ examination objective: *Given a scenario, perform server hardware maintenance.*

Out-of-band management

An activity is out-of-band when it occurs outside of standard practice. In this case, **Out-Of-Band Management (OOBM)** refers to system and server administration and management performed over a telecommunication link rather than a direct link or in-house. An OOBM system allows an administrator to access, configure, and manage network resources remotely, working outside an organization's production systems. *Figure 3.1* illustrates the fundamental differences between an in-band and an out-of-band management system. The in-band system connects to a remote system using the network links within the organization. The out-of-band system uses a console server to connect to a remote system through an Internet (WAN) link or a telephone system dial-up link. Assuming that the in-band network is an organization's production or live system, the out-of-band approach avoids conflict with the production systems.

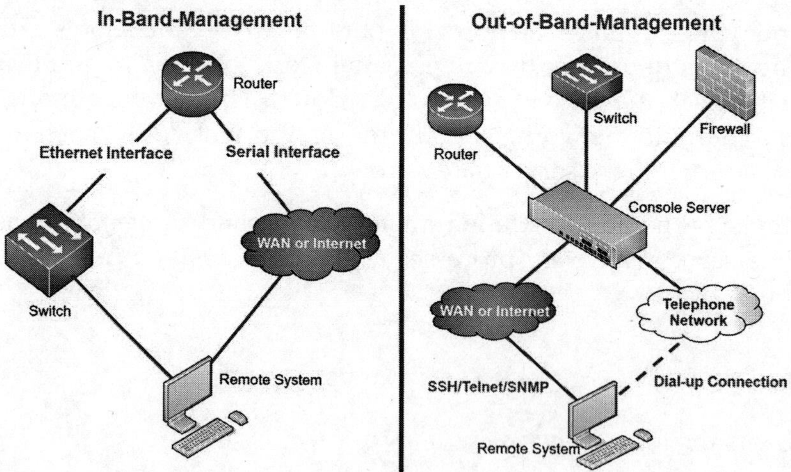

***Figure 3.1**: Comparison of an in-band management system to an out-of-band management system*

One of the benefits provided by an OOBM interface is that it can be used when the production network is down or when the target device is powered off, in sleep mode, or inaccessible over the production network. OOBM can reboot remote devices that have crashed or exhibit operational problems. An OOBM allows administrators to perform reboots, shutdowns, power on, hardware monitoring, software installation, configure BIOS/UEFI settings, and use a KVM over IP (IP KVM) to enter commands and receive feedback.

Local hardware administration

System and network administrators must rely on various monitoring, error notification, and troubleshooting guides to identify problems on network devices, including servers and internetworking equipment, like routers, firewalls, switches, etc. On many large-scale and enterprise networks, fault tolerance and high availability are hardware administrators' primary objectives, and downtime is not an option. The following sections describe many tools hardware administrators can use to keep the network and systems available:

Keyboard-Video-Mouse (KVM)

A **keyboard-video-mouse** (**KVM**) switch is a device that allows one set of input/output and control devices to be switched to interface with one of the multiple devices. In a server room with several server hardware units and support devices, a single set of I/O devices can be switched to work with any connected device as if they were directly connected solely to that device. A KVM switch eliminates the need for each device to have a dedicated keyboard, video, and mouse. *Figure 3.2* illustrates using a KVM in a data center or server room environment.

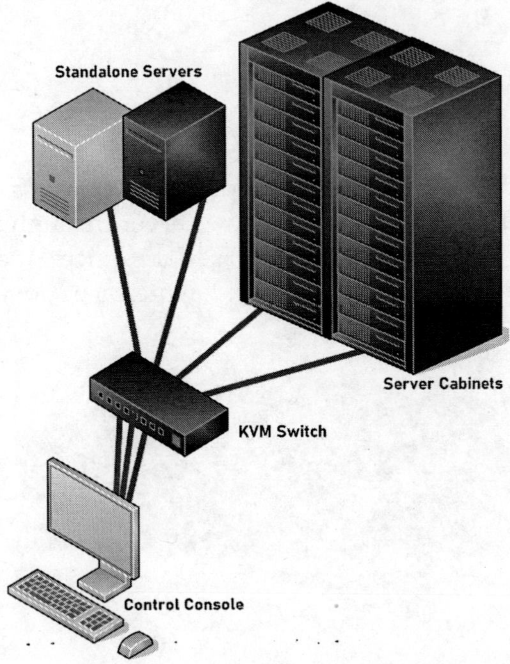

***Figure 3.2**: A KVM switch allows one control console to connect to multiple servers*

Crash cart

While a crash cart is associated primarily with life-threatening medical emergencies, its basic need applies to server room and data center emergencies. A medical crash cart contains all the equipment and medications needed to treat a patient in the first 30 minutes of an emergency. Likewise, the primary purpose of a data center or server room crash cart is to allow an administrator to deal with system or hardware emergencies.

A crash cart and its equipment provide a secured and reliable workstation that an administrator can use to install and configure servers, internetworking equipment, hardware, and software. Administrators can directly connect with the problem devices in a rack or cabinet using the crash cart. At a minimum, it includes a secured laptop computer, a KVM unit, an external hard disk, backup drives and media, and a workspace for opening manuals and reference materials. The cart should be mobile and ergonomic so that the administrator can sit or stand while using their equipment.

Virtual administration console

Virtualized systems, especially servers in a virtual environment, can be administered and maintained through a virtual administration console. These tools include the **VMware Remote Console (VMRC)**, the RedHat OpenShift Container Platform, and the **Microsoft System Center Virtual Machine Manager (VMM)**. Using these tools, an administrator can create, stop, start, restart, delete, and configure virtual machines and servers through a console display or web browser.

Serial connectivity

At one time, keyboards and mouse units connect to a computer through a serial connection. This is no longer true, as these devices are now primarily wireless or connected through a KVM unit. However, serial links can be made to a server through a serial device server if needed or desired. It provides a bridge between serial services, including RS-232 and RS-422, and TCP/IP communication and provides data interface conversion. *Figure 3.3* shows an example of a 4-port serial device server:

Figure 3.3: A serial device server [1]

1. Image courtesy: Digi International Inc.

Console connections

Another serial communication application is a console server, which provides a link over which a remote administrator can access any device (that has an IP address) in a server room or data center through a server console. It is connected to a local network like any other device, and its serial ports are connected to a serial console port on a server, and then it is connected to the local network. Each port on the console server is assigned an IP address and an SSH or Telnet session address, or any IP address to connect to a remote device via the serial connection. The administrator connects to the console server through a TCP/IP connection remotely or at some point other than in the server room.

Drive maintenance

The reliability of the data storage drives is essential to the availability and security of a network. Whether the drives are directly connected to a server or standalone systems on a network (NAS or SAN), the drives must be maintained to be operational and error-free. Maintaining hard disk drives is simple, and little physical work is involved. Most of the maintenance activities for disk drives are things that should not be done, such as:

- **Secure installation**: Consider using anti-vibration mounting to minimize motion and sudden stops (such as dropping the drive or its computer) to avoid the possibility of the read/write heads contacting the disk's platters.
- **Minimize motion**: Never move or shake a disk drive (or its computer) while powered on. Turn it off if you need to move it.
- **Do not obstruct the air hole**: Encased hard disk drives have an air hole that equalizes the air pressure inside the disk to that outside the disk. Covering up this hole, even inadvertently, can impact the function of the read/write heads. *Figure 3.4* shows an example of the air hole on a hard disk drive:

***Figure 3.4**: The air hold on a hard disk drive should never be covered*

There are also a few things that should be done, including:

- **Trusted sources**: Application software installed on a server's or network's storage drives should always be from a trusted source.

- **Apply patches and updates**: Update the operating system after you receive a notification of a patch or update. The problem or issue being fixed could affect the disk drives.
- **Uninstall unused applications**: If an application is no longer used, it should be removed to free up disk space.
- **Defragmentation**: Running defragmentation on active storage devices can help an HDD operate more efficiently. There is no benefit for defragmentation on an SSD drive. *Figure 3.5* shows the Windows **Optimize Drives** app used to defragment drives:

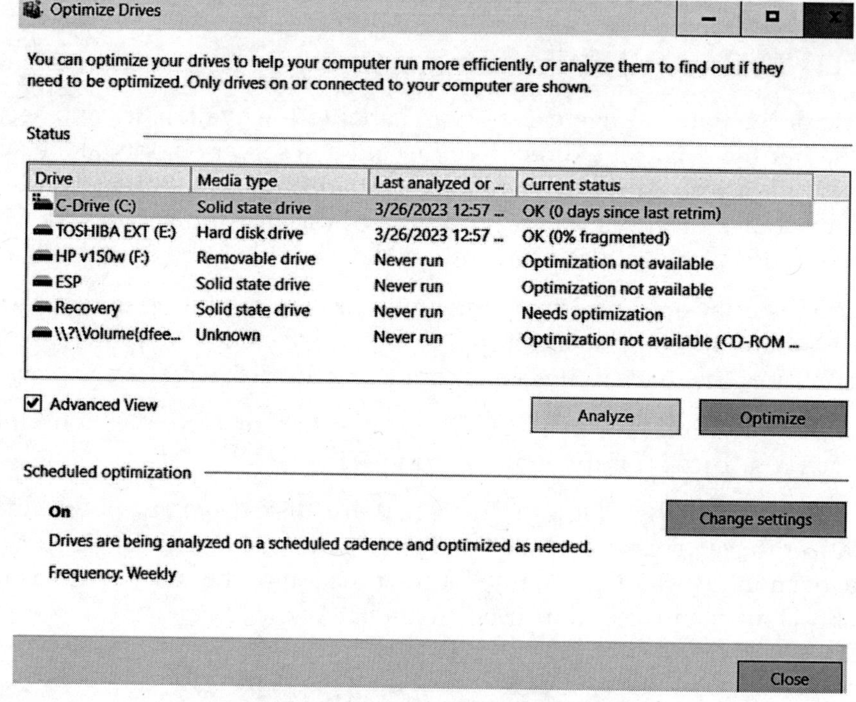

***Figure 3.5**: The Windows 11 optimize drives app*

- **Clean the drive**: The exterior of a hard disk drive should be cleaned regularly to remove dust and debris that could impair its airflow.
- **Minimize start-ups**: Powering up and down can be hard on a disk drive and should be done as little as possible. It is better to put the computer into sleep or hibernate mode when it sits idle for extended periods.
- **Protect against power surges**: A surge protector or a UPS protects a computer system, especially its power supply and hard disk drives.

Hot-swappable hardware

A **High Availability (HA)** strategy should address server availability and failed component replacement. On the Server+ exam, expect questions on component replacement, especially the difference between hot-swappable and non-hot-swappable devices.

The terms hot-pluggable and hot-swappable are commonly used interchangeably. Hot-pluggable devices connect to a system through Plug and Play and usually require an additional step to complete their installation. A hot-swappable device installs on a running system and is immediately usable. A non-hot swappable device, also called a cold-swappable device, is its replacement and requires the system to be powered down before it can be inserted or removed.

Hot-swappable devices

Some examples of hot-swappable devices are:

- **Audio devices**: Most audio devices and the ports they connect are hot-swappable, including speakers, microphones, headsets, and more.
- **USB devices**: All USB ports and devices are hot-swappable, along with Firewire and Thunderbolt ports and devices.
- **Displays: Video Graphics Array** (**VGA**), **Super Video Graphics Array** (**SVGA**), **Extended Graphics Array** (**XGA**), and **High-Definition Multimedia Interface** (**HDMI**) ports and devices are hot-swappable.
- **Network adapters**: RJ-45 connections can be made at any time.
- **Hard disk drives**: All SATA, SAS, NVMe, HDD, and SSD drives are hot-swappable. However, it is the best practice to shut down the disk drive before swapping it out.
- **Cages, backplanes, and racks**: Many RAID disk drives are installed in a backplane module that is designed to allow individual disk drives to be easily hot-swapped. Some cages also include a RAID controller, and most also include cooling. *Figure 3.6* shows an example of a SATA RAID hot-swap rack.

Figure 3.6: *A SATA RAID hot-swaps rack* [2]

2. Image courtesy: KWI Technology Inc.

Cold-swappable devices

Cold-swappable devices include:

- **Power supply unit (PSU)**: It may be obvious, but a PSU should never be worked on, removed, or installed while a computer runs. There is a risk of electric shock, and the sudden power interruption may damage other components.
- **Cooling fans**: Any cooling fans inside a computer case, including those in PSUs, should not be removed or installed. At the same time, the system is powered on to avoid damage to the fan and, depending on the amount of time involved, heat damage to other components.
- **Internally installed devices**: While a particular device may be hot-swappable if it is installed inside the system case, the computer should be powered down before it can be safely installed or removed.
- **Expansion cards**: Any device controller, sound, video, and other cards should not be removed or inserted while a computer runs.
- **IDE interface devices**: Hard disk drives, CD-ROM, DVD, and other internal devices connected with an **Integrated Drive Electronics (IDE)** interface are not hot-swappable.
- **Serial and parallel interfaces**: Serial and parallel ports and devices should not be disconnected while a computer runs.

Firmware upgrades

Security upgrades should not be the only reason to upgrade a server's firmware. The same goes for operating system patches, fixes, and upgrades. Firmware upgrades and updates can add capabilities to a system, such as support for new technology on an older system. However, some firmware updates may not be needed or may not apply to every server or network and, if possible, should be tested in a non-production environment. A firmware update that fixes one problem could introduce other bugs or issues.

When building up a system to host one or more servers, all applicable firmware should be updated to the latest versions for no reason other than to establish a baseline. Consider updating the firmware when the applicable manufacturer releases an update. The process for updating firmware can vary with the device and the manufacturer, so verify the process through the manufacturer's website before applying the update each time.

BIOS/UEFI maintenance

The **Basic Input/Output System (BIOS)** and the **Unified Extensible Firmware Interface (UEFI)** are firmware-level utilities that provide configuration support when a computer boots up. BIOS is on its way out, and UEFI is its replacement. Which, if not both, is used as a function of the chipset version on the computer.

BIOS and UEFI are updated somewhat irregularly, but when an update is issued, in either case, the update is applied through a process called flashing. It is the process of installing or updating the firmware of a device stored in its flash memory. The processes used to update BIOS and UEFI are slightly different.

Flashing BIOS

Not all BIOS versions are updateable; check with the CPU manufacturer to ensure the version in use can be updated. A BIOS update has two primary files: a text file detailing the upgrades or fixes and an executable file (**`.exe`**) that performs the BIOS update. The **`.exe`** file cannot be executed but must be flashed. The process for flashing the BIOS should be outlined in the update's text file or can be accessed on the manufacturer's website.

Flashing UEFI

Updating a UEFI BIOS is simpler but involves a few more steps. The most common method for updating a UEFI BIOS has four stages:

1. Download the compressed update file from the manufacturer's website.
2. Uncompress the download file onto a USB drive.
3. Reboot the computer.
4. Access the UEFI menu during the **power-on self-test** (**POST**) process.

The method for accessing the UEFI BIOS and installing the update can vary with the manufacturer, so follow the instructions in the system's documentation or the manufacturer's website.

Some manufacturers provide a USB device with a motherboard that can be used to update the UEFI BIOS from Windows or utility software for downloading and installing the update to the USB drive. Some motherboards have a designated port and indicator LEDs for the update process.

Note: Regardless of which BIOS/UEFI is being updated, ensure that the electrical power to the computer is not interrupted during the update process. The computer will likely not be used if an interruption occurs during the update.

Conclusion

Server hardware maintenance keeps the components and peripheral devices of a server up to date, operating properly, and minimizes downtime and data loss. Regular server maintenance helps to avoid network issues, including complete or partial failure. Server maintenance includes properly setting the hardware configuration, monitoring a server's performance, and identifying potential security vulnerabilities, among others. Performing regular server maintenance helps to extend the service life of a server's hardware and to reduce server outages.

In the next chapter, we look at the operating systems that run on servers, their minimum hardware requirements, and the structures and formats of filesystems. The operating system running on server hardware is a vital part of every server.

Points to remember

- OOBM is server administration performed over a telecommunication link.
- The tools hardware administrators use to keep systems available are KVM, crash cart, virtual administration console, serial connectivity, and console connections.
- The maintenance activities for disk drives include secure installation, minimized motion, an unobstructed air hole,
- To keep a server secure, application software should be from a trusted source, update the OS, uninstall unused applications, run defragmentation, clean the drive, minimize start-ups, and protect against power surges.
- Hot-pluggable devices connect through Plug and Play. A hot-swappable device is installed and is immediately usable. Hot-swappable devices include audio devices, USB devices, display monitors, network adapters, data storage drives, rackmount cages and backplanes.
- Cold-swappable devices include PSUs, cooling fans, and internally installed devices.
- A firmware update that fixes one problem could introduce other bugs or issues.
- The **BIOS** and **UEFI** provide configuration support when a computer boots up.
- Flashing BIOS/UEFI varies with the manufacturer, following the documentation.

Part - 2
Server Administration

The individual generally responsible for server administration is, you guessed it, a *server administrator*. The duties of a server administrator vary with the size of the organization and its computing resources, but, for the most part, it includes implementation, monitoring, optimizing, troubleshooting, communicating, and working as a part of a team. The specific knowledge and skills a server administrator must possess are reviewed in the chapters in this part of the book.

The chapters included in Part 2 are:

- Chapter 4 - Server Operating Systems
- Chapter 5 - Network Infrastructure
- Chapter 6 - Server Configuration
- Chapter 7 - High Availability
- Chapter 8 - Server Virtualization
- Chapter 9 - Scripting
- Chapter 10 - Server Planning
- Chapter 11 - Licensing

CHAPTER 4
Server Operating Systems

Introduction

A computer network becomes an integral part of an organization's culture almost immediately after it is deployed. It is an essential work tool; an essential communication device and system; and without it, the pace of work slows down. One of the most critical parts of a computer network, if not the most important part, are the servers. The server hardware may be the most important part of a server.

This chapter reviews the administration, management, and preventive maintenance of local and remote server hardware processes and procedures that you need to know for the CompTIA Server+ exam.

Structure

The chapter covers the following topics:

- Minimum hardware requirements
- Operating system installations
    - Installation types
    - Partition and volume types
    - File system types

Objective

By the end of this chapter, you will be able to identify and describe the sub-objectives of the following Server+ examination objective: *Given a scenario, install server operating systems.*

Minimum hardware requirements

An **operating system (OS)** is a very important computer program. In fact, it is the most important software on virtually any computer. However, for an OS to completely function as it should, (over all its functions) it requires certain levels of hardware and operational functionality. To ensure an OS has the hardware baseline it needs, its developer provides a minimum hardware requirement for each OS version.

Windows Server 2022

The hardware requirements for Windows Server 2022 are as follows:

- **Processor**: 1.4 GHz x86-64 processor.
- **RAM**: A minimum of 2 **gigabytes (GB)** of RAM.
- **Storage**: A minimum of 32 GB HDD or SSD.
- **System firmware**: UEFI 2.3.1c system and Secure Boot capability.
- **Graphics**: A display with 1024 x 768 resolution.
- **Security**: Trusted Platform Module 2.0.
- **Network**: An IEEE 802.11 wireless adapter or a 1 Gbps Ethernet adapter.

Comparatively, the hardware requirements for a Windows Server 2022 system may seem to be somewhat less than those for a Windows 11 desktop. Remember that these are the minimum, and the hardware required is a function of what services and demands are on the server.

Windows 10/11

Microsoft sets the following minimum hardware requirements for the Windows 10/11 OS:

- **Processor**: An Intel Core i5 or Core i7 CPU or an AMD Ryzen 2000, or newer CPUs from either manufacturer that provides 1 **gigahertz (GHz)** or faster with two or more cores on a compatible 64-bit processor or **system on a chip (SoC)**.
- **RAM**: A minimum of 4 GB of RAM.
- **Storage**: A minimum of 64 GB HDD or SSD.

- **System firmware**: UEFI and Secure Boot capability.
- **Graphics card**: Must be compatible with DirectX 12 or later with a **Windows Display Driver Model (WDDM)** 2.0 device driver.
- **Security**: Trusted Platform Module 2.0.
- **Display**: A video display at least 9-inches diagonally with 8-bits per color channel and a minimum of 1280×720 resolution.
- **Internet**: Microsoft 11 requires an Internet connection for all its versions. A Microsoft account is required to configure the system.

Yes, these requirements are specific, but the OS would not run properly, even if it can be installed, on a computer that does not meet these minimums.

The Windows 11 requirements above are those for desktop systems and not necessarily those for a network server.

Linux distros

In contrast to the requirements for Windows 11 and Server 2022, the following are the recommended hardware requirements for a RedHat Linux distribution on a server:

- **Processor**: An Intel Core i5, AMD Ryzen 5, AMD-V, or newer with at least 4 cores.
- **RAM**: To properly run a Linux OS server and all its add-in software and utilities requires at least 16 GB of RAM, and more is better.
- **Storage**: A minimum of 250 GB HDD or SSD.
- **Graphics**: Minimum of 1280x1024 for text display and 1600x900 for graphical display.
- **Network**: Wire-connected **Gigabit Ethernet (GbE)**.

Some Linux distros have slightly different minimum hardware requirements with some requiring more resources and some less. In any case, be it a windows, windows server, or Linux OS, always check with the OS provider to ensure the hardware on which the OS is to be installed meets its recommended requirements.

Note: A Wi-Fi interface is not included in the official requirements and is especially not recommended for a server environment.

Hardware compatibility list

The minimum hardware requirements for any software, whether it is system software (operating system, device drivers, etc.) or application software, are listed in an associated **hardware compatibility list (HCL)**. An HCL specifies the internal and peripheral hardware and system software compatible with the system to be installed. It is commonly associated only with operating systems, but many system and application software packages also issue an HCL. *Figure 4.1* shows an HCL for VMware:

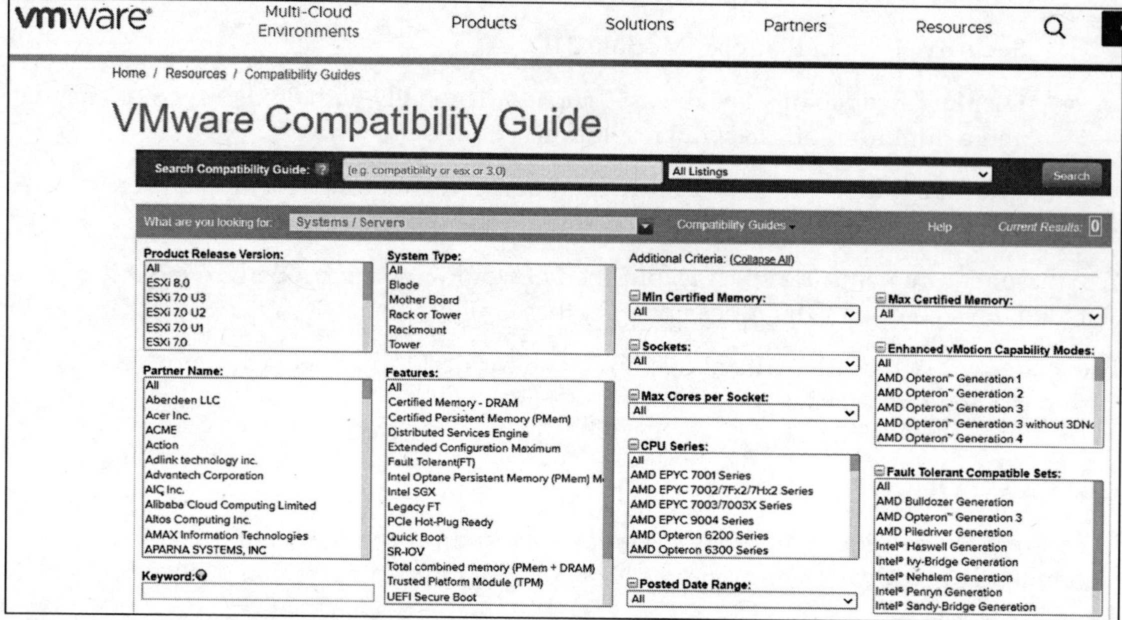

***Figure 4.1**: An example of the VMware Compatibility Guide*

An HCL provides guidance on what hardware and system components are required by the software to operate as it should. In some cases, the software will check for certain components or configurations it requires, and if they are not found, the software will abort its installation.

Operating system installations

In the sections that follow, the various installation or configuration processes involved with setting up a network or a networked server are discussed. The first few sections deal with the types of OS installations, which are then followed by the inclusion and configuration of OS features.

Installation types

The OS versions that include the **graphical user interface** (**GUI**) and other user-oriented software are the most commonly installed version, but typically only at an organization's data center or server room.

OS Core

Server OSs, like Windows Server 2022 and some Linux distros, have installation options for a smaller core system or a larger fully featured system. Often, the difference is whether user interface graphics and other features are included in the installation. A **server core** version has only the minimum of base or essential elements required for the OS to support the server roles. A server core option is installed primarily on remote servers that are managed remotely, eliminating the need for a GUI. Server management in enterprise environments through a **command line** interface (**CL**) is preferred as it is more efficient and faster.

Bare Metal

In the computing and networking worlds, the term **bare metal** has different meanings. It can refer to a computer that has no OS and runs functions from firmware. Or it can be a type of virtualized server installation. In the context of a server, it can be the server hardware before an OS is installed.

It is common for server hardware that is built to a buyer's specific configuration to be shipped without an operating system. The buyer organization boots the system from its firmware, installs the preferred OS, and configures the software for the task or role the server is to fill.

Virtualized

A virtualized server is one of many possible isolated software-based standalone servers running on a physical computer. Each **virtual server** can run a different OS and be configured uniquely. There are three basic types of virtualized servers:

- Full virtualization: On a fully virtualized server, a **hypervisor** services **virtual machine** (**VM**) requests for data and CPU services. The hypervisor interacts with the physical host computer's components as needed for the requested data or service. The hypervisor returns the response back to the requesting VM. A downside to a full virtualization is that the hypervisor requires resources from the physical computer as well.
- **Paravirtualization**: The OS running on a virtual machine is explicitly recompiled for the configuration of the VM. Like full virtualization, the VM (or guest) OS runs on the hypervisor, which is running on the host OS.
- **OS-level virtualization**: This type of virtualization runs on a host computer's OS virtualization features, which emulate the role of a hypervisor. The host system creates partitions (a.k.a. containers) in which each separate virtual machine runs. Each of the partitions must run on the host OS.

Note: ***Chapter 8, Virtualization*** **provides a detailed look at server virtualization.**

Remote Server Administration

The **Remote Server Administration tools** (**RSAT**) is a suite of administration and management tools that provide the capability for a server administrator to remotely manage a Windows Server OS. The administrator may access and work on a remote Windows Server system from a Windows 10 or Windows 11 workstation. The RSAT bundle includes the Server Manager, **Microsoft Management Console** (**MMC**) snap-ins, PowerShell cmdlets, and **command-line interface** (**CLI**) tools for the administration and management of server roles and features. *Figure 4.2* shows the Server Manager app included in the RSAT bundle:

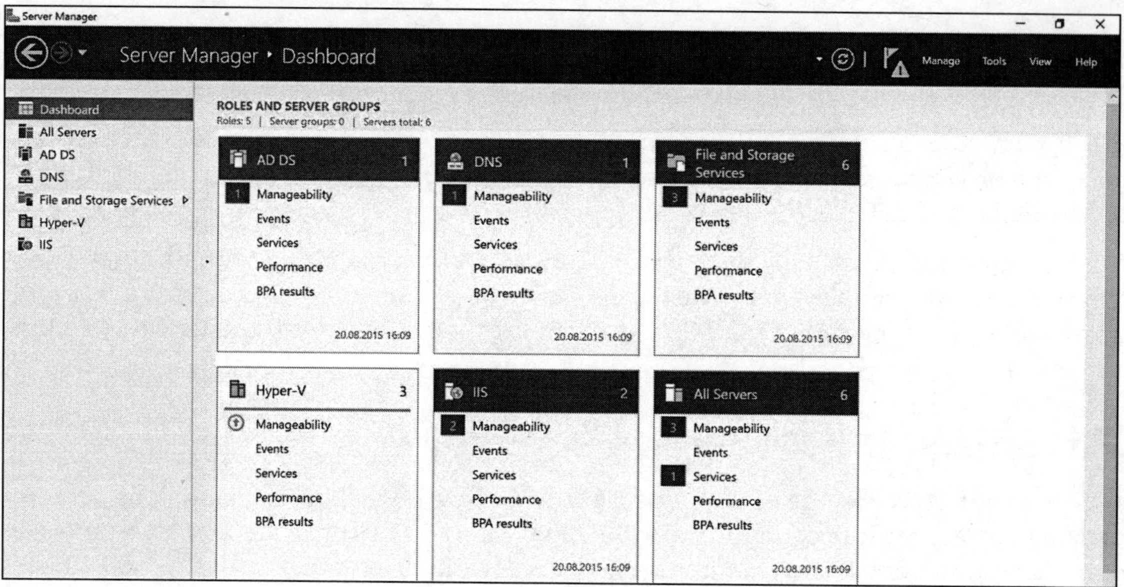

Figure 4.2: The RSAT Server Manager

On both windows and Linux systems, a remote server can be accessed and administered using one of three ways:

- **The Secure Shell (SSH) protocol**: Not only is SSH the easiest way to access and manage a remote system, it is also the fastest and the most secure. The PowerShell command used to connect to a remote server is:

```
ssh -v -l remote_username@remote_host
```

- **Remote desktop software**: There are a variety of third-party programs for viewing and managing remote systems. A few of the leading packages are VNC Connect, Remmina, and Vinagre. These, and several other options, provide good interfaces and functionality. Most are customizable and support multiple sessions simultaneously. Security and privacy vary, but there is a package to fit each situation. *Figure 4.3* shows an example of the Remmina open-source remote desktop app:

***Figure 4.3**: The Preference page of the Remmina remote desktop viewer*

- **TeamViewer**: TeamViewer is a proprietary remote administration package that provides an administrator with complete control of a remote server or desktop system that has the TeamViewer client installed. *Figure 4.4* shows the startup page of the TeamViewer app:

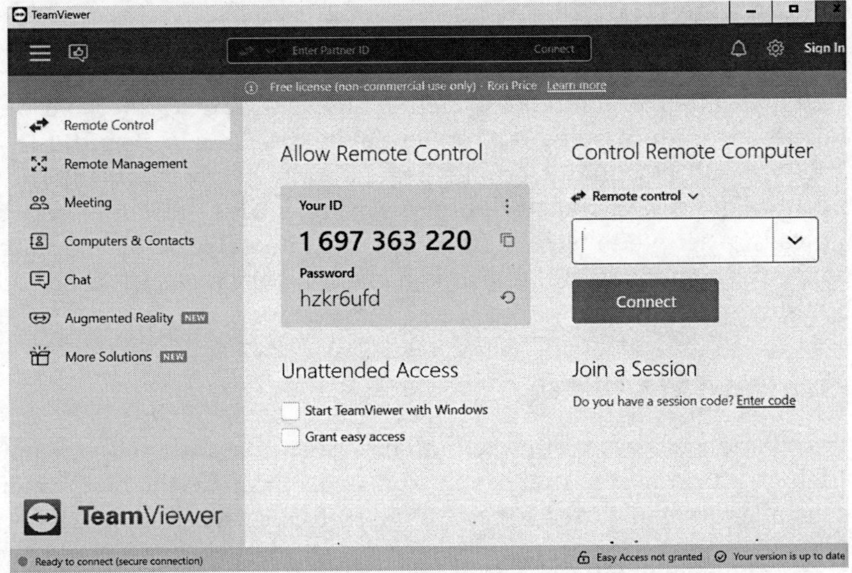

***Figure 4.4**: The startup page of the TeamViewer remote administration app*

Slipstreaming

In many cases, the installation medium or files for an OS is the original version licensed by an organization when it was released or initially purchased. Since the time when the install medium was obtained, there have likely been multiple updates, upgrades, fixes, and patches. So, when a new server system is configured, the OS is installed, and each of the sequential updates are applied. Depending on the release date of the OS and the number of updates, this entire process can be tedious and time-consuming.

One method used to make this process more efficient is called slipstreaming. **Slipstreaming** combines the downloaded update files with the installation files onto a new installation medium. The new installation medium, typically a CD or DVR disc, can then be used to initialize or re-install the OS and its updates in one operation. Slipstreaming can be a more efficient way to setup new systems, especially when there are several systems to be initialized or refreshed.

Unattended installations

This process, as its name suggests, is used to install software on a server or host without any intervention by an administrator. Many OS and utility packages include support for an unattended or silent installation. To perform an unattended installation, a distribution server or file server provides the installation files for the installed software. In many cases, the responses to any questions or options, such as clicking **Next** or **OK**, during the installation process are stored in a separate file and fed to the installation software when needed.

Scripted installations

Two additional methods for installing software on either a local or remote computer are, using a scripted installation or loading a system image (see *Imaging* later in the chapter). A scripted installation is performed by the sequential instructions in a script file. The setup files for most software are essentially scripted installations. A **scripted installation**, because it is a script, can be specific to the location of a system, such as different departments or functions. Typically, a scripted installation runs from a bootable setup medium or a **pre-boot execution environment** (PXE), which is a client-server interface used to book host systems from a server.

Installation media types

Whether an installation process is attended, unattended, scripted or slipstreamed, the OS or software files are introduced to the system from an external (to the new system) source. The primary installation media used for installing software on a system are:

- **Network**: An installation file stored on a network can be used to install software, system, or application, to a network-connected host or server. For Windows 10 or earlier systems, the installation process is managed through the **Windows Deployment Services (WDS)**. Windows 11 introduced The **Windows Assessment and Deployment Kit (Windows ADK)** for installation.

- **Optical media**: Optical media, which includes CDs, DVDs, and Blu-Ray discs, can contain scripted installation files, network installation boot files, or, most commonly, disk images of an entire system. Disk images stored on optical media are commonly in one of the following file formats:
    - **International Standards Organization (`.ISO`)**: This is perhaps the most common of the disk image file formats. ISO is a standard defined in ISO 9660.
    - **`.IMG`**: This file type contains raw disk image files.
    - **`.BIN` and `.CUE`**: These two file formats contain a binary data image of a system and a cue sheet file that details the structure of the binary data.
    - **Media Disk Image File (`.MDF`)** and **Media Descriptor File (`.MDS`)**: These optical disk file formats contain the image (MDF) and the header and track information (MDS).
- **USB**: A USB installation disk has been created through the utilities of an OS or through third-party software. A USB drive can be a copy of a software package's proprietary installation medium or contain a disk image.
- **Embedded**: An embedded system is a computer system, but one with a specified, limited, or dedicated purpose. It exists within a larger system and, to function as a software installation source, is one of two types:
    - **Standalone embedded system**: This type of embedded system is independent, even within another system. A standalone system can initiate an action, such as a software installation, and produce outputs without assistance from another system.
    - **Network embedded system**: This type of embedded system must communicate with a web or network server to operate.

Imaging

An image file is essentially a snapshot or backup of a base or standard system that can be copied to other systems to provide uniform configurations. An image file that is to be used for initializing new systems typically contains the OS, applications, system utilities, system states and configurations, and the data associated with each.

Cloning

Cloning copies the contents of one HDD to another and creates a duplicate of the drive. The clone then provides a fallback should the source drive be corrupted or fail. A major problem with cloning is that any additions, deletions, or updates to the original drive will not be reflected in the clone.

A clone can be made by a direct transfer from one drive to another in a system with two HDDs. Or a single internal HDD can be cloned to an external HDD SATA drive that can be installed into a computer when needed.

Physical-to-Virtual clone

Although copying one HDD to another creates a physical clone of the source drive, a physical computer system can also be cloned to a virtual machine by a **physical-to-virtual (P2V)** conversion utility. Software tools like VMware vCenter Converter and Paragon Go Virtual, convert physical systems into virtual machines. Drive imaging software, such as Symantec Ghost or Acronis True Image, will image a physical HDD to an empty VM virtual HDD.

Virtual Machine (VM) cloning

A VM can be backed up by taking a snapshot. A snapshot captures the memory, the state of the VM, and its power settings. However, a snapshot is not a clone. A VM clone can be used to create a new VM that matches the source VM at the point the clone was created.

Instant cloning is very convenient for large-scale application deployments because it ensures memory efficiency and allows for creating numerous virtual machines on a single host. VMware's Instant Clone and Azure's VM Image Capture, make an image copy of a VM and customize the image to assign unique MAC and IP addresses to setup a destination VM on a virtual network.

Software deployment templates

Software deployment templates are scripts that help to ensure that software bundles and updates are installed properly and completely. The template packages programs, setup processes, and silent switches and parameters together, especially when software from multiple sources are being installed. It is common that software requires some support services to be installed and configured correctly. A deployment template creates an installation wizard that eliminates the possibility of installation errors or missing support. The automation of software deployment facilitates the installation of software to multiple systems that runs unattended.

Partition and volume types

The method used to prepare an HDD for an OS installation depends on the system configuration firmware and the boot process of the hardware. BIOS creates a **master boot record** (**MBR**) and UEFI creates a **Globally Unique Identifier** (**GUID**) partition table, also known as a **Universally Unique Identifier** (**UUID**). GUIDs/UUIDs are 128-bit hexadecimal ID numbers that are almost guaranteed to be unique in the universe.

As would seem logical, MBR creates BIOS partition tables and GPT creates UEFI partition tables. Both MBRs and GPTs use a relative addressing scheme of **logical block addressing** (**LBA**) rather than the physical **cylinder-head-sector** (**CHS**) addressing of an HDD.

Note: Understand that MBR and GPT apply to hard disk drives only and not to solid-state drives.

Master boot record

Master boot record (**MBR**) is located in the first sector of a hard disk volume. The MBR includes the number and sizes of the partitions on the volume and which partition contains the boot data. The MBR is created when a drive is formatted and partitioned. However, the MBR is not in a partition, but at the very beginning of the storage space in Head 0/ Cylinder 0/Sector 1.

The MBR contains the data needed by the OS to boot up a computer:

- **Master partition table** (**MPT**): Contains information on the types and sizes of the HDD's partitions. The MPT is limited to 64 bytes and since each partition entry in the MPT is 16 bytes in length, only four physical partitions can be defined on the drive. However, the physical partitions can be divided into logical partitions.
- **Disk signature**: This is a unique ID number assigned to the HDD that is used by the OS to identify the storage devices on a system.
- **Master boot code** (**MBC**): The first set of instructions for booting the system. The MBC typically takes up over 80% of the 512-byte MBR.

The largest HDD that can be specified in a BIOS MBR is 2 **terabytes** (**TB**). If the HDD's storage capacity is larger than 2TB, only the first 2TB of the drive will be accessible.

GUID partition

In contrast to the BIOS MBR, a UEFI GUID partition table (GPT) is not limited to four HDD partitions and can address 4 TB or larger HDDs. A GPT partitioned disk can have up to 2^{64} – 512-byte sectors, which is about nine **zettabytes** (**ZB**) (1 ZB is equal to 1,000,000,000,000 GB) in 128 physical partitions.

A GPT partition table is made up of the following elements:

- **Primary partition table**: The first sector of a GPT contains three parts:
    - **Protective MBR**: The first sector of a GPT disk is structured like an MBR disk. This is to keep BIOS utilities from corrupting the GPT partitions. The protective MBR is stored at LBA 0.
    - **GPT header**: The GPT header contains a hexadecimal "signature" that identifies the disk as a GPT disk and that this is the GPT partition table. The GPT header is in LBA 1.

- **Partition table**: This element contains the location addressing for the partitions on the disk.

- **Data partitions**: These are the physical locations on the disk that contain files and data.
- **Backup partition table**: A backup of the GPT header and partition table is kept to protect against the loss or corruption of the primary partition table.

Dynamic disk

A dynamic disk is an HDD configuration in windows systems that is formatted in volumes rather than partitions. A dynamic disk uses the **Logical Disk Manager** (**LDM**) to manage volumes. The LDM, is located at the end of a dynamic disk and stores the information relating to each volume in the dynamic disk, including the volume's drive letter, label, size, and file system. Dynamic disks can contain multiple volumes, each of which is assigned a unique drive letter. Theoretically, a dynamic disk can hold up to 2,000 volumes, but limiting them to 32 volumes is recommended. Dynamic disk can be formatted with the **File Allocation Table** (**FAT**), **FAT 32-bit** (**FAT32**), or the **New Technology File System** (**NTFS**).

A dynamic disk can contain five different volume types:

- **Simple volume**: This is essentially the same as a standard basic volume.
- **Spanned volume**: This type of volume can be made up of merged areas of unallocated spaces on multiple dynamic disks.
- **Striped volume**: This type of volume should not be confused with RAID 0 striping. A dynamic disk striped volume can be made up from free space on different dynamic disks but does not provide fault tolerance.
- **Mirrored volume**: This is a copy of another dynamic disk volume.
- **RAID-5 volume**: This type of dynamic disk volume is striped to three or more dynamic disks to provide fault tolerance and improved disk performance.

Logical volume management

Logical volume management (**LVM**) is a data storage management method for Linux systems. Like the windows dynamic disk system, LVM creates logical volumes that can be mounted and used in a file system in place of partitions. However, there is one exception to their use: an LVM volume cannot be used for the boot files or the `/boot` directory.

An LVM disk can have three components:

- **Physical volumes**: These are the primary logical units of LVM. A physical volume can be an entire HDD or a disk partition.

- **Volume groups**: A collection of physical volumes is a volume group, which can combine the disk space of multiple HDDs.
- **Logical volumes**: A logical volume is similar to a disk partition and is contained within a volume group.

Note: the Linux utilities for creating, managing, and removing the three components of an LVM are easily identified. The utilities for physical volumes begin with the letters "pv," as in *pvcreate, pvchange,* and *pvdisplay.* This same pattern holds true for volume groups (vgcreate, vgs, vgrename, etc.) and logical volumes (lvcreate, lvs, lvreduce, etc.).

File system types

While there are many different file systems defined for each of the major operating systems, the Server+ exam objectives name only the ext4, NTFS, VMFS, ReFS, and the ZFS. Each of these file systems is unique in their application and functions. But, they generally cover the general structure and operations of the file systems found on modern systems, especially those on a server or networked storage unit.

However, before looking at each of these file systems more deeply, we should set a baseline on just what a file system is.

File systems

In general, a file system has four primary functions or components:

- **Application programming interface (API)**: In the context of a file system, an API is a utility program that interfaces with and passes requests made to a file system. Windows provides APIs for NTFS and the FAT file systems. Linux distros commonly include APIs for ext2, ext3, ext4, and others.
- **Data storage**: This is the primary task of any file system. A file system provides a structured environment for the storing and retrieving data from a storage device.
- **Namespace**: While some file systems have stricter rules than others for naming files and directories, a file system defines the structure, length, and format of file and directory names.
- **Security**: A file system defines a scheme for access and authorization for its files and directories.

ext4

The extended file system – four (ext4) is a Linux-based file system that was the successor to the ext, ext2, and ext3 file systems. The ext4 file system has a maximum file size of 16 TB and supports volume sizes of up to 1 exabyte (one million GB). The ext4 file system is a journaling file system that uses inodes and extents for file and directory identification and addressing. Let us look at each of these concepts.

Journaling

A journaling file system keeps a log (journal) of file and directory changes (adds, rewrites, deletions, etc.) that were made but not yet committed to the file system. In other words, journaling keeps track of pending actions to the file system. If the system crashes, there is a power failure, or some other type of catastrophe, a journaling file system, like ext4, is less likely to be corrupted.

Inode

As far as anyone knows, Inode is the short form of Index Node, which is a Linux data structure that stores information about a file. A "file" can be a directory or a data file. Each file is referenced with an inode number and the file's name. The inode number is used to retrieve the metadata from the inode table.

An inode contains metadata for each file in a directory. The metadata includes the size, owner, location, access permissions of the file, and the location of the file in the partition. The metadata does not include the file name or its data. An inode references one file and every file has an inode. *Figure 4.5* shows the results of a *stats* command on a file that shows the contents of an inode:

```
rgilster_su $ ls -i    Display the inode of each file in the current directory
83691 test.txt
rgilster_su $ stat test.txt    Display the stats for test.txt file
  File: test.txt
  Size: 1048576         Blocks: 192          IO Block: 4096   regular file
Device: 820h/2080d      Inode: 83691         Links: 1
Access: (0666/-rw-rw-rw-)  Uid: (    0/    root)   Gid: (    0/    root)
Access: 2023-03-31 22:21:48.441524700 -0500
Modify: 2023-03-31 22:13:58.421524700 -0500
Change: 2023-03-31 22:21:08.771524700 -0500
 Birth: 2023-03-31 22:08:48.981524700 -0500
```

Figure 4.5: The information stored in a Linux system inode

Extents

On a physical storage medium, such as an HDD, the available storage space is divided into fixed-sized units or extents. An extent is the smallest amount of storage space that can be allocated to a file. A physical volume has physical extents, and a logical volume has logical extents that are the same size as the physical extents, which by default is 4 MB. Files stored on a disk, for example, use one or more extents.

Extents reduce the amount of data stored in a file's metadata. Instead of recording the number of every disk block in a file, two numbers representing the first and last blocks (extent) in the file requires much less space in the metadata.

NTFS

The **New Technology File System (NTFS)** is a file system through which a Windows OS stores, organizes, and retrieves files from an HDD. NTFS provides the following characteristics and attributes:

- **Journaling**: NTFS keeps an audit log of files added, modified, or deleted from the file system in the **Master File Table (MFT)**.
- **Access control**: NTFS support access and use rights and permissions on folders and files that restrict what can be done with a file or folder and who can access, manipulate, or remove it.
- **Recoverability**: Since NTFS uses transaction logging and recovery processes, it is able to restore itself using the information in the MFT.
- **Compression**: NTFS supports file compression and encryption which increases both the storage space available and its integrity.
- **Disk quotas**: NTFS supports the application of disk quotas that control how much data (and therefore how much disk space) a user use in an NTFS file system volume.

Virtual Machine File System

Also known as the VMware File System, the **Virtual Machine File System (VMFS)** is a cluster file system that runs on virtual machines for storing files on **virtual machine disks (VMDKs)**. VMFS is proprietary to VMware systems that also functions as a volume manager and stores the files from multiple VMs in datastores or logical containers. The VMFS datastores hide the physical storage devices from the VMs and a datastore can store multiple VMs. The files of each VM is encapsulated in a separate directory. VMFS allows multiple VMs to concurrently read and write to the same shared storage resources.

VMFS containers, with either GPT or MBR, can be created on directly connected SCSI and SAS disk drives. They can also be generated on block storage devices accessed by iSCSI and Fibre Channel. VMFS volumes can be up to 64 TB and a VMDK file can be as large as 2 TB.

Resilient File System

The **Resilient File System (ReFS)** is a fault-tolerant storage technology that maximizes data availability, scalability, and data integrity. ReFS has been a part of the **Storage Spaces** feature in windows since Windows 8 and is included in Windows 10 and Windows 11, as well as the Windows Server versions beginning with Windows Server 2016.

ReFS supports a mind-boggling amount of storage space with a maximum volume size of 1 yobibyte (YiB – 2^{80} bytes or 1,208,925,819,614,629,174,706,176 bytes) and a maximum file size of 16 exbibytes (EiB – 2^{60} bytes or 1,152,921,504,606,846,976 bytes.) ReFS stores checksums and metadata for maintaining data integrity on each partition. During read/write operations, corrupted files are detected immediately.

Storage Spaces

Storage Spaces is a Windows system feature that allows for two or more physical disk drives to be combined into a storage pool. ReFS works with the Storage Spaces service to prevent file corruption. A storage pool can be used to create three types of spaces:

- **Simple spaces**: A simple space provides the largest amount of space, but that space is unprotected against drive failures or corruption. Only a single copy of a file is stored in the space and if one of the physical drives fail, the data could be lost or corrupted. A simple space is best used only for temporary data stores.
- **Mirror spaces**: Similar to the methods of a RAID 1 system, a mirror space stores multiple copies of a file to protect the data against a disk drive failure.
- **Parity spaces**: A parity space stores a single copy of a file along with parity data that can be used to reconstruct the file should there be a hardware failure. However, parity spaces are slower than either simple or mirror spaces. This type of space is best suited for archives or data that is not frequently in use.

Z File system

The **Z file system (ZFS)** is an open-source LVM for Linux systems. ZFS is a 128-bit file system that can manage several ZB of data (the source of the "Z" in its name). All ZFS file functions use checksums to maintain file integrity and makes data repairs on files when corruption is suspected. ZFS is highly scalable. When more disk space is required, an additional hard disk can be added. No formatting, partitioning, or prepping is required.

ZFS is commonly used on larger servers because of its capabilities to preserve data integrity and prevent data corruption. ZFS is considered to be the best filesystem for storage enterprise solutions. A minimum of 2 GB of free memory is required to run ZFS, but 8 GB is recommended.

ZFS supports a variation of RAID called RAIDZ, which defines variations of the standard RAID schemes as RAIDZ (RAID5), RAIDZ2 (RAID6), RAIDZ3 (triple parity), and Stripe+Mirror (RAID 10).

Conclusion

In this chapter, we reviewed the services and functions of a server operating system. The major areas we reviewed were the minimum hardware requirements and compatibilities, and the various types of OS installations. We also looked at data storage methods supported by Windows and Linux and the file systems each supports.

In the next chapter, we will look at the configuration and components of network infrastructures.

Points to remember

- Developers set minimum hardware requirements for their OSs that can specify the processor, RAM, storage, firmware, graphics card, display, and networking.
- An HCL specifies the internal and peripheral hardware and system software compatible with the system to be installed.
- A server OS core has only the minimum of base or essential elements required for the OS to support the server roles.
- There are three basic types of virtualized servers: full virtualization, paravirtualization, and OS-level virtualization.
- RSAT provides a server administrator with the ability to remotely manage a Windows Server OS. The RSAT bundle includes MMC snap-ins, PowerShell cmdlets, and **command-line interface** (**CLI**) tools.
- A remote server can be accessed three ways: SSH, remote desktop software, and TeamViewer.
- Slipstreaming combines update files with installation files to an installation medium.
- Scripted installations are performed by the sequential instructions in a script file.
- The primary installation media for installing software are network, optical media, .ISO files, and USB,
- Cloning copies the contents of one HDD to another and creates a duplicate of the drive.
- Software deployment templates are scripts that help to ensure that software bundles and updates are installed properly and completely.
- MBR is located in the first sector of a hard disk volume.
- GPT can address 4 TB or larger HDDs.
- A dynamic disk is formatted in volumes rather than partitions.
- LVM is a data storage management method for Linux systems.
- A file system has four components: API, data storage, namespace, and security.
- ext4 is a Linux-based file system.
- A journaling file system keeps a log of file and directory changes that are made but not yet committed to the file system.

- NTFS is a Windows file system that stores, organizes, and retrieves files from an HDD. NTFS supports journaling, access control, recoverability, compression, and disk quotas.
- VMFS is a cluster file system that runs on virtual machines for storing files on VMDKs.
- ReFS maximizes data availability, scalability, and data integrity.
- Storage Spaces allows for two or more physical disk drives to be combined into a storage pool.
- ZFS is an open-source LVM for Linux systems.

CHAPTER 5
Network Infrastructure Services

Introduction

Almost immediately after it is deployed, a computer network becomes an integral part of an organization's culture. It is an essential work tool; an essential communication device and system; and without it, the pace of work slows down. The servers are one of the most critical parts of a computer network, if not the most important. What may be the most important part of a server is the server hardware.

This chapter reviews the administration, management, and preventive maintenance of local and remote server hardware processes and procedures that you need to know for the CompTIA Server+ exam.

Structure

This chapter covers the following topics:

- IP configuration
- Virtual local area networks
- Default gateways
- Addressing protocols
- Firewalls

Objective

By the end of this chapter, you will be able to identify and describe the sub-objectives of the Server+ examination objective: *Given a scenario, configure servers to use network infrastructure services.*

IP configuration

Virtually no two servers and the networks they serve are configured the same. How a network is configured when it is installed is very likely to be different from how the same network is configured some time later. It is imperative that a server or network administrator can display the current configuration of a network and, especially, be able to understand and interpret the information displayed.

The configuration of a network, including its server, hosts, networking, security, and internetworking devices, is much more than whether these devices are plugged in and turned on (but that's a good start). The configuration of any network connected device includes, but is not limited to, the following elements and settings:

- Device name
- Network adapter/NIC information
- Description
- Physical address (MAC)
- Configuration protocol settings
- IP addressing
- DHCP configuration and lease information
- Gateway address
- DNS server address

This information can be displayed using the IP configuration command **ipconfig** (Windows) or **ip** (Linux), which replaced the now deprecated **ifconfig** command. Examples of each of these commands are shown in *Figure 5.1*:

Windows: *ipconfig /all*

```
Wireless LAN adapter Wi-Fi:

   Connection-specific DNS Suffix  . :
   Description . . . . . . . . . . . : Intel(R) Wi-Fi 6 AX201 160MHz
   Physical Address. . . . . . . . . : 44-AF-28-B3-D4-09
   DHCP Enabled. . . . . . . . . . . : Yes
   Autoconfiguration Enabled . . . . : Yes
   Link-local IPv6 Address . . . . . : fe80::d0ad:4520:902c:3553%5(Preferred)
   IPv4 Address. . . . . . . . . . . : 192.168.0.79(Preferred)
   Subnet Mask . . . . . . . . . . . : 255.255.255.0
   Lease Obtained. . . . . . . . . . : Friday, March 31, 2023 12:26:34 PM
   Lease Expires . . . . . . . . . . : Sunday, April 2, 2023 9:30:09 AM
   Default Gateway . . . . . . . . . : 192.168.0.1
   DHCP Server . . . . . . . . . . . : 192.168.0.1
   DHCPv6 IAID . . . . . . . . . . . : 71610152
   DHCPv6 Client DUID. . . . . . . . : 00-01-00-01-29-A4-43-35-44-AF-28-B3-D4-09
   DNS Servers . . . . . . . . . . . : 208.67.222.222
                                       208.67.220.220
   NetBIOS over Tcpip. . . . . . . . : Enabled
```

Linux: *ip a*

```
1: lo: <LOOPBACK,UP,LOWER_UP> mtu 65536 qdisc noqueue state UNKNOWN group default qlen 1000
    link/loopback 00:00:00:00:00:00 brd 00:00:00:00:00:00
    inet 127.0.0.1/8 scope host lo
       valid_lft forever preferred_lft forever
    inet6 ::1/128 scope host
       valid_lft forever preferred_lft forever
2: bond0: <BROADCAST,MULTICAST,MASTER> mtu 1500 qdisc noop state DOWN group default qlen 1000
    link/ether 4e:47:1e:f7:8f:ef brd ff:ff:ff:ff:ff:ff
3: dummy0: <BROADCAST,NOARP> mtu 1500 qdisc noop state DOWN group default qlen 1000
    link/ether 86:89:05:eb:f0:ca brd ff:ff:ff:ff:ff:ff
4: tunl0@NONE: <NOARP> mtu 1480 qdisc noop state DOWN group default qlen 1000
    link/ipip 0.0.0.0 brd 0.0.0.0
5: sit0@NONE: <NOARP> mtu 1480 qdisc noop state DOWN group default qlen 1000
    link/sit 0.0.0.0 brd 0.0.0.0
6: eth0: <BROADCAST,MULTICAST,UP,LOWER_UP> mtu 1500 qdisc mq state UP group default qlen 1000
    link/ether 00:15:5d:d6:54:a6 brd ff:ff:ff:ff:ff:ff
    inet 172.27.95.55/20 brd 172.27.95.255 scope global eth0
       valid_lft forever preferred_lft forever
    inet6 fe80::215:5dff:fed6:54a6/64 scope link
       valid_lft forever preferred_lft forever
```

***Figure 5.1**: The IP configuration displays the Windows ipconfig (top) and the Linux ip (bottom)*

The Windows ipconfig command

The ipconfig command is the primary tool for viewing, setting, or managing the IP configuration of any network-connected device. As shown in *Figure 5.1*, this command can display the configuration information for all interfaces, physical and virtual, on a system using the **`/all`** parameters. *Table 5.1* lists the ipconfig command parameters you should know for the Server+ exam, along with some included in the "DNS" section below:

Command	Use
`ipconfig`	Display the details of active interfaces.
`ipconfig -a`	Display the information for all network interfaces (active or inactive).

Command	Use
ipconfig Wi-Fi	View the settings of a specific interface.
ipconfig /release Wi-Fi	Discards the existing DHCP configuration for an interface.
ipconfig /renew Wi-Fi	Requests new DHCP configuration of an interface.

Table 5.1: *Basic ipconfig commands and parameters*

An administrator often uses the *ipconfig* command to troubleshoot various issues, primarily those involving the **Domain Name System** (**DNS**), **Dynamic Host Configuration Protocol** (**DHCP**), and possibly an IP address. Let us look at each of these areas.

DNS

DNS provides a very valuable service to users and site addressing. It works like any indexing system: it translates a name into an address. The site a user wants is the BigBlueButton.tv website (fictional), which should not be too hard to find. After all, it is a unique name on the Internet. Unfortunately, much like the postal service, computer networks need addresses, preferably numeric (binary). It is unreasonable to expect humans to remember the binary address of every website they wish to visit, which is where DNS comes in.

DNS takes in requests to translate text **fully qualified domain names (FQDNs)** and **uniform resource locators (URLs)**, like BigBlueButton.tv, and cross-references them to the registered IP address of each website. The IP address is returned to the requester to communicate with the site at that address. *Figure 5.2* shows one example of a DNS request in action:

```
PS C:\> ping bpbonline.com

Pinging bpbonline.com [23.227.38.65] with 32 bytes of data:
Reply from 23.227.38.65: bytes=32 time=48ms TTL=56
Reply from 23.227.38.65: bytes=32 time=42ms TTL=56
Reply from 23.227.38.65: bytes=32 time=43ms TTL=56
Reply from 23.227.38.65: bytes=32 time=44ms TTL=56

Ping statistics for 23.227.38.65:
    Packets: Sent = 4, Received = 4, Lost = 0 (0% loss),
Approximate round trip times in milli-seconds:
    Minimum = 42ms, Maximum = 48ms, Average = 44ms
```

Figure 5.2: *A ping command uses DNS to convert a URL to an address*

The **ping** command in *Figure 5.2* identified the target site with a URL (bpbonline.com). However, it needed an IP address, so it sent a request to the DNS site listed in the IP configuration to obtain the site's IP address. DNS returned the address 23.277.38.65, the address used in the packets sent out to the Internet.

In *Figure 5.1*, two DNS addresses are listed:

```
DNS Servers . . . . . . . . . . . : 208.67.222.222
                                    208.67.220.220
```

Should an administrator wish to change the DNS servers used by an organization, the changes are entered through the Network and Internet Settings app. However, there are ipconfig commands for other maintenance and troubleshooting actions, as shown in *Table 5.2*:

Parameter	Purpose/Action
`/flushdns`	Clears the DNS resolution cache. Used when the content of the DNS cache is corrupted to resolve problems, increase security and speed up Internet requests.
`/registerdns`	Renews all DHCP leases and DNS name registrations. Resolves dynamic update problems between a client and the DNS server. Used to renew the settings to resolve connection problems.
`/displaydns`	Displays the DNS resolution cache

***Table 5.2**: The DNS action parameters for the ipconfig command*

Hosts

When a URL is entered into a browser, it needs to convert the URL into an IP address. However, before it sends out a DNS request, it may first look in the Windows **hosts file** to see if a user has assigned a specific IP address to that domain. The hosts file is often used to block websites. If a website has an entry in the hosts file that directs to a non-existent IP address, such as 256.0.0.0, the browser displays that the website is unreachable. This same feature can also connect directly to a website for maintenance. *Figure 5.3* shows a standard hosts file on a Windows 11 system:

```
# Copyright (c) 1993-2009 Microsoft Corp.
#
# This is a sample HOSTS file used by Microsoft TCP/IP for Windows.
#
# This file contains the mappings of IP addresses to host names. Each
# entry should be kept on an individual line. The IP address should
# be placed in the first column followed by the corresponding host name.
# The IP address and the host name should be separated by at least one
# space.
#
# Additionally, comments (such as these) may be inserted on individual
# lines or following the machine name denoted by a '#' symbol.
#
# For example:
#
#      102.54.94.97     rhino.acme.com          # source server
#       38.25.63.10     x.acme.com              # x client host
# localhost name resolution is handled within DNS itself.
#    127.0.0.1       localhost
#    ::1             localhost
```

***Figure 5.3**: A sample of a Windows 11 hosts file*

DHCP

If a computer is not connected to a network, there is no need for it to have an IP configuration, including no DNS or DHCP. But, since virtually all of an organization's computers are connected to a network of some type, each time they boot up, they need to be configured to communicate on the network.

DHCP is a server function that services requests from client hosts to provide each with a unique IP address and other relevant information needed by the host to connect to a network. When a network host boots up, it transmits a DHCPDiscover request to the network since it does not know the address of the DHCP server at that time. When the DHCP server discovers the request, it offers an IP address to the host. If the host accepts the offer, it sends a DHCPRequest message to the server that responds either with an **acknowledgement** (ACK) and the configuration data or a **non-acknowledgement** (NAK) if, for some reason, it denies the host's request.

APIPA

Automatic Private IP Addressing (APIPA) is an OS feature that enables a network computer to automatically configure its IP address and related information when either the DHCP server is not reachable, or the server denies its configuration request. APIPA addresses are in the range of 169.254.0.1 to 169.254.255.254. Along with the APIPA address, the subnet mask is set to 255.255.0.0, and the default gateway address is set to 0.0.0.0. An APIPA address allows the host to communicate on a local network using either its MAC address or the APIPA address if other hosts on a local network are also configured with APIPA addresses.

The Linux ifconfig command

Older versions, and a few current versions, of Linux distros included the workalike of the Windows ipconfig command: **interface configuration** (**`ifconfig`**). Like its Windows counterpart, ifconfig operates with or without parameters. When the command is executed without parameters, the response (see *Figure 5.4*) includes only the enabled interfaces:

```
su_demo $ sudo ifconfig
eth0: flags=4163<UP,BROADCAST,RUNNING,MULTICAST>  mtu 1500
        inet 172.27.82.241  netmask 255.255.240.0  broadcast 172.27.95.255
        inet6 fe80::215:5dff:fed6:56e5  prefixlen 64  scopeid 0x20<link>
        ether 00:15:5d:d6:56:e5  txqueuelen 1000  (Ethernet)
        RX packets 192  bytes 274001 (267.5 KiB)
        RX errors 0  dropped 0  overruns 0  frame 0
        TX packets 42  bytes 3538 (3.4 KiB)
        TX errors 0  dropped 0 overruns 0  carrier 0  collisions 0

lo: flags=73<UP,LOOPBACK,RUNNING>  mtu 65536
        inet 127.0.0.1  netmask 255.0.0.0
        inet6 ::1  prefixlen 128  scopeid 0x10<host>
        loop  txqueuelen 1000  (Local Loopback)
        RX packets 0  bytes 0 (0.0 B)
        RX errors 0  dropped 0  overruns 0  frame 0
        TX packets 0  bytes 0 (0.0 B)
        TX errors 0  dropped 0 overruns 0  carrier 0  collisions 0
```

Figure 5.4: An example of the output from the ifconfig command in Linux

Its parameter set can be used to display or maintain the configuration and settings of an interface. The parameter set of the **ifconfig** command are listed and described in *Table 5.3*:

Command	Use
ifconfig	Display the details of all active interfaces or check the IP address assigned to a server
ifconfig -a	Display the information for all network interfaces (active or inactive).
ifconfig eth0	View the settings of a specific interface.
ifconfig eth0 up	Enable an interface (activate)
ifconfig eth0 down	Disable an interface (deactivate)
ifconfig eth0 192.168.0.125	Assign an IP address to an interface
ifconfig eth0 netmask 255.255.255.224	Assign a netmask to an interface
ifconfig eth0 broadcast 192.168.0.254	Assign a broadcast address to an interface
ifconfig eth0 mtu 1000	Change the **maximum transmission unit** (MTU) for an interface
ifconfig eth0 promisc	Enable promiscuous (accept all messages) mode on an interface
ifconfig eth0:0 192.168.0.127	Add an alias interface to an existing interface
ifconfig eth0 hw ether <MAC address>	Change the MAC address of an interface

***Table 5.3:** ifconfig commands and parameters*

One major difference between the ipconfig and the **ifconfig** commands (other than the operating system) is the configuration of DHCP. The **ifconfig** command can only assign a static IP address to an interface. Another Linux command, **dhclient,** is used to configure DHCP.

The Linux ip command

Some Linux distros continue to offer the Linux equivalent of the ipconfig command: **ifconfig**. However, many latest releases have deprecated that command in favor of the **ip** command. The **ip** command is very different from the ifconfig, which, like the ipconfig command, uses switches and parameters to set the command object. The **ip** command has a **command/sub**-command structure that makes it a bit more complex, but with more display options. *Figure 5.1*, earlier in this chapter, shows an example of the display of an ip command.

Each of the **ip** command's sub-commands works with an object, which are addresses, routes, links, and neighbors. Each of the objects has several options for viewing and configuring the option.

Addresses

To list the IP addresses configured on a computer, use the ip command with the address object with the sub-command **show**.

```
ip address show
```

The sub-command **show** is the default and does not need to be included. The object **address** can be shortened to **addr** or just **a**. In fact, the command above can also be entered in one of the following variations to produce the output shown in *Figure 5.5:*

```
ip address show
ip addr show
ip addr
ip a
```

```
1: lo: <LOOPBACK,UP,LOWER_UP> mtu 65536 qdisc noqueue state UNKNOWN group default qlen 1000
    link/loopback 00:00:00:00:00:00 brd 00:00:00:00:00:00
    inet 127.0.0.1/8 scope host lo
       valid_lft forever preferred_lft forever
    inet6 ::1/128 scope host
       valid_lft forever preferred_lft forever
2: bond0: <BROADCAST,MULTICAST,MASTER> mtu 1500 qdisc noop state DOWN group default qlen 1000
    link/ether 4e:47:1e:f7:8f:ef brd ff:ff:ff:ff:ff:ff
3: dummy0: <BROADCAST,NOARP> mtu 1500 qdisc noop state DOWN group default qlen 1000
    link/ether 86:89:05:eb:f0:ca brd ff:ff:ff:ff:ff:ff
4: tunl0@NONE: <NOARP> mtu 1480 qdisc noop state DOWN group default qlen 1000
    link/ipip 0.0.0.0 brd 0.0.0.0
5: sit0@NONE: <NOARP> mtu 1480 qdisc noop state DOWN group default qlen 1000
    link/sit 0.0.0.0 brd 0.0.0.0
6: eth0: <BROADCAST,MULTICAST,UP,LOWER_UP> mtu 1500 qdisc mq state UP group default qlen 1000
    link/ether 00:15:5d:d6:54:a6 brd ff:ff:ff:ff:ff:ff
    inet 172.27.95.55/20 brd 172.27.95.255 scope global eth0
       valid_lft forever preferred_lft forever
    inet6 fe80::215:5dff:fed6:54a6/64 scope link
       valid_lft forever preferred_lft forever
```

***Figure 5.5:** An example of the output produced by the ip address shows the command*

Figure 5.3 lists six address objects and their information. IP addresses are always associated with a network interface, physical or virtual. The first IP address listed is the **loopback address (lo)**, also called the **localhost address**, is the internal communication port. In the example shown in *Figure 5.5*, the address objects 2 through 5 are operating system interfaces and beyond the objectives of the exam. Address 6 is a wireless NIC that connects the computer to a **wireless local area network (WLAN)**. The information included for **Ethernet port 0 (eth0)** is:

- **`<BROADCAST,MULTICAST,UP,LOWER_UP>`**: These are the interface capabilities configured to the interface.
- **`mtu 1500`**: The maximum transmission unit (packet) size for this interface is 1500 bytes.
- **`Qdisc`**: This is a queuing function that schedules packet transmissions. The next parameter following qdisc is the queuing discipline in use. In *Figure 5.3*, the discipline is "mq," which represents multi-queuing. Other options are "noqueue," pfifo (First-in/First-out), **Stochastic Fair Queuing** (**SFQ**), **Generic Random Early Drop** (**GRED**), and **Token Bucket Filter** (**TBF**).
- **`state`**: An interface can be "UP," "DOWN," or "UNKNOWN." The unknown state indicates the interface is up, but there is no connection.
- **`group`**: The value "default" indicates that the interfaces have not been grouped logically.
- **`qlen`**: This indicates the maximum number of packets that can be held in the transmission queue. In the example, the qlen is 1000.
- **`link/ether`**: The MAC address of the interface adapter.
- **`inet`**: The IPv4 address and its **Classless Inter-Domain Routing** notation (**CIDR**)
- **`brd`**: The broadcast address for the interface's subnetwork.
- **`scope`**: This indicates the validity of the interface's IP address: "host" indicates the address is only valid within the computer, and "global" is, well, global.
- **`<eth0>`**: This is the interface ID to which the IP address is associated.
- **`valid_lft`**: This is the valid lifetime of the IP address.
- **`preferred_lft`**: This is the preferred (default) lifetime of the IP address.
- **`inet6`**: The IPv6 address, scope, and lifetimes.

Routes

The route object of the **`ip`** command is used to view and manage the IP/kernel routing table in Linux, mostly to configure static routes associated with an interface. A **route** indicates the interface that should be used to transmit a packet toward its destination IP address.

To view the route table on a Linux computer system, enter the following command: **ip route**. The output from this command should be something like *Figure 5.6*:

```
su_demo $ ip route
default via 172.27.80.1 dev eth0
172.27.80.0/20 dev eth0 proto kernel scope link src 172.27.82.241
```

***Figure 5.6**: Sample output from the ip route Linux command*

Another command that will display the IP/kernel routing table is **route** (see *Figure 5.7*):

```
su_demo $ sudo route
Kernel IP routing table
Destination     Gateway         Genmask         Flags Metric Ref    Use Iface
default         DESKTOP-5I0RQST 0.0.0.0         UG    0      0        0 eth0
172.27.80.0     0.0.0.0         255.255.240.0   U     0      0        0 eth0
```

***Figure** 5.7: Sample output from the route Linux command*

Comparing the **ip route** output with the **route** output in *Figure 5.5* and *Figure 5.6*, there is more detail provided in the **ip route** command, including such information as the default gateway, the interface associated with the route, and more.

To add a static route to a network host, the command is something like this:

```
ip route add 192.168.0.151 via 192.168.0.1 eth0
```

In the above command sample, a route to the IP address 192.168.0.151 is through the device with the IP address of 192.168.0.1 or interface **eth0**.

Links

The **link** object of the **ip** command is used primarily to view the state of the network interfaces and to bring an interface up or down. The **ip link** object differs from the **address** and **route** objects, since the **show** command does not provide information about any IP addresses associated with a particular interface or device.

Neighbors

The **ip neighbors** object provides almost the same information and actions as the **Address Resolution Protocol** (**arp**) command and, in fact, uses the same **arp table**. The output of the **ip neigh** command (shown in *Figure 5.8*) and the output of the **arp** command (see *Figure 5.9*) contain essentially the same information. The **ip neighbors** object provides commands to add, change, delete, and show the entries in the ARP table:

```
su_demo $ ip neigh show
172.27.80.1 dev eth0 lladdr 00:15:5d:18:4a:4c STALE
```

***Figure** 5.8: The ARP table, as displayed by the ip neighbors shows the command*

```
su_demo $ sudo arp
Address                  HWtype  HWaddress           Flags Mask            Iface
DESKTOP-5I0RQST          ether   00:15:5d:18:4a:4c   C                     eth0
```

***Figure** 5.9: The ARP table as displayed by the arp command*

Virtual local area networks

A **virtual local area network (VLAN)** is an internal logical network configuration that provides benefits to both administrators and network users. A VLAN organizes two or more network workstations and devices into a logical network. A logical network is virtual by its nature. Typically, a logical network, and especially a VLAN, is created by logically combining nodes from one or more physical networks into what appears to network users to be a single network. The nodes included in the logical or virtual network remain a part of their physical network. *Figure 5.10* illustrates how a logical network is constructed on top of a physical network:

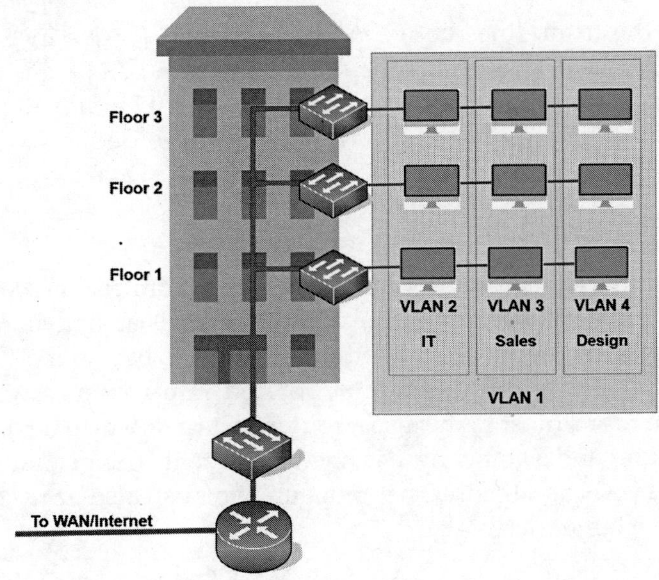

Figure 5.10: The VLAN structure in an organization

Figure 5.10 shows an example of how a physical network distributed over three floors of an organization's business can be configured into three VLANs. VLAN 1 is the default VLAN for any organization, so VLANs 2, 3, and 4 are configured for the IT, Sales, and Design functions, respectively, from each of the three floors.

A VLAN is one of two types:

- **Static VLAN**: A static VLAN is a port-based VLAN that is configured on one or more network switch ports. A device connected to a static VLAN port is automatically included in the VLAN.
- **Dynamic VLAN**: A node on a physical VLAN is identified by its MAC address. A **VLAN Member Policy Server (VMPS)** file contains a list of nodes that belong to each dynamic VLAN. This data is used by a network switch to manage the VLAN.

A VLAN is a broadcast domain and virtually breaking up a network can improve its overall performance. VLAN nodes do not have to be in the same physical location, like the constraints of a LAN. VLANs do have security issues though. One common problem is **VLAN hopping**, which is an attack method that sends packets to a port from within one VLAN to gain access to the other VLANs on the same network. Of course, for this to happen, the attacker must first breach the security on one VLAN.

VLANs are defined in the IEEE 802.1Q standard. Each VLAN is identified by a number, called **Vlan ID (VID)**, ranging from 1 to 4094 (0 and 4095 are reserved for specific purposes). VLANs are integrated into a logical environment through **trunking**, which is a technique that provides access by sharing several lines or frequencies with multiple users.

Messages sent over the trunk lines between switches and VLANs include a **VLAN tag** that identifies the message's source VLAN by number. The VLAN tag is a 12-bit field that is added to the message frame. The tag contains the VLAN ID indicating the origin of the message and the VLAN to which any response is to be forwarded.

Default gateways

A router that is the primary link for an internal network to connect and communicate with an external network can be its **default gateway**. A gateway is actually a network protocol converter that connects one network to another and sets its boundary. Gateways are not independent network devices. They are incorporated into routers, switches, and even some computers. Therefore, most LANs use a router as its gateway. The default gateway is then a designated router and a static route is configured to it. The primary use of a default gateway is between a LAN and the internet, but gateways can also be used to interconnect sub-networks within a larger network.

Addressing protocols

The TCP/IP protocol suite includes three primary protocols that define and use network node addresses: **media access control** (MAC), **Internet protocol version 4** (**IPv4**), and **Internet protocol version 6** (**IPv6**).

MAC addressing

When a network addressable device or component is manufactured, a number code is burned into its electronics. This number has two parts: a number code that identifies the manufacturer and a serial number assigned by the manufacturer. The manufacturer is identified by a 24-bit hexadecimal **organizationally unique identifier (OUI)** code obtained from the **Institute for Electrical and Electronics Engineers (IEEE)**. The 24-bit hexadecimal serial number component is generated by the manufacturer and is unique within the OUI. *Figure 5.11* depicts a MAC address and its components:

MAC Address

OUI - Serial Number

06-F3-7A - 84-BB-8E

***Figure 5.11**: The components of a MAC address*

A MAC address is also called a hardware address, a physical address, and a Data Link or Layer 2 address. Every network adapter or NIC in use to connect nodes to a local network has a MAC address. Within a local network, this address can be used to communicate with the other nodes on the same network. A MAC address cannot be used to communicate beyond the local network.

MAC addresses can be represented in a variety of ways, including the following:

- No separating symbol – 007A0EBF274C
- Spaces after two or four digits – 00 7A 0E BF 27 4C or 007A 0EBF 274C
- Colons after two or four digits – 00:7A:0E:BF:27:4C or 007A:0EBF:274C
- Dashes after two or four digits – 00-7A-0E-BF-27-4C or 007A-0EBF-274C

Internet Protocol addressing

The purpose of the **Internet Protocol** (**IP**) is to define a method for navigating through the nexus of computing and routing devices that make up the unstructured network that is the Internet. Achieving this goal has led to the development and evolution of the IP's flexible addressing schemes. Currently, there are two IP standards (versions) in use: **IP version 4** (**IPv4**) and **IP version 6** (**IPv6**).

IPv4

The IPv4 address is 32-bits in length and is divided into four 8-bit octets (groups of eight). The octets are expressed in a **dot-decimal** format that inserts a dot (period) between the octets (see *Figure 5.12*), whether expressed in binary or decimal.

```
Binary value:   10101001.1110011. 00011001. 11011010
Decimal value:    169   . 115  .    25    .   218
```

***Figure 5.12**: The dot-decimal format for IPv4 addresses.*

An octet may be any binary value between 00000000 and 11111111 or 0 to 255 in decimal. *Figure 5.13* illustrates the range in binary values of IPv4 addresses.

```
00000000.00000000.00000000.00000000 (decimal 0.0.0.0)
to
11111111.11111111.11111111.11111111 (decimal 255.255.255.255)
```

***Figure 5.13**: The binary range of an IPv4 address*

A significant number of the addresses in this range are set aside for special purposes. This means that not all the addresses in the range are available for assignment to network nodes.

Classful IP Addressing

When IPv4 was first adopted, its available addresses were divided into five classes, each with an intent for various purposes. The first three classes, A, B, and C, were issued to Internet providers and users, and the last two classes, D and E, were designated for multicasting and R&D, respectively.

Table 5.4 lists the separate classes and the span of IP addresses each includes:

Address Class	First IP Address	Ending IP Address	Subnet Mask	Networks	Hosts per Network
A	1.0.0.0	126.255.255.255	255.0.0.0/8	126	16,777,214
B	128.0.0.0	191.255.255.255	255.255.0.0/16	16,682	65,534
C	192.0.0.0	223.255.255.255	255.255.255.0/24	2,097,150	254
D	224.0.0.0	239.255.255.255	Not defined	Reserved	
E	240.0.0.0	254.255.255.255	Not defined	Reserved	

***Table 5.4**: IPv4 Address Classes*

LAN addressing

Eventually, there were not enough IPv4 addresses and IPv6 was just beginning its development. To avoid completely running out of IPv4 addresses, some innovative developments emerged to help minimize the impact of the declining number of addresses. This included private IP addresses, subnetting, CIDR, and others.

Modifications, revisions, or new technologies or methods applied to the Internet must go through a review and examination process. The lead agency guiding these actions is the **Internet Engineering Task Force (IETF),** along with a few other agencies. The IETF reviews request for changes or additions and, if approved, issues a **request for comments (RFC)**. For example, RFC 1918 was issued for the proposal to designate and use private addresses.

Private addresses allow nodes on a LAN to communicate within the nodes on the LAN. However, private addresses cannot be routed and are not valid beyond an organization's gateway router. Private addresses can be used on any LAN without restriction. Since they are not seen on the internet, there is no issue with their use on multiple networks. A block of addresses from each of the primary address classes were set aside for use as private addresses. *Table 5.5* lists the private addresses designated from address classes A, B, and C:

Address Class	Private Address Range	Addresses Available
A	10.0.0.0 – 10.255.255.254	16,777,216
B	172.16.0.0 – 172.31.255.254	1,048,576
C	192.168.0.0 – 192.168.255.254	65,536

Table 5.5: *IPv4 Private Addresses*

Network and Host IDs

An IPv4 address has two parts: a network ID and a host ID. The number of bits used to identify each of these elements varies with the address classes. *Table 5.6* lists the number of bits in each class for the network ID and the host ID:

Address Class	High-order Bits	Address Pattern	Network ID Bits	Host ID Bits	Default Net-mask
A	0	n.h.h.h	7	24	255.0.0.0
B	10	n.n.h.h	14	16	255.255.0.0
C	110	n.n.n.h	21	8	255.255.255.0

Table 5.6: *Net ID, Host ID, and bit constructs of IPv4 address classes*

The high-order (or first) bit or bits of the left-most octet identify the address class of an IPv4 address. This lets a router or other internetworking device determine the network mask to apply to extract the network ID.

A router and other internetworking devices only care about the network ID of an IP address because that is the destination to which it is forwarding a message. The host ID of an IP address will be considered by the gateway router of the destination network, so routing on the Internet is all about the network IDs.

To extract a network ID from an IPv4 address involves **Boolean algebra** and the application of the bitwise AND operator to the address using the **network mask** appropriate for the address class. In very simple terms, the extraction process is performed on each bit position, and only the matches between the address and the mask are kept. Mismatches are discarded and replaced with a zero value.

The masking process works like this:

- The IPv4 address (10.25.115.88) is fetched - 00001010.00011001.01110011.01011000
- The first bit is a zero, indicating a class A address
- The class A default network mask is applied - 11111111.00000000.00000000.00000 000
- The ANDing operation yields the Network ID – 00001010.00000000.00000000.000 00000

- The network ID is 10.0.0.0 (see *Figure 5.14*):

```
 10 = 0 0 0 0 1 0 1 0
255 = 1 1 1 1 1 1 1 1
      ---------------
      0 0 0 0 1 0 1 0
```

***Figure 5.14**: The bitwise AND operation of an IPv4 address and address mask*

After the network mask is applied and the network ID is revealed, the message can be forwarded toward its destination, meaning the router or device with the extracted network address.

IPv6

Internet Protocol version 6 (IPv6) was developed to replace IPv4 before it ran out of assignable addresses. However, many small businesses and homes are reluctant to replace their existing systems or reassign their IP addresses, so the conversion from IPv4 to IPv6 is slow to complete. Because of this, virtually all modern computers and devices, including smartphones, can work with both IP versions.

An IPv6 address is much longer than an IPv4 address, provides for exponentially more IP addresses, and identifies network and host IDs in a slightly different way. An IPv6 address has 128-bits and the addresses are stored in hexadecimal values that use 4-bits each. This results in an IPv6 address having 32 hexadecimal numbers. The address is divided into two 64-bit network ID and host ID sections (see *Figure 5.15*):

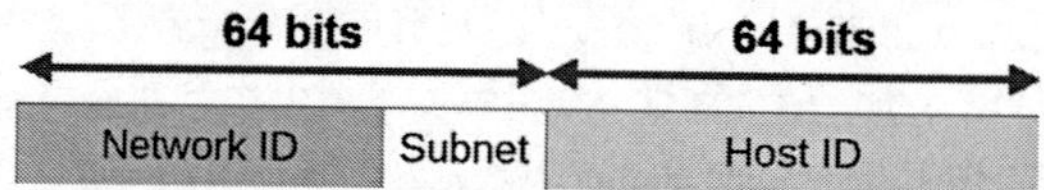

***Figure 5.15**: The basic structure of an IPv6 address*

A standard format for an IPv6 address is **2001:0db8:0000:0000:0000:ff00:0042:8329**. The hexadecimal numbers are grouped as 8 blocks of 4 values separated by colons. As you can see in this example, an IPv6 address can contain a fair number of zeroes. The standard provides shortening methods to reduce the length of the address by compressing the zeroes. Two rules can be applied to remove the zeroes from the address:

- **Rule 1**: Compression: Consecutive zeroes can be compressed by substituting a double colon (::) for them. For example:

  `Before: 2001:0db8:0000:0000:0000:ff00:0042:8329`

  `After:  2001:0db8::ff00:0042:8329`

- **Rule 2**: Leading zeroes: The leading zeroes in each block are removed.

```
Before: 2001:0db8:0000:0000:0000:ff00:0042:8329

After:  2001:db8::ff00:42:8329
```

An IPv6 address is split into two parts, like the IPv4 address: network and host. Like the IPv4, the network portion is used for routing a message to its destination. However, the host portion of an IPv6 address is taken from the host's MAC address using the IEEE **extended unique identifier** (**EUI-64**).

Firewalls

A network **firewall** is a hardware or software device that examines incoming (and possibly outgoing) message traffic and allows only authorized traffic to pass in or out. The criteria used by a firewall to determine whether a message is allowed to pass is defined by an administrator and possibly organizational policies.

Firewall types

There are three different types of firewalls:

- **Software firewalls**: Also called host firewalls, this type of firewall is just what its name implies – a software application. A software firewall protects only the host its on, and like all software, it competes for the CPU, memory, and storage resources.
- **Hardware firewalls**: This type of firewall is a network appliance typically positioned on the perimeter of a network. Hardware firewalls are primarily packet-filtering systems. Newer firewalls, especially those classified as **Next-Generation Firewalls (NGFWs)**, are **unified threat management (UTM)** devices that include additional features, such as antivirus, content filtering, email & web filtering, and more. NGFWs use packet-filtering, stateful inspection, **intrusion detection systems** (**IDS**), and **intrusion protection systems** (**IPS**). Packet data is analyzed using pattern matching, protocol, heuristic, and anomaly detection methods.
- **Cloud firewalls**: Also called **Firewall-as-a-Service** (**FaaS**), this cloud-based service is provided by a **cloud service provider** (**CSP**) who offers all the services.

Firewall methods

Firewalls provide protection in a variety of different methods, including:

- **Packet-filtering firewalls**: The majority of network firewalls are this type, which examines a packet header against a ruleset, primarily in **access control lists (ACLs)** entered by an administrator. This type of firewall is the fastest and most affordable.
- **Circuit-level gateways**: Also known as session gateways, this type of firewall examines each of the steps in a **Transmission Control Protocol (TCP)** handshake to allow a connection to be established (nailed up), operate, and end (torn down). The

handshake elements are compared against predefined session rules to determine if the connection is permitted.

- **Stateful inspection firewalls**: This firewall type inspects incoming and outgoing packets against a ruleset defined by an administrator. A **stateful firewall** monitors the status of active network connections and inspects message traffic for potential risks.
- **Proxy firewalls**: Also known as application gateways, this type of firewall uses **deep packet inspection (DPI)** or packet sniffing to examine all the data in a packet. A **proxy firewall** sets up connections to each of the two communicating stations to manage the connection and the traffic.

Firewall ports

Incoming and outgoing message traffic through a firewall is identified in three ways: IP addresses (destination and source), service, and port. A **service** is a protocol-based function, such as web access using **Hypertext Transfer Protocol** (**HTTP**), email using **Simple Mail Transfer Protocol** (**SMTP**), and others. Ports, in the context of firewalls (routers, switches, etc.), are logical constructs that indicate which application is to process the contents of a message. It works something like this: An incoming HTTP (service) message indicates port 80, which, in turn, indicates a web browser.

In total, there are 65.535 ports identified by the **Internet Assigned Number Authority (IANA)**. Of these, there are only about 20 or so that are used for the most part. *Table 5.7* lists the most commonly used ports:

Port Number	Protocol or Usage
20	File Transfer Protocol (FTP) Data Transfer
21	FTP Command Control
22	Secure Shell (SSH)
23	Telnet
25	Simple Mail Transfer Protocol (SMTP) email routing
53	DNS
67	DHCP Server
68	DHCP Client
80	HTTP
110	Post Office Protocol (POP3)
161	Simple Network Management Protocol (SNMP)
162	SNMP agent
443	HTTP Secure (HTTPS)/HTTP over TLS/SSL

***Table 5.7**: Commonly used ports*

A port can be either open (allow) or closed (deny). An open port is listening for incoming traffic to be serviced by its associated application. However, an open port is also an open door that could allow unauthorized entries because anything with its number is allowed. On the other hand, a closed port is just that – closed with nothing listening. The bottom line is to close any port not in use, which is easily done on virtually all firewalls (routers, switches, etc.).

Conclusion

The configuration of a server and the networking devices that support and protect it is extremely important to the operation, reliability, and security of not only the server but the network as well. The infrastructure of a network, and its servers and hosts can be exposed and subject to hardware, software, and security failures. A certified server administrator must know how to apply the best practices and settings to ensure the continued operation of the network and its components.

In the next chapter, we look at some of the different roles servers can have, the importance of connectivity to directory services, storage management, administrative interfaces, and server monitoring. In addition, we'll discuss data migration methods.

Points to remember

- The configuration of any network-connected device includes device name, network adapter, MAC address, IP addressing, DHCP configuration, gateway address, and DNS address.
- The Windows ipconfig command is used for viewing, setting, or managing the IP configuration of any network-connected device. It is also used to troubleshoot issues involving DNS, DHCP, and IP addresses.
- DNS translates a domain name into IP addresses.
- DHCP provides network hosts with a unique IP address and information the host needs to connect to a network.
- APIPA enables a host to automatically configure its IP address should the DHCP server be unreachable.
- ifconfig is a workalike of the Windows ipconfig command that operates with or without parameters.
- The `ip` command has a command/sub-command structure that works with the objects' addresses, routes, links, and neighbors. The ip neighbors object manages the ARP table.
- A VLAN organizes network workstations and devices into logical networks. A VLAN is static or dynamic.

- A default gateway is the primary link for an internal network to connect and communicate with an external network.
- The protocols that define network node addressing are MAC, IPv4, and IPv6.
- A MAC address has two parts: the OUI and serial number.
- IPv4 addresses are 32-bits in length and are divided into four 8-bit octets in a dot-decimal format. An octet may be a value between 00000000 and 11111111 or 0 to 255 decimals. IPv4 is a classful protocol.
- A proposed modification to the Internet is released on an RFC.
- Private addresses cannot be routed but can be used on any LAN without restriction.
- An IP address has two parts: a network ID and a host ID. A network mask is used to extract the network ID.
- IPv6 addresses have 128-bits divided into 4-bit hexadecimal values, resulting in 32 hexadecimal numbers. IPv6 addresses can have shortening methods applied to reduce the length of the address by compressing zeroes.
- A network firewall is a hardware or software device that examines network traffic and allows or denies packets to pass. The three types of firewalls are software, hardware, and cloud.
- Firewalls use different methods, including packet-filtering, circuit-level, stateful inspection, proxy, and NGFW.
- Firewalls identified message traffic using IP addresses, services, and ports.

CHAPTER 6
Configure Network Servers

Introduction

A computer network becomes an integral part of an organization's culture almost immediately after it is deployed. It is an essential work tool and communication device and system. Without it, the pace of work slows down. One of the most critical parts of a computer network is the server. The most crucial component of a server is the server hardware.

This chapter reviews the administration, management, and preventive maintenance of local and remote server hardware processes and procedures you need to know for the CompTIA Server+ exam.

Structure

The chapter covers the following topics:

- Server roles and requirements
- Storage management
- Server monitoring
- Monitoring

- Data migration and transfer
- Administrative interfaces

Objective

By the end of this chapter, you will be able to identify and describe the sub-objectives of the following Server+ examination objective: *Given a scenario, configure and maintain server functions and features.*

Server roles and requirements

We established in *Chapter 1, Physical Hardware* that a server is the software, not the hardware it runs on. However, we only briefly discussed the different server types or roles commonly part of a network. In this section, we look at the server types you should expect to encounter on the Server+ exam: print, database, file, web, application, and messaging servers.

Print server

A **print server** is typically a part of an **Operating System (OS)**, or it can be added to a system as a software application, a network appliance, a cloud service, or a networked computer that accepts print requests, manages the print queue, and directs print jobs to the appropriate printing devices. In larger organizations, a print server can serve as a go-between for users and multiple printers. However, in a SOHO situation, one with two or more printing devices, a print server can be an expansion board in the server hardware, or a small appliance. In even smaller situations, the OS is often the print server.

A print server, in any form, is a client-server device. Requests for printing from network clients are queued for the request printer, the print job's status is fed back to the requestor, and the print job is forwarded when the appropriate printer is available. In addition, some print servers may be able to manage specialized functions and fonts on specific printers using different protocols. The protocols in the print server process fall into three categories:

- **Dedicated**: These protocols are specifically for printing. The AppSocket, Jetdirect, and the **Line Printer Daemon (LPD)** are examples.
- **Generic**: These protocols treat printers as a remote network device, much like scanners and multimedia devices, including multi-function printers. Examples include Telnet and **Server Message Block (SMD)**.
- **Wireless**: These protocols apply a **Zero-configuration networking (zeroconf)** mechanism, typically in conjunction with another printing protocol. Zeroconf provides automatic addressing and locating services for printer devices. Examples of wireless printing protocols are the Apple AirPrint and the Mopria Alliance.

- **Internet printing**: Several Web-based services incorporate the **Internet Printing Protocol (IPP)** into their services.

Database server

It may be obvious, but a database server manages a **Database Management System (DBMS)** and services database requests, such as access, retrieval, and update, for network clients. A database server consists of both, the software, and the hardware as a specialized unit. Since database software requires large capacity processing, and data storage, the hardware is generally a dedicated high-performance computer. Database servers are commonly used for handling large databases and data requirements, ensuring the integrity and security of the DBMS and the data in the database, and managing concurrent client access.

File server

A file server is like a database server without the DBMS software. They store data, typically in filesystems on direct- or network-attached storage devices. It provides security against two data storage weaknesses: sensitive or classified digital data stored in multiple locations and the difficulty of sharing scattered and isolated data resources. A file server resolves these issues by storing sensitive and shareable data in a central store to which network clients have access. *Figure 6.1* illustrates a basic file server arrangement:

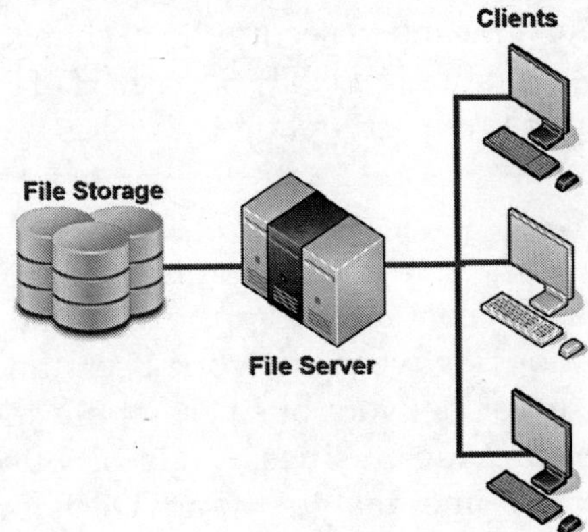

***Figure 6.1**: A basic file server setup*

File servers are available as network appliances, specialized software, and cloud services.

Web server

A web server does the following:

- Store website content along with front-end and back-end design and data services that support the website.

- Fulfill authorized requests from client web browsers for the stored website files. In plain language, a web server hosts website definition and execution files and the data used to populate the site.

A web server works as follows:

- The web server receives an HTTP/port 80 request for a website's files. This request is typically in the form of **http://www.MyWebSite.com/index.html,** a Uniform Resource Locator (URL), which contains the protocol/scheme (http), the sub-domain (www), the second-level domain name (MyWebSite), the top-level domain (com), and the file requested (index.html).
- If the file requested, `index.html` is present on the web server, it is transmitted back to the requester's browser.

This process may seem simple, and it is for webpages with **static content** like **Hypertext Markup Language (HTML)** and image files. However, dynamic content complicates the process a bit. A webpage with dynamic content is created or modified, on the fly, in reaction to a user's input or choices.

One of the early standards for dynamic content, which is still in use somewhat, is **Common Gateway Interface (CGI)**. It defines how information is transferred between web servers, databases, and CGI programs (scripts). It accepts and returns data allowing a web server to interact with a user's input and their browser. Most e-commerce websites have dynamic content. They also incorporate a means to secure the exchange of data between the user and the web server, which is commonly HTTP, Secure (HTTPS). This protocol provides secure transmissions between the web server and the user's browser.

Application server

Where a web server provides web content, an **application server**, which can also deliver web content, enables interactions between network users and server-side applications (programs). An application server delivers business applications via a communication protocol. Application servers provide **business logic** or **business intelligence**, which generates dynamic content, real-time analytics, and **Decision Support System (DSS)** information.

Application servers are generally placed physically or virtually between a database server and a web server to support client requests. Many application servers use a feature called servlets. A **servlet** is a Java programming language methodology that improves the function of client-server or **request-response** actions on an application server. A servlet provides support for mixing static and dynamic content on a webpage, such as a retail e-commerce site that shows which items are currently in stock.

Messaging servers

An **Instant Message (IM)** service provides a means for two users to communicate online in real-time. It works like a telephone call, but instead of voice, the communication is text-based. At one time, IM was a standalone app. However, it is now incorporated into social media sites, e-commerce, and online customer service interactions. IM communications are conducted on the **Extensible Messaging and Presence Protocol (XMPP)**.

Although IM is much like a phone call, it requires the use of a server. The server would not be necessary if all users had permanent IP addresses, like phone numbers. However, very few do. An IM server facilitates IM communications using the temporary IP address each user is assigned when they boot a computer onto a network.

Server baselining

A baselining process sets a standard inventory and performance record as a point of reference against which future measurements can be compared. In several areas, the performance of one year becomes the baseline to which the following year is compared. When a new server is built and configured, its performance measurements form the baseline against which any future measurement is compared. A baseline removes the guessing and perceptions that a system may not perform as it should. However, if the configuration or the hardware components of a computer system change, a new baseline must be established.

It is very important that all aspects of a baseline measurement be documented. Without a record of all of the aspects that may be compared in the future, there can be no certainty of any comparison. The baseline itself should be specified and documented as a series of performance metrics. Essentially, performance metrics provide a standard for measurements:

- **Count**: The number of occurrences of an event.
- **Duration**: How long in time did each occurrence run, or what was the timing of the occurrences.
- **Amount**: What was the size, volume, or output of the occurrences.
- **Rate**: How many occurrences happen in a time period, such as a second or a minute, etc.

These performance metric characteristics are not intended to be necessarily troubleshooting measurements, but they can be. When a baseline is established, they are what they are.

Directory connectivity

Connectivity to the **Active Directory** (**AD**) is uniquely a Windows OS issue. It stores user account login data and information on other network resources. It is a repository of the information about the authorized users and devices and what each can do. The AD stores an **object** for each network resource, including users, computers, printers, shares, applications, and groups. Objects are organized in domains that establish security boundaries around the objects.

When properly implemented, the AD becomes the key structure in an organization's IT operations. It is the primary resource for authentication and authorization of user and device accounts. So, it is easy to see why connectivity to the AD is highly important.

There are several utilities and PowerShell commands that can be used to test the connectivity between a server or host and a domain controller, and the AD. The two PowerShell commands that can be used to test the connectivity to an organization or an IP address are **`Test-Connection`** and **`Test-NetConnection`**. Both these commands send **Internet Command Message Protocol** (**ICMP**) echo request packets, or the equivalent of a ping command, to one or more target computers using a URL, computer name, or IP address. *Figures 6.2* through 6.5 show examples of the use of these commands:

```
PS C:\> Test-Connection 10.131.0.1 -Count 2 -BufferSize 128 -Delay 3

   Destination: 10.131.0.1

Ping Source           Address                    Latency BufferSize Status
                                                    (ms)        (B)
---- ------           -------                    ------- ---------- ------
   1 DESKTOP-5I0RQST  10.131.0.1                      14        128 Success
   2 DESKTOP-5I0RQST  10.131.0.1                      14        128 Success
```

***Figure 6.2**: Test-Connection has a variety of switches that can customize the test*

The test shown in *Figure 6.2* sets the Count to two tries, sets a test packet to **`BufferSize`** of 128 bytes, and a 3 second delay between attempts. Refer to *Figure 6.3*:

```
PS C:\> Test-Connection 10.131.0.1 -Quiet
True
```

***Figure 6.3**: A quiet connection test returns True if the connection is valid*

The test in *Figure 6.3* shows the **`Quiet`** option that returns only **`True`** or False to reflect the validity of the connection between the testing station and the target address. Refer to *Figure 6.4*:

```
PS C:\> Test-NetConnection 10.131.0.1
Test-NetConnection :: 10.131.0.1 [Ping/ICMP Test
```

***Figure 6.4**: The initial response of the Test-NetConnection command*

Refer to *Figure 6.5*:

```
PS C:\> Test-NetConnection 10.131.0.1

ComputerName           : 10.131.0.1
RemoteAddress          : 10.131.0.1
InterfaceAlias         : Wi-Fi
SourceAddress          : 192.168.0.79
PingSucceeded          : True
PingReplyDetails (RTT) : 15 ms
```

***Figure 6.5**: The results of the Test-NetConnection command*

Figure 6.4 and *Figure 6.5* show the initial response and its completion of a **`Test-NetConnection`** PowerShell command.

Other PowerShell commands that test a connection to the AD or a domain are:

- **`Test-ComputerSecureChannel`**: It tests the channel to a domain controller.
- **`PortQry`**: A Windows Server command-line utility used to troubleshoot the connectivity for Windows components and features.
- **`DCDiag`**: A utility that checks the health of a domain controller.

Storage management

Storage management is a broad spectrum of policies, procedures, and actions that optimize, manage, and secure data stored electronically throughout an organization. A storage management program focuses on the user or computer-generated data stored on fixed and removable storage devices.

Processes

In general, storage management programs should address six process categories:

- **Provisioning**: Assessing and assigning storage capacity to host computers, servers, and other devices.
- **Compression**: The process of freeing up drive space, closing storage gaps, reducing data retrieval times, and otherwise maximizing storage capacity.
- **Migration**: The process of transporting or transmitting data from one storage location to another.
- **Replication**: The process of taking snapshots, backups, and data mirroring, redundancy, resilience, and reliability.
- **Automation**: The tools and techniques used to create simple scripts to DevOps for automating data storage processes.

- **Disaster recovery**: The tools, planning, policies, and procedures for restoring operations in the aftermath of a disaster.

Virtualization and containerization are other areas that can be included under storage management processes. Virtualization is the process of using **Virtual Machines (VMs)** to leverage hardware and software resources. Containerization is another approach to virtualization for decoupling applications from an OS.

Formatting

Windows systems require at least one disk drive volume with a file system and drive letter before the drive can be accessed or used for data storage. While the majority of HDD and SSD drives are pre-formatted and ready for use, there are occasions when you need to reformat and allocate a storage drive.

Windows systems include the **Disk Management** tool. This tool is used to manage both internal and external disk storage. It has tools to create new volumes, perform formatting, adding or changing labels and drive letters, applying data compression, and modifying the size of a volume. *Figure 6.6* shows an example of the **Disk Management** tool and its option for formatting a selected drive:

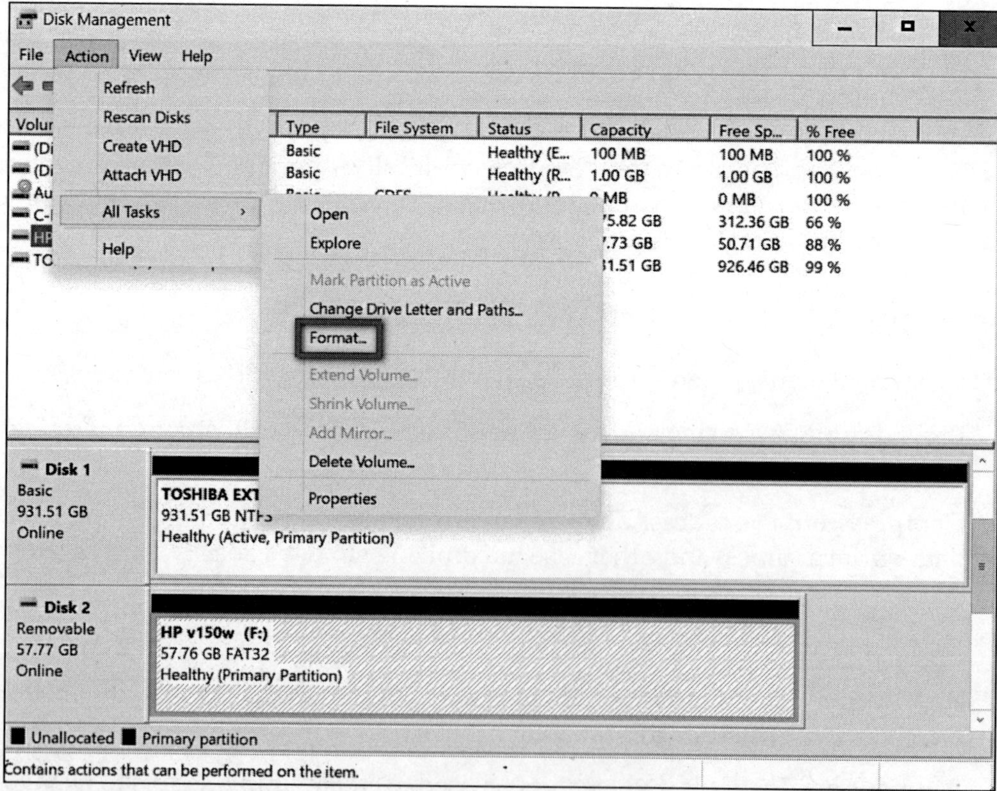

Figure 6.6: The disk management utility can be used to format a selected disk drive

Partitioning

To use the disk management app to create a new partition on a disk drive, click into an unallocated space on the drive to be partitioned, right-click to display a pop-up menu, and choose **New Simple Volume** (see *Figure 6.7*). This will open the new simple volume wizard which will guide you through setting the size, assigning a drive letter, and formatting the new partition.

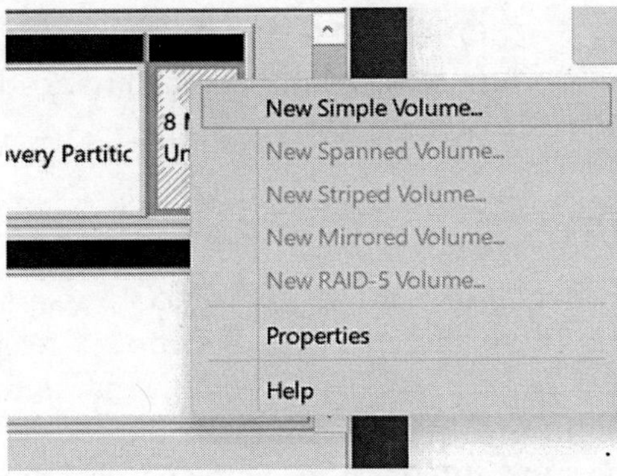

***Figure 6.7**: The new simple volume selection is used to create a new partition on a disk drive*

There are a number of third-party disk management applications that can also be used to partition and format a disk storage drive, such as Partition Magic, AOMEI Partition Assistant, and Gparted for Linux systems.

Paging

Active programs and files are stored in RAM by the OS because RAM is much faster to work with than repeatedly fetching it from a disk drive. However, sometimes there is not enough space in memory to hold all that is needed at a certain point. The OS has two choices: discard something in RAM that is not being used at that instant or temporarily store that same content somewhere safe to be brought back to RAM later. The second choice is the better one.

Windows

All versions of Windows systems use paging files, also known as swap files, which is a disk file located at `C:\pagefile.sys`. You may not see this file because, by default it is hidden. There may also be more than one if the system has multiple disk drives. To view and possibly change the size of the page file, use the following process:

1. Right-click the start icon and choose settings from the power user menu.
2. On the systems page, select the advanced systems settings option to display the system properties dialog box.

3. On the advanced tab, click the settings button in the performance area to display the performance options dialog box.

4. On the advanced tab, the size of the paging file is included in the virtual memory area.

5. If you wish to change the size of the paging file, click on the change button to open the virtual memory dialog box.

If you decide to change the size of the paging file, the rule of thumb is that the minimum size should be 1.5 times the amount of RAM in the machine, and the maximum should be no more than three times the size of the RAM.

Linux and macOS

Linux and UNIX-based systems, like the Apple macOS, use swap spaces instead of a paging file. In these systems, there are two types of swap space: swap partitions and swap files. Linux systems create a swap partition by default that is designated as the primary swap space. However, if sufficient space is not available on the storage drive for a swap partition, a swap file can be substituted as the swap space. If the RAM size is greater than 2GB, the swap space must be the RAM size plus 2GB.

Scratch space

A scratch space is a dedicated space on a disk drive or even in RAM that is set-aside for use as temporary storage. Scratch space is used when both RAM and swap space are full or when insufficient space is not available for a large application object, such as an image or video. Perhaps the most common method used to create scratch space is creating an empty partition on the primary storage device.

On a virtualized system, swap space can be allocated, but should it be necessary to troubleshoot a VM, a scratch partition can be used to store the contents of a VM's VRAM. It is common that when a virtualized system is initialized, a scratch partition is created. If no scratch space is available when needed, a host computer's space is used.

Disk quotas

Disk quotas limit the amount of disk storage space a user has available. When a disk quota is set, users cannot store data in a designated space that exceeds the limits of that space. In most applications, the administrator can set points of capacities that trigger warnings to users to avoid any surprises when the quota space fills up. Disk quotas can be set for drives and partitions, but not on folders or files.

On Windows systems, disk quotas can only be set on NTFS systems, meaning they cannot be set on FAT, FAT32, or exFAT file systems. To set a disk quota on a Windows system, use the following steps:

1. Open the file explorer and right-click on the disk drive on which the quota is to be applied.
2. From the pop-up menu, click on properties to display the drive properties dialog box.
3. Click on the **Quota** tab and then click the show **Quota Settings** button to display the **Quota Settings** for the drive selected (see *Figure 6.8*):

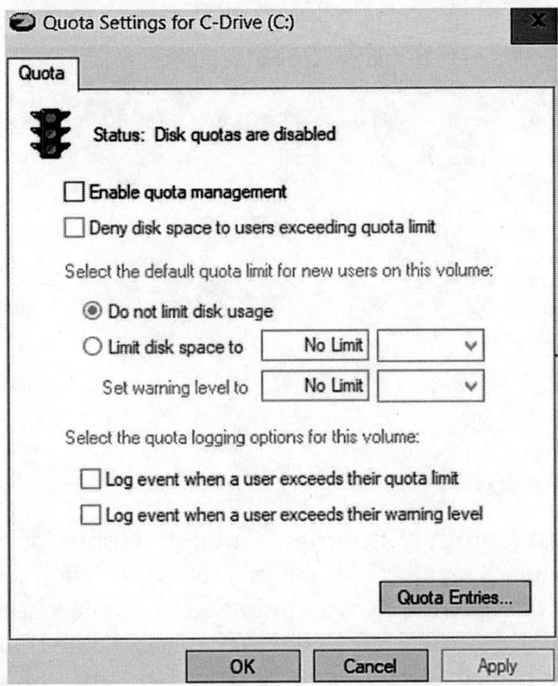

***Figure 6.8**: The quota settings dialog box of Windows system*

To set user disk quotas on a Linux distro involves editing the **`/etc/fstab`** file or the installation of the **`quota-tools`** package.

Compression

Most data files, especially text documents, have relatively predictable content, including strings of repetitive characters that can be compressed. The compression of a file or document is performed with a variety of algorithms that reduce the size of the file and free up storage space. There are two basic types of compression algorithms: lossy and lossless.

Lossy compression

Lossy compression gets its name from the fact that to compress data, it discards some of the data. The compression algorithm selects needless or redundant data and omits it (the loss) from the compressed file. Lossy compression is used for digital media, including audio, video, images, and streamed data. These media have sequences of empty spaces or repeated elements that can be omitted from the compressed file without materially altering the media's reproduction. For example, a `.jpeg` image file can be reduced to 20 percent of its original size without dramatically altering the image's quality. However, the quality of the resulting image or sound depends on the compression ratio used on the data. Higher compression ratios can affect the quality of the object when decompressed. *Figure 6.9* illustrates the effects of lossy compression:

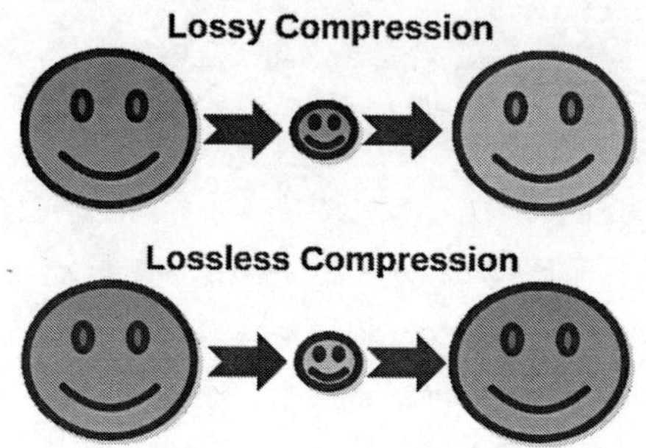

***Figure 6.9**: Illustrations of the effects of lossy and lossless compressions*

Lossless compression

Lossless compression can reproduce the original object without loss and remove repeating elements in a file to produce a smaller file. The elements removed from the file are replaced with placeholders that describe what was removed. The placeholders are then used to reconstruct the object. For example, a placeholder can indicate that 250 white spaces are in a certain area of the object, which were removed during compression and inserted when it is decompressed. *Figure 6.9* illustrates the difference between lossless and lossy compression.

Windows file compression

Data compression on data files on a Windows NTFS system uses lossless compression. Redundant data, such as repeating characters or spaces, are replaced with placeholders. On a Windows 11 system, applications can access the compressed files, yet use them if they were uncompressed.

To apply file compression on a Windows 11 system, use the following steps:

1. On the file explorer, right-click on the folder or file and choose properties from the pop-menu.
2. On the properties dialog box, select the general tab and click the **Advanced** button to display the **Advanced Attributes** box (see *Figure 6.10*):

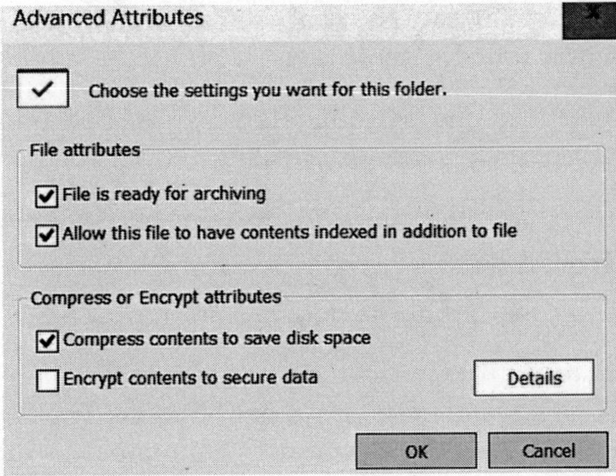

***Figure 6.10**: The advanced attributes dialog box for a file or folder*

3. In the **Compress or Encrypt attributes** area, check the box associated with **Compress contents to save disk space**. This choice and the choice to **Encrypt contents to secure data** are mutually exclusive on this dialog box and cannot both be checked.
4. Click **OK** to apply compression to the file or folder selected.

All the files in the folder you chose to apply compression to are now compressed, and any file you place in that folder will become compressed. However, if you only compressed one or more individual files, only those files will be compressed.

If you wish to apply compression to an entire disk drive, these steps are essentially the same as those above for compression of a file or folder,

Linux file compression

On a Linux system, file compression is primarily performed to save space on backups or archives. Several commands can be used to apply different compression algorithms, including **`tar`**, **`gzip`**, **`bzip`**, **`xz`**, and **`tar`** with either **`gzip`** or **`bzip`**. Another command, **`lrzip`**, is a large file or source file compression tool. For file compression on a HDD or SSD, it needs to be applied through a file system. The **Better Filesystem** (**BTRFS**) supports file compression similar to that of a Windows system. For read-only data stores, the **SquashFS** file system compresses all files, but does not allow updates or writes.

Deduplication

Duplicate or multiple copies of data or files can eat up storage space and perhaps result in erroneous or expired data being used. The deduplication process seeks to identify and remove all duplicate data. Some deduplication software looks only for duplicated files, while others seek out duplicated data in databases and data files. There are two different ways that the deduplication process is applied:

- **In-line**: As data is written to a storage device, it is scanned for duplications, and if any are found, a reference to the duplicated data is stored.
- **Post-process**: The deduplication process is applied at a later time after data is written to a storage device.

There are also two different ways that the deduplication process is performed:

- **Source deduplication**: It is performed inside a file system. The file system scans recently stored files and creates a hashing of the file. The hash is then compared to hashes that the file system has previously generated. If duplicates are found, the newest copy is deleted.
- **Target deduplication**: It reduces duplicated data on backups and archives. Target deduplication is performed by specialized backup software or hardware.

There are two deduplication platforms:

- **Software-based**: Software-based deduplication scans data on the system on which it is running. If duplicates are found, user-specified actions are taken.
- **Hardware-based**: Hardware deduplication occurs on storage devices that perform target deduplication. This feature is found on hardware systems for virtual tape libraries, **Network-Attached-Storage** (**NAS**) systems, and some backup appliances.

Server monitoring

A server monitor can provide an administrator with automated and on-demand reporting, device checking, and alerts should a device or system reach a user-defined threshold. Server monitoring systems perform checks and measurements on the systems and components of a server, including:

- **CPU usage**: High levels of CPU usage may impact response times and productivity.
- **Disk IOps**: **Input/output operations per second (IOPS)** measure the efficiency of a storage device.
- **Hard disk space**: The amount of available disk capacity can indicate utilization may be too high. Low storage space may contribute to reduced performance, fragmentation, and slow searches.

Note: Remember that defragmentation is effective only on HDD and not SSD.

- **Hardware status**: A poor performing hardware component can slow or halt a server.

- **Network**: Network monitoring allows administrators to see the status and performance of a network's connected devices and traffic load.
- **RAM utilization**: RAM utilization can be an indicator of several issues that may cause reduced runtimes, throughput, and the need for additional memory.
- **Uptime**: The availability of a system to users and perhaps subscribers is typically the key to a **service level agreement (SLA)**.
- **Virtual machine performance**: Active VMs counters can track activity and performance levels, like IOps on a virtual disk and network volume.

Log files

Log files hold a record of events, warnings, and errors caused, initiated, or captured from the action of users and applications. These records are valuable in the investigation or troubleshooting of system issues.

Windows logs

A Windows system records a variety of events, actions, and errors in several default log files, some of which are shown in the left pane of the Windows **Event Viewer** (see *Figure 6.11*). The Windows system log files are categorized as **Custom Views**, **Windows Logs**, **Application and Services Logs**, and **Subscriptions** (see *Figure 6.11*):

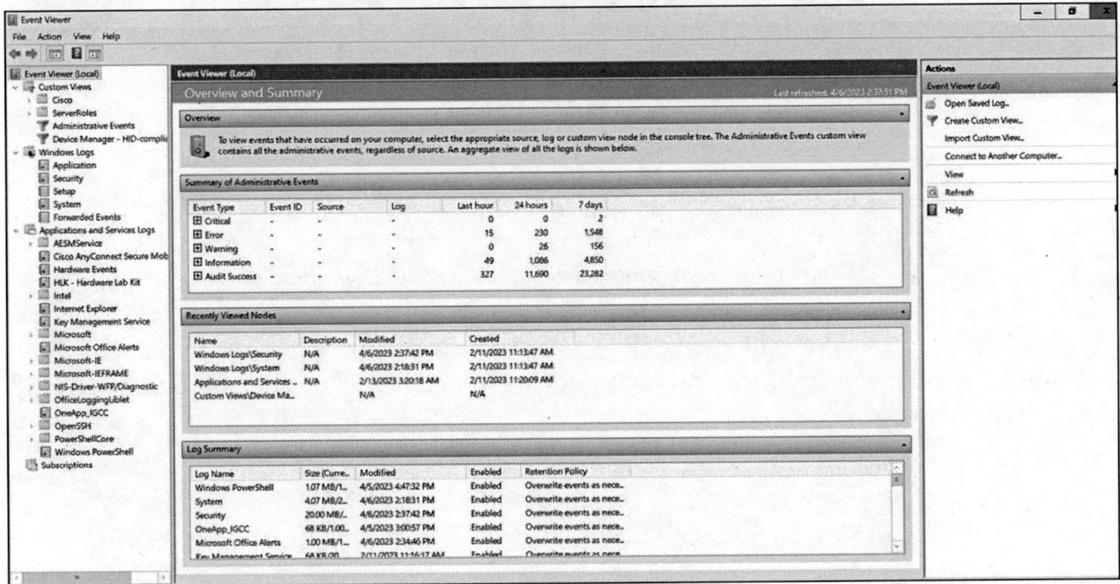

Figure 6.11: The Windows event viewer

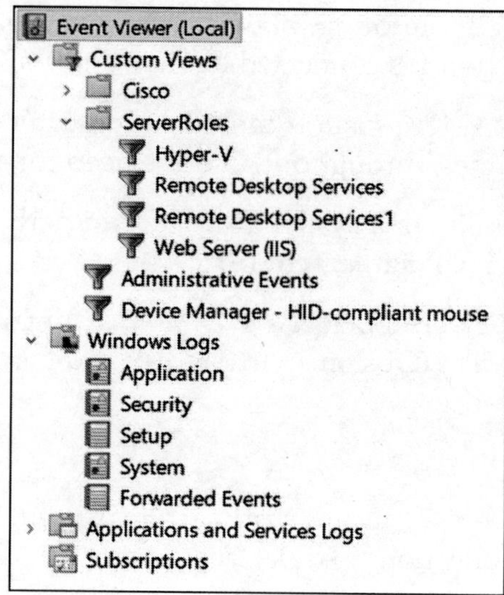

Figure 6.12: The navigation pane of the Windows event viewer

The **Windows Logs** group of log files contains log entries on virtually every important action, event, or error occurring on a system. As shown in *Figure 6.13*, the log entries concern activities in **Administrative** and **Operational** events associated with actions of the Windows OS:

Windows Logs

Name	Type	Number of Events	Size
Application	Administrative	7,483	6.07 MB
Security	Administrative	23,340	20.00 MB
Setup	Operational	226	1.00 MB
System	Administrative	7,077	4.07 MB
Forwarded Events	Operational	0	0 Bytes

Figure 6.13: The inventory list for the Windows Logs group

Figure 6.14 shows the details of a log entry in the **Windows Log/Security** log file. This is an example of the detailed information recorded in log entries. The information varies with the system area.

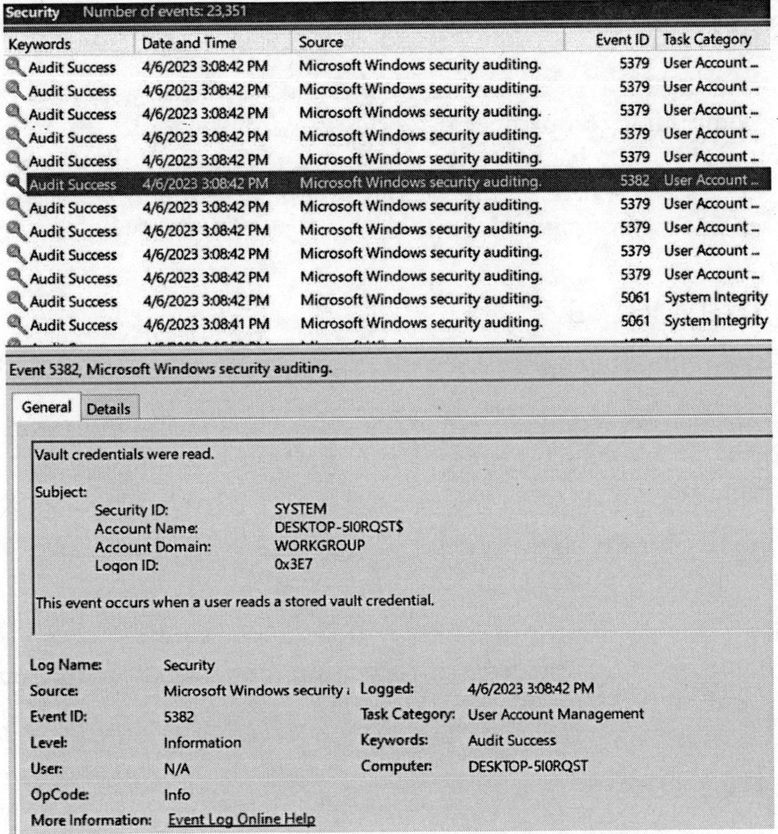

Figure 6.14: The details of a Security log entry

Linux logs

On a Linux or macOS system, system log files are stored in the **/var/log** directory. *Figure 6.15* shows the log files in the **/var/log** directory. There are also third-party software packages for viewing and analyzing log files on all three operating systems.

```
test_su $ls -l
total 1672
-rw-r--r-- 1 root               root             63575 Apr  5 14:23 alternatives.log
drwxr-x--- 2 root               adm               4096 Apr  5 14:22 apache2
drwxr-xr-x 2 root               root              4096 Apr  5 14:33 apt
-rw-r--r-- 1 root               root             90763 Dec 26 05:45 bootstrap.log
-rw-rw---- 1 root               utmp                 0 Dec 26 05:44 btmp
drwxr-xr-x 2 root               root              4096 May 23  2022 cups
-rw-r--r-- 1 root               root           1455118 Apr  5 14:33 dpkg.log
-rw-r--r-- 1 root               root             32032 Apr  5 14:27 faillog
-rw-r--r-- 1 root               root              5879 Apr  5 14:33 fontconfig.log
drwxr-sr-x 2 root               systemd-journal   4096 Dec 26 05:45 journal
-rw-rw-r-- 1 root               utmp            292292 Apr  5 14:27 lastlog
drwxr-xr-x 3 root               root              4096 Apr  5 14:20 runit
drwxr-x--- 2 root               adm               4096 Aug  9  2022 samba
-rw-r--r-- 1 sddm               sddm                 0 Apr  5 14:22 sddm.log
drwx------ 2 speech-dispatcher root               4096 Nov 30 14:10 speech-dispatcher
drwxr-x--- 2 root               adm               4096 Feb 19  2021 unattended-upgrades
-rw-rw-r-- 1 root               utmp                 0 Dec 26 05:44 wtmp
-rw-r----- 1 xrdp               adm                  0 Apr  5 14:27 xrdp.log
-rw-r----- 1 root               adm                  0 Apr  5 14:27 xrdp-sesman.log
```

Figure 6.15: The log files in the Linux directory /var/log

Monitoring

Server monitoring is the use of software packages and processes to assess that an organization's computing resources are working as they should. In small and SOHO installations, monitoring can be simply by eyesight and hopefully, not by smell. However, in larger data centers and server rooms, monitoring has become of major importance and a valuable tool in the battle against downtime.

Monitoring types

The basic types of monitoring are:

- **Availability**: Also called system monitoring, this is the most common type of monitoring. It involves tracking a set of performance measures, such as uptime and throughput.
- **Performance**: This type of monitoring focuses on the performance of user- and customer-facing applications, including websites.
- **Security**: This type of monitoring looks for potential data breaches and vulnerabilities using **Security information and event management (SIEM)** policies and procedures.

Monitoring tools

Monitoring software and tools are categorized into three groups:

- **Observational**: These tools are used to observe IT resources, including hardware, software or IT services, and measure their operational effectiveness. Included in this group are tools for availability monitoring, infrastructure monitoring and management, application performance monitoring, and web performance monitoring.
- **Analysis**: These tools analyze the data collected from observation to identify where problems may originate and why the problems are occurring.
- **Engagement**: The tools in this group act on the information developed in the observational and analytical processes. If the analysis indicates action is required, administrators are notified with an alert and possibly trouble-tickets. Some versions of these tools can act on their own to reboot or perform probing tests.

Performance monitoring

The overall mission of a data center should be focusing on the monitoring procedures and actions applied to servers. The primary objective of this monitoring is to determine whether the systems are able to handle the workload now and possibly in the future.

We discussed baselines in an earlier chapter, and that baseline is the basis on which performance measures are compared.

To measure the performance of a server, there are four primary measurements that should be taken, analyzed, and acted upon, if necessary:

- **CPU utilization**: Gilster's law (You never can tell, and it all depends) applies here. Which measurements or counters are included will depend on how the server is used. The processor's manufacturer most likely has some recommended measurements and counters, each with a specific purpose. Commonly, the following metrics are the key elements determining the load placed on the CPU:
  - **% processor time**: The percentage of uptime a CPU executes commands, which should be 85 percent or less.
  - **% user time**: The percentage of uptime a CPU spends executing commands from an application. This percentage should not be higher than the baseline percentage. If it is, an application or service is tying up the CPU.
  - **% interrupt time**: The percentage of time a CPU spends servicing hardware interrupts in a sample time period. This should always be 15 percent or less, otherwise there is likely a hardware issue to investigate.
  - **Processor queue length**: The number of threads in the processor queue should never be more than twice the number of CPUs. If it is, the system isn't able to handle its workload.
- **Memory utilization**: The more commonly used counters and metrics for monitoring RAM are:
  - **% committed bytes in use**: This metric measures how much virtual memory is used. If it is more than 80 percent, the need for additional memory is indicated.
  - **Available MB**: This metric measures how much RAM, in MB, is available (not in use). If it is less than 5 percent of the total RAM, more memory should be added.
  - **Virtual memory paging**: Depending on the OS, virtual memory paging may have a number of different metrics or counters available, including:
    - **Free system page table entries**: A paging table typically has space for thousands of entries. If the free entries space is less than 5,000, it can indicate a **memory leak**, which means applications or services are not returning memory allocations to the system to be allocated to another process.
    - **Pages per second**: This measures the read/write rate for memory pages. This value should be less than 1,000. Otherwise, there is excessive paging or a memory leak.

- **Network adapter/NIC**: The performance of network interfaces can be monitored using metrics, including:
    - **Bytes total/sec**: This metric indicates how much of a network adapter's bandwidth is being used. More than 70 percent may mean the interface is overloaded.
    - **Output queue length**: If there are more than 2 packets in the output queue, the adapter is unable to handle the workload.
- **Disk IOps**: This metric represents the number of read/write operations that can be completed in one second. The manufacturer of the disk drive should have the specifications available, and this metric should be included in the system baseline.

Data migration and transfer

There is a difference between data migration and data transfer. One involves moving and possibly converting data from one system to another and the other is simply moving the data from one system to another.

Data migration is a process that may involve conversion of the data as it is moved from one location to another or from one system to another. For example, moving systems and their associated data from an in-house operation to cloud-based services. Data migration is more than just moving the data. It involves a series of steps, each focused on ensuring the data retains its integrity, security, and usability. The steps in a data migration process are: cleansing, profiling, mapping, backup, testing, and a timeline for retention and expiration.

Maintaining the integrity of data being migrated requires that data infiltration and data exfiltration are considered and guarded against. **Data infiltration** occurs when unauthorized data from an external source is introduced into a system. For example, a new employee is hired who previously worked for a competitor and brings proprietary and sensitive data. **Data exfiltration** is what that employee did to gain the information brought to the new employer.

Data transfer is the process that collects and duplicates datasets from one system to another. The data can be from an active system to a **disparate system**, which is essentially a read-only environment, such as a data warehouse or a reference database, or to a recovery system as a part of a disaster recovery plan. Some of the tools available to copy data for transfer are:

- **Robocopy**: This Windows command-line utility is used to copy large data volumes.
- **File transfer**: There are several file transfer systems available both online and for installation. A few of these products are: pCloud, SpiderOak, and Citrix Sharefile. These products vary in features, but they all provide secure file sharing and transfer.

- **FastCopy**: Claimed to be the fastest copy and backup software for Windows systems, this product copies large file volumes with several filters and switches fast and efficiently. *Figure 6.16* shows the criteria page of this software:

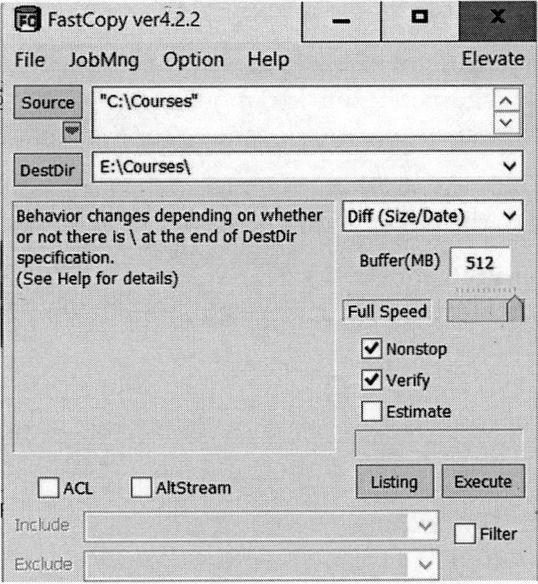

***Figure 6.16**: The FastCopy file transfer tool.*

- **Secure copy protocol (SCP)**: It is used to transfer data between computers, local or remote, securely. SCP is based on the SSH protocol. SCP is being deprecated in favor of **Secure FTP (SFTP)** or on Linux systems, the **rsync** command.

Administrative interfaces

Administrators need access to server operating systems, services, and application software to effectively do their jobs. In a large data center or server room, local or remote, how an administrator interfaces with any one of the server systems can depend on several factors, but mostly proximity. A server may have a standard keyboard, mouse, and video device directly connected, have a KVM switch connected to multiple servers, or use a console server to provide a connection to an entire server room.

A **console**, in the context of servers and computers, is the combination of a keyboard, monitor, and probably a mouse, which may be connected to computers and servers over a network. Consoles are used for system administrators to manage and monitor the devices on a network.

KVM interfaces

A **Keyboard-Video-Mouse (KVM)** switch facilitates a single set of input/output devices, namely a keyboard, video monitor, and mouse, to interface with remote computers on a network as if connected directly to the remote unit (for more information on KVM switches, see *Chapter 1, Physical Hardware*.

Network-based interfaces

Network-based administrative interfaces provide a centralized administrator with the capability to remotely manage, configure, and monitor local and remote servers. Examples of the network-based tools an administrator can use for system administration are:

- **Remote Server Administration Tools (RSAT)**: This Windows tool provides an administrator with the ability to manage Windows Server systems.
- **Remote Desktop Protocol (RDP)**: This Windows tool provides an administrator with remote access to network-connected systems through a GUI interface that gives full access to that system.
- **Secure Shell (SSH)**: SSH is a software utility used to connect to remote systems for administration and file transfers over an encrypted remote connection, including all authentication, commands, output, and file transfers.
- **Virtual Network Computing (VNC)**: It provides a GUI desktop through the **Remote Frame Buffer (RFB)** protocol that provides an administrator with the ability to control and manage a remote system over a network. VNC sends all keyboard and mouse actions to the remote system and displays the resulting video display on the monitor of the controlling system.
- **Web interface**: There are a variety of web-based applications that provide administrative access and control to any networked server, including the Web-console and Windows Admin Center for Windows systems, the Red Hat Web Console, and the Cockpit project for Linux.

Conclusion

Configuring a network server has many considerations, which can include the role the server is to play in a networked environment, its directory organization and connectivity, its data storage technology and type, how the system is to be monitored, the process with which data is to be migrated or transferred, the level of availability and fault tolerance required, and the administrative methods and tools to be used. Each of these areas is a vital element of a server, regardless of its purpose in its network.

In the next chapter, we will look at the techniques and devices that provide fault tolerance and high availability.

Points to remember

- The role of a server can be one of any number, including print server, database server, file server, web server, application server, or messaging server, among others.
- A server baseline sets a standard inventory and performance record as a point of reference against which future measurements can be compared. Common performance metrics are: count, duration, amount, and rate.
- On Windows network, connectivity to the AD must be maintained and tested regularly.
- Storage management encompasses policies, procedures, and actions that optimize, manage, and secure user or computer-generated data stored on both fixed and removable storage devices. The categories of a storage management system are provisioning, compression, migration, replication, automation, and disaster recovery.
- Virtualization is the process of using VMs to leverage hardware and software resources.
- Containerization is another approach to virtualization for decoupling applications from an OS.
- Disk management activities include formatting, partitioning, and paging (swapping).
- Disk quotas can limit the amount of disk storage space a user has available.
- Data, file or folder compression is performed by algorithms that reduce the size of the file and free up storage space. The two basic types of compression algorithms are lossy and lossless.
- Deduplication identifies and removes duplicated data in one of two ways: in-line and post-process.
- Server monitors perform reporting, device checking, and can produce alerts for devices that may be reaching a pre-defined threshold.
- Log files hold a record of events, warnings, and errors caused, initiated, or captured from the action of users and applications.
- Server monitoring assesses an organization's computing resources for availability, performance, and security.
- Data migration moves and possibly converts data from one location to another. Data transfer collects and duplicates datasets from one system to another.
- Administrators access servers and their OSs, services, and software for management and monitoring through an administrative console.

Join our book's Discord space

Join the book's Discord Workspace for Latest updates, Offers, Tech happenings around the world, New Release and Sessions with the Authors:

https://discord.bpbonline.com

CHAPTER 7
High Availability

Introduction

In most organizations, there is not enough for the data systems, servers, and network to be available. These resources need to be highly available. The difference between available and high available (other than the word *high*), is *available* which might mean that the systems, network, and its resources are accessible to customers only during a set number of hours and not outside that time. On the other hand, *high availability*, in the context of servers and networks, generally means that the systems, networks, and resources are available for customer access whenever a customer/subscriber may need to access them. High availability sets an expectation of service-level quality and performance. This chapter discusses the technologies and methods you may encounter on the Server+ exam, namely, fault tolerance, clustering, load balancing, and redundancy.

Structure

The chapter covers the following topics:

- High availability
- Fault tolerance
- Clustering
- Load balancing

Objective

By the end of this chapter, you will be able to identify and describe the sub-objectives of the following Server+ examination objective: *Explain the key concepts of high availability for servers.*

High availability

High availability (HA) is the ability of a system or component to ensure high performance without interruptions over a particular time period to avoid a single point of failure (SPOF). An SPOF is any system component that could fail, is likely to fail, and should be backed by a redundant component to prevent a break in availability. HA is an extremely important quality for a network server and all other network-connected devices. An HA server and network is committed to operate properly and be available as needed by customers or users. Typically, this commitment is expressed as a percentage, made up of a series of nines that increase in value as the decimal place moves right. *Table 7.1* lists what is called the Nines, which is commonly used to express a committed level of availability. However, as you can see in the table, the availability level is expressed in the amount of downtime allowed. For example, the 4-nines level is common in many **service level agreements (SLAs)** between a service provider and a subscriber. At this level, the service provider is committing to no more than 52.6 minutes of downtime in an entire year.

Availability	Common name	Downtime/ year	Downtime/ month	Downtime/ week	Downtime/ day
99.9999999%	9-nines	31.6 ms*	2.6 ms	604.8 μs*	86.4 μs
99.999%	5-nines	5.3 min*	26.3 sec*	6.1 sec	864.0 ms
99.99%	4-nines	52.6 min	4.4 min	1.0 min	8.6 sec
99.9%	3-nines	8.7 hrs*	43.4 min	10.1 min	1.4 min
99%	2-nines	3.7 days	7.3 hrs	1.7 hrs	14.4 min

***Table 7.1**: HA measures with their time equivalents*

* ms = milliseconds
* **μs = microseconds**
* sec = seconds
* min = minutes
* hrs = hours

The different values associated with each of the *nines* in *Table 7.1*, indicate that what high availability means can vary with the service provider, the purpose, and the use of the service. However, in a system that must be reliable and available, each critical device, such as RAID, NAS, SAN, FAX, RRAS, etc., is expected to be highly available. Achieving the goal of *9-nines* may seem impossible to some, but some data centers reach that level of availability.

Most SLAs and customer or subscriber support commitments are typically three-, four-, or five-nines. In the context of service commitments, downtime does not have to mean not operational. It could just mean off-line. There are all sorts of reasons that a server or a network's resources may be unavailable, such as power, weather, war, and other forms of catastrophic events. As we will discuss in *Chapter 19, Troubleshooting Methods,* a disaster recovery plan can be an integral part of any high availability scheme.

Fault tolerance

Fault tolerance practices are the means to achieve high availability. **Fault tolerance** is the capability for a system or component to continue its normal operations upon a system or major component failure. The capability to tolerate a fault or failure and continue running with no loss of service or data is essential to any high availability system, its organization, and users.

Fault tolerance is not an all-or-nothing function. Its level depends on the device, its use, and how critical it is, or in the case of a disk drive, its contents are to a service or an organization. Generally, there are four levels of fault tolerance:

- **Power issues**: The lowest level of fault tolerance is the capability of a system to continue operations in case of a power event, that is, black out, brown out, failure, surge, etc.
- **System failures**: In the event that a production system fails, a ready back-up system can come online immediately.
- **Partial failure or device degradation**: This level is also called enhanced faulty tolerance. If a critical component fails or begins to fail, redundant devices pick up the processing to avoid a shutdown and loss of service.
- **High-level fault tolerance**: Multiple processors work together to examine incoming and outgoing data for errors that are corrected immediately.

Fault tolerance principles say that a program on any level must have two characteristics:

- **Component failures would not cause downtime**: If a component fails, replacing it should not require any or all the systems to be powered down.
- **Component failures would not cause loss of data or processing**: Any fault or failure can be easily identified and remedied without data loss or interrupted processing.

The level of application for the preceding principles to any system depends on how critical the system is, its continued operations, and the resources available. Not all problems are necessarily fire drills or *the sky is falling*, but many can be. Therefore, there should be a formal plan and procedure for any component that details how expeditiously a failed or failing component must be replaced, and this plan should be followed.

Swaps

There are three general types of hardware and power component changes that can be included in a fault tolerance and high availability program:

- **Hot swap**: Immediate switchover or physical replacement while a system is running and operational. There are three basic types of hot swaps:
    - **Basic**: The hardware component can be replaced with a hot swap, but any software configuration must be done by the administrator.
    - **Full**: A micro-switch provides the signal to connect to a new device, including any software configurations needed for continuity.
    - **High-availability**: This full hot swap system uses device controllers and software to control the mechanical, hardware, and redundancy systems.

      Examples of hot swap devices, called **hot spares**, are audio devices, displays, USB devices, SATA drives, and network connections.
- **Warm swap**: A **warm swap** requires the system or, at least, the failed component to be idle while the switch is made. Warm swaps are used for media, backup, or archive changes and are typically not an entire component.
- **Cold swap**: A **cold swap** requires the entire system to be powered down before upgrades, replacements, or repairs can be applied.

Clustering

A server is generally server software running on a single computer. A **server cluster** is two or more interconnected servers operating as a single unit. The cluster shares the processing load under the control of a load-balancing controller. The purpose of this arrangement is to improve throughput and response to users.

The processing issues that server clustering helps solve are:

- **Expansion**: Additional servers can be added to the cluster should network or user demand exceed the capabilities of an existing cluster.
- **Availability**: The failure of a single server in a server cluster can be tolerated more easily than the failure of a single standalone server.

- **Maintenance**: The maintenance of a single server typically requires downtime, while maintenance on a server in a cluster has only a limited impact on processing.

Server clusters

The two primary configurations for server clusters are:

- **Active/active**: This server cluster configuration interconnects two or more computers running the same processes. All the connected servers are active, and the load balancing hardware/appliance manages assignments to the servers attempting to optimize the throughput time.
- **Active/passive**: This server cluster configuration can have one or more active servers sharing the processing load with one or more failover, backup, or standby servers, ready to replace a failed server or one taken out of service for maintenance as a hot spare.

Load balancing

Load balancing distributes incoming client requests to a cluster of servers. Load balancing can direct the requests based on a port, specific software, or a hardware appliance. The distribution attempts to evenly assign requests to an available and appropriate server in the cluster, sometimes acting like a router. However, where a router directs network traffic using the best path to a destination, a load balancer directs requests to a server with the appropriate software, data, or the best available server. *Figure 7.1* illustrates the basic concepts of a load balancer placed before a server group:

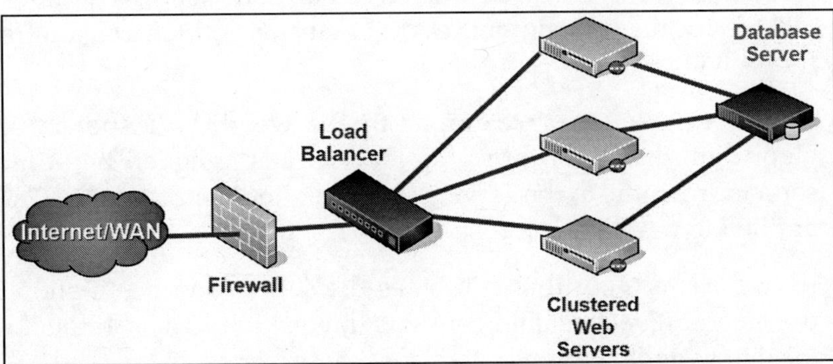

***Figure 7.1**: A load balancer forwards a message to the best available server*

Load balancers use a variety of algorithms to determine which server is best to process a request. These algorithms are divided into two groups:

- **Dynamic load balancing algorithms**: Dynamic algorithms distribute requests based on the status of each server in the cluster. Dynamic algorithms include:

- **Least connection**: A request is assigned to the server with the fewest number of connections (requests being processed) at a given time, under the assumption that all requests require about the same processing duration.
- **Weighted least connection**: Requests are assigned based on the least connection state and the weights (priorities) assigned to each server.
- **Weighted response time**: This algorithm keeps an average of the response time of each server and combines it with the least connection state to distribute a request. This method helps ensure faster turnaround time for users.
- **Resource-based**: This algorithm determines the server to which a request is sent using feedback from status indicators (agents) running on each server. In effect, this algorithm performs a health-check on a server before forwarding traffic to it. In this approach to load balancing, traffic is distributed by analyzing current server loads. Specialized software called an agent runs on each server and calculates the use of server resources, such as computing capacity and memory. The load balancer then checks with the agents, looking for sufficient free resources before distributing the traffic to a server.

- **Static load balancing algorithms**: Static algorithms distribute traffic without using adjustments. Generally, a static algorithm distributes the same amount of traffic to each server in a cluster, in either a specific order or randomly.
  - **Round robin**: This algorithm distributes requests to a server in a group in a rotation using DNS. The active DNS nameserver has multiple address records for the domain of the server cluster and returns a different address for each DNS query.
  - Weighted round robin: Similar to the weighted response time dynamic algorithm, this algorithm uses the weights assigned by administrators to send more traffic to the servers that can handle more traffic. The weights are applied to the DNS records.
  - IP hash: This algorithm combines the source and destination addresses of the incoming request and converts the result into a hash total, which is then used to assign the request to a specific server.

Path selection policy

Path selection, whether in routing or virtualized systems, can be either static or dynamic. Dynamic path selection uses a variety of routing protocols to determine the best available path to a destination. An administrator configures a static path to fix the path to be taken. In the context of load balancing, a static path sets which server in a cluster is to be used for a particular request. However, another approach for forwarding messages to the best server for processing is **most recently used (MRU)**. MRU assumes that the last forwarding decision is the best current decision for a request.

NIC teaming and redundancy

Network Interface Card (NIC) teaming groups physical NICs into one **virtual NIC (vNIC)**. The benefits of NIC teaming are, improved performance and network adapter redundancy. In addition, teaming can also provide load balancing. As many as 32 physical NIC connections can be made to one vNIC. The vNIC is seen by a server's OS as a single network adapter, with a single IP address. All network traffic generated through the OS is sent to the vNIC and load-balanced on the teamed adapters. The benefits of NIC teaming include:

- **Load balancing**: Network traffic is statically-balanced to all active NICs in the team cluster on a round-robin basis.
- **Fault tolerance**: Should one or more of the teamed NICs or its connection fail, traffic is moved to another NIC in the team cluster.

On a Linux system, NIC teaming is referred as **NIC bonding**. The network switch to which the physical NICs are bonded must support the EtherChannel link aggregation architecture.

NIC teaming modes

NIC teaming can be implemented in one of two modes, which are:

- **Switch independent**: In this mode, NICs can be independently connected to different switch ports or switches. MAC addresses are used to distribute incoming requests.
- **Switch dependent**: All the NICs in a teaming implementation are connected to the same physical network switch that determines how traffic is distributed to NIC team members. This mode has two sub-modes:
    - **Static teaming**: The NICs and network switches are manually configured into a **Link Aggregation Group (LAG)**. The configuration must be the same on the host and switches to identify which links are in the teaming group.
    - **Link aggregation**: The **Link Aggregation Control Protocol (LACP)** must be enabled on each of the members of a teaming group. LACP provides load balancing and failover protection for incoming and outgoing network traffic.

Conclusion

High availability means, in the context of network servers, that a server and its components operate in a fault tolerant way and are continuously available to network users, without the intervention of an administrator for a predetermined period of time. A high-availability infrastructure delivers consistent, high-quality performance and continues to operate through low and high processing loads and component failures with a minimum of system downtime.

In the next chapter, we look at the concepts and applications of virtualization and its use in a data center and the cloud.

Points to remember

- High availability SLAs typically express the uptime commitment as a percentage.
- Fault tolerance is the capability of a system or component to continue its normal operations in the event of a system or major component failure.
- The three types of hardware that can be included in a fault tolerance and high availability program are; hot swap (basic, full, and HA), warm swap, and cold swap.
- A server cluster is two or more interconnected servers operating as a single unit. A server cluster shares the processing load under the control of a load-balancing controller.
- The two primary configurations for server clusters are active/active and active/passive.
- Load balancing distributes incoming requests to a server cluster to evenly distribute them to the best available server.
- Load balancers use algorithms to determine which server is best to process a request.
- Load balancer algorithms are in two groups: dynamic and static.
    - Dynamic load balancing algorithms distribute requests based on the status of servers in a cluster. Dynamic algorithms include least connection, weighted least connection, weighted response time, and resource based. Dynamic path selection uses a variety of routing protocols to determine the best available path to a destination. An administrator sets static paths to fix the path to be taken.
    - Static load balancing algorithms distribute traffic without adjustments to servers in a cluster, in a specific order or randomly, using round robin, weighted round robin, and IP hash algorithms.

- MRU assumes that the last forwarding decision is the best current decision for a request.
- NIC teaming groups physical NICs into a vNIC, which is seen as a single network adapter with a single IP address. The benefits of NIC teaming are load balancing and fault tolerance. On a Linux system, NIC teaming is NIC bonding.
- NIC teaming can be implemented in two modes: switch independent and switch dependent. Switch dependent has two sub-modes: static teaming and link aggregation.
- LACP provides load balancing and failover protection for incoming and outgoing network traffic.

Chapter 8
Virtualization

Introduction

Virtualization is the process of defining and creating a virtual version of an IT resource. This can include the virtualization of hardware, **operating systems (OSs)**, storage devices, network adapters, and other network resources. Using virtualized systems, a company can reduce the number and power of the physical computing assets needed for its application workload. This chapter discusses the fundamentals of virtualization and its use in a networking environment. The chapter also includes a quick overview of the basic cloud computing delivery models.

Structure

This chapter covers the following topics:

- Virtualization
- Host vs. guest
- Resource allocation and provisioning
- VM testing
- Cloud models

Objective

By the end of this chapter, you will be able to identify and describe the sub-objectives of the following Server+ examination objective: *Summarize the purpose and operation of virtualization.*

Virtualization

A virtual environment contains virtual versions of devices, resources, and operating environments that reside on a physical computing platform, the host system, and possibly an OS. The virtual environment consists of one or more software-defined execution spaces or guest systems. A guest space is commonly referred as a **virtual machine** (**VM**). To the user and the application running in it, a VM appears for all intents and purposes to be a physical machine.

Host vs. guest

In a virtualized environment, there are hosts and guests, which are different types of OS implementations. The same OS can be used in either case, but the difference is in the configuration and structure of the virtualized device.

A host OS runs as the primary system software on a computer, and the hypervisor or **virtual machine manager** (**VMM**) runs as a process or application on top of the OS. This system can now support multiple VMs, each of which can run a guest OS installed into the VM to service it alone. Each VM can run a different guest OS than other VMs on the same host machine. Where a host OS interacts directly with a computer's resources and devices, a guest OS interacts with the hypervisor or VMM, which, in turn, interacts with the host OS. Virtualization types

Virtualization is applied to many computing technologies to define almost any component of a computer system, but especially several of the major network components:

- **Server virtualization**: Also known as hardware virtualization, server virtualization defines one or more logical execution spaces on a physical computer. Server virtualization can be implemented in one of three ways:
  - **Full virtualization**: This type of server virtualization is also known as Type 1 or a Bare Metal implementation. As shown in *Figure 8.1*, the hypervisor is installed directly on the physical hardware in place of an operating system. Under this approach, each application is isolated in its own logical space and runs on a unique OS rather than other VMs on the system. This virtualization type requires host control software, such as a VMM or a hypervisor, which creates and controls the VMs and their resource requirements. *Figure 8.1* illustrates the structure of a fully virtualized system:

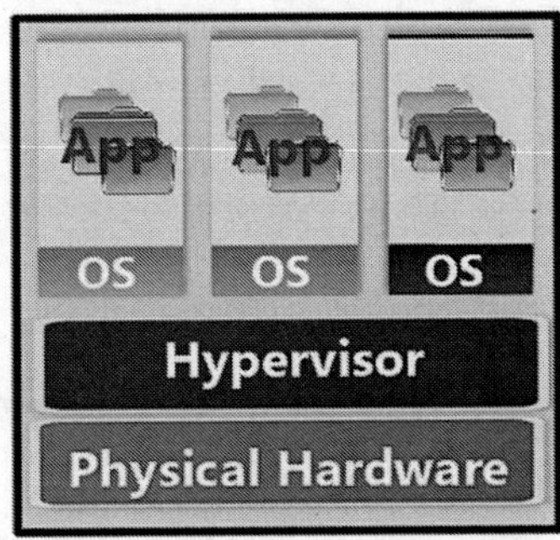

Figure 8.1: Full virtualization

- **Para-virtualization**: In this type of virtualization, the guest OS is modified to interact with a VMM (or hypervisor) for memory management, interrupt handling, and clock functions using non-standard commands called **hypercalls**. The VMM provides programming interfaces (APIs) that allow a guest operating system to access the host system's physical hardware. *Figure 8.2* illustrates an example of para-virtualization:

Windows 11 App	Linux App	Windows 7 App
Hypercalls	Hypercalls	Hypercalls
VM	VM	VM
Virtual Machine Monitor (VMM)		
Physical Hardware		

Figure 8.2: Para-virtualization

- **OS virtualization**: This type of virtualization creates independent virtual servers that share the OS kernel of the host system. Each guest server shares the same OS kernel as the host system. This is also called "hosted" virtualization since the guest servers run as a software layer on other computer programs. Oracle Virtualbox, and VMware workstation are examples of what is also called *Type 2* virtualization. *Figure 8.3* illustrates this type of virtualization:

Virtual Server	Virtual Server	Virtual Server
Shared OS	Shared OS	Shared OS
Shared OS		
Physical Hardware		

Figure 8.3: OS virtualization

- **Storage virtualization**: **Storage virtualization** logically combines multiple storage devices into a single virtual device. Storage virtualization creates a mapping between the logical and physical storage. *Figure 8.4* illustrates how storage virtualization works. **Input/output (I/O)** requests are made to the storage virtualization manager, who looks up the logical data block and maps it to a physical location in storage.

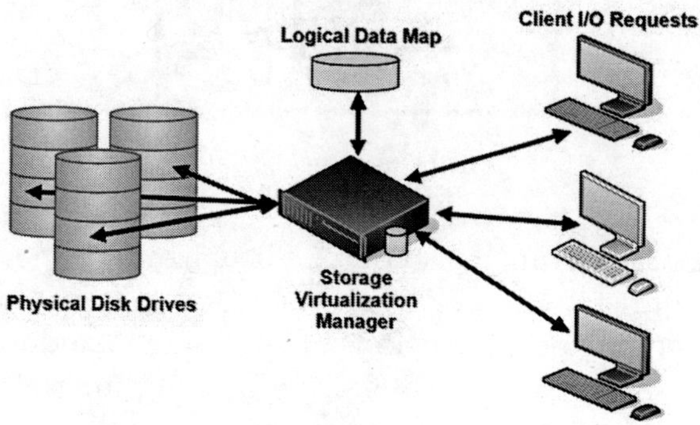

Figure 8.4: Storage virtualization

- **Application virtualization**: Application software is encapsulated by the host operating system that includes virtual support services that interact with the host OS services and data storage systems as needed. *Figure 8.5* illustrates application virtualization:

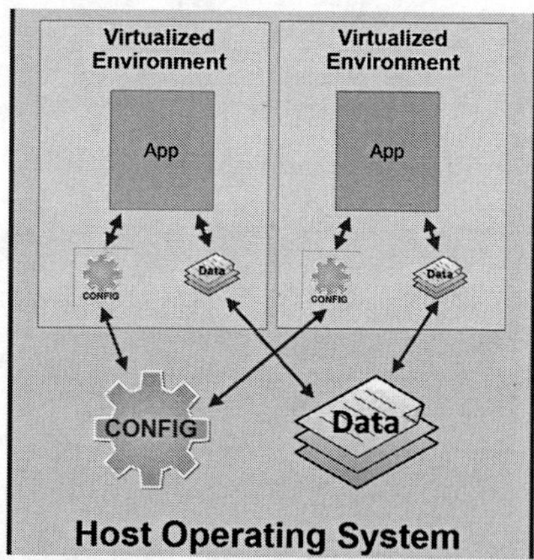

Figure 8.5: Application virtualization

Virtual networking

Physical networks connect workstations and other devices using cabling or **radio frequency (RF)** signaling. A virtual network connects its devices through software that emulates physical devices with virtual switches, network adapters, and more. When a VM is created, it can be configured to function solely as a network node on a LAN, be secured behind a firewall and router, or be a part of a customized full-blown enterprise network. The following sections discuss some features commonly available to VMs in a virtualized network.

Network address translation

Network address translation (NAT) is a protocol service that provides a means for private IP addresses to be transmitted over the Internet. IPv4 private addresses cannot be, by definition, routed outside of their local network. NAT associates a pre-defined public IP address with a private source address and forwards its message to the Internet or an external network. For example, if an internal node has an IPv4 private address of 192.168.0.15 and wishes to access a website, it issues an HTTP request to its edge router. The router, enabled with NAT service, sees the source address as unrouteable and replaces it with either its own public-facing address or one from a configured list, such as 23.227.38.65. The original source address, the new source address, and the destination address are recorded in a NAT table for referencing and redirecting the returned webpage. Often, a NAT extension, **Port Address Translation (PAT)**, is used to add additional information to the outgoing request and its response. When a VM issues a request for content from an external network, two translations occur before the message is sent out. The first translation replaces the VM's private address with the private address of the host system, which is then replaced with a NAT address for transmission to the external network. Each of the translations is recorded for use in forwarding the returned content.

Direct access

Also called bridged mode, **direct access** allows a VM to communicate directly with external services through the host device's network interface. A VM with direct access communicates directly with the router and is seen as a standalone device with an IP address and port number identity. Bridged mode is commonly used in virtual server environments.

Virtual switch

Like all virtual devices, a **vSwitch** is a software program that provides an interface that allows a VM to communicate with another VM or to a physical network. A vSwitch can connect to one or more port groups or connections. Each port group has a network ID that is associated with the host server. The vSwitch detects which port groups connect to a VM and forwards network traffic using that information either internally between VMs or to a link that connects to an external network.

Virtual NIC

Virtual NIC (vNIC) is a software that emulates the functions of a **network interface card** (NIC) or network adapter. A vNIC is associated with a VM, which essentially sees this virtual device as a **physical NIC (pNIC)**. A vNIC connects a VM to a virtual switch (vSwitch). The vSwitch or a vSwitch group typically connects to a host system's pNIC. *Figure 8.6* illustrates this series of connections. The pNIC then connects to a physical Ethernet switch or router.

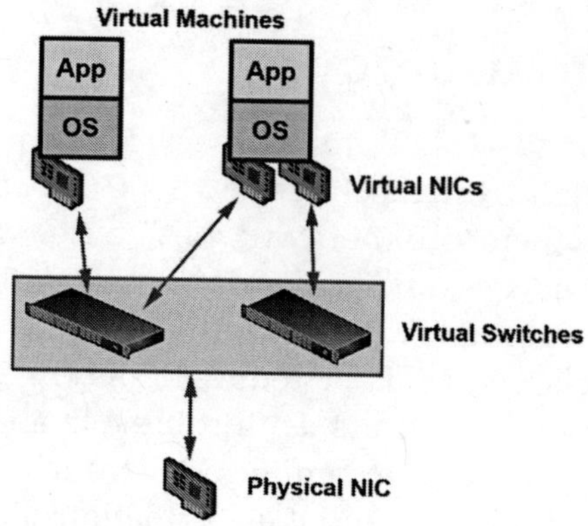

Figure 8.6: A vNIC connects to a vSwitch that then connects to a pNIC

Resource allocation and provisioning

Various methods are used to create a relationship between a physical resource and any virtual versions of it. A virtual environment is created through the virtualization and allocation of physical resources. The physical resources available to be allocated facilitate the virtual existence and independence of VMs, especially CPUs, memory, and storage. Like a physical machine, these components are essential to the virtualized environment.

Key configuration elements of device allocation to a VM are:

- **Resource shares**: This setting sets the priority or comparative importance of a VM or a resource pool. A VM with a **High** resource share has twice as many shares of a particular resource than a VM with a **Normal** resource share. It can also consume two times more resources, should the two VMs compete for it. The same holds true for the Normal resource share in comparison to a VM with a **Low** resource share. The ratio of High to Normal to Low is 4:2:1. However, a **Custom** resource share can be used for setting a relative weighting to a VM.

- **Resource allocation**: Resources are allocated to VMs based on resource shares, **resource allocation reservations** that set the minimum allocation, and **resource allocation limits** that set the maximum allocation. These factors are used in combination to set the relative priority of VMs competing for a resource.

CPU allocation

Most of today's virtualized environments run on systems that have a **symmetric multiprocessing (SMP)** CPU, also known as a multicore CPU. SMP multiprocessors contain two or more processors (cores). On SMP multicore processors, each core functions as a separate processor that can independently process a different program from other cores, while sharing common system services. CPU allocations are typically made as a part of the creation of a VM. *Figure 8.7* illustrates the basic structure of an SMP microprocessor:

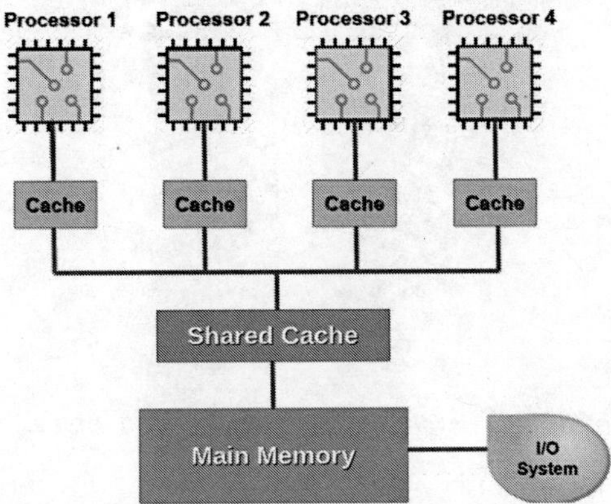

***Figure 8.7:** The structure of an SMP microprocessor*

Applications running in VMs are often dependent on multithreaded and multicore processors. Each of the cores of a multicore CPU can have multiple **virtual CPUs (vCPUs)** assigned through *hyperthreading*, which means that a single physical core can support two logical or virtual cores. A vCPU is essentially a time allotment on a core. A physical core can support up to eight vCPUs. However, A VM cannot be assigned for more than four vCPUs. A vCPU assigned to a VM is exclusive to that VM when it starts up, while it is running, and even when idle. vCPU and VM mapping are performed by the hypervisor.

Memory allocation

A virtualized environment may contain virtualized memory, which can be allocated to a VM. **Memory virtualization** occurs when an operating system combines the main memory of networked servers into a single memory pool that any application running on networked resources can share. Allocating memory to a VM is a virtual environment configuration setting. The memory allocation for a VM is specified in its configuration as the amount of memory the VM is to be allocated when it starts up. There are limits, and the administrator must know the amount of physical memory available. A VM cannot be allocated more memory than actually exists.

Disk allocation

There are two approaches for allocating any resource, including data storage, in a virtualized environment. **Thick provisioning** allocates the amount of a resource that a process actually uses. **Thin provisioning** allocates less of a resource than the total amount allocated to it. Thick provisioning is usually the least flexible solution, but it can be the best performing provisioning method. This is because the hypervisor doesn't need to recalculate the actual size of the space used. *Figure 8.8* illustrates the basic difference between thick provisioning and thin provisioning of a storage space:

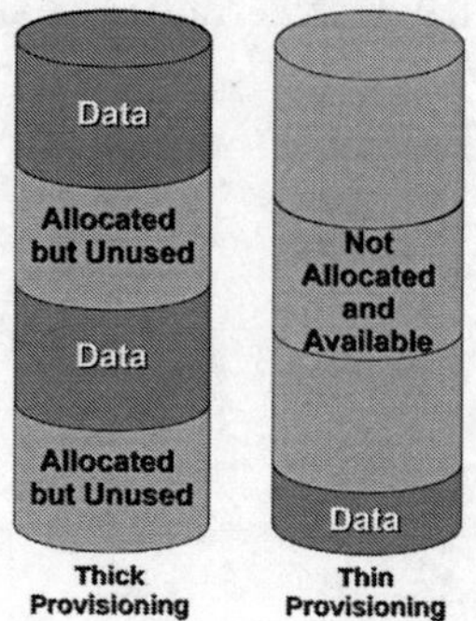

***Figure 8.8**: Thick provisioning allocates a set storage space, and thin provisioning allocates space as needed*

Overprovisioning

A common problem with virtualized environments that grew rapidly is that the resources that were initially allocated and provisioned in excess of their actual needs are now hoarding the resources needed by the additional processing. Similar to the issues shown in the previous section, disk, memory, CPUs, and other physical and virtual devices that were allocated in full to one or more VMs may now not be available to other processes. Another type of overprovisioning can be in the resource allocation reservations and limits being set too high. However, setting the allocations too low can also impact processing efficiencies.

VM testing

There are a variety of performance tests that can be used to measure the efficiency of a virtual environment, especially where the configuration of the VMs is standard. However, the three primary test categories that should be performed regularly in a highly active virtual environment are:

- **Performance testing**: The purpose of this type of testing is to monitor the performance of a VM under different situations or demands. The performance tests of a VM should be to measure the reliability, resource utilization, and scalability of its configuration and resource allocations. The tests typically used include:
    - **Spike testing**: This is a test of the performance of an application running in a VM with a rapid change in traffic volumes, high and low.
    - **Endurance testing**: This is a test of how a VM performs under a high-volume load for an extended time.

- o **Scalability testing**: This is a test of how a VM or an application performs with a slowly rising increase in processing volume.

- **Load testing**: This is similar to both spike and scalability testing, but with the objective of measuring the performance of a VM as it nears its allocation limits. Load tests look to identify issues or potential problems with memory mismanagement, buffer overflows, allocation capacities, bandwidth, load balancing, and other areas.
- **Stress testing**: This type of testing attempts to identify possible conditions that could cause a system to fail by increased volumes. A variation of stress testing is to reduce the resource allocations while the VM is running to find its minimum stress level. To avoid tests with unexpected errors, never go below the pre-established minimum requirements for each technology, operating system, or installed application.

VM management interfaces

The VM management software helps administrators manage, monitor, and configure virtualized environments. In addition, these software tools provide functions for allocating resources, troubleshooting problems, and monitoring the performance of virtual machines. There are several VM management software packages available, both proprietary and open-source. The capabilities of these systems commonly include creation, editing, and removal of VMs, management of virtual disks and vNICs, creation, and restoration of VM snapshots (backups), troubleshooting, monitoring, and threshold-based alerts. *Figure 8.9* shows a screen capture of a VM management system display:

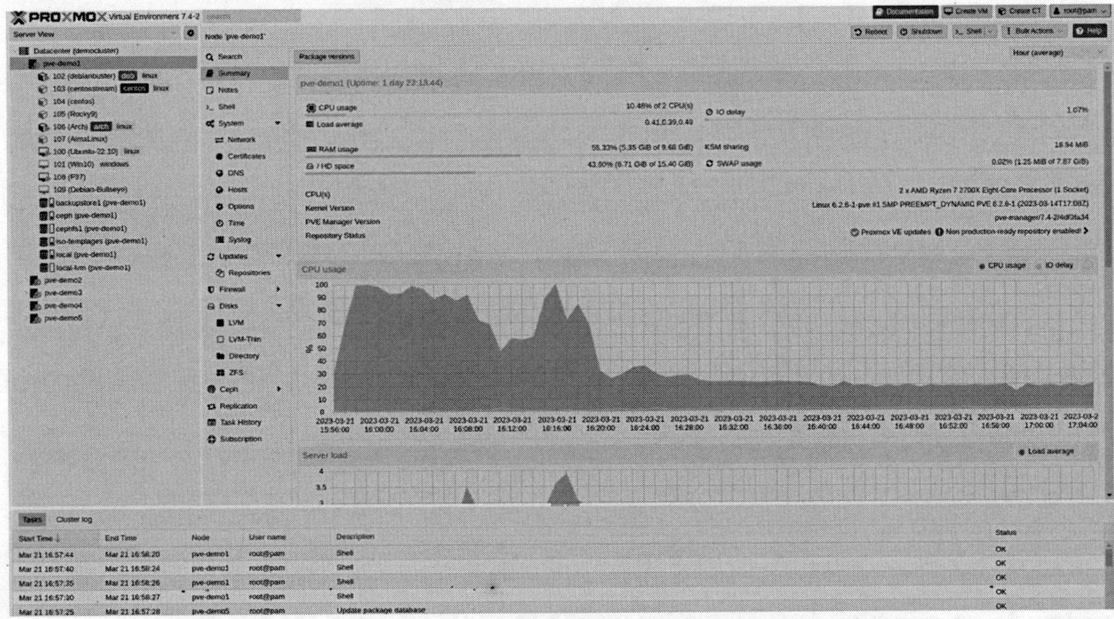

***Figure 8.9**: An example of a VM management software system*

Cloud models

Cloud computing services are available for private or public use in a range of offerings that are, for the most part, available for just about anyone at anytime. Cloud services generally fall into one of the four model categories: private, public, hybrid, and community.

Private cloud

A **private cloud**, also known as, an internal cloud or a corporate cloud, is a completely proprietary computing network architecture that is specific to an organization and its users (see *Figure 8.10*). In that, a *cloud* is generally external to an organization's computing resources, whereas, a private cloud is not exactly a cloud. In most cases, a private cloud is a virtualized computing resource, such as a network or intranet, which is available only to an organization's internal users. A private cloud can be a proprietary entity or provided by a **cloud service provider** (**CSP**), or a combination of both.

A private cloud should not be confused with a personal cloud, which is a limited form of a private cloud. However, unlike a private cloud, a personal cloud may or may not include a firewall or any other security devices. A personal cloud, which is also called MiFi, a short form for "My Wi-Fi," is a wireless network router that serves as a mobile hotspot. A MiFi device is commonly a dedicated wireless appliance, but many smartphones also have this capability.

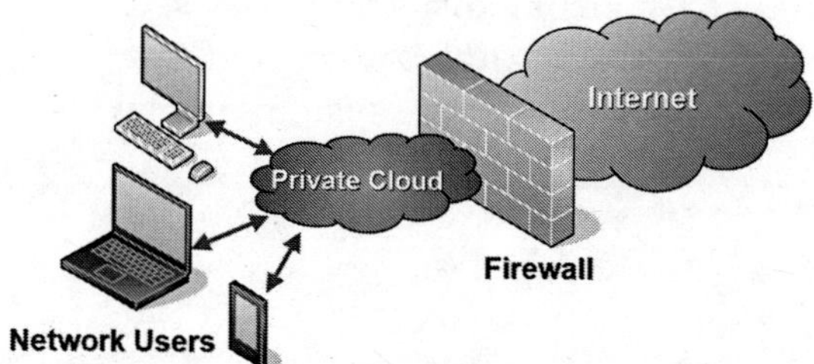

Figure 8.10: A basic private cloud model

Public cloud

A **public cloud** allows an organization or private party to subscribe to one or a set of software-based services that are accessed on the Internet from a CSP. *Table 1.1* compares the attributes of a public cloud to those of a private cloud:

Characteristic	Public Cloud	Private Cloud
Host	CSP	Organization
Access	Multiple entities	Single entities
Shared/Unshared	Shared	Unshared
Connection	Internet	Intranet or Internet

Characteristic	Public Cloud	Private Cloud
Security	Not secure for sensitive data	Secure for sensitive data
Expense	Less than private cloud	Organization bears the total cost

Table 8.1: *Comparison of Public and Private Cloud Models*

The facilities and services of a public cloud are the property of the CSP. The subscribing organization, or party, is essentially renting the hardware and software provided. The benefit of a public cloud service is that it can provide an effective and cost-beneficial alternative to a company that needs to expand a network, purchase new application software, or replace a data center it has outgrown. The benefit of a public network can also be realized by a company that is downsizing.

Hybrid cloud

A **hybrid cloud** model (see *Figure 8.11*) combines the private cloud of an organization with any of the services available on the public cloud. A hybrid cloud contains at least one private cloud application and at least one public cloud service. This combination results in some computing resources that are managed in-house and some that are acquired by subscription from a CSP. For example, a company might use a cloud data storage service like pCloud International to store and archive its general data but elect to manage its sensitive data in-house.

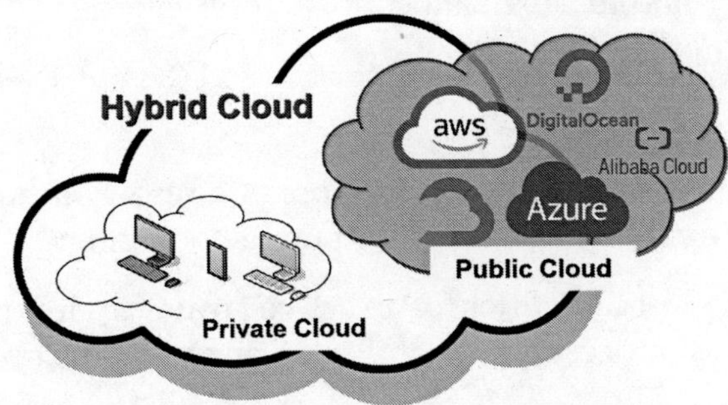

Figure 8.11: *A hybrid cloud combines private cloud and public cloud services into a single infrastructure*

Community cloud

A **community cloud** is an environment in which several companies, associations, clubs, or individuals, share the benefits of a public cloud, but with the control and security of a private cloud. Community clouds are multi-tenancy environments, meaning they can be shared by multiple subscribers simultaneously. Community clouds are often used as an excellent way for multiple individuals or companies to collaborate on a development, document, or project. A community cloud can be managed by one or more of the cloud members or by a third-party CSP.

Conclusion

Virtualization provides a means for organizations to leverage their IT investments to be more productive. A virtual environment extends physical computing devices to support multiple abstracts of the devices, resources, and operating environments. A virtual environment consists of one or more guest systems or VMs that reside on a host system. The administration of a VM specifies its allocations, configuration, and monitoring systems.

In the next chapter, we look at the use of scripting to create efficient blocks of commands for administration, configuration, and operations.

Points to remember

- Virtualization defines three types of virtualized systems: server virtualization, full system virtualization, and para-virtualization.
- Component virtualizations include OS virtualization, storage virtualization, and application virtualization.
- Virtualized networks commonly included NAT, PAT, direct access, and one or more vNICs and vSwitches.
- Key elements of resource and device allocations to a VM are resource shares (High, Normal, or Low), and resource allocations (reservations and limits).
- Virtual device allocations are made for SMP CPUs (vCPUs), memory, and disk space.
- Overprovisioning involves allocating more of a resource than is needed by a VM or setting the minimums and maximum limits too high.
- The three primary test categories for an active virtual environment are performance testing (spike, endurance, and scalability testing), load testing, and stress testing.
- VM management software is used to manage, monitor, and configure virtualized environments, as well as allocate resources, troubleshoot problems, and monitor VM performance.
- Cloud service models are private, public, hybrid, and community.
- A private cloud is a proprietary network architecture specific to one organization.
- A public cloud allows an organization or private party to subscribe to one or a set of software-based services that are accessed on the Internet from a CSP.
- A hybrid cloud combines a private cloud with the services of the public cloud.

On a community cloud, several organizations or individuals share a public cloud with the control and security of a private cloud.

Chapter 9
Scripting

Introduction

Among the essential skills a system or network administrator should possess, the two most important are: a basic knowledge of computer programming concepts and a working knowledge of a scripting language. Writing an administrative script is a form of programming, but not all programming languages can be used to write scripts. Programming creates new programs from scratch. Scripting defines a sequence of tasks (commands) that automate an action or activity. Programming languages are complex and can be difficult to learn. Scripting languages are generally simple and easier to learn.

This chapter looks at how scripts are used in system and network administration, along with the various types of scripting, what a script can do, the contents of a script, and some scripting examples.

Structure

The chapter covers the following topics:

- Scripting in server administration
- Script types
- Basic scripting constructs

- Scripting terminology
- Basic data types
- Windows environmental variables
- Script comments
- Linux environmental variables

Objective

By the end of this chapter, you will be able to identify and describe the sub-objectives of the following Server+ examination objective: *Summarize scripting basics for server administration.*

Scripting in server administration

Scripts provide a means for automating repetitive tasks. **Scripting languages** are indeed a type of programming language. However, a script is interpreted each time it is executed. Unlike C, Java, and other high-level programming languages, scripts are not compiled and stored as machine language executable files. Scripts are intended for use in runtime environments to automate functions, integrate systems, and possibly communicate with an **operating system** (**OS**) or another programming language.

Some of the important characteristics of a scripting language are:

- Open source
- Simple, not complex, and easy to learn
- Few data types and structures
- Faster to develop than using a programming language to develop a program

Script uses

There are several uses for scripts, and their effectiveness for a particular task or application depends directly on the type of scripting language used. Some of the common uses for scripts are:

- **Task automation:** Scripts can be used to automate tasks that are performed through a series of related commands.
- **Command sequences:** Command series that are used frequently or repetitively can be condensed into a file for execution as needed.
- **Data extraction:** A script can be used to extract data from a dataset, log file, or archive to be used for analysis, statistics, or troubleshooting.

- **System and network administration:** Scripts provide administrators with the ability to pull data or track activities from specific systems, logs, or metrics to monitor system or network performance.

Script types

There are two basic types of scripting languages:

- **Server-side:** This type of scripting language is executed on a web server. Server-side scripts are not visible to web users and are used to deliver content to HTTP requests. Some examples of server-side scripting languages are:
  - ASP.NET
  - Java
  - Node.js
  - Perl
  - PHP
  - Python
  - Ruby
- **Client-side:** This type of scripting is executed by a web browser on a host client. Examples of client-side scripting languages are:
  - HTML
  - CSS
  - JavaScript

Two other basic scripting types available that are dedicated to operating systems:

- **Bourne Again Shell (BASH):** This is a Linux **command line interface (CLI)**. Commands that would normally be entered one at a time at the CLI can be sequenced into a text document to be executed as a batch. The file containing the commands can then be shared with others or used as needed.
- **PowerShell:** This is a scripting language for automating tasks on Windows systems. PowerShell has an extensive library of commands and applets for system and network administrative tasks, such as administering the active directory and configuring network interfaces.

Note: The Server+ exam objectives include a reference to Virtual basic scripting (VBS), which is likely to mean VBS. Visual basic scripting was Microsoft's answer to JavaScript and was primarily supported by the Internet Explorer (IE) browser, which is now deprecated. VBS can still be used as the Edge browser will interpret it in IE mode. However, VBS has been unsupported since 2019 and is fading away.

Basic scripting constructs

Virtually all forms of programming are formed around three basic construct types:

- **Sequence:** This is the order in which instructions or commands are listed and executed. This is the standard for scripts.
- **Selection:** This is the process path taken when the script is executed. Scripts are primarily straight-line.
- **Iteration:** This is any repetitive steps performed by the script based on the conditions that arise. There are two types of iteration, which are also called loops:
    - **Definite:** This type of iteration is controlled by a count.
    - **Indefinite:** This type of iteration is controlled by a logical condition.

Scripting terminology

Like most programming languages, scripting languages have terms that reference or represent the elements it uses. Here are the primary terms you should know:

- **Syntax:** This can be defined as the rules or grammar of any scripting language. It sets the order in which the commands, variables, and operators are used.
- **Variable:** As in all programming languages, a variable is a uniquely named memory location in which data is stored during processing.
- **Operator:** Operators are mathematical or logical symbols that indicate the type of operation to be performed. For example, a plus sign (+) indicates addition, a minus sign (-) indicates subtraction, and a double-equal set (==) indicates a comparison.
- **Conditionals:** These constructs are used to compare values for a relational condition to one another. The result of a conditional statement is either or . *Table 9.1* lists the conditional operators available in most scripting languages:

Operator	Symbol	Syntax
Less than	<	a < b
Greater than	<	a > b
Less than or equal	<=	a <= b
Greater than or equal	>=	a >= b
Equal	==	a == b
Not equal	!=	a != b

Operator	Symbol	Syntax
String is not empty	-n	-n string1
String is empty	-z	-z string1

Table 9.1: Conditional operators in scripting languages

- **Assignment:** When data is stored in or transferred out of a variable, it is assigned to another variable or used as a parameter to a command. The assignment operator is an equal sign (=).
- **Comparators:** This type of construct is used for profiling datasets, such as comparing old and new datasets for differences, datasets with different formats, columns of a dataset, or searching for specific data in a dataset.
- **Construction:** A scripting language may be user-friendly, but it still requires its syntax, commands, and sequence to be valid and presented in the correct order expected by the interpreter.

Basic data types

Scripting languages, like all programming languages, define some basic data types each recognizes and works with. These basic data types are known as primitives. For example, scripting languages generally define the following primitive data types:

- **Number:** Any numerical data value, with the exception of very large data values, such as integers and real numbers (numbers with decimal values) falls in this data type. The number data type stores real numbers as a 64-bit binary value that can range between 2^{-1074} and 2^{1024}. Integer values are limited to the range of $-(2^{53} - 1)$ and $2^{53} - 1$ or ± 9,007,199,254,740,991.
- **String:** Test strings of any makeup, including embedded alphabetical, numerical, and special characters enclosed in quotation marks, are data type string.
- **Boolean:** A Boolean data type holds only one of two values, which can be represented as a 1 (one) or 0 (zero), True or False, Yes or No, etc.
- **Null:** The value zero (0) is a numerical value and should not be used to test for the absence of a value. This is what the non-value null is intended for. Testing for null is testing for a non-value.
- **Array:** This data type is used to organize data into a list form. An array is useful in a script for supplying strings of values or parameters to a command.

Server administration scripting

The process for creating or modifying a script file is essentially the same in all operating systems. It is the content of the script that varies. Windows scripts are primarily written with PowerShell **`cmdlets`** but a script of CLI commands can also be created. Linux scripts, called shell scripts or bash scripts, contain standard Linux commands that could be entered individually at the command prompt. In any case, script files provide the means to save a series of commands that collectively perform a task. These commands can be used again or repetitively.

Any **`cmdlet`** or command that can be issued from a command prompt can be included in a script file. Virtually any multiple command task can then be entered into a script file. This alleviates the need to enter each command separately by running the script file. So, an administrator can create scripts for a variety of regularly performed tasks. In fact, cmdlets typically return a value or an object that can be passed on (piped) to a subsequent command through a pipeline.

For the Server+ exam, you should know some of the basic tasks for which scripts can be used, including startup, shutdown, user account creation, login and logout, and starting and stopping processes and services. Examples of these scripts are included in the upcoming sections.

Windows scripts

On a Windows system, several routine task scripts can be created through the Local Group Policy Editor, a text script, or as a PowerShell script.

Windows startup scripts

Startup scripts are run as a part of a Windows system boot cycle. Scripts should be placed in the **`Startup`** folder. This folder is reached through the following pathname:

```
C:\Users\<username>\AppData\Roaming\Microsoft\Windows\Start  Menu\Programs\Startup
```

`<username> in this pathname is the user account name of the current user.`

After creating the script file, copy (or move) it into the Startup folder. To create a script file, use any text editor, such as the Windows Notepad or Notepad++, and enter the commands you wish to run at startup. Startup scripts can be used to display information, open files, startup applications, and any number of other tasks that you wish to have performed automatically when the system starts up. For example, the following startup script displays a variety of system status messages. See *Figure 9.1* for your reference:

```
:: Thanks to Mauro Huculak at WindowsCentral.com
@ECHO OFF
:: This batch file details Windows, hardware, and networking configuration.
TITLE My System Info
ECHO Please wait... Checking system information.
:: Section 1: Windows information
ECHO ==========================
ECHO WINDOWS INFO
ECHO ============================
systeminfo | findstr /c:"OS Name"
systeminfo | findstr /c:"OS Version"
systeminfo | findstr /c:"System Type"
:: Section 2: Hardware information.
ECHO ============================
ECHO HARDWARE INFO
ECHO ============================
systeminfo | findstr /c:"Total Physical Memory"
wmic cpu get name
wmic diskdrive get name,model,size
wmic path win32_videocontroller get name
wmic path win32_VideoController get
CurrentHorizontalResolution,CurrentVerticalResolution
:: Section 3: Networking information.
ECHO ============================
ECHO NETWORK INFO
ECHO ============================
ipconfig | findstr IPv4ipconfig | findstr IPv6
START https://support.microsoft.com/en-us/windows/windows-11-system-
requirements-6d4e9a79-66bf-7950-467c-795cf0386715
PAUSE
```

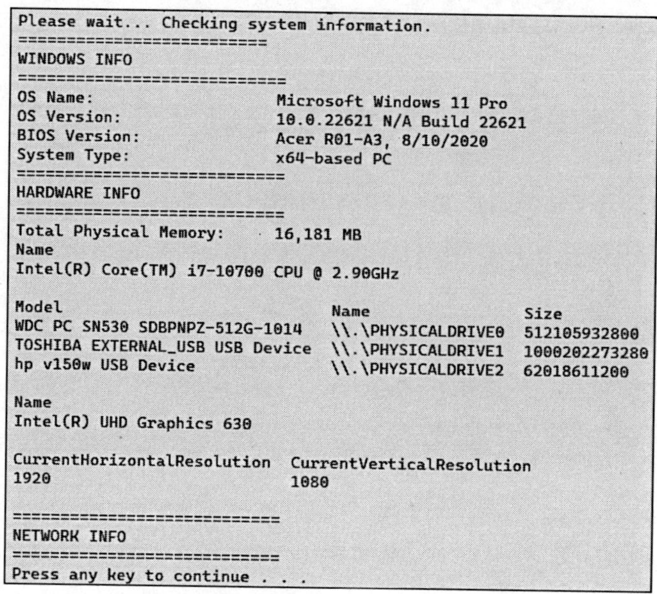

Figure 9.1: The results of a startup script

Startup scripts can also be added through the Local Group Policy Editor. To add a script, use the following steps:

1. Press the *Win+R* keys to open the run box, enter **gpedit.msc** in the **open** box and click on **ok** to display the Local Group Policy Editor (see *Figure 9.2*):

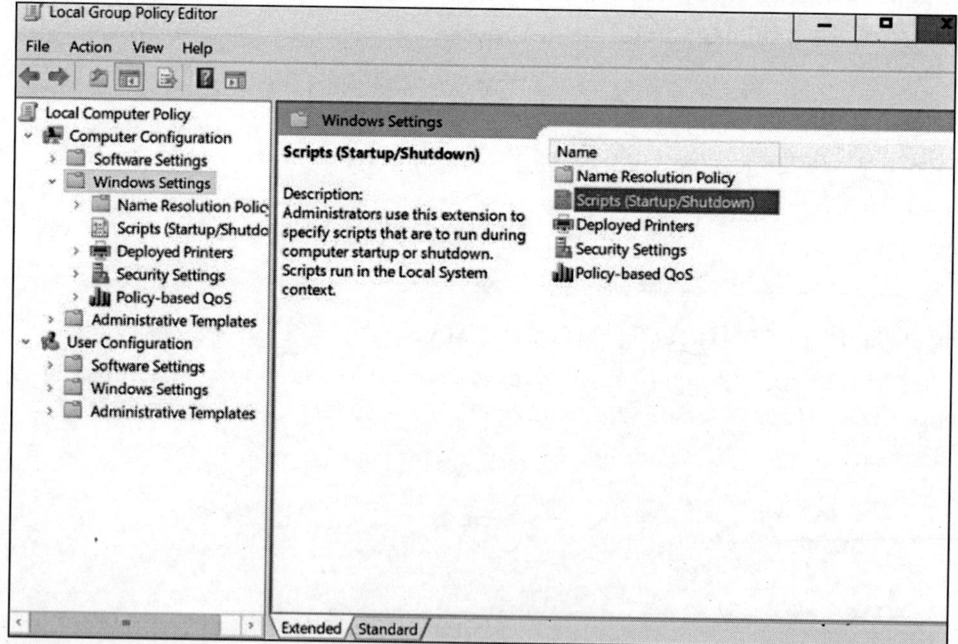

Figure 9.2: The Local Group Policy Editor

2. Double-click the (Startup/Shutdown) option.
3. At the bottom of the pane (left side), select the tab.
4. Click on the type of script you wish to add (Startup or Shutdown) to open the dialog box for that script type (see *Figure 9.3*):

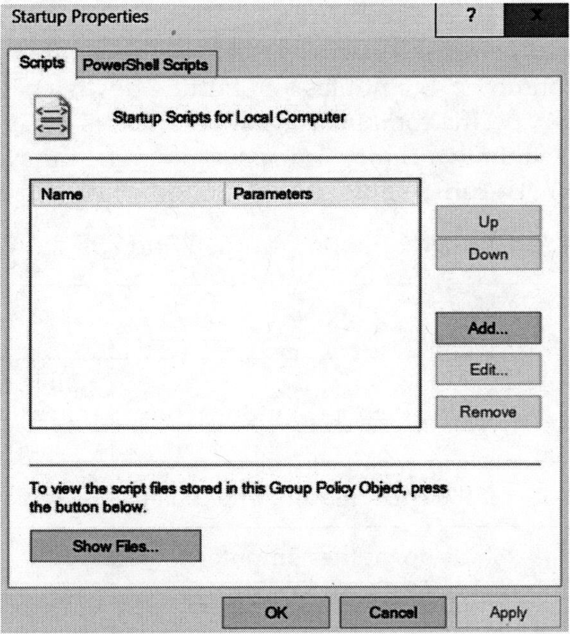

Figure 9.3: *The Startup Properties dialog box of the Windows Local Group Policy Editor*

5. Copy the script file from its current location and click on the button to open the **`C:\WINDOWS\System32\GroupPolicy\Machine\Scripts\Startup`** folder. Paste the script into this folder and close the page.
6. Click on the button on the dialog box to display the dialog box.
7. In the box, enter the script's name. Use the button to locate a script you wish to add, remove, or modify.
8. In the box, enter the parameters exactly as they would be entered following the script name on the command line. For example, if you wish to provide a count or size, you might enter **`//8`** or to run in interactive mode, **`//i`**. If there are no parameters to enter, leave the box empty.
9. Click on the button and then the button.

Note: Use one or the other of the two methods above to add a Startup script. Using both may cause the script to run twice, which may or not be a problem.

Windows shutdown scripts

The procedure outlined above for creating a startup script is the same process you will use to create a Shutdown script. The major difference is that where a startup script runs immediately after the boot process, a shutdown script runs right before the shutdown occurs.

The windows shutdown command has a variety of options that can be configured for virtually any type of shutdown. Script files for shutting down a system or remote devices are typically created for specific combinations of parameters or situations. A script could shutdown all systems without warning, issue a warning that the system will shutdown in a number of minutes or at a certain time, or just shutdown certain devices.

Table 9.2 lists some of the parameter options for the Windows shutdown command:

Parameter	Action	Comments
/i	Displays the Remote Shutdown box.	Must be the first parameter after the command, all other options are ignored.
/l	Logs off the current user immediately.	No time-out period.
/s	Shuts down the computer.	
/r	Restarts the computer after shutdown.	
/f	Forces all running applications to close without warning users.	Could result in the loss of unsaved data.
/m	Specifies a target computer for shutdown.	Can't be used with the /l option.
/t <xxx>	Sets the time-out period until shutdown to xxx seconds.	The default is 30.
/c <comment>	Enables upto 511 character comment in quotes; usually about the reason for the shutdown.	

Table 9.2: *Windows shutdown command parameters*

Start/stop services

A script to start or stop a single service on a Windows system is a bit of an overkill and can easily be done in the **services.msc** app, through the , or by running a command at a CLI. However, if there is a need to start or stop several services, especially if this is required repeatedly, a script can be perhaps more efficient.

The commands for stopping and starting a service are: **NET STOP <SERVICE_NAME>** and **NET START <SERVICE_NAME>**, respectively. Any combination of these commands can be included in a script file that is executed *ad hoc* or as a part of a startup or shutdown.

User logins

Login scripts are executed immediately after the authentication process when a user successfully logs onto a computer or network. These scripts are frequently used to modify settings in the OS, file and program permissions, map network drives, or simply to display a welcome message that may be specific to a particular user or group. Login scripts can be associated with user and group accounts and multiple login scripts can exist.

Account creation

By far the easiest and most efficient way to create a script for adding user accounts is through PowerShell. Adding a single user may not always be the best use of a script, but if the command parameters remain constant, it can be easier to edit the name parameters and run the script. For creating multiple user accounts from a script, the name parameters would need to be edited. To create a PowerShell script, the commands are entered into a text file that is saved with a **.PS1** file extension.

The PowerShell **cmdlet** used for creating a new local user is **New-LocalUser**. This **cmdlet** creates the user account with an option to also set a password, if desired. *Table 9.3* lists a few of the more commonly used parameters for this command:

Parameter	Action
-Name	Assigns an up to 20 character login name
-Password	The secure string
-Description	A description of the account
-AccountExpires	DateTime the account expires
-AccountNeverExpires	The account never expires
-Disabled	Disables the account
-PasswordNeverExpires	The password never expires
-UserMayNotChangePassword	User cannot change the account password

Table 9.3: *New-LocalUser parameters*

A **New-LocalUser** command set may look like this:

```
$password = Read-Host -AsSecureString
New-LocalUser -Name “NewUser” -Password $password -FullName “New User”
```

In these statements, the user is prompted to enter a password that is encrypted **(-AsSecureString)** and then inserted into the **New-LocalUser** command. The password is optional and can be edited later or set to a default password in this command.

Windows environmental variables

An environment variable, in any OS, are values that define the operating environment for apps and programs. These values provide parameters, data, and general information of the system and the OS. On a Windows system, environment variables have labels and store the value to which they are set.

On a Windows system, environment variables are grouped under three scopes: system (machine), user, and process. These are listed in a top/down order. The system scope is the parent to the user scope, which is parent to the process scope. The system scope has the environment variables that are associated with the system and Windows. Anyone can look at these variables, but administrator privileges are required to change them. The user scope environment variables are associated with the current user and can override some of the system scope variables that have the same names. The process scope has the environment variables associated with the currently run processes. These variables include some system and user variables as well as some dynamic variables related to each process.

Environment variables are stored in the Windows registry. User environment variables are stored in the **HKEY_CURRENT_USER\Environment** registry key. System environment variables are stored in the **HKEY_LOCAL_MACHINE\SYSTEM\CurrentControlSet\Control\Session Manager\Environment** registry key. *Table 9.4* lists a sampling of the environment variables on a Windows system with example settings:

Name	Value
ALLUSERSPROFILE	C:\ProgramData
APPDATA	C:\Users\bpbonline\AppData\Roaming
APPDATA	C:\Users\bpbonline\AppData\Roaming
CommonProgramFiles	C:\Program Files\Common Files
CommonProgramFiles(x86)	C:\Program Files (x86)\Common Files
ComSpec	C:\WINDOWS\system32\cmd.exe
DriverData	C:\Windows\System32\Drivers\DriverData
FONTCONFIG_FILE	C:\Windows\fonts.conf
HOMEDRIVE	C:
HOMEPATH	\Users\bpbonline

Name	Value
LOCALAPPDATA	**C:\Users\bpbonline\AppData\Local**
NUMBER_OF_PROCESSORS	16
OS	Windows_NT
PATH	**C:\Program Files\PowerShell\7;C:\Program Files**
PATHEXT	**.COM;.EXE;.BAT;.CMD;.VBS;.VBE;.JS;.JSE;.WSF;.WSH;.MSC;.CPL**
PROCESSOR_ARCHITECTURE	AMD64
SystemDrive	**C:**
windir	**C:\WINDOWS**

Table 9.4: *Examples of Windows environment variables.*

To manipulate the environment variables from a script requires that the current user has the appropriate privileges to make the changes to the variables in the script. The best choice is to run scripts that affect the environment variables from an administrator account.

To display the current settings of the environment variables, enter the commands **dir env:** or **Get-ChildItem -Path Env:** at the PowerShell CLI. To display the settings of a particular environment variable, use the command **Get-ChildItem -Path Env:\<variable name>**.

The standard PowerShell **cmdlet** for managing an environment variable is:

```
Set-Item -Path Env:<variable-name> -Value ($Env:<variable-name> + ";<new-value>")
```

An example of this command is:

```
Set-Item -Path env:UserRole -Value "Administrator"
```

In addition to the **Set-Item cmdlet**, there are the Remove-Item, Clear-Item, and Rename-Item cmdlets that can be used to delete, assign a blank name, or to change the name of a variable, given the appropriate user privileges.

Script comments

As you have probably noticed in the scripts shown earlier in this chapter, comments were indicated in a couple of different ways. In some scripts, a comment was marked with a double colon **(::)** and in PowerShell scripts with either a hashtag **(#)** or a bracketed hashtag **(<# comment #>)**. Depending on the scripting language used, comments can be marked off with a variety of characters. You can research to know which characters are used in each case.

Linux scripts

In the Linux/UNIX world, **shell scripts** are commonly used to execute command strings rather than one-by-one at a command prompt. Like Windows scripts, virtually all administrative tasks can be done through a script, which are also called **batch files**.

Linux startup scripts

Linux scripts, as far as their content is concerned, are much like Windows scripts. However, one large difference is when and how a Linux script executes. Linux uses the **`cron`** utility to run a program, utility, or script without operator intervention. Cron is short for chronological, meaning time-based. Cron allows you to set a specific day, date, and time for a process to run unattended in either foreground or background, something similar to using the Task Manager in Windows.

Note : If there are one or a few commands that need to be executed with every startup, these commands can be inserted into the /etc/rc.local script.

Crontab

A script can be set to run at a specific time by an entry in the crontab (cron table). As shown in the figure below, an entry in the crontab can be scheduled by minute, hour, day of the month, month of the year, or day of the week. Processes can also be scheduled to run on certain events, such as **`@yearly`**, **`@monthly`**, **`@weekly`**, **`@daily`**, **`@hourly`**, or the one used for startups, **`@reboot`**. *Figure 9.4* shows the help file information for a Linux crontab:

```
└─$ cat crontab
# /etc/crontab: system-wide crontab
# Unlike any other crontab you don't have to run the `crontab'
# command to install the new version when you edit this file
# and files in /etc/cron.d. These files also have username fields,
# that none of the other crontabs do.

SHELL=/bin/sh
PATH=/usr/local/sbin:/usr/local/bin:/sbin:/bin:/usr/sbin:/usr/bin

# Example of job definition:
# .---------------- minute (0 - 59)
# |  .------------- hour (0 - 23)
# |  |  .---------- day of month (1 - 31)
# |  |  |  .------- month (1 - 12) OR jan,feb,mar,apr ...
# |  |  |  |  .---- day of week (0 - 6) (Sunday=0 or 7) OR sun,mon,tue,wed,thu,fri,sat
# |  |  |  |  |
# *  *  *  *  * user-name command to be executed
17 *    * * *   root    cd / && run-parts --report /etc/cron.hourly
25 6    * * *   root    test -x /usr/sbin/anacron || ( cd / && run-parts --report /etc/cron.daily )
47 6    * * 7   root    test -x /usr/sbin/anacron || ( cd / && run-parts --report /etc/cron.weekly )
52 6    1 * *   root    test -x /usr/sbin/anacron || ( cd / && run-parts --report /etc/cron.monthly )
#
```

Figure 9.4: Linux crontab information

The crontab can be edited through the command **`crontab -e`**, which lists the text editors available on the system. Choose the editor you wish to use and add a table entry for an **`@ reboot`** item (see *Figure 9.5*) as shown:

```
# m h  dom mon dow   command
@reboot /home/bpboline/Desktop/test.sh
```

***Figure 9.5:** A crontab entry to run test.sh at reboot.*

Permissions

Linux shell scripts must be given permissions to execute, just like in any other OS. This is done through the **chmod** (change mode) command. This command is used to set the permissions for the owner, group, and others to execute, read or write (which includes delete) for a file or directory. Without going very deep into all of the actions of this command, to change a script file to be executed by the system, the owner permissions should include execute. To do this, the command is **chmod 754 /home/bpbonline/Desktop/test.sh**. This command assigns full permission to the owner, executes and reads to the owner's group, and only reads permissions to all others.

Cross reference: More information on Linux file and directory permissions, see Chapter 22 – "OS and Software Issues."

Linux shutdown scripts

Shutdown scripts can be used for any number of actions that are to take place before a system shuts down. All that is needed to have this happen is to create the script, apply its permissions, and then place it in the **/usr/lib/system/system-shutdown/** folder.

Linux start/stop services

There are two ways to start or stop a single service on a Linux system. Either run the service's **/etc/init.d** script with a start parameter: **/etc/init.d/<service> start** or run the service command with the start parameter: **service <service> start**.

For example, to run the **hwclock.sh** script, the commands would be:

/etc/init.d/hwclock.sh start and **service hwclock.sh start**

To stop a service, either of these commands can be used with a stop parameter replacing the start parameter.

User logins/logouts

There are default scripts that are executed whenever a user logs into a Linux system. These scripts can be modified to perform fewer or additional tasks, start specific programs, start or stop services, and set environment variables.

Linux systems typically have four login scripts, each of which is used at different times or under different conditions. These scripts (including their paths) are:

- **/etc/profile**: This script is run by the root system immediately after a boot process completes.
- **~/.bash.profile**: This script is also executed by the root system after a boot process completes.
- **~/home/.bashrc**: This script is executed after a login by a specific user.
- **/etc/bashrc**: This script is processed after the login by a specific user.

Similarly, there are two scripts that run at user logout:

- **~/.bash_logout**
- **/etc/bash.bash_logout**

All these scripts can be edited and have additional functions inserted or existing functions idled by being converted into comments.

Account creation

Adding a single user to a Linux system is a relatively simple process. However, on the other hand, adding multiple user accounts can be tedious and could be error-prone. The surest way to add multiple user accounts is to create a shell script to guide the process.

The command to add a single user is **useradd -m <username>**. For example, to add a user account for Jane D, the command would be **useradd -m janed**. The -m parameter is a flag to create a home director for the username.

To create multiple user accounts, either the **useradd** commands can be listed in a script or just the usernames, one in a line, for processing by the script. The script statements for processing a list of names are more like a program than just a string of commands. The following statements are one example of the script coding:

```
for user in `more user-list1.txt`
do
    echo "$user"
    useradd $user
    echo "$passw0rd!" | passwd -- stdin "$user"
    chage -d 0 $user
done
```

The above script reads in each of the usernames, adds the user account, assigns a default password, and sets the password expiration.

> **Note: The adduser command, which can be added to most Linux distros, can also be used to add new user accounts.**

Linux environmental variables

An environment variable, in any OS, are values that define the operating environment for apps and programs. These values provide parameters, data, and general information of the system and OS. On a Linux system, environment variables have labels and, like any variable, store a value to which they are set.

The most commonly used environment variables on a Linux system are:

- **EDITOR**: The current default text editor.
- **HOME**: The pathname of the current user's home directory.
- **HOSTNAME**: The network hostname of the PC.
- **LOGNAME**: The user's name.
- **MAIL**: The user's mail directory name.
- **PWD**: The present working directory (active directory).
- **SHELL**: The current shell type (bash, zsh, c, etc.)
- **UID**: The user's unique identifier.

Environment variables can be set temporarily, meaning until the system is shutdown or rebooted or permanently. The command to temporarily set an environment variable is

```
[VARIABLE_NAME]=[variable_value]
```

For example, to change the HOSTNAME variable, the command is **HOSTNAME = "MySystem"**

To permanently change the setting for a Linux environment variable, the command is

```
export [VARIABLE_NAME]=[variable_value]
```

To permanently change the **HOME** variable, the command is **export HOME = "~/student"**

These commands can be included in a shell script if several of the environment variables need to be set either temporarily or permanently.

Linux script comments

Like a Windows script, comments in a Linux shell script are indicated with a hashtag (#) in its first position. A comment can be inserted at any point: on a new line or following text on a line. For example:

```
# This is an example of a Linux shell script comment
# And this is another one.
```

Conclusion

System or network administrators must be able to deal with any unusual or extraneous configuration, definition, or operational settings and conditions that may occur on the systems. One of the best ways to do so is often through an administrative or shell script. In this chapter, we reviewed the various types of scripts and their constructs, data types, and uses. We also looked at ways to use scripts to perform repetitive and routine tasks.

In the next chapter, we will look at an important part of a server administrator's job – asset management.

Points to remember

- Scripts automate repetitive tasks and are used on runtime environments to automate functions, integrate systems, and possibly communicate with OSs. Scripting languages are open-source, simple, have few data types and structures, and are faster to develop.
- Common uses for scripts are task automation, command sequences, data extraction, and system and network administration.
- There are two basic types of scripting languages: server-side and client-side. Two basic scripting types that are dedicated to OSs are bash and PowerShell.
- Programming statements have three basic construct types: sequence, selection, and iteration.
- Some scripting terms to know are syntax, variable, operator, conditionals, assignment, comparators, and construction.
- Scripting language define primitive data types, including numbers, strings, Boolean, null, and array.
- Scripts can be used for basic tasks, including startup, shutdown, user account creation, login and logout, and starting and stopping processes and services.
- Windows startup/shutdown scripts can be added with the Local Group Policy Editor.
- On a Windows system, environment variables are under three scopes: system (machine), user, and process. Environment variables are stored in the Windows Registry.
- On Linux, shell scripts are used to execute command strings.

CHAPTER 10
Asset Management

Introduction

Asset management in the context of computing and **Information Technology (IT)** is the tracking and management of IT assets to guarantee that all assets are used properly, maintained, and upgraded during their useful life and disposed of properly at the end of their lifecycle. IT assets include more than just physical equipment. Perhaps, data is the most valuable and important asset in any organization. Another asset, although often overlooked, is the documentation of the hardware, software, policies, and procedures of the IT function.

However, there is a difference between the security of assets and their management. This chapter looks at the process of asset management, including the management and storage of system documentation.

Structure

This chapter covers the following topics:

- Asset management
- Documentation management
- Change management
- Policies and procedures

Objective

By the end of this chapter, you will be able to identify and describe the sub-objectives of the following Server+ examination objective: Explain the importance of asset management and documentation.

Asset management

Information Technology asset management (ITAM) involves the tracking, maintenance, monitoring, and disposal of the IT assets used in the processing and reporting of data and information in an organization. An IT asset is any unit of data, information, software, or hardware involved in the computing processes of an organization. Assets can be physical assets, such as computers, storage devices, and other equipment, or intangible assets, such as software, licenses, and electronically stored data. An asset's type does not necessarily have a bearing on its worth.

The asset management process involves more than just an asset inventory. While it is good to know what you have, it is better to know its worth, usefulness, and currency. With this information about each asset involved in the production processes of a business or organization, it is easier to minimize the risk of failures and disruptions, make the best use of existing resources, and plan for upgrade and replacement assets.

Asset management process

An asset management process has four major parts:

- **Asset identification**: In order to effectively manage the assets, it is essential to have a clear understanding of their nature and characteristics. A detailed and complete inventory of all assets must be taken and maintained with assets classified by type.
- **Asset tracking:** For every asset, there is a comprehensive record that includes information such as cost, contractual agreements, warranty, usage, location, condition, and relevant service dates, if applicable.
- **Asset maintenance**: A record is maintained to track the lifecycle of each asset, including any maintenance, repairs, upgrades, or refurbishments.
- **Asset disposal**: Depending on the asset type, many jurisdictions have requirements for the disposal of some IT assets. This would also include the retention and destruction of data assets.

Asset lifecycle

The ITAM processes also must take into consideration the lifecycle of an asset. Every IT asset, regardless of its nature (physical or functional) or value and currency, has a finite lifecycle. An IT asset's lifecycle has the following stages, refer to *Figure 10.1*.

- **Planning**: This involves determining the need for a particular asset and the best way to fulfill that need. Typically, this can be a make/buy or a purchase/lease decision.
- **Acquisition**: IT assets, especially intangible assets, can be acquired in any number of ways, including licensing, cloud applications, leasing, or purchasing.
- **Deployment**: This stage determines how an asset will be used or integrated into the current environment and supported.
- **Maintenance**: A procedure should be developed that outlines how the asset should be maintained, upgraded, or managed and by whom.
- **Disposal**: All assets have a serviceable lifespan, after which the asset should be retired or replaced. A procedure for the verification of end-of-life and the disposal method of the asset should be developed when the asset is first deployed.

Take a look at the following figure for a better understanding:

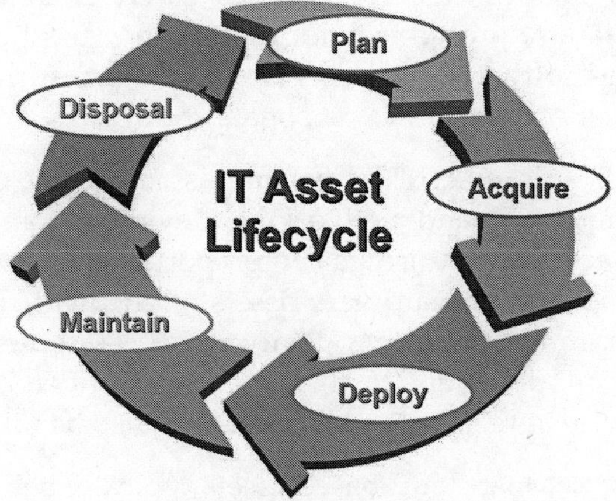

Figure 10.1: *IT Asset Lifecycle*

Asset labeling

Not all IT assets can be labeled. Software assets, acquired on a physical media or boxed set can be labeled, but the actual asset, the software stored in a computer, can only be labeled electronically, using metadata that details its information. Physical hardware devices can certainly be labeled or tagged, as it is referred to.

Asset tagging involves affixing an identifying tag or label physically on a piece of equipment or a device that identifies what it is, where it should be, any identifying numbers, and any other pertinent data. *Figure 10.2* illustrates one example of what an asset tag might look like:

Figure 10.2: An example of an IT asset tag

Asset classification

Grouping assets into asset classes is recommended to facilitate their management and administration, as it allows the organization of similar assets together. There are basically four general asset classes for IT resources:

- **Software assets:** This asset class includes **Intellectual Property (IP)**, such as design documentation, procedural documentation, and licensing. Of course, this class also includes software programs and packages, such as operating systems, middleware, server software, and personal productivity applications.
- **Hardware assets:** This asset class encompasses all the computing, peripheral, storage, communication, and networking devices of an organization. All the equipment in a server room or data center, portable devices, cell phones, tablets, notebooks, and so on, are hardware assets, along with their power cords and charging devices. Internetworking devices, such as routers, switches, hardware firewalls, bridges, modems, and the like, are also included in this class. In addition, any pre-paid service agreements or licenses will also be included in this class.
- **Cloud-based assets:** Most cloud-based assets typically belong to the cloud service provider. Various organizations store data in the cloud, and this asset must be monitored and accounted for.
- **Data assets**: In most cases, the data assets of an organization are likely the most valuable of all their IT assets. Their management is more of a security matter, but its accounting, administration, and safeguarding are an important part of any asset management system.

Documentation management

Document management in the context of an IT organization is the processes, procedures, and resources applied to the organization, storage, and maintenance of the plans, designs, records, and history of the hardware and software assets it employs. The documents may be hardcopy, digital, and perhaps even audio/video recordings, and represent contracts, forms, designs, implementations, purchases, employee records, and more.

Internal documentation

Internal documentation refers to the collection of records and documents used in an organization's decision-making processes. Internal documentation varies based on the specific needs of each organization and can encompass various types of documents. These may include plans, schedules, policies, directives, and other relevant materials. However, in general, internal documentation is of three types, as mentioned here:

- **Team documentation:** This includes records and documents generated before and during the development and design phases of a project, including goals, plans, schedules, reports, meeting minutes, and so on.
- **Reference documentation:** This type of documentation includes policies, operating procedures, guidelines, sample forms, and so on.
- **Project documentation:** This type of documentation consists of individual records of ongoing or completed projects. It may also include the team documentation from the project, along with proposals, product requirements, design guidelines, sketches, roadmaps, and so on.

The primary value of documentation is communication. In many cases, when a team looks to upgrade or replace an existing system, none of the original development teams are still with the company. Hence, without adequate documentation, any work on the system would be guesswork and delay the project.

Documentation updates

Documentation that is not kept up-to-date with changes in the operating environment, modifications to the programming, or any other alternation that may affect it; ceases to hold its value to the organization. Any change that impacts the correctness and completeness of documentation should be immediately incorporated into the document. A log or record should also be maintained to indicate when and who made the changes. Documentation that is not maintained and updated properly can be the cause of misconfiguration, and erroneous assumptions, and lead to other problems.

Documentation content

What is included in a particular set of documentation is completely dependent on the nature of the object, project, tasks, procedure, etc. being documented. However, for the Server+ certification examination, the following lists include the documentation types you are likely to encounter on the exam.

- **Architecture diagrams**: Also called **Software Architecture Diagrams (SADs),** this documentation provides a graphic representation of the order of events in a software project. The purpose of these diagrams is to show the structure, processes, procedures, methods, and/or database of the project.

- **Baselines:** A baseline is a set of fixed reference measurements and metrics against which future measurements can be compared. Documentation should also include any measurements compared to the baseline.
- **Recovery processes**: Also called a **Disaster Recovery Plan (DRP),** this documentation provides a roadmap and detailed procedure for the actions to be taken for the recovery of computing services following a natural disaster or catastrophic event.
- **Server configurations**: Just like a baseline, the documentation for different server hardware and software configurations should be diligently maintained. Any settings changes, new hardware upgrades, firmware upgrades, OS upgrades, and so on, should be documented with an explanation of the change and its date.
- **Network diagram**: This is an illustration of the physical topology of a network that shows how the network devices are connected. Another important network illustration is a logic diagram that depicts the flow of information through the network. Where appropriate, these diagrams should also identify subnets, network masks, IP addresses, active ports, VLANs, routing protocols in use, and more.
- **Service manuals**: Many peripheral and standalone systems can be serviced independently of the system. To facilitate ready access to the product guides, service manuals, and user guides for these components, as well as the **heating, ventilation, and air conditioning** (HVAC), security, and other environmental systems in a server room or data center, this documentation should be kept near the equipment.
- **Workflow diagrams**: This documentation is an extension of the architectural diagrams of a system and provides a detailed visual layout of the individual processes of a project in the form of a flowchart diagram. Workflow diagrams also incorporate the roles and duties of users and integrated processes.

Document availability

Documentation is only as good as it is up-to-date and accurate. However, even the best documentation can be worthless if it is not available when needed. Documentation, in general, is typically hardcopy, in binders, and one copy is located in a cabinet in the data center or server room.

Documentation should be available where it is likely to be needed. This may mean that there should be more than one copy, or it should be available electronically. Access to the documentation should be on a need-to-know basis and restricted to those who could require its information as a part of their assigned duties. Depending on the content of the documentation, the principle of least privilege should be used to determine who should have access to it.

In some cases, system or network documentation may require secure storage, especially if proprietary information, such as administrator passwords and encryption information is documented.

Change management

Changes are inevitable in any organization, especially in their systems. Managing change is a way to lessen the impact it has on the organization's resources. A part of managing change is documenting the change process in detail. Every organization should have a standard process for documenting not only the change management process, but its products as well.

Every change that makes an impact on a project, an existing system, or process, should be thoroughly documented. This documentation should include, at minimum, the following eight areas:

- **Communication**: Have all the required stakeholders and policy makers approved of the proposed change?
- **Cost**: How will the proposed change affect the budget or funding of the project, or is the proposed change financially feasible?
- **Procurement**: Will the proposed change impact the materials and resources already bought, or any new resources required by the change be available?
- **Quality**: Will the proposed change alter the overall quality of the project, or will the proposed change create an environment for defects to occur?
- **Resources**: Are new human and material resources required by the proposed change, and are these resources available?
- **Risks**: Are there any potential logistical, financial, or security risks involved with the proposed change?
- **Schedule**: How will the proposed change impact the current schedule of a project, or what are the time constraints of the proposed change?
- **Scope**: How will a proposed change affect the existing scope of the affected system or project?

In addition to managing and documenting proposed changes, approved, or denied, version control should also be applied. The purpose of **version control** is to limit access to making documentation changes to one or a few individuals and avoid multiple conflicting changes.

Policies and procedures

Among the important areas to be documented are the policies and procedures on disaster or catastrophic events and the recovery from these events. Exactly what should be covered in the policies and procedures related to the recovery of a severe failure of an organization's systems depends on the nature of the organization and its operations. There is no one-plan-fits-all solution.

For the Server+ exam, the objectives list many of the key components that a disaster and recovery plan should address, and you should know about the following:

- **Business impact analysis (BIA)**: This is a study or exercise that projects the impact of a disruption to an organization's normal operations, such as weather, labor strikes, raw material shortages, war, or a natural disaster. A BIA is typically the precursor to developing a **Business Continuity Plan (BCP)** or a DRP.
- Business disruption/disaster recovery plan metrics:
    - **Mean time between failures (MTBF)**: This metric represents the average amount of time between recoverable failures in a system, network, or component. The ideal MTBF is a higher number, which represents a longer period between failures.
    - **Mean time to recover (MTTR)**: This metric can represent any one of four different measurements, all roughly about the same meaning: mean time to repair, recover, respond, or resolve. MTTR is the average time required to put a failed component back in service, including the time to resolve the problem and complete any testing.
    - **Recovery point objective (RPO)**: This is less a metric and more of a relative point in time for the point at which operations can resume. For example, if a catastrophic event disrupts normal system operations, the RPO may be six hours before failure. The RPO of an organization sets many policies, such as when backups are created and the RTO for restoring the systems. *Figure 10.3* illustrates the difference between RPO and RTO.
    - **Recovery time objective (RTO)**: This metric states the goal for a recovery process to complete and restore the operations of a failed system or component. The RTO must address all possible actions required to restore normal business operations.

Take a look at the following figure:

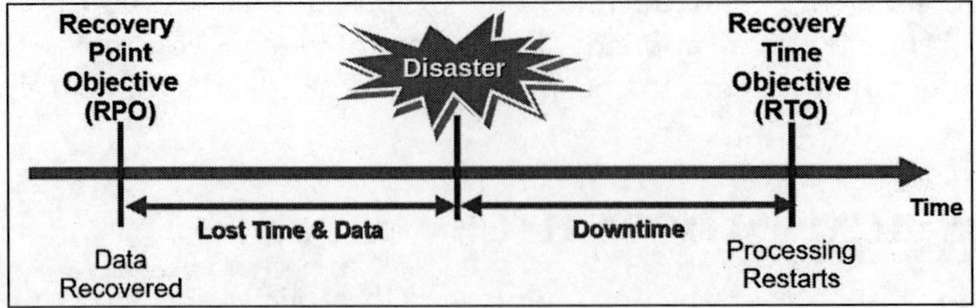

***Figure 10.3:** RPO is the point of recovery, and RTO is the time required to recover*

Note: The objectives list two other items in this area: service level agreements (SLAs) and uptime requirements. Both these areas are discussed in *Chapter 7, High Availability*.

Conclusion

The duties and responsibilities of a server or network administrator also include the acquisition, installation, maintenance, and retirement of hardware and software components of a system or network. This includes the stewardship of the computing and IT assets and the system, network, along with operational plans and procedures' documentation.

The next chapter covers the various aspects and types of software licensing.

Points to remember

- ITAM involves the tracking, maintenance, monitoring, and disposal of the IT assets used in the processing and reporting of data and information in an organization.
- Assets can be physical assets or intangible assets.
- Asset management has four parts: asset identification, asset tracking, asset maintenance, and asset disposal.
- An IT asset lifecycle includes planning, acquisition, deployment, maintenance, and disposal.
- Asset tagging affixes an identifying tag or label physically on a piece of equipment or a device that identifies it.
- There are basically four general asset classes for IT resources: software assets, hardware assets, cloud-based assets, and data assets.
- Document management in an IT organization is the storage, and maintenance of plans, designs, records, and history of the hardware and software assets it employs.
- Internal documentation is records and documents used in an organization's decision-making processes. Internal documentation has three types: team documentation, reference documentation, and project documentation.
- Documentation can include architecture diagrams, baselines, recovery processes, server configurations, service manuals, and workflow diagrams.
- An organization should have a standard change management process.
- Documentation of changes should include communication, cost, procurement, quality, resources, risks, schedule, and scope.
- The policies and procedures for disaster or catastrophic events and recovery should address: a BIA and business disruption/disaster recovery plan metrics, including MTBF, MTTR, RPO, and RTO.

Join our book's Discord space

Join the book's Discord Workspace for Latest updates, Offers, Tech happenings around the world, New Release and Sessions with the Authors:

https://discord.bpbonline.com

CHAPTER 11
Licensing

Introduction

Software can be free to try, share, or licensed for a fee. In every case, the software may be copyrighted and provided for use by a consumer under no, some, or restricted conditions. This chapter looks at the various types of software versions along with the conditions and rights a software provider grants its users.

Structure

The chapter covers the following topics:

- Software licensing
- Licensing agreements
- Licensing models
- Version compatibility

Objective

By the end of this chapter, you will be able to identify and describe the sub-objectives of the following Server+ examination objective: *Explain licensing concepts.*

Software licensing

When you obtain a software, your right to use it on a computer, server, network, etc., is granted under one of five general licenses:

- **Freeware**: This type of software is copyrighted but made available to anyone who wants it free of charge, typically for an unlimited time. Freeware is not a *free software*, that is, it is copyrighted and has restrictions.
- **Shareware**: Like freeware, shareware is a copyrighted software shared by the copyright holder for demonstration or trial use, usually at no cost or a small price. Shareware generally is intended to generate a revenue stream at some point.
- **Trialware**: Also called demoware, this form of shareware is typically a limited version of a software package that can be used for a limited period of time as a *try before you buy* demonstration.
- **Open-source**: This freeware software includes its source code, which users can add or modify without restriction.
- **Licensed**: Commercially available software is not purchased in ownership. Rather, it is licensed, which means a user is buying a right to use the software as it is.

Licensing agreements

Software licensing agreements, also called **end-user licensing agreements (EULAs)**, are legal contracts between a software developer or publisher and an end-user purchasing a use license for a software package. A EULA specifies how the software can be used, the number of times the software can be installed, the limitations for copying, modifying, or sharing the software, and any other restrictions the developer chooses to enforce. EULA is typically a separate document in the retail packaging of a software product. However, if the license is purchased online, users must accept the EULA terms as a part of the purchase or accept its terms as a part of the software's installation process.

A software license agreement creates an agreement between the software developer and the end-user on two major points:

- The software developer retains all rights of ownership to the software.
- The end-user's rights are limited to those specifically included in the licensing agreement.

Licensing models

A license model is the structure and process that a software developer uses to generate revenue for its software product. The software industry uses over a dozen licensing models, but any one software publisher may support only a few, depending on its product lines and customer base. Microsoft supports eight different licensing approaches ranging from Enterprise licensing to specific plans for government and educational bodies. What software is included in a license and the type and availability of technical support, training, and other product-oriented offerings can also vary.

Licensing models, especially large-volume or bulk licensing models, set licensing fees on a variety of units. The following are the ones you may encounter on the Server+ exam:

- **Per subscriber**: A separate license is required for each user or device that accesses and uses a licensed product.
- **Per instance**: This licensing model is commonly used in virtualized environments. A product license is required for each virtual guest (VM) running on the host, as well as a license for the physical host (hypervisor).
- **Per processor/per server**: A processor license covers unlimited network users who can access and use the licensed software. Processor licenses cover individual software packages.
- **Per core**: A core license supports unlimited users to access and use server-based software running on a set number of processor cores.
- **Per concurrent user**: This licensing model provides a fixed number of licenses that can be accessed by that number of users concurrently. For example, if a network has 30 workstations, but only 20 licenses are purchased, only 20 users can use the software concurrently.
- **Per socket**: This licensing model bases its fees on the number of CPU sockets on a computer's motherboard. If a computer has two CPU sockets available, but only one CPU is installed, only one per socket license is needed. Two licenses are required if two CPUs are mounted on a computer's two sockets.
- **Site-based**: A site-based license allows a software package to be installed or accessed by an unlimited number of users concurrently.
- **Node-locked**: In this licensing model, software is assigned and limited to specific hardware (nodes, mobile devices, IoT, etc.). This model is designed to limit software to specific hardware devices and capabilities. During product setup, nodes are assigned a device fingerprint or hardware ID code that authorizes the software to run on that device.
- **Digital signatures**: Perhaps the most secure method for verifying licensed software installed on an end-user's computer is digitally signed licenses. This method uses an encrypted public/private key pair and a passphrase issued by a server-side process controlled by the software provider. The digital signature license is verified at startup and, in some cases, frequently while the software is in use.

Subscriptions

Much like a magazine subscription, the software licensing model known as *software as a subscription* provides users with the ability to pay to use a particular software program or package and continue using the software as long as they pay the subscription fees. Subscribed software, also known as **Software as a Service** (**SaaS**), is accessed via the Internet on a cloud service provider's system.

However, there are several different types of software subscriptions offered to users, including:

- **Consumptive**: This type of subscription is based on the number of uses (consumptions) a user purchases in advance. Several methods can be used to measure the consumption, including the number of input/output operations, executions, running time, and more.
- **Freemium**: This is a hybrid of a software licensing type and a subscription method in which users have access to a limited version of a software package at no cost. Additional features can be accessed for a subscription fee that may also include other services, such as technical support and upgrades.
- **Metered**: Under this subscription type, usage of the software is automatically recorded and charged against a pre-paid amount or a billed amount. This method allows users to limit the cost of the software based on its registered use.
- **Project-based**: This subscription method facilitates the use of a software package by a project team or group. The subscriber purchases a primary license and is then able to provide access to a fixed number of team members.
- **Use-time**: This subscription method gives a user a specific period during which the software can be used. After the subscribed period expires, the software is not accessible. To regain access to the software, the user must purchase another time block or subscribe to a version with no time constraints.
- **Perpetual licensing**: In this type of subscription, customers purchase a never-ending software license. Typically, customers pay for the license only once, but may have to pay a yearly maintenance fee. The advantage of perpetual license for customers is that the upfront license fee eliminates being surprised by increasing license fees for renewals.

Software license and maintenance agreements

A **software license and maintenance agreement** (**SMA**) is an agreement that the software publisher commits to provide technical support, fixes, and updates for its product. This agreement assures the consumer that the software provider can be held accountable for their products. The content of an SMA can vary, but for the most part, it details the software license, what and when updates are available, and the miscellaneous legal terms of the agreement.

An SMA primarily defines the software support services the provider is committing to provide. In general, these services cover technical support and product fixes and upgrades, although it is not unusual for upgrades to require a fee. The services provided may include remote troubleshooting, access to **frequently asked question** (**FAQ**) databases, and voice or messaging user assistance.

Volume licensing

Most software providers offer some form of a volume licensing program, which is intended for organizations requiring multiple licenses for individual or network users. A volume license provides activation keys but not the packaging and documentation usually provided in a retail **full packaged product** (**FPP**). The benefits of a volume license are typically a lower price per unit, permission to duplicate the media, and extended product licensing and support agreements. At one time, volume licensing required volume license keys or one product key per unit. These have largely been replaced in most volume license agreements with an umbrella activation key or a key management server key set.

The size of a volume license typically depends on four factors:

- The size of the organization
- The organization type
- The licensed product
- How the product is to be used

Software providers will usually tailor a volume license agreement to the needs of specific organizations, such as federal, state and local governments, along with agencies, schools and colleges, large manufacturing facilities, and geographically dispersed organizations.

These license agreements can be either perpetual or non-perpetual:

- A perpetual license is never-ending and remains in force as long as both parties abide by the license agreement and its terms.
- A non-perpetual license agreement, which is essentially a subscription, is temporary, specific to certain software, and has an end-date.

License validation

Volume license agreements, such as the Microsoft **Enterprise Agreement** (**EA**), can require **license validation**. This means that a process must be in place on the consumer's systems to verify that its software licenses are current and valid, and are used as per the EULA or user agreements.

In most situations, all that the consumer is required to do is to make sure that the system, network, or workstations are connected to the Internet when the validation process runs.

How often the validation runs can vary with the software provider, the software itself, or the size of the license agreement. In general, the validation process runs each time a product key is entered for a licensed product. When the validation takes place, the information sent to the software provider's validation software includes the name of the license holder, the number of units in the license, the license key, the OS version, and a serialized control number. This information is used only to validate the license.

Microsoft requires that its EA customers provide certain information at the end of each year of the volume license agreement. Microsoft calls this process *True-Up*. This information is to include an inventory of any new hardware or software installed during the previous year of the agreement, in the form of:

- A statement saying that either no changes have been made to the qualified hardware, software, or online services since the last anniversary, and if applicable, the number of licenses to be reduced from the agreement (a minimum of 500 user subscription licenses is required).
- A true-up order that lists any additional qualified hardware, software, or online services since the last anniversary for which new licenses are to be subscribed, subject to the minimum requirement.

The inventory must include the number of each of the following items:

- Qualified desktops with the date each was put into service.
- Qualified users with the date each became a qualified user.
- Operating system installations running on either physical or virtual devices.
- CPUs on which the software is running with the date each was put into service.
- Operating system installations on desktop computers with the date each was put into service.
- New devices added requiring user **client access licenses** (**CALs**).
- Servers with access to external users with the date each was put into service.

Failure to complete the Microsoft True-Up could result in additional fees for the licensing agreement renewal.

Version compatibility

As new or revised versions of the software are released, there can be concerns about whether it will work with the data files of an older version or whether its files may be compatible with future versions. These issues are backward and forward compatibility, respectively. They are especially important in computing and telecommunications.

- **Backward compatibility** is a condition or property of software and hardware technologies that provides a newer version of a product to be interoperable with one or more previous or legacy versions of that product. A product release that is not backward compatible can create data and process issues that typically require some form of file conversion or procedure revision to resolve.

- **Forward compatibility** is a less common problem. A forward compatible product can accept data in a format that will be a part of a future version. In effect, forward compatibility in an older version requires a newer version to be backward compatible.

The Windows OS provides backward compatibility for programming developed for older Windows versions. While most programs created for earlier Windows versions will run on Windows 11, some require **compatibility mode** to run at all. However, to do so, you will need to know the Windows version of the older program.

There are two compatibility modes that can be configured: the current user and all users. To enable or disable compatibility mode, follow these steps:

1. In the **File Explorer**, navigate to the folder holding the older software.
2. Right-click on the file and choose **Properties** to display its properties dialog box, as shown in *Figure 11.1*:

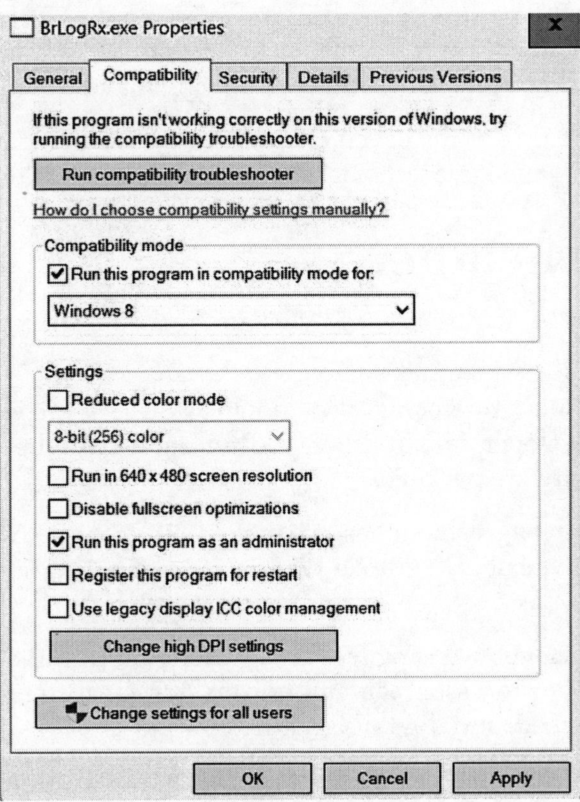

***Figure 11.1**: The Properties/Compatibility dialog box of a legacy application*

3. If this adjustment is strictly for the current user, no other actions are needed. However, if this is to apply to all users, click on the **Change settings for all users** bar.
4. To enable compatibility mode for this file, check the checkbox in the **Compatibility mode** area associated with the **Run this program in compatibility mode for:** and use the pull-down list to choose the legacy Windows version.
5. Select the adjustments required in the **Settings** area.
6. Click the **Apply** button and then the **OK** button.

Note: Whether backward or forward compatibility, it's essential that the minimum requirements of the software, such as the OS version, the amount of hardware required, the software libraries, additional drivers, and so on, are always met.

Conclusion

Software developers and providers issue licensing agreements to protect their rights of ownership and copyright. In order to acquire and use this software, consumers must agree to the terms of the software licenses and usage agreements. There are several types of software licenses and end user agreements, including single-user licensing, subscriptions, and volume licensing. Enterprise and volume licensing may be subject to validation.

The next chapter is the first of the seven chapters in the Security and Disaster Recovery (*Part 3*) part of the book and covers the data security objectives of the Server+ exam.

Points to remember

- The five general software license types are freeware, shareware, trialware, open-source, and licensed.
- Software licensing agreements, also known as EULAs, are legal contracts between a software developer or publisher and an end-user who is purchasing a user license for a software package.
- A software license agreement has two major points: the software developer retains all rights of ownership, and the end-user's rights are limited to the licensing agreement.
- Licensing models set licensing fees on a variety of units, including per subscriber, per instance, per processor/server, per core, per concurrent user, per socket, site-based, node-locked, and digital signatures.
- Software subscription types include: consumptive, freemium, metered, project-

based, and use-time.

- An SMA is an agreement that the software publisher commits to providing technical support, fixes, and updates for its product.
- The size of a volume license depends on four factors: the size of the organization, the organization type, the licensed product, and how the product is to be used.
- A perpetual license remains in force as long as both parties abide by the license agreement and its terms. A non-perpetual license agreement is temporary, specific to certain software, and has an end-date.
- The Microsoft **Enterprise Agreement** (**EA**) requires license validation that verifies that the software licenses are current and valid and are used per the EULA or user agreements.
- The license validation sends the name of the license holder, the number of units in the license, the license key, the OS version, and a serialized control number.
- A true-up inventory includes: qualified desktops, qualified users, OS installations, CPUs, OS desktops, new devices added, and servers with external users.
- Backward compatibility is when a newer version of a product is interoperable with previous versions of a product.
- A forward compatibility product can accept data in a format that will be a part of a future version.

Part - 3
Security and Disaster Recovery

One of the most important responsibilities of a server or network administrator is the **Confidentiality, Integrity, and Availability** (**CIA**) of the data and information while it is at rest, in-transit, or in use. This part of the book covers the various aspects of this responsibility and the policies and procedures that are employed to protect the data assets.

Part 3 includes the following chapters:

1. Chapter 12 - Data Security
2. Chapter 13 - Physical Security
3. Chapter 14 - Access Management
4. Chapter 15 - Risk and Mitigation
5. Chapter 16 - Server Hardening
6. Chapter 17 - Server Decommissioning
7. Chapter 18 - Backup and Restore
8. Chapter 19 - Disaster Recovery

CHAPTER 12
Data Security

Introduction

In today's information and computer technology environments, security has become one of, if not the most important parts of a system or network administrator's responsibilities. Protecting the data assets in each of their states, along with the issues of access, both physical and logical, is an absolute requirement for any system or network. This chapter looks at the methods, processes, and concepts that you should know and understand for the Server+ certification exam.

Structure

The chapter covers the following topics:

- Encryption
- Data retention policies
- Data storage
- Data protection and data
- Business impacts

Objective

By the end of this chapter, you will be able to identify and describe the sub-objectives of the following Server+ examination objective: *Summarize data security concepts.*

Encryption

Throughout history, we have wanted to keep our communications private and confidential. Whether this was war plans, affairs of state, secrets, or messages that were just not anybody's business, it needed to be secured. To do this, methods were developed to alter the body of a communication to make it unreadable, except for those who knew how to unalter the message. These methods are called **ciphers**. A cipher is a process or an algorithm that changes plain text into an unreadable coding that hides the original message from prying eyes. The application of a cipher to plain text is encryption. *Figure 12.1* illustrates this process. Encryption is used to keep private and confidential messages private. In computing, the primary use of encryption is to secure data in each of its states.

Figure 12.1: *The encryption/decryption processes*

There are two primary types of encryption algorithms:

- **Symmetric encryption**: This type of encryption uses the same password or encryption key to both encrypt and decrypt data.
- **Asymmetric encryption**: This type of encryption uses two keys: one, a public key that is shared, is used to encrypt data; and two, a private key, which is not shared, is used to decrypt data.

An **encryption key** is a string of alphanumeric data that is applied by the encryption algorithm to encrypt plain text into cipher text or decrypt cipher text back to plain text.

Data encryption

Data encryption is the process of applying an encryption algorithm to make data unreadable for storage, transmission, or use. Encrypted data can only be decrypted by users having the appropriate access and an encryption key. Encryption has three primary objectives: **confidentiality, integrity, and availability** (**CIA**), which is known collectively as the **CIA Triad**. The CIA Triad is the basis for the authentication, authorization, and non-repudiation processes that are the basis for user access to data. Encryption fulfills the integrity and confidentiality protection of data.

Data in computing exists in three states:

- **Data-at-rest** : This is data stored on a secondary storage device, such as a **hard disk drive** (**HDD**), a **solid state drive** (**SSD**), or some form of removable media. Data-at-rest is the primary target for attacks and breaches.
- **Data-in-transit**: This is data in transmission between one station and another. This data is subject to interception, especially on wireless networks. Data-in-transit needs protection from a variety of interception techniques while it is being transmitted. Equal, if not more robust, protection is also a requirement for data on a storage media, such as an HDD, SSD, flash drive, optical media, or a magnetic tape.
- **Data-in-use** : This is the data in primary memory or RAM, the data moving between a storage device and memory, and data on the system bus structures. Data-in-use is decrypted and copied to memory for a logical operation.

Data-at-rest

Data-at-rest is inactive data stored as a digital value. This type of data is not currently in use by any programs and is not being requested. Data-at-rest is essentially a sitting duck for an attacker. It has a logical structure, an identifying filename, and can contain proprietary, confidential, and valuable information, which can include financial data, intellectual property, contracts and agreements, employee information, and planning documents.

Encryption applied to data-at-rest on a storage device can have different levels of security. Encryption can be applied to all data levels, including an entire storage device or removable media. **Full-disk encryption** (**FDE**) creates a conduit between a storage device and RAM. Data is encrypted as it passes to storage and is decrypted as transfers from storage to memory. The encryption/decryption process can be applied to protect a partition, an entire filesystem, or an individual file.

Data-in-transit

Data-in-transit is data that moves between two nodes on a network, such as email, transferred files, a downloaded webpage, or an instant messenger message. Data-in-transit can be transmitted on a public network, such as the internet, or within a private network, like a corporate LAN. Data in motion is vulnerable to attack through eavesdropping attacks, such as man-in-the-middle, snooping, or sniffing. Data missent to an unknown or erroneous destination creates data leakage and may lead to an **advanced persistent threat** (**APT**), like ransomware.

Encrypting data before it is in-motion converts the data from plaintext to ciphertext, which can reduce its disclosure if intercepted or captured. With the data in an encrypted form, an attacker or any other third-party who intercepts the data, either maliciously or accidentally, is unable to open, decrypt, read, or change it without the associated decryption key.

Some best practices for encrypting data-in-transit are:

1. Applying SSL/TLS encryption on email and messaging.
2. Implementing **Virtual Private Networks (VPNs)**.
3. Sending data only to secure websites with HTTPS., SSH, TLS, SFTP, and other secured protocols.
4. Using **confidential computing** which isolates data-in-transit and data-in-use during processing.

Data-in-Use

Data-in-use is the type of data being processed, modified, deleted, read, or written by the system in response to requests from applications or services. This data is moving, but only within a computer. Data-in-use may be in RAM, before or after its use or in a database or a file actively being accessed. Unlike data-at-rest and data-in-transit, traditional encryption doesn't protect data-in-use. It is typically stored as clear text in RAM during its usage, which makes it the most vulnerable form of data. Unfortunately, encryption methods of data-in-use aren't yet available.

Data retention policies

It is well established that data is by far one of the most, if not the most, valuable assets an organization holds. According to the search technology firm *Lucidworks*, about 7.5 septillion (7,700,000,000,000,000,000,000) **gigabytes (GB)** of data is generated worldwide onto the internet every day. All this data is subject to the laws and rules that define how data should be managed.

Data retention is the application of an organization's policies and governmental laws and regulations, as well as guidelines of trade and industry associations. An organization's **data retention policy** prescribes exactly how its data should be stored and secured and the length of time the data is to be kept. These policies also typically prescribe the recommended or lawful way data and the media on which it is stored is to be destroyed.

A data retention policy defines what data will be kept and for how long. The policy should define the following:

- The data to be retained.
- The format in which the data is to be stored.
- The length of time the data is to be retained.
- Is the data to be archived or destroyed at the end of its retention period?

- Which organization has the authority and responsibility for the retention and disposal of the data?
- What constitutes a policy violation, and what is the recovery procedure?

A data retention policy should also address several business operations areas, including:

- The applicable laws, regulations, and legal obligations that apply to some or all data.
- The business requirements for keeping data.
- The membership of a company data retention policy team.
- Specific policies for different data types and formats.
- The detailed policies and procedures for data backup and restoration, including RTO and RPO expectations.
- A precise schedule for data retirement that includes the method of archival or destruction.

Data storage

The **Storage Networking Industry Association** (**SNIA**) defines **data storage security** as:

"Storage security: Application of physical, technical, and administrative controls to protect storage systems and infrastructure as well as the data stored within them. Storage security is focused on protecting data (and its storage infrastructure) against unauthorized disclosure, modification or destruction while assuring its availability to authorized users. These controls may be preventive, detective, corrective, deterrent, recovery or compensatory in nature."

The SNIA's definition focuses on protecting data and its storage location, where the data is stored which can provide a *last line of defense* against the loss or destruction of this valuable asset. Stored data, regardless of its physical or electronic location, must be protected and secured from unauthorized access to preserve its CIA.

Data protection and data security

Data protection and data security are different in their focus and application. Both aim to guard private and sensitive data and keep it away from unauthorized access and manipulation.

Data protection

Data protection focuses on data being available or being restored in the event of an attack, a catastrophic event, or a natural disaster. Ensuring data is protected requires the development and implementation of specific policies, procedures, and practices for the continued availability or restoration of data. Some of the important elements that should be included in a data protection program are:

- **Limit access**: Unrestricted access and little or no monitoring of who is accessing what is often the cause of a data breach. Attackers can often take advantage of open access controls to access an organization's data.
- **Consistent policies**: Organizations often apply protective controls too loosely or tightly, which leads either to wide open access or strict protection measures that hinder productivity. The data protection policies should seek to provide a balance of protection and availability.
- **Least privilege**: The principle of least privilege says that a user should have access to the data required for that person to perform his or her duties – and no more. If privileges are too strict across the board, productivity is affected. On the other hand, privileges for data not required by the user can lead to protection issues.
- **Protect only what needs protection**: Not everything stored on network servers or storage devices requires the same level of protection. Some documents and files are kept for convenience and do not need protection. Remember that even if a document is protected against changes, if it can be viewed, it can be captured by a screenshot or a cell phone camera.
- **Protect data-in-transit**: Even if in-house systems are well-protected and the cloud storage service to which it is backed up is very secure, data can be exposed to interception in transmission. Encrypt data-in-transit or use a VPN service for its transmission.
- **Backups**: A well-defined data backup plan should be developed and implemented. The frequency of backups depends on the nature of the organization. For instance, an online sales back-end database may need to be backed up every few hours while a data warehouse can be backed up once a week.
- **Storage**: Backups should be stored in a location that is secure, safe, and accessible, should the backups be needed for recovery.

Data security

The policies and procedures of a data protection plan should be incorporated into an organization's data security policies and procedures. **Data security** focuses on assuring the principles of the CIA Triad, preventing unauthorized access and attacks, breaches, and malware. *Figure 12.2* illustrates the differences and similarities in data security and protection:

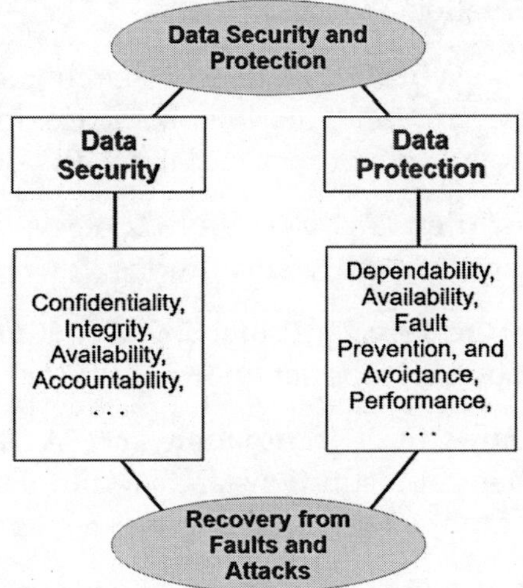

Figure 12.2: Security and protection are essential parts of a data security policy

A data security policy should include the following elements:

- **Formal policies**: An organization should develop a formal written policy that details the security required for the different data types requiring security. The policies should detail the security measures required for data in every storage location.
- **Access control**: A security policy should detail the **role-based access control (RBAC)** for the employee positions requiring access to secured data. This policy should specify the **authentication, authorization, and accounting (AAA)** measures to be implemented.
- **Encryption**: The policy must define the encryption methods to be applied to data-at-rest, data-in-transit, and, if applicable, data-in-use. The policy should define the encryption key management process to be used.
- **Backup and recovery**: A detailed data backup program should be defined in the organization's security policies. The program details should include the backup media, the schedule for backup actions, off-site and on-site storage locations, a **disaster recovery plan (DRP)**, and procedure.

Data security compliance

Many organizations belong to what are called regulated industries. These organizations are required to comply with the laws, regulations, and guidelines that define how they are to secure their data. There are many international, federal, state, and general data security and privacy laws in effect, with more in development. The following list mentions many existing laws concerning data security and privacy.

- Federal laws and regulations:
  - **Sarbanes-Oxley Act (SOX)**: Protects shareholders and the general public from accounting errors and fraudulent practices in publicly traded companies by requiring increased accuracy and reliability of corporate disclosures.
  - **Gramm-Leach-Bliley Act (GLBA)**: Protects the consumers' personal information held by financial institutions.
  - **Children's Online Privacy Protection Act (COPPA)**: Governs the online collection of personal information from children under 13.
  - **Fair and Accurate Credit Transaction Act (FACTA)**: Established provisions that require financial institutions and creditors to implement identity theft prevention programs.
  - **Federal Information Security Management Act (FISMA)**: Federal agencies must implement programs to secure their information and information systems.
- Industry-specific guidelines and requirements:
  - **Payment Card Industry Data Security Stand**ard **(PCI DSS)**: Defines the cybersecurity controls and business practices that must be implemented by companies accepting credit card payments.
  - **Health Insurance Portability and Accountability Act (HIPAA)**: Requires the adoption of standards for electronic health care transactions and code sets.
  - **The Health Information Technology for Economic and Clinical Health Act (HITECH)**: Adds new requirements concerning privacy and security for patient health information to HIPAA.
- U.S. state laws:
  - **California**: **Consumer Privacy Act (CCPA)**: Allows any consumer to see the information any company has on them, as well as a list of the third parties with which the data has been shared.
  - **Maine**: Act to Protect the Privacy of Online Consumer Information: Prohibits Internet providers from *"using, disclosing, selling or permitting access to customer personal information unless the customer expressly consents to that use, disclosure, sale or access."*
  - **Virginia**: **Consumer Data Protection Act (CDPA)**: Defines a framework for how companies control or process personal data.

- International laws:
    - **Canada: Personal Information Protection and Electronic Documents Act (PIPED)**: Defines how public and private organizations collect, use, and disclose personal information.
    - **European Union: General Data Protection Regulation (GDPR)**: Requires businesses to protect the personal data and privacy of EU citizens for transactions that occur within EU member states.
    - **Mexico**: Law on the Protection of Personal data held by private parties: Requires organizations to have a lawful basis, such as personal consent or a legal obligation, to collect, process, use or disclose personally identifiable information.

Storage security

Storage is anywhere data is stored. Data does not necessarily mean electronic data. It can also be paper documents, microfilm, presentation slides, and other physical forms. Storage security is the policies, procedures, and storage media or facilities that define the security measures applied to secure data. This can include computer hardware, physical hardware (cabinets, shelving, etc.), network security controls, physical access security, user access security, and organizational policies.

The primary focus of storage security is to protect stored data from cyber threats, such as malware, attackers (internal and external), and loss. The security measures that protect data on a computer or network must be implemented to protect the data. However, storage security also includes the protection and preservation of data outside of a computer or a network. Typically, this means that the data, on a backup media, is stored in a physical location, either on-site or off-site. A physical storage location is an area set aside to store and possibly archive records and data backups. Preferably, a physical storage location can be locked or secured.

On-site storage

As it sounds, on-site data storage is within an organization's physical location. The location may be a computer room, data center, or an adjacent space where backups and sensitive records are stored. When considering an on-site storage location for data backups and archives, the following should be addressed:

- **Time**: On-site storage of data backups reduces the time needed to acquire and restore systems should the need arise.
- **Cost**: It is likely that an internal space is less costly to keep than the subscription fees for an off-site storage location. However, if a secure space is not available, the cost could be in lost data.

- **Safety**: Backups stored in an on-site location are exposed to the same natural and man-made threats of the entire facility. Fire, earthquakes, hurricanes, war, and severe weather can damage or destroy the building, along with the data backups needed to restore operations.
- **Security**: The security of data backups in an on-site storage location is more easily controlled than with an off-site location. The security considerations for an on-site storage space should include preventive measures against theft, heat, fire, and other environmental threats.

Off-site storage

Off-site data storage is physically separate and at a distance from an organization's primary facilities. The reasons for storing data backups in an off-site storage location are primarily safety and recovery. Should a catastrophe occur that destroys an organization's computing capabilities, data stored in an off-site location may not have been effected by the event. If necessary, replacement systems can be obtained, the backup data loaded, and processing resumed. An off-site storage location allows an organization to safely secure copies of its operational files in the case of a business disruption.

There are many ways to store data in an off-site location besides storing physical media, such as a magnetic tape, optical media, or other removable media. Data can also be stored off-site in a private or public cloud storage system or copied to a remote backup server. The primary types of off-site data storage are:

- **Tape and optical media**: Magnetic tapes have been a primary media for data backups for some time. Tape provides long-term data storage. However, tape reels and cartridges must be physically transported and stored and could be damaged, lost, or destroyed. The same issues apply to external disk drives, optical discs, and virtually all removable media.
- **Cloud backup services**: A data backup on a cloud service is commonly a mirror image of an organization's data. The data is stored on a service provider's system, which provides the storage medium, security, and an expandable capacity. Since the cloud storage service is geographically remote to an organization, recovering data from the cloud is generally assured.
- **Hybrid cloud backup services**: Neither a backup on local media nor to a cloud service is without risk. A hybrid approach combines a local backup with a backup to a cloud service. This provides double assurance that the data backup should be available when needed. This approach looks to provide recovery if either backup cannot be accessed.

System passwords

In addition to the OS, network, and possibly application passwords used to secure software on a computer, other passwords are intended to protect the physical configuration of the machine, as well as how it starts up. These passwords, which may or may not be available on every system, are the **Basic Input/Output System** (**BIOS**), **Unified Extensible Firmware Interface** (**UEFI**), and Bootloader passwords.

BIOS/UEFI passwords

BIOS and UEFI are firmware stored on a motherboard ROM chip. Not all systems have both and UEFI is the replacement for BIOS in newer systems.

BIOS/UEFI is the first set of instructions to run when a computer is powered on and provides the hardware configuration settings of a system. The configuration settings specify the date, time, the priorities of the storage devices to be used to boot the system, the memory size, and others. The first task performed is the **Power-On Self-Test** (**POST**). This test procedure verifies if the devices configured in its configuration setup are present, active, and operating. After completing the POST, control is passed to the system bootloader that loads and starts the operating system.

Adding a password to BIOS/UEFI adds another layer of security to a system. If a password is assigned in the BIOS/UEFI, without it the BIOS/UEFI configuration settings cannot be accessed or changed. There are three passwords that can be set in BIOS/UEFI:

- **System or user password**: This password controls access to the BIOS/UEFI settings, the boot menu, and the boot process that loads the operating system. This password is intended to prevent an unauthorized user from accessing the setup configuration and the OS.
- **Setup or administrator password**: This second-level password must be entered to modify the configuration settings in the BIOS/UEFI. If this password is enabled, an unauthorized user may open the BIOS/UEFI settings but must enter this password to change the settings.
- **HDD password**: If this password is used, it must be entered so that the BIOS/UEFI can access the HDD and complete the boot process.

Bootloader password

When a computer starts up, it goes through four stages to complete the boot process. These stages are, in order:

1. **BIOS/UEFI**: This firmware performs the POST and loads the bootloader from the master boot record (MBR – BIOS) or the GUID Partition Table (GPT – UEFI).
2. **Bootloader**: This is a small program that loads the OS kernel into RAM.

3. **Kernel**: The primary purpose of the OS kernel is to initialize installed devices and RAM and then load the init (initialization) program.
4. **Init**: This Linux utility starts the essential services configured to start at boot up.

On a Windows system, the bootloader is a small program named the **`Winload.exe`** or the Windows Boot Loader. This program was started by the Windows boot manager in Windows versions starting with Windows Vista and later. Winload.exe loads the essential device drivers and the Windows kernel, **`ntoskrnl.exe`**. Prior to the Windows Vista version, the boot manager was the **`ntldr`** utility. Winload.exe does not support a password.

Linux systems have two primary bootloaders: **Grand Unified Bootloader** (**GNU GRUB**) and GRUB2. Other bootloaders are available, such as **Linux Loader** (**LILO**) and Syslinux, but GRUB or GRUB2 are commonly released in most distros. GRUB/GRUB2 provides a text-based menu that allows the user to choose which OS is to boot, provided multiple OSs are installed on the system, and then performs the process as described for the Windows bootloader. *Figure 12.3* shows an example of a GNU GRUB menu:

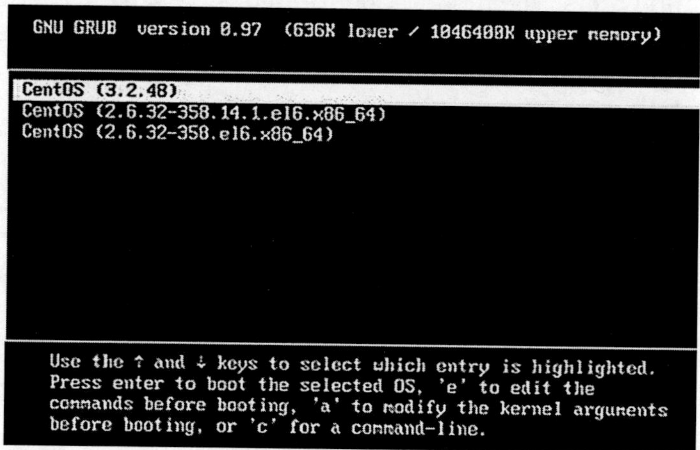

***Figure 12.3:** An example of a GNU GRUB menu*

To prevent someone from gaining bootloader access to a PC, extra security can be enabled by adding a password to the GRUB Bootloader. A GRUB password prevents an unauthorized user from booting a Linux system. It will also prevent him or her from accessing single user mode and possibly resetting the root password and login. However, there is one definite caveat: if you forget a GRUB password, you would not be able to boot into the system.

Business impacts

Data is a valuable asset. However, like all assets, data's value to an organization comes from the information that can be generated from it. Data must be converted into meaningful information before it can truly have a value-based impact on a business. For data to provide a measurable financial impact on a business, it must be associated with cost reduction, revenue generation, or profits.

Data value prioritization

The value of data is a function of an organization's data strategy, meaning, where and how it is used. Storing data is not without cost. Collecting, transmitting, standardizing, and storing data can be costly. On a cost-benefit basis, data must reduce costs, increase revenues, or generate income to offset its cost.

Data prioritization is especially important in security programs, especially since there are many inputs as to what is important. A security administrator focuses on the details of day-to-day events and the upper management may react to something in the news. The priorities, and the data required to deal with them, must be centered on the needs of the most critical threats and risks to the organization. The goal of data prioritization is to decide which projects are of the most value and to gather and align the data related to each project.

The value of the data is in how relevant it is to the decisions to be made in each project. Data volume is not the same as data quality. The quality of the data, its value, lies in its usefulness and relevance to the decisions to be made. To ensure the data quality, the data should be filtered to remove the data that is not related to the decisions and organize the remaining data around the goals of the organization.

Data life-cycle management

Data life-cycle management (**DLM**) is a process that manages the data lifespan from its creation to its disposal. This includes its storage, accessibility, and security to ensure its CIA. The data life-cycle consists of a sequence of phases. The number of phases in this life cycle varies from three to eight, with the most common definitions identifying five phases (see *Figure 12.4*):

1. **Capture**: Data in virtually all forms are facts. A datum (a single piece of data) can be almost anything: a number, a name, a color, even a symbol. When a fact is collected and entered into a computer, it becomes data. It is at this point that the data life-cycle begins. Not all data needs to or should be captured. The quality and relevance of the data collected to the organization should be the guiding factor.

2. **Storage**: Data can be stored as structured or unstructured. Structured data is organized, such as in a relational database and unstructured data is non-relational and often stored in flat file formats. Regardless of its formatting, data stored on secondary storage devices requires protection to ensure it remains safe, available, and accessible by those who are authorized to access, use, modify, or delete it. This phase of the data life-cycle must also address the retention of backup data images that may be needed to restore operations.

3. **Usage**: Once the data is captured and stored securely, it can be accessed and shared by authorized users for reporting, analysis, visualizations, dashboards, and more in support of decision-making.
4. **Archival**: At some point, data can cease being relevant. However, this does not necessarily mean the data has lost all its value. Data can be archived in case it may later be of use or filtered into a data warehouse for analytical and comparative reporting.
5. **Deletion**: Some data can become obsolete and should be purged from storage and destroyed. Data can have a definite and prescribed retention period or is no longer of value or purpose to the organization. Data should be removed and destroyed securely and completely.

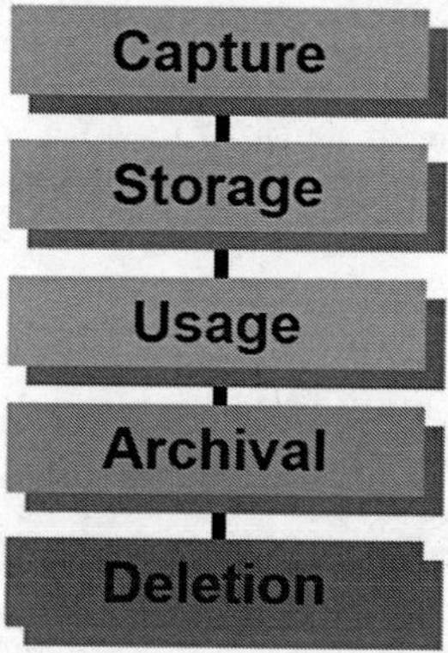

Figure 12.4: *The phases of data life-cycle management*

Cybersecurity costs versus risks

For any organization, the cost of applying cybersecurity measures varies with a number of factors. These factors include the industry or type of business the organization is in, the quantity and types of data the organization keeps, the extent of the findings of a security or risk assessment, the size of the IT and security budgets, the availability of cybersecurity professionals, and the requirements of security and privacy regulations or laws affecting the business. In any case, an organization has the choice between avoiding a cybersecurity event or cleaning up the aftermath of one.

A cybersecurity risk has three basic parts:

1. **Threats**: The possibility of any unauthorized physical or logical event or action that attempts to discover, obtain, destroy, manipulate, or use private or confidential data from an organization for illegal purposes occurring is a **threat**. A threat can be posed by employees, criminals, countries, hackers, script-kiddies, and even by inadvertent and unintended actions.

2. **Vulnerabilities**: A **vulnerability** exists whenever and wherever there is a weakness, flaw, error, or omission in the physical or logical security measures of an organization and its computing resources. A vulnerability can be an open or unlocked door, or it can be a weakness in a password policy or access created through malware. In other words, a vulnerability is a means for an attacker to penetrate the security of a system.

3. **Result**: The potential damage or loss that may occur from a threat actor exploiting a vulnerability is the **result** or consequence that defines risk.

The cost of security measures to prevent or mitigate the projected result of a risk should determine if the cost/result comparison justifies the expenditure. In some instances, the cost to repair or mitigate a vulnerability may be such that a newer model or an upgraded version of the device or system may be a better investment.

Conclusion

The elements and components of the security for data stored on a server or a network device must include or at least consider the use of data or file encryption, data retention policies, the types and methods of data storage devices and formats, the use of low-level passwords, and the overall impact of data and data loss on the operations of a business.

In the next chapter, we look at physical security and the practices and measures that can be applied to protect against the physical intrusion, harm, or theft that may result from unauthorized entry.

Points to remember

- A cipher is a process or an algorithm that changes plaintext into an unreadable ciphertext.
- The two types of encryption algorithms are symmetric encryption and asymmetric encryption.
- An encryption key is applied by an encryption algorithm to encrypt plain text into cipher text or decrypt cipher text back to plain text.
- Data encryption is the process of applying an encryption algorithm to make data unreadable for storage, transmission, or use.
- Data exists in three states: data-at-rest, data-in-transit, and data-in-use.
- Data retention prescribes the length of time data is to be kept.
- Data storage security is the "application of physical, technical and administrative controls to protect storage systems.

- Data protection focuses on data being available.
- Data security focuses on preventing unauthorized access and attacks, breaches, and malware.
- Regulated industries are required to follow the laws, regulations, and guidelines that define how they are to secure their data.
- Storage security protects stored data from cyber threats and loss.
- On-site data storage is within the physical location of an organization.
- Off-site data storage is physically at a distance from an organization's primary facilities.
- Three passwords can be set in BIOS/UEFI: system or user password, setup or administrator password, and an HDD password.
- A computer goes through four stages in the boot process: BIOS/UEFI, bootloader, kernel, and init.
- On Windows, the bootloader is Winload.exe. Linux systems use GNU GRUB and GRUB2. A password can be added to the GRUB Bootloader.
- The value of data is a function of an organization's data strategy, meaning where and how it is used.
- The goal of data prioritization is to decide which projects are of the most value and to gather and align the data related to each project.
- DLM manages the data lifespan from its creation to its disposal. Its phases are capture, storage, usage, archival, and deletion.
- Cybersecurity risk has three parts: threats, vulnerabilities, and results.

CHAPTER 13
Physical Security

Introduction

Physical security is the first line of defense for servers, data centers, server rooms, or any IT facility. The objective of physical security is to keep assets functioning, secure, and protected from unauthorized intruders. In addition to locked doors, access controls, and other physical barriers, environmental systems and controls are important to an organization's security policies and infrastructure. This chapter looks at the physical security approaches, devices, and environmental controls an organization can install to protect its systems.

Structure

The chapter covers the following topics:

- Access controls
- Architectural security reinforcements
- Authentication factors
- Environment controls

Objective

By the end of this chapter, you will be able to identify and describe the sub-objectives of the following Server+ examination objective: *Summarize physical security concepts.*

Access controls

In general, **access control** allows an authorized individual to enter, use, or access a secured entity. It is also the denial of access to an unauthorized individual. There are two types of access control: physical access and logical access.

Physical access

Physical access controls prevent unauthorized entry or access to a secure space. This can include permitting or denying physical access to a building, a room, a cabinet, or any physical structure. Physical access controls regulate who can and cannot access physical areas or resources. For the most part, these controls are physical barriers, such as doors, locks, fences, signs, cameras, and security guards.

External perimeter security

Physical and logical security starts at the perimeter of an organization's property or operational space. Whether this is the property lines of a plant or office building or leased space in a building, whoever enters that space should be subject to the policies, devices, and controls of a physical security program.

For an outdoor space, there are a variety of ways to prevent unauthorized access:

- **Alarms:** A siren, claxon, or other loud sound, especially when coupled with lighting and other warning devices, can encourage an intruder to leave the premises.
- **Fences**: A fence can deter or at least delay an unauthorized intruder. Although a fence can be cut, broken, or climbed, doing so takes time and exposes the intruder to detection.
- **Security cameras:** The presence of a security camera can be a deterrence, especially if the camera is working and can detect the intruder.
- **Security lighting**: Motion-detecting lights can expose an intruder and deter further entry into the premises. Lighting also helps to improve the effectiveness of cameras and guards.
- **Warning signs:** Although a sign that warns against intrusion and specifies the actions to be taken on unauthorized intruders, is subjective, an intruder may be deterred from avoiding these actions. This is especially true if signs warn of video surveillance or the presence of guards or guard dogs.

In addition to preventing unauthorized entry, a perimeter security system must permit authorized entries. This requires that a controlled entryway be included in the perimeter security system. This could be facilitated with a badge reader, a biometric scanner, or a security guard who verifies ID cards. This does not mean that authorized entry should be less controlled than the denial of unauthorized entry. These two processes should be applied in balance.

Bollards

A bollard is a post that is either embedded or installed in a street or sidewalk to mark a boundary, set a perimeter, and prevent the entry of motor vehicles. Bollards are not new. They have been around since the Roman empire, where they separated walkways from horse-powered vehicles. A bollard can be a solid metal, concrete, plastic, or a plastic tube, depending on the strength required by its purpose. Some bollards also operate on hydraulics to raise and lower as needed. *Figure 13.1* shows bollards used to protect a building:

Figure 13.1: *Bollards protecting the exterior of a building* [1]

Architectural security reinforcements

The layout and materials used in the architectural design of a building can add to its physical security by deflecting radio frequency signals, obscuring the view of its interior, and hiding or camouflaging security devices.

Signal blocking

A commonly overlooked security vulnerability is the signal range of an organization's wireless **radiofrequency** (**RF**) network signals. With ranges that can extend to as much as 30 meters (about 100 feet) indoors and 250 meters (820 feet) outdoors (Wi-Fi 7), someone parked in a building's parking lot could intercept the signal and disrupt the wireless signal with a frequency disturbance method, such as jamming. Another possibility is a rogue AP or an "evil twin" AP inserted into the wireless network.

1. Image courtesy of Ontario Bollards, Inc.

The construction design and the materials used in the walls, floors, and ceilings of a building can help to contain the RF signals of a Wi-Fi network. When an RF signal comes into contact with any surface, the signal is affected in one of three ways:

- **Refraction:** The signal passes through the surface.
- **Reflection**: The is reflected, typically at an angle.
- **Absorption:** The surface absorbs the signal.

These three results occur depending on the composition of the surface. Wi-Fi signals can penetrate many solid objects, depending on the size and closeness of the atoms or the thickness (width) of the material. Another factor in the range of a Wi-Fi signal is called attenuation, which is the loss of energy over distance. The range of an RF signal is affected by its attenuation point. For example, a Wi-Fi signal in a space that is enclosed by relatively thick cement walls, there isn't likely to be any signal reaching outside the walls (absorption), or if you are beyond the attenuation point of the signal, you may get a small bit of the signal or none. However, most commercial space walls are not too thick or made of signal-blocking materials. The RF signals can pass through the walls, perhaps with a slight bit of absorption. *Figure 13.2* shows how some common building materials affect an RF signal:

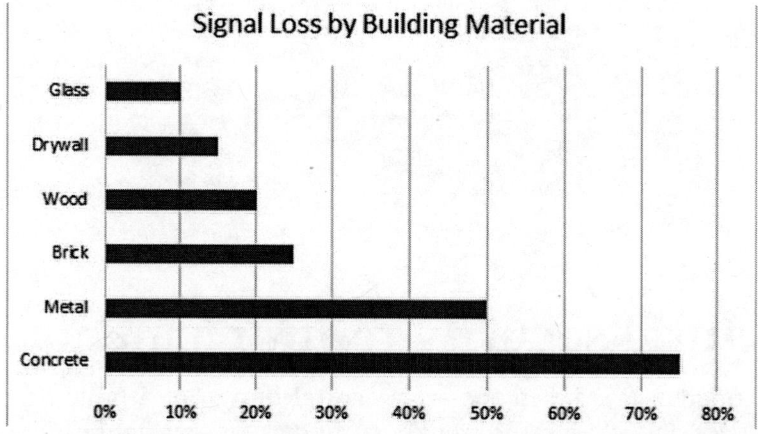

***Figure 13.2:** The impact of common building materials on an RF signal*

If the goal is to contain the Wi-Fi signal, there are materials and fabrics that can be used. These materials can keep signals in the building, and externally-source signals, such as RF signals, from penetrating outer walls and windows. RF shielding materials used in clothing or window coverings are commonly a thin metallic mesh, typically silver or copper. For the interior of a wall, sheets of galvanized steel or aluminum can be inserted into its core. These materials do not block the RF signals but attenuate the signal essentially to zero.

Reflective glass

There are window and wall glass products and coatings that prevent RF signals from Wi-Fi networks and even cellular telephones from passing through. These products absorb and reflect RF signals as well as most **electromagnetic** (**EM**) radiation and **ultraviolet** (**UV**) rays but allow visible light to pass through.

A common type of window or wall glass used is Low-e glass. The **e** stands for emissivity, which is a material's capability to radiate heat. So, a Low-e product has a lower capability for radiating heat, which also includes reflecting RF signals. This also means that Low e glass can cause reception problems for both, cell phones and Wi-Fi reception inside a building.

Window films can also be used to block RF signals, as well as **infrared** (**IR**) signals. These products, when applied to a window's interior surface, attenuate the RF signals to prevent interception or eavesdropping by external receivers.

Data center camouflage

Many data centers can appear to be anything but a high-tech facility housing sophisticated computing and network systems. This is a form of industrial camouflage. A non-descript building, warehouse, or even a seemingly residential home can house a data center that may be overlooked by an intruder. Because these facilities do not advertise what they are, they must beef up their access controls.

Security fencing

The right type of fencing around a facility can be both a deterrent and an obstacle to an intruder. Depending on the area, building, or materials to be protected, the height and structure of a security fence can vary. It can also be enhanced with materials and devices to increase its protective capabilities.

A standard perimeter fence is commonly 4 to 6 feet in height. Security fences are 8 to 10 feet tall to increase the deterrence factor. Some fences can be up to 14 to 16 feet tall, if appropriate to what's contained inside its perimeter. A security fence can also have barbed wire or razor wire added to its top to further discourage intruders. Perimeter fencing is typically wood, vinyl, or metal, such as chain-link fencing. Fences enhanced for security are generally steel or aluminum with sturdier posts, rails, and thickness to prevent its destruction.

Security fences can be supplemented with additional security devices, including security cameras, and sensors, such as seismic, infrared, vibration, and photoelectric. Lighting is commonly placed strategically along security fencing as well. In areas where an automobile or truck may have a path to the fence, bollards can be installed for protection.

Security cameras

Video cameras can either be security cameras or surveillance cameras – there is a difference. A **security camera** is visible and intended to deter intrusion, theft, or damage to a facility. **Surveillance cameras** are hidden and used to monitor the activities of specific areas. Which of these security cameras is best for an organization depends on its location, the nature of its business, and who has access to its assets. If the property to be protected is in a high-crime area, security cameras would certainly be a good idea. However, if a facility stores highly valuable or sensitive products, surveillance cameras are probably in order.

Externally mounted security cameras should be weather-resistant, if not weather-proof. Security cameras should have a wide-range lens and be mounted where the full range of view avoids blind spots. *Figure 13.3* shows outdoor security cameras mounted on a pole.

***Figure 13.3:** Outdoor security cameras* [2]

A surveillance camera is typically installed inside a facility and is often hidden from sight. Depending on the business, surveillance cameras can prevent theft, such as shoplifting in a retail operation, improve productivity because people tend to work better when they know they are being watched, and they can provide evidence of an intrusion, employee theft, or a workplace accident.

The security cameras, whether exterior or interior, can be either wired or wireless. Besides the wire, the two camera types have other differences, as shown in *Table 13.1*:

Attribute	Wired	Wireless
Reliability/Signal	More reliable	Less reliable
Cost	More expensive	Less expensive
Installation	More expensive	Less expensive
Image	Less pixelation	More pixelation due to bandwidth issues
Power source	Cable	Batteries

***Table 13.1:** Comparison of wired vs. wireless security cameras*

2. Image courtesy of Harvard Kennedy School's Shorenstein Center

Additional equipment is required for the video equipment in order to get all the benefits it provides in the way of security. This equipment includes monitors for viewing the captured video, video recorders to store the captured video to provide as a record and, perhaps, evidence. In larger spaces, the capture range of the surveillance cameras should overlap. This helps to detect tampering and provide expanded coverage of the premises. Depending on the size of the facility and its premises, more than one of these devices could be required. In addition, a best practice is to connect all of the security and surveillance equipment to **uninterruptible power supply** (**UPS**) units to provide power in the event of a power source failure.

Locks

Minimum physical security is easily implemented simply by locking doors. What kind of lock you use depends on the level of security whatever is behind the door requires. There are several different types of locks, including key-operated, combination, cylindrical, deadbolts, drop-bolts, mortise, biometric, RF identity readers, and more. While any lock can provide some level of security, some are just not worth the effort. Locks that use keys or remembered combinations or codes require keys to be managed and accounted for, and combination numbers or codes have to be changed every time an employee leaves the company. For these reasons, locks on doors, cabinets, fence gates, and any other secured area are less about physical key entry and more about the person wanting into the building.

Key cards

Key cards have many different names, including proximity cards, PIV cards, key fobs, and smart cards. Key cards are security instruments used by authorized card holders to gain entrance into a secure building. The one assumption for this form of access control is that only the authorized individual will have this identity card, and only that person will use it.

To gain access, the card holder presents the card to a reader by passing the card over or in front of the device, which is located very near a door. The key card is an electronic device with the unique identity credentials of the card holder stored on it. When the card is passed by the reader, a magnetic field, an RF signal, or a Bluetooth signal is picked by sensors and passed to a controller. The controller then authenticates the credentials by comparing them with a database, usually on a server to which the reader is connected. If the credentials on the card are matched to an entry in the database, access is authorized, and the door is unlocked, usually with a buzzer sounding.

There are two basic types of key cards:

- **Proximity cards:** This type of key card transmits credentials to the card reader using an **RF identification** (**RFID**) signal. The card does not need to contact the reader as long as it is within 4 to 6 inches of the device. RFID cards are often confused with **near-field communication** (**NFC**) devices, which use a completely different technology. Two NFC devices must each have transceivers and must be extremely close to communicate. Credit cards that feature a tap feature are NFC devices.

- **Swipe cards:** A swipe card must be passed through a magnetic reader slot that reads the information stored on the magnetic strip located on the back of the card. The magnetic strip has three tracks. Tracks 1 and 2 hold the core information, such as the card holder's name, the credit card account number, the expiration date of the card, and the **card verification value** (**CVV**). The third track is not always used, but it can hold information like the currencies in which the card can be used and other information the issuer wishes to include.

Authentication factors

The security process involved with allowing access to a secured space is **authentication**. The person seeking admission must authenticate (prove) that they are someone who has been authorized to gain access to the secured space. To be authenticated, the person must present what are called **factors** that can be used by the security system to recognize the individual and permit his or her entry.

There are five standard physical security factors applied to authentication:

- **Something you have:** This would be a physical item. It could be a standard lock key, but it could also be a proximity card, a smart card, a **personal identity verification** (**PIV**) card, a key fob, or a flash drive. *Figure 13.4* shows an example of a PIV card:

Figure 13.4: A personal identity verification card [3]

3. **Image source: U.S. General Services Administration - https://piv.idmanagement.gov/elements/**

- **Something you know:** This would be something memorized, such as a password, PIN code, number sequence, or perhaps even a spoken pass phrase.
- **Something you are:** This type of factor is known as **biometrics**, or some physical human body element or pattern, such as a fingerprint, a retinal scan, a handprint, facial recognition, and a few others.
- **Somewhere you are:** This factor relates to the physical location of the person, or the device being used to gain access. This factor is used less for building access and more for accessing network resources. It may use the user's IP address or the MAC address of their computer, tablet, or smartphone for authentication.
- **Something you do:** This factor is not commonly used. It observes an action performed by the requester, such as a gesture, touches on a picture, or even how the person walks. The authentication process used to determine if a request to access a webpage is a human or a computer, a captcha, is a form of this factor.

Mantraps and tailgating

Organizations that use key cards must be alert for unauthorized persons entering a door unlocked by an employee, usually immediately following the employee through the door. This is a **tailgating attack** and the reason that building security includes turnstiles to make sure only one person at a time passes through an entry point.

A turnstile is a form of a **mantrap**, which is an area between two entry doors that separates a secure area (inner door) from an exterior (outside) door. Only one of the doors of a mantrap can be open at a time. Usually, the outer door is unlocked. However, the inner door requires a key card or biometric device to unlock, if the outer door is closed.

Multifactor Authentication

Authentication can be much stronger when multiple factors must be verified before access is granted to a secure space. It is becoming more common for multifactor authentication to be required for a variety of activities. To extract money from a bank account through an ATM, in addition to a valid debit card (something you have), a PIN code must also be entered (something you know). Access to a secure work area might require the input of a specific code and a fingerprint scan.

A single factor could be compromised by someone stealing or finding a keycard or shoulder-surf a PIN code and used to gain access to a secure facility. Requiring two or more authentication factors raises the difficulty of someone being able to break through an authentication system. The use of **two-factor authentication (2FA)** or **multiple-factor authentication (MFA)** provides an additional level of security to the authentication process. 2FA is a subset of an MFA. An MFA may have three or four factors in the authentication process.

Environmental controls

Environmental controls set and maintain the operating environment of the devices contained in a space. The components of the environmental controls include:

- **Heating, ventilation, and air conditioning (HVAC)**: The purpose of HVAC systems is to maintain a constant temperature and humidity level for an entire space. An HVAC system should be interconnected to a fire control system, so that in case of a fire in a space, the HVAC can be shut down and not feed oxygen to the fire.
- **Room, row, and rack temperatures:** As discussed in *Chapter 1, Physical Hardware*, large data centers install servers and peripheral devices in open racks or enclosed rackmount cabinets. Rackmount cabinets typically have on-board airflow, but open racks require airflow from the HVAC system. The HVAC system can direct cooling to one row and warmer air to another using airflow baffles and rack blanking panels that create open spaces between rack-mounted devices.

Environmental monitoring

This environment of a server room or data center can be difficult to balance because of changes in the external weather, air quality, the facility's general HVAC system, and the HVAC system dedicated to the data center.

To ensure that the operating conditions of a server room or data center are within the recommended ranges, an environmental monitoring system should be used to detect, and report the following conditions:

- **Temperature:** The recommended operating temperature range for computer rooms and data centers is 68 to 77 degrees Fahrenheit or 20 to 25 degrees Celsius. If the ambient temperature is below or above this range for an extended period, the electronic components of the systems could be damaged.
- **Humidity:** Humidity can be a major problem in a data center, depending on its location. If the humidity is too high, oxidation and corrosion of the electronic circuits and components can occur. If the humidity is too low, static electricity may become a problem and cause electrical shorts and component failures. The standard recommended range for relative humidity in a data center is between 45 percent to 55 percent.
- **Voltage and power:** Voltage sensors and power monitoring sensors should be used in larger centers to monitor the voltage levels of the electrical power sources for exceeding or falling out of high and low voltage limits. Power backups, such as **uninterruptible power supplies (UPSs)** and generators, should be in place to absorb brown outs, and power outages.

- **Smoke:** Smoke and carbon monoxide fumes are dangerous to humans working in a closed space. Smoke alarms and chemical detectors, interconnected to the power and environmental monitoring systems, should be set to shut off the power and trigger alerts when smoke or fumes are detected.

Environmental threats

Environmental threats are external events, such as weather, natural disasters, catastrophic events, and other natural world events. They include:

- **Dust:** Airborne dust particles can cause electrical problems in a computer, including clogging the airflow and cooling of the motherboard and CPU.
- **Earthquake:** An earthquake typically causes structural damage to buildings but may also cause damage or failures in the electrical, plumbing, and ventilation systems.
- **Extreme weather:** Catastrophic weather events, such as high winds, heavy rain, tornados, hurricanes / typhoons, ice, snow, hail, etc., can cause structural damage to a facility, its surroundings, and the infrastructure of the power, water, and other utilities.
- **Fire/Explosion:** Fire or a blast can destroy computing equipment. However, damage could also be caused by the chemicals in the retardants, suppressors, extinguishers, and water.
- **Floods:** Floods are often caused by weather events, such as heavy rain, hurricanes, and storm surges. A flooded computer facility is not likely to operate properly, not to mention the risk of electrical shock.
- **Lightning:** An electrical storm is a serious threat to the electrical supply of a building. A direct lightning strike to a data center is likely to send an extreme electric spike through even protected equipment.
- **Pests:** A mouse chewing through a communication cable or power cable can introduce hard-to-detect failure or intermittent power issues for a server and its nodes.

Conclusion

Physical security prevents unauthorized individuals from entering or accessing the private or secured areas of an organization's operations and facilities. In this chapter, we covered the application of physical access controls, architectural reinforcements, surveillance and monitoring equipment, locked or secured entryways, and environmental controls. We also looked at authentication factors and how they are applied. Physical security plays a huge role in the safety, operations, and continuity of an organization's physical assets.

In the next chapter, we look at the methods and processes involved in access management, which controls the who and what of user authentication and authorization.

Points to remember

- Access control allows authorized individuals to enter or use a secured entity and denies this access to unauthorized individuals. The two types of access control are physical access and logical access.
- Physical access controls prevent unauthorized entry or access to a secure space. These controls include doors, locks, fences, signs, cameras, and security guards.
- Security starts at the perimeter. Someone entering that space is subject to the policies, devices, and controls of the organization's physical security program.
- There are several ways to prevent unauthorized access, including alarms, fences, security cameras, security lighting, and warning signs.
- A bollard is an embedded or free-standing post on a street or sidewalk that marks a boundary or sets a perimeter and prevents the entry of motor vehicles.
- Signal blocking materials can keep RF signals in a building and keep out external signals.
- A data center may appear to be other than a high-tech facility through industrial camouflage.
- Fencing around a facility can be a deterrent and an obstacle.
- Security cameras are visible and can deter intrusion, theft, or damage to a facility. Surveillance cameras are hidden and monitor specific areas. These cameras can be wired or wireless.
- Key cards can be proximity cards, PIV cards, key fobs, and smart cards. There are two basic types of key cards: proximity cards and swipe cards
- Authentication factors are in five categories: something you have, something you know, something you are, somewhere you are, and something you do.
- Tailgating occurs when an unauthorized person enters by immediately following an employee through the door.
- A mantrap is an area between two entry doors that separates a secure area (inner door) from an exterior (outside) door.
- The use of a two-factor authentication (2FA) or multiple-factor authentication (MFA) provides an additional level of security to the authentication process.

- Environmental controls maintain the operating environment of the devices contained in a space. The operating temperature range for data centers is 68 to 77 degrees Fahrenheit. The standard range for relative humidity is between 45 percent to 55 percent.
- Voltage sensors and power monitoring sensors monitor electrical power sources for high and low voltage limits.
- Environmental threats include dust, earthquakes, extreme weather, fire, floods, lightning, and pests.

CHAPTER 14
Access Management

Introduction

Access management (**AM**) is primarily an information security, IT, and data governance process used to grant and prohibit access to valid users and invalid users. Typically, AM is used in conjunction with **identity access management** (**IAM**). Identity management creates, provisions and controls different users, roles, groups, and policies, whereas AM ensures that these roles and policies are followed. An AM-based application/system stores the different user roles and their profiles, and process user access requests based on the data/profile/roles.

Structure

The chapter covers the following topics:

- User accounts
- Access controls
- Permissions
- Auditing
- Single sign-on

Objective

By the end of this chapter, you will be able to identify and describe the sub-objectives of the following Server+ examination objective: *Explain important concepts pertaining to identity and access management for server administration.*

User accounts

To protect sensitive data stored on a computer or network, it is necessary to authenticate anyone seeking access to the system and its resources. This is the primary reason behind user accounts. A user account provides a first level of authentication by requiring the entry of, at minimum, a username and password that are used to verify an authorized account.

On a standalone Windows system, the user accounts created on that device are **local accounts**. The rights and permissions of these accounts are applied only to a particular computer. In effect, local accounts provide access control to a single computer and its resources. Local user accounts include some default accounts, which are created automatically when the OS is installed. These accounts cannot be used to gain access to a network and cannot be deleted.

Default local accounts

The default local user accounts created automatically on a Windows system are:

- **Administrator**: This local user account is provided for system administration. An administrator account has full control of files, folders, services, and other resources but only on a local device. An administrator account can create local user accounts and assign rights and permissions.
- **DefaultAccount**: This local user account is also known as the **Default System Managed Account** (**DSMA**). A DSMA account can run **multi-user-manifested-apps** (**MUMAs**), such as Xbox apps.
- **Guest**: This local user account is provided for infrequent users who do not have a user account on a particular computer. Guest accounts have limited user rights and permissions. By default, guest accounts are not enabled and do not have a password assigned. A guest account is anonymous as it can be a security risk, so it is best to leave it disabled.
- **HelpAssistant**: This local user account is created by default but is enabled only when a Remote Assistance session is activated, in which a remote support person takes control of the local computer. HelpAssistant accounts are disabled when no Remote Assistance sessions are running.
- **Local service**: This is a default local user account that is used by the Windows SCM. The local service account has the minimum rights and privileges.

- **Network service**: This is a default local account that is used by the Windows **service control manager (SCM)**, which presents the computer's credentials to remote servers.
- **System**: A system account is a default account type that is used by the OS and running services to sign-in. A system account has the same rights and permissions as an Administrator account.

Note: The default local user accounts can't be removed or deleted and don't provide access to network resources.

Local user account types

User accounts can have different levels of access based on the account type. There are several user account types on a Windows system, including:

- **Standard**: Standard accounts are the most basic user accounts. A standard user account can do anything a user would normally need to do, including running software or personalizing a desktop.
- **Standard with family safety**: This is a standard user account with parental controls. Standard accounts can be created for each family member and website restrictions, time on site limits, and other settings can be set per user in the Family Safety settings of the Windows Control Panel.
- **Guest**: This account type is intended for users needing temporary access to a system. This account is normally disabled for security purposes.
- **Microsoft account**: This account type uses an email address to access many Microsoft devices and services. A Microsoft account can sign-in on a local computer, an Xbox console, the Microsoft Store, and more, which is not possible with a local user account.
- **Privileged account**: This is a user account category that includes administrator accounts with high-level rights and privileges. If they remain unprotected, they can be used to access, modify, or destroy data, change the system configuration, or install or remove software and malware. Privileged accounts should be closely monitored.

User groups

On a Windows system, a user group contains one or more user accounts that share the same permissions and security rights. There are three general types of Windows user groups:

- **Local groups**: Local user groups are defined on a single computer. They are managed through the Local Users and Groups utility (lusrmgr.msc), shown in *Figure 14.1*:

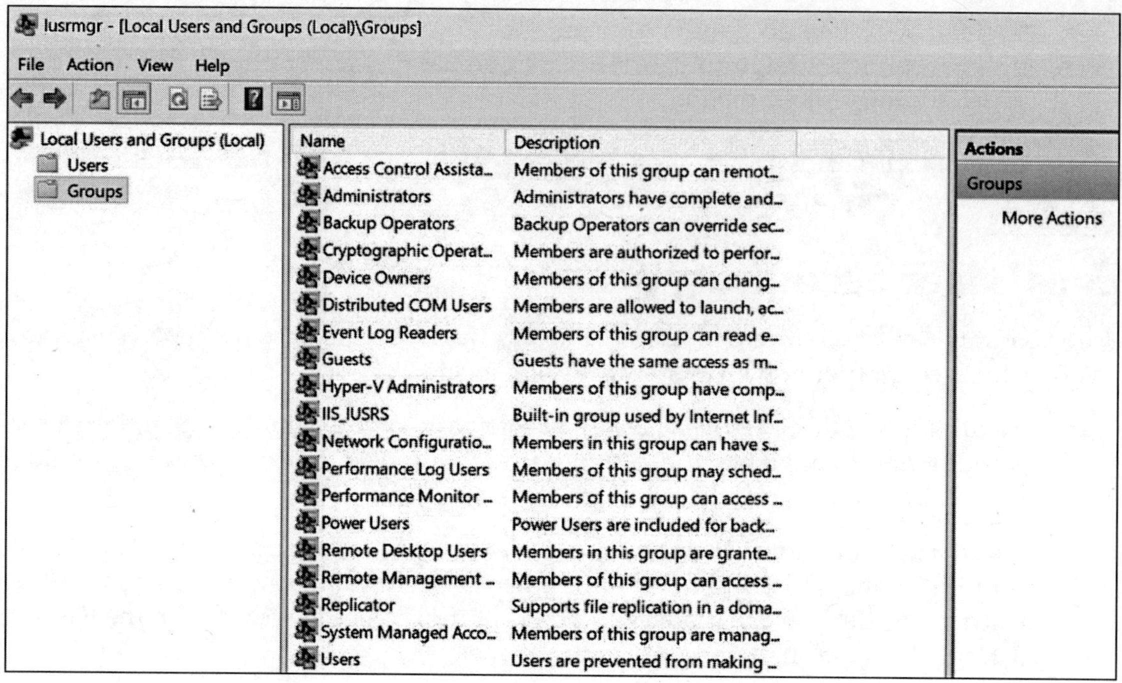

***Figure 14.1**: The Local Users and Group app*

- **Security groups**: These user account groups have security information defined in their configuration. This type of group is used in **Windows Active Directory** (**AD**).
- **Distribution groups**: This user group type is used to create distribution lists of AD users for email.

Linux user accounts

A Linux user account is the same as a user account in any OS. A user account is a way for the system to control access to its resources. It provides a means for a system to track and monitor system resource use. Linux user accounts have two unique identifiers: username and a **user identity number (UID)**. When a user account is created with a username, it is mapped to a unique UID. The username on an account can be changed but must remain unique to the system. However, the UID cannot be changed and remains with the user account.

There are three types of user accounts in Linux:

- **Root**: This is the equivalent of an administrator account of a Windows system. It is automatically created during installation and has the highest rights and privileges of any user account.

- **Regular**: This could be called a normal or default account type. One regular account is created as a part of a Linux installation, but any number of other regular accounts can be created after the installation is complete. This is the account type used for routine activities..
- **Service**: Service accounts are created by applications or services when they are installed on a Linux system and are used by the apps or services to run associate processes and functions.

Linux user groups

Linux collects user accounts into groups for administrative purposes. User groups are an essential part of Linux file and data security. Groups are used to limit the actions and to specify the permissions of their user accounts. User groups are based on the roles of user accounts. Linux defines two types of user account groups: primary and secondary.

Primary user groups are the default group type for user accounts. All user accounts belong to a primary group, which is the group associated with the user account in the **`/etc/passwd`** file. Secondary user groups allow a user account to belong to other groups besides a primary group. A user account can be added to as many as 15 secondary groups but is not required to belong to any secondary groups.

Access controls

Access control is the process of authenticating and authorizing users, groups, software and systems to gain access to resources on a network or computer. Access control uses file and folder permissions, ownership, inheritance, user rights and permissions, and object auditing to approve or deny access to a resource. The access to and the uses of resources are controlled through the interrelated processes of authentication and authorization. Once a user is authenticated (verified), the OS uses the defined rights and permissions of the user and the resource to determine what actions the user is authorized to perform on a resource. The actions a user could perform on a resource (object) include read, write, modify, or all of the above (full control). Objects are files, folders, printers, registry keys, and more. Either the object owner or an administrator assigns the permissions to groups, but they can also assign permissions to individual users.

Permissions

As a part of securing files and object, least privilege should be a guiding principle, which says that a user only needs the permissions and rights on a file or object that permit him or her to do their job. However, the access to and the permissions and rights of an object can be based on an individual's role or job function, access rules based on company policies, or an application scope. Let us look at each of these:

- **Role-based access control (RBAC)**: Also called role-based security, RBAC assigns permissions and rights to users based on their role within an organization. For example, data files and folders that an administrator may use in the performance of their job would not be accessible by a standard user account.
- **Rule-based access control**: In this form of access control, access to resources is allowed or denied based on a set of rules pre-defined by an administrator or a resource owner. For example, the files of an accounting system can only be accessed by a user designated with an accounting role.
- **Scope-based access control**: A scope defines the actions an application can perform on behalf of a user. Scopes are resource permissions an application wants to exercise. Scopes are specific to the OAuth 2.0 authorization and used in applications like Slack, GitHub, Google, and others.
- **Mandatory Access Control (MAC):** This security model is regulated by a central administrative authority that assigns access control to system resources in which the OS controls the operations an account can perform on an object. MAC grants or denies access to objects based on the security settings of a user account or device.

Delegation

In the context of access control and authentication, delegation is the process of one user assigning his or her credentials to another user. This is most common in RBAC authentication and authorization models. The delegation can transfer the role or the specific permissions of the assigned user.

Password policies

A username is only the first step in an authentication process, that is, identification. In fact, a username is a reference value used to look up the stored information associated with the username, such as a password, account type, and more. The password and username together create a **single-factor authentication** (**SFA**) token. The username is used to lookup its associated password, and if the password entered by the user matches the one paired with the username, access is granted to the user.

However, passwords are subject to discovery and no longer secure. Password crackers, social engineering, malware, and other attack methods are able to expose passwords, which can lead to several security problems accessing the user's personal data. An improvement to SFA is to implement **multiple-factor (multifactor) authentication** (**MFA**).

Multifactor credentials add another layer of verification to the authentication process. This makes the brute-force discovery of a password an almost useless exercise since there is yet another factor to be entered.

MFA combines two or more identification factors to the authentication of a user attempting to access a system or network. This process combines two or more factors to uniquely identify a user. MFA factors fall into five general categories, which are:

- Something you know
- Something you have
- Something you are
- Somewhere you are
- Something you do

Note: Remember that a username and password combination is only a single authentication factor.

See *Chapter 13, Physical Security* for more information on each of the above authentication factors.

Separation of duties

Another part of access control is to separate the control of an asset from a single authority. This means that an organization's policies and procedures prohibit a single employee or department from being in a position to conceal unauthorized modifications or fraudulent actions that occur as a part of their duties. The **separation of duties** control recommends that certain duties be separated into discrete tasks, each of which are performed by different individuals. Specifically, separation of duties involves the authorization or approval of related or associated transaction that affect assets, the control of assets, and the reporting or record-keeping of transactions related to the assets. For example, the purchasing agent should not be the one who records the receipt of goods or the one who pays the invoices.

The individuals to whom the separation of duties policy would apply are:

- **Individuals**: This is the basic level of duty separation. The tasks in a process are performed by separate individuals.
- **Departments**: The same department should not have authority or perform all of the tasks involved in a transaction. The purchasing, receiving, and accounting scenario earlier is an example of this level.
- **Organizations**: Operating units within an organization should have their asset-involved actions reviewed by a higher authority.

Auditing

Access management consists of the processes that issue policies, enforce rules, and audit results of an organization's identification and access control procedures. Questions concerning who has access to the system, who has access to what data, is the access control working as it should, and are the activities good or bad being logged and monitored, among others, are within the scope of access management and its auditing procedures.

Access control audits

The objective of auditing the access control policies and procedures is to verify that the implemented controls are in effect and protect the system's resources. The procedure for auditing access controls includes the following steps:

1. **Create or review the security policies**: Prior to conducting an audit, develop or review the security policies on the whole, but especially the policies affecting user access controls.
2. **Develop a formal plan**: The audit team roles should be clearly defined and state what actions each team member is responsible for conducting and reporting findings. The plan should include the detail of the tests and reviews to be conducted. The audit plan should be developed around **policy-based access control (PBAC)**.
3. **User review**: Users should be interviewed to learn what permissions and rights they are able to exercise. This review could identify user access controls that are too open or are too low. Users should also perform a monitored test in which they attempt to access unauthorized areas or data.
4. **Assign privileges**: The audit team should develop a user access control profile for each user and group account that implements least privilege and review it with users and managers. The agreed upon profiles should then be implemented for the applicable users.
5. **Separation of duties**: The process in-place for processing financial and asset records and transactions are to be reviewed to ensure that they implement a separation of duties program that prevents any one employee or department from performing actions without oversight.
6. **Close unused or inactive accounts**: Guest accounts, generic accounts, and user accounts of past employees who are no longer with the company should be disabled and where possible, deleted.
7. **Document the audit**: The results of the audit and its findings, improvements, and corrections should be formally documented. Changes to policies should be added to or removed from the official policy documentation. User training on any changes to the policies and procedures should be conducted to ensure they are understood and applied.

In addition to formal audit programs, administrators should regularly review and monitor the event log files created and updated by the operating system. Failed attempts to login to a system should be reviewed and followed up.

User activity audits

There are some audit, review, or monitoring activities that should be done regularly to see if there are events occurring that may indicate malware, attempts for unauthorized access, and errors in the user account permissions. The log files of the operating system keep a record of administrative, user, and security events, as well as other events an administrator wishes to track.

On a Windows system, log files can be reviewed using the **Event Viewer** (see *Figure 14.2*). The Windows OS has a variety of default event logs to track user activities, login attempts, application issues, and file and folder actions. The following sections describe some of the audit tracking functions available:

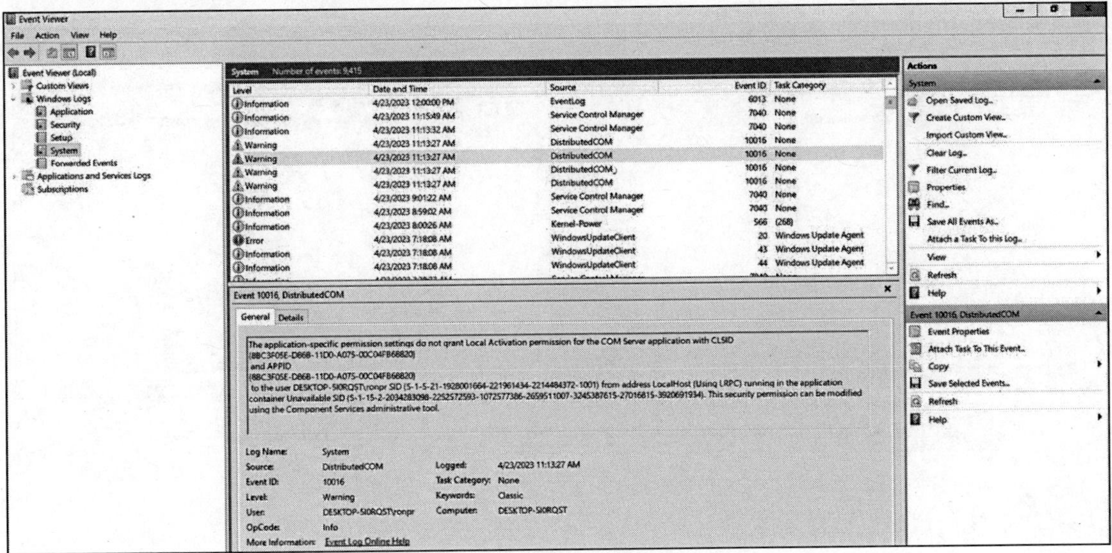

Figure 14.2: The Windows Event Viewer

User account management

The **Audit User Account Management** policy generates audit events when certain actions or tasks are performed by a user account. This audit policy can be set to audit changes to user accounts, including:

- Actions taken to create, change, delete, rename, lock/unlock, enable/disable a user account.
- The password of a user account is set or changed.
- The rights and permissions of a user account are changed.
- A user account's group membership is changed, or the user account is added to a group.

- User account credentials are backed up or restored by the Credential Manager.

Specific audit events are defined through the **Local Security Policy** app (**`secpol.msc`**), as shown in *Figure 14.3:*

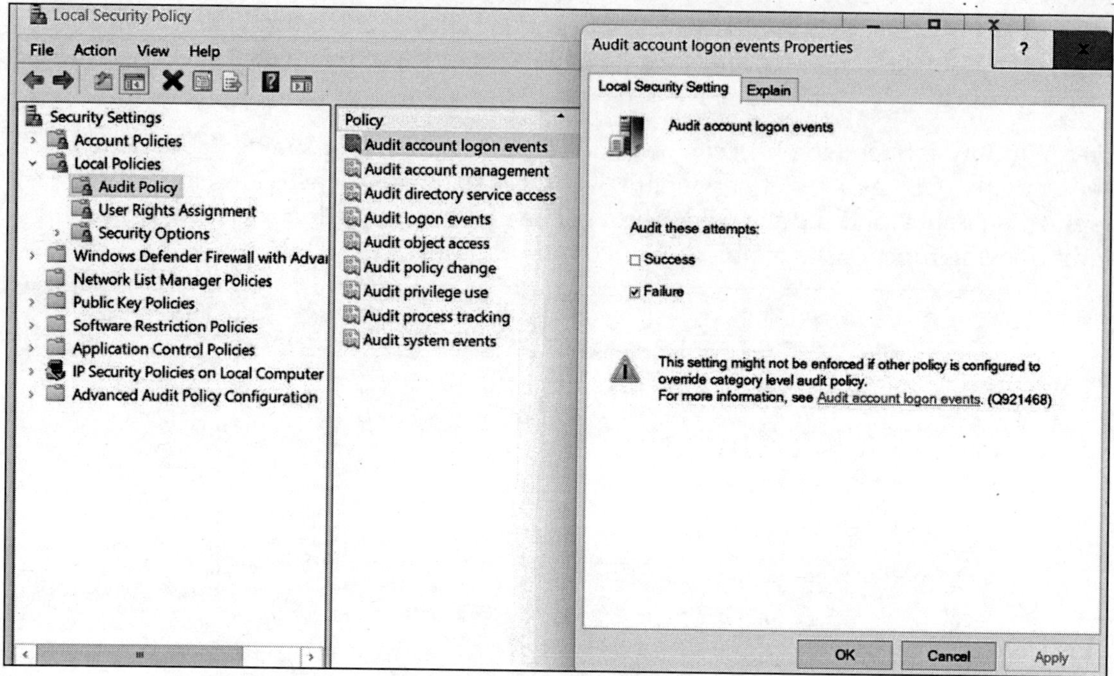

Figure 14.3: *The Local Security Policy app with an audit event properties dialog box*

User account logins

A variety of user account audits that can be set to capture event logs when certain actions occur, are included in the audit events list under **Audit Policies** in the **Local Security Policy** display. *Figure 14.3* shows the settings for failed user account logins. User account login event log file entries are generated when a user either logs into a domain controller or are authenticated on a local computer. Both successful logins and failed logins are tracked. The events generated from this policy include:

- **Pre-authentication failed**: It is a user entered an incorrect password.
- An account was successfully mapped to a domain account.
- Logon failure to a domain account logon was attempted.

Group memberships

There are two levels of group membership policy settings: one that resides on a domain controller that applies audit policies to the domain members and a local machine policy, which applies only to a single device. In either case, group membership audit policies are managed through the Group Policy Management console on a domain controller or the **Local Group Policy Editor (`gpedit.msc`)** on a local computer (see *Figure 14.4*):

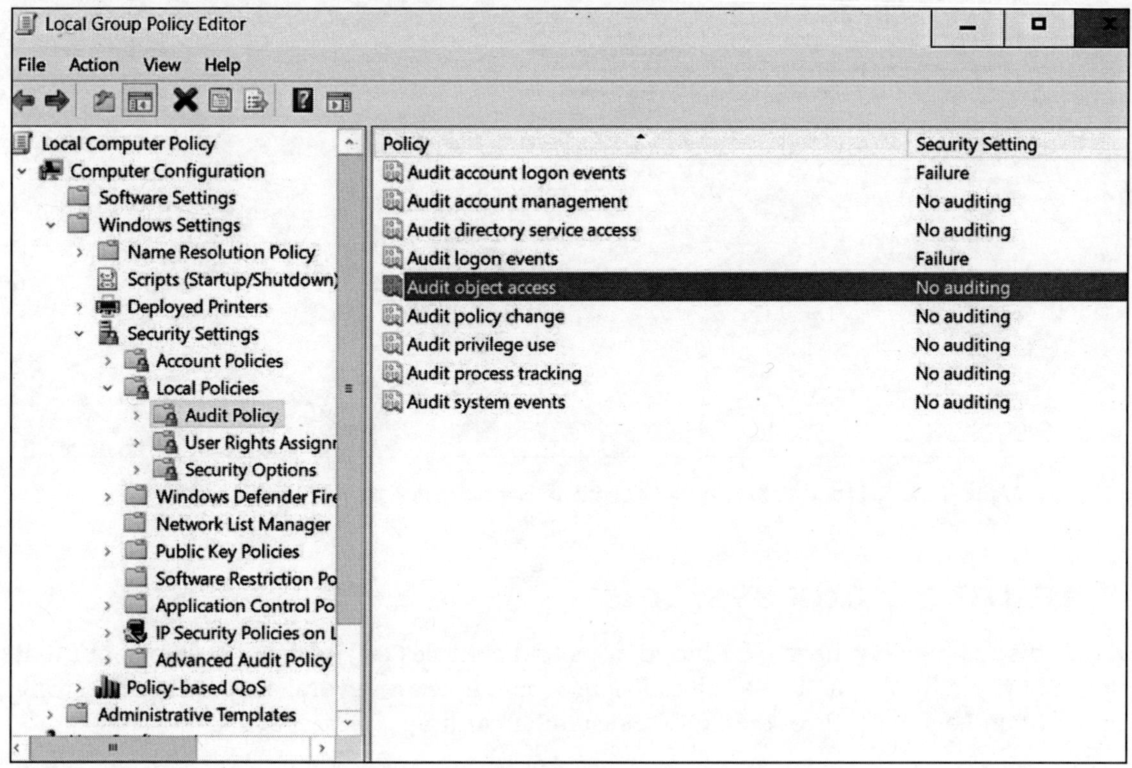

***Figure 14.4:** The Local Group Policy Editor.*

Deletions

Filesystem, folder, and file deletions are not normal operating events. So, when something is deleted from a filesystem, it should definitely be reviewed. In order to know about this action, an audit policy should be configured so that an event is generated when any changes occur to the files and folders within the filesystem. Windows does not provide an audit policy specifically for file deletions but does have one to track changes in a filesystem. Using the **Local Group Policy Editor**, the **Audit File System** policy can be set to generate events on either **Success**, **Failure**, or both.

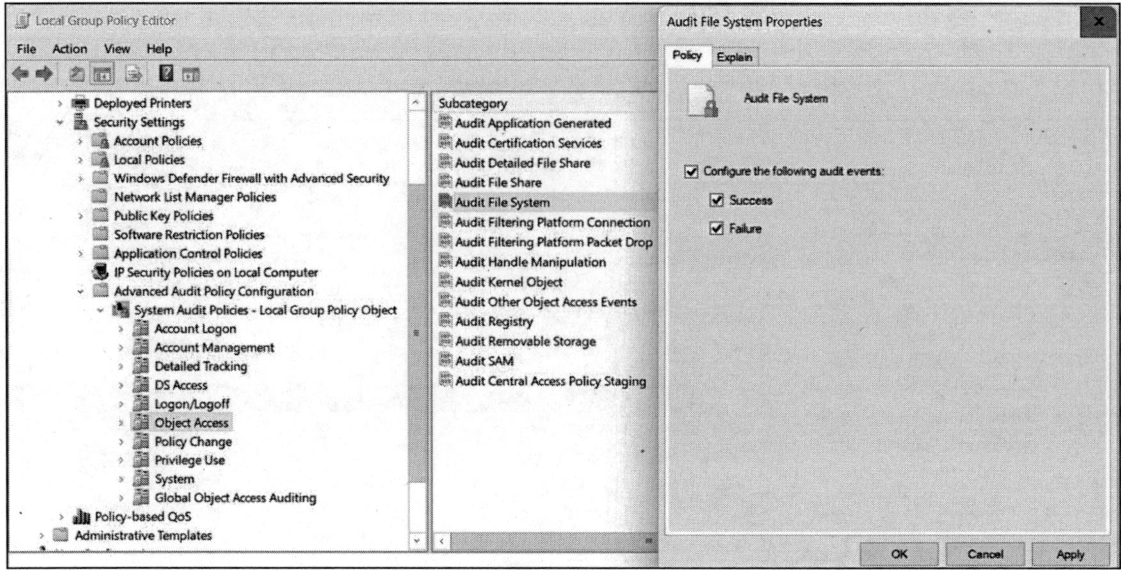

***Figure 14.5:** The Local Group Policy Editor with the Audit File System Properties dialog box*

Auditing Linux systems

Linux distros may not have GUI-based apps and consoles of Windows systems, but that does not mean they cannot be audited just as well. There are several approaches to setting up audit and event captures on a Linux system, including:

- **Script**: The **`script`** command opens a capture file, named typescript, in which all terminal activities are recorded. This includes everything displayed on the terminal, including any inputs or outputs. This command is best used to record the sessions of the active user. *Figure 14.6* shows the command line and response for the script command.

```
root@bpbonline #script
Script started, output log file is 'typescript'
```

***Figure 14.6:** The Linux script command*

- **Audit daemon (auditd)**: The Linux **auditd** utility can be configured with rules and properties to log information about the actions and events taking place on a system. The audit records can be viewed with the ausearch or aureport utilities. The configuration of the auditd is done through the auditctl utility. The rules are defined in the **`/etc/audit/audit.rules`** and the **`auditd.conf`** files. When an auditd session starts, the **`audit.rules/auditd.conf`** files are loaded into the kernel. *Figure 14.7* shows the contents of an **`auditd.conf`** file. Auditd stores its log entries in **`/var/log/audit/audit.log`**:

```
# This file controls the configuration of the audit daemon
#

local_events = yes
write_logs = yes
log_file = /var/log/audit/audit.log
log_group = adm
log_format = ENRICHED
flush = INCREMENTAL_ASYNC
freq = 50
max_log_file = 8
num_logs = 5
priority_boost = 4
name_format = NONE
##name = mydomain
max_log_file_action = ROTATE
space_left = 75
space_left_action = SYSLOG
verify_email = yes
action_mail_acct = root
admin_space_left = 50
admin_space_left_action = SUSPEND
disk_full_action = SUSPEND
disk_error_action = SUSPEND
use_libwrap = yes
##tcp_listen_port = 60
tcp_listen_queue = 5
tcp_max_per_addr = 1
##tcp_client_ports = 1024-65535
tcp_client_max_idle = 0
transport = TCP
krb5_principal = auditd
##krb5_key_file = /etc/audit/audit.key
distribute_network = no
q_depth = 1200
overflow_action = SYSLOG
max_restarts = 10
plugin_dir = /etc/audit/plugins.d
end_of_event_timeout = 2
```

Figure 14.7: *The audit configuration in the auditd.conf file*

The **auditd** utility creates a variety of log files. The following are the most common log files it creates:

- **System log**: Tracks authorizations, system messages, and the actions of system daemons.
- **Authorization log**: Tracks password prompts, sudo commands and remote logins.
- **Daemon log**: Tracks daemons running in background, such as SSH sessions, print services, Bluetooth, and more.
- **Kernel log**: Tracks the actions of the Linux kernel.
- **System log**: Tracks information on system activities and miscellaneous events.
- **Login logs**: There are several logs that track user account logins, including the login failures log, the last logins log, and the login records log.

Note: If for any reason, auditd does not run, the kernel audit messages are sent to rsyslog.

Single sign-on

Single sign-on (SSO) authentication facilitates a user to sign into two or more applications or website through the entry of one set of credentials. SSO is a part of **federated identity**, which covers several concerns of user logins, including authentication, authorization, user attribute exchange, and user account management. We have covered authentication and authorization before, attribute exchange shares user data across the user management systems to which the user is being validated. In addition, user account management is also a sharing of data that allows the separate administrators to manage account across domains and systems.

SSO operates on a trust relationship between an application and an identify provider, such as OneLogin or Auth0. The identity provider issues a digital certificate to the service provider (application). The certificate is used to digitally sign the information being shared to certify that it is coming from a trusted source. The identity data, such as email addresses or usernames, in SSO is contained in tokens.

The steps in the SSO login process are:

1. The user navigates to the application or website (service provider) to which he or she wishes to access.
2. The service provider sends a token with user information to the SSO system (the identity provider).
3. The identity provider checks if the user is already authenticated and if so, grants access.
4. If the user has not been authenticated, the user is prompted to enter the required credentials.
5. If the identity provider is able to authenticate the user, a token is sent to the service provider that the user is authenticated.
6. The user is given access to the service provider (application or website).
7. If the user accesses a different application or website that has a trust relationship with the SSO system, the authentication on the new site would follow the same process.

Conclusion

User accounts management is the first-level security by authenticating a user's credentials. The rights and permissions of user accounts may apply to a local computer or to a network or domain. Access control is the process of authenticating and authorizing users who wish to access resources. What a user is permitted to access and what he or she can do with the accessed object is controlled by the rights of the user and the permissions assigned to the object. The access, use, and manipulation of data resources should be audited to protect against theft, alterations, and destruction from both interior users and exterior attackers.

In the next chapter, we look at the risk of vulnerabilities and threats and the methods that can be applied to mitigate any potential attacks and harm to an organization's assets.

Points to remember

- Authentication requires the entry of user credentials, typically a username and password.
- The user accounts, on a standalone Windows system, are local accounts.
- Windows default local accounts are categorized as administrator, guest, HelpAssistant, local service, network service, and system.
- User accounts on a Windows system include standard, Microsoft account, and privileged account.
- A user group contains one or more user accounts that share permissions and security rights. The three general user groups are local groups, security groups, and distribution groups.
- Linux user accounts have two unique identifiers: username and UID. The three types of user accounts in Linux are root, regular, and service.
- Linux groups are used to limit the actions and to specify the permissions of their user accounts. The Linux group types are primary and secondary.
- Access control is authenticating and authorizing users, groups, software and systems to gain access to resources on a network or computer.
- The least privilege principle is that a user needs only the permissions and rights on an object that permit him or her to do their job.
- RBAC assigns permissions and rights to users based on their role within an organization.
- Scope-based access control defines the actions an application can perform on behalf of a user.
- Delegation is a user assigning his or her credentials to another user.
- MFA combines two or more identification factors for authentication. MFA factors have five categories: something you know, something you have, something you are, somewhere you are, and something you do.
- The separation of duties control recommends certain duties be separated into discrete tasks, each of which are performed by different individuals.

- Access management includes issuing policies, enforcing rules, and auditing the results of an organization's identification and access control procedures.
- The objective of auditing is to verify controls are in effect and protect resources.
- The Linux auditd utility logs information about the actions and events taking place on a system.
- **Single sign-on** (**SSO**) authentication facilitates a user to sign into two or more applications or website through the entry of one set of credentials. SSO is a part of federated identity.

CHAPTER 15
Risk and Mitigation

Introduction

In the context of physical and logical security, virtually everything related to a network server is at risk. These valuable assets could be damaged, stolen, destroyed, or simply fail to operate as they should. The measure of this risk is the impact these events could have on the organization and its continued operations. The latest version of the Server + certification exam has placed a higher emphasis on the overall security of servers. This chapter discusses the risks to which servers are exposed, how those risks may be mitigated, and the regulatory and legal constraints that must be incorporated into an organization's security program.

Structure

The chapter covers the following topics:

- Security risks
- Data theft
- Mitigation strategies
- Security information and event management
- Regulatory constraints

Objective

By the end of this chapter, you will be able to identify and describe the sub-objectives of the following Server + examination objective: *Explain data security risks and mitigation strategies*.

Security risks

Due of the importance to their organization, the level of investment in their assets, and their dependence on physical and logical security, server rooms and data centers are subject to high levels of risk. The application of risk management is crucial to the protection and continued operation of a data center.

Risk management involves four primary activities: identifying and classifying assets, defining the security measures to protect each of the asset classes, implementing the security measures, and performing regular reviews of their effectiveness. A proactive risk management program can be a **Vulnerability Risk Management (VRM)** that identifies and mitigates (resolves) vulnerabilities before they become threat targets and create a risk.

A security risk is a vulnerability (weakness) that could be exploited (attacked) by a threat actor (attacker) who has specific motivation to cause damage, destruction, or loss (harm). Risk, which is two-fold, is the probability (chance) of an attack, the impact on operations, and the value of the harm (cost). *Figure 15.1* illustrates these elements of risk:

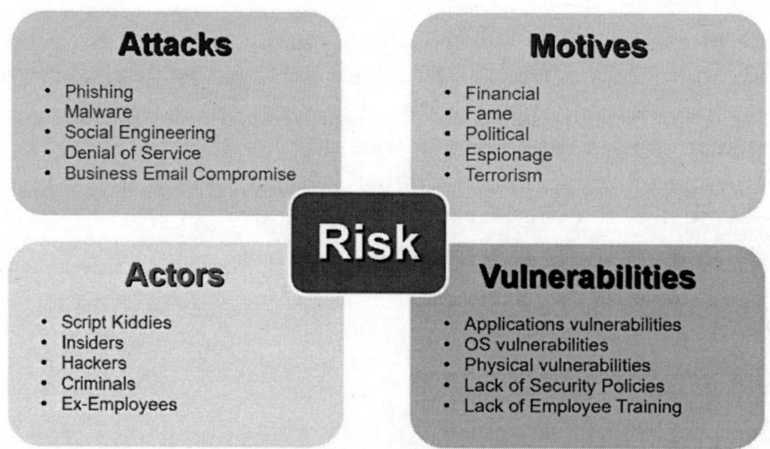

***Figure 15.1**: The elements of risk*

There are essentially two general types of risk to a data center:

- **Physical risks:** Weather, power, and catastrophes (see *Chapter 13, Physical Security*, for more information on physical security)
- **Logical risks:** Applications, operating systems, data storage, and communications

Logical risks are the result of the existence of a vulnerability that could potentially be exploited by an attacker with the intent of doing harm. In the section that follows, we look at each of these elements.

Vulnerabilities

A vulnerability in server security is a flaw or weakness on a network host or server. This could be a missing software update or fixing a poorly configured system, or the general lack, or inattention to needed security measures. Vulnerabilities pose the danger of being exploited by a threat actor and should be viewed as an open door through which an attack can occur. All vulnerabilities are within the control and responsibility of the organization operating the data center. The attacker, or criminal, can seize this as an opportunity. The organization is responsible for removing the vulnerability and the opportunity for an attack.

In any server room or data center, several common vulnerabilities can exist; here are a few:

- **Configuration errors:** Settings and configurations are servers' most common source of exploitable vulnerabilities. This is primarily caused by mistyping or data entry errors by administrators.
- **Excessive permissions:** The principle of least privilege should be applied for user permissions, ensuring that employees are granted access to resources only at the level necessary to perform their job duties. User accounts with excessive permissions can be exploited for identity-related attacks and data breaches.
- **Unpatched application software:** Software developers release updates and patches according to their schedule, which can cause problems for system administrators, who can fall behind in keeping the software up-to-date. Attackers track software patches and updates and attempt to take advantage of software that has not been updated.
- **User credentials:** The security level of user credentials can create a vulnerability if the credentials are weak. This is primarily an issue with user account passwords, which are often easily hacked, just like they are easily remembered. A weak password, something like "password" or the like, is an easy target for a brute force or dictionary password attack.
- **Zero-day flaws:** A zero-day vulnerability is typically a software flaw unknown to the developer before it is discovered and exploited by a threat actor.

Threat actors

Several names are used for the individuals or groups who exploit data center or server vulnerabilities, and just as many motivations for why they do it. These people are known as hackers, cybercriminals, attackers, crackers, and black hats, among other names, but in the terminology of cybersecurity, they are **threat actors**. However, some threat actors perpetrate specific types of attacks. A security program must identify the types of threat actors and their motivations to attack the organization. Here are some more active threat actor types:

- **Cybercriminal:** This threat actor could be operating independently or as a part of an organized crime group to steal sensitive data, money, **Personally Identifiable Information (PII)**, and identities. Their sole motivation is money.
- **Cyberterrorist:** The primary objective of this threat actor is to cause as much harm and destruction as possible, typically related to a social or political cause.
- **Hacktivist:** The title for this threat actor is a blend of the two words, hacker, and activist. Their motivation is to share secret documents with the public that expose the truth about the government or an agency.
- **Insider:** The first threat actor to any organization is an employee who inadvertently or maliciously shares, steals, or destroys an organization's data.
- **Script kiddie:** This threat actor typically tries out someone else's attack software, primarily to see what it does.
- **State-sponsored:** This type of threat actor may be employed or sponsored by foreign government espionage agencies with the purpose of obtaining, stealing, or destroying intellectual property, classified information, and even money.

Threat actor motivations

Except script kiddies, threat actors exploit and attack vulnerabilities for one reason or another. The motivations of any threat actor can be anything. However, for the most part, their motivation will be somewhere close to one of the following:

- **Fame and reputation:** If you have seen the movie *Hackers*, you know that threat actors can be motivated by gaining fame and street cred.
- **Political and economic:** State-sponsored, cyberterrorist, and hacktivist threat actors either work for a cause or are trying to promote a cause. A cybercriminal may also be motivated by politics or sociological ideals to steal data or money.
- **Profit and gain:** This may be the most common motivation for a threat actor. Cybercriminals, hacktivists, insiders, and state-sponsored threat actors can be motivated by financial gain in addition to their political agenda.
- **Revenge and pay-back:** Threat actors motivated by seeking revenge or "getting back" at someone who is known to their target, such as employees of the same company or members on the same social network.

Common attacks

While there are hundreds of different types of attacks that a threat actor (attacker) can launch against a system's vulnerabilities, if they exist, The following are the most common types of attack an organization may experience:

- **Malware**: Malware is a shortened version of "malicious software," that includes spyware, ransomware, viruses, and worms, among others. Malware attacks a system through a vulnerability, commonly when a user clicks on a malicious link or opens an email attachment. This action causes the malware to be installed on the system. Once it is on a system, malware may do one or more of the following:
    - Use ransomware to block access to key components or data
    - Install malware or other harmful software
    - Activates spyware that steals and transmits information to the attacker
    - Causes system disruptions or makes it inoperable
- **Phishing**: An attacker sends fraudulent communication, typically via email, which appears to have come from a reputable source. The attacker's objective is to obtain or steal sensitive data like credit card and login information or to install malware on the victim's machine.
- **Man-in-the-middle attack (MitM)**: This type of attack, also known as eavesdropping, occurs when attackers insert themselves into a two-party communication to filter and steal data. Using a MitM attack, an attacker can steal sensitive information and impersonate one or both parties to gain access to sensitive information. There are two common points of entry for MitM attacks:
    - Attackers can insert themselves between a visitor's device and the network access point or router on an insecure public Wi-Fi hotspot. Unaware of the attacker's presence, the visitor passes information through the MitM attacker.
    - An attacker can install malware that captures and transmits a victim's information to the attacker.
- **Denial-of-service (DoS)**: This attack floods systems, servers, or networks with **Internet Control Message Protocol (ICMP)** requests that exhaust resources and bandwidth. This results in the target system begin unable to fulfill legitimate requests. The attack may use multiple compromised devices to launch this type of **distributed-denial-of-service (DDoS)** attack.
- **SQL injection**: This type of attack occurs when an attacker inserts malicious code into a file, program, or webpage that causes it to reveal information it would ordinarily not share. A common SQL injection attack method is the attacker submits malicious code into a vulnerable website search box.
- **Zero-day exploit:** This type of attack occurs most commonly after a network vulnerability is announced but before a fix can be implemented.

Data center risks

Attacks perpetrated by outsider threat actors are constant in any data center or server room. An organization's security policies and programs should concentrate on mitigating the vulnerabilities that expose the servers to these attacks. However, several vulnerabilities within the data center can put the systems at risk. While many situations can cause a vulnerability, the server + certification exam objectives list the following as the ones you should know:

- **Hardware failure:** When a hardware component fails, production, security, or both can be impacted. For example, an authentication server's failure or a biometric device's misfunction could create an exploitable vulnerability.
- **Malware:** Malicious software or malware is an umbrella term for software specifically designed to attack, damage, or destroy a system or stored data in such a way that it becomes unusable.
- **Data corruption:** Corrupted data, which results from an attack by a threat actor or malware, is a permanent data loss. While a data breach is considered a more severe attack, data corruption can lead to legal or economic problems for an organization, as well as possible interruptions in business continuity.

Data theft

Data theft is stealing data or digital information from an organization's servers, networks, and computers to gain sensitive and private data. The motivation behind data theft can be any of those listed earlier. Still, it is typically done to assume the identity of an individual or to sell corporate secrets or PII. In most cases, the data is not actually stolen, rather, it is duplicated or copied. Regardless, data theft compromises the data and the organization.

Data breach and data leak are commonly used interchangeably with data theft, which is somewhat true. However, data breaches and data leaks are a bit different.

- **Data breach:** A data breach is an intentional attack by an unauthorized threat actor to view or harvest confidential, sensitive, or private information. It results from weaknesses in an organization's or a person's technology or behaviors.
- **Data leak:** In contrast to a data breach, a data leak is not usually intentional. Data leak is the accidental exposure of confidential, sensitive, or private information. A data leak can become a data breach if an attacker obtains the exposed information. Data leaks typically happen on the internet, logged-in workstations, or discarded storage devices.

Data theft can occur in several ways, including:

- **Social engineering:** There are a variety of social engineering attacks, all of which aim to gain data and information from an individual. The attacker uses a false narrative to get a victim to disclose PII or to perform an act that often leads to a data breach. A social engineering attack aims to get the targeted individual to disclose their login credentials, send money to the attacker, install malware, or unknowingly launder money.

- **Weak password:** As discussed earlier, passwords that are simple to guess or are used on multiple accounts, not all of which may have adequate security, can be almost like an open door to an attacker who is seeking to steal data.
- **Insider threats:** Disgruntled employees can copy, alter, or steal data because they have access rights and privileges above what they may need. Insider threats can also come from ex-employees and external companies or partners to whom access to the internal systems was granted.
- **Human error:** Data leaks that become data breaches can result from user errors, such as sending sensitive information to an unintended recipient, attaching the wrong document to an e-mail, or giving a removable device with sensitive data to someone not authorized to access that information. Human error can also be caused by misconfiguration or omission, like a database without a password assigned.
- **Compromised downloads:** A user may download infected programs or data that provide a threat actor to gain access to a system from which they can steal data.

The data that can be the potential target for data theft can be almost anything. For example:

- Credit card or debit card information
- Customer records
- Human resource records and employee data
- Login credentials such as usernames and passwords
- PII
- Private documents stored on computer computers
- Proprietary process descriptions and operating methodologies
- Source code

Data loss prevention

Data loss prevention (DLP) is an overall data security strategy focused on detecting and preventing data leaks, data breaches, and unauthorized use of stolen data. A DLP program provides visibility of all the data on a network, including data-in-use, data-in-transit, and data-at-rest (see *Chapter 12, Data Security* for more information on these data states).

There are four types of DLP approaches:

- **Network DLP:** This type of DLP monitors an organization's network activity on traditional networks and in the cloud. This includes tracking e-mail, messaging, and file transfers for critical data that may be sent in violation of an organization's security policies. **Network DLP** manages an activity database in which it records the access of sensitive or confidential.
- **Endpoint DLP:** Endpoint DLP monitors all network servers, cloud services, computers, cell phones, and other devices that use or save data to prevent data leaks, loss, or misuse.
- **Cloud DLP:** An extension of endpoint DLP, **cloud DLP** scans and audits data in the cloud to detect and encrypt sensitive information before it is stored in the cloud. It also maintains a list of applications and users authorized to access the data and logs when data is accessed and by whom.
- **Data-centric DLP:** Where the other types of DLP primarily monitor data, **data-centric DLP** protects data at rest on a database or file server. Data-centric DLP is typically implemented by software integrated with the data storage systems to encrypt and control access to the data through user credentials and other authentication factors.

Data duplication

The unneeded and unwanted duplication of data on a system generally occurs when the same data is recorded in multiple files or as separate entries in the same file. Having duplicate data can cause issues in a business, such as multiple addresses, phone numbers, or other information for a customer that has moved, revised contract information or terms, and conflicting product information from different suppliers.

Data duplication does not happen intentionally. It results from a lack of planning, attention to detail, and poor systems design. Since it can create inefficiencies and confusion in an organization's operations, duplicated data should be identified, analyzed, and removed.

Data deduplication is a process typically performed by software that removes unwanted duplicated data. This process searches for duplicates using several different methods and then deletes them. The goal of data deduplication is to delete only the data that will not impact the applications using that data. Some data deduplication services deduplicate data and store it as a backup. The different deduplication methods that can be used are described in the following sections:

In-line and post-process deduplication

In-line deduplication occurs when a data block is written on the storage device. The storage system searches for a duplicate of the incoming data block, and if one is found, a reference is created that points to the existing data block, and the new data block is discarded. The **post-processing deduplication** method essentially does the same thing, only later. The new data block is stored on the storage device. At a later time, the device is scanned for duplicates. If one is found, a reference is created, and the duplicate data is removed.

Source and target deduplication

Source deduplication is performed by the file system, which scans a new file and creates a hash total of the file. This hash of the new file is then compared to the hashes of existing files. If a match is found, the new file is referenced to the older file and is discarded. Source deduplication has flaws, especially if either the old file or the new file is altered, or a copy is created, such as on a backup.

Target deduplication does not involve a file server or storage system in its process. However, it may have more data being transferred across the network because checking for duplicates occurs at the storage solution, which could be a burden on network resources.

Hardware-based and software-based deduplication

Hardware-based deduplication services use a separate hardware device to inspect data and remove duplicates. Hardware deduplication has better performance but can be more expensive than a software-based solution, which is why it is better for organizations with large amounts of data.

Software deduplication occurs locally on the computer on which the data originated. The software scans the data, and if a duplicate is found, a pointer to the older version is created. A software solution is generally less expensive but more difficult to install and manage.

Data publication

Data captured illegally or protected as confidential or sensitive can be used as an inducement for an individual or a company to pay a ransom (as in the case of ransomware attacks), perform an illegal act or disclose additional information. There have been several well-publicized cases of data being published or broadcast without official authorization by media outlets. For example, the data obtained by *Daniel Ellsberg* (Pentagon Papers), *Julian Assange* (WikiLeaks), *Edward Snowden* (NSA), and *Bradley Manning* (US Army) were released nefariously on the internet or in the press. Most definitely, the authorities responsible for these documents and data did not want it to be released.

The data privacy laws in the US and around the world (see *Chapter 12, Data Security*) set regulations and guidelines for the storage and retention of individuals' PII. Laws also exist that make data theft illegal and punishable. However, the publication of stolen data is not prohibited by law. In fact, it is a protected right under the First Amendment of the US Constitution as the Freedom of the Press.

The data privacy and protection laws around the world are basically uniform in their protection of private and business confidential information, including likenesses and intellectual property. This data cannot be published without permission of the person. In some privacy laws, this permission must be in writing, but nonetheless, permission must be given. There are two types of data publication restrictions:

- **Publication of private facts:** This is actually categorized as an invasion of privacy in most cases. The publication of PII or confidential data that would be offensive to a reasonable person is prohibited.
- **Publishing the name or likeness of another person:** This also includes publishing information that claims that an attacker is actually the person whose data is published. Under the privacy laws, this is considered a breach of the right to publicity. Identity theft comes under the laws in this area.

Unwanted access methods

Chapter 13, Physical Security, covered many access methods used by unauthorized persons to gain access to a secured facility. However, there are a few that bear repeating:

- **Tailgating:** When one or more unauthorized people enter a door or portal by following an authorized person, commonly an employee, very closely. Typically, this means that the tailgater(s) move through the door before it closes and locks. It is not unusual for an employee to unwittingly hold the door open for an unauthorized individual(s) as a courtesy.
- **Forcing (levering) doors open:** Unless a door is specially designed to prevent someone from prying or levering it open, it may be easy to open it with a small tool, like a screwdriver or pry bar.
- **Keys:** Door, panel, and even locker keys can become stolen, lost, or borrowed. A physical key is nearly impossible to keep track of once it is out of the possession of its rightful owner. A lost or missing key can set up a serious security vulnerability that may require the locks of a building to be rekeyed.
- **Access cards:** An electronic access card is far better than a physical key, but it can also be lost, stolen, or loaned to another person, who just might be otherwise unauthorized.
- **Social engineering:** As mentioned earlier in this chapter, social engineering is an attack form that seeks to get private or confidential information from a target. If the information gained this way includes a passcode, password, or a borrowed access key or card, the attacker has gained access to a secured facility or system.

Backdoor

A backdoor, although it sounds like a physical rear entryway, is actually a malware type that allows an attacker to remotely access a computer totally without your permission and, in most cases, your knowledge. A backdoor can be hardware, firmware, or software that is installed on a system, typically through other malware. Once the backdoor is installed, an attacker can access a computer for data theft, sabotage the system, or launch a bigger malware attack.

A hardware or firmware backdoor are modifications made to the hardware or ROM that provides remote access to a computer. Software backdoors are malware routines that hide its identity so that the operating system does not see an additional user login. There are several types of backdoors, all of which are malware that opens access to a system, including rootkits, trojans, keyloggers, worms, and ransomware.

In order for a backdoor to be added to a system, the attacker must gain access. This access is commonly through an open TCP/UDP port, out-of-date applications, poorly configured firewalls or routers, and, of course, weak passwords. The more common forms of backdoors include:

- **Trojans:** A trojan is a malware file that acts like a legitimate or safe file to gain access to or infect a system. Trojan backdoors allow attackers to access folders and files and install additional malware on the system.
- **Rootkits:** A rootkit is a malware that can hide its actions from the operating system and gain advanced security privileges and permissions. Through a rootkit, an attacker can remotely access a system, modify its data, and alter its configuration.
- **Hardware backdoors:** A hardware backdoor is typically a firmware modification that provides attacker access to a device, including smartphones, IoT devices, routers, and computers. A hardware backdoor, which can be malware or have an intended benign purpose, can be installed prior to shipment or during a maintenance procedure.
- **Cryptographic backdoors:** A crypto backdoor is more of a key than a door. This backdoor unlocks any data transmitted in or out of a system that is encrypted with a particular encryption algorithm.

Identifying and disclosing data breaches

According to *IBM's 2022 Cost of a Data Breach Report*[1], it took an average of 277 days, or about 9 months, for an organization to discover it had suffered a data breach and an additional 73 days to contain the breach. A data breach in which the data copied is difficult to detect unless the activities on storage devices is closely monitored. However, there are several steps that may be needed to detect that a data breach has occurred. These steps are:

1. Source: IBM Corporation, "Cost of a data breach 2022," https://www.ibm.com/reports/data-breach

- **Define the data breach:** To determine whether a data breach has happened, the first step is to identify the data that may have been compromised. This step of the process involves the examination of two components, lead and indicators, which can help to verify a data breach has occurred and what data was the target. Leads are entries in log files that indicate a data breach has occurred. Log files can also contain indicators, such as buffer overflows on database servers, failed login attempts from unauthorized user or unidentified networks, and the like.
- **Make no changes:** Once it is determined that a data breach has occurred, no changes should be made to the affected systems. Changing anything could alter evidence of the breach or make the situation worse. However, if the breach is still happening, a priority should be made to stop the data outflow.
- **Implement emergency intervention:** In this step of the process, facts and evidence are gathered, including the date and time the breach was detected and the internal stakeholders were notified, document the process used to interrupt the data outflow (if necessary), and conduct the tasks of an emergency case intervention, such as a risk assessment and recording as much information regarding the breach as possible.
- **Collect evidence:** Immediately after the discovery of a data breach, the person who discovered the breach should be interviewed, the security measures that may have allowed the breach should be reviewed, and the elements involved in the data transfer, such as log files, network ports, memory and storage device usage, active network connections, and logged in user accounts.
- **Analyze the data breach:** After gathering the evidence, analyze the data and information available regarding unauthorized activity, escalated permissions and data access, and unknown applications or services used in the breach.
- **Inform stakeholders:** Many national, state, and local data privacy laws require that a government authority be notified within 72 hours of the discovery of the breach. Notifications to individuals whose data may have been compromised must be notified without delay. Stakeholders that may be affected by a data breach are employees, clients, users, customers, and suppliers.

Mitigation strategies

Risk mitigation (resolving) is the application of security policies and procedures that eliminate or reduce the risk or harm of a threat. Risk mitigation has three primary components:

- **Prevention:** There are several approaches to risk prevention, but the following two are typically included in virtually all risk prevention programs.
    - **Prevention by design:** The most effective type of risk prevention is one that is designed into a system from the beginning of the development effort.

  - **Prevention by layering:** Security measures are applied at separate points of a system or network, such as firewalls, encryption, and authentication. This type of risk prevention is also called **defense in depth**. An attacker must penetrate each of the layers separately.
  - **Intrusion Prevention System (IPS):** An IPS can be installed as a standalone network device – **network IPS (NIPS)** – and as a software application on a local host – **host IPS (HIPS)**. An IPS detects, flags, and blocks any detected malicious activity, although it can be prone to false positives. An IPS can also **correct cyclic redundancy check (CRC)** errors and help avoid TCP packet sequencing problems.
- **Detection:** An **Intrusion Detection System (IDS)** or monitoring software can identify an attack and take preventive steps to block it by shutting down the system, logging off users, triggering an alarm, or alerting an administrator.
- **Remediation:** This is the process in which potential threats are identified and preventive measures are applied. With existing vulnerabilities known, new gaps or flaws are easier to detect and remediate.

Proactive strategies

Risk management should be proactive and include strategies that are appropriate to the organization. The strategies most commonly used are:

- **Conduct a risk assessment:** In order to resolve a potential threat and its risk, it must be known. A risk assessment can discover gaps or flaws in an organization's security measures and controls. The assessment identifies the assets that should be protected and measures the effectiveness of any security controls that are in place.
- **Establish controls:** Once you have identified the assets at risk and the impact on the organization if they are exploited, the security controls and measures that mitigate the threats and risks are implemented.
- **Install firewalls and malware software:** The installation of preventive and blocking devices and software provides an additional layer of protection to a system or network.
- **Implement a patch management program:** The patches, fixes, updates, and version releases of system and application software should be applied as soon as possible to stay ahead of the threat actors. The best practice is to install and test the patches on a non-production system before applying them to the production system.
- **Monitor network traffic:** Being proactive is the best risk mitigation strategy. Monitoring server and network activity and traffic. There are several third-party security monitoring software tools available to continuously monitor systems and networks and provide a comprehensive view of their activities.

- **Define an Incident Response Plan:** Should a serious security event occur, the affected employees in the organization must know what each of them is to do and what their responsibilities are. An **Incident Response Plan** (**IRP**) enables the organization to respond proactively and quickly to remediate any attack issues.

Attack surfaces

Another risk mitigation strategy that should be included by all organizations is to minimize the attack surface. An attack surface is a general name for an organization's vulnerabilities or attack vectors (entry points) that an attacker may exploit. To minimize the attack surface, an organization should assess the potential risks in the following:

- **Physical:** The **physical attack surface** of any organization is the assets that could be exploited if the attacker gains access to its premises or buildings.
- **Digital:** The **digital attack surface** consists of any assets that can be exploited over the internet or beyond a firewall, such as servers, DMZ, and honey pot devices.
- **Social engineering:** The **social engineering attack surface** is an organization's employees, partners, or contractors that could be manipulated into disclosing private, sensitive, or confidential information or data about themselves or the organization.

Security information and event management

Security information and event management (SIEM), the combination of **security events management (SEM)** and **security information management (SIM)**, enables an organization to identify potential vulnerabilities and threats before an attack can occur. SIM collects and manages system log files and security data. SEM is the analysis and reporting of data collected, primarily in log files, from security events.

SIEM gathers log and event data from the various components of an organization's systems, including applications, servers, internetworking, and security devices. This data is then sorted, categorized and scanned for anomalies from predefined rules aimed at identifying potential threats, such as malware activities or failed logins. In other words, SIEM helps identify potential vulnerabilities and threats before they can be exploited.

SIEM systems, although they vary in their total capabilities, typically do provide most of the functions described in the following sections.

Log management

Log management involves organizing, storing, processing, and analyzing log file and other system information with the objective of improving system operations, identifying any technical issues, managing system resources, and strengthening security. Log management is more about analyzing events recorded in log files than it is about managing the log files. **Log Management Systems (LMSs)** are softwares that perform these tasks to store log data and event data in a central location.

Log management systems perform the following actions:

- **Collection:** Log management tools gather data from the operating system, applications, servers, users, endpoints, or other relevant sources
- **Monitoring:** Log monitoring tools track event activity
- **Analysis:** Log analysis tools analyze logs to identify bugs, vulnerabilities, threats, and other possible issues
- **Retention:** Log retention tools manage how long log data is retained
- **Indexing:** A log management tool filters, sorts, and searches across all log files
- **Reporting:** Log management systems automate reporting on operations, resource allocations, and security

Two-person integrity

Demonstrations of this security approach are common in movies and shows in which a nuclear intercontinental missile is being fired in active aggression of some sort. Two individuals must enter separate codes or insert and turn separate keys to launch the missile. In any case, this is a demonstration of the two-person control. The secrecy of the process and the codes or keys is **two-person integrity**.

Split encryption keys and tokens

A variation on the two-person integrity or control rules is splitting an encryption key and storing each part in a different location. For an attacker to get one part of the key might not be too difficult, but getting the second, third, or more parts can be much more difficult.

A **split key** or token can also be integrated into a two-person approach with an administrator and a user each having a part. This requires some coordination, much like that used to fire the missile, but the security is much higher. Encryption keys and **Password-Based Encryption (PBE)**, which converts a password into a symmetric encryption key, can be split into two or more parts with SQL or **Java Naming and Directory Interface (JNDI)** programming.

Separation of roles

The separation of roles, more formally known as the **separation or segregation of duties (SOD),** is a commonly used internal control that is an essential element of a risk management strategy. The basic premise is that each of the separate responsibilities in a business process is performed by a different department or individual under distant supervision. The idea is to prevent unilateral fraud or theft that could result from one or more employees colluding with a scheme to provide what looks like official records or actions.

Regulatory constraints

More and more governments and trade associations are enacting laws, regulations, or bylaws intended to protect themselves, the organizations they govern, their members, and, in virtually all cases, private citizens. These laws, regulations, and guidelines set, prescribe, or recommend how data is to be secured, managed, processed, and retained. The data that is the focus of the majority of these requirements is data that can be used to identify a specific person, which is called **Personally Identifiable Information (PII)**. More than any other types of data, except for highly classified government and military documents, PII is specially protected by law. Another classification of personal data is **Individually Privileged Information (IPI)**. IPI is information about an individual that is created and retained by medical, legal, and other professionals. This means that a person's medical records (HIPAA), education records (FERPA), and consumer information (CCPA and GLBA) are protected by law. *Table 15.1* lists some of the major laws that govern the privacy and protection of personal and private data:

Law or Regulation	Coverage
California Consumer Privacy Act (**CCPA**)	Privacy rights and consumer protection
Children's Online Privacy Protection Act (**COPPA**)	Regulates online collection of a child under 13 years of age's PII
Federal Information Security Modernization Act of 2014 (**FISMA**)	Requires all federal agencies to protect their information systems
Gramm-Leach-Bliley Act (**GLBA**)	Companies must secure the private information of clients and customers
Health Insurance Portability and Accountability Act (**HIPAA**)	Governs electronic data and protects the privacy of patients
Sarbanes-Oxley Act (**SOX**)	Public companies must retain financial records for 7 years
The **Family Educational Rights and Privacy Act** of 1974 (**FERPA**)	Protecting student records

Table 15.1: *US laws affecting data*

Table 15.1 is far from a complete list. Beyond the laws and regulations it lists, there are data security standards for specific industries, payment card processing, and data privacy protections. The following sections describe three of these laws: the **Payment Card Industry Data Security Standard (PCI DSS)**, the European Union's **General Data Protection Regulation (GDPR)**, and a data protection standard called the **Red Flag Rules**.

Payment Card Industry Data Security Standard

The PCI DSS specifies the requirements for processing payment cards (credit cards) and the security of cardholder data. The **PCI Security Standards Council** (**PCI SSC**), with members representing the major payment card companies, develops and issues the PCI DSS standard. The PCI DSS applies to the organizations that accept credit card payments, regardless of whether the transactions are in-person or online. The PCI DSS is designed to mitigate the risks of storing, processing, and transmitting payment card and cardholder data.

General Data Protection Regulation

The General Data Protection Regulation (GDPR) defines the regulations governing the collection and use of PII for the citizens of the **European Union** (**EU**). The GDPR also applies to any website that an EU citizen might access, regardless of where its server is located. The GDPR requires that a website must inform any EU visitor of his or her consumer rights and provide disclosures on what the site can and cannot do with his or her PII. This includes an explanation of the data collected, how and where the data is stored, and how he or she is to be notified in the event of a data breach. The GDPR includes photographs and likenesses, IP addresses, and any information stored in a cookie as PII.

The Red Flags rule

The **Red Flags rule** is a government regulation enforced by the Federal Trade Commission (US) to prevent identity theft. The Red Flags rule says that businesses that accept payment cards must implement a written identity theft prevention program designed to detect the red flags of identity theft in their day-to-day operations, take steps to prevent the crime, and mitigate its damage.

Red flags are questionable or possibly illegal actions that may appear to be identity theft. Such actions raise a red flag indicating that something is not right in the actions of a customer or client. Examples of what may raise a red flag are a lost or stolen debit card used at an ATM, a thief gaining access to an account through a stolen debit card and attempts to change the account holder's mailing address, e-mail address, or password.

Data retention

A data retention plan defines how an organization will collect, store, and protect specific types of data. As covered earlier in this chapter, PII data is governed by laws and regulations, which also define how it is to be stored and how long it must be maintained and protected. An organization may have other confidential or sensitive data that may also be regulated by law or guidelines. Any organization that deals with large volumes of data should have a well-defined data retention plan that details how data is managed from its collection to disposal.

Table 15.2 lists a sampling of data types and their recommended or legally required retention periods. However, an organization should keep records or data for as long as it is useful, regardless of the recommended period. Also, should data be subpoenaed to a court case, the subpoena can request the data needed, even if the data's retention period is exceeded.

Data Type	Retention Period
Employee benefits records	6 years after the creation
Employee drug tests	Up to 5 years after the test
Employee payroll records	3 years after the creation
Employee personnel records	1 year after the creation
Personal Health Information (PHI)	6 years after treatment
Personally Identifiable Information (PII)	No legal restriction
Tax records	4 years after the end of the year.

Table 15.2: *Examples of data retention periods.*

Conclusion

Risk is the projected harm or impact of a security event measured by its likelihood of occurring and the possible monetary damage it may cause. Risk is based on the chance that a threat actor will exploit a vulnerability to harm. In physical and logical security, virtually everything may be at risk for damage, theft, or destruction. An organization must assess the risk to its systems by identifying its weaknesses and flaws, mitigating these vulnerabilities, and complying with the laws, regulations, and guidelines that apply to its operations.

In the next chapter, we look into the hardening process that can be applied to protect servers and hosts. The chapter also covers the methods used to decommission a server from a network.

Points to remember

- Risk management involves identifying and classifying assets, defining security measures, implementing security measures, and regularly evaluating effectiveness.
- Risk is the probability that an attack could occur and the impact on operations and the value of the harm. There are two types of risk: physical risks and logical risks
- Common vulnerabilities are configuration errors, excessive permissions, unpatched software, user credentials, and zero-day flaws.
- Threat actor types include cybercriminals, cyberterrorists, hacktivists, insiders, script kiddies, and state-sponsored. Threat actor motivations include fame, politics, profit, and revenge.
- A data breach is an intentional attack by an unauthorized threat actor to view or harvest confidential, sensitive, or private information. A data leak is the accidental exposure of confidential, sensitive, or private information.
- Data theft can occur in the form of social engineering, weak passwords, insider threats, human error, or compromised downloads.
- **Data loss prevention (DLP)** is a security strategy that focuses on detecting and preventing data leaks, data breaches, and unauthorized use of stolen data. There are four types of DLP approaches: network DLP, endpoint DLP, cloud DLP, and data-centric DLP.
- Data deduplication removes duplicated data by deleting the data that won't impact applications using that data. Data deduplication can be in-line, source, target, and hardware or software-based.
- Unauthorized access methods include tailgating, levering doors, lost or stolen keys and access cards, and social engineering.
- A backdoor is malware that allows an attacker to remotely access a computer without permission. Common forms of backdoors include trojans, rootkits, hardware backdoors, and cryptographic backdoors.
- Risk mitigation eliminates the risk or harm of a threat. Risk mitigation has three primary components: prevention, detection, and remediation.
- SIEM identifies potential vulnerabilities and threats before an attack can occur by gathering log and event data from the various components of an organization's systems, including applications, servers, internetworking, and security devices.
- Two-person integrity defines the process and codes or keys used in a two-person program.

- The separation of roles requires each separate responsibility in a business process to be performed by a different department or individual under additional supervision.
- Governments and trade associations issue laws, regulations, or bylaws that govern how data is secured, managed, processed, and retained. These requirements focus on PII.
- The PCI DSS specifies payment card processing and security for cardholder data.
- The GDPR defines regulations for the collection and use of PII for the EU.
- The Red Flags rule is intended to prevent identity theft.
- A data retention plan defines how an organization will collect, store, and protect specific types of data.

CHAPTER 16
Server Hardening and Decommissioning

Introduction

Protecting a server's hardware and software involves the hardening process, which is closing any open doors that an attacker could use to exploit the system or gain access to its network. In addition, keeping the operating system and applications up-to-date with fixes, updates, and patches is important to the effectiveness and security of both servers and workstations. These and other issues, including backup media retention, dealing with wire and cabling issues, and recycling or repurposing computer hardware, are covered in this chapter.

Structure

This chapter covers the following topics:

- Hardening
- Patch management
- Change management
- Server decommissioning
- Media destruction
- Media retention requirements

- Cable remediation
- Electronics recycling

Objective

By the end of this chapter, you will be able to identify and describe the sub-objectives of the following Server + examination objective: *Given a scenario, apply the server hardening method and summarize proper server decommissioning concepts.*

Hardening

Hardening increases security by reducing the vulnerability of a workstation, server, and network. On the Server+ exam, you should expect to encounter questions regarding OS hardening, workstation hardening, application hardening, and hardware hardening.

Server OS hardening

There is a difference between hardening a server **Operating System (OS)** and the OS on a workstation. Hardening a server OS involves four steps:

- Disabling unneeded services,
- Disabling unused TCP/UDP ports,
- Only software needed for the tasks supported should be installed, and
- The OS should be kept up to date through patches and updates.

The following are considerations appropriate to the hardening of an OS:

- **Unused software:** Software that is no longer in use can create a vulnerability that would allow a way in for an attacker. Any unused or unneeded software should be removed from the server. A policy should be enforced that restricts users from installing non-standard software.
- **Group and user accounts:** A common vulnerability on servers is caused by administrator errors giving users access to confidential or private information they do not need during their jobs. User passwords, both in content and expiration, should follow a password policy. Administrators should regularly review the permissions and rights assigned to all groups and user accounts.
- **Patch management:** It is the best practice to keep the S current with the latest patches, error fixes, service packs, and updates. However, not all fixes may be appropriate for a particular server. Patches, fixes, and updates should be tested before they are applied to a production system.

- **Establish and monitor baselines:** A baseline establishes a standard level of performance for an OS and a server's components. An operational baseline created at an initial installation that is updated after modifications set the basis for comparing current performance levels.

Firewall and Router hardening

The firewalls and routers that precede a server in a network configuration should also be hardened. This can help to avoid issues on the servers and workstations by denying access to the network to unauthorized messages.

Firewall hardening

Firewall rules should be reviewed by asking some difficult questions:

Why does a rule exist?: If a rule has no purpose, it should be removed. However, one rule that an edge firewall (and router) should include is a "deny all" safety net. This rule, placed as the very last rule, denies any message that was not explicitly allowed by a previous rule. If a message falls to the "deny all" rule, it is blocked by default.

Are source and destination addresses too expansive?: The fewer workstations addressed, the better. Limiting the scope of a rule can make it difficult for insiders or attackers to set up rogue workstations and attack the network.

Are only the required ports or services enabled?: Only the ports or services required for network operations should be active. All others should be disabled.

Are all messages being logged?: The actions applied to pass and deny message traffic should be recorded in a log file. Should a breach occur, this can be vital information.

Router hardening

Many router systems have software utilities that recommend hardening actions. However, the result, whether performed automatically or manually, should include:

- **Unused router interface ports:** If a router interface port is not in use, meaning that nothing is plugged into it, it should be disabled (shutdown).
- **Unused services:** Any services not in use should be disabled. Commonly this includes BOOTP, FTP, TFTP, and others.
- **Unused management protocols:** Any management protocols not in use on the router should be disabled. This is commonly SNMP, HTTP, and Telnet. Any deprecated protocols or services should also be disabled and removed from the system. In many cases, they are insecure and don't implement encryption.
- **Redirects:** Router features that are used to redirect message traffic should be disabled, including ICMP redirects, and IP source routing.

Workstation hardening

Workstation hardening improves the security of network nodes. While the specific hardening steps used on any workstation can vary with its OS and applications, some hardening steps apply to every workstation. The hardening steps for a network workstation include:

- **User account policies:** Password policies should require regular password changes on a specific number of days, password reuse should be limited, and login repeated failure lockouts should be enabled.
- **Physical security:** Users should know the physical security policies that apply to their workstations, including the control of entrances and exits and a clean desk policy, which secures access to physical documents and computer access.
- **Logging:** All system and network interactions, including login and logouts, applications and data accessed, and any security-related program or data access attempts, successes, and failures should be recorded in log files.
- **Automatic patch application:** Typically, fixes and patches to a workstation's OS and most applications can be applied automatically. These actions should be logged and regularly reviewed for compliance.
- **Disable sharing:** File and device sharing services should be disabled to prevent network access through shared systems.

Application hardening

Application hardening uses several techniques to protect applications from attacks, including:

- **Code obfuscation:** This cloaks the binary executable code of an application so that it is not comprehendible.
- **White-box cryptography:** This process combines encryption and obfuscation and embeds secret keys in application code. The objective is to protect an application from reverse engineering and modification.
- **Polymorphism:** This method alters the code of an application to prevent reverse engineering.

Host security

Securing a network host and providing protection to it can also be considered as hardening. Like all forms of hardening, the general purpose of **host hardening** is to reduce its vulnerability to possible attacks. The following are commonly a part of hardening a network host:

- **Antivirus and antimalware software**: The prevention of viruses and malware on a host can not only protect the host from the loss of data, function, and availability, but can also contribute to the protection of the network as a part of its defense-in-depth strategy.
- **Intrusion detection and prevention**: **Host intrusion detection software** (**HIDS**) and **host intrusion prevention software** (**HIPS**) systems run on a local host to detect and/or prevent an attack or other malicious network traffic transmitted over an internal network.
- **Unused applications**: The number of processes, services, and apps running on a host computer is typically and surprisingly large. It can be difficult to know which ones to disable, enable, or remove completely. Many of the services are a part of the OS. Others, including applications, may have found their way onto the host without the user's knowledge. The system administrators should assist users in identifying the services and applications that should be disabled or removed from each host.
- **Patches and updates**: A host computer's OS and applications should be included in the organization's patch management system. In a SOHO environment, users should be aware of patch and update releases and apply them as they are released.
- **Monitor network services**: The data, services, or applications being accessed from network servers or services by a host should be monitored for appropriateness. Using role-based access control and the application of the principle of least privilege, the data and apps accessed from a host are controlled, but an anomaly should cause an alert.
- **Check for open ports**: Related to monitoring network services is the use of a port scanner, such as Nmap, to see which ports are active on a host. The active (enabled) ports should correlate to the services and apps used by the host.

On a Windows system, there are some older or deprecated services that can hang around even after the OS is upgraded. **`NetBIOS`** and **`WINS`** services should be disabled if they are active. Remote services like remote desktop protocol (RDP), any terminal services, and remote Registry utilities should also be disabled. On a Linux system, legacy remove services, including **`rlogin`**, **`rsh`**, and **`Telnet`**, should be disabled.

Hardware hardening

In addition to OS and application hardening, hardening the hardware of a server or workstation can improve its security. Hardening hardware on a workstation or server is mostly done in the BIOS/UEFI configuration settings.

Setting a BIOS/UEFI password to prevent unauthorized access to the configuration settings, disabling the **Wake on LAN (WOL)** feature, and removing a remote boot initiation from the boot device sequence are just three settings that help to prevent an intrusion. Disable all unused peripherals from the BIOS/UEFI and use USB port blockers to avoid the unauthorized insertion of USB drives or other potentially infected peripherals. While antivirus software can be set to automatically scan any newly inserted removable drives, it may not be enough to increase security.

Patch management

Patch management controls the processes of identifying and deploying updates to OSs, system software, and applications. Under a patch management program, updates are applied to workstations, servers, and network devices. A **patch** is a change to specific software that can fix an existing bug, flaw, or vulnerability. Patches may also apply additional features and functions to the effected software. Patches are short-term solutions to correct software errors and add features for use until the next software release.

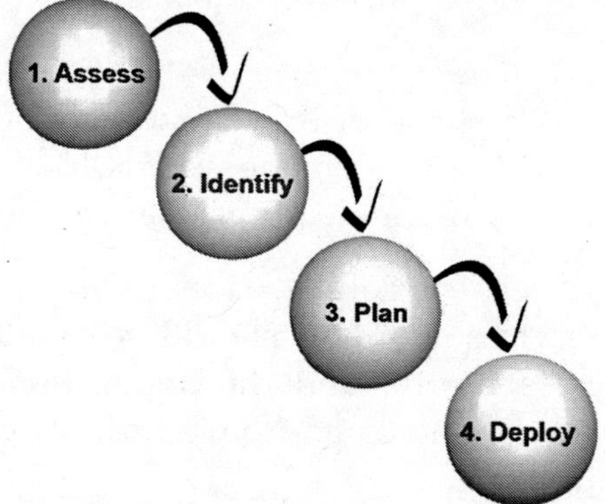

***Figure 16.1:** The flow of a patch management process*

- **Assessment:** A review of the patch, update, or fix to determine if it is applicable to the organization's systems and should be applied immediately or at a later time.
- **Identification:** Does the patch resolve an issue or vulnerability specific to the organization and if so, how will it impact the processes and procedures currently in use?
- **Plan:** A testing plan should be developed to ensure that the patch will not cause other problems with the affected system. Patches should be tested on a non-production system prior to applying them to the production system. If the patch affects only an application installed on a workstation, it should be tested on a test workstation.
- **Deploy:** If the testing proves that the patch does not cause additional problems or issues, the patch can be applied to the production system and any procedures or documentation related to the change or fix should be updated.

Change management

Often assumed to be the same as patch management, the objective of change management is to define a process for implementing required changes that also minimizes service disruptions. An IT change management program should provide an organization with the following controls:

- The prioritization of changes and the allocation of resources
- Gathering the information relevant to the change
- Implementing a process for verifying the source and reasons for proposed changes
- Establishing a framework and procedure for managing the change process
- Implementing an approval process that is effective for the entire organization
- Reducing system downtime

Server decommissioning

There are many reasons why a server might be removed from service and decommissioned. The processing has been completely moved to the cloud or the portion of the business that a particular server or servers supported is no longer operating, or a major upgrade is being installed. Whatever the reason, it is not a matter of taking a backup and pulling the plug.

Servers tend to be very central to the design and operations of a network. Pulling a server out of a network or a load balancing system could cause a loss of data, creating unforeseen vulnerabilities and inadvertently causing configuration issues on the network. When the need for decommissioning an active service arises, there are three primary concerns to be considered:

- **Security holes:** All connections, interfaces, and shared services must be addressed to ensure no security hole or vulnerability is created when a server is removed. Firewalls, especially any **Access Control Lists** (**ACLs**) defined on them, and the configuration of subnets and **Virtual Local Area Networks** (**VLANs**) should be examined.

- **Time:** On a larger network, the process of decommissioning a server should not be rushed. In many cases, the whole process can take a couple of weeks or longer. Removing a server permanently may not take as long as the process involved with replacing server hardware with new equipment. A formal schedule should be developed that addresses required milestones, licensing, removing the stored data, and verifying all stored data is removed from the server.

- **Upgrades:** Decommissioning and replacing server hardware has been a part of the IT lifecycle. However, cloud computing has become the replacement system in many cases. Regardless, the upgrade or transition should not be assumed to be a matter of loading up the data and continuing running. Hardware upgrades are a fact of life for a data center and must be planned well in advance. That planning should also include the decommissioning of the equipment being replaced.

In addition, the plan for removing a server (or a data center for that matter) should address the following as well:

- **Company policies:** If a company policy does not exist, one should be created. This policy should detail the individuals responsible for each of the steps involved with decommissioning the servers and other equipment, if needed.
- **Non-utilization:** Data should be captured and reported that verifies the server to be removed is, in fact, not being used. If a replacement system is being added, the verification should also verify that the new server is able to manage the processing load of the replaced system.
- **Documentation:** All the planning, the plan itself, a record of the actions performed, and any measurements or verifications made as a part of the decommissioning process should be formally documented and approved.
- **Asset management:** Server hardware are assets and its removal and disposition must be reflected in the organization's asset management system.
- **Change management:** As discussed earlier in this chapter, change management should be applied to control the changes made to the IT infrastructure of the organization. Removing a server from service is definitely a change that could affect the entire organization, so it should be managed through the organization's change control process.

Media destruction

Media destruction boils down to data destruction, although the storage device (media) is typically destroyed right along with the data. There are a variety of services that destroy both media and data through industrial shredders and the like. However, there are some actions that an organization can do if it desires. Understand that no particular destructive method is absolutely perfect, but one or more of the following methods is suitable in many cases. These methods include:

- **Degaussing:** Degaussing has been used to remove data from magnetic media since magnetic tape reels were the primary data storage media. Degaussing removes data by passing a high-power magnet over the media, which scrambles the magnetic field of the stored data and effectively destroys it. However, along with the data, degaussing can also destroy the media, especially hard drives, which means that the destruction of the data cannot be verified.
- **Delete/Reformat:** Deleting a file from a disk drive only removes its reference information but does not actually remove it from the media or destroy the data. Otherwise, restore commands would not work. Data stays on the hard drive until

it is overwritten or degaussed. Reformatting the storage devices does not wipe out the data either. The reference tables are replaced with new ones, but the files and their data remain where they were. Some utilities can restore a data file from a reformatted disk.

- **Erasure:** In effect, this method, along with data overwriting and data wiping, accomplishes essentially the same results as the delete and reformat functions. The difference is that erasure is typically performed by a vendor who erases the data and provides a certificate of destruction that states the data was successfully destroyed.
- **Incineration:** Burning a storage device at accelerated temperatures will definitely destroy the unit and any data stored on it. However, in the process, toxic fumes are usually emitted from the process.
- **Overwriting data:** The process of overwriting the data on a storage device involves writing (storing) ones and zeros (binary values) over any existing data. The pattern of these bit values can be random or set by the users. In most cases, overwriting a disk one time is sufficient. However, suppose there is a certainty that must be achieved, such as a storage device that held highly sensitive data. In that case, multiple passes can ensure that all data is completely destroyed and no bit shadows can be detected. An issue with overwriting data and data wiping (see below) is what bit shadows can occur. A **bit shadow** is the leftover electrical charge of the bit that can be sensed with highly sophisticated equipment. In high-security situations, bit shadows can be a concern, but in most other cases, not so much.
- **Physical destruction:** Degaussing is one form of physical device destruction, but there are many other ways to physically destroy a storage device. Physical destruction provides the highest assurance that the data on a device is destroyed and cannot be accessed. Some of the methods used in physical destruction are:
    - **Shredding:** This destructive method shreds a disk drive into small pieces, which makes any data on the drive unreadable. A shredder may also compress the drive's pieces into a compact lump for ease of disposal. This process is also known as electronic shredding, which means that electronics are shredded.
    - **Crushing:** Crushing a drive, also called mangling, involves stamping the disk with enough force to break down the casing and crush the disk platters inside the drive.
    - **Disintegration:** This method can also be called slicing. A storage device is sliced into small pieces that cannot be reassembled.
    - **Melting:** Storage drives are dipped into a hydrochloric or nitric acid solution that melts the casing and the platters or circuits. While highly effective, this method is hazardous to use.

- **Drilling:** Using a substantial drill bit, drilling holes in a storage device damages its platters or circuits to the point that the drive is unusable and its data is unreadable. Another method included under this destructive method is to use a nail gun or a hammer and a large nail to penetrate the drive.

- **Wiping:** Data wiping overwrites data on a storage medium, which renders the data unreadable. Data wiping is not a fast solution; on an average disk drive, the process can take as long as an entire day. Data wiping is not a practical solution for a business but it can be helpful for an individual.

Media retention requirements

How long an organization retains its backup files depends on various issues, including the type of backup schedule, the cost of off-site storage and the media itself, and the overhead of managing the backup media and the data on them. There is not one answer that fits every situation. However, before storing backup media, we review the elements that go into a backup program.

Backup media

There are three primary magnetic mediums used for backup storage. They are:

- **Linear access:** The only type of linear access medium is magnetic tape because it is a beginning-to-end, front-to-back type of serial access. Magnetic tape is the most commonly used medium for data backups. Also, it is the least costly of the standard backup media and can be the easiest to store.

- **Random access:** Archiving data and backing up data are two different functions. Tape media is better suited for archiving data because of its longer storage life and the fact that archives are usually restored completely. External magnetic disks or **solid-state drives (SSD)** are better for backing up data that could be restored soon. Disk storage also provides access or restoration to only some of the data on the backup.

- **Removable media:** The medium type that is best for backing data is removable media, including magnetic tape, external drives, optical media (DVD, **write-once-read-many** [WORM]), and USB-connected flash memory devices.

Backup media retention

Many backup strategies include a rotation schedule that reuses the backup medium after a certain period. For example, depending on the rotation plan, a backup created on a Monday could be used again in three days or even after two weeks, depending on the data, how often backups are taken, and the volatility of the data itself. Rotating medium helps to reduce the cost and storage requirements.

Because of legal and regulatory requirements, an organization may retain different backups for varying lengths of time and store them in different places. Typically, the decision to be made in a retention policy is how long full backups will be kept, even after being replaced with later backups. However, how long a backup is retained is a balance of the cost to store the backups and the benefit of having the backup available.

Cable remediation

The cabling and wiring in a home or office can develop problems over time. Depending on the age of the building, it may have very old wiring techniques (knob and tube, for example), aluminum wiring (the 1970s and later), rodents or pests chewing through or exposing the wire core, or even poor workmanship when the home or office was built. Regardless of the cause, wiring problems can be identified specifically and remediated (repaired) by a licensed electrician. The homeowner can usually repair problems with the cabling in a computer network or an in-house technician.

Electrical wiring

Once pulled into the walls, electrical wiring remains intact, which means no chewing, stapling, cutting, or yanking, should continue to provide good electrical power to a building. However, the electrical service wiring of a building can cause problems, especially if the building was built in the 1960s or 1970s.

In the 1960s and 1970s, aluminum wiring was used in construction as a less expensive alternative to copper wiring. At that time, there were no known problems with the aluminum wiring, but over time problems appeared. One problem is aluminum can corrode where it connects to an outlet or switch. A corroded aluminum wire can cause loose connections and arcing (electrical sparks from one wire to another), which can cause an electrical fire. Currently, the building codes across the US, and much of the world, require copper wiring in new construction. The remediation for aluminum wiring is called **pigtailing**, which means a length of copper wire is attached to the end of an aluminum wire and then connected to the outlet or switch.

Most electrical service problems in buildings occur in the main circuit box or at power outlets or light switches. If electrical problems develop, a licensed electrician must be brought to identify the issue and make necessary remediations.

Computer cabling

A computer and network cable can develop many of the same problems but a few others as well. Computer cables are exposed and can be stepped on, tripped on, inadvertently yanked or pulled, or have heavy objects placed on them. Most computer cable problems are with the connections, either through stress or improper installation. However, a computer cable can be chewed, cut, crushed, or otherwise damaged. Here are some of the common cable issues:

- **Electromagnetic interference (EMI):** If the display screen on a network workstation become scrambled or looks strange or some workstations lose their network connections, the problem could be EMI. Network cabling should be at least 12 inches from an unshielded electric wiring or an EMI source (such as an electrical motor).
- **Loose connections:** This is the most common cause of cable issues. If connection issues occur, check the connections for loose wiring or pining, not just at the workstation but at any connection points between the workstation and the server, switch, or router.
- **Cable loops:** While this is an easy fix, it can be overlooked as a source of a problem. Copper cabling that is coiled or looped can cause interference issues on the cable. If there is an excess length in a cable, it is better to use a shorter cable.
- **Pinches or breaks:** A cable that is bent too sharply or shows a cut or break can cause intermittent communication issues. A pinched cable, such as when a computer is pushed up against a wall, can cause one or more of the interior core wires to break. Provide space around cable connections and eliminate tight cable bends.

Electronics recycling

Electronic devices that are useless and can be discarded are referred to as **e-waste**. This can include cell phones, computer equipment, scanners, and fax machines, among others. The reasons these devices are no longer needed can be outdated technology, replaced equipment, or equipment no longer used.

E-waste recycling does not necessarily mean finding a new use for these devices, although that could be a solution. Rather, it means that the electronics of these devices are removed and separated into component groups, such as precious metals, wiring, plastic, and toxic materials. In any computer system and especially on the motherboard, there are gold, silver, copper, and other metals or minerals that have worth. However, there are also heavy metals and toxic materials, such as lead, mercury, and cadmium. US and many other countries worldwide have made dumping electronic devices in trash or random sites illegal.

In some cases, recycling electronics and computer equipment may require the donor to pay a fee, but there are also certain retailers and manufacturers accepting recycled components for free, including cell phones, computers, laptops, display monitors, UPS batteries, and networking devices. However, a fee may be charged for recycling projection devices, keyboards, printers, scanners, and speakers.

Internal vs. external recycling

Recycling can be divided into internal and external. **Internal recycling** involves reusing excess or waste materials in a process as raw material back into the process. This is a common practice in the metals and distilling industries. Metal trimmed from a finished product can be melted down and recast. Aluminum cans are melted down to make new cans or other aluminum products.

External recycling deals with products and materials that are no longer usable, worn out, or have become obsolete, such as newspapers turned into pulp and used to manufacture new paper products. Another example is glass containers, which can be returned for a deposit refund, dropped off at a recycling center or picked up curbside by a waste management company.

Repurposing

An alternative to recycling or trashing a computer or its peripheral devices is to repurpose it. Repurposing finds a new home or uses for a computer that still works rather than throwing it out or breaking it up in recycling. An older computer in reasonably good condition can be traded on a new system, sold online, or donated to a school, nursing home, or charitable association. Another alternative is to give it a new role, such as a video conferencing unit, streaming video player, or an online recipe station in the kitchen.

Conclusion

This chapter covered the importance of the hardening processes on servers and workstations to the overall security of a network. Another aspect of server security covered was change and patch management. Certified systems administrators must deal with the policies and procedures involved with backup media, wire, and cabling issues, and what to do with old or obsolete computer hardware.

In the next chapter, we will also look at the processes, methods, and media involved in creating backups and archives. We also look at restoring backed up data and the retention cycles of backup media.

Points to remember

- Hardening increases security by reducing the vulnerability of a workstation, server, and network.
- Hardening a server OS involves disabling unneeded services, and disabling unused ports, only software used for supported tasks is installed, and the OS is up-to-date with patches and updates.
- The hardening of a workstation includes user account policies, physical security, logging, patch application, and disabling sharing.
- Application hardening uses code obfuscation, white-box cryptography, and polymorphism.

- Hardware hardening is done in the BIOS/UEFI configuration settings.
- In a patch management program, updates are applied to workstations, servers, and network devices.
- Change management is a process for required changes that minimize disruptions of service.
- Server decommissioning has concerns for consideration: security holes, time, and upgrades.
- Media destruction methods include degaussing, delete, erasure, incineration, physical destruction, shredding, and wiping.
- There are three primary magnetic medium types: linear access, random access, and removable media.
- The remediation for aluminum wiring is "pigtailing."
- Common cable issues include EMI, loose connections, cable loops, and pinches or breaks.
- Internal recycling reuses waste materials in a process as raw materials back into the process.
- External recycling deals with products and materials that are no longer usable, worn out, or have become obsolete.
- Repurposing finds a new home or uses for a computer that still works rather than throwing it out or breaking it up in recycling.

CHAPTER 17
Backup and Restore

Introduction

Data backups are essentially insurance assets. A server or its operating system could crash, a user could inadvertently or maliciously corrupt or destroy valuable data, or catastrophic weather wipes out the facility and the systems. In any of these situations, a backup that can be restored to provide a restart point is a very good operational policy. This chapter will examine the various aspects and practices of a backup and restore policy, including the different types of backups and their management.

Structure

This chapter will cover the following topics:

- Backup and recovery methods
- Restore methods
- Backup validation

Objective

By the end of this chapter, you will be able to identify and describe the sub-objectives of the following Server + examination objective: *Explain the importance of backups and restores*.

Backup and recovery

Data as an asset class is among the most valuable in any organization. Like all other assets, data must be protected and safeguarded. Aside from the threats to data-at-rest in data centers from threat actors, data is exposed to the same threats, physical security and operations of the organization. In case of an event that disrupts a business, restoring data backups can provide a fast return to normal operations. Data backup and recovery is an essential part of any organization's business continuity plan.

Backup methods

Backup software uses the archive bit of a file to determine if the file is to be included in a backup. When its **archive bit** is set **on**, a file must be included in a backup. As discussed below, not all backup methods set the archive bit **off** after copying a file to the backup medium.

Backup types

Not every data backup needs to be a complete copy of a system. The different types and levels of backups can be used in a backup strategy to serve the needs of the organization best. Whether a file is to be included on a backup is indicated by the file's archive bit.

The most common types of backups are:

- **Full backup:** This backup copies all the data on the storage media. Full backups turn-off the archive bit.
- **Copy backup:** This backup method creates an archival copy of all or part of the data stored on a storage device.
- **Incremental backup:** This backup contains only the data that has been added or changed since the last backup, which could be either a full or **incremental backup**. An incremental backup resets the archive bit to **off**. *Figure 17.1* illustrates the cycles of an incremental backup:

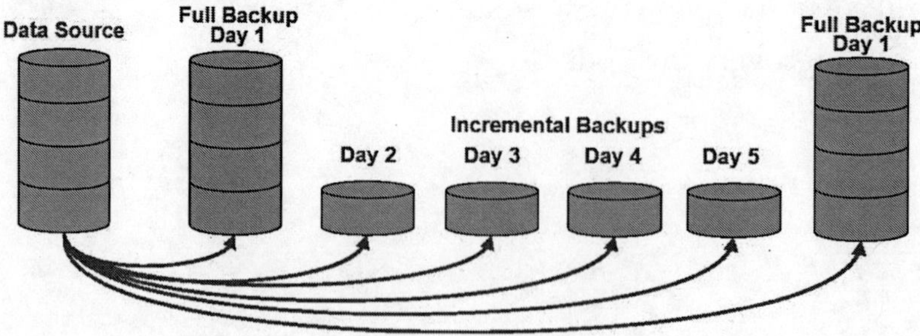

Figure 17.1: *The cycles of an incremental backup*

At the beginning of a cycle, a full backup is created. On each successive day of the period, an incremental backup is made. At the end of the period, which is the beginning of the next period, another full backup is created, and the cycle starts over.

- **Differential backup:** This backup contains all the data added or changed since the last full backup. A **differential backup** does not reset the archive bit, leaving that to the next full backup. *Figure 17.2* illustrates the cycles of a differential backup:

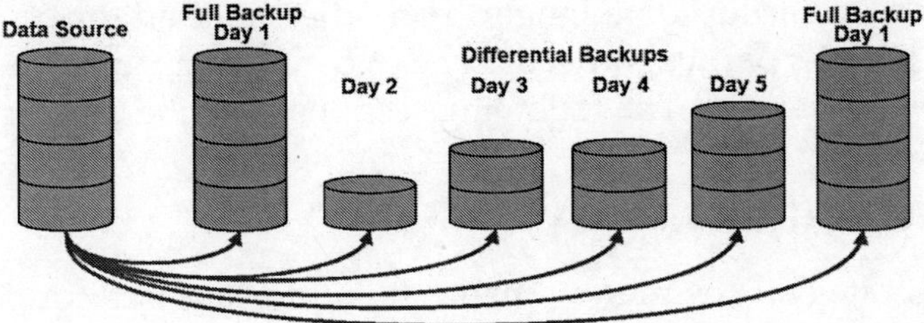

***Figure 17.2:** The cycles of a differential backup*

As depicted, a full backup is created at the start of a period, and then a differential backup is created for each of the days of the period. At the beginning of the subsequent period, another full backup restarts the backup cycle. The primary difference between differential and incremental backup programs is in their restoration. To completely restore an incremental backup on day 4 of a cycle requires the last full backup to be restored. Then, each incremental backup in the current period created to the recovery point must also be restored. With the differential backup program, only the last full and last differential backups need to be restored.

Tip: If the volume of data to be backed up is relatively small, incremental backup is the more efficient method, which is why it is widely used in those instances.

- **Snapshot backup:** This backup type, also called an **image**, captures the state of a system at a specific point—a storage.
- .e snapshot contains the information required to restore data to a recovery point, typically when the snapshot was taken. A snapshot, as the illustration in *Figure 17.3* shows, does not copy the data; it contains the data locations and its organization:

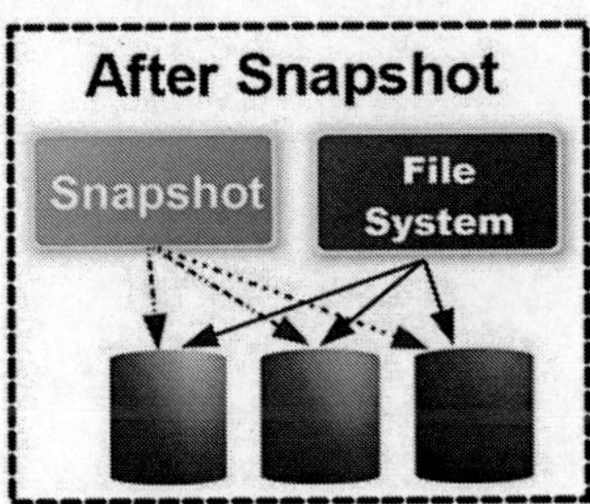

***Figure 17.3:** A snapshot only captures where data is located and how it is organized*

- **Synthetic full backup:** This backup type builds on the last full backup by applying all of the incremental backups since that full backup to create a new full backup. The only difference between this backup type and a full back is how it is created.

Backup strategies

An organization's backup strategy is a factor in how long the backup media is kept. Some backup strategies keep backup data longer than others and an organization may alter a standard strategy to fit its particular needs. The two major backup strategies are the 3-2-1 and the grandfather-father-son. The following sections describe each of these strategies.

The 3-2-1 backup strategy

The 3-2-1 backup strategy is the predominant minimum standard for IT backups. Simply put, it recommends that an organization keep three copies of its data. Two copies are stored locally on different devices and media, and one copy is stored securely off-site. Locally stored backups are readily available should they be needed. Those stored off-site provide security though redundancy. *Figure 17.4* illustrates the concept of the 3-2-1 strategy:

Figure 17.4: *The 3-2-1 backup strategy*

Grandfather-father-son backups

The **grandfather-father-son (GFS)** backup strategy combines full and incremental backups into a strategy that minimizes the time required to create the backup and can reduce the media required as well. An example of the grandfather-father-son strategy (see *Figure 17.5*) works is:

- **Grandfather:** A monthly full backup is stored off-site or in the cloud.
- **Father:** A weekly full backup is stored locally or in the cloud.
- **Son:** Daily incremental backups are stored locally or in the cloud with the current father's backup.

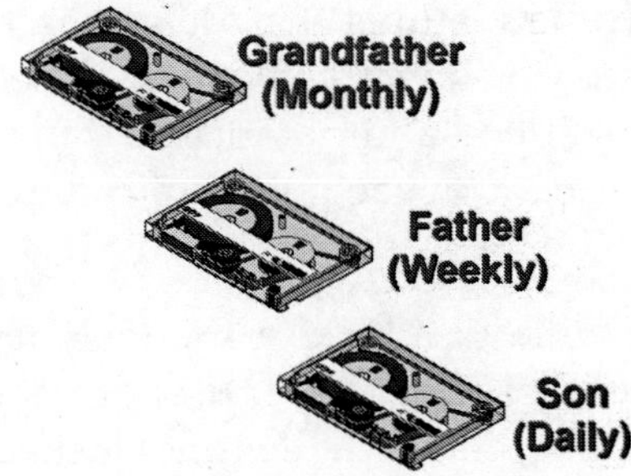

Figure 17.5: The grandfather-father-son backup strategy

In many uses of the GFS backup method, the daily backup (Son) media is reused for each backup taken on the days of a week, such as Monday through Friday. The Parent backup media which holds the backup taken at the end of the week, is stored in a secure location, either on-site or off-site. At the end of a month, or after four weeks, the Grandfather backup, which contains the backup taken at the end of the period is then stored off-site. Depending on the cycles and the retention of the backup media, the GFS strategy can require from 8 to 22 backup medium units. In a standard implementation, in which 4 weekly and monthly backups are created, 21 backup medium units are required.

Archive vs. Backup

Although many believe a data archive is the same as a data backup, that is not the case. The difference is in their purposes. A **data archive** may not include all of the data that is included on a data backup. Rather, an archive contains older, inactive data that an organization wishes to keep available just in case it is required in the future, but no longer needs to occupy space on its active systems. Typically, archives are created because of legal requirements, law or regulation compliance, or historical purposes. An archive can be retained for extended periods, depending on the nature of the organization and the data.

A **data backup** is a stop gap measure that provides a restart point in the event of data loss, destruction, or corruption. Backups are short-term data recovery resources, which are generally not used (restored) and are overwritten in the next cycle.

Open files

Many backup utilities and applications skip over any open file when the backup is being created. If a backup is created at the same time of the day each time and the same files are open at that time of the day, such as a log file or the like, then the open files may never be backed up.

On a Windows system, the **Volume Shadow Copy Service (VSS)**, can be used to create a snapshot of a storage volume that a backup can use as its base. However, VSS is not an option on a server that is running Linux, for example.

Some backup applications include features that delay the backup of an open file for a specific time (minutes or seconds) to allow the file to be closed. If the time expires without the file being closed, the file is skipped and not included in the backup. On a system that may have many open files, the delay on each of them can extend the time for the backup to complete.

Some files are opened with or without a lock. A **file lock**, if engaged, blocks other users from updating the file while it is in use by another user or application. Backup applications can be configured to detect the file lock. If the file is not locked, the backup application can lock the file, preventing changes to it, copy the file to the backup media, and then release the lock. However, if the file is actually in use without a lock, this process could interfere with the activities of a user or application or perhaps cause the application to crash.

Another option for backing up open files is to include them on the backup media as they are at the time they are accessed. The risk in this option is that condition of the file will be unknown and could be corrupt if a file write occurs coincidently with the copy action.

In many organizations, the IT department creates its backups at a time of low activity on the network or system. In many of these cases, users are asked to log off or are automatically logged off to prevent having any open files while the backup process runs. However, even this approach has problems in an organization that operates around the clock.

File-level vs. system-state backup

If backups are for the sole purpose of restoring one or more files or to set a recovery point, then file-level backups should be created. A **file-level backup** is best for capturing still (not open) files, each of which can be quickly restored. However, if the purpose of creating a backup is to capture a complete copy of the entire contents of a storage device, a system-level backup is a better choice. A system-level backup contains the OS, applications, APIs, DLLs, data, configuration settings, and everything else. System-level backups are used to recover a failed system to meet the RTO and RPO points.

Restore methods

There can be some confusion over using the terms **recover** and **restore**. While both these terms refer to copying one or more files from a backup media, there are some differences between them. Recovering a file refers to salvaging a deleted, corrupted, or destroyed file. Restoring a file refers to replacing a file on a storage device with a copy from a backup media, regardless of the condition of the file being replaced. However, recovery usually applies to single files or folders and restoration replaces an entire system, hard drive, volume, or partition from a complete system backup or image. In simple terms, the **`undelete`** command performs a restoration activity and the **System Restore** utility recovers all or part of a Windows system.

Overwrite

When recovering a file (or folder, partition, volume, etc.), you may or may not actually want to overwrite the file version currently on the disk, (writing the recovered file over the version on the disk. It could be the case that since the backup was captured, additional transactions or updates may have been applied to the file version on the disk. The `restore` command options in most backup and restore software typically include controls that allow the user to indicate which file is to be restored from the backup media, where it is to be placed on the disk, and whether or not the user should approve the action before it happens. The options available also include unconditional overwrites (don't ask; just do it), prompt before overwriting (ask for permission to proceed), and don't overwrite an exact match (skip the recovery if the files are the same).

Side by side

The **Windows Side by Side (WinSxS)** folder is one of the biggest folders on a Windows system, both in terms of the number of items it contains and the disk space it occupies. It is found at `C:\Windows\WinSxS` and holds essential software components for installing, updating, and customizing the operating system. This includes files which need to switch Windows editions, recover missing or damaged system files, and data for added or removed Windows features.

Notice the and quantities and the count of the items in this folder. *Figure 17.6* shows the folder properties dialog box for a `WinSxS` folder:

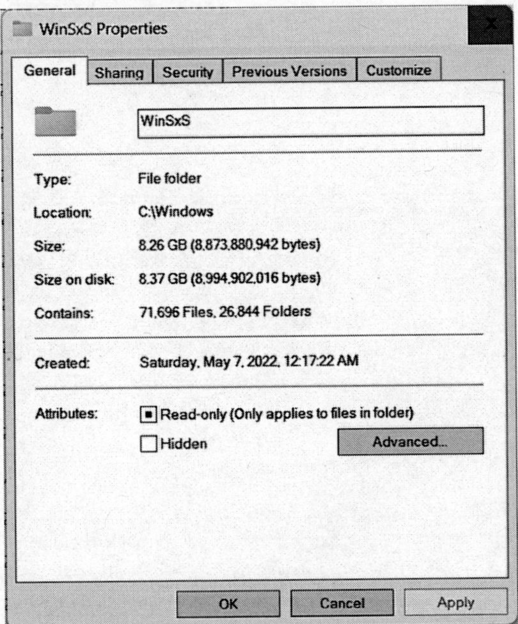

***Figure 17.6:** The properties dialog box for the WinSxS folder on a Windows 11 system*

When you need to recover system files or when you add or remove Windows features (through the Control Panel), the **`WinSxS`** folder is where Windows looks for the files it needs to perform that action. Because of this, the folder is also referred to as the **component store**. WinSxS starts out relatively large in size and then continues to grow as more components and component versions are added to the system.

Including the WinSxS can slow a full system backup, and incremental or differential backups as well, due to its ever-increasing size. However, at any time, the **`WinSxS`** folder can also include unneeded files that can be cleaned up to reduce its size. In the following sections, the primary methods that can be used to clean up the WinSxS are described.

Task Scheduler

The StartComponentCleanup task is available by default in the Windows 10/11 versions. This task can be used to automatically clean up component versions when the system is not in use. When the StartComponentCleanup task, which is a parameter of the DISM. exe command runs automatically, it waits 30 days after the component version is updated to remove any previous component versions. However, running this task from the Task Scheduler eliminates the 30-day wait period.

1. To run the StartComponentCleanup task from the Task Scheduler, use the following steps: Execute **`taskschd.msc`** with the Run dialog box (<u>*Win+R*</u>) to open the app, see *Figure 17.7*:

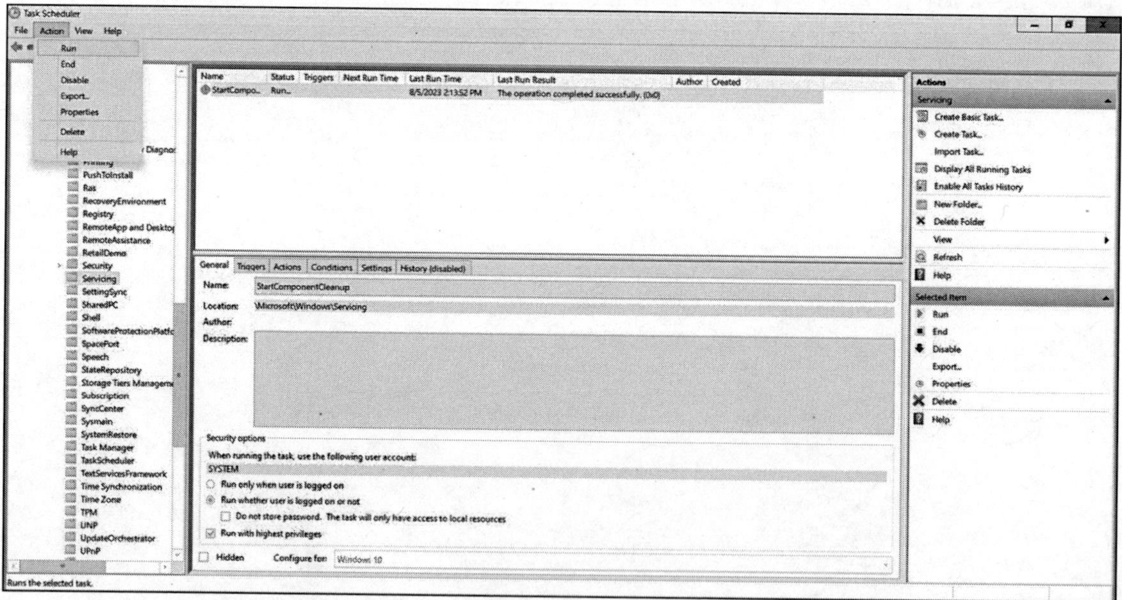

Figure 17.7: The StartComponentCleanup task can be executed from the Task Scheduler to clean the WinSxS folder

2. In the Navigation pane (left side), expand the folders to select | | | . The display shown in *Figure 17.7* should appear.

3. Select the option for in the top center pane and click on in the list in the pane (right side bottom).

4. The immediately begins cleaning the **WinSxS** folder. Depending on its age and the level of activities on the system, this process may take anywhere from a few seconds to some minutes to complete.

Disk Cleanup

Windows also includes the **Disk Cleanup** tool that can reduce the size and contents of the WinSxS folder. Disk Cleanup can also be used to tidy up extraneous or no longer needed system files and other unnecessary files. To clean the WinSxS folder using Disk Cleanup, use the following steps:

1. Execute **`cleanmgr`** with the Run dialog box (*Win+R*) to open the dialog box, see *Figure 17.8*:

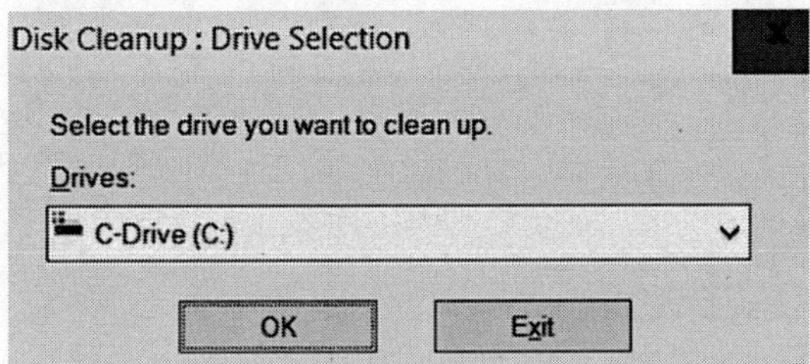

***Figure 17.8:** The Disk Cleanup: Drive Selection dialog box*

2. From the pull-down list, select the disk drive to be cleaned.

3. On the (the drive selected), click on the button near the bottom left corner of the window. Confirm the disk drive to clean when the box reappears.

4. The **Disk Cleanup for** (the drive selected) redisplays, but with fewer options. You can select any of the options listed in the list box, but to clean WinSxS, select any dealing with or , see *Figure 17.9*:

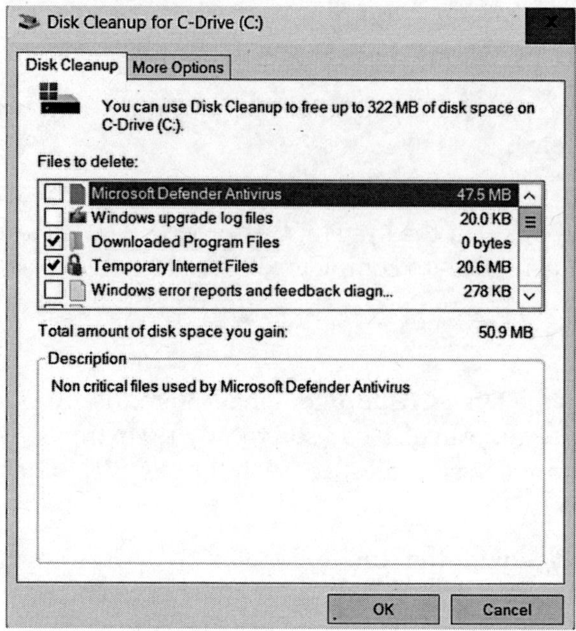

Figure 17.9: *The Disk Cleanup System Options dialog box*

5. Click on the button to start .

Backup validation

Backup validation is a process used to verify the integrity of the data copied to a backup media. This process is an essential part of any data security or disaster recovery policy or plan. The purpose of backup validation is two-fold: verify that the data backup contains all the data it should, and that the data is valid and can be restored, if required. Another result of a backup validation procedure is awareness of any possible data loss.

Media integrity

Verifying the integrity of backup media is crucial to business continuity and disaster recovery programs. The process involved in verifying the usability of backup media for restoring single files, folders, volumes, or systems, is as simple as creating checksums (hash totals) of both the backup and the corresponding files on the storage device. To do this manually, the only way to verify a backup is to restore random files and examine the restored data. However, software backup verification packages exist, such as the **Handy Backup** application, which can verify the backup against the original files.

In addition to verifying the integrity of the backups, physical checks should also be performed on the backup media. These checks include the security and safety of where the media are stored, meaning that they are protected against heat, humidity, light, and dust hazards, and, in most secure locations, restrictions on who can access or handle them.

Backup storage devices

A **backup storage device** is identified by the medium to which it writes data. In large data centers, such as found at the enterprise-level, a backup storage device is both the hardware appliance and the software that performs the backup, restoration, and other file operations. The hardware media provides the space in which the backed up data is stored and the software executes the policies that control data transference from secondary storage to external storage.

In many enterprise data centers, the backup storage devices can be DAS, NAS, SAN, or a **tiered storage system**, a storage arrangement in which data is stored in a hierarchy on the storage media based on its required availability, performance, and its ease of recovery. In small to medium businesses, the backup storage devices can be tape cartridges, optical disc, external SSD drives, and the like. The important characteristics of these devices are capacity and speed of operation. Cloud backups are considered to be backup storage devices as well.

Regular testing intervals

As a part of verifying both the backup storage device and the backup media, testing on both elements should be performed on a regular basis. The frequency of the testing program should be consistent with the business cycles of the organization and be frequent enough to provide assurance and confidence that in the event of a disaster or catastrophic event, the backup device and the media will be usable and retain the integrity of the data.

Media inventory before restoration

It is a best practice for system administrators to regularly verify that all of the units of each backup are on-hand, available, and stored safely. The restoration of an organization's automated operations is dependent on all the tapes, discs, or other media being available, functional, and without corruption at the exact moment they are needed. Many the higher-end backup and restore applications include cataloging and inventory application.

Conclusion

Data backups are crucial to an organization's data recovery, disaster recovery and business continuity programs. Each organization must determine the best option for the type of backups it creates and the type of rotation method it uses, where the backup media is to be stored, and the guidelines and procedures for restoring data. Data backup should be formalized into a backup and restore policy and plan.

In the next chapter, we look at the policies, processes, and requirements for restoring operations after an interruption in system services and the development of a disaster recovery plan.

Points to remember

- Data backup and recovery is an essential part of any organization's data recovery, disaster recovery, and business continuity plans.
- Backup software uses the archive bit of a file to indicate a file to be included on a backup.
- The most common types of backups are full, copy, incremental, differential, snapshot, and synthetic full.
- The major backup strategies are 3-2-1 and grandfather-father-son.
- A data archive contains older, inactive data that an organization wishes to keep. A data backup is a stop gap measure that provides a restart point.
- VSS creates a snapshot of a storage volume including open files.
- A file lock is used to block other users from updating a file while it is in use.
- File-level backups are used to restore files or set a recovery point. A system-level backup contains the OS, applications, APIs, DLLs, data, configuration settings, etc.
- Recovering a file is the salvage of a deleted, corrupted, or destroyed file. Restoring a file is replacing a file on a storage device with a copy from a backup media.
- Overwrite options are unconditional overwrites, prompt before overwriting, and do not overwrite an exact match.
- The Windows WinSxS folder contains a variety of vital software components for installing, updating, backing up, and customizing the OS.
- Backup validation verifies the integrity of a backup media.
- Verifying the usability of backup media for restoring single files, folders, volumes, or systems compares checksums of the backup and the storage device.
- A backup storage device is a hardware appliance and the backup software. In enterprise systems, backup storage devices can be DAS, NAS, SAN, or a tiered storage system. In SMB, backup storage devices can be tape cartridges, optical disc, external SSD drives, and the like.
- As a part of verifying both the backup storage device and the backup media, testing on both elements should be performed on a regular basis.
- System administrators should regularly verify that all backup units are stored safely.

CHAPTER 18
Disaster Recovery

Introduction

Disaster recovery is a planned exercise in which an IT organization executes predetermined actions to fully and promptly restore its computing and business operations. Before any disaster or catastrophic event occurs, the organization should have a complete plan, and the appropriate personnel should know their role in the recovery effort. This chapter discusses the elements and actions that may be included in a disaster recovery plan.

Structure

This chapter covers the following topics:

- Disaster recovery planning
- Recovery sites
- Replication
- Testing
- Failovers and failbacks
- Testing: production vs. non-production

Objective

By the end of this chapter, you will be able to identify and describe the sub-objectives of the following Server+ examination objective: *Explain the importance of disaster recovery.*

Disaster recovery planning

In the event of a complete disruption that halts business operations, having pre-planned measures in place—knowing the necessary actions, responsibilities, and recovery logistics—would undoubtedly be beneficial for any organization.

Without a plan, the chaos of the situation would make the recovery process very difficult.

A disaster does not need to be a major force, such as a bomb, fire, hurricane, tornado, earthquake, or the like. It could be as simple as someone tripping on the power cord of the network server, a water pipe running over the data center bursting, or the local power grid being sabotaged. Whatever causes the interruption of the organization's normal operations, especially if the interruption lasts for some time, can be a disaster.

To prepare for the possibility of requiring a disaster recovery plan, it is essential to conduct a planning exercise well in advance of any actual need for recovery measures. The objective of the disaster planning process is the development, approval, and general agreement on a **Disaster Recovery Plan** (**DRP**). The DRP for an organization is likely to be unique to its structure, staffing, products or services, and information systems technology. Several sources on the internet and web provide templates and guidelines for developing a DRP. Regardless of its format or style, the development project and the finished DRP should include the following:

- **Management commitment**: The organization's senior management must fully support and be actively involved in both the development of the DRP and its contents.
- **Planning committee**: All functional areas of the organization should be represented by the planning committee, especially the operations manager and the information system manager.
- **Risk assessment**: The planning committee should identify the possible disasters that could befall the organization. A risk analysis and a **Business Impact Analysis** (**BIA**) should be performed for each of the potential disasters identified. Every department or function within the organization should analyze the consequences to the department in the event of a projected disaster. Any vulnerabilities identified should be prioritized for mitigation.
- **Recovery priorities**: Each department should identify the assets, working materials, and services needed to operate and the period in which it can effectively operate without them.

- **Recovery strategies**: The planning committee develops the recovery strategy detailing the logistics, services, and equipment required to return the organization to normal operations.
- **Develop the written plan**: After an outline of the DRP is approved, the members of the planning committee should develop the formal plan and submit it for approval by senior management.
- **Testing procedure**: Even the best DRP could fail if it had never been tested. A test plan should be developed that tests each of the recovery actions. A test of the plan should be conducted on a regular schedule.
- **Adjustments**: Any corrections or adjustments identified during the plan's testing should be made to the DRP. The plan should be resubmitted for approval.

Recovery sites

If a disaster destroys the building in which the computing equipment is housed and results in a total loss of computer-based services, an alternative operating location will become necessary, particularly in the short-term. Depending on several factors, an organization has different options for the characteristics of a disaster recovery site or a temporary location for its computing services.

A disaster recovery site is any location an organization uses to restore its IT operations. There are three general categories of disaster recovery sites (see *Figure 18.1*):

- **Cold site**: This type of facility may have office space with basic utilities and services, such as power, HVAC, telephone, and the like. These sites typically do not have computing equipment, which must be brought in and set up before systems and data can be loaded and operations restarted. In general, cold sites require more time to get up to speed than the RTO and RPO of the disaster recovery plan allows. Companies requiring a relatively short recovery period will typically opt for warm or hot site.
- **Warm site**: This type of facility has the needed computing, network, and communication equipment pre-installed. In most cases, the configuration of the equipment of a warm site is likely different from what the organization is using for its primary computing services. Systems, applications, and data is synchronized on a regular basis, commonly weekly. Warm sites work for organizations that can tolerate some downtime, but not as much as would be required by a cold site.
- **Hot site**: This facility could also be called a mirror site because it is the duplicate of an organization's production systems. A **hot site** is an active backup or replication of the operational system, applications, and services. In the event of a disruption of service to the primary systems, operations can be switched to the secondary (hot) site with only a minimum delay.

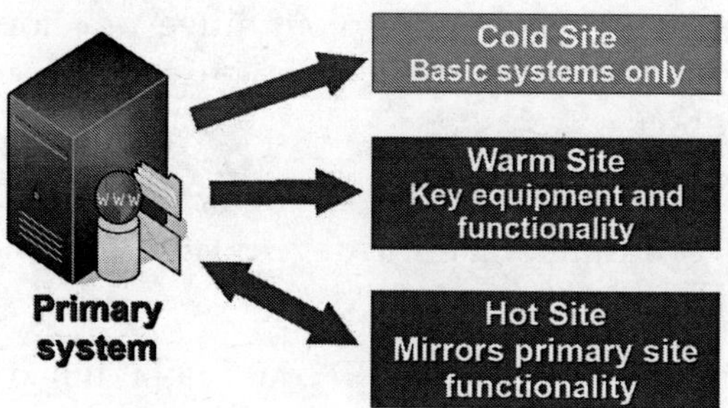

Figure 18.1: Disaster recovery site types

A recovery site can be located in the same facility as the production systems. However, the recovery site would be subject to the same disruption or disaster elements and may not be serviceable when needed. It's common for a recovery site to be located at a distance from a main facility, which could mean crosstown, across a county or state, or at some greater distance. For example, a Web hosting service located in Toronto, Ontario, Canada, has a hot site located in Miami, Florida, USA.

The cloud is becoming a popular disaster recovery site location. Depending on the needs of the organization, a cloud service may be **Software as a Service (SaaS)**, **Platform as a Service (PaaS)**, or **Infrastructure as a Service (IaaS)**. In any of these delivery models, the subscribing organization remains responsible for restarting its operations, the security of the data-in-transit, and the configuration of a PaaS, IaaS, or **Disaster Recovery as a Service (DRaaS)** system. Mostly, data backups to the cloud are subscription-based applications. However, if the SaaS for backups is through a different cloud service provider than the platform or infrastructure provider, the backed-up data must be transmitted from one provider to another.

Replication

One strategy against the loss of data due to a disaster, hardware failure, power loss, or perhaps ransomware, is data replication. It can mirror a storage device to another system or distribute parts of a database to multiple storage units spread out geographically. Data replication assures an organization that one or more copies of its data are up-to-date and available as a protection against data loss.

Replicated data does not have to be a complete copy of the database. It can be a snapshot or a duplicate that is stored on-site, off-site, or in the cloud. The replicated data serves as a failover backup to the production systems and in a disaster recovery action, the data can be restored to a production system or serve as a hot site.

Data is replicated using either a synchronous or asynchronous method. **Synchronous replication** writes data for the primary storage, and each of its replica stores in the same operations. **Asynchronous replication** stores data in the primary storage but updates the replica stores at some future time. *Figure 18.2* illustrates the difference between these two replication types:

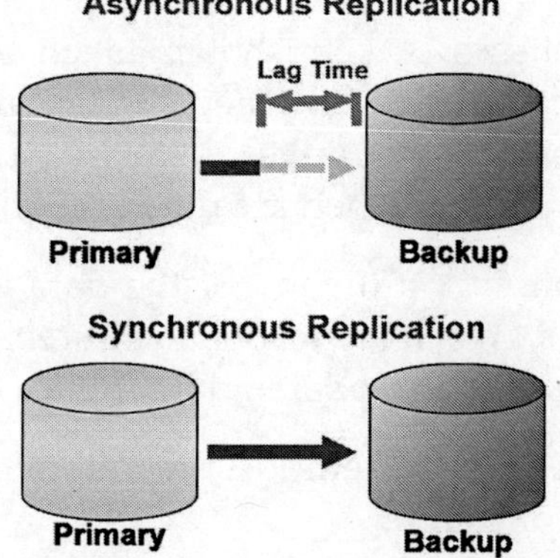

Figure 18.2: The difference between asynchronous and synchronous replication

Synchronous replication, of the two options, is the most widely used. It involves the replication of data and systems on both primary and secondary sites. Every block written locally is also copied to a second remote array. This technique guarantees extremely rapid restart, with very low RTO and RPO and high levels of reliability. Its disadvantage is that it's expensive and that its costs can depend on the quality of the storage on both the primary and secondary sites.

In asynchronous replication, distance problems are not critical. After storage on the primary site is completed, writing and propagation takes place on the secondary site. This method is meant to overcome the distance between the two sites. However, the misalignment of the two storage processes can make it impossible for exact duplicate or identical copies to be available in real-time. In asynchronous replication, the array controller comes into play and must be able to manage a cache and an important data flow.

The two types of replication can also be used in a mixed or hybrid way. This approach focuses on the selection of systems and data, between critical and non-critical ones, and designates which should be processed with a synchronous replication method and which should use an asynchronous replication mode. In this way, even in the event of a major disaster, the critical data is available and not affected.

There are a variety of data replication process methods, including:

- **Constant replication**: Also called **continuous replication**, this replication method is always running, unless configured to not run, and creates and maintains a backup of data files.
- **Heterogeneous replication**: This type of replication is used to create data replicas on data servers with different operating systems and devices. For example, data from an SQL server can be replicated to a non-SQL server.
- **Merge replication**: This replication method allows multiple users to actively post changes to the data. Conflicting updates or changes are discovered and addressed.

- **Snapshot replication**: This method is most commonly used as the replication method between databases. A snapshot is taken of a primary database at the beginning of the replication process. Then changes made to the primary database (the publisher) are copied to the replica database (subscriber) at regular intervals. This type of replication is best when the data is changed infrequently.
- **Transactional replication**: A full copy of the data is updated by transactions to the primary data stores, which are also made in real-time to the replica data. This replication method ensures an updated data replica of the primary data.

In addition to the different replication methods, the following are other types of methods and processes used for data replication:

- **Application-consistent**: Also called **application-aware**, this is a file copy method that uses Microsoft VSS to capture data in memory and in any pending I/O actions. The VSS writer creates shadow copies, which are current transactionally, when the backup process encounters a locked file. A **shadow copy** is a history of a file or folder maintained by the system restore function.
- **File-locking**: File-locking locks out any other users when one user is updating a file. The purpose is to prevent interceding updates. Some backup processes and applications will attempt to backup a locked file by idling it for a specific time to await the removal of the lock. If the lock is not removed at the end of the wait time, the file is skipped. Most OSs now support record-locking, which locks individual records within a file, and allows users to proceed with their processes.
- **Bi-directional**: Copying data from a hard disk to a magnetic tape is a backup process called **unidirectional synchronization**. With more and more collaboration projects being worked on simultaneously, **bidirectional synchronization** ensures that any changes made by one collaborator are also made to the document copies of the other collaborators. This same concept can also be applied to the replication of active databases and files.

Testing

Every disaster recovery plan should be tested to verify its effectiveness and completeness and to add or remove any missing or unnecessary steps. In many organizations, having a DRP is perceived as sufficient effort, and testing the plan is often viewed as resource-intensive for something that may not be necessary in the end. Every organization must address the risk of a disaster potentially disrupting its operations and system access. However, Investment in testing the plan to ensure it will not fail when such situation arises will be a wise decision.

A testing procedure for a DRP should at least test the intra-team and external communication, and the system, application, and data recovery. The specific testing procedures performed are dependent on the organization's **Recovery Point Objective** (**RPO**) and **Recovery Time**

Objective (**RTO**). However, the test should also prove the reality of the RPO and RTO expectations.

There are three types of DRP testing:

- **Plan review**: This is a read-through of the DRP by the planning committee and stakeholders to determine if there are missing areas or inconsistencies in the plan.
- **Tabletop exercise**: This test is a step-by-step walk-through review of the DRP under a generic disaster scenario. It is called a tabletop, because it is conducted as a meeting and simulates the activities of the planning team, employees with assigned responsibilities, and management to judge the effectiveness of the plan.
- **Simulation**: A simulation can be something like a tabletop exercise using a specific threat to demonstrate the DRP under certain conditions. A DRP for a building fire and flood will be different. The objective of the simulation is to test the plan and determine whether the business operations and computer services are restored in a timely manner.

Failovers and failbacks

There are actually two disaster recovery mechanisms that can be used as a part of the service restoration process in the event of an interruption or outage: failover and failback. Briefly, a **failover** is a switching process that transfers active processing from the primary system or device to a backup system or device. **Failback** is used to return to the primary system from the failover system. *Figure 18.3* illustrates failover and failback.

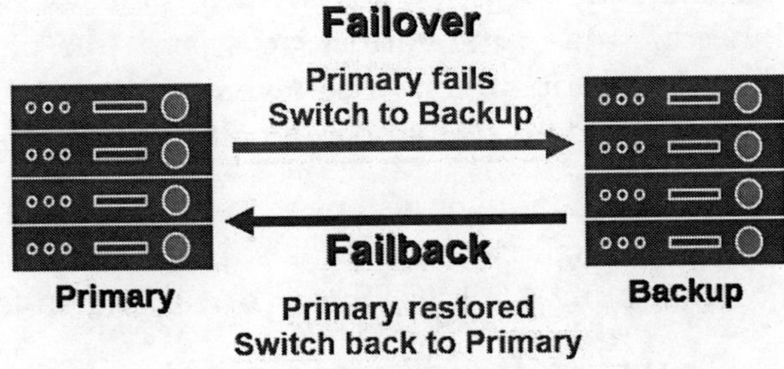

Figure 18.3*: Failover and failback*

Failover

Failover is a mechanism used to provide continuous availability to a network and its resources in the event of an unexpected security issues, weather, or disaster event, or perhaps for the downtime of a planned maintenance activity. A failover requires that a replicated system, either full-scale or virtual, be available to immediately replace the primary system. In most cases, the backup system tracks the heartbeat or pulse of the primary system and when prescribed thresholds are reached, it automatically issues the failover process.

Failovers can be either **active-active** or **active-passive**, which is also called **active-standby**. These failover methods require at least two systems, either full-scale or virtual, that have identical configurations and software.

- **Active-active**: In this failover setup, two or more systems are running synchronously, sharing the workload. If one system fails, its workload is taken up by the other node(s) until the failed unit becomes active again.
- **Active-passive**: This failover setup also uses two or more systems, but all the systems are not active at one time. If an active system fails, a passive (idle) system is activated and issues a failover. If the failed system becomes active again, the backup system issues a failback to return operations back to the primary system.

Failback

Failback returns the processing control back to the primary site after unplanned or planned interruption of services is resolved. However, in some cases, the failback can be made permanent and the backup system can become the primary system.

During a failover, all processing occurs on the backup system. Any changes made to the system or the data are stored in a temporary file as change data. When the failback is executed, the change data is copied to the primary system to be processed, eliminating the need for transfer of a copy to the backup system.

Failover simulation

Before performing any testing that involves a failover or failback simulation, first verify that all cables and connectors are in the correct jacks, and free of defects and, that all devices involved in either of these operations are powered up and functioning. This visual inspection may eliminate any roadblocks that could halt the test unexpectedly.

There are several ways to initiate a failover test, nearly all of which involve disrupting the system or network to simulate a failure that initiates the failover process. The following are the primary forms of evaluating a failover through a simulated failure.

- **Planned failover**: The process for a planned or **scheduled failover** first synchronizes the data of the primary and secondary systems before switching the backup system into the primary role. Planned failovers simulate the switch from production to backup systems in a disaster recovery plan. For a planned failover, the failure point should be located at a networking device that connects the two systems, not at the primary server. The test plan should also include a planned failback.
- **Unplanned failover**: Also called **forced failover**, this testing method simulates a sudden loss of the primary system and switches to the backup system without synchronization. Typically, this type of failover testing, unless tightly controlled, results in the loss of some data. A failback should also be included in the testing plan.

Testing: Production vs. non-production

Everyone involved with software development, patch management, and production system administration are likely to respond to the question of testing in a live production environment with a resounding, "NO!" There are many reasons why they may feel this way, but the underlying reason is mostly fear. Fear that data will be corrupted, the software may have bugs that crash the system, or an unfavorable event may occur. Their recommendation is to test the software or patch in a non-production environment, a sandbox, on a backup failover system that is not active.

A non-production system provides the assurance that live production data will not be affected. Any problems or bugs in the application or system being tested should not affect the live systems or its users. However, a non-production system is safe and can be restored to its state before the test, but there are some drawbacks to testing in this environment. The main limitation is that it does not replicate the production environment. In the non-production environment, none of the production applications and services are competing for system resources, which the system will encounter in production.

In many medium-large organizations, there can be a greater segregation of environments, as explained in the following:

- **Test environment**: After an application or test has been developed to an agreed stage, it is released into the test environment. This is where testers ensure the quality of the application and methods, open bugs, and review bug fixes. This environment must accurately resemble the production environment, as this is the last safe place to find and fix environment-related bugs.
- **Staging environment**: The staging site is used to assemble, test, and review new versions of a solution before it goes into production. The staging site is often different from the development site and provides a final QA area separate from the development or production environments.
- **Production environment**: This is where the application technology goes out into the world and becomes production. Content can be updated from the staging environment to the production environment when available, as well as the release of new application features and bug fixes from UAT or the staging environment.

A testing plan should consider the security of the systems and data. Initial testing should be desktop run-throughs, also called bug hunts. Then, process testing on a non-production system using simulated live data should be conducted. After issues are corrected and retested in the non-productive environment, test on a production system will be attempted.

Conclusion

Disaster recovery should be a planned procedure in which all the necessary actions, resources, and processes required to reinstate the operations and systems are executed.

The processes of a disaster recovery plan are designed to re-establish the organization's business operations completely within the time frame. Disaster recovery planning should be completed and tested before any disaster or catastrophic event occurs. The incident response team should understand their role in the recovery effort. The continuity or restoration of the computing systems should be an integral part of the disaster planning. The details of how the restoration of services is to be accomplished is vital to the recovery.

In the next chapter, we begin looking at the various troubleshooting processes and methods you will likely encounter both on the Security+ exam and as a server administrator.

Points to remember

- The development and approval of a DRP should be priority for any organization, which includes management commitment, planning committee, risk assessment, recovery priorities, recovery strategies, and a testing procedure.
- A disaster recovery site is any location an organization uses to restore its IT operations. The three general types of disaster recovery sites are cold, warm, and hot. The cloud is a disaster recovery site location.
- Data replication mirrors a storage device to another system or distributes parts of a database to multiple storage units. Data replication is synchronous or asynchronous.
- Data replication process methods include constant replication, heterogeneous replication, merge replication, snapshot replication, and transactional replication. Other types of data replication are application-consistent, file-locking, and bi-directional.
- DRP testing verifies the effectiveness of the plan.
- A testing procedure for a DRP should test the intra-team and external communication, and the system, application, and data recovery. There are three types of DRP testing: plan review, tabletop exercise, and simulation.
- A failover is a switching process that transfers active processing from the primary system or device to a backup system or device.
- Failback is used to return to the primary system from the failover system.
- Failovers are active-active or active-passive.
- The primary forms of evaluating a failover through a simulated failure are a planned failover and an unplanned failover.
- A non-production system provides the assurance that no live production data will be affected. A production environment provides applications and services competing for system resources.

Part - 4
Troubleshooting

Part 4 includes the following chapters:

- Chapter 19 – Troubleshooting Methods
- Chapter 20 – Common Hardware Issues
- Chapter 21 – Storage Issues
- Chapter 22 – OS and Software Issues
- Chapter 23 – Network Connectivity Issues
- Chapter 24 – Security Issues

Chapter 19
Troubleshooting Methods

Introduction

This chapter reviews the methods recommended for troubleshooting a failure or fault in any general hardware, software, network, storage device, and security policies or devices. This chapter precedes the other four chapters in this part of the book. The following chapters cover common issues and the appropriate troubleshooting methods for hardware, storage, operating systems and software, network connectivity, and security.

Structure

The chapter covers the following topics:

- Troubleshooting step
- Identifying the problem and determining the scope
- Establishing a theory of probable cause
- Testing the theory to determine the cause
- Establishing a plan of action to resolve the problem
- Verification and prevention
- Performing Root Cause analysis
- Document findings, actions, and outcomes throughout the process

Objective

By the end of this chapter, you will be able to identify and describe the sub-objectives of the following Server+ examination objective: *Explain the troubleshooting theory and methodology.*

Troubleshooting step

Troubleshooting is a structured step-by-step process used to identify, isolate, and resolve performance issues. This process can be used on standalone computers, server hardware and software, networking devices, or any other computer technology or information processing system. Regardless of the use or location of a failing device, it is likely to prevent a user from performing their job in some way. The system administrator's responsibilities to the user and the organization are straightforward: identify the problem, resolve it, and document all the processes and actions involved.

A search on the web for troubleshooting methods would likely return several different versions with varying steps. However, for the most part, all the versions are focused on the same thing: finding the problem and fixing it. The questions on the Server+ exam that concern the troubleshooting method are based on the steps included in the exam objectives for this certification. The steps in this troubleshooting method are as follows:

1. Identify the problem and determine the scope
2. Establish a theory of probable cause (question the obvious)
3. Test the theory to determine the cause
4. Establish a plan of action to resolve the problem
5. Implement the solution or escalate
6. Verify full system functionality and, if applicable, implement preventive measures
7. Perform a root cause analysis
8. Document findings, actions, and outcomes throughout the process

Using all the above steps is not always essential in any particular troubleshooting situation. Some problems are apparent, some may not call for troubleshooting, and most often require each of the troubleshooting steps to be performed at least once.

Soft skills

The use of the troubleshooting method and its steps supplement and guide the existing knowledge and skill of the administrator or technician. The technical knowledge provides a basis for any decision-making involved in determining the specific issue. As important as technical skills and knowledge may be, the professional's **interpersonal skills** can be just as important. Interacting calmly with a frustrated or flustered user, supervisor, or customer and effectively listening to learn the issue is essential to successfully resolving the problem. In addition, remember that the person's work habits and ethics are on display, and are being watched carefully by the user throughout the troubleshooting and repair processes. The work performed should be efficient, effective, and correct.

A system, server, or network administrator may or may not come into contact with network users in the organization directly. However, the administrator must remember and appreciate that the users are in fact his or her customers. End-users see any problem that is preventing them from doing their work as a big problem with their workstation. Keep in mind that for non-technical users, their network workstation is the system. Above all else, be as patient and helpful, as possible.

Identifying the problem and determining the scope

The objective of the immediate response to an issue should be to verify that there is a problem. While that may seem simple enough, what the problem may look like, sound like, or even smell like, may not be the underlying cause (if any) of the apparent issue. The best way to be sure that the issue or problem experienced or observed still exists is to recreate it. However, on a server, this is not always the safest bet. This is where the administrator must apply his or her knowledge and experience. Typically, a problem may be destructive when reproduced is likely to be documented somewhere. If it is a hardware issue, check the manufacturer's documentation or website. If it is a software issue, check the developer's documentation, or the community blog or the FAQs on their website for similar occurrences. If the only source for a problem is a user, use interview tactics to learn what he or she believes to be the problem. Remember that users typically do not have the same technical knowledge and often cannot recreate what was seen, heard, or smelled; only describe it.

Regardless of the problem's source or cause, protect the user, the system, and the organization by backing up the data, software, and settings of the device before beginning any work that requires the covers of a device to be removed. Remember that this should be preceded by disconnecting the system from its power source.

Hardware or software?

While this may seem like a simple question, some problems are hard to identify using only their symptoms. A problem that appears to be software issue may, in fact, be a hardware issue to which the software is reacting. If the underlying problem is not apparent, draw on your knowledge and experience to begin troubleshooting to what you believe is the issue. Remember that most problems occur immediately after a hardware or software change. Installing new hardware inside the system case may inadvertently loosen adjacent connectors, cause electrical grounding issues, and the like. New software can have bugs, incompatibilities, or resource conflicts with other processes. It is always best to back up any system before adding, or even removing, hardware or software from a system.

Hardware problems

The systematic approach of the troubleshooting steps can help determine if a reported problem is a hardware or software issue, which is really a hardware issue. For example, Blue Screen of Death. Most hardware problems are caused by loose connectors, dirty fans and components, or a hardware component that is in the process of wearing out due to a very limited number of moving parts. With any hardware problem, deal with the obvious issues first, whether they have anything to do with the reported problem. For example, if the insides of the system case look like it has not been cleaned for a while, that problem needs to be dealt with before anything else. A clean area is so much better to work in.

Hardware component areas where problems commonly occur includes:

- Main memory
- Power supply
- Cooling fan
- Hard disk drive
- Video or graphics card
- Expansion cards, slots, and ports
- Cable connections

Note: Hardware troubleshooting and common hardware problems are covered in more detail in *Chapter 20, Common Hardware Issues.*

Software problems

Software problems occur more frequently than hardware problems probably because hardware tends to stay the same. Software has three general categories: system software (for example, Operating Systems), application software (for example, Microsoft Office), and utility software (for example, device drivers). Each category has its own particular set of problems as follows:

- **Operating systems (OS):** OS problems are commonly improper or erroneous configurations, settings, or compatibilities that may require a minor adjustment or, in its extreme, a complete reinstall or upgrade.
- **Application software:** Problems in an application can be similar to those of the OS or can be caused by the OS. However, most application problems are caused by a resource allocation issue (for example, not enough memory, a disk drive full, etc.)

or a bug in the application itself. Many application problems are resolved through an update or patch from the developer, or an adjustment to its settings.

- **Utility software:** The issues with most device drivers and system utilities and apps are caused by out-of-date versions that are solved by installing an updated version.

Some of the most common software issues are:

- Missing or corrupted system files
- Errors or missing configuration settings in BIOS/UEFI
- Malware attacks or virus infections
- Improperly installed or removed software
- Corrupted filesystem configuration or registry entries
- User permissions: rights to the software or the files it uses.

Note: Software troubleshooting and common software problems are covered in more detail in *Chapter 22, Storage Device Issues and Solutions.*

Establishing a theory of probable cause

What the user explains as the problem or what sounds or looks like the obvious problem may not be the problem, but its symptoms. There are situations where the actual problem is obvious, such as when smoke is pouring out of the case, or when the system starts up, it sounds like metal on a grinding wheel. However, a system that would not complete its boot cycle or one that starts up and shuts down after a short time may need further consideration.

Identifying the underlying cause of an issue can be more problematic. Even if there are several causes to a problem, each should be considered, tested, and either eliminated or resolved. Establishing a probable cause is a process used to:

- Identify possible sources of a problem
- Analyze the probability of a source causing the problem
- Determining the cause(s) for further investigation

This troubleshooting step aims to identify any possible causes for the problem. After identifying the possible causes to be investigated, prioritize them by likelihood with the more likely causes at the top.

Testing the theory to determine the cause

In order to prove the possible causes identified in the previous troubleshooting step, each must be tested. Chances are that the most likely cause, which is at the top of the list, is the actual cause, but all the possible causes should still be tested to positively identify the most likely cause of the problem.

Test each of the possible causes on the list to prove or disprove that it is or could be the cause of the problem. After testing each listed possibility, retest the one that proved to be the most likely cause. As each of the possible causes is tested, document the test and its results. If a decision is made as to whether it may be the cause of the problem, document why the outcome was chosen.

The testing process for each of the possible causes can be unique to the component, system, or software. In many instances, the developer or manufacturer may have a test procedure it recommends in its documentation or on its website. Another source can be the question and answer websites, like Stack Overflow (**www.stackoverflow.com**) and Microsoft Support (**support.microsoft.com/**). Most likely, the issue being tested has happened before, and a solution was provided.

However, if none of the possible causes on the list proved to be the cause of the problem, reconsider the problem and, if possible, use the outcomes of the tests performed to develop a new list of probable causes, which is likely to be much shorter. If all possible causes have been eliminated as the actual cause, it may be necessary to escalate the investigation to a specialist technician or perhaps the developer or manufacturer's helpline.

Note: Remember that all the actions, decisions, tests, and test results are to be documented.

Establishing a plan of action to resolve the problem

Now that the actual cause of the problem is, hopefully, identified, before fixing it, a plan must be thought out and documented. The reason for a plan is to be sure that the steps required to resolve the issue do not introduce other issues. A carefully thought out plan can ensure that all of the required steps are included, in the correct sequence, and that all required materials, contacts, or permissions are identified.

Repair work plan

The work plan can be simple, but it must be complete. It will be included in the documentation for the repair activity, so it should be at least legible. The following list of steps is an example of what might be in the repair plan for replacing a hardware component, such as a damaged cable:

1. Power down the server
2. Remove all power connections
3. Remove housing
4. Loosen cable connections
5. Remove the cable
6. Insert new cable
7. Snug up cable connections
8. Replace power connections
9. Power up the server
10. Test connected device
11. Power down the server
12. Replace housing
13. Power up server
14. Document repair process

The repair plan can be more complicated and take much more time, especially if the impact of the repair effects other operations, local or remote, or outside vendors or service people. In either case, a written repair plan is an essential guide.

Identifying potential effects

One of the best ways to avoid causing any other problems while resolving a problem is to identify beforehand anything that could possibly go wrong, be affected, or should be avoided. For example, if repairs are to be made to the server hardware that hosts the main DHCP server for a local network, there is a possibility that network users could be affected. Or, if a step in a repair process requires that a network device be power-cycled, what is the possible impact to the network if the device is turned off and back on? Identifying the effects of the actions in the repair plan can save many headaches down the road. Once the possible effects of the repair plan are identified, the end-users and stakeholders who could be affected should be notified. This should be documented.

Implementing the solution or escalate

The repair plan was developed for a purpose and not just for the documentation. The plan should be followed, step-by-step. After completing a step, its outcome should be verified. For example, in the plan included in the previous section, the second step was to *Remove all power connections*. To prove that this step was completed, attempt to power up the device.

As you proceed, each subsequent test step retests each of the preceding steps, and the sequence of the work becomes accumulatively compatible. After making the change or one of a series of changes, the problem still exists, or new problems have appeared, reverse the changes made to that point and reconsider the solution.

If the repair requires multiple components to be installed or replaced, each component placement should be individually completed and tested before proceeding to the next component. There may be some components that must be installed together, but each completed step should be tested to ensure its fit and function.

After completing the repair and successfully testing it, notify its user or stakeholder and brief them on the cause of the problem, how you identified the cause, what you did to resolve the problem, and how you tested the solution.

Some problems can be outside the experience and knowledge of an administrator. It is best to know this and not try to bluff through the issue and possibly damage the system further. In these cases, the problem should be escalated to someone with the knowledge or expertise to resolve the issue. This could be another in-house administrator, outside technician, or manufacturer's representative.

Verification and prevention

This step in the troubleshooting method is several steps combined into one. Even though the problem has been resolved and tested, its functionality needs to be verified with the end-user and possibly other administrators. If the problem is one that could reoccur, can preventive measures be implemented to prevent the reoccurrence? Let us discuss this further.

Verifying full system functionality

Although the repair made was tested, which is usually a test to make sure it solved the problem, everything associated with the system, application, or component repair or resolved must also be tested. It needs to be verified that everything is back to normal, if not better than before. In some cases, resolving one problem uncovers another problem that was unreported or had not been discovered. In such a case, treat the newly discovered issue as a standalone problem and start the troubleshooting process from the beginning.

Implementing preventive measures

After the problem has been resolved, give some thought to how it may have been prevented. While not all hardware and software issues can be prevented, most can be anticipated. Preventive measures can be improvements to the backup procedures, adjusting the HVAC system, checking the UPS, or a plan for replacing the entire system or moving to the cloud.

Manufacturers of hardware components typically publish guidelines on the length of service for their products as a **Mean Time Between Failures (MTBF)**. This can be used as a part of a preventive maintenance plan to check on components that have lower MTBFs or a history of failures. Software makes it harder to predict problems, but a dedicated patch management system can help prevent problems and crashes.

Another important preventive measure is user awareness training. Users should be aware of the warning signs that a problem exists or is beginning. Users should also be trained to observe, report, and document problems and issues on their workstation or the network. A user should know which types of problems should be reported.

Performing Root Cause analysis

This step is performed after the repair or fix has been applied and is less of an integral part of the troubleshooting process and more of an investigative step to identify areas that may be future issues. This step aims to find the primary underlying cause(s) for the problem just addressed or a group of similar problems that have occurred in a short period. This process is called a **Root Cause Analysis (RCA)**. RCA is used to identify the primary source of frequent hardware or software malfunctions or failures. It is intended to determine what happened, why it happened, and is there a way to prevent it from happening again.

RCA is performed after the fact; after a repair or fix has been applied and tested. If a root cause is identified, a proactive action should be started to correct the issue causing the problem(s). RCA provides a follow-up review to repair activities to ensure that the repair activities are not dealing with the symptoms of a larger issue.

Document findings, actions, and outcomes throughout the process

The documentation process of any troubleshooting and repair procedure begins before any troubleshooting or repair work takes place. The initial report of the problem and any investigative effort to determine where and what the problem may be must be documented.

The documentation of individual workstations, servers, network devices, and their software must include all repair and maintenance actions performed, beginning with their installation. This record should detail all troubleshooting actions, repairs, upgrades, patches, fixes, and components or software added to or removed from each system. This information is extremely important because the administrator or technician of one instance may not be the one handling the next instance.

The documentation should include a written record of all reported problems and the correction, component, or fix applied. This information provides a history and a starting point for administrators or technicians who work on the system or component in the future. This information should include, for each diagnostic or repair instance:

- The date, location, and the name of the person reporting the problem
- A description of the problem, as reported
- A detailed description of the troubleshooting steps performed and result of each step
- A detailed description of the repair or fix applied, if any, including any components replaced, added, or removed
- A detailed description of any software changes applied, including updates, configurations, installation, or removals
- The details of testing performed and the results of each test
- A description or list of any additional or suspected issues or any potential maintenance or repair issues that should be considered

Conclusion

The troubleshooting process is structured to identify, isolate, and resolve a system performance issue, software problem, or malfunctioning hardware component. While knowing computer systems is important when dealing with a customer or end-user's problem, interpersonal skills are also important. Following a structured approach when troubleshooting a problem, regardless of its nature or complexity, helps to ensure that nothing is overlooked. Documentation should be recorded at every step of the process.

The next chapter begins our look into the specifics of server-related issues and problems by discussing some of the more common hardware issues.

Points to remember

- Troubleshooting is a structured step-by-step process used to identify, isolate, and resolve performance issues.
- The Server+ examination objectives define the troubleshooting steps as identify the problem and determine the scope, establish a theory of probable cause, test the theory to determine the cause, establish a plan of action to resolve the problem, implement the solution or escalate, verify full system functionality and if applicable implement preventive measures, perform a root cause analysis, and document findings, actions, and outcomes throughout the process.
- A professional's interpersonal skills are important.
- The objective of the response to an issue should be verifying the problem.
- It is best to back up any system before adding, or removing, hardware or software.

- The systematic approach to troubleshooting helps determine if a problem is hardware or software.
- The common component areas where problems commonly occur are main memory, power supply, cooling system, hard disk drive, graphics card, expansion cards, slots, ports, and power and device connectors.
- Software has three general categories: system, application, and utility.
- OS problems are commonly erroneous configurations, settings, or compatibilities.
- Application software problems are commonly resource allocation issues.
- The issues with most device drivers and system utilities and apps are caused by out-of-date versions.
- Common software issues are missing or corrupted system files, configuration settings in BIOS/UEFI, malware attacks, improperly installed or removed software, and corrupted configuration or registry entries.
- A probable cause is a process used to identify possible sources, analyze a source causing a problem, and determine causes for further investigation.
- A work plan should be developed so the steps required to resolve the issue don't introduce other issues.
- To avoid causing problems, identify anything that could be affected or should be avoided during the repair action.
- The repair plan should be followed step-by-step.
- After completing the repair and successfully testing it, notify its user or stakeholder and explain the cause of the problem, how it was identified, what was done to resolve it, and how it was tested.
- If a problem is beyond the experience and knowledge of an administrator, it should be escalated to someone with the knowledge or expertise to resolve the issue.
- Everything associated with the system, application, or component repair or resolved must be tested.
- Preventive measures that may prevent the issue from reoccurring should be made.
- An important preventive measure is user training.
- RCA is used to identify the primary source of frequent hardware or software malfunctions or failures.
- The documentation process begins before any troubleshooting or repair work takes place.
- The documentation should detail all troubleshooting action, repairs, upgrades, patches, fixes, and components or software added to or removed from each system.

Join our book's Discord space

Join the book's Discord Workspace for Latest updates, Offers, Tech happenings around the world, New Release and Sessions with the Authors:

https://discord.bpbonline.com

CHAPTER 20
Hardware Issues

Introduction

Hardware components can and do have problems, usually somewhere between disruptive and catastrophic. An administrator's ability to troubleshoot, resolve, and document hardware issues can directly affect how disruptive a hardware issue might be and provide the knowledge and skills measured on the Server+ exam. This chapter looks at the hardware problems that can occur on server hardware, the problem scenarios you are likely to encounter on the Server+ exam, and what you will likely see in your role as a certified server administrator.

Structure

The chapter covers the following topics:

- Common hardware problems
- Memory issues
- Common problem causes

Objective

By the end of this chapter, you will be able to identify and describe the sub-objectives of the following Server+ examination objective: *Given a scenario, troubleshoot common hardware failures.*

Common hardware problems

Computer hardware problems are usually caused by a fault in an electrical or electronic component, or possibly the setup, installation, or configuration of a device, any of which can lead to the failure of a device and possibly an entire computer. Some of what may appear to be hardware problems may be a problem with software. However, a software problem can be solved through a patch or a configuration change, but most hardware problems require that a computer's case be opened or removed. The following sections describe the common hardware problems you will probably encounter on the Server+ exam.

Predictive failures

There are two categories of failures on a computer system: soft failures and hard failures. A soft failure is typically caused by data, of a non-catastrophic design defect or failure in the software or hardware. **Soft failures** may indicate that something is wrong somewhere in the system, but the system overall is still reliable. A soft failure can occur at the chip-level or at the system-level. Chip-level defects, caused at manufacturing, can intermittently cause errors in data or instructions stored on a defective chip. System-level defects are typically the result of data or instructions moving on the internal bus of the motherboard being altered by electrical noise or EMI or possibly overheating. However, errors in the programming of an application can also cause soft failures. An app that for some reason always locks up if a certain account number is being processed at a particular time of day, is also a type of soft failure. For the most part, the causes of soft failures cannot be easily isolated or readily fixed. In the worst case, recovery from a soft failure requires a restart of the system.

A hard failure is way more obvious. **Hard failures** are serious malfunctions of the electronics or mechanical devices of a computer, typically inside the computer case. A hard failure of a device or component requires a repair or replacement, after troubleshooting of course.

There is really no way to predict soft failures; they happen generally without warning or any pattern. However, there are ways to predict hard failures and avoid the problems associated with the downtime of a server. **Predictive Failure Analysis (PFA)** can be used to predict the failure of CPUs, memory, I/O devices, and data storage devices. PFA analyzes corrected problems in a component or device to predict a possible failure in the future. Most PFA systems are specific to a component or device, such as the CPU, memory, or hard disks.

Memory issues

A computer has several components without which it cannot function properly. One of the more essential components is memory or RAM. If there is a suspected problem with RAM, before trying to isolate the cause, there are general troubleshooting steps (see the following section) that can be used to find and fix most memory issues.

Memory troubleshooting

After the power cord is removed from the computer and the system case is opened, follow the given steps to troubleshoot a memory issue:

1. Verify that the memory modules are snuggly inserted into the memory slots and that the locks are engaged. *Figure 20.1* shows a memory module being reinstalled.
2. Check that the memory slots are populated in the correct order, such as slots 1 and 2, 1 and 3, or 2 and 4. This check verifies that the memory cards were installed in the correct sequence, which allows the multi-channel technologies of the memory circuits to function properly. Depending on the manufacturer some memory cards use dual or triple channels to allow greater performance and stability. Check the motherboard's documentation for this information.
3. Verify that the memory modules are the same size, speed, and manufacturer's brand. Mixed memory modules typically will not work correctly. If the memory modules are compatible, test each module one at a time to see if there is a bad one.

***Figure 20.1:** A memory module being reinstalled to ensure it is properly installed* [1]

4. Access the BIOS/UEFI settings and verify the RAM amount. If this setting is incorrect and the RAM is inserted properly, a BIOS/UEFI update is likely needed.
5. On a Windows system, use the **`resmon`** utility, and on a Linux system, use the **`memtester`** utility to check for possible memory leaks.
6. Restart into safe mode and run the anti-malware application to ensure no virus or malware exists and is causing problems.

1. Image courtesy of Enrico Signoretti (juko.it)

7. Check with the operating system developer for updated device drives or updates that may address the problem.

Common memory errors and failures

The following sections describe the memory (RAM) errors and faults you can expect on the Server+ exam. You may encounter these errors or problems as a part of a scenario question that begins, "Given ..." or "You are called to ..." or something similar.

Blue Screen of Death

Although it is technically a stop error code message screen, it is known far and wide as the **Blue Screen of Death (BSOD)**. BSOD is unique to Windows and its purpose is to inform the user that something very critical has gone wrong with the system. In most cases, the problem is with a hardware device, a bad or obsolete device driver, or a problem with Windows itself. *Figure 20.2* shows an example of a BSOD:

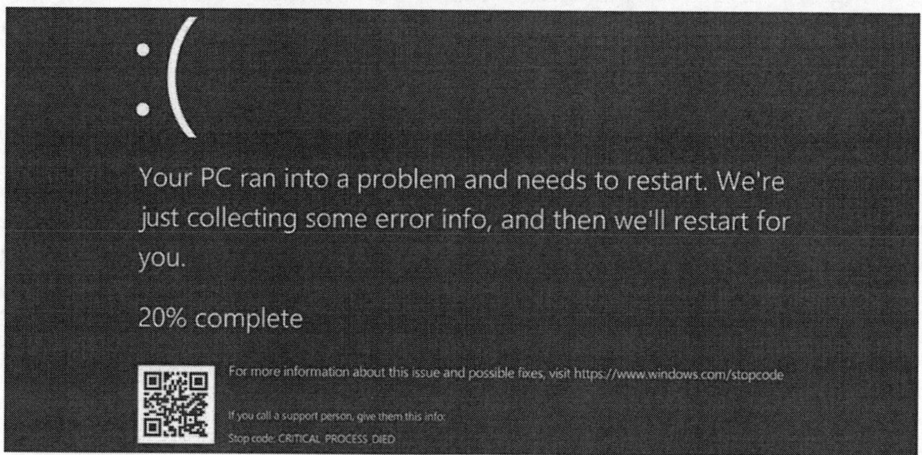

***Figure 20.2:** An example of a Windows system "Blue Screen of Death."*

A BSOD is generally the result of a **STOP Error**, of which there are over 260 different stop error codes. *Table 20.1* lists just a few of the codes as examples:

Stop code	Description	Detail/Message
0x000000C4	Fatal errors found by Driver Verifier.	"DRIVER_VERIFIER_DETECTED_VIOLATION"
0x0000003F	System has performed too many I/O actions	Resulted in fragmented system page table entries (PTE). "NO_MORE_SYSTEM_PTES"
0x000000C9	Driver Verifier I/O violations.	"DRIVER_VERIFIER_IOMANAGER_VIOLATION"

Stop code	Description	Detail/Message
0x000000E6	Driver Verifier DMA violations	"DRIVER_VERIFIER_DMA_VIOLATION"
0x00000024	Problem occurred in ntfs. sys	"NTFS_FILE_SYSTEM"
0x000000EF	Critical process died	"CRITICAL_PROCESS_DIED"
0x000000DC	Driver accessed stack address below stack's thread.	"DRIVER_INVALID_STACK_ACCESS"
0x00000076	Driver failed to release locked pages after I/O operation	"PROCESS_HAS_LOCKED_PAGES"

***Table 20.1:** BSOD Stop Codes*

When a stop error is generated on the system, the CPU halts operations, which appears to users as a crash. All that can be done at that point, is to restart the system, which clears the error. However, because the stop is more sudden than a shutdown or hibernation, files that were opened by applications may have data loss. Windows automatically creates a dump ("minidump") file with information about the system's state at the time of the stop error. Dump files can be read using the WinDbg app to learn more about the stop error's cause.

Purple screen

Although it is sometimes called the "**purple screen of death**" or PSOD, it is mostly just the purple screen, which is a bit less common than its blue cousin. In any case, this screen shows up only on systems running the VMkernal on a VMware ESX/ESXI host computer.

The cause for a PSOD on a Windows system can be an outdated graphic card device driver, an overclocked processor, errors or misconfiguration of the VMkernal, hardware problems, and incompatible settings in interacting software. Like the BSOD, a restart is the best solution, but if that does not solve the problem, remove all external devices and add them back one at a time, upgrade the graphics card device driver, and/or remove the overclocking on the CPU. Concerning the overclock: when a computer is overclocked, the hardware operating rate and voltage generate more heat than the system was designed to handle. This could make the CPU or the graphics processor unstable and result in a PSOD.

Memory utilization

Memory usage, or more formally known as memory utilization, should be monitored. This is especially true for systems that run several large applications and occasionally all or many at the same time. When the server hardware gets low on available memory, it will noticeably slow down and may eventually crash.

On a Windows system, there are several ways to check memory utilization. Two simple ways to check memory usage are to use the Task Manager to view both total memory use and the memory use of individual processes. A third, slightly more complicated way, is to use the **systeminfo** command at a command prompt. The following sections describe each of these methods.

Using Task Manager to check memory

The Windows Task Manager is a handy utility that can be used for a variety of purposes, including killing problem processes, checking on CPU utilization, memory use, data storage, and network utilization.

To check on total memory usage, use the following steps:

1. Open the by right-clicking the Task Bar and choosing from the pop-up menu.
2. Click on the icon on the left side of the window (See *Figure 20.3*).
3. Select the option in the options list.
4. Beneath the usage graph, the shows the total memory usage.

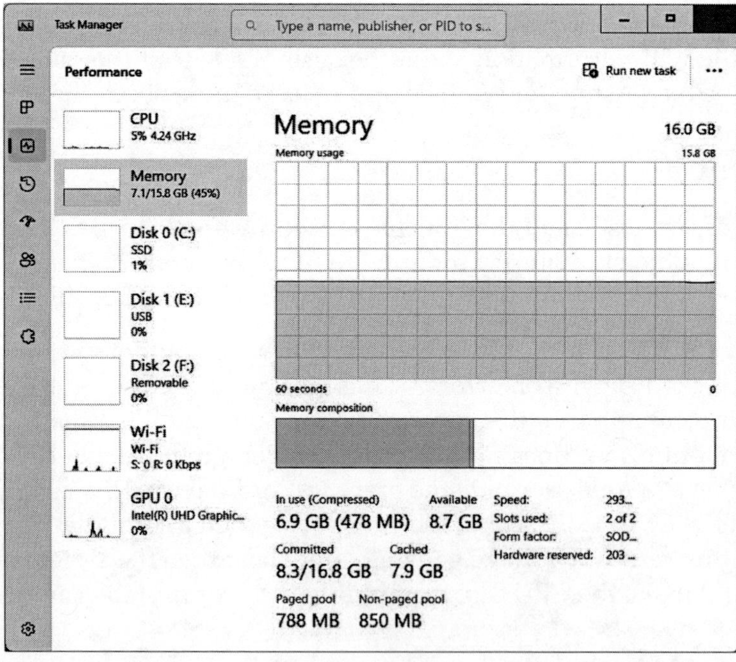

***Figure 20.3:** The Windows Task Manager Performance page showing memory utilization*

To check the memory use of an individual process, select the view and use the column to see the memory usage of each process, along with its CPU, disk, and network usage. Click on the column heading to sort the column high to low or low to high. *Figure 20.4* shows the Processes view of the :

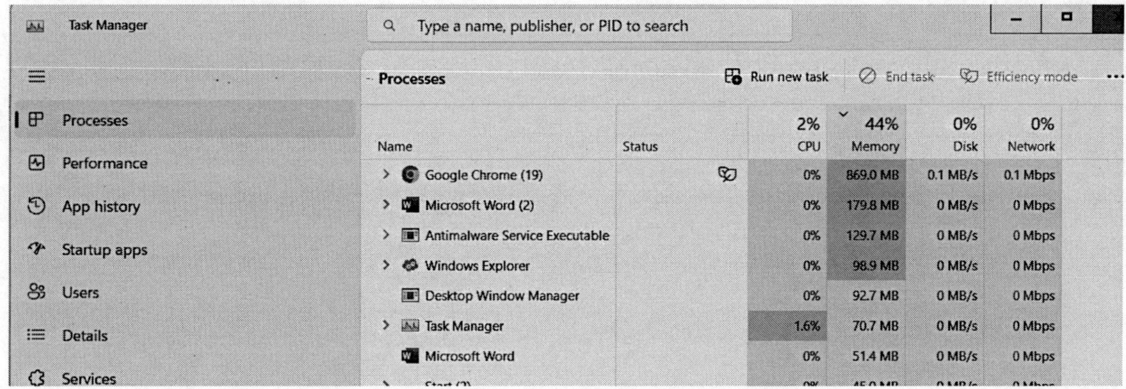

Figure 20.4: Processes view of the Windows Task Manager

Command to check memory utilization

To use the **systeminfo** command at a command prompt in the Windows Terminal, use the following steps:

1. Right-click on the Start icon and select the option on the Power User menu, (see *Figure 20.5*).

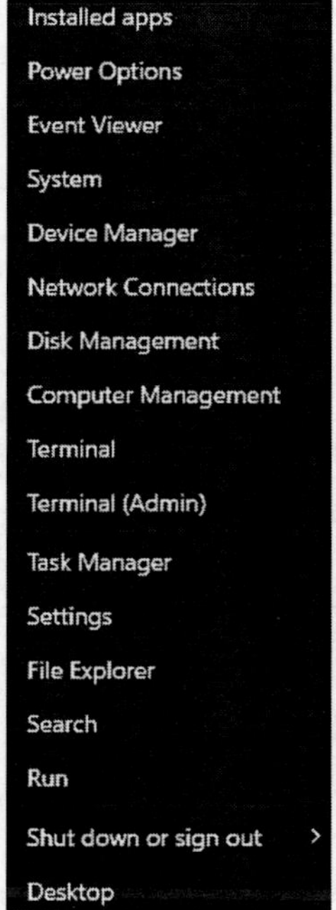

Figure 20.5: The Windows Power User menu

- At the command prompt, enter the following command and press *Enter*.

  systeminfo | find "Available Physical Memory"

- The command returns the available (unallocated) memory. To get the total memory in use, subtract the available memory from the total memory, as shown in *Figure 20.6*:

```
PS C:\> systeminfo | find "Available Physical Memory"
Available Physical Memory: 8,792 MB
PS C:\> |
```

***Figure 20.6:** The **systeminfo** command displays the available memory on a Windows computer*

Another command line entry that will list the top ten memory usage processes by memory use size (see *Figure 20.7*) is the following:

```
Get-WmiObject WIN32_PROCESS | Sort-Object - Property ws -Descending |
        Select-Object -first 10 ProcessID,Name,WS
```

```
PS C:\> Get-WmiObject WIN32_PROCESS | Sort-Object -Property ws -Descending | Select-Object -first 10 ProcessID,Name,WS

ProcessId Name                      WS
--------- ----                      --
     5536 WINWORD.EXE        496996352
    15244 chrome.exe         422739968
     3104 Memory Compression 400986112
    14548 chrome.exe         381337600
     9384 explorer.exe       306405376
     7492 SearchHost.exe     305713152
    14748 chrome.exe         271863808
    15904 chrome.exe         257363968
     4860 MsMpEng.exe        256061440
    17276 chrome.exe         200040448
```

***Figure 20.7:** The PowerShell **Get-WmiObject** cmdlet can be used to display the memory use of processes*

POST errors

The **power-on self-test** (**POST**) process runs almost immediately after a computer is powered on. The POST verifies that the physical devices configured in the BIOS or UEFI are attached, powered, and read for use. POST tests are run independently of the OS. No matter what OS is installed, the hardware and firmware runs a POST process. While the POST is running, a failure caused by a missing device or a misconfiguration can halt the POST and the error detected is signaled.

Most POST systems use audible beep codes to indicate the problem encountered, primarily because the system speaker is the only output device available. The patterns of the beep codes vary by manufacturer of the motherboard and, in some cases, by the developer of the boot firmware and BIOS/UEFI. However, the beep codes generally involve a pattern of long beeps (about two seconds long) and short beeps (about 1 second in length). *Table 20.2* lists some generic POST failure beep codes:

Beep Code	Meaning
1 short	Memory refresh fault
2 shorts	POST fault
4 shorts	System timer fault
5 shorts	CPU fault
8 shorts	Video adapter fault
10 shorts	CMOS fault
1 long, 3 shorts	Memory fault
1 long	POST successful

Table 20.2: *Examples of POST beep codes*

Random lockups

A computer system is locked up or frozen when it does not respond to either the keyboard or the mouse and nothing moves on the display. It is just not working at all. This is a fairly common problem and can happen intermittently on any computer. One of the more common causes for a computer lock up is memory or the lack of available memory to allocate to a process. However, many other components and devices can also cause a system to lock up, including the **power supply unit** (**PSU**), loose power connections, overheating components, dust and debris inside the case, incompatible hardware and software, and out-of-date device drivers. The list of actions that can help to prevent lock ups includes:

- **Update device drivers:** Verify that the device drives for all installed components are up-to-date. Replace any out-of-date or obsolete drivers.
- **Clear temp tiles:** If the space for temporary files fills up, it can cause Windows to freeze up. Regularly clear the temp files or expand its disk space.
- **Modify virtual memory:** The virtual memory settings for a Windows computer should be 1.5 times the size of a computer's RAM. If the setting is selected, clear the selection.
- **System files:** If one or more system files (and there are a bunch) are missing or have been corrupted, Windows will randomly lock up. To check if this could cause

lock ups, run the System File Checker (sfc /SCANNOW), which finds and corrects any system file problems. *Figure 20.8* shows the results of the **`sfc.exe`** command:

```
PS C:\Users\> sfc /scannow

Beginning system scan.  This process will take some time.

Beginning verification phase of system scan.
Verification 100% complete.

Windows Resource Protection found corrupt files and successfully repaired them.
For online repairs, details are included in the CBS log file located at
windir\Logs\CBS\CBS.log. For example C:\Windows\Logs\CBS\CBS.log. For offline
repairs, details are included in the log file provided by the /OFFLOGFILE flag.
```

***Figure 20.8:** The sfc /scannow command results*

- **Faulty memory module:** A faulty memory module or a module that is not properly seated in its expansion slot can cause frequent lockups. If the physical mounting is proper, run a memory check using the Windows **`mdsched.exe`** command. Run this command in the Run box (*Win+R*). When it starts, it offers two options: "" and "." Choose the option desired. The results of the test are displayed after the test is complete (either option). *Figure 20.9* shows the process and results screen for this command:

```
(P) Pause (X) Exit (T) Run standard tests          | Windows Memory Diagnostic

 Test name:          MATS+ (cache disabled)            Pass: 1 Test: 7 of 11
 Test description:   Identifies most basic faults using walking ones
                     and zeroes.
 Pass progress:      |=========|                                          |
 Test progress:      |==========                                          |
 Range progress:     |==============================/                     |

Pass     Test       Cache                       | System memory map
------------------------------------------------|----------------------------
1        Stride6    On      Succeeded           | [00030000 - 0009e800]
1        WMATS+     On      Succeeded           | [00100000 - 00400000]
1        WINVC      On      Succeeded           | [004de000 - dfee0000]
1        MATS+      Off     Active              | [dfee3000 - dfef0000]

Results  Pass    Test        Cache   Address    Expected   Actual
-----------------------------------------------------------------------
62957    1       MATS+       Off     3fcf40a0   ffffffff   ffffefff
62958    1       MATS+       Off     3fcf4080   ffffffff   ffffefff
62959    1       MATS+       Off     3fcf4020   ffffffff   ffffefff
62960    1       MATS+       Off     3fcf4000   ffffffff   ffffefff
```

***Figure 20.9:** The display of the Windows Memory Diagnostic tool*

Run a disk check: This diagnostic tool is executed from the properties dialog box of a disk drive. To run the check, open the **Windows File Explorer** and click on **This PC**. Right-click on the device to be checked and choose **Properties** from the pop-up menu. Select the **Tools** tab and click the **Check** button (see *Figure 20.10*). If there are no issues with the drive, a message will tell you that. Otherwise, the Check will run.

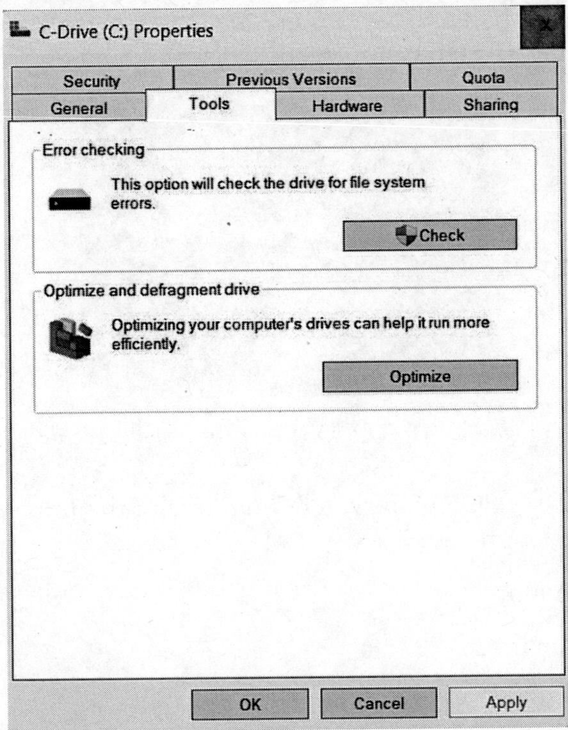

Figure 20.10: *The Properties dialog box and Tools tab for a hard disk drive*

Kernel panic

The equivalent of the BSOD on a UNIX/Linux system is the **kernel panic (KP)**. A KP is issued by the OS kernel if a fatal system error is detected that cannot be recovered or processing continued without an increased risk of data loss. Linux systems have a preliminary event that can precede a full-on KP called a **kernel oops**. If an error condition is detected, but the overall system can continue to run with the problem process stopped, a kernel oops is issued. However, if the condition reoccurs, kills the problem process, or causes some resources to be unavailable, it can become a full kernel panic, which is signaled to the user by flashing the keyboard LEDs.

CMOS battery failure

Complementary metal-oxide semiconductor (CMOS) is a battery-powered RAM chip on computer motherboards that stores about 256 bytes of information that ranges from system time and date to the computer's hardware settings. Like all RAM, CMOS loses the information it stores if the battery that provides its constant power goes dead. The **CMOS**

battery is a coin-sized cell battery (see *Figure 20.11*) that normally lasts up to 10 years, but in some instances, it may need to be replaced depending on how the computer is used.

***Figure 20.11**: A CMOS battery on a motherboard* [2]

On many systems, if the CMOS battery is failing, one of the following messages may be displayed during the boot process:

- CMOS battery failure
- CMOS checksum error
- CMOS read error
- System battery voltage is low

Common symptoms of CMOS failure (battery failure) are a computer having problems booting up, it will not connect to the Internet, device drivers disappearing, external devices stop responding, or the system date and time being incorrect and must be reset frequently. Another not so common problem is a CMOS Checksum error, an incompatibility conflict between the CMOS and BIOS that occurs when the computer is booting. This problem can be resolved by rebooting the computer, flashing a BIOS update, resetting the BIOS configuration, or simply replacing the CMOS battery.

Fault and device indication

Most PCs, notebooks, and laptops display some form of a visual signal or indicator when a problem is detected during the boot sequence in addition to the POST process' beep codes. PC manufacturers often provide details on their websites about their systems' faults and warning LEDs. Typically, LED fault indicators fall into two groups: power button LEDs and diagnostic indicator LEDs. *Figure 20.12* shows a capture of the Dell Technologies' Knowledge Base website showing a few of the LED codes for a particular system:

2. Image courtesy of ASUSTeK Computer Inc.

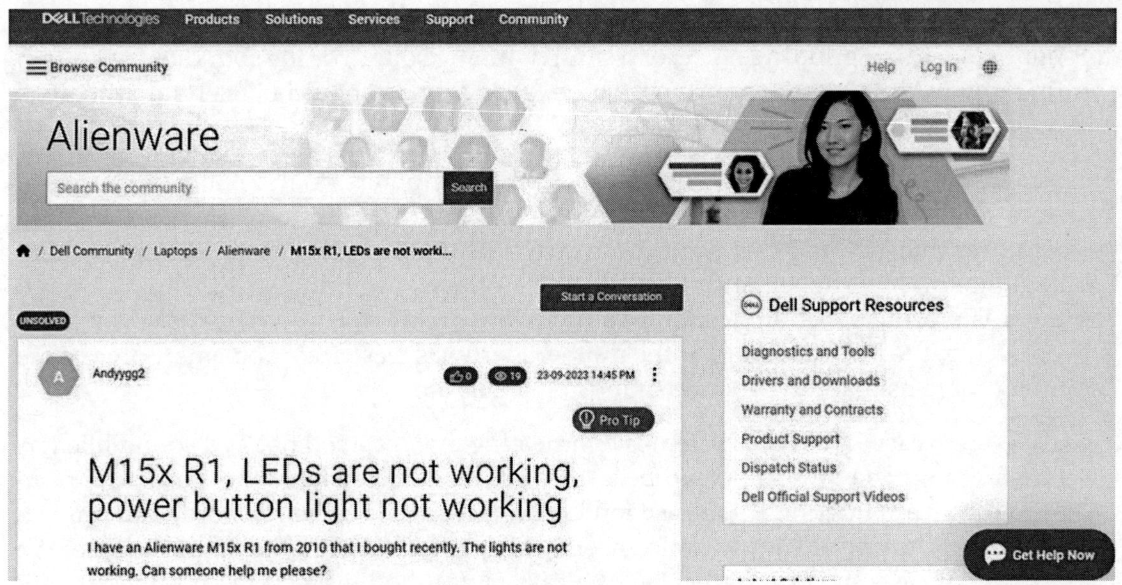

Figure 20.12: Diagnostic LED website for Dell Technologies

Another way that the conditions of a desktop or server computer can be monitored is by installing an LCD either inside the system case or on its exterior. These displays (such as the one shown in *Figure 20.13*) can display information on the condition of the system, including the system operating temperatures and the status of the CPU, GPU, RAM, disk drives, and the PSU:

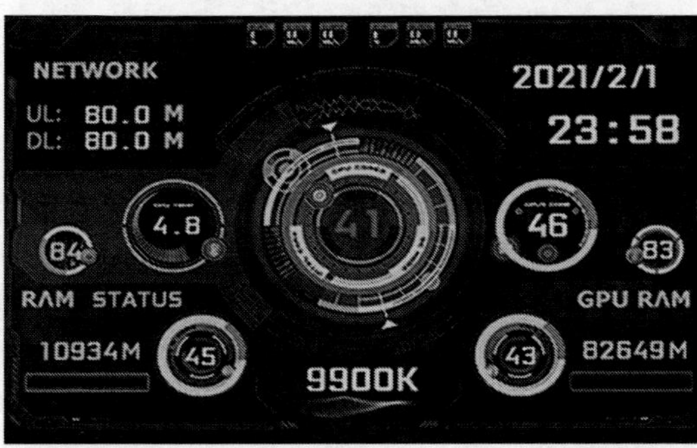

Figure 20.13: An LCD monitor inside a PC system case [3]

Problem sounds and smells

If something does not sound or smell right from a computer, regardless of its size, shape, or model, there is probably something wrong going on with it. Computers have sounds, like the sound of the hard disk, the sound of the cooling fans, and the sounds generated

3. Image courtesy of ASHATA Electronics.

from mouse clicks or touches on icons, plus a few other normal sounds. However, there are sounds, such as a grinding noise, or a sharp whining sound, or the sound of the system shutting down, that are not so normal. These latter sounds should be alerts that there is definitely something wrong.

The same can be said for smells. For the most part, computers do not really have smells. You can smell the case materials and perhaps the odor produced by the operating temperatures, but nothing that should concern a user, unless the smell is of something burning, like plastic, rubber, and other alarming odors. A burning smell coming from a computer is most likely an indication of a hardware problem. It could be that the system is overheating, the PSU is failing, or the motherboard has electrical problems. Some of the common problems that can produce sounds or smells are:

- **System case fan:** If the system is overheating, it may smell hot and sound like it is straining. The problem could be a dirty or clogged case fan, which can also mean a dirty case interior. If the case fan is failing, it needs to be replaced, and if it is a part of the power supply, it also needs to be replaced. Regardless, the inside of the system case must be kept clean, the case fan(s) should be clean and uncluttered, and component assemblies and wiring should be kept clean.

- **Power supply unit:** If the case is clean and clear and the fans are operating as they should, overheating and sluggish performance could be caused by a failing PSU. The number one failing component in a PC is its PSU.

- **CPU fan:** A common cause for system overheating and intermittent performance issues is the cooling system of the CPU. If the CPU has a fan (as many do these days), and the fan is not rotating, clean the fan with a soft brush or compressed air. If that doesn't do the trick, replace it immediately.

- **LCD monitor:** LCD monitors, especially those in an All-in-One PC can produce a burning odor from its filament. If there is a burning smell, the monitor must be replaced.

- **Hard disk drive:** An HDD that is failing can produce grinding or high-pitched noise and perhaps a burning odor. A failing HDD overheats, which causes its components to produce smoke. The drive needs replacement, right after you attempt to create a backup.

If the sound or smell cannot be pinned to a particular component, the best action is to shut the system down and initiate a full troubleshooting procedure to isolate the cause. The problem may be severe enough to call the manufacturer's maintenance service to avoid invalidating the warranty, if applicable.

Misallocated virtual resources

In the context of computing and servers, the term *virtual* has two common meanings, both of which mean the same thing, although they are applied differently. The two virtuals are virtual memory and virtualization, as in virtual machines.

Virtual memory is a portion of a hard disk drive set aside as a temporary storage space to hold idled pages of main memory (RAM) when more space is needed in memory. Virtual memory can cause a computer to run slower because the CPU must wait for data to be swapped out to the hard disk from RAM. Hard disk drives have much slower access and transfer speeds than RAM, which causes the slowness.

A virtualized environment creates virtual machines, several of which can operate on a single computer. Like a physical computer, a needs a sufficient allocation of resources to run its operating system, applications, and services. The allocation of resources, physical or virtual, required depends on the systems running on the VM. Resources are allocated to a VM through reservations, or resource commitments reserved for the VM to use as needed. Common issues with misallocations of resources include:

- A VM is not receiving its full reservation.
- A VM's resource pool limit is too restrictive for its processing demands.
- The physical host on which a VM is running has insufficient resources or a VM's share priority lets other VMs have a greater share of the resources.
- The resources on the host computer are oversubscribed.

Common problem causes

Although the reliability of computing equipment has vastly improved over the years, a computer is still an electronic device with literally hundreds of components all of which are at the mercy of the quality of the electricity they run on. Some of these components are electromechanical, which means in addition to its electronics, they also have moving parts, such as a hard disk drive. Because the environments and conditions in which computers are used are extremely varied, all of the components are stressed, have wear and tear, and deal with vacillating electrical power. The following sections describe the common problems for the major component areas of the hardware on which server software runs.

Power supply unit

A computer does not work at all without a fully functional **power supply unit (PSU).** A computer and its electronics are powered differently than electrical devices. Although a computer plugs into an electrical outlet that provides 110 or 220 volts of **alternating current** (AC) electricity, the internal components of the computer operate on +/- 3.3 volts,

+/- 5 volts, and +/- 12 volts of **direct current** (**DC**) power. It is the job of the PSU to make the conversion from the AC power to the DC power used by the computer's components.

The PSU has the highest failure rate of all the electrical components in a computer. Problems with a PSU can cause serious problems with a computer's other internal components. Troubleshooting a problem related to a faulty PSU is sometimes more difficult to isolate because it could be the source of any electronic problems. Signs that a PSU is faulty or may be failing include:

- Unusual sounds coming from the back of the system case.
- The computer does not power up when the power switch is moved to the on position. Instead, an LED begins flashing on the front or the back of the computer.
- The computer starts up fine, but after a short time, powers itself off.
- The computer powers off suddenly without warning and possibly displays the BSOD.
- The video display is distorted because the PSU's wattage and amperage are too low for graphics card.
- When the computer starts up, the hard disk drive and the cooling system do not power on, and this causes the system to lock up.
- Touching a metal system case causes an electrical shock.

Malfunctioning fans

As odd as it may seem, heat inside a computer's system case can cause the case fan to develop problems. After all, is not that what the fan is about, cooling the system? Yes, but as the temperature inside the case rises, cooling fans run faster to compensate, which may not be enough to cool the system and could damage the fan itself.

Cooling fans

The computer hardware used for servers typically has more than one fan. In fact, there are several different fan applications that could be in place, including:

- PSU fan: Nearly all PSUs include a cooling fan, which is not intended to be a case fan.
- CPU fan: In older systems, a CPU fan was used to cool the heat sink of the CPU to prevent the CPU from overheating. Newer CPU fans incorporate the heat sink and provide more cooling capabilities, as shown in Figure 20.14:

Figure 20.14: *CPU fan assembly* [4]

- Graphics card fan: The fan or fans on a graphics card cool the CPU heat sink and its memory. Figure 20.15 shows a graphics card showing its cooling fans:

Figure 20.15: *A GPU card showing its cooling fans* [5]

- **Chipset fan**: This fan is typically only on the north bridge of a chipset on a motherboard of a computer that is over clocked. On those systems where much of the chipset features are integrated into the processor, this fan is not needed in most cases. *Figure 20.16* shows an example of a chipset fan:

Figure 20.16: *A chipset fan.* [6]

4. Image courtesy of DeepCool Industries Co., Ltd
5. Image courtesy of NVIDIA Corporation
6. Image courtesy of Conrad Electronic International GmbH & CoKG

Common fan issues

The most common problems with the cooling fans inside the system case, regardless of their specific application include obstructions, dust or debris accumulations, poor ventilation, BIOS/UEFI in need of update, and physical damage. A fan will be noisy, erratic, or not working in nearly all these instances.

In addition to poor or erratic power issues, any fan inside the computer case cannot properly cool its component is the case air vents are blocked or clogged with dust or debris. The case air vents provide the input and exhaust of the airflow, which is the general cooling source for everything inside the case. Blocked air vents can increase the operating temperature inside the case, which if excessive could cause heat-related damage or problems.

Overheating issues

The most common cause of overheating in a computer is neglected preventive maintenance. Dust build up on air vents and grills of the system case can block or limit the airflow that should provide cooling for the heat-emitting components inside the case. Heat that builds up beyond its safe operating levels can deteriorate electronic components on the motherboard and installed devices. Dust on electronic components creates an insulating layer that traps heat and blocks the airflow that would help to cool them.

Overheating problems can also be caused by location and the lack of ventilation. A computer, especially a server, should be placed in a well-ventilated space with good airflow. Other factors can include direct sunlight, closeness to exterior windows, or furniture or objects obstructing airflow.

The simple solution to an overheating problem on a computer is to remove or reverse the conditions causing the problem. Clean the inside of the system case with compressed air to blow dust away from any cooling system vents, fans, heat sinks, and air passages. Do not try to blow air from your mouth because the moisture in your breath can cause even more problems. You can vacuum up the dust but be sure to use a vacuum cleaner specifically designed for computer cleaning (one that does not create or emit static electricity).

Heat sink issues

Basically, a heat sink is a metal component that is placed on top of computer chips, such as the CPU, to draw heat away from the chip and dissipate it with a series of fins. Heat sinks can be passive (like the one in *Figure 20.17*) or active. A **passive heat sink** has no moving parts, such as a fan. An **active heat sink** can be combined with a fan or a liquid cooling radiator.

Figure 20.17: *Examples of passive heat sinks.* [7]

An overheating CPU can result from a heat sink that is not properly installed or seated. The process to install a passive heat sink on a CPU is as follows:

- If the heat sink has thermal past pre-applied, remove the plastic covering before installing it. If the heat sink does not have the thermal compound applied, there should be a small packet or tube of the thermal paste.
- A heat sink without thermal paste applied needs the paste applied to either the top of the processor or the bottom of the heat sink. In either case, apply small dabs of the paste to either surface. The paste dabs should be about the size of a rice grain. Place the paste dabs in the corners but closer to the middle of the device.
- If the heat sink has a back plate, install it on the motherboard per its instructions.
- The heat sink must be snuggly attached to the top of the processor and should resist movement with slight pressure. Tighten the mounting screws but not overly tight. Connect the power cord to the CPU fan header and remember to set the BIOS/UEFI settings for it.

Improperly seated expansion cards

Expansion cards are used to add features, functions, and devices to a computer either in addition to or in replacement of elements of its standard configuration. Common expansion cards inserted into a computer are graphics cards, sound cards, network interface cards, and special function cards, like video adapters, FM tuners, TV tuners, and more.

Server and desktop computers commonly have several expansion slots, often two or three different expansion bus standards. Some even include expansion slots of older standards to provide backward compatibility. The expansion bus connects the slots and the inserted cards to the system bus.

A common problem with an expansion card not performing as it should be that the card is not properly installed in the expansion slot. A card of a particular bus standard has a unique

7. Image courtesy of Kimsen Industrial Corporation

edge connection pattern that fits a slot of the same standard. Suppose the edge connections are not completely inserted into the slot or the card is inserted into a different standard. In that case, the card may not work, work intermittently, or may possibly be destroyed.

Another common problem with some expansion cards is *chip creep*. This condition, which is also called *power creep*, is a result of temperature cycles of the metal connectors of the card and the expansion slot. If the cooling in the system case fluctuates, eventually, an expansion card may work its way partially out of the expansion slot, which can either stop the card's functions altogether. To resolve this issue, during preventive maintenance on the interior of a system case, all expansion cards should be checked for proper installation.

An expansion card that has functioned correctly starts to have problems. The likely causes are heat and power. Overheating damages components on the card, and a failing PSU can cause damage to the circuits on the card. On some systems, a conflict can exist between an expansion card and the motherboard and chipset that have the same function as the card.

Component incompatibility

In instances where several components of a computer are replaced, such as the motherboard, PSU, disk drives, and perhaps the CPU, or these components are used to build a PC; there is the chance that some of the components may not be compatible with each other. In most cases, the root of the problem is the motherboard and typically the CPU. Not all CPUs are compatible with all motherboards. Many components, including the CPU, have specific requirements, characteristics, and compatibilities that will work with only certain other devices. For example, an Intel CPU will not fit into an AMD CPU socket and motherboard.

The motherboard can also limit the options for memory, PSU, expansion cards, and perhaps the disk drives. Whenever the motherboard is replaced or installed as a part of a new computer system, its specifications and requirements must be carefully checked before either choosing it or the other components. Some of the things to verify when replacing parts in an existing system or building a new computer system are:

- The motherboard, CPU, and CPU socket are compatible.
- The RAM modules are compatible with the motherboard, CPU, and bus speeds.
- The motherboard supports the graphics card desired.
- The form factor, size, and dimensions of the system case are compatible with the components to be installed.
- The PSU provides sufficient voltage and amperage for the internal components and the connectors necessary to provide power to the devices installed inside the system case.

Backplane failure

A backplane expansion card typically contains either a number of expansion slots of one or more standards. Backplanes are used to expand the capabilities of a computer system by adding additional expansion slots or device connections to develop computer systems. *Figure 20.18* shows an example of a backplane card:

Figure 20.18: An 8-slot single segment ISA passive backplane [8]

Two types of backplanes can be added to a computer: passive and active. The difference is that a passive backplane does not have active bus circuitry and an active backplane buffers data for the bus. Passive backplane are generally more reliable due to less complicated structures. However, either backplane type can fail on the whole if the backplane's card connectors are damaged or become corroded. Individual slots on the backplane can suffer the same problem if the connection slots or the expansion card connectors are damaged.

Firmware incompatibility

In any computer, notebook, tablet, or even smartphone, there is more than one device or component that has firmware to start it up, set its configuration, and perhaps guide its operations. When we talk about firmware, there is a need to be somewhat specific. On most electronic devices that have firmware, there is typically not much that can physically change, so the only element that requires, if ever, an update is the firmware. In these instances, the firmware is by default, compatible with the device.

Computers of any size or style can develop incompatibilities in a variety of ways. It is common for the BIOS/UEFI configuration settings to be incompatible on some overclocked systems, especially those with non-standard or non-conforming devices installed. In many cases, a setting in the BIOS/UEFI may be incompatible with the hardware it was intended to enable. In these situations, the boot process may fail to complete the POST process.

Incompatibility problems can also be caused by out-of-date firmware. The BIOS/UEFI system is firmware that can be reinstalled, updated, or replaced. If newly installed devices are causing unexpected problems, it could be time for an update. On the other hand, it could be time to reset the BIOS/UEFI settings back to their defaults and reset the configuration. Many motherboards include a BIOS reset button on their I/O panels, but regardless, refer to the motherboard documentation for the specific process for resetting their firmware.

Windows event logs

When anything that should be recorded happens on a Windows system, such as a system action or error, a hardware action, a security event, or an application issue, the Windows OS

8. Image courtesy of Advantech Co., Ltd.

records it in a log file. The entries in the various log files provide a detailed chronological record of these events. The log files are valuable records that an administrator can use to determine the cause or source of a system issue.

The Windows OS maintains the following log files by default, as can also be seen in *Figure 20.19*:

- Application: The entries in this log file are related to any application or third-party utilities installed on a local computer. Any major problem with an application, such as I/O errors or crashing, is recorded in this log.
- Security: The entries in this log file are created when an event defined in the OS audit policies occurs, such as failed login attempts, resource accesses, and authentication actions.
- Setup: The entries in this log file relate to the control of Active Directory activities on domain controllers.
- System: The entries in this log file relate to events associated with the Windows OS.
- Forwarded events: The entries in this log file relate to actions on other network devices that are being recorded on a computer maintaining multiple log files.

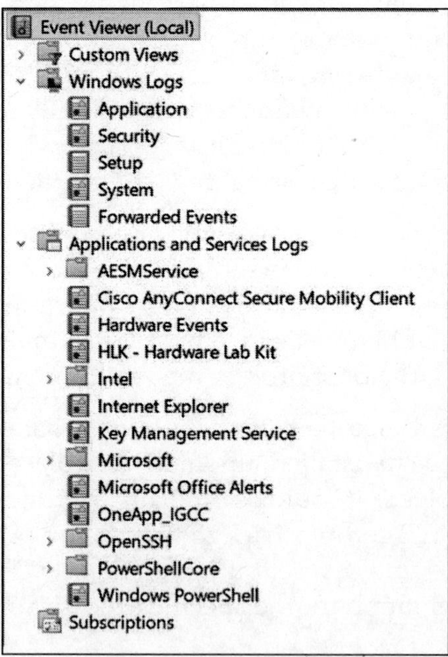

Figure 20.19: *The log files maintained by the Windows OS shown in the Event Viewer*

Log file entries are relatively uniform in their formatting. In general, a log file entry contains:

- **Level:** This indicates the severity of an event. The level could be one of the following:
    - **Information:** These events are recorded as non-issues.
    - **Verbose:** These events are recorded to record the successes or progress of a particular action.
    - **Warning:** These entries are intended to flag events that indicate a potential issue or something that should be reviewed.
    - **Critical:** These events indicated serious system problems that should be acted upon immediately.
- **Date and Time:** The date and time of the event.
- **Source:** The program, device, or component associated with the event.
- **Event ID:** An identification number that indicates the type of event that occurred. For example, in *Figure 20.20*, the Error event shown has an event ID of 10010, which indicates that an application or component failed to register with the **Distributed Component Object Model** (**DCOM**) and could not communicate.

System Number of events: 11,777

Level	Date and Time	Source	Event ID	Task Category
Information	5/22/2023 6:59:09 AM	Service Control Manager	7040	None
Information	5/22/2023 6:55:05 AM	HttpService	113	HTTP Configuration Property Trace Task
Information	5/22/2023 6:55:05 AM	HttpService	114	HTTP Configuration Property Trace Task
Information	5/22/2023 6:55:05 AM	HttpService	113	HTTP Configuration Property Trace Task
Information	5/22/2023 6:55:05 AM	HttpService	114	HTTP Configuration Property Trace Task
Information	5/22/2023 6:54:41 AM	HttpService	113	HTTP Configuration Property Trace Task
Information	5/22/2023 6:54:41 AM	HttpService	114	HTTP Configuration Property Trace Task
Information	5/22/2023 6:54:41 AM	HttpService	113	HTTP Configuration Property Trace Task
Error	5/22/2023 6:50:56 AM	DistributedCOM	10010	None
Information	5/22/2023 6:50:26 AM	Kernel-General	16	None
Information	5/22/2023 6:49:14 AM	Kernel-General	16	None
Warning	5/22/2023 6:49:09 AM	Netwtw10	6062	None
Information	5/22/2023 6:49:08 AM	Power-Troubleshooter	1	None
Information	5/22/2023 6:49:07 AM	Winlogon	7001	(1101)
Information	5/22/2023 6:49:07 AM	Kernel-Power	566	(268)
Information	5/22/2023 6:49:07 AM	Kernel-Power	566	(268)

***Figure 20.20:** A sampling of the log entries in the System log file*

Tip: For more information on the Windows Event ID codes, go to

https://www.windows-security.org/windows-event-ids

Note: The event logs can be viewed using the Windows Event Viewer from the Power User menu, by running eventvwr in the Run box (Win+R) or running wevtutil from a command line.

Hardware diagnostics

On a Windows system, a built-in set of tools, the Troubleshooter utilities, can be used to identify various system and hardware problems. To run the troubleshooter for a particular device:

1. Select the **Settings** option from the **Power User** menu (right-click the Start icon)
2. Scroll down in the options list and select **Troubleshoot**.
3. Click on **Other troubleshooters**.
4. Pick the component or device you wish to troubleshoot from the list provided, as shown in *Figure 20.21*:

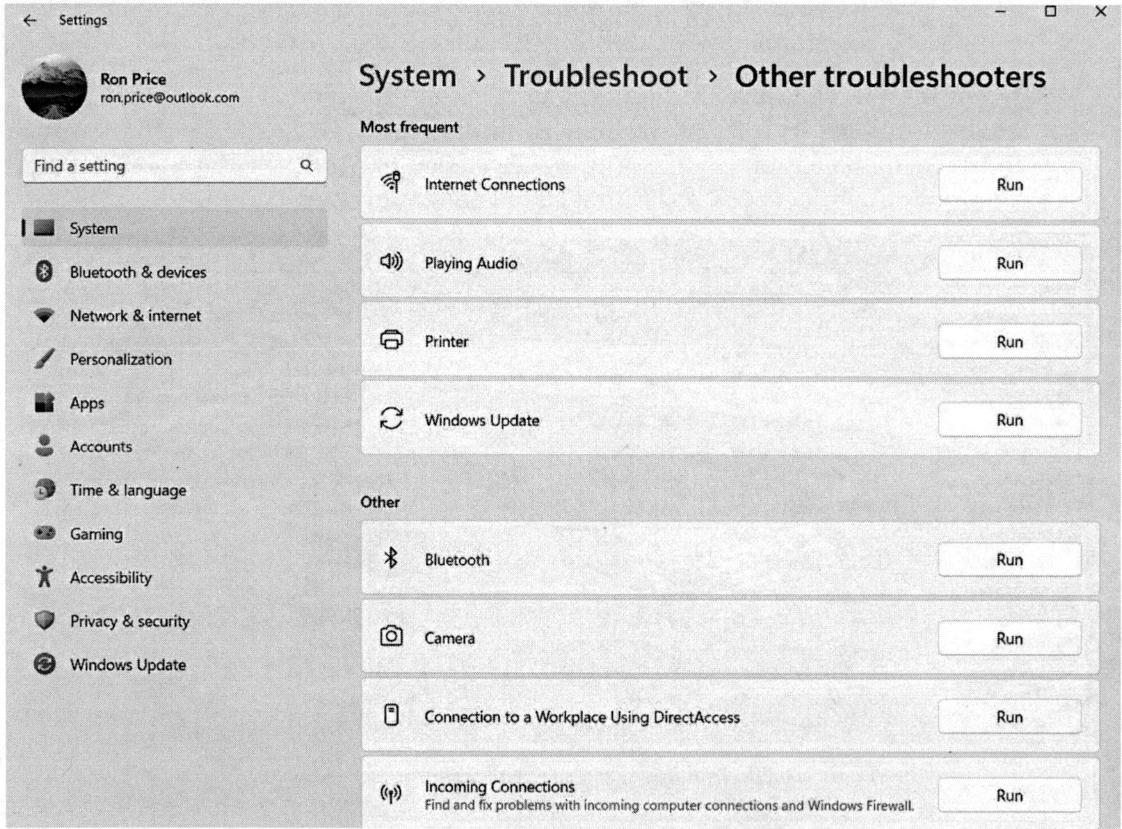

***Figure 20.21**: The Other troubleshooters page*

Electrostatic discharge equipment

Static electricity is a fixed charge that can occur from friction, such as when two different materials are rubbed together. Friction causes one of the materials to become positively charged and the other becomes negatively charged. It is the positively charged material that has an electrostatic charge that transfers to other materials, such as door knobs, electronic components, and humans, on contact. This transfer is **electrostatic discharge (ESD)**. An example of static electricity and ESD is the charge that is generated when you walk on carpets, work in an ungrounded area with low humidity, or perhaps petting a dog or cat. If the next thing touched is something metal, like a door knob, you will be electrically shocked with around 3,000 volts of ESD.

The components on a motherboard run on ± 3, ± 5, or ± 12 volts of DC electricity. A human will not feel an ESD that is less than 2,500 volts and will only see a blue spark from an ESD when the discharge is more than 20,000 volts. As little as 30 volts of ESD is enough to damage or destroy the electronic components of a computer.

The electronic components in a computer run on 3 to 5 volts of electricity and, for the most part, as little as 30 volts of ESD can damage or destroy them. Consider that you cannot feel ESD of less than 2,500 volts and that the blue spark of ESD is only visible when a discharge of 20,000 volts or more is involved. When an ungrounded technician touches any electronic component inside a computer, it is likely that ESD with enough voltage to cause damage can happen without him or her feeling a shock.

When working in or around computer systems, and especially inside the system case, certain precautions can be taken to prevent damage from ESD. Using an anti-static wrist strap, a work area grounding mat on the workbench surface, or a grounded workbench can greatly reduce the risk of ESD. However, even with anti-static devices in use, some ESD preventive practices can also be used:

- **Grounding:** Before working inside a system case, touch and continue to be in contact with an unpainted metal surface of the computer's chassis or the housing of the power supply unit.
- **Standing:** Always stand when working inside the system case. Sitting on a chair can generate static.
- **Clothing:** Do not wear fabrics that conduct electrical charges, such as wool, and do not wear jewelry on your hands or body.
- **Weather:** Do not work on a computer if there is an electrical storm in the area.

As a general rule, at the least wear an anti-static ESD wrist strap, use an anti-static mat under the computer case, and keep a hand or forearm in contact with the computer's inner chassis when touching any of the computer's electronic components. Refer to the following figure:

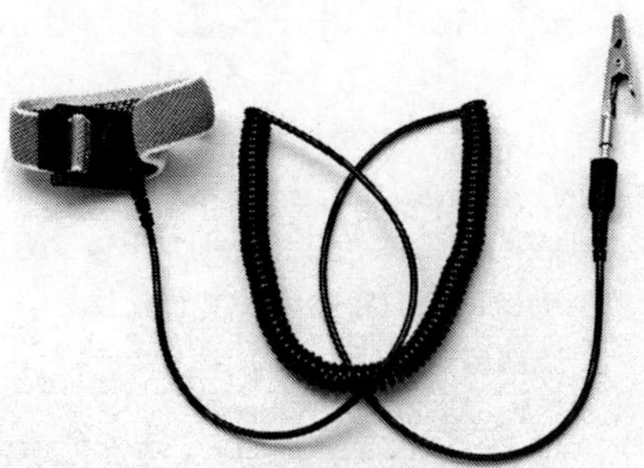

Figure 20.22: Anti-static wrist strap protects against ESD [9]

Conclusion

Hardware components problems are, at best, disruptive but can also be destructive. A technician's ability to troubleshoot, resolve, and document hardware issues can directly affect the amount of disruption or damage a hardware issue may cause. The technician's knowledge and skills, measured by the Server+ exam, are applied to resolve, repair, or mitigate hardware problems. In this chapter, we looked at common hardware problems that can occur on server hardware, and the problem scenarios you are likely to encounter on the Server+ exam and on the job.

In the next chapter, we will look at the common problems in data storage systems.

Points to remember

- Computer hardware problems are usually caused by a fault in an electrical or electronic component, or setup, installation, or configuration of a device.
- The two categories of failures on a computer system are, soft and hard failures.
- A stop error code message screen, BSOD, informs a user of a critical error with a system.
- The PSOD shows up only on systems running the VMkernal on a VMware ESX/ESXI host computer.
- Memory utilization should be monitored. On a Windows system, use Task Manager or the **`systeminfo`** command.
- POST runs after a computer is powered on and verifies that the physical devices configured in the BIOS or UEFI are attached, powered, and ready for use. POST uses audible beep codes to indicate a problem.
- A common cause for a computer lock up is the lack of available memory to allocate to a process. Other causes for a system lock up are PSU, loose connections,

9. Image courtesy of Carl Berkeley on Flickr.com

overheating, case debris, incompatible hardware and software, and out-of-date device drivers.

- On a UNIX/Linux system, a **kernel panic** (**KP**) is the equivalent of a BSOD.
- CMOS stores information such as system time and date and a computer's hardware settings.
- LED fault indicators groups are power button LEDs and diagnostic indicator LEDs.
- Virtual memory is space set aside on a disk drive for temporary storage to hold idled pages of RAM when more space is needed.
- A **virtual machine** (**VM**) needs sufficient resources to run its operating system, applications, and services.
- Major hardware components with common problems include the PSU, cooling fans, overheating motherboard components, expansion cards, incompatible hardware, backplanes, and firmware.
- System actions or errors, hardware actions, security events, and application issues are recorded by the Windows OS in its log files, which are viewed using the Event Viewer.
- On a Windows system, the Troubleshooter utilities are used to identify a variety of system and hardware problems.
- ESD is a fixed charge that can damage internal components of a computer when transferred from a human to its electronics.

Chapter 21
Storage Issues

Introduction

Unfortunately, data storage technologies that can withstand corruption, accidental or malicious erasure, or physical damage do not exist, so far. Disks, solid-state electronics, tape, and optical storage devices can and do have problems. This chapter looks at data storage devices, their issues and causes, and the processes used to detect them that you are likely to encounter on the Server+ exam.

Structure

The chapter covers the following topics:

- Common storage device problems
- Causes of common problems
- Causes of common storage problems

Objective

By the end of this chapter, you will be able to identify and describe the sub-objectives of the following Server+ examination objective: *Given a scenario, troubleshoot storage problems.*

Common storage device problems

Data storage devices store an organization's most valuable asset (data), which we hope is a reliable and safe electromagnetic, optical, or electronic device. This device is subject to power issues, viruses, malware, physical damage, and software errors, not to mention humans. The result is that despite our best intentions and actions, storage devices can have problems.

Note: Although there are several types of large-capacity data storage devices used, such as hard disk drives (HDD), solid-state drives (SSD), magnetic tape, optical discs, and flash drives, with desktops, notebooks, and server computers, the term "disk drive" is used throughout this chapter to represent any and all of these devices.

Table 21.1 lists some general failure causes of data storage devices you should know for the Server+ exam:

Problem	Cause	Recovery
Deleted files, formatted drive	Human error	Good
Database or file corrupted or missing	Malware, software errors	Good
Filesystem corrupted	Media logical fault	Good
Corrupted data	Mechanical failure or malfunction	Fair to Poor
Cannot access disk drive or garbled data	Media physical fault – heads, spindle motor, actuator	Fair to Good
Device water damaged	Natural disaster	Fair
Damaged device	External drive or laptop computer dropped	Fair
Flash media fails	Flash device overwrite limit exceeded*	Fair
Stored data garbled	Magnetic tape media degradation, failure, or damage*	Fair
Stored data unreadable	CD/DVD medium failure*	Poor
The medium in some data storage units, such as flash, tape, and optical, wears out and degrades over time to the point that anything stored on the medium becomes garbled, unreadable, or not there at all.		

***Table 21.1**: Common failure causes of data storage media*

Common disk drive problems

It can be difficult to identify some disk drive problems. A failing disk drive can exhibit symptoms similar to a malware attack, memory problems, a failing power supply, or appear generally slow, such as when too many downloads are running simultaneously. When dealing with a suspected disk drive, some of the problems you should look for are as follows:

- **Operating system not found:** During the startup process, the BIOS/UEFI loads the **operating system (OS)** kernel from a disk drive into memory to start the system. If the OS is not found or is corrupted, this error occurs, indicating three possible causes: a serious BIOS/UEFI error, a faulty disk drive, or a corrupt or missing **Master Boot Record (MBR) or GUID Partition Table (GPT)**.
- **Slow file access:** There are several reasons why a drive can run slower than usual when accessing, reading, writing, or transferring data to memory, including:
    - **Lack of sufficient space:** On Windows systems, this condition is usually warned with an error message display, stating that a given disk drive is running out of disk space, as shown in *Figure 21.1*. Some processes that use secondary storage cannot execute properly if there is not enough disk space available for their needs.

Figure 21.1: *Windows low disk space warning box*

    - **Corrupted data:** Corrupted data on a disk drive could cause slow data transfers. If corrupted data is suspected or to troubleshoot the slow performance, open the **Properties** dialog box for the drive and on the Toolstab, click on the **Check** button to check for corrupt data. Refer to the following figure:

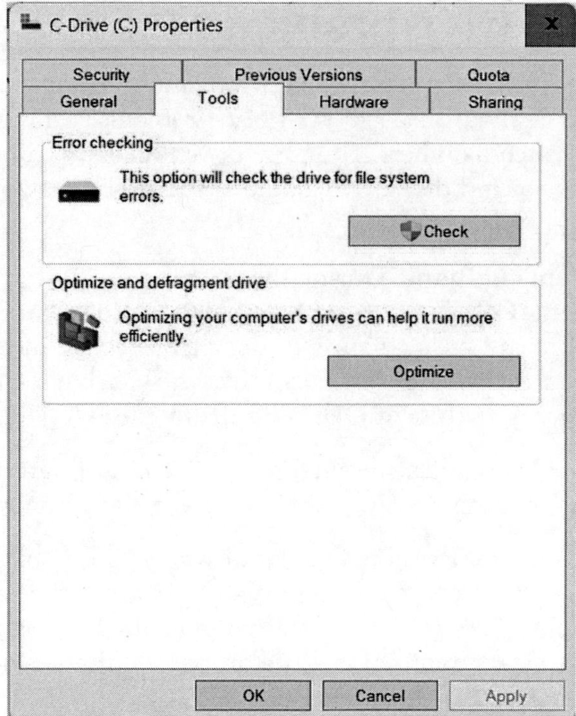

Figure 21.2: Windows Properties dialog box and Tools tab

- **File/data/object unavailable:** There are several possible causes for this problem, such as:
    - **Automatic OS updates:** Automatically downloaded and applied upgrades or fixes may remove desktop files or installed applications, depending on their storage locations.
    - **Malware/virus:** Malicious software can delete or hide systems, application, or personal files.
    - **User rights:** Users with multiple user credentials may log into a system with different credentials, each of which may or may not have permissions or rights to a given folder or file.
    - **Disk drive failing:** The disk drive may be logically or mechanically failing. Always assume this to be true and create a backup immediately.
- **Disk drive logical problems:** There are several possible causes why you may not be able to access a file system, file, or data:
    - **Drive letter missing:** The drive designation (such as "C:") is missing from a disk drive partition. This may be the result of a virus or an inadvertent user error.

- **Hidden partition:** A user can hide a partition to protect personal or sensitive files, and to access its contents, the file system must be unhidden.
- **Partition inaccessible:** There are three possible causes for this condition which are:
    - The user access permissions of a partition are corrupted.
    - The OS detected an error in the **cyclic redundancy check (CRC).**
    - The **Master File Table (MFT)** or the **File Allocation Table (FAT)** is corrupt.
- **RAW partition:** A RAW partition is not formatted as a standard partition, like an NTFS, ext4, or others. What was previously a formatted filesystem can become a RAW partition through malware or a failure during its formatting.
- **Unallocated partition:** An electrical problem, such as a power surge could damage the logical partitioning of a disk drive and change a partition to unallocated.

- **Backup/restore problems:** Backup media can fail or become damaged, such as when the power fails, or another event causes an interruption in the backup process. Unfortunately, a failed backup may not be discovered until it is needed to restore files.
- **Cache failure:** Caching, here, refers to **disk cache** (disk buffer or cache buffer), which is a small amount of reserved space on a disk drive. When the drive is busy, the disk cache receives and holds data until the read/write operations are available. Disk cache failure can be the result of a power failure, or any sudden system stop error, like kernel panic on a Linux or Mac OS system or the BSOD on a Windows system. When a disk cache error occurs, the cache empties, and the data is lost.
- **Multiple disk drive failure:** There are two possible causes for this error condition: the failure of individual disk drives one-at-a-time in series; or an array of disk drives, such as RAID, NAS, or SAN, all failing at once. In most cases, the source of the problem is the power supply.
- **Status/error lights**: Most rackmount and tower servers have LED lights on their front panels to indicate the activity or anror status of the disk drives. Disk drive caddies and multiple drive cages for NAS or SAN, have LEDs to provide the status of each bay independently. Table 21.2 shows a sampling of these LED light patterns and their meanings.

Pattern	Color	Meaning
Off	-	Empty slot
Steady	Green	Online
Flashing slow	Green	Drive administration in progress
Flashing fast	Yellow	Drive has failed
Flashing very slow	Alternating Green/Yellow	Drive failure imminent

Table 21.2: *Common disk drive status light colors, patterns, and meanings*

Causes of common problems

Finding the cause of a device problem involves identifying a set of symptoms related to a common system problem. Fortunately, on a storage device, there are a limited number of things that can go wrong. This section looks at common storage device problems you should expect to see both on the Server+ certification exam and on the job.

Virtual memory problems

Swap files, page files, and scratch files are other names for what is generally known as **virtual memory (VM)** management. **Swap files**, the most commonly used name, are system files used as temporary storage on disk drives for memory pages swapped out of RAM when additional memory space is required. A swap or scratch space can be an entire disk drive, a partition, or a large file space. While swap files, or virtual memory, provides many advantages to the user, they can also have a few problems, such as:

- **System slowdowns:** If the configuration of the swap space is too small or too large, the time required to swap out memory pages can slow other processes. Disk drives are much slower than RAM.
- **Low virtual memory:** The Windows system can sense when additional virtual memory is required to prevent thrashing (excessive swapping of memory pages) and display a message like "Your system is low on virtual memory. Windows is increasing the size of your virtual memory paging file." If this happens, you should check the virtual memory settings to review the changes.
- **Out of virtual memory:** In this situation, Windows displays the message "Out of Virtual Memory: Your system is low on virtual memory. To ensure that Windows runs properly, increase the size of your virtual memory paging file." Access the virtual memory settings and increase the size of the virtual memory allocation.

Media failures

The storage medium of any data storage device is where the data is actually stored. This medium is encased in a chassis, inside an enclosure, or embedded in a multilayer unit. We have to trust that it will remain safe, sound, and without flaws. However, that is not always the situation.

Hard disk media

Although it is encased in what looks like a rugged metal case, a hard disk drive is a relatively fragile device. Its internal components operate extremely close together at high speeds. Any shock or sudden jolt to the drive or the system in which it is installed, can cause damage to the internal disk platters and read/write heads. A read/write head that contacts the disk surface can scratch the ferrous oxide material on the platter and corrupt or destroy any data in that area.

A common disk medium failure is caused by bad sectors appearing on the device. There are two types of bad sectors:

- **Physical bad sectors:** This type of bad disk sector is caused by the read/write head contacting the disk medium or by a contaminant inside the disk's housing, such as dust, hair, and so on, which is rare. **Physical bad sectors** cannot be used and are not usually repairable.
- **Logical bad sectors:** Unlike a physical bad sector, logical or soft bad sectors are accessible but can cause I/O problems, such as increased access latency or read errors. Logical bad sectors are repairable, typically with system utilities. However, if these tools are not sufficient to repair the problems, low-level formatting using tools provided by the device manufacturer can be used to reset the whole device, including any bad sectors.

SSD media

An advantage of an SSD over a hard disk drive is its lack of moving parts, which eliminates head crashes, vibration, overheating, and contaminant problems. An SSD is an electronic device with an error-free storage medium, although its electronics can be its weakness. Capacitors, circuits, and their power source can fail and if this happens, the SSD fails as well.

SSD drives do not have bad sector problems like a hard disk, but they can have bad blocks. Here are a few of the symptoms to look for:

- Writes to or reads from the storage medium fail.
- I/O intensive applications freeze up.
- System errors occur when copying or moving files.
- Longer than normal time is required to access larger files.

Magnetic tape media

Magnetic tape is one of the most commonly used backup media. A backup tape must be reliable because when it is needed for restoring data; it is an essential asset. Mag tape (as it is commonly referred to) can have problems though. Here are the common issues you may see on the Server+ exam:

- **Human errors:** Technicians and system administrators often cause problems with magnetic tape. Forgetting to change or load a tape, using the wrong tape for a cycle, using a tape beyond its service life, and improperly storing tapes are only some of the problems a human can cause.
- **Script errors:** Instead of using a third-party backup application, some organizations use a system script to automate the creation of their backups. Errors in the script statements, SAN or NAS addressing errors, or folders or files missing or not available, can result in incomplete backups that may not restore the system completely if needed.
- **Hardware errors:** Tape drives and magnetic tape media can and do fail. A tape drive issue can affect the spooling of the tape medium, which can stretch, tear, or unravel the tape, usually outside the cartridge. Disk drive read errors can cause missing or corrupted data on the backup media as well.

Causes of common storage problems

Although we have discussed a few causes for storage device problems above, let us focus now on specific causes of specific device or component failures. We have categorized the problem causes into four groups: drive and connector failures, controller and cache failures, and RAID and array failures.

Disk space utilization

Running out of data storage space on a disk drive can be a major problem, especially if it occurs when a critical application is updating essential files. The following are some of the disk space issues related to the utilization of data storage space.

- **Incorrect disk space reports:** Several system files, typically hidden, can take up a considerable amount of disk space but are not included in the calculation of the amount of free disk space available. Some of these files and objects are:
    - **System restore points:** The Windows System Restore tool can take up a large amount of free space to create restore points. The problem is that old restore points are not removed when new ones are created.
    - **System bugs:** A bug in the system maintenance process causes the free space to be estimated incorrectly. This problem can be fixed by running the

System Maintenance Troubleshooter. Another bug, affecting only version 1803 (Windows 10) causes the free space to be reported incorrectly.

 - **Hidden files:** Windows may have created large hidden files in one version that were not removed when a newer version is installed. Unfortunately, a third-party disk maintenance utility is required to track these files down.

Drive and connector failures

A storage device problem is possible at any point in the device's installed life. Installing a disk drive can introduce problems that are not immediately noticeable and can grow into serious issues. Even in normal usage, several problems can cause a storage device to become unavailable, perform erratically, or fail altogether. The following sections detail a few of these problems.

Disk drive problems

Beyond human error, power, physical damage, and a few other issues, disk drive problems can cause issues with the OS, application software, and any process that interacts with a storage device. The causes for some of these problems are:

- **Corrupt or missing MBR:** If the MBR on the boot disk is corrupted or missing, the boot process ignores the drive and moves to the next boot device listed in the BIOS/UEFI configuration settings. An MBR can be missing or corrupted by malware, a process overwrote it, or the disk drive physically or logically losing the clusters that included the MBR or the disk drive completely failed.

- **Corrupt filesystem table:** The MBR contains a filesystem table and an MFT or GPT, which describes the logical partitions on a disk. *Table 21.3* shows the contents of a BIOS MBR's filesystem table. Any damage to an MBR would likely also affect the filesystem table:

Byte	Length (Bytes)	Contents
0	1	Active boot indicator
1	3	Cylinder-Head-Sector (CHS) starting values
4	1	Partition Type
5	3	CHS ending values
8	4	First sector
12	4	Partition size in sectors

Table 21.3: The contents of the 16-byte filesystem table entry

- **Insufficient disk space:** A disk drive can have two partition types: a system partition and one or more data partitions. The system partition holds the OS, commonly designated as the C: drive. A data partition can store anything else and be designated with any other alphabetic letter, such as D, E, F, etc. Each of the data partitions should be thought of as an independent device with a fixed size. If a partition fills up, the OS will display "insufficient disk space." This warning, which is common to all operating systems, is an alert that the size of a partition may be incorrect.

Cable and connector problems

In most server rooms or data centers, rackmount disks and disk arrays connect to a network through either an Ethernet or **Serial Attached SCSI (SAS)** connector. Standalone servers, whether free-standing (tower) or rack-mounted, generally have an onboard disk drive inside the system case and may also connect to a SAN or NAS system on a network. Regardless of how a computer connects to its storage drives, problems can occur with the connectors and the cabling. The causes of these problems tend to be the same and can include:

- **Configuration issues:** If a server is not seeing a storage device, the problem can be either a BIOS/UEFI configuration setting is incorrect or a connector problem (see the next bulleted item). Boot into the BIOS/UEFI and correct the disk drive settings.
- **Connector issues:** An RJ-45 jack fits into its port in only one way. If this Ethernet connection is used, ensure that the jack is snuggly in the connection. If an SAS connection is in use, it must be oriented correctly for the connection to be made. As shown in *Figure 21.3*, the tab (typically a blue tab), item 1 in the drawing, should be on the top of the connector. The SAS cable and connector (2) is pushed into the port (3) until a click is heard or felt. A loose or not completely seated connection acts as no connection.

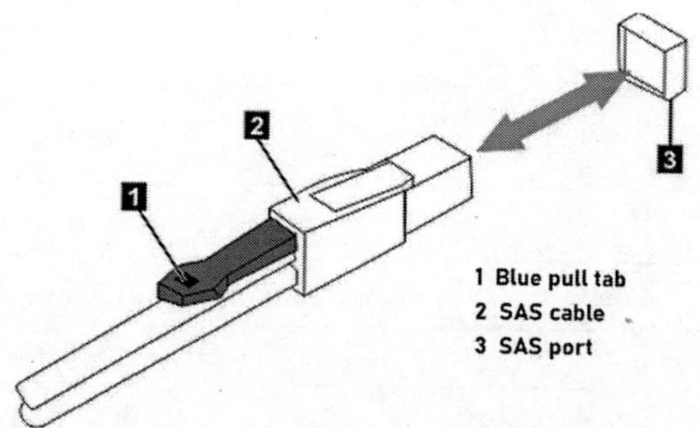

***Figure 21.3:** The orientation and connection of an SAS connector* [1]

- **Cable issues:** As the interior of a computer's case heats up and cools down as it operates and shuts down, respectively, a cable's contacts can oilcan (wiggle) itself out of a connector. A cable with faults, cuts, or other damage can cause intermittent problems.

1. **Image courtesy of IBM Corp.**

- **Improper termination:** This issue is associated with SCSI and SAS devices and the "chain" that interconnects them. To prevent a signal from bouncing back onto the chain and creating "ghost devices," properly terminate each end of a SCSI and SAS chain.
- **SATA connectors:** There are multiple **Serial Advanced Technology Attachment (SATA)** drive standards. To add to the confusion, there is also a **Parallel ATA (PATA)** drive. Each of the SATA and PATA drive standards uses a unique connector. The good news is that all the SATA connectors, regardless of version, are interchangeable. However, you should match the cables to the specific drive manufacturer and model. The cabling should not be more than one meter in length to avoid intermittent problems, and like all connections, make sure that they are clean and snugly inserted.

Storage system issues

Data storage device failures are in one of two general problem types: software-caused failures and hardware-based failures.

Software-caused failures

Data on a storage device (that is, data-at-rest) can be affected by a variety of software-related factors that may alter its quality, usability, and availability. Common software-caused or logical data issues include:

- **Formatting:** Formatting a disk drive deletes its partition and filesystem tables and the file location information. The data itself remains intact, but accessing it is difficult since, in effect, we lost the map.
- **Deleted data:** A file, folder, or filesystem deleted by a user, whether the action was intentional, remains on the storage medium, and the data is recoverable. Deleting a filesystem removes the file indexing used to find and access a folder or file; in most cases, this is also recoverable.
- **Corrupted data:** Data can be corrupted, which means that it no longer is the same data and may be unintelligible. This can be caused by malware, or just plain bad programming, and hardware issues, like a head crash. In most cases, the data must be restored from a backup.
- **Hard disk controller:** The controller is an embedded system on a disk drive that facilitates communication with the motherboard, which then converts the transmitted data and passes it on to the CPU. If the disk controller fails, the disk drive is unable to communicate with the system and will not be seen by the POST or boot process. The drive may spin up, but an error about the boot device not found will be indicated.

Hardware-based issues

Hardware or mechanical problems of disk drives most commonly occur during the boot and startup processes. You should expect to see questions on the Server+ exam regarding hardware-related disk drive problems and their effect on data stored on the drive, including questions about:

- **Host bus adapter (HBA) failure:** The HBA connects computers with a **fiber channel** (FC) SAN, NAS, RAID, or an on-board data storage device. An HBA is similar to a network adapter in that it connects the data storage system to a server or host. The common problems related to an HBA are caused by improper setup and configuration during installation, a failed component on the HBA board, or the failure of a storage system's controller. Some of the more common HBA problems are:
    - **Incorrect HBA for the OS:** HBAs are configured to work with specific operating systems. The HBA for one OS may not work with even another version of an OS. The HBA used must be matched to the OS and device drivers running on the host or server.
    - **Incorrect HBA for the hardware:** Some HBAs are compatible with the hardware of a particular computer but not with the hardware of another manufacturer, even if they both are running the same OS. Make sure that the host or server is compatible with the HBA before installing it.
    - **Configuration for a storage system:** The HBA needs to be configured properly to work with a SAN or other storage system, especially for the link speed between the HBA and the storage system.
- **Disk caching off:** By default, **disk buffering** or **disk caching** is enabled and it assists a disk drive by temporarily storing data received from the system to be written to the disk, while the drive is busy with other tasks. Refer to *Figure 21.4*. If you disable this feature on an internal HDD, I/O speeds may be slow. On external drives, disabled disk caching is the default.

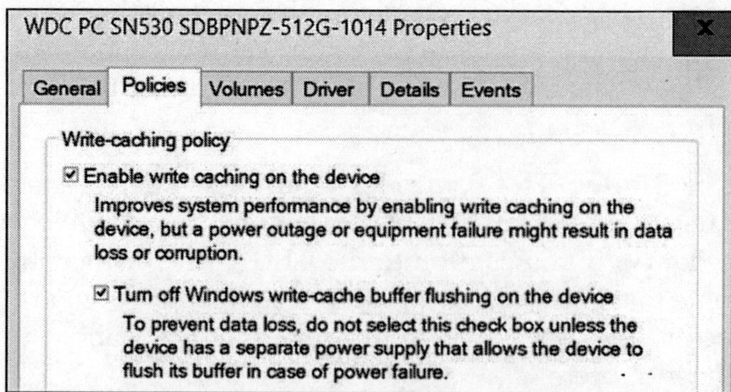

Figure 21.4: *The Write-caching policy settings in the Windows Device Manager*

- **Cache battery failure:** The write cache memory of a RAID system is powered by a battery, which allows the system to clear the cache before it shuts down. Should the battery weaken or fail, any data in the cache is gone.

Storage array issues

Although the devices and controllers for storage arrays and networks are relatively problem free, improper configuration, incompatible devices, or disk drive issues can create operational problems. Specific issues that can arise on storage arrays and networks are:

- **Improper RAID configuration**: **Redundant Array of Independent Disks** (**RAID**) is a data storage technique that combines disk drives into a system configured to prevent data loss and improve data availability, integrity, and redundancy. RAID systems can be configured for performance or the prevention of data loss. Both are possible, but one is emphasized at the expense of the other. The rule of thumb for the configuration of a RAID arrangement is that the configuration priority should align with the objectives of the organization.
- **RAID rebuilds:** A very good feature of most RAID systems is that if a storage device configured into a RAID system fails and a failover drive is available, RAID will move the failed device onto the replacement. The downside is that, unfortunately, while this happens users will experience higher than normal latency.
- **Mismatched drives:** On a NAS or SAN, a variety of differently sized disk drives will work together as well as identical drives. However, a RAID system requires that all the disk drives have the same capacity. When differently sized disk drives are configured into a RAID array, all disk drives, regardless of their capacity, will be limited to the storage space of the smallest drive.
- **Backplane failure:** RAID is commonly implemented through a backplane circuit or enclosure. Each disk drive blade connects into a slot on the backplane. This eliminates the cabling clutter normally associated with multiple disk drives in one system. If one backplane connector fails, only the disk drive in that slot is inaccessible. However, if the entire backplane chassis fails, all the disk drives are unavailable. The drives themselves are okay though.

Administrative tools

A systems administrator is concerned with data's capacity, technology, configuration, and security and the data storage devices connected to a server. To accomplish this, a single server or a data center often requires administrative software tools. A variety of disk or storage management software packages are available that have the functions necessary to perform the tasks described in the following sections.

Disk management

Disk management is a utility feature of the Windows OS. The **Windows Disk Management** utility shown in *Figure 21.5* supports the creation, modification, removal, extension, and redesignation of disk volumes and partitions. There are also third-party software for this purpose, like the MiniTool Partition Wizard and the AOMEI Partition Assistant. On a Linux system, the **`fdisk`** and **`disk`** commands provide many of the same features, and the open-source **Gnome Partition Editor** (**GParted**) is also an excellent disk management tool.

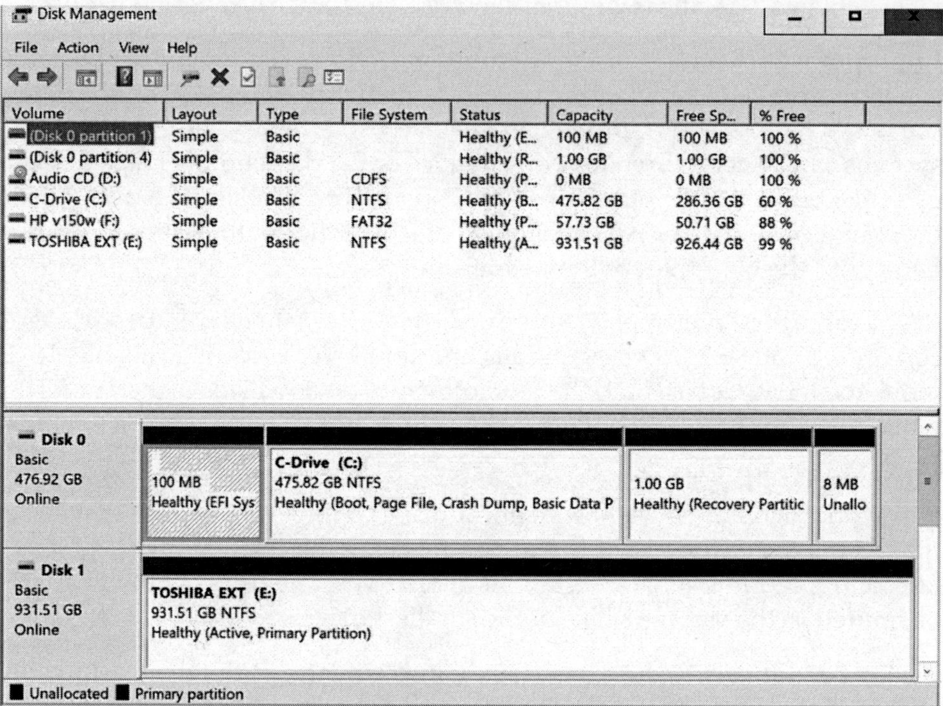

Figure 21.5: The Windows Disk Management utility

Map, mount, and net use

Mapping a network resource is different from mounting a storage device or creating a share. However, these actions are often confused. Let us look at each one separately:

- **Drive mapping:** Mapping a disk drive involves assigning a drive identity, such as "E:" and making the drive available to the local network. Drive mapping essentially creates a share for network users. However, the same can be accomplished by adding a shortcut to the drive in the Windows File Explorer's Network folder.
- **Mount command:** Both Windows and Linux use the **`mount`** command to connect a storage device or a filesystem to the directory structure, and make it available to users.

- **Net use:** The **`net use`** command is used to create, configure, or remove connections to shared resources on a network, such as disk drives, external devices, and printers. The Linux **`mount`** command has options that make it the equivalent of the Windows **`net use`** command.

Disk arrays

A disk array or storage array combines multiple disk drives into a single data storage system that can operate independently of network servers. Storage arrays centralize disk drives for resource management. Storage arrays are the foundation of SANs and NAS. Disk array manufacturers typically provide storage management software for their products. Several third-party storage management software packages are available. *Figure 21.6* shows a screen capture of a disk array management system:

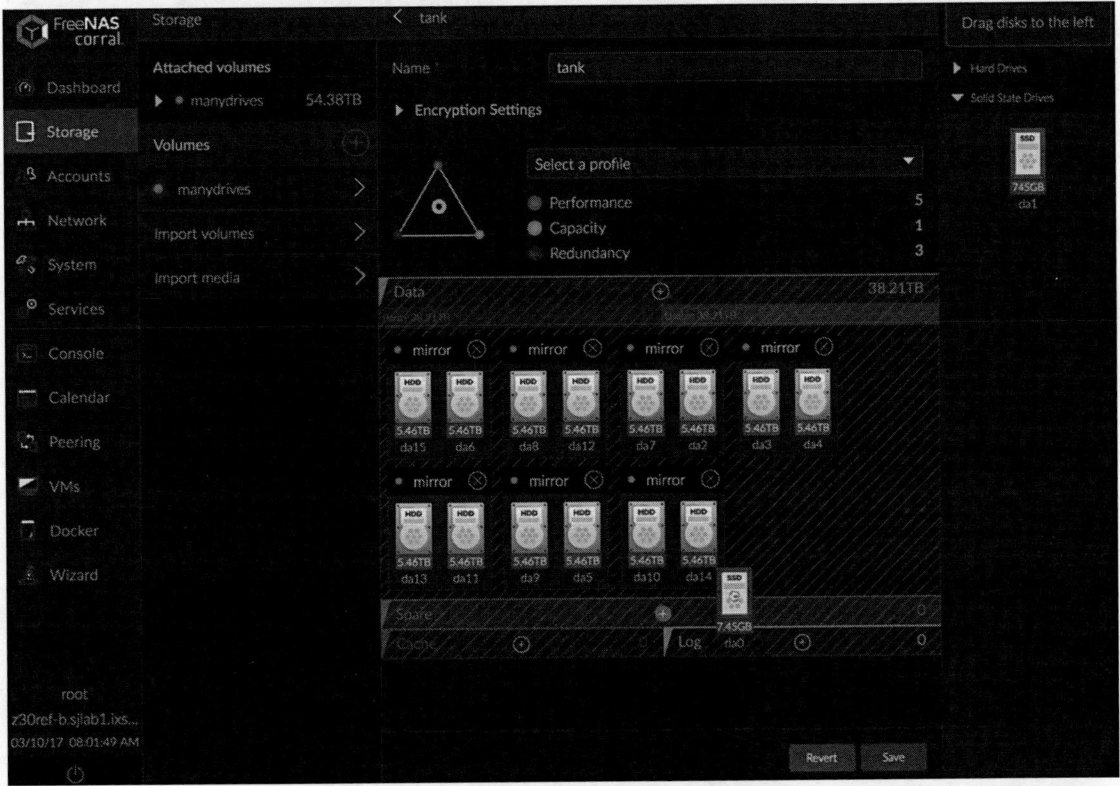

Figure 21.6: FreeNAS is an example of disk array management software

RAID arrays

RAID is another type of storage device array and there are specific software management tools for RAID implementations. On a Linux system, RAID management is through the **`mdadm`** command. *Figure 21.7* shows the **`-help`** information for the **`mdadm`** command:

```
bpbonline: $mdadm --help
mdadm is used for building, managing, and monitoring
Linux md devices (aka RAID arrays)
Usage: mdadm --create device options...
            Create a new array from unused devices.
       mdadm --assemble device options...
            Assemble a previously created array.
       mdadm --build device options...
            Create or assemble an array without metadata.
       mdadm --manage device options...
            make changes to an existing array.
       mdadm --misc options... devices
            report on or modify various md related devices.
       mdadm --grow options device
            resize/reshape an active array
       mdadm --incremental device
            add/remove a device to/from an array as appropriate
       mdadm --monitor options...
            Monitor one or more array for significant changes.
       mdadm device options...
            Shorthand for --manage.
Any parameter that does not start with '-' is treated as a device name
or, for --examine-bitmap, a file name.
The first such name is often the name of an md device.  Subsequent
names are often names of component devices.

 For detailed help on the above major modes use --help after the mode
 e.g.
         mdadm --assemble --help
 For general help on options use
```

Figure 21.7: *The help display for the mdadm Linux command.*

On Windows Server and other 64-bit Windows versions, utilities like the HP Array Configuration Utility, shown in *Figure 21.8*, support the creation, administration, and monitoring of RAID and other disk arrays:

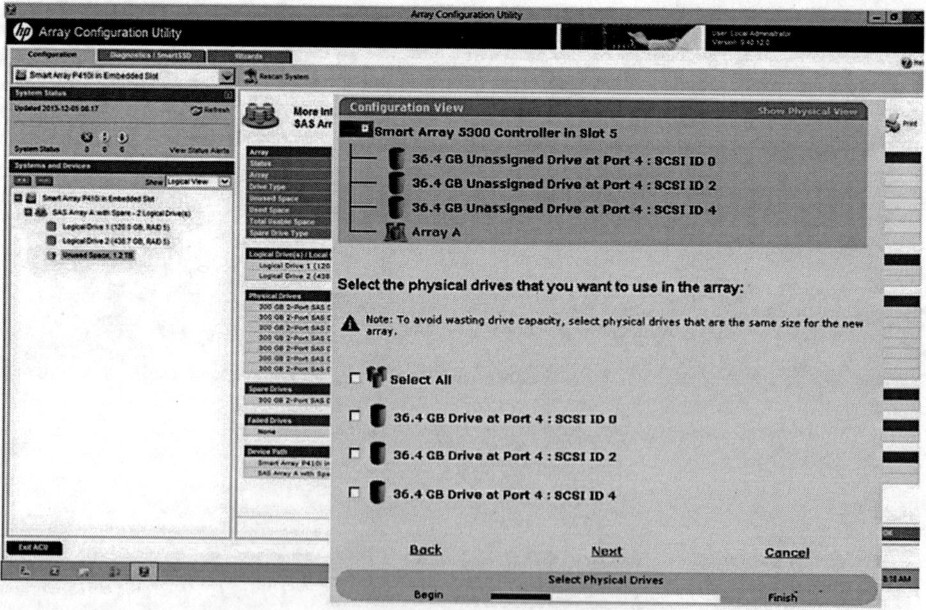

Figure 21.8: *The HP Array Configuration Utility is an example of RAID array management software*

Storage monitoring tools

All operating systems record log file entries which provide information, caution, and error level events in system log files. On a Linux system, log files are in the **/var/log** directory. *Figure 21.9* shows a display of the log entries in the **sysinfo.log** file, which contains entries for the general activities of the system. The Windows Event Viewer can be used to view, manage, archive, and customize the content and display of each of the log files.

```
2019-02-02 12:49:07,285 ERROR    Network plugin raised an exception.
Traceback (most recent call last):
  File "/usr/lib/python3/dist-packages/landscape/sysinfo/sysinfo.py", line 99, in run
    result = plugin.run()
  File "/usr/lib/python3/dist-packages/landscape/sysinfo/network.py", line 32, in run
    for info in self._get_device_info():
  File "/usr/lib/python3/dist-packages/landscape/lib/network.py", line 181, in get_active_device_info
    speed, duplex = get_network_interface_speed(sock, interface)
  File "/usr/lib/python3/dist-packages/landscape/lib/network.py", line 261, in get_network_interface_speed
    raise e
  File "/usr/lib/python3/dist-packages/landscape/lib/network.py", line 253, in get_network_interface_speed
    fcntl.ioctl(sock, SIOCETHTOOL, packed)  # Status ioctl() call
OSError: [Errno 22] Invalid argument
2019-02-02 12:58:57,199 ERROR    Network plugin raised an exception.
Traceback (most recent call last):
  File "/usr/lib/python3/dist-packages/landscape/sysinfo/sysinfo.py", line 99, in run
    result = plugin.run()
  File "/usr/lib/python3/dist-packages/landscape/sysinfo/network.py", line 32, in run
    for info in self._get_device_info():
  File "/usr/lib/python3/dist-packages/landscape/lib/network.py", line 181, in get_active_device_info
    speed, duplex = get_network_interface_speed(sock, interface)
  File "/usr/lib/python3/dist-packages/landscape/lib/network.py", line 261, in get_network_interface_speed
    raise e
  File "/usr/lib/python3/dist-packages/landscape/lib/network.py", line 253, in get_network_interface_speed
    fcntl.ioctl(sock, SIOCETHTOOL, packed)  # Status ioctl() call
OSError: [Errno 22] Invalid argument
2019-02-02 13:00:09,923 ERROR    Network plugin raised an exception.
Traceback (most recent call last):
  File "/usr/lib/python3/dist-packages/landscape/sysinfo/sysinfo.py", line 99, in run
    result = plugin.run()
  File "/usr/lib/python3/dist-packages/landscape/sysinfo/network.py", line 32, in run
    for info in self._get_device_info():
  File "/usr/lib/python3/dist-packages/landscape/lib/network.py", line 181, in get_active_device_info
    speed, duplex = get_network_interface_speed(sock, interface)
sysinfo.log
```

Figure 21.9: *The contents of a Linux sysinfo.log file*

Several third-party systems are available for log file monitoring, analysis, and reporting. *Figure 21.10* shows a screen capture of an event log analysis tool. Monitoring a server's log files is an important task. As Pascual said, "The Devil is in the details," and it most certainly is in the log files.

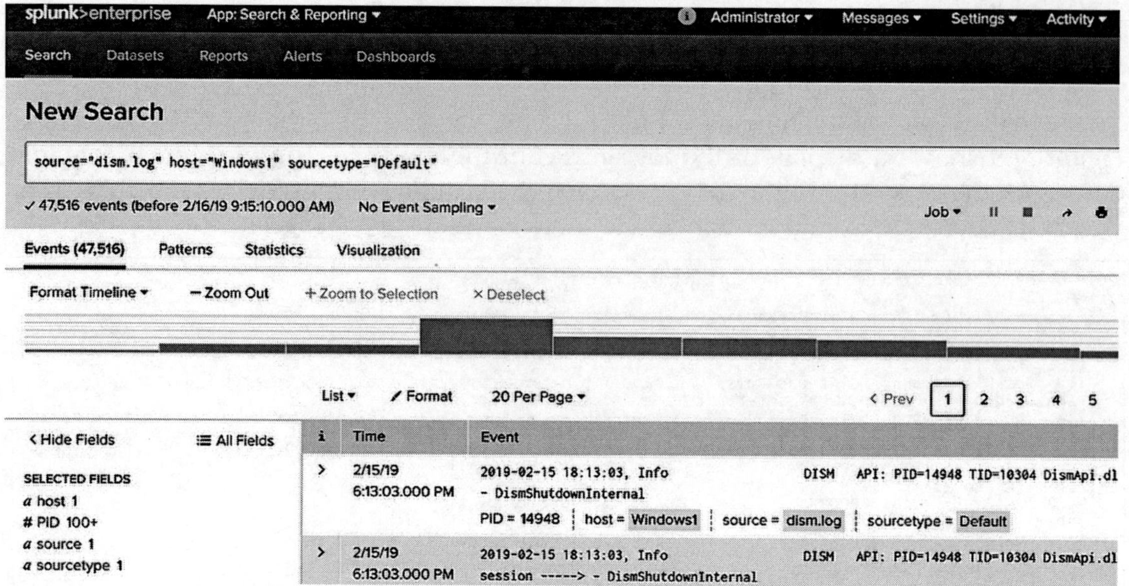

Figure 21.10: The Splunk Enterprise log file analysis tool

Visual and auditory inspections

Preventive maintenance is a regular and routine maintenance process performed on the components and devices of a computer system. Its purpose is to reduce the chance of failure and unplanned downtime. Key activities within a preventive maintenance program are visual and auditory inspections and, in some cases, tactile inspections of the essential parts of a system. These inspections should be performed as standard activities in the formal inspection policies. Preventive maintenance is essentially a condition monitoring activity that checks the status and condition of a component or device to determine its health.

The primary steps in a condition monitoring process are:

1. **Detection:** Using your senses of sight, hearing, and feel, you can detect damaged, corroded, and failing or failed components and devices. Once detected a problem can be further identified and verified by further testing.

2. **Analysis:** The objective of this step is to identify the underlying cause of a detected problem. Once the cause is identified and the analysis is completed, the results should be recorded and communicated.

3. **Correction/improvement:** Depending on the nature or severity of the problem, a replacement component or device, a correction in the configuration or settings, or perhaps even the elimination of the part causing the problem can be accomplished and tested.

4. **Verification:** It is essential to verify that the corrective action continues to solve or improve the initial situation. Further testing should be performed sometime after the correction is made and initially tested.

Visual inspections

Visual inspections are always subjective. However, if something looks wrong, you should trust your *gut* and check it out. Remember that in most cases, the underlying problem may not be obvious visually and further diagnosis may be required. Visual inspections are excellent for detecting conditions like cleanliness, damage, improper or poor connections, and observing LED status lights. Of course, a visual inspection can also detect smoke and fire if present.

Auditory inspection

If something does not sound right – you guessed it! Any loud, unusual noise, such as a grinding, high-pitched whine, clicking, or the like, must be investigated. Normally, during a preventive maintenance process, severe problems like those mentioned would have already been dealt with when they first occurred. However, a low volume sound can indicate a growing problem that should be resolved.

Tactile inspection

This type of inspection is pretty simple. It amounts to placing your hand on a computer case to see if it feels hot to the touch, or is vibrated excessively, or perhaps the reverse of these two conditions: too cold or no vibrations at all. Like the other sensory inspection types, how a computer feels is subjective, but it may alert you to a potentially catastrophic problem.

Conclusion

Data storage devices hold one of the most valuable assets of any organization. Unfortunately, these devices can have problems and can be damaged. Dealing with these devices' symptoms, problems, and conditions is an essential knowledge of a system server administrator. The server administrator is the steward of the organizations' data store and its integrity, availability, and security. He or she must be able to recognize and resolve common storage device problems, identify the underlying causes of storage device problems, and apply the appropriate tools and techniques to resolve storage device problems.

The next chapter deals with problems that can occur with operating systems and application software.

Points to remember

- A failing disk drive can exhibit symptoms similar to a malware attack, memory problems, a failing power supply, or appear generally slow.
- Common disk drive problems include operating system not being found, slow file access, lack of sufficient space, corrupted data, and file/data being unavailable.

- Causes of the common disk drive problems include automatic OS updates, malware, user access rights, disk drive failing, drive logical problems, drive letter missing, and partition inaccessibility.
- A RAW partition is not formatted as a standard partition.
- A cache failure can be the result of a power failure, or any sudden system stop error.
- Swap files, page files, and scratch files are other names for **virtual memory** (**VM**).
- A read/write head that contacts the disk surface can scratch the ferrous oxide material on the platter and corrupt or destroy any data in that area.
- Physical bad sectors are not repairable. Logical bad sectors are repairable.
- SSD drives can have bad blocks.
- Magnetic tape is a common backup media.
- Disk drive problems can cause issues with the OS, application software, and any process that interacts with a storage device because of corrupt or missing MBR, corrupt filesystem table, and insufficient disk space.
- Disks and disk arrays connect through an Ethernet or **Serial Attached SCSI** (**SAS**) connector.
- Data storage device failures are in one of two types: software-caused failures and hardware-based failures.
- Hardware or mechanical problems can include HBA failure, incorrect HBA, incorrect configuration, and disk caching.
- Storage array issues include improper RAID configuration, mismatched drives, and backplane failure.
- Mapping a disk drive involves assigning a drive identity and making the drive available to the local network.
- The net use command is used to create, configure, or remove connections to shared resources on a network.
- A storage array combines multiple disk drives into a single data storage system that can operate independently of network servers.
- Preventive maintenance is a regular and routine maintenance process performed on the components and devices of a computer system.
- Visual, auditory, and tactile inspections can sense existing or potential problems.

CHAPTER 22
Operating System and Software Issues

Introduction

Many software problems result from hardware issues. However, software can create, cause, or generate its own problems, faults, and errors related to or completely independent of hardware issues. In this chapter, we will review common software problems, their causes, and some of the tools and utilities used to troubleshoot them.

Structure

The chapter covers the following topics:

- Common OS and software problems
- Causes of common problems

Objective

By the end of this chapter, you will be able to identify and describe the sub-objectives of the following Server+ examination objective: *Given a scenario, troubleshoot common OS and software problems.*

Common OS and software problems

In a production or live environment, the system software running on a server has been tested in a non-production environment and on a replicated production system, and then implemented on the production system under strict monitoring. This is the ideal process in a perfect world. Although this is what should happen, it is common that some, if not all, these steps are omitted, and server system software is installed, with possible bugs. There can be logic errors or interface misalignment, and software problems may be hardware problems. Another scenario may be that the software may not be compatible with hardware and software.

The cause of software problems may be misconfigured, improperly installed, or incompatible system software, device drivers, utility apps, or diagnostic and analysis software. Common software problems can be separated into hardware-related and operating system problems.

Hardware-related software problems

Common hardware-related problems that can look like software issues include:

- **Blue Screen of Death (BSOD):** A BSOD is a Windows display screen, as shown in *Figure 22.1*, that appears when a stop error condition occurs and halts the OS. The cause of the error could be a specific hardware component, a device driver, or a component of the OS kernel. Application software does not typically cause BSOD errors. However, some applications can cause other errors resulting in a BSOD display, such as a buffer overflow. A BSOD is more often the result of a hardware or OS error.

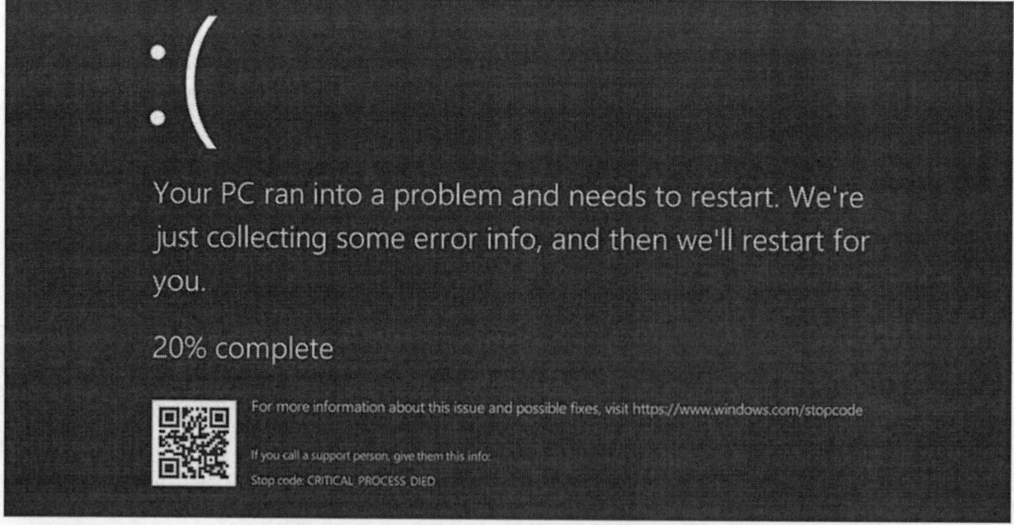

***Figure 22.1:** The BSOD display of a Windows system*

- **Boot disk failure:** The most common cause of this is when the boot sequence in BIOS/UEFI indicates that a CD or DVD is the primary boot device and the drive is empty or does not have a boot disk. The solution is to change the disk or modify the BIOS/UEFI boot device priorities and restart the computer. Other possible issues can be problems with the disk drive or the drive not being connected to power.
- **Cannot mount drive:** On a Windows system, this problem is typically a hardware issue with a USB porter and an external drive. On a Linux system, the problem could be filesystem corruption or an error in the filesystem table file (`fstab`).

Common OS problems

An operating system can have problems and produce errors, especially when encountering incompatible resources. The common OS problems and errors you are likely to see on the Server+ exam are as follows:

- **User is unable to login:** User login problems are pretty much the same on all operating systems, as discussed:
    - **Windows:** See *Table 22.1* for the common Windows OS user login problems.
    - **Mac OSX:** The macOS recommends users create a password for logins but does not require one. If the password is used and forgotten, then this password or username can be reset in Admin mode, Single User mode, or via the Apple ID account.
    - **Linux:** Most Linux distributions (distros) incorporate the **Pluggable Authentication Module (PAM)** for authenticating username and password credentials. If a user is unable to login, the PAM table may be reconstructed with the **`pam-auth-update -package`** command.

Refer to the following table:

Message	Problem
Windows cannot sign into your Account.	Password changed or upgrade installed.
Windows cannot login with a password.	Password on file is different from the one entered.
We cannot sign into your account.	User profile is missing or corrupted. Windows upgrades can cause user login problems.
The User Profile Service failed the sign in; user profile cannot be loaded.	User profile is missing or corrupted.
No login screen is displayed	This is likely a startup (boot) problem.

Table 22.1: *Common Windows user login errors and possible causes*

- **User cannot access resources:** A user is denied access to resources on a single computer or a shared network resource. In most instances, this is a permissions problem for that specific user account or the group of the user. If the user is denied access to a resource on a peer-to-peer network, the problem may be a TCP/IP configuration issue or a browser error.
- **Users cannot print:** This condition may be caused by an incorrect printer driver on a computer or a group policy issue.
- **Driver issues:** Often, this issue is caused by a newly added device, using the device driver of a previous model. Driver issues are commonly compatibility problems. However, driver problems may also be caused by BIOS/UEFI configuration errors.
- **Cannot write to system log:** A user must have authorization to access (read/write) system log files. On a Windows system, to grant permission to a user, this is done in the log file's entry in the Registry's `HKEY_LOCAL_MACHINE\SYSTEM\CurrentControlSet\Services` key. On a Linux system, create a log file directory owned by the user.
- **Slow OS performance:** An OS slows down when the system resources, primarily the CPU, memory, and disk drives, are dominated by one or more programs. Using Windows **Task Manager**, macOS **Activity Monitor**, or the Linux `systemctl` command, end the processes that are not critical. You should also review the startup programs and disable unnecessary processes.
- **Runaway process:** A process that gets stuck in an infinite loop (no stop condition) is a runaway. On Windows, open the **Task Manager** and end the process. On macOS, use the **Activity Monitor** to end the process. On Linux, use the `ps` or `kill` command to end the process.
- **Patch update failure:** After applying an OS patch, if a component, service, or application has problems and you are sure that a recently applied update or patch is causing the problem, use a **backout utility** to revert to a previous state. In Windows, this is the Go back to a previous version of the app on the **Settings** menu. On a macOS system, run the **reinstall macOS** utility from **Recovery Mode**. Use the **Last-Known Good** option on the **GRUB** menu on a Linux system.
- **Service will not start:** The message **"The service cannot be started, either because it is disabled or because it has no enabled devices associated with it"** indicates one or more services, programs, or scripts failed to start. Isolate the service and reload it or a new version.
- **Hangs no shut down:** An OS fails to shut down typically because of one of three issues:
    - A process or service will not end.
    - A device driver is holding a device open.

- Malware is causing the operating system to hang.
- Hardware failures or misconfigurations can prevent the computer from shutting down properly.

- **Memory leak:** When a program fails to release its allocated memory, a memory leak occurs. This problem can also happen when an object in memory cannot be addressed by programming code. The Windows **Memory Diagnostic** utility, as shown in *Figure 22.2*, can help resolve these errors:

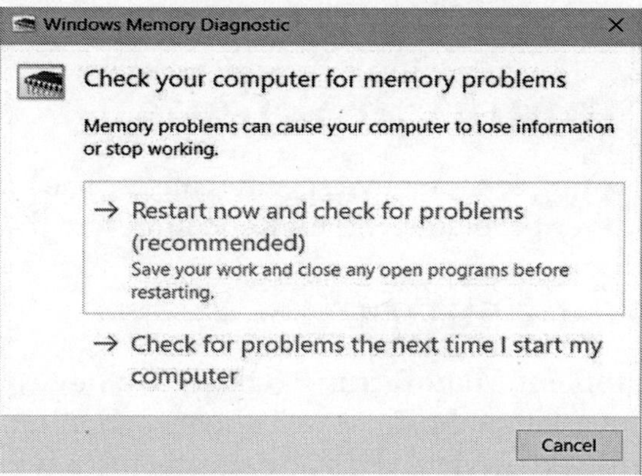

***Figure 22.2:** The Windows Memory Diagnostic utility*

- **System or application hanging:** There can be multiple reasons a system hangs or freezes up. Some of the possible causes are:
  - **Memory is low:** When there is insufficient memory, including virtual memory, a computer can run slower than usual and hang up or freeze. Windows can warn that it is running out of memory through a warning box notification, as shown in the following *Figure 22.3*:

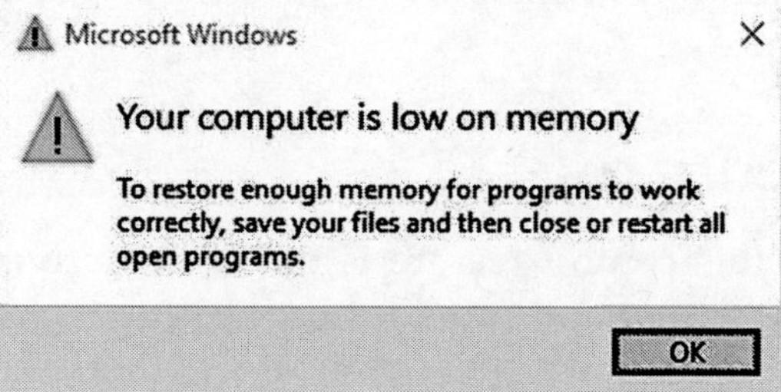

***Figure 22.3:** Windows low memory warning*

  - **Program requiring excessive processor or resource utilization:** Although a computer configuration meets the minimum system resource requirements for an application, there are instances when one of the required resources may not be available. The application may hang up or cause the whole system to run erratically. Typically, you must uninstall the application to restore normal functions.

- **Malware:** A computer running slow or hanging up can be caused by malware. Malware can attack various parts of a computer; the symptoms are often strictly a hardware or OS problem.
- **A program is not responding:** Perhaps the most common causes for a computer to hang up or freeze are the programs or apps that for one reason or another, are unable to run at the same time.

Causes of common problems

The problems in the preceding section have specific causes. The following sections discuss the causes of common server problems you may encounter on the Server+ exam.

End of life/end of support

When the **Original Equipment Manufacturer** (**OEM**) of a device declares an **End of Life** (**EOL**) for the device, it means that the OEM will not be marketing, selling, or updating the device to be effective on a certain date. This also means there will be no future firmware, fixes, patches, or upgrades for that device. The OEM may offer service packages for maintenance after the EOL date or recommend a third-party maintenance company for the device. **End of Support** or **End of Service** (**EOS**) essentially means the same as an EOL. However, it does indicate that the OEM will no longer provide any support or maintenance for the device. If maintenance is desired for the device, a third-party company will need to be used.

In situations where one or more hosts or servers must remain in production after an EOL/EOS is announced, additional security measures should be applied to the systems, such as device or system segregation, system hardening, and the strict application of the principle of least privilege to its users.

User account controls

On a Windows system, this control feature is the **User Account Control (UAC)**. On a Linux computer, the **sudo** command provides user control elevation one command at a time. UAC (and **sudo**) restrict system changes to only authorized users. Generally, system changes are the responsibility of an administrator with a supervisor-level account. With UAC enabled (or when using **sudo**), a user must enter an administrative password. UAC can be set at one of four levels, which range between "Always notify" and "Never notify," as shown in *Figure 22.4*. Depending on the UAC level, the user may be required to enter a password ("Always notify") or is not required to do so ("Never notify"). If the UAC setting is too high, it can lead to installation mistakes, malware, and serious application or system errors. On the other hand, a low setting may create vulnerabilities.

Refer to the following figure:

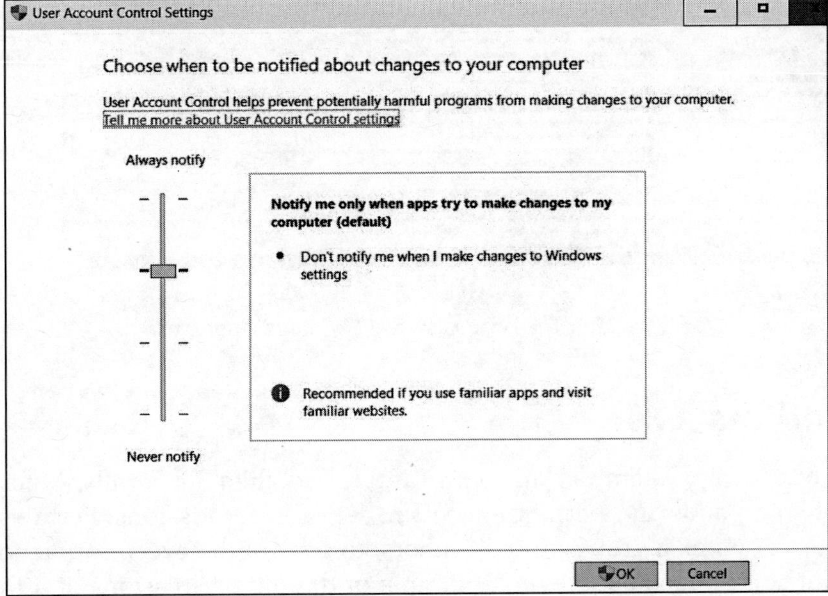

Figure 22.4: The UAC control sets the level of control for changes to the system

Access control

Although they use slightly different formats, Windows, Linux/UNIX, and Mac OS use the same access permission structure. Access rights and permissions are specified on three levels: the owner (creator), the owner's group, and everyone else. Linux and the Mac OS, which are built on a UNIX-like foundation, use the same permissions scheme. However, Windows is similar, but it presents itself much differently.

Windows

On a Windows 10 system, the equivalent of an **Access Control List** (**ACL**), that defines what a user or group can access, open, modify, write, or delete, is defined in the user's or group's permissions. The **Advanced Security Settings** dialog box provides access to the existing permissions of all users or groups, and access to administrators to modify the permissions. On a Windows 11 system, the command `lusrmgr.msc` executed from the Run box, opens the Local Users and Groups app, as shown in *Figure 22.5*. This app is used to manage users and the groups to which they belong. In either case, permissions for files, folders, and apps are set on each object.

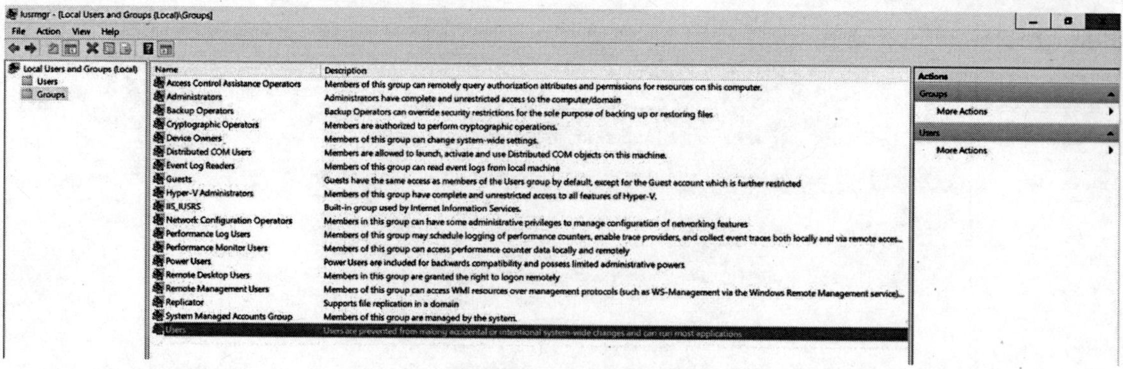

Figure 22.5: The Windows Local Users and Groups app

Linux and macOS

The macOS operating system is built on a Linux workalike. Generally, Macs and Linux use the same commands and permission sets to set user permissions. Permissions can be set for the object owner, a group, and all others, to control the execution, read, and write (including delete) for each user level. A sample of the file permissions of a Linux/UNIX file or directory is shown in *Figure 22.6*:

```
bpbonline: $ls -l
total 1332
-rw-r--r--  1 root root     2981 Dec 26 05:45 adduser.conf
-rw-r--r--  1 root root      185 May 25 10:44 aliases
drwxr-xr-x  3 root root     4096 Apr  5 14:15 alsa
drwxr-xr-x  2 root root    12288 May 25 10:44 alternatives
-rw-r--r--  1 root root      401 Feb  6  2021 anacrontab
-rw-r--r--  1 root root     4185 Jul 29  2019 analog.cfg
drwxr-xr-x  8 root root     4096 Apr  5 14:22 apache2
-rw-r--r--  1 root root      433 Aug 23  2020 apg.conf
drwxr-xr-x  2 root root     4096 Apr  5 14:21 apparmor
drwxr-xr-x  7 root root     4096 Apr  5 14:23 apparmor.d
-rw-r--r--  1 root root      769 Jun 22  2021 appstream.conf
drwxr-xr-x  7 root root     4096 Dec 26 05:44 apt
drwxr-xr-x  3 root root     4096 Apr  5 14:22 avahi
-rw-r--r--  1 root root     1994 Mar 27  2022 bash.bashrc
drwxr-xr-x  2 root root     4096 Apr  5 14:22 bash_completion.d
-rw-r--r--  1 root root      367 Sep 22  2022 bindresvport.blacklist
drwxr-xr-x  2 root root     4096 Aug  7  2022 binfmt.d
drwxr-xr-x  2 root root     4096 Apr  5 14:21 bluetooth
-rw-r--r--  1 root root     7374 Feb 10  2021 bogofilter.cf
drwxr-xr-x  3 root root     4096 Apr  5 14:11 ca-certificates
-rw-r--r--  1 root root     5662 Apr  5 14:11 ca-certificates.conf
-rw-r--r--  1 root root      119 Sep 13  2017 catdocrc
drwxr-s---  2 root dip      4096 Apr  5 14:21 chatscripts
```

Figure 22.6: Directory file list showing type, permissions, owner, group, size, and creation information

Figure 22.7 shows the entry for the "**alsa**" directory:

```
drwxr-xr-x  3 root root    4096 Apr  5 14:15 alsa
```

Figure 22.7: An example of a Linux permissions entry

For each item in this directory, the first ten characters (**`drwxr-xr-x`**) are divided into four sections. Reading from the far left to the right, we have:

- The file or directory indicator is a single character of a "**`d`**" (directory) or a "**`-`**" (file).
- Next are three sets of three character permission sets:
  - The first character set has permission from the file owner. For example, for the "**`alsa`**" directory, the owner (root) has "**`rwx`**" permissions, meaning the owner has read, write, and execute permissions. For a directory, the execute permission applies to the files in the directory through inheritance.
  - The second set of permissions ("**`r-x`**") is for the group of the owner, meaning the permissions for everyone in that group. In this case, the group has read and execute permissions, meaning no write permissions.
  - The third set of permissions ("**`r-w`**") is for all other users (not the owner or the group), who have read and executed permissions.

Corrupted files

Unfortunately, not all corrupted files are recoverable. Although many are, it depends on the damage and its cause. There are cases in which data was recovered from hard disk drives that had suffered bent or broken platters, heavy water or fire damage, and other catastrophes. Typically, it is destroyed and unrecoverable data is confined to a single partition or sector.

Windows file recovery

There are three ways to recover files on Windows systems:

- **System File Checker (SFC): `sfc.exe`** scans the hard disk for corrupted system files and folders. The SFC utility works with **Windows Resource Protection** (**WRP**), which protects Registry and system files. SFC can be executed in **Safe Mode** to eliminate contention with third-party software. *Figure 22.8* shows an example of the output from **`sfc.exe`**:

```
PS C:\> sfc.exe /scannow

Beginning system scan.  This process will take some time.

Beginning verification phase of system scan.
Verification 100% complete.

Windows Resource Protection did not find any integrity violations.
```

Figure 22.8: The output of the SFC utility

- **Replace the corrupted file**: Providing there is a backup that contains a last-known good copy of a corrupted file, simply overwrite the bad file with the good copy. Remember that you may need to take ownership (**`takeown`**) and gain full administrative rights (**`icacls`**) of the corrupted file on a Windows system.

- **Restore system:** If you fail to recover a corrupted file or several corrupted files, a filesystem, or a partition, you will most likely need to restore the system from a backup to its last known good point.

Linux file recovery

There are several data and file recovery utilities available for Linux systems. These tools range from finding and copying retrievable data and files from a corrupted partition or volume to a good storage medium, such as *ddrescue*. Others attempt to repair the structure and retrieve the data of a corrupted files and images, such as TestDisk. Many of the same utilities that run on Linux are also available for the Mac OS.

Log files

Operating systems keep log files, which is a good thing. Log files provide a running history of the events, actions, errors, actions deserving a warning, and some good things. Troubleshooting an operating system or an application problem should typically start with a look and some analysis of one or more of the system's log files. *Figure 22.9* shows the Windows Event Viewer that provides a look at the contents of a variety of system log files:

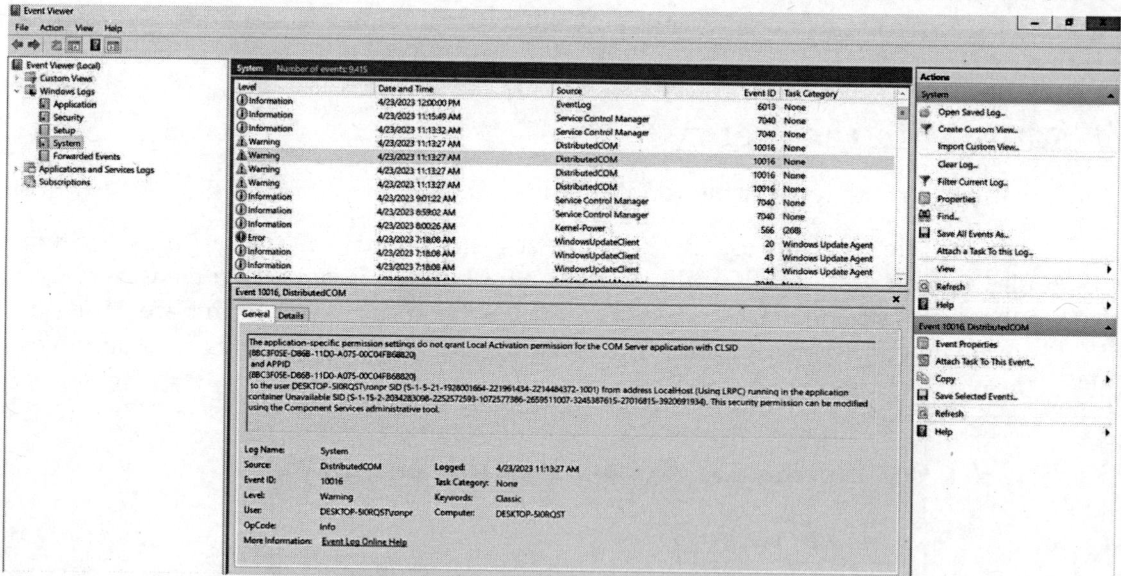

***Figure 22.9:** The Windows Event Viewer*

On a Linux system, system logs are in the **`/var/log`** directory. *Figure 22.10* shows the command prompt entries to list and then displays one of the log files on a Linux system:

```
bpbonline: $pwd
/var/log/apt
bpbonline: $ls -l
total 1008
-rw-r--r-- 1 root root 119888 Jun  1 05:42 eipp.log.xz
-rw-r--r-- 1 root root 148485 Jun  1 05:43 history.log
-rw-r----- 1 root adm  750022 Jun  1 05:43 term.log
bpbonline: $sudo more history.log

Start-Date: 2023-04-05  14:09:23
Commandline: apt upgrade -y
Requested-By: ron (1000)
Upgrade: tzdata:amd64 (2021a-1+deb11u8, 2021a-1+deb11u9), libssl1.1:amd64 (1.1.1n-0+deb11u3, 1.1.1n-0+deb11u4), sudo:amd
64 (1.9.5p2-3, 1.9.5p2-3+deb11u1), libgnutls30:amd64 (3.7.1-5+deb11u2, 3.7.1-5+deb11u3)
End-Date: 2023-04-05  14:09:24

Start-Date: 2023-04-05  14:11:32
Commandline: apt-get install curl wget -y
Requested-By: ron (1000)
Install: libssh2-1:amd64 (1.9.0-2, automatic), libcurl4:amd64 (7.74.0-1.3+deb11u7, automatic), libnghttp2-14:amd64 (1.43
.0-1, automatic), libldap-common:amd64 (2.4.57+dfsg-3+deb11u1, automatic), libsasl2-modules:amd64 (2.1.27+dfsg-2.1+deb11
u1, automatic), libsasl2-2:amd64 (2.1.27+dfsg-2.1+deb11u1, automatic), librtmp1:amd64 (2.4+20151223.gitfa8646d.1-2+b2, a
utomatic), libsasl2-modules-db:amd64 (2.1.27+dfsg-2.1+deb11u1, automatic), libldap-2.4-2:amd64 (2.4.57+dfsg-3+deb11u1, a
utomatic), wget:amd64 (1.21-1+deb11u1), publicsuffix:amd64 (20220811.1734-0+deb11u1, automatic), ca-certificates:amd64 (
20210119, automatic), libbrotli1:amd64 (1.0.9-2+b2, automatic), curl:amd64 (7.74.0-1.3+deb11u7), libpsl5:amd64 (0.21.0-1
.2, automatic), openssl:amd64 (1.1.1n-0+deb11u4, automatic)
End-Date: 2023-04-05  14:11:33
```

Figure 22.10: *A Linux log file displayed from the command prompt*

Incompatible drivers

Often, when a device is not operating as it should, it is not really the device that is the problem. In a majority of these instances, the problem is the device driver. Moreover, in virtually all these instances, some change has been made, such as installing a replacement for an older device, a physical change to the switches or jumpers on the device, or perhaps the driver was inadvertently deleted or corrupted.

On a Windows system, to view the information of the driver for any device (not all devices require drivers though), access the device's properties through the Device Manager, by following the given steps:

1. Right-click the **Start** icon on the **Task Bar** and select the **Device Manager** from the **Power User** menu.
2. On the Device Manager, as shown in *Figure 22.11*, click on the device type of the device you wish to view. For example, to view an internal SSD disk drive, click on **Disk Drives** to expand the type to show all of the installed devices of that type.

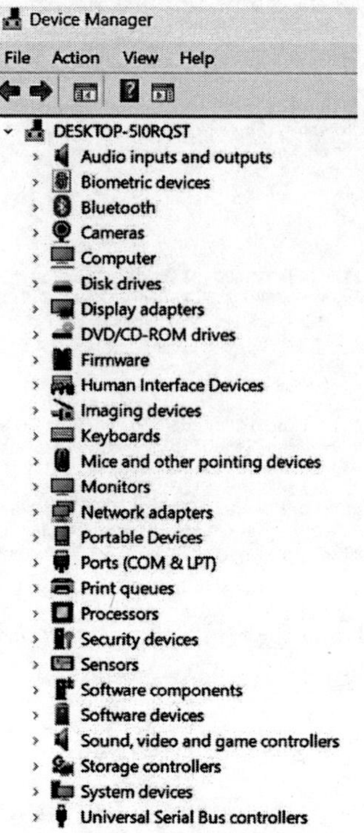

Figure 22.11: The drives types shown in the Device Manager

3. Right-click on the device you wish to check and choose **Properties** from the pop-up menu to open the **Properties** window for that device. *Figure 22.12* shows the **Properties** window for an internal disk drive:

Figure 22.12: The Properties window for a disk drive

4. Select the **Driver** tab. Click on the **Driver Details** button to view the driver files in use.

5. If you have to update the driver, select the **Update Driver** button and follow the instructions on the **Update Drivers** dialog box.

Improperly applied patches

Although not often, the processing to apply a patch to an operating system or an application can fail or be interrupted. In either case, it is most likely that a partial patch could even be worse that the problem it was fixing. This could also be true for some whole patches.

Generally, patches and updates are applied by an automated and reliable service, such as the Windows Server Update Services. However, even these reliable services cannot recover from a communication interruption while downloading the patch to be applied. Should the update not be received in total, you can skip applying it and wait for the next update or install the patch manually. Some additional problems with patches and updates are insufficient disk space to receive the update, the firewall may not allow the update files to pass, and the update received is corrupted. These issues must be corrected, the update downloaded again and then applied.

Server not joined to a domain

The first thing to check whenever you have a problem with a Windows server not joining a domain, is the **Domain Name System** (**DNS**). The heart of the Windows Active Directory services is DNS and without it or if it is not reachable for some reason, a server not joining a domain may not be your only other problem. Check the DNS for the following:

- Are the DNS server IP addresses correct?
- If multiple DNS domains exist, is the DNS suffix search order correct?
- Are there duplicate or erroneous DNS records for the same device?
- Does a reverse DNS lookup provide a different domain name that the A record?
- Can the domain name, the **Domain Controllers** (**DC**), and the DNS servers all be pinged?
- Check DNS records for conflicts, especially for the specific server having the connection issue.
- View the **`C:/Windows/debug/netsetup.log`** file on the Domain Controller for domain join issues.

Clock skew

First, skew is the difference between the readings of two devices. Clock skew, also called timing skew, occurs on synchronous circuits, like those in a computer, when a clock signal is received by different components or devices at differing times, due to latency caused by the signal's propagation on a wire.

The "clock" in a computer is an electronic signal, that sets the pace for the devices and components on a circuit. The clock signal is generated by a single source and distributed electronically to the components on a particular circuit. This includes the CPU, memory chips, graphics processor, CMOS, and more. As data or instructions move from one component to another, such as from the chipset Northbridge to the CPU, the distance between the devices on the circuit can introduce very small amounts of delay.

Buffer overrun

A **buffer overrun** or **buffer overflow** occurs when a process writes data into an allocated memory space, called a buffer, and the data is too large for the space and overflows into the memory space of another process. If data or instructions are overwritten in the adjacent memory space, memory errors, processing errors, and program crashes can occur. Buffer overruns are a relatively common vulnerability exploit in which an attacker submits data too large for a buffer.

A buffer is an area of RAM, allocated as a working space to a process running on the computer. Buffer space is assigned in memory to a process for holding data being moved from one part of the program to another or other programs or processes.

Insecure dependencies

Software dependencies are often the largest attack surface because their coding bugs often go unnoticed. Software dependency attacks have been used to compromise assets and steal user credentials. An application dependency is a technology component, another application, or a server on which an application relies to perform certain of its functions. When an application is developed, the software developer can have a technology stack he or she commonly uses. The technology stack can include operating systems, database engines, and development frameworks, such as Node.js, Angular, or Spring. The stack may also include **Application Programming Interfaces (API)**, which are used primarily to accept data from users and external services. All the elements in this technology stack are dependencies that an application requires to run correctly.

APIs are typically used as a backend framework for mobile and web applications. As such, they transfer what could be sensitive data, which must be protected and secured. **Representational State Transfer (REST)** is the commonly used security for APIs. Using REST API security, the data accessed by the API is controlled by a **Hypertext Transfer**

Protocol (**HTTP**) and **Uniform Resource Identifier** (**URI**). REST API security prevents attacks containing malicious data introduced through an API.

Version management

Version management, also called version control and source control, is a system or practice for tracking and managing changes to software programming code and releases. A version management program typically includes the creation, submission, analysis, modeling, approval, development, testing, and release of software source code or procedural documents. The objective of a version management system is to track each version of a software product by documenting any modifications made to the code, including who, when, why, and evidence of what of the change. Version identity provides for a concise record of its functions for customer support and documentation.

Version control systems are software applications that provide the capability to record changes, log version changes, and identify who has made certain changes to a previous version, when the changes were made, and who authorized the changes and approved the results. There are basically three types of version control systems:

- **Centralized Version Control System (CVCS):** Under this type of version control system, a server acts as a centralized repository, in which every version of a system's source code is stored. This version control type is excellent for small teams, in which team members can easily coordinate to avoid working on the code at the same time. However, CVCS can be a **Single Point of Failure** (**SPOF**).
- **Distributed Version Control System (DVCS):** In this type of version control system, each developer has their own repository and working copy. Changes committed to a private repository must be pushed to a central repository before other developers have access to them. The most popular DVCS are Git and Mercurial. These systems and others help to eliminate the SPOF problems.
- **Local Version Control Systems (LVCS):** This type of version control system is simple. It tracks file versions and patch sets (differences between files) in a special format on a disk drive. This type is also error prone which means that the chances of accidentally writing to the wrong file are higher.

Architecture

There are essentially two processor architectures used in the computer hardware that could possibly be used as server platforms: 32-bit and 64-bit. Realistically, only a 64-bit architecture is appropriate for use as a server host. The 64-bit architecture is much more efficient, especially when it is mated with 64-bit compatible operating systems. A 64-bit processor will run 32-bit applications, but the reverse is not true. A 32-bit processor will not run 64-bit applications or operating systems.

There are three primary CPU architectures:

- **X86:** Its name comes from the first series of CPUs for PCs (8086, 80286, 80386, and 80486). X86 architectures are 32-bit, with the exception of the 8086, which was a 16-bit architecture.
- **X64:** This architecture supports 64-bit CPUs, which support more memory space (RAM and virtual) for software.
- **Advanced RISC Machine (ARM):** This is a series of **Reduced Instruction Set Computing** (**RISC**) architectures that require fewer resources than either x32 or x64 architectures. ARM CPUs are used in tablet computers, smartphones, and other mobile devices.

Missing updates

You should keep your software up-to-date when a fix, patch, or update is available. Keeping your software updated is a best practice for no other reason than security, among others. This is especially true for OS updates, not that application software updates are not very important. It is very likely that the problem, vulnerability, or flaw being fixed is already known to threat actors who are eager to exploit it. Software developers issue patches, fixes, and updates for various reasons, but for nothing more important than to mitigate security issues in their products. Not applying fixes and updates to your software when they are issued can not only keep vulnerability in your systems, but, because it has now been publicized, it also increases the threat that your systems will be exploited.

On a Windows system, there is a PowerShell command that checks for missing Windows updates on a local computer:

```
(New-Object -ComObject Microsoft.Update.Session).CreateupdateSearcher().
Search("IsHidden=0 and IsInstalled=0").Updates|Select-Object Title
```

It looks more complicated than it is. *Figure 22.13* shows a sample of its output:

```
PS C:\> (New-Object -ComObject Microsoft.Update.Session).CreateupdateSearcher().Search(("IsHidden=0 and IsInstalled=0")).Updates | Sele
ct-Object Title

Title
-----
2023-05 Cumulative Update Preview for .NET Framework 3.5 and 4.8.1 for Windows 11, version 22H2 for x64 (KB5026515)
Security Intelligence Update for Microsoft Defender Antivirus - KB2267602 (Version 1.391.1030.0)
ACER Inc. - Firmware - 5.39.11.10
```

Figure 22.13: *Sample output of the PowerShell command to list missing updates*

Another approach that can be used is to list any available updates that have not been applied. To do this, you have to follow a series of commands to install the Windows Update module. If this module is already in your system, you can skip to step 6.

1. Open PowerShell with Administrator rights.

2. Enter **`Install-Module PSWindowsUpdate`** at the command prompt to install the Windows Update module.

3. A fairly long message displays. Enter "**`Yes`**" or "**`Y`**" to proceed. (The PS module may take some time to complete).

4. Next, an "**`Untrusted repository cmdlet`**" confirmation message is displayed. Enter "**`Y`**" to continue.

5. When the previous step is completed, enter **`Import-Module PSWindowsUpdate`** to import the Windows Update module. If an error occurs while importing the module, you may need to change PowerShell's execution policy. Enter **`Set-ExecutionPolicy unrestricted`** and re-enter the Import-Module command.

6. Enter **`Get-WUList`** to list the available and pending Windows updates.

Figure 22.14 provides a sample of the output for this series of commands:

```
PS C:\> Install-Module PSWindowsUpdate

Untrusted repository
You are installing the modules from an untrusted repository. If you trust this repository, change its InstallationPolicy value by
running the Set-PSRepository cmdlet. Are you sure you want to install the modules from 'PSGallery'?
[Y] Yes  [A] Yes to All  [N] No  [L] No to All  [S] Suspend  [?] Help (default is "N"): Y
PS C:\> Import-Module PSWindowsUpdate
PS C:\> Set-ExecutionPolicy unrestricted
PS C:\> Get-WUlist

ComputerName Status     KB          Size Title
------------ ------     --          ---- -----
DESKTOP-5I0… -------    KB5026515   56MB 2023-05 Cumulative Update Preview for .NET Framework 3.5 and 4.8.1 for Windows 11, version 2…
DESKTOP-5I0… -------    KB2267602  992MB Security Intelligence Update for Microsoft Defender Antivirus - KB2267602 (Version 1.391.103…
DESKTOP-5I0… -------                 9MB ACER Inc. - Firmware - 5.39.11.10
```

Figure 22.14: *The output of the Get WUList cmdlet shows any pending updates*

Downstream failures caused by updates

A small company may have only one server that connects to the Microsoft Update services using the **Windows Server Update Service** (**WSUS**). In this basic setup, updates are downloaded directly from Microsoft to the server. However, large data centers with multiple servers are configured into a hierarchy with an upstream server, one or more connected downstream servers, and perhaps one or more disconnected (downstream) servers.

The upstream server downloads updates directly from the Microsoft Update site and passes updates downstream to other servers. A downstream server receives the updates from an upstream server directly and does not interface with Microsoft Update. There are two standard configurations for downstream servers:

- **Downstream replica server:** Replica servers are centrally administered and inherit updates (and their approvals) from an upstream server.

- **Downstream autonomous server:** Autonomous servers are not centrally administered and are passed updates by an upstream server to be applied locally.

A disconnected downstream server may be connected to the Internet or a WAN, but typically is not connected to the internal intranet. These servers are updated manually using updates extracted from an upstream server.

If the passing of updates in the server hierarchy is interrupted or fails, it is possible that the downstream or disconnected servers may receive an incomplete or corrupted update. In addition, if the update package has errors, bugs, and mistakes, those will be passed downstream and installed on each of the servers in the hierarchy.

Improper CPU affinity and priority

The Windows OS provides the capability for setting the affinity and the priority of a process. The affinity setting controls which CPU or core(s) are dedicated to a process. The priority setting controls the ranking of running processes for the allocation of processor resources.

CPU affinity

CPU affinity, which is also called processor affinity or cache affinity, is a configuration setting that allows the system to designate which CPU or processor core(s) a process or application is executed. After the affinity is set, the process executes only on the designated CPU or core. The processes in the system queue have a kin processor tag, and if a processor has an affinity setting for a particular processor or core, the process will be assigned to it. The Windows OS can set processes to use only one or two processor cores instead of assigning them to the least-busy processor, which is the default setting.

Processor or CPU affinity can improve performance by reducing caching in a particular process. In programs like video editing or rendering, assigning a specific core to the task means that whenever the process is opened, the assigned core will be dedicated to it. However, if a process is best served by multiple or all the cores available and affinity has been assigned to only a single core. In that case, the performance of that process may be degraded, which may affect other processes as well.

The CPU affinity can be set on a Windows OS through the Task Manager, by following the given steps:

1. Right-click on the **Task Bar** and choose **Task Manager** or right-click on the **Start** icon and select **Task Manager** from the **Power User** menu.
2. On the **Task Manager** app, select the **Details** tab.
3. Right-click the process you wish to configure affinity on and select **Set affinity** from the pop-up menu to display the **Processor affinity** configuration box, as shown in *Figure 22.15*:

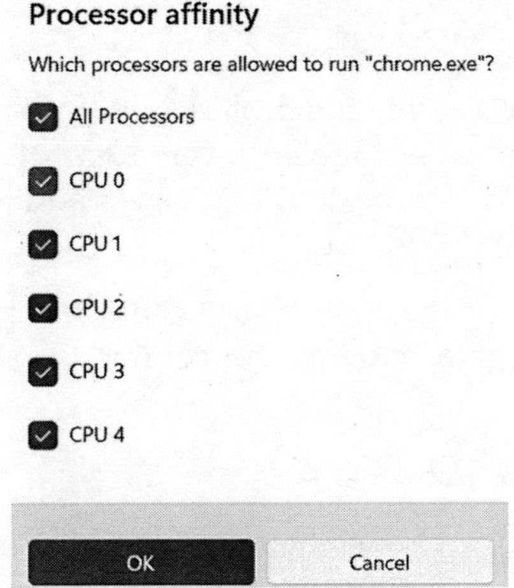

Figure 22.15: *The Processor affinity configuration box*

Priority

The Windows OS shares processor resources to a running process based on the priority level of the process. A process is assigned a priority when it is added to the process queue. The default is Normal, but the priority of any process can be changed to one in the range of Realtime to Low, as shown in *Figure 22.16*.

Higher priorities get a larger share of processor resources, which can improve its performance. A change to a process' priority is temporary and is not carried forward to the next time that the process is executed. The wrong priority may crowd out other processes or push a process to be the least in line for resources.

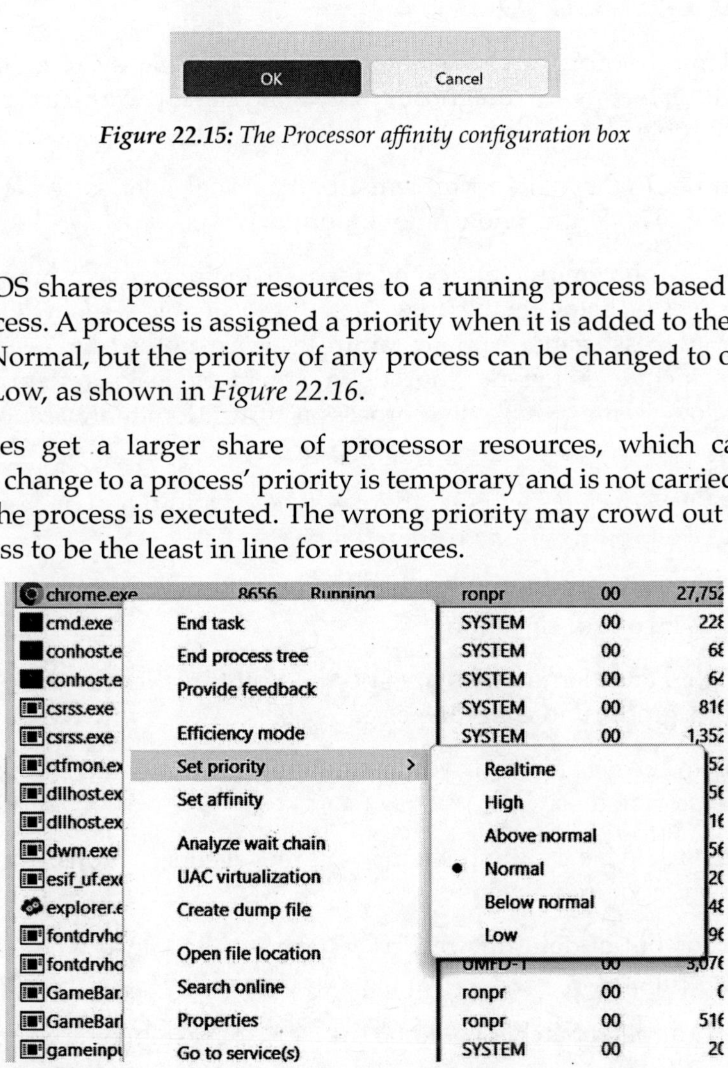

Figure 22.16: *The priority of a process can be changed through the Task Manager*

Conclusion

This chapter discussed common issues and problems with operating systems, applications, and system software and their causes. It also covered how to troubleshoot, diagnose, and resolve them. This information is important to a server administrator on the job and as a part of your preparation for the Server+ exam.

In the next chapter, we look at the tools and techniques that can be used by a server administrator to prevent, mitigate, and monitor common problems with server software.

Points to remember

- Misconfigured, improperly installed, or incompatible system software, device drivers, utility apps, or diagnostic and analysis software can be the cause of software problems.
- Common hardware-related problems that can look like software issues include BSOD, boot disk failure, and cannot mount drive.
- Common OS problems include being unable to login, access resources, print, driver issues, as well as being unable to write to the system log, a slow OS performance, runaway process, patch update failure, service not starting. Moreover, other problems include hangs-no shut down, memory leak, system or application hanging, low memory, excessive processor utilization, malware, non-responding process, malware, and non-responsive process.
- When an OEM declares an EOL, there will be no additional marketing, selling, or updating of a product after a certain date.
- User account control on a Windows system is UAC and on a Linux computer, *sudo* provides user control elevation.
- Access rights and permissions are specified on three levels: the owner (creator), the owner's group, and everyone else.
- The ways to recover files on Windows systems are the SFC utility, replacing the file, and restoring the system.
- Log files provide a running history of the events, actions, errors, warnings, cautions, and required actions.
- Improper or out-of-date device drivers can be the cause when a device is not operating properly.
- Improperly applied patches could be the cause of system or application problems.
- DNS issues can cause a Windows server not joining a domain.

- Clock skew occurs on synchronous circuits when a clock signal is received by different components or devices at differing times due to latency.
- Buffer overrun occurs when a process writes data too large for a buffer.
- Insecure software dependencies are when one application depends on another to perform specific functions and errors or flaws exist in the providing application.
- Version management tracks and manages changes made to programming code and software releases. Version identity provides for a concise record for customer support and documentation.
- Two processor architectures are used in computer hardware: 32-bit and 64-bit. There are three primary CPU architectures: x86, x64, and ARM.
- Not applying fixes and updates to your software when they are issued can keep vulnerabilities but can increase the threat that it will be exploited.
- If downloading of updates in a server hierarchy is interrupted or fails, it is possible that the downstream or disconnected servers may receive an incomplete or corrupted update.
- CPU affinity allows the system to designate which CPU or processor core(s) a process or application is executed.

CHAPTER 23
Software Tools and Techniques

Introduction

The previous chapter identified common problems and issues that can occur on a server system. This chapter looks at the tools and techniques available to resolve and fix those problems and issues, along with a few more. Knowing which tool, method, or technique to use when dealing with software issues is a vital skill of a server administrator and one that is key to success on the Server+ exam.

Structure

The chapter covers the following topic:

- Tools and techniques

Objective

By the end of this chapter, you will be able to identify and describe the sub-objectives of the following Server+ examination objective: *Given a scenario, troubleshoot common OS and software problems.*

Tools and techniques

This section provides a definition, description, and example, for the OS, software, techniques, procedures, and tools listed in the Server+ exam objectives. These are presented in alphabetical order, which means that no emphasis has been placed on just one of these elements.

Adding or removing ports

Transmission Control Protocol (TCP) and **User Datagram Protocol** (UDP) operate through ports. On a computer or internetworking device, such as a router or switch, a port is a virtual addressing indicator for where a specific network connection starts and ends. A port is software-based and managed by the device's OS. Virtually, every port is associated with a specific process, protocol, or service, as shown in *Table 23.1*. Ports allow networked devices and computers to determine to which process or application an incoming message is to be forwarded for processing.

TCP/UDP Port Number	Application, Protocol, or Service
20 and 21	**File Transfer Protocol (FTP)**
22	**Secure Shell (SSH)**
25	**Simple Mail Transfer Protocol (SMTP)**
53	**Domain Name System (DNS)**
80	**Hypertext Transfer Protocol (HTTP)**
443	**HTTP Secure (HTTPS)**

Table 23.1: *A sample of TCP/UDP Port Numbers*

On a Windows system, ports are enabled and disabled through the Windows Defender Firewall. To add or enable a port, use the following steps:

1. Open the Windows Control Panel and select the **Windows Defender Firewall.**
2. On the "Help protect your PC with Windows Defender Firewall" page, click on the **Advanced Settings** option in the left-side options list to display the **Windows Defender Firewall with Advanced Security** window, as shown in *Figure 23.1*:

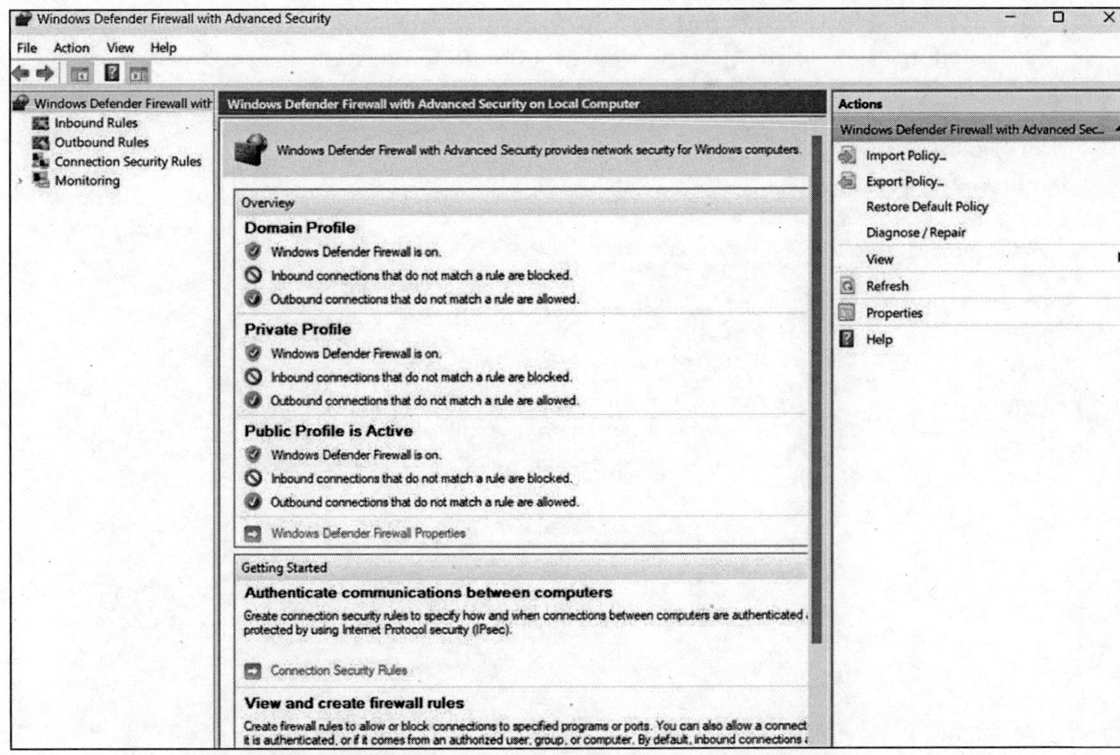

Figure 23.1: The Windows Defender Firewall with Advanced Security window

3. Choose **Inbound Rules** from the left-side navigation menu. The center pane will display the existing inbound rules. If you modify an existing rule, you can find it in the **Name** list. Right-click it to display a pop-up menu. Select **Properties** and make

the changes. However, if you are adding a new rule, click on **New Rule** in the right-side **Actions** pane to display the **New Inbound Rule Wizard**, as shown in *Figure 23.2*:

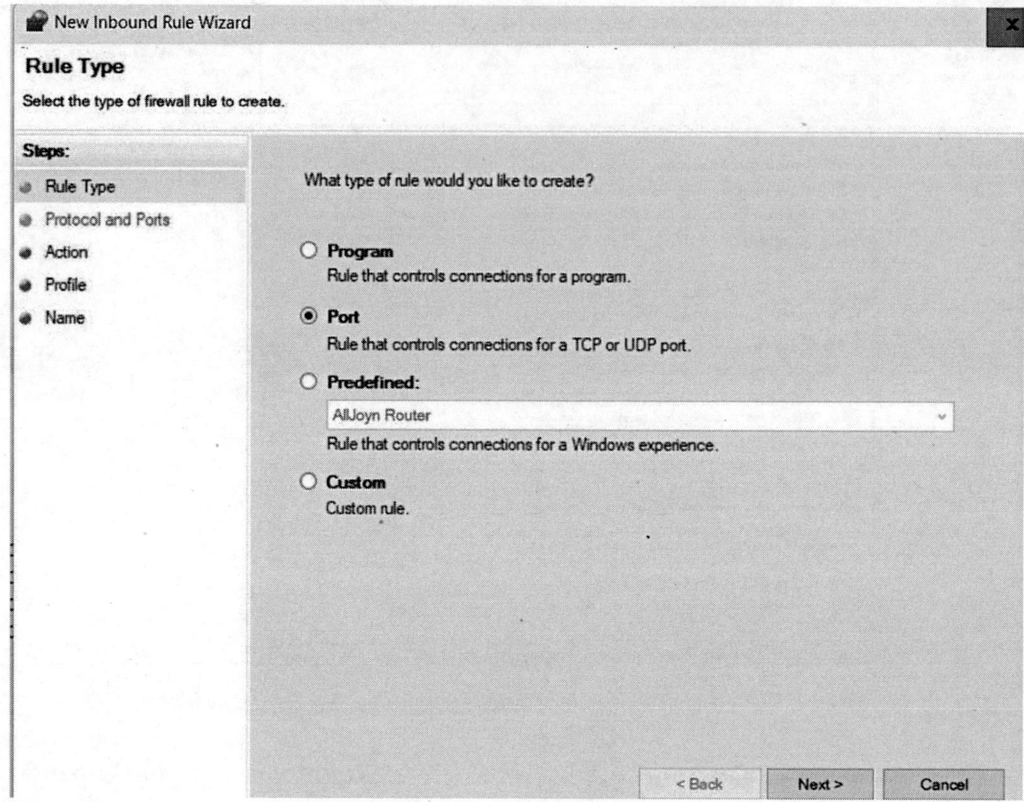

***Figure 23.2:** The New Inbound Rule Wizard*

Note: Most port assignments are inbound designations but can also be applied to an Outbound rule if desired.

4. Select the radio button associated with Port on the Rule Type page and click **Next**.
5. On the Ports and Protocols page, indicate whether the port is TCP or UDP, enter the port(s) for which you are creating a rule in the Specific local ports box, and click **Next**.
6. Select the action you wish to take on the Action page for the ports identified on the previous page. Your choices are to Allow the connection (allow the traffic to pass), Allow the connection if it is secure (allow the traffic to pass if it is secured), or Block the connection (deny passage to the traffic with the indicated port(s). Click **Next**.
7. On the Profile page, select the area to which the rule applies. Your choices are Domain, Private, and Public. You may choose any or all of the areas.

8. On the Name page, give the rule a short, but descriptive name and provide a brief description of its purpose. Click **Finish** to complete the Inbound Rule definition.

To disable a rule, find it in the appropriate rule category, right-click it, and choose **Disable rule** from the pop-up menu.

Boot options

On a Windows OS system (specifically Windows 11, 10, and 8), the **Advanced Startup Options (ASO)** menu, as shown in *Figure 23.3*, provides the various boot options available. The options available on the ASO menu all relate to diagnostics, repair, and troubleshooting, such as **Reset This PC**, **System Restore**, **Command Prompt**, **Startup Repair**, and **Startup Settings**, which is where **Safe Mode** is included.

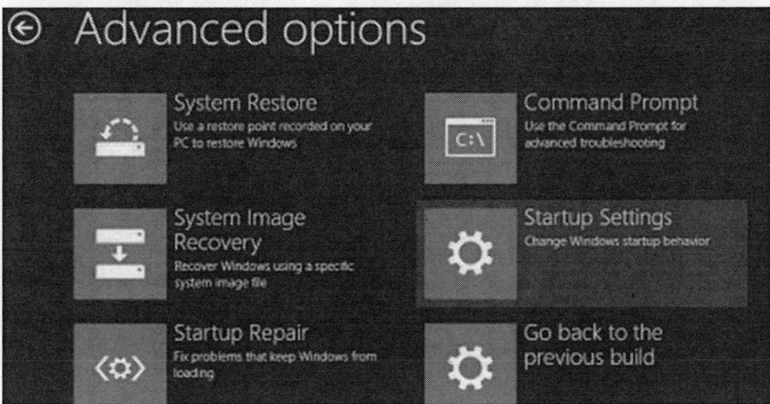

Figure 23.3: *The Advanced Startup Options menu*

The ASO menu will automatically display in the event of two startup errors in a row. However, there are several other ways to display it. Three of the easiest to use are as follows:

- **Shift key + Restart**
    - Click on the **Start** button to display the **Start** menu.
    - Click on the **Power** button (lower right corner).
    - While holding down a **Shift** key (either one), select **Restart** from the **Power** button menu.
    - After a few seconds you should have access to the **ASO** or the **Boot Options** menu.
- **Run box**
    - Open the Run box (*Win* + *R*), enter **shutdown /r /o** in the Open box and click *Enter*.
    - When the "You're about to be signed out" message box appears, click the **Close** button.

- After a few seconds, you should have access to the ASO or the Boot Options menu.

- **Windows Settings**
    - Right-click the **Start** button to display the Power User menu.
    - Choose **Settings** to open the **System Settings** app.
    - Select the **Recovery** option in the **System Settings** list.
    - On the **System | Recovery** page, find the **Advanced Startup** option in the **Recovery Options** section.

Tip: A word of caution here - be sure that any open files or documents are saved before you click on the Advanced Startup option. You won't have another chance to save them after you do.

The computer will display a series of blue screens with a few options on them. Follow the given steps:

1. On the first screen, choose the **Troubleshoot** option..
2. On the next blue screen, choose **Advanced Options** to display the **Advanced Options** screen, which has different utilities available, including **Startup Repair** and **Command Prompt**.

Clocks

Not counting any clock apps running on the Desktop, there are two clocks in a computer: the **Real Time clock** (**RTC**) and the **Software clock**. The real time clock is a battery-powered integrated circuit on a computer motherboard that continues to keep the time even when the main power is off. The RTC provides the timing for the system functions, as well as the system clock.

The system clock uses the RTC to set the synchronization and scheduling of tasks and processes, settings, timers, and system interrupts. The system clock begins providing time in binary code to represent microseconds and seconds in the boot process. The components on the motherboard uses the system clock to synchronize their actions using the up (binary 1) signal.

There is an additional clock in the electronics of a computer: the CPU clock. The CPU clock does what the system clock does, but only within the CPU itself. The timing of the CPU clock is a multiple of the system clock, meaning that the CPU clock multiplies the signal of the system clock by some variable, which can be modified to overclock or underclock the CPU.

Configuration management

Configuration management is the collection of procedures involved in establishing and maintaining computer hardware, servers, and software in a preferred and constant configuration. The configuration of a computer and its resources provides an administrative guide for what the system is to do and how it should perform.

Configuration management begins before the settings on a computer system are set. The first step is to identify the settings required and the values or settings to be applied and to then apply this design to the system. The tools used to monitor and assess the configuration of computer systems are primarily configuration assessments and drift analysis.

Configuration assessment

There are two types of configuration assessments that are popular with enterprises: computer system configuration assessments and **Security Configuration Assessments** (**SCA**). In the context of Server+, the one you should be aware of is the first one. On a Windows system, the Windows Assessment Toolkit can be used to assess the performance, reliability, and function of the OS on a local host. This app includes tools to assess the computer, display the results, diagnose any problems, and apply improvements. The Windows Assessment Toolkit includes:

- **Windows assessment console:** A GUI display used to group assessments and to create, run, and view a test assessment job.
- **Assessments:** Files that can be used to establish states, measure, and record the activity, and store the results.
- **Assessment platform:** A tool for developing and running assessments.

Drift analysis

The configuration of a computer system has drifted when its actual configuration differs from the designed and intended configuration. Understand that this does not just happen on its own. Configuration drift occurs when changes are made between the design of the configuration and the actual application of the configuration settings on the system. In effect, configuration drift can also happen after the configuration is implemented, if any changes are made to the system, without reviewing whether or not these changes had an effect on the configuration.

Some of the most common causes for configuration drift are as follows:

- **Changes made by users:** It is a fact that users make changes, which are almost always unauthorized.
- **Documentation:** One of the last actions of any project, change order, or system modification is updating the documentation if it is done at all. Documentation

commonly has a much lower priority than any other part of a project and is often "something we will do later."

- **Hardware upgrades:** When a new device is added to a system or network, which is usually an emergency or against a deadline, updating the configuration and the documentation is either not updated or poorly done.
- **Poor communication:** Configuration drift can result from two types of inadequate communication. The first is when a change is made without communicating the fact to anyone or without documenting the change. The second is that the configuration design as not good to begin with and changes are being made to correct the configuration by various technicians.
- **Software/firmware patches:** While applying patches and updating devices is important, doing so can lead to the need for configuration changes or unknown configuration changes.
- **Troubleshooting and remediation:** When the network servers or a user's computer can have problems, the objective is to correct them and get them back to work. Quick or ad hoc fixes or changes made to remedy a problem can change the configuration and increase the chances for configuration drift.

Chef, Puppet, and Ansible

Three of the more popular configuration management tools are:

- **Chef:** A system configuration management tool for managing an infrastructure. Chef, or Progress Chef, allows users to create system configurations, which it calls recipes. A recipe describes the preferred state of an infrastructure, including which software should be running on which server, which software should be installed on a particular device, and the files that should be created or updated by an application. Chef ensures a system is configured correctly and can automatically adjust for resources not running properly.
- **Puppet:** Another popular server configuration management tool, Puppet can configure and monitor multiple servers simultaneously. Puppet uses a proprietary declarative language to define system configurations and is considered to be very user friendly.
- **Ansible:** Ansible is a Red Hat product that is gaining in popularity. Ansible supports automated software provisioning, configuration management, and application deployment. Ansible uses YAML to define system configurations and describing the optimal state of an infrastructure.

Downgrades

Downgrading an OS or an application implies removing a previous upgrade and reinstalling the older version that the upgrade replaced. But one might wonder, why would you do such a thing? Maybe the upgrade had functional problems or would not completely install. Whatever the reason, most systems do not really support downgrades and if they do, like Microsoft, there is a short time limit for when it can happen. For example, downgrading to Windows 10 after upgrading to Windows 11 must be done within 10 days of the upgrade.

Upgrade software (setups) are developed strictly to do exactly that, that is, upgrade. There is no code in the upgrade script or software to support a downgrade. If you do decide that you wish to downgrade a newer version back to its predecessor, hopefully you gave this some thought before making the upgrade. Before upgrading, you should make a backup of the downgrade system, so that if you wish to return to it, you can restore it. Otherwise, you may have no recourse. However, some Linux distros have utilities or downloadable available that can help you out. Before performing a downgrade operation, you should evaluate any new updates or revisions to the systems that may have remedied the problem being avoided.

Tip: In production environments, system (server) rollbacks should be considered to be an eventuality. Before making any major changes to a system, including a rollback, always back up the system, take a snapshot, or create an image, along with verifying all existing restore points.

Group Policy Object

The **Group Policy Object** (**GPO**) is a Windows snap-in that consists of a collection of group policy settings that set the rights and privileges of a defined user group. Group policies are defined as one of three types:

- **Local GPOs:** Local GPOs are settings that apply only to user accounts on a local computer. Local GPOs exist by default on all Windows computers.
- **Non-local GPOs:** Non-local GPOs apply to one or more Windows system and their users that are linked to Active Directory objects, such as sites, domains, or organizational units.
- **Starter GPOs:** Starter GPOs are templates for Group Policy settings that an administrator can use to create pre-configured group settings for any future policies.

Group policies are managed through a snap-in named the **Group Policy Management Console** (**GPMC**), shown in *Figure 23.4*. GPOs are linked to Active Directory containers, including sites, domains or **Organizational Units** (**OU**). Through the GPMC, you can create GPOs for registry-based polices, and security, software installation and maintenance, scripts and folder redirection options.

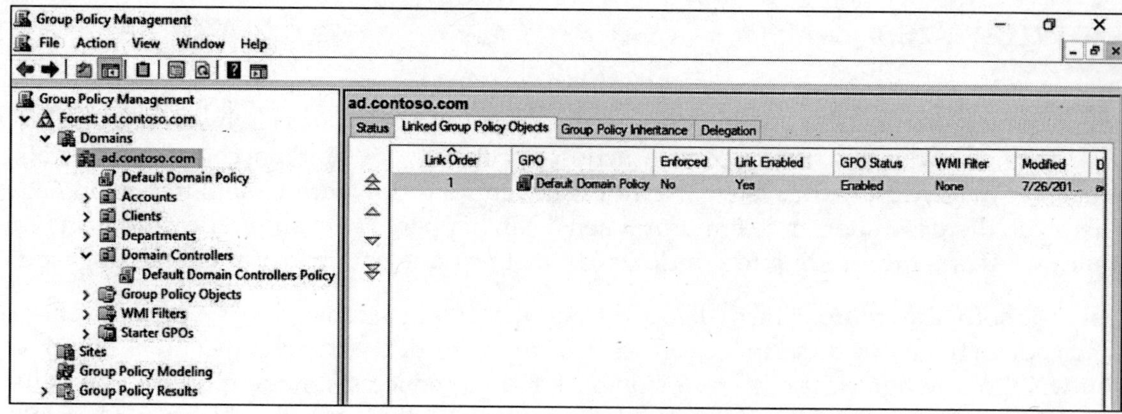

Figure 23.4: The Group Policy Management Console

Network time protocol

The **Network Time Protocol** (**NTP**) provides clock synchronization in a computer system. NTP relies on the **coordinated universal time** (**UTC**) from individual clients and servers. NTP synchronizes system clocks at nanosecond levels interacting with any of the dozens of primary time servers on the Internet. Many Internet-oriented organizations provide public NTP servers, including Google (*time.google.com*), Cloudflare (*time.cloudflare.com*), Apple (*time.apple.com*), and the NIST (*time-a-g.nist.gov*). The underlying time sources, which are atomic or radio clocks, provide accurate time to the primary time servers and are made available to private networks.

Package management

A **package management system** consists of software that can automate the installation, upgrade, configuration, as well as removal of computer programs and applications from a system. Package managers work with software packages that contain software and data stored as archives. The package also includes metadata that identifies the software, its purpose, version, developer, the dependencies required for the software to execute properly, and a hash total. The package management system stores the metadata in a package database that also tracks the dependencies and release information. The purpose of a package management system is to provide automatic installations and updates on local and remote systems.

Patching

A patch consists of one or more files that contain updates, fixes, or additions to an operating system or an application. Patches are commonly used to remediate system vulnerabilities as well. A patch is applied to a system by an automated process or under the control of a system administrator. Most patches are permanent fixes but can also be stop-gap or temporary. Some patches can be poorly designed and, while fixing one problem, can create problems in an unrelated area.

Privilege escalation

Privilege escalation is a form of cyberattack that seeks to gain not only access to a system, but to gain elevated privileges on that system. A **privilege escalation attack** typically begins with some form of social engineering, such as phishing or shoulder surfing. Once the attacker has a set of valid network user credentials, they have access to the network, but only at the privilege level of that particular user.

Privilege escalation attacks can take one of two forms:

- **Horizontal privilege escalation:** Also called an account takeover, in this type of privilege escalation attack, the attack gains access to a standard user account and then moves laterally through the system to find accounts with elevated access privileges.
- **Vertical privilege escalation:** After gaining access to a standard account, the attacker looks for user accounts with higher privileges, such as an **Administrator** or **root** account.

Reloading an OS

Although it may be a last resort solution, major problems on a computer, if bad enough, may require a complete reload of the operating system. Any number and type of problems can be wiped away when the OS is re-installed, including refreshing the boot sector and any system files that became corrupted, damaged, or went missing. The process involves two primary steps:

1. **Backup:** The first step in the process of reloading the OS is to back up all user files, which the reinstallation process will destroy. You may even want to perform a data cleanup before creating the back up.
2. **Installation or restore media:** Boot the computer from the restore disk that should have come with the OS. If not, you can also use the installation disk to restore the system. However, if neither is available, you can use the product key or the product number to create a restore disk. Search the OS developer's website for these instructions.

Run as command

The Windows Run As command is used when a user needs to run a program or command under the account of a different user. The most common usage of this command is the "**Run as administrator**" option that appears on a program's pop-up (right-click) menu. Refer to the following *Figure 23.5*:

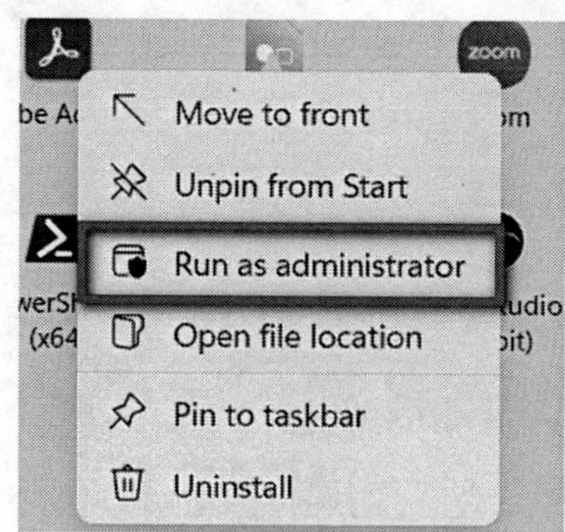

***Figure 23.5:** The Run as Administrator option for a program*

The **Run As** command is most commonly used by administrators to execute commands requiring administrator privileges when they are logged in with a standard user account. However, most users can also use this command to run a program as a different user. When you enter the **Run As** command with another user's username and enter the account's password, another **Command (cmd)** window opens, as shown in *Figure 23.6*. Any command to be entered as the Run As user, is entered into the new shell. For example, the command **`Runas /user:User1 cmd`** will ask for User1's password and then open a new window for that user.

```
cmd (running as DESKTOP-5I0RQST\User1)
Microsoft Windows [Version 10.0.22621.1702]
(c) Microsoft Corporation. All rights reserved.

C:\Windows\System32>_
```

***Figure 23.6:** A cmd window opened by the runas command*

The Run As command has a number of options that can be selected through its parameters. The more commonly used are listed in the following *Table 23.2*:

Parameter	Description
`/user`	The user account that you want to use
`/noprofile`	Do not load a user profile (the application will load faster). /profile is the default
`/netonly`	Use credentials for remote access only
`/savecred`	Save login credentials for later use
	Display the available trust levels

***Table 23.2:** Run As command parameters*

On a Linux system, root is the equivalent of the Windows Administrator account. The root user account has the rights and privileges to all files and programs in every directory and every mode. To access the system as the root or "superuser," you must either log into the system as the root or use one of the following commands:

- **su (superuser)**: The **su** command can switch to the root account or execute a command using root permissions and privileges.
- **sudo (superuser do)**: The **sudo** elevates the execution of a single command to root privileges.
- **doas**: The **doas** command is used to run a command using the privileges of another user account. It is the equivalent of the **runas** Windows command.

Safe mode

On a Windows system, you can boot up in a diagnostics "safe" mode. **Safe Mode** provides an alternative startup when Windows does not start in its normal mode. Safe Mode can also fix many OS problems and remove PUPs and malware. Safe mode differs from a normal mode by loading only the essential elements of the OS and the device drivers for only the display and data entry devices. Most operating systems offer some version of a safe mode.

Safe mode on a Windows OS is accessed through the Startup Setting menu, as shown in *Figure 23.7*. Safe mode is available in three options:

- **Safe Mode (standard):** Starts up Windows with minimum drivers and services, including no local or Internet networking.
- **Safe Mode with Networking:** Starts up Windows in Safe mode with networking services available.
- **Safe Mode with Command Prompt:** Starts up Windows in Safe mode at a command prompt.

Refer to the following figure:

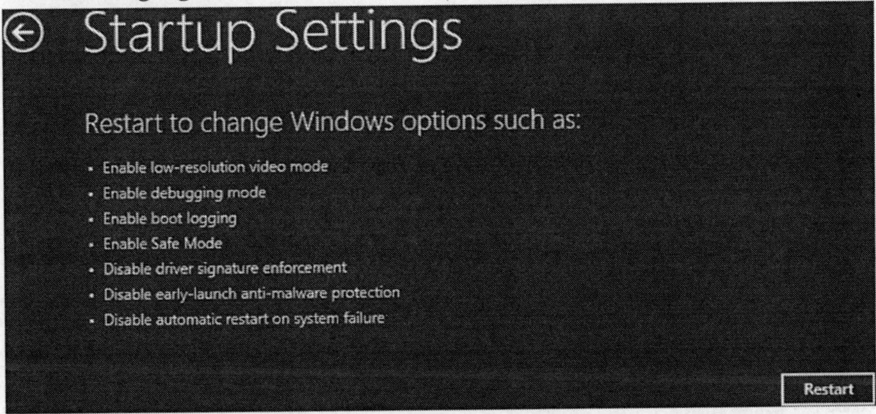

Figure 23.7: *Safe mode can be started through the Startup Settings menu*

The equivalent to Safe Mode on a Linux system is **single-user mode**. Only the root (administrator) can log into this system mode to make corrections, do repairs or maintenance, and reset passwords. On a macOS system, **Safe Boot** is the equivalent of the Windows Safe Mode.

Scheduled reboots

For many reasons, systems should be restarted or shut down on a regular basis, if for no other reason than to flush temporary data in RAM, cache, and files. All OSs provide a means to schedule a system restart or shut down.

Windows OS

On a Windows system, the **Task Scheduler** can be used to shut down, restart or execute commands at a specific time, on a schedule, periodically, or just once. To setup a regularly scheduled restart of a Windows system, use the following steps:

1. Open the Run box (*Win+R*), enter **`taskschd.msc`** in the Open box and press *Ctrl+Shift+Enter* together to run the Task Scheduler as an administrator. Refer to the following figure:

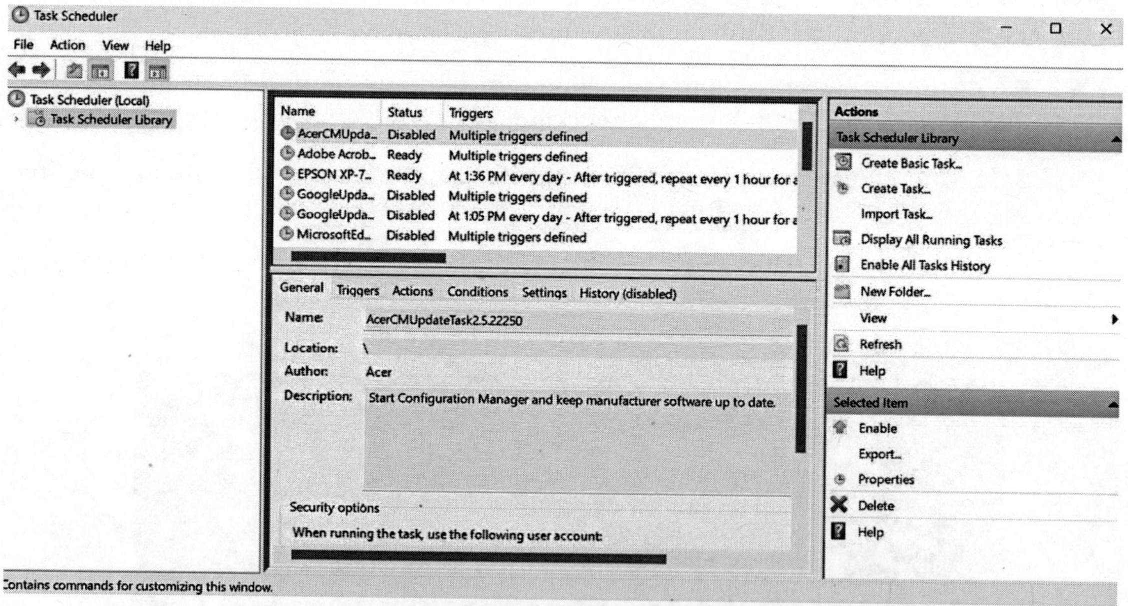

Figure 23.8: The Windows Task Scheduler

2. On the Task Scheduler app, shown in *Figure 23.8*, click on **Create Basic Task** in the right-side pane to open the **Create Basic Task Wizard**. Refer to the following figure:

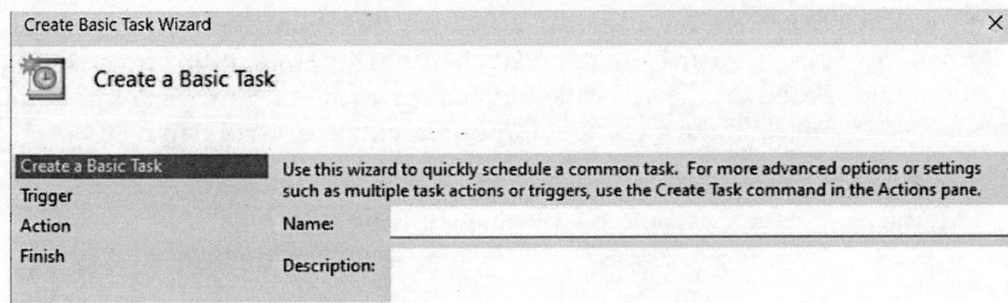

***Figure 23.9:** The Create a Basic Task Wizard*

3. Enter a descriptive **Name** for this task and an optional short description, and then click **Next**.
4. On the **Task Trigger** page, click on the radio button associated with the frequency this task is to execute. Click **Next**.
5. On the page for the frequency selected on the previous page, set a **Start** time, how often the task is to reoccur, and the day of the week it is to run (for other than daily). Click **Next**.
6. On the **Action** page, select the **Start a program** option and click **Next**.
7. On the **Start a program** page, enter **`shutdown`** in the **Program/script** box and enter the parameters **/s `/f /t 0`** in the **Add arguments** box. Click **Next**.
8. On the **Finish** page, review the **Task** and its settings and click **Finish** to record and schedule the task.

Figure 23.10 shows the entry added to the Task Scheduler for the reboot.

***Figure 23.10:** The reboot task added to the Windows Task Scheduler*

Linux OS

To schedule a reboot on a Linux system, you have two options: one to set a later time on the same day for the reboot and the other, for scheduling a reboot at some point in the future on a regular schedule. These options are outlined as follows:

- To reboot the system at a certain time later in the same session, use the following command:

  ```
  shutdown -r 0:00
  ```

  In the above **`shutdown`** command example, the "**`-r`**" option indicates a reboot and the time (0:00) indicates that this action will occur at midnight.

- To reboot the system on a regular schedule, the **`cron`** utility is used to execute scheduled jobs from the **`/etc/crontab`** file. The **cron** utility runs scripts and commands based on the schedule defined for each entry in the **crontab** file. The schedule for a job in the crontab is indicated with a series of parameters.

  For example, to schedule a reboot of the system to run weekly on Fridays at 10:00 PM, the crontab entry would be like that shown in *Figure 23.11*:

```
00 22 * * 5   root   shutdown -r
          |____ day of week (0-6) (0 is Sunday)
        | _____ month (1-12)
      |   _____ day of month (1-31)
    | _________ hour (0-23)
  |___________ minute (0-59)
```

Figure 23.11: *The format of a Linux crontab entry*

On a macOS system, a reboot is scheduled through the **Energy Saver** app on the **System Preferences** page.

Software firewalls

First, do not confuse "software firewall" with "firewall software." The first is a software system that runs on server hardware, virtual machine, or a network host with functions that emulate a hardware firewall. The second one, "firewall software," is an OS running on a **next-generation firewall** (**NGFW**).

A **software firewall**, such as the Windows Defender Firewall with Advanced Security, Comodo Internet Security, and the open-source pfSense system works and is configured in much the same way as a hardware firewall. Software firewalls protect data, applications and communications in situations where a hardware firewall is difficult or impossible to deploy. Software firewalls are commonly used in **Software-Defined Networks** (**SDN**), virtualized data centers, branch offices, and hybrid and multi-cloud environments.

Status identification

In the context of network servers, status indication can reflect the operating condition of a server and its major components, or it can report on the state of a remote server, such as a web server. Several server monitoring systems scan the components and processes of a server to identify potential problems or failures, such as Paessler PRTG, Netwrix Auditor, and Nagios. However, if you only wish to know the state of a remote server, you can use several online server status checkers for that purpose. *Figure 23.12* illustrates an example of the RecordMetrics.com Server Status Checker (**https://recordmetrics.com/tools/server-status-checker**):

Server Status Checker

Result Status of each sites

No.	URLs	HTTP Code	Response Time	Status
1	23.227.38.65	403	0.00 Sec	Online
2	54.239.28.85	unknown	No Response Sec	Offline
3	67.222.36.113	unknown	No Response Sec	Offline

Figure 23.12: *The output of a Server Status Checker online app*

Stopping: kill a stuck service

Occasionally, a service gets stuck in "Starting" or "Stopping" status for longer than either should take. The easiest way to resolve the issue is to restart the system, but that option is not always available. The other ways to end (kill) a stuck service are detailed in the next section.

Windows

On a Windows system, the steps to kill the service are:

1. On the Task Manager's Services tab, identify the service that has been in the status of either **Starting** or **Stopping** for an extended time.
2. Get the PID. Using the service's Name from the Task Master list, enter the following command at a command prompt or in PowerShell to get the **process id (PID)** of the service (the Name from the Task Manager's Services tab is the **`System_Name`** of the service):

   ```
   sc queryx <System_Name>
   ```

3. In the output of the **`sc`** command, find the service's **PID**, as shown in the following figure:

```
SERVICE_NAME: AdobeARMService
        TYPE               : 10  WIN32_OWN_PROCESS
        STATE              : 2  START_PENDING
                                (STOPPABLE, NOT_PAUSABLE, IGNORES_SHUTDOWN)
        WIN32_EXIT_CODE    : 0  (0x0)
        SERVICE_EXIT_CODE  : 0  (0x0)
        CHECKPOINT         : 0x0
        WAIT_HINT          : 0x0
        PID                : 7876
        FLAGS              :
```

Figure 23.13: *The output of the sc queryx command*

4. Using the PID, stop the service with the following command:

   ```
   taskkill /PID 7876 /F
   ```

The response from the command should be: "**`SUCCESS: The process with PID 7876 has been terminated`**."

Linux

On a Linux system, there are occasions where there are stopped processes in RAM, that should be eliminated to free up any resources they are holding. The command to kill only stopped (terminated or suspended) processes on a Linux system is:

```
kill -9 $(jobs -p)
```

Figure 23.14 illustrates the sequence of commands used to kill stopped, terminated, and suspended processes. In the first **`ps -l`** (list processes) command, the PID 204 has been terminated (Status = "T"). The kill command is entered and the subsequent **`ps -l`** command shows this process has been killed.

```
bpbonline: $ps -l
F S   UID   PID  PPID  C PRI  NI ADDR SZ WCHAN  TTY          TIME CMD
4 S  1000   197   196  0  80   0 -  1790 do_wai pts/1    00:00:00 bash
0 T  1000   204   197  0  80   0 - 96236 do_sig pts/1    00:00:00 gnome-mahjongg
1 T  1000   209   196  0  80   0 -  2518 do_sig pts/1    00:00:00 dbus-launch
0 R  1000   272   197  0  80   0 -  2419 -      pts/1    00:00:00 ps
bpbonline: $kill -9 $(jobs -p)
bpbonline: $ps -l
F S   UID   PID  PPID  C PRI  NI ADDR SZ WCHAN  TTY          TIME CMD
4 S  1000   197   196  0  80   0 -  1790 do_wai pts/1    00:00:00 bash
0 R  1000   278   197  0  80   0 -  2419 -      pts/1    00:00:00 ps
[1]+  Killed                  gnome-mahjongg
```

Figure 23.14: *The steps in killing a terminated process*

TIP: The Linux top command allows you to see if there are suspended, sleeping or zombie processes along with their resource usage.

System Center Configuration Manager

The Microsoft **System Center Configuration Manager (SCCM)** is a Windows tool that allow an administrator to manage, deploy, and secure system hardware and software locally or remotely across an enterprise network. Some of its most common uses are endpoint protection, patch and update management, and software configuration and installation. SCCM allows an administrator to manage systems from a central location. Some of the features in SCCM are Windows management, endpoint protection, system reporting, OS deployment, and system health monitoring.

Note: The Microsoft Endpoint Configuration Manager (MECM), which is a part of the InTune suite, has recently replaced the System Center Configuration Manager (SCCM).

Zones

On a Windows system, there are two types of zones: security zones and DNS zones. DNS zones also apply to Linux and macOS, but the Windows security zones are unique. Let us deal with the DNS zones first.

DNS Zones

DNS zones are designated areas assigned to a person, organization, or corporation for administration and maintenance. Zones also include responsibilities for the authoritative servers and other DNS components in an area. When you enter a URL for a website, your browser issues a DNS request to convert the URL into an IP address. The request first performs a DNS zone lookup and is then sent to the DNS authoritative server for the zone in which the website is located. The authoritative server provides the IP address for the URL.

DNS is layered in domain levels: **Top Level Domains** (**TLD**) like .com, .org, .net; second-level domains like bpbonline.com, and subdomains or domains within domains, like support.bpbonline.com. Each of the domain levels can have a DNS zone. This means that a root domain like bpbonline.com may be delegated to the BPBOnline company and it takes on the responsibility for setting up the authoritative DNS server for that domain. Each level of the DNS system has a nameserver that includes a zone database that contains the DNS records for the zone.

The hierarchy of the DNS zones is as follows:

- **Root zones:** The root zone is the absolute top level of the DNS hierarchy. Essentially, it is represented by the dot (period) between the domain name and the TLD, as in bpbonline.com. The root zone is distributed to 13 organizations, including the U.S. Army's Research Labs, **National Aeronautics and Space Administration** (**NASA**), and Verisign. A DNS request or query first contacts one of the root servers for information on the TLD level, the next level down.

- **TLD zones:** Each of the TLDs, of which there are more than 1,500, are the extensions that are intended to indicate the type of website or operator included in the zone, such as ".com," ".org," or ".info." There are also country TLDs, such as ".uk (United Kingdom)," ".cn (China)," ".in (India)," and ".tv (Tuvalu*)*.

- **Second-level domain zones:** The domains on this level, which are domains assigned to individuals and organizations, are separate DNS zones. An organization can operate and maintain its own DNS name server or assign it to an external DNS services provider.

- **Subdomains:** A subdomain is a part of its parent domain zone by default but can be separated as its own DNS zone.

Security zones

Windows OSs predefine a set of four security zones: Internet, Local Intranet, Trusted Sites, and Restricted Sites. The security zones are accessed through the Windows Control Panel and the Internet Options icon, which open a dialog box entitled **Internet Properties**, as shown in *Figure 23.15*. The security levels can be set for each zone independently using the slide scale in the middle of the dialog box. Here is a bit more about each of the security zones:

- **Internet zone:** This zone contains external websites that are not on local servers or on the internal intranet of an organization or individual. A website may also be included in the trusted sites zone.
- **Local intranet zone:** This zone sets Web content permissions on your local area network.
- **Trusted sites zone:** This zone contains the website that have been designated as safe and trusted.
- **Restricted sites zone:** This zone is the opposite of the trusted sites zone in that it contains the websites designated as unsafe and untrusted.

Refer to the following figure:

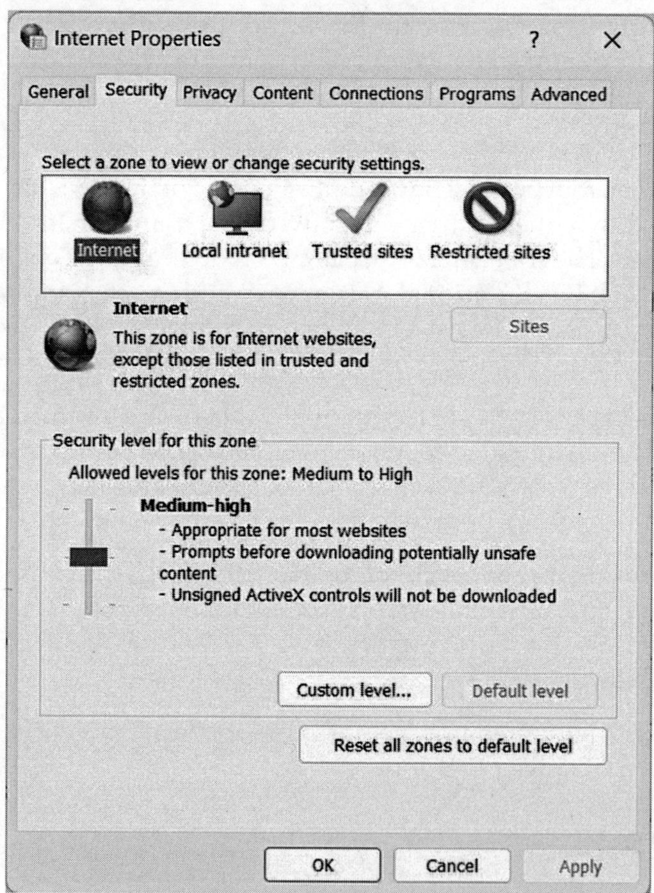

Figure 23.15: The Internet Properties dialog box

Conclusion

The tools and techniques discussed in this chapter provide both investigative and verification of system problems on a network server. System administrators used these tools and techniques, as well as many others, to monitor, troubleshoot, and mitigate operational, configuration, and throughput problems on a server, host, or networked device. For the Server+ exam, the successful certification candidate knows the right tool or technique to diagnose, monitor, or fix any potential problem.

In the next chapter, we will look at the problems and issues that can impact the connectivity and communication of a network server and its hosts.

Points to remember

- A port is a virtual addressing indicator for where a network connection starts and ends as well as the process, protocol, or service to which it is associated.
- The options on the ASO menu relate to diagnostics, repair, and troubleshooting: Reset This PC, System Restore, Command Prompt, Startup Repair, and Startup Settings, which is where Safe Mode is included.
- A computer has two clocks: the **Real Time Clock** (**RTC**) and the Software clock.
- Configuration management includes the procedures involved in establishing and maintaining computer hardware, servers, and software versions in a preferred and constant configuration.
- There are two types of configuration assessments: computer system configuration assessments and **Security Configuration Assessments** (**SCA**).
- Configuration drift occurs when changes are made between the design of the configuration and the actual application of the configuration settings on the system.
- Three popular configuration management tools are: Chef, Puppet, and Ansible.
- Downgrading an OS or an application removes a previous upgrade and reinstalling the older version that the upgrade replaced.
- The **Group Policy Object** (**GPO**) is a collection of group policy settings defining the rights and privileges of a defined user group. Group policies are one of three types: Local GPO, Non-local GPOs, and Starter GPOs.
- NTP provides clock synchronization in a computer system.
- A package management system is software that automates the installation, upgrade, configuration, and removal of computer programs and applications from a system.

- A patch is a set of files that contain updates, fixes, and additions to an OS or an application.
- Privilege escalation is a cyberattack that seeks to gain elevated user account privileges on a system. Privilege escalation attacks have two forms: horizontal privilege escalation and vertical privilege escalation.
- The Windows Run As command allows a user to run a program or command as a different user. On a Linux system, to access the system as a superuser use *su, sudo,* or *doas*.
- Safe Mode is an alternative startup for Windows in normal mode. It has three options: Safe Mode, Safe Mode with Networking, and Safe Mode with Command Prompt. The equivalent to Safe Mode on a Linux system is single-user mode. On a macOS system, Safe Boot is the equivalent of the Windows Safe Mode.
- All OSs provide a means to schedule a system restart or shut down.
- A software firewall is a software system that runs on server hardware, virtual machine, or a network host to emulate a hardware firewall.
- Status indication reflects the condition or state of a server and its major components.
- To resolve a process stuck in start or stop, kill the PID.
- DNS zones are designated areas assigned to a person, organization, or corporation for administration and maintenance. The hierarchy of the DNS is root zones, TLD zones, and second-level zones.
- Windows defines four security zones: Internet, Local Intranet, Trusted Sites, and Restricted Sites.

CHAPTER 24
Network Connectivity Issues

Introduction

Businesses and organizations rely on computer networks for information, applications, communication, and interchange in the form of analysis, reporting, email, Web access, and personal productivity. It is common for the organization's computer network to be so integrated into its operations and culture that its availability is assumed. Therefore, when a technical problem causes the network to be unavailable, network and system administrators are responsible for identifying and resolving the problem, and reassuring the integrity of the network. All this must be done in as little time as possible. This chapter identifies the common problems, issues and their causes on a computer network.

Structure

The chapter covers the following topics:

- Common network problems
- Causes of common problems

Objective

By the end of this chapter, you will be able to identify and describe the sub-objectives of the following Server+ examination objective: *Given a scenario, troubleshoot network connectivity issues.*

Common network problems

What may be a "common" network problem or issue to one organization, may be something that another organization has never experienced. The hardware, software, and configuration issues that can occur, depend not only a function of the size and complexity of the network, but on the age of the equipment and systems and how they are used. However, in general, and on the Server+ exam, the problems and issues listed in the following sections are the ones you should know and recognize for the exam.

Internet connectivity

In some organizations, those that rarely access sites beyond their local networks, losing connectivity to the Internet may not be too much of a problem. However, in organizations that work with applications, systems, databases, and other resources in the public, private, or perhaps a hybrid cloud, the loss of Internet connection can be almost catastrophic.

The communication link between a local network and a **Wide Area Network (WAN)** or Internet, includes a variety of devices and software, any of which could cause the link to fail. The following are the elements of the connection to the world outside a **Local Area Network (LAN)** and its potential to cause a break in the connectivity to the Internet:

- **Power:** Firstly, verify that the problem device has electrical power. Check the electrical cord and plugs.
- **Cables:** On wired networks, lose or faulty connectors can cause connectivity problems. Ensure that there are no sharp bends, pinches, or breaks in the sheathing of the cables.
- **Connections:** On wireless networks, if a node is not able to associate with an access point or router, check the connection settings on the node. Verify that the node is within the wireless standard's range and that no materials near the node may be blocking the signal. You should also check to see that no other high-power RF devices operating nearby, such as a radio transmitter, could interfere with the Wi-Fi signal.
- **Network adapters:** If a Windows host is configured with an **Automatic Private IP Addressing (APIPA)** address (169.254.0.1 to 169.254.254.255), it is an indication that the host failed to connect with the **Dynamic Host Configuration Protocol (DHCP)** server when it booted up. The issues here may be that the

Network Interface Card (**NIC**) is faulty; the DHCP server is misconfigured, or anything in-between. If the NIC is suspected as the source of the problem, use the PING command as an attempt to reach the localhost IP (127.0.0.1). If this fails, the NIC may be the problem. You may also want to check the status of the NIC and its driver in the **Windows Device Manager**.

- **Gateway device and its configuration:** The gateway device is typically a router, bridge, modem, or the like, depending on the type of connection (cable, wireless, telephone, and so on). Suppose a host cannot reach its gateway device and you are sure it has power and is working. In that case, the problem may be the IP configuration of the host or the gateway's configuration has become changed, corrupted, or the device may need to be reset.
- **Communication service:** If a node is unable to connect to the Internet and all else is working, the problem is either that the gateway device is faulty or there is a problem with the service provider. If all subscriber-side devices are working, the ISP service is most likely down.

Network resource unavailable

Should a warning message box (as shown in *Figure 24.1*) display a message indicating that a feature or object is unavailable on the network, it could mean that the object has either been moved to a new location or the object or its folder has been deleted, among several other less frequent causes.

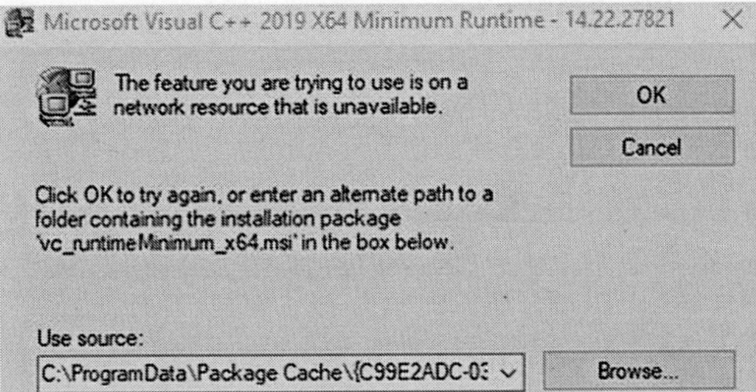

Figure 24.1: *A message box stating that a network resource is unavailable*

Some of the causes behind a **network resource unavailable error** are:

- **Firewall rules:** A network or host firewall can block access to some network resources either intentionally or unintentionally.
- **Antivirus and anti-malware:** An antivirus or an anti-malware application can block access to a network resource because of false positive virus detection.
- **Network connection:** A faulty Internet connection will cause file downloading problems.

Configuration problems

Errors and omissions in the configurations of the various components, both hardware and software on a network, can cause several network issues. The configuration of the **Network Operating System** (**NOS**) hosts and their operating systems, the NICs or network adapters in any network device, and the interconnecting switching and routing devices, must all be compatible and configured to function in support of the network and its users.

The following sections are the common configuration issues on a network.

DHCP server

There are two common issues for a host failing to receive its IP configuration: no network connectivity or DHCP server issues. When a host boots up, it first establishes a connection with the network and then broadcasts a DHCPDISCOVER packet on the network. Suppose it does not receive a DHCPDISCOVER packet in response. In that case, the host configures its IP configuration with an **Automatic Private IP Addressing** (**APIPA**) default network address (as discussed in the following section). A network host can boot and join a LAN without receiving a configuration from a DHCP server. However, configured with an APIPA address, the host cannot access any addresses outside of the local network.

DHCP server issues

The issues common to a DHCP server are typically caused by errors in its configuration. Common DHCP server problems are:

- **Duplicate IP configurations:** When multiple devices (router, switch, or network server) have an enabled DHCP server function with overlapping address scopes or ranges and issue duplicate IP configurations to two or more hosts.
- **Exhausted address pool:** When the address pool of a DHCP server is exhausted (assigned), the next host request is denied and the host must configure itself with an APIPA address.

DHCP servers allocate network configuration to hosts in one of three ways:

- **Automatic:** This form of address allocation designates an IP address to a host from its address pool with an "Unlimited" lease period, which indicates that the address is a permanent IP and will not expire.
- **Dynamic:** This address allocation option assigns an IP address from a pre-defined address scope (pool) for a preset lease period (duration). Dynamic address assignments can be renewed.
- **Static:** A static IP address is a Reserved address, permanently linked to a host's MAC address. A network administrator assigns a static address to a specific host. When the host requests its configuration, the DHCP server includes the static address in

the configuration that it sends to the host. The Static DHCP address allocations are permanent and remain with the host even if it reboots. Static addresses are most commonly used for network peripheral devices, such as printers, storage units, etc.

APIPA

As mentioned earlier, if a host has an established network connection, but cannot connect to a DHCP server, it is automatically configured with an APIPA address from the range of 169.254.0.0 to 169.254.254.255. The APIPA address is verified as available and unique through the **Address Resolution Protocol (ARP)** before the host can use it. A host assigned an APIPA address sends a discover message to the DHCP server periodically (typically every 5 minutes or so) to see if the DHCP server can service requests and provide a configuration. A host can communicate on a LAN using an APIPA address. However, routers will not forward APIPA addresses and may require network switches to be configured for these addresses.

Destination host unreachable

The **Destination host unreachable** error (as shown in *Figure 24.2*) is typically a response of a ping (Packet Internet Groper) command, but it could also result from an IP address entered into the address bar of a browser. The cause of this error could be cable connection problems or even a proxy server or firewall that is configured too strictly. However, in most cases, the gateway router of the local network is replying that it is unable to forward the ping request message to its destination. There is a difference between a Destination host unreachable error and a **Request timed out** response. The first is likely an error or misconfiguration on a network, and the second is caused by a bad or unassigned IP address.

```
Microsoft Windows [Version 10.0.19044.2006]
(c) Microsoft Corporation. All rights reserved.

C:\Users\Administrator>ping 192.168.1.101

Pinging 192.168.1.101 with 32 bytes of data:
Reply from 192.168.1.206: Destination host unreachable.
Request timed out.
Request timed out.
Request timed out.

Ping statistics for 192.168.1.101:
    Packets: Sent = 4, Received = 1, Lost = 3 (75% loss),
```

Figure 24.2: *A ping command with a Destination host unreachable error*

Unknown host

A few Windows and Linux commands can result in the error message referring to an "Unknown host." The more common of these are:

- **Ping:** Cannot resolve or find the host. The error message shown in *Figure 24.3*, indicates that the hostname entered is not associated with an IP address. This could be for one of three common reasons:
    - o The default DNS server may be misconfigured or may be unreachable.
    - o The host name is not registered in a DNS server.
    - o The host name may no longer exist, never existed, or was entered incorrectly.

```
PS C:\> ping bpbpbonline.com
Ping request could not find host bpbpbonline.com. Please check the name and try again.
```

Figure 24.3: The unknown host message in a ping command

- **Linux `hostname -i`:** The Hostname unknown error indicates that DNS is unable to resolve the hostname into an IP address. The problem could be either with the DNS server or the hostname of the host not being correctly configured.

Unable to reach remote subnets

Suppose a host on one network or subnet wishes to communicate with a host on another network or subnet, especially a remote network subnet. In that case, there must be an entry for the destination address in the local device's routing table (also known as forwarding information base or MAC table). This entry includes the remote host's network address, a subnet mask (either dotted decimal form or a **Classless Inter-Domain Routing** (**CIDR**) suffix), and the interface on the gateway router through which the remote host's network or subnet can be reached. Without this entry, the remote host cannot be reached.

The primary issues to check include:

- **Addressing:** Check that the respective source and destination addresses are configured to pass in edge router and firewall devices.
- **Routing:** The gateway router of the sending host must have an active route to the remote subnet.
- **Firewall and routing policies:** If policy routing or filtering is used, create a policy route to the source and destination subnets.
- **VPN:** If a **Virtual Private Network** (**VPN**) is in use, for LAN to VPN, **Network Address Translation** (**NAT**) should be disabled. For VPN to LAN, **Port Address Translation** (**PAT**) should be enabled.

Failure of service provider

Although it is rare, ISPs can suffer outages or even system problems. If the Internet service to a home or office is suddenly out, first try to reset the router, bridge, or modem. If that fails to restart the service, check the ISP's website, social media page, or use a service status checker site, such as *downdetector.com*.

Another issue that can impact an Internet service connection is network congestion. While it can interrupt your service intermittently, it is more common that it just slows it down. Internet services on cable, **Digital Subscriber Line** (**DSL**), satellite, and 5G home Internet are the most susceptible to network congestion.

Cannot reach server

A hostname is the identity of a network node (sales) or in the wide world of the Internet, the name of a Web server (www). The domain of a website is the part issued and registered by the **Internet Corporation for Assigned Names and Numbers** (**ICANN**) that identifies the site along with its **top-level domain** (**TLD**), such as bpbonline.com. Combine the hostname and the domain name, in that order, and the **Fully Qualified Domain Name** (**FQDN**) is formed, as in *sales.bpbonline.com*.

DNS record types

The content and accuracy of the information stored in the records of a DNS server are important for addressing or connecting with a local or remote device. A DNS server holds several different types of records, each of which serves a purpose in supporting the translation of domains and FQDNs into IP addresses. DNS records are text files in the DNS syntax. *Table 24.1* lists the more common DNS record types and their purposes:

Type	Name	Purpose
A	**Address record**	Translates domain names and IPv4 addresses.
AAAA	**Address record**	Translates domain names and IPv6 addresses.
CNAME	**Canonical name**	Used in place of an A record when a domain or subdomain is an alias. Point to a domain name and not an IP address.
HINFO	**Host information**	Details about the hardware and operating system the host is using. On local DNS servers only.
NS	**Nameserver**	Indicates the server containing the DNS records for a domain. A nameserver is a DNS server containing all DNS records for a domain.
PTR	**Pointer record**	Reverse of A or AAAA records that map IP addresses to domain names. IPv4 and IPv6 addresses are saved with the segments in reverse order.
TXT	**Text**	Store descriptive text in combination with other record types.

Table 24.1: *DNS record types that affect name resolution*

Address lookup

Three basic commands can be used to look at the information stored in a DNS server:

- **dig:** This command displays the IPv4 information in an A record for a domain. *Figure 24.4* shows the output of a dig command on a Linux system:

```
bpbonline: $ dig bpbonline.com

; <<>> DiG 9.16.37-Debian <<>> bpbonline.com
;; global options: +cmd
;; Got answer:
;; ->>HEADER<<- opcode: QUERY, status: NOERROR, id: 4758
;; flags: qr rd ad; QUERY: 1, ANSWER: 1, AUTHORITY: 0, ADDITIONAL: 0
;; WARNING: recursion requested but not available

;; QUESTION SECTION:
;bpbonline.com.                 IN      A

;; ANSWER SECTION:
bpbonline.com.          0       IN      A       23.227.38.65

;; Query time: 0 msec
;; SERVER: 172.20.16.1#53(172.20.16.1)
;; WHEN: Fri Jun 16 09:58:09 CDT 2023
;; MSG SIZE  rcvd: 60
```

Figure 24.4: *The output of a dig command on a Linux system*

Figure 24.5 shows the equivalent command output on a Windows system:

```
PS C:\> Resolve-DnsName -Name bpbonline.com -Type A

Name                                           Type   TTL   Section    IPAddress
----                                           ----   ---   -------    ---------
bpbonline.com                                  A      7833  Answer     23.227.38.65
```

Figure 24.5: *The output of the Resolve-DNSName PowerShell command on a Windows system*

- **nslookup:** This command displays the information in a PTR record for a domain. *Figure 24.6* shows the results of a **nslookup** command:

```
PS C:\> nslookup bpbonline.com
Server:  dns.opendns.com
Address:  208.67.222.222

Non-authoritative answer:
Name:    bpbonline.com
Address:  23.227.38.65
```

Figure 24.6: *The results of a nslookup command*

- **ping:** This command typically uses Windows name resolution, which can use DNS, NetBIOS, WINS, and other services, if available. To resolve a hostname, Windows performs the following steps in order:

1. Check to see if the host name is its name.
2. Searches the local Hosts file, which is a list of IP addresses and names on the local host.
3. DNS server resolution is requested using the information in A records.
4. If the name is not resolved at this point, the NetBIOS or WINS is used.

Figure 24.7 shows the output of a ping command:

```
PS C:\> ping bpbonline.com

Pinging bpbonline.com [23.227.38.65] with 32 bytes of data:
Reply from 23.227.38.65: bytes=32 time=24ms TTL=57
Reply from 23.227.38.65: bytes=32 time=23ms TTL=57
Reply from 23.227.38.65: bytes=32 time=23ms TTL=57
Reply from 23.227.38.65: bytes=32 time=23ms TTL=57

Ping statistics for 23.227.38.65:
    Packets: Sent = 4, Received = 4, Lost = 0 (0% loss),
Approximate round trip times in milli-seconds:
    Minimum = 23ms, Maximum = 24ms, Average = 23ms
```

Figure 24.7: *The results of a ping command*

Tip: A ping command on some Linux distros may continue to run until you cancel it with either a Ctrl+Z or a Ctrl+C entry.

Cannot reach server using hostname

If an **nslookup** command finds the server, but a ping or dig does not, and you are unable to connect to the server, the issue is likely that there is a problem with the DNS records for the server or the hostname itself. Changing to a different DNS server, such as Google at 8.8.8.8 or Cloudflare at 1.1.1.1 may resolve the issue. Otherwise, the local DNS server will need to be edited, or a second record PTR record will be added to point back to the hostname from the server.

Cannot reach server using FQDN

This error is commonly resolved by flushing the DNS cache on the local machine. To do so, run the **ipconfig/flushdns** command on a Windows system or the **system-resolve --flush-caches** on a Linux system. If this does not resolve the issue, try switching to a different DNS server and try it again. For a last resort, edit the local DNS database.

Causes of common problems

In reality, there are not many common problems with computer systems. Any computer's problems can reflect its use, location, maintenance, manufacturer, and, most importantly, its user. However, CompTIA includes a list of *common problems* in the Server+ exam objectives, which are covered in the following sections.

Improper IP configuration

On most networks, a DHCP server provides the IP configuration settings to the network nodes. Unless the DHCP server is misconfigured, it is not likely that the node will have an improper IP configuration. However, it does happen. After booting up a computer attached to a network, some common problems could occur:

- **Cannot access the Internet:** If a node can connect to other devices on a local network but cannot access a WAN or the Internet, the DHCP server could be down or unreachable. The node is configured with an APIPA address.
- **Cannot access the LAN:** Chances are that the NIC in the host has failed or is in the process of doing so. If you can **`ping 127.0.0.1`** or **`ping localhost`**, the problem lies elsewhere, such as the cable or connector on the network link, or an intermediary device, such as a switch or hub, may be down.
- **IP configuration is incorrect:** This can happen. For whatever reason, the IP configuration of a network node, whether wired or wireless, has an IP configuration that is incompatible with the network it is trying to join. The best recourse is to reboot the device and let it pick up a fresh IP configuration from DHCP.

Another reason why a computer may not connect to a network is that certain required services may not be enabled and running. Use the Windows Task Manager or the Services app to ensure that the following services are set to start automatically and are running:

- TCP/IP NetBIOS Helper
- Wired or Wireless AutoConfig
- DHCP Client
- DNS Client
- Function Discovery Resource Publication
- SSDP Discovery
- UPnP Device Host

IPv4 vs. IPv6 misconfigurations

The transition from IPv4 to IPv6 has been slowly advancing for over 20 years with IPv6-only networks beginning to appear more frequently. In most cases, networks are referenced with IPv4 and IPv6 records (A and AAAA, respectively). Any errors made in the IPv6 records might not be noticed because the IPv4 records are backing them up. IPv6-only networks generate the AAAA records, and an error in these records can defeat a connection to a remote site. Given the length of the IPv6 address, it is common for transpositions of numbers and improper zero reductions to result in an unreachable address.

One growing misconfiguration error in DNS records is when the IPv4 records (A) and the IPv6 records (AAAA), which should point to the same site, give addresses to different sites. This may occur when a server is moved to a new IP address and one or the other DNS record is updated and the other is forgotten. The solution is to make sure the A and the AAAA records are referencing the same site.

Network port security

By default, all the interfaces (ports) on a network switch are enabled, but not secured. Port security is applied through the configuration settings of each port on the device. The objective is to limit the devices that defined with specific MAC addresses, can access an individual port. Without this configuration, any network node can access the port and possibly send and receive data through the port. Applying port security limits unauthorized access to network resources and the flow of data.

The principle tools in port security are **Access Control Lists** (**ACL**), firewalls, and VLANs, along with authentication protocols such as RADIUS, DIAMETER, and TACACS+. Through the proper configuration of these resources, network traffic from certain source and destination addresses can be limited on the network.

The security on an individual port can be configured to one of three violation modes:

- **Protect:** Any packet with an unknown or unrecognized source address (not identified as secure or valid) is discarded. No log entries are created.
- **Restrict:** Any packet with an unknown source address is dropped, a log entry is created, and a security violation alert is made.
- **Shutdown:** Any packet with an unknown source address is dropped, a violation alert is made, and the port is disabled. The administrator must re-enable the port manually. Shutdown is the default violation mode.

Component failures

Hardware failures are, for the most part, component failures, which can be caused by a wide variety of events or conditions. These causes include electrical spikes or surges, humidity and water damage, age, and uneven or poor maintenance. Component failures can lead to hardware failures, which, in turn, can lead to server failures. When a server goes down and offline, its services are unavailable to users and other network resources until either the failed component is replaced or a high availability or fault tolerant failover is up and running. However, some components must be replaced to restore the server, such as motherboards, CPUs, and cooling systems. A thorough preventive maintenance program with specific attention to these components, as well as **Power Supply Units** (**PSU**) and storage devices, should be formalized and performed regularly, perhaps even daily.

Incorrect OS route tables

First of all, let us look at routing tables in general. Routing tables contain rules, each of which determines where data frames are to be sent to reach their destination addresses. A routing table, regardless of its device (router, switch, server, and so on) has the same format essentially, but the routing data it contains is relative to its location and network environment. On a local network server or host, a routing table is relatively simple.

Routing tables

The entries in routing tables are generally added dynamically as frames are created and forwarded to different destination addresses. However, static routes can be added manually. The entries in a Windows routing table can be viewed using either the **`route print`** or the **`netstat -rn`** commands. *Figure 24.8* and *Figure 24.9* show the contents of the routing tables for IPv4 and Ipv6 addresses, respectively using **`route print`** commands on a Windows network host. To view the routing table on a Linux system, use the command **`ip route`**.

```
Administrator: PowerShell 7 (x64)
PS C:\> route print
===========================================================================
Interface List
  9...98 ee cb d3 de d5 ......Intel(R) Ethernet Connection (11) I219-LM
 19...46 af 28 b3 d4 09 ......Microsoft Wi-Fi Direct Virtual Adapter
 21...44 af 28 b3 d4 0a ......Microsoft Wi-Fi Direct Virtual Adapter #3
  5...44 af 28 b3 d4 09 ......Intel(R) Wi-Fi 6 AX201 160MHz
  1...........................Software Loopback Interface 1
 46...00 15 5d ee 18 c3 ......Hyper-V Virtual Ethernet Adapter
 58...00 15 5d dc 46 e5 ......Hyper-V Virtual Ethernet Adapter #2
===========================================================================

IPv4 Route Table
===========================================================================
Active Routes:
Network Destination        Netmask          Gateway       Interface  Metric
          0.0.0.0          0.0.0.0      192.168.0.1    192.168.0.79     30
        127.0.0.0        255.0.0.0         On-link        127.0.0.1    331
        127.0.0.1  255.255.255.255         On-link        127.0.0.1    331
  127.255.255.255  255.255.255.255         On-link        127.0.0.1    331
      172.20.16.0    255.255.240.0         On-link      172.20.16.1   5256
      172.20.16.1  255.255.255.255         On-link      172.20.16.1   5256
    172.20.31.255  255.255.255.255         On-link      172.20.16.1   5256
      172.28.48.0    255.255.240.0         On-link      172.28.48.1   5256
      172.28.48.1  255.255.255.255         On-link      172.28.48.1   5256
    172.28.63.255  255.255.255.255         On-link      172.28.48.1   5256
      192.168.0.0    255.255.255.0         On-link     192.168.0.79    286
     192.168.0.79  255.255.255.255         On-link     192.168.0.79    286
    192.168.0.255  255.255.255.255         On-link     192.168.0.79    286
        224.0.0.0        240.0.0.0         On-link        127.0.0.1    331
        224.0.0.0        240.0.0.0         On-link     192.168.0.79    286
        224.0.0.0        240.0.0.0         On-link      172.28.48.1   5256
        224.0.0.0        240.0.0.0         On-link      172.20.16.1   5256
```

Figure 24.8: *The IPv4 routing table entries on a Windows system*

Refer to the following figure:

```
PS C:\> route -6 print
===========================================================================
Interface List
  9...98 ee cb d3 de d5 ......Intel(R) Ethernet Connection (11) I219-LM
 19...46 af 28 b3 d4 09 ......Microsoft Wi-Fi Direct Virtual Adapter
 21...44 af 28 b3 d4 0a ......Microsoft Wi-Fi Direct Virtual Adapter #3
  5...44 af 28 b3 d4 09 ......Intel(R) Wi-Fi 6 AX201 160MHz
  1...........................Software Loopback Interface 1
 46...00 15 5d ee 18 c3 ......Hyper-V Virtual Ethernet Adapter
 58...00 15 5d dc 46 e5 ......Hyper-V Virtual Ethernet Adapter #2
===========================================================================

IPv6 Route Table
===========================================================================
Active Routes:
 If Metric Network Destination      Gateway
  1    331 ::1/128                  On-link
  5    286 fe80::/64                On-link
 46   5256 fe80::/64                On-link
 58   5256 fe80::/64                On-link
 46   5256 fe80::1bc5:b0e7:f5da:c05e/128
                                    On-link
 58   5256 fe80::c97c:a39:5396:c14e/128
                                    On-link
  5    286 fe80::d0ad:4520:902c:3553/128
                                    On-link
  1    331 ff00::/8                 On-link
  5    286 ff00::/8                 On-link
 46   5256 ff00::/8                 On-link
 58   5256 ff00::/8                 On-link
===========================================================================
```

Figure 24.9: *The IPv6 routing table entries on a Windows system*

The fields in a routing table are fairly consistent across all OSs. These fields are:

- IPv4 routes
  - **Destination:** This is the IP address of the destination network or host of a packet.
  - **Subnet mask (netmask):** The binary mask is applied through a Boolean ANDing operation to extract the network address.
  - **Gateway:** The address or link to the gateway router or edge router for the host.
  - **Interface:** The Ethernet interface address for forwarding outgoing messages.
  - **Metric:** The value or ranking of a route. If there is more than one route to a destination network, the path with the lowest metric is given precedence.
- IPv6 routes
  - **If (interface):** The interface number from the Interface list.
  - **Metric:** The value or ranking of a route. If there is more than one route to a destination network, the path with the lowest metric is given precedence.
  - **Destination:** This is the IP address of the destination network or host of a packet.

   - **Gateway:** The address or link to the gateway router or edge router for the host.

Routes

Routing table entries (routes) can be created in a variety of ways, including:

- **Interface enabled:** When an interface (NIC, port, and so on) is enabled, a route may be automatically created for it and any address range reachable through it.
- **Static routes:** An administrator adds a static route to a gateway device (router, modem, bridge, and so on).
- **DHCP gateways:** If an interface port uses a DHCP server for its configuration, a default route may be created to the default gateway.
- **Point-to-point routes:** Interfaces using a **Point-to-Point Protocol** (**PPP**) may create a default route to the end of the link.

Routing table errors

Routing table entry errors are the result of entry or content errors made when administrators create entries. However, errors in the configurations of interfacing devices can also cause errors in the routing table as well. Errors in routing table entries can cause message traffic to be forwarded to the wrong port or interface on a switch or router. On a multi-homed server, a routing error could forward traffic through the wrong NIC. Moreover, an error in a routing table entry could cause a message to not be forwarded when it should or maybe not at all.

Troubleshooting tools

The tools most commonly used to troubleshoot issues with a routing table on either a Windows or Linux system are the **`ping`** and **`traceroute/tracert`** commands. The **`ping`** command will tell you whether the issue is a destination address that is down, unavailable, or perhaps in error. The **`traceroute`** command (**`tracert`** on Windows) can indicate where in the path to the destination a problem may exist. A **`traceroute`** command can also show a routing loop in which the path returns to a previously passed router repeatedly.

Device misconfiguration

A misconfigured device, component, or server can either have no effect or bring down a network. On the Server+ certification exam, you can expect to encounter questions concerning misconfigured devices, services, and protocols. The following sections discuss the issues you may see:

Misconfigured NIC

Although a NIC, USB, or an integrated network adapter is relatively reliable, they can fail. When they do fail, the issue is likely to be one of two problems: the NIC is bad or the OS is not allocating the system resources the NIC needs to function properly.

Most NICs have LED lights on their mounting plates to indicate whether they are working properly. When a system is connected to a network, if the status lights on the NIC are not green, there is a problem. *Figure 24.10* shows the LED lights on a NIC expansion card. A problem with a NIC does not necessarily mean that NIC itself is bad and must be replaced. The NIC may need to be reseated, or a jumper block or switch setting on the NIC may be incorrect or incompatible with other changes made to the host computer. Check the documentation for these possibilities.

Figure 24.10: *The LED lights on a network interface card* [1]

The other issue involves a NIC being allocated some or all the same system resources (see the next section) as another device. On a Windows system, the system resources assigned to a device can be viewed through the device's properties and the **Device Manager**. *Figure 24.11* shows the system resources allocated to a NIC on the **Properties** dialog box

1. Image source: Durgtech.com

and **Resources** tab. If there were any conflicts in the resources assigned to the NIC, that information would be included in the **Conflicting device list**.

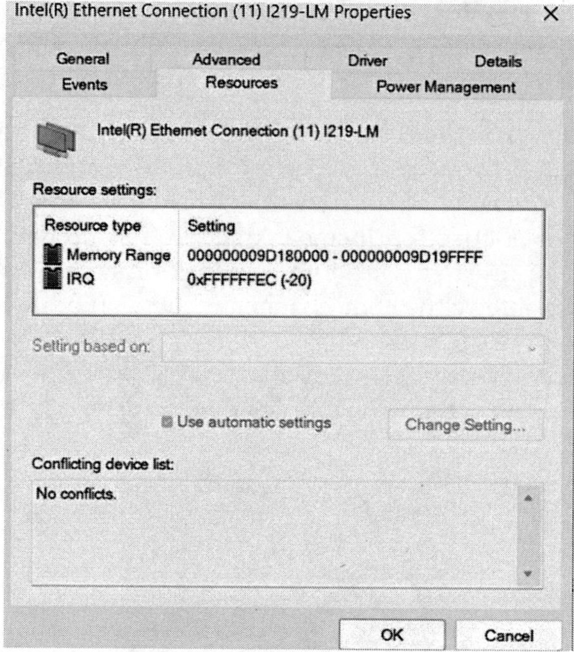

Figure 24.11: The Resources tab of the Properties dialog box of a NIC on a Windows system

Tip: The Windows Device Manager can also display the properties of a built-in network adapter on the motherboard.

System resources

On a Windows system, many settings and components are referred to as system resources, typically related to RAM. However, in the strict use of that term, system resources are features and allocated space through which the OS communicates with hardware devices.

The four system resource types are:

- **Direct memory access (DMA):** DMA is a feature that allows **input/output (I/O)** devices to directly access RAM without going through the CPU.
- **I/O port address:** This feature, also called a port address, is a memory space on a peripheral device controller to pass control signals and data.
- **Interrupt requests (IRQ) line:** When a computer component or peripheral, such as a NIC, wants attention from the CPU, it generates a signal on its assigned IRQ.
- **Memory address range:** A process running on a computer may need to pass or receive data from other processes. To facilitate this, each process is allocated a certain amount of memory in which it can place the data or receive the data.

There is generally one type of error associated with system resources: "Insufficient system resources exist to complete the requested service." What this means typically is that there is not enough memory to load the process, but it could also indicate a conflict in one of the other resource allocations. The simplest resolution of this problem is to end unneeded processes to free up resources or, in the worst case, reboot the system.

VLAN configuration errors

A virtual LAN is a logically-created broadcast domain that is configured on a network switch. A VLAN is designated to one or more interface ports on a switch. Specific network nodes are then associated with the port as members of its VLAN.

As shown in *Figure 24.12*, hosts located on different LAN segments can also be on a VLAN. This figure also shows the trunk lines that interconnect the networking devices (switches and router) through trunk ports:

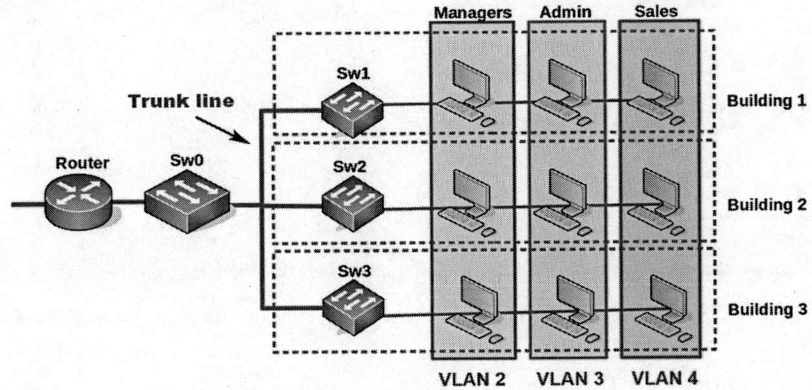

***Figure 24.12:** The configuration of multiple VLANs*

Common VLAN problems include:

- **Incorrect IP addresses:** A network host configured with an incorrect IP address, such as an APIPA or an erroneous subnet address or mask, cannot access the network and VLAN.
- **Port configuration:** An incorrectly configured or unconfigured interface port cannot support a VLAN or does not see it as a network segment or subnet.
- **Disabled VLAN:** A VLAN was configured but left in a "down" state.
- **Trunking protocol:** A VLAN's trunk ports must all be running the same trunking protocol and be configured as either "tagged" or "untagged."
- **Authorized VLAN:** A VLAN must be authorized to access a particular trunk port.
- **Trunk port "flapping:"** Flapping is a hardware failure that causes a port to intermittently power on and off.

Default gateway not available

This is a common network connection problem with causes that are not obvious, and most have nothing specific to do with the gateway device. The problem manifests itself as a sudden loss of access to the Internet and the message **The default gateway is not available**. Refer to the following *Figure 24.13*:

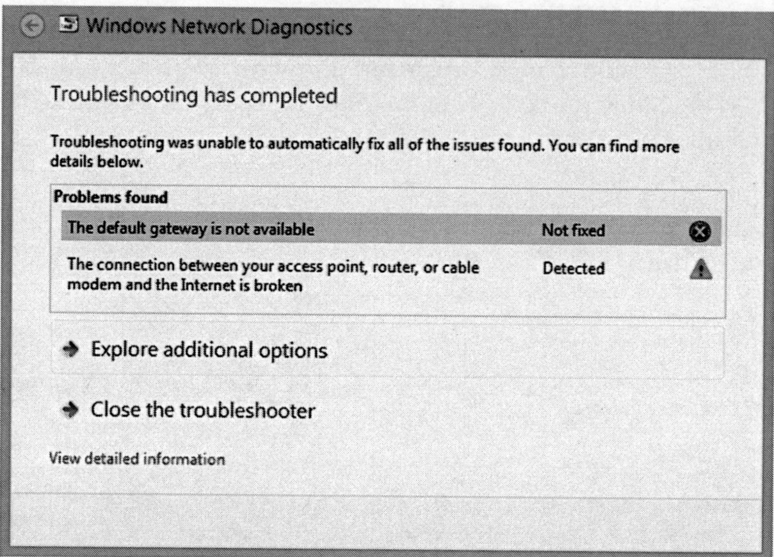

***Figure 24.13:** The Windows Network Diagnostics showing a default gateway issue*

Here are common causes for this issue:

- **Antivirus or anti-malware software:** This software can change the network configuration of a host, including its default gateway. Reset the default gateway configuration by rebooting the computer to refresh the DHCP configuration.
- **Outdated network adapter drivers:** An out-of-date or obsolete device driver for the NIC or network adapter can interfere with a network connection. Check the default gateway connection (ping or traceroute) after applying each of the following fixes until one resolves the problem: reinstall the drivers, update the drivers, and replace or add-in a network adapter.
- **Windows auto-login:** This feature can alter the IP configuration of a host, including the default gateway's address. Disable the auto-login feature and set the login to require a username and password or PIN.

Firewall failure

A firewall can be a specific hardware device, a service provided by a router, or software. Regardless of its form, the purpose of a firewall is the same: protecting a network, server, or host from intrusion or attack. A firewall is essentially the drawbridge at the main gate of the castle. However, much like all components of a computer, a firewall can have problems. Here are just a few:

- **Configuration issues:** A firewall configured primarily from the default configuration is likely not specific enough to meet the needs of any particular organization. A default configuration can be too broad in scope and not specific in detail. The rules and configuration of a firewall should be based on an organization's security policies.
- **Currency issues:** A firewall should not be a "set it and forget it" device. The security settings of a firewall require monitoring and maintenance to keep its rules current to the security needs of its network.
- **Processing power:** Software firewalls must always have sufficient resources in order to handle their peak loads. Removing or un-configuring unnecessary features and functions from a firewall is one way to reduce its resource requirements.
- **IP address validity:** Hackers can send packets to an external-facing firewall with a bogus source or destination IP addresses to test the firewall's rules and ACL. If the packet is allowed to pass, the hacker knows that incoming traffic with dubious addresses can penetrate through to the internal network.

Power supply issues

The **Power Supply Unit** (**PSU**) is the computer component with the highest fail rate. Given that it provides the interface between the external power source, which can be 115 volts (V) or 220 V of **Alternating Current** (**AC**), and the power required by the internal devices and components of a computer that range from ±3 V to ±12 V of **Direct Current** (**DC**), it is constantly in use. Generally, when a PSU begins to fail or does fail, the best solution is to replace it. However, knowing that a PSU is failing, is not always easy. Here are few of the signs that a PSU may be failing:

- **Smoke or burning smells:** If you smell or see smoke, it is beyond the point that the PSU should be replaced.
- **Shocks:** Not talking about ESD shocks, but rather real, lasting, dangerous electrical shocks, which is an indication that the protective shielding and electrical grounding of the PSU and the computer have failed somewhere. Change out the PSU and retest. If the problem persists, begin checking all the power connections and wires.
- **BSOD, kernel panic, or generic error screen:** If the reason behind the system shutting down and displaying a stop error or fault cannot be found, chances are the problem is the PSUs fluctuating voltages and shutting itself down.
- **Boot failure:** If the system crashes or halts intermittently right after booting up, the problem is either a temperature overheat issue or a failing PSU. Check the PSU first.

- **PSU noise:** Any noise above the vibrations of the PSU's normal operational sounds is a clear indication of a problem. Regardless of whether the fan is making grinding noises, or a high-pitched whine or buzzing, the PSU should be replaced.

Conclusion

Knowing what to do, how to do it, and where to look are as important with network issues as they are with server and host issues. When a technical problem causes the network to be unavailable, network and system administrators must identify and resolve the cause and results of the problem, apply preventive measures to keep it from reoccurring, and restore and reassure the network's integrity. This chapter identified the common problems and issues that occur on a computer network and their causes.

The next chapter continues this discussion by looking into the tools and techniques used to troubleshoot, isolate, and correct network problems and issues.

Points to remember

- The communication link between a LAN and a **WAN** can include various devices, software, and services, including: power, cables, connections, network adapters, gateway devices, and communication services.
- An object that is flagged as being unavailable or not found can mean it was moved or deleted, among other causes, including firewall rules, antivirus/anti-malware software, or network connection problems.
- Common DCHP server issues are duplicate IPs and exhausted address pools. DHCP servers allocate host configurations automatic, dynamic, or static. A host unable to connect to a DHCP server is configured with an APIPA address.
- Unknown host errors can be caused if a hostname does not have an IP address, the default DNS server is unreachable, or the hostname is not registered or no longer exists.
- To reach a remote subnet, a routing entry must be in the routing table. Issues may include addressing, routing and firewall policies, or VPN use.
- DNS record types include A, AAAA, CNAME, HINFO, NS, and PTR.
- The three basic commands that used reference information in a DNS server are, dig (command line), Resolve-DNSName (PowerShell), and nslookup (command line).
- Flushing the DNS cache can resolve the "Can't reach server using FQDN" error.
- A server may not connect to a network because one or more required services may not be running. These include: TCP/IP NetBIOS Helper, Wired or Wireless

AutoConfig, DHCP Client, Function Discovery Resource Publication, SSDP Discovery, and UPnP Device Host

- By default, all ports on a network switch are enabled, but not secured. Port security tools are ACLs, firewalls, VLANs, and authentication protocols RADIUS, DIAMETER, and TACACS+.
- The security on an individual port can be one of three violation modes: protect, restrict, or shutdown.
- A thorough preventive maintenance program should be developed and executed on a regular basis.
- Routing table entry errors are the result of entry or content errors or misconfiguration of interfacing devices.
- The software utilities used to troubleshoot routing issues are **`ping`** and **`traceroute/tracert`** commands.
- The four system resource types are DMA, I/O port address, IRQ line, and memory address range.
- Common VLAN problems include: incorrect IP addresses, port configuration, disabled VLAN, trunking protocol, and trunk port "flapping."
- Causes for a default gateway not available error include, antivirus/anti-malware software, outdated network adapter drivers, and the auto-login feature setup.
- Firewall problems can include: configuration issues, currency issues, processing power, and IP address validity.
- Signs that a PSU may be failing include: smoke or burning smells, shocks, BSOD, boot failure, and noise.

CHAPTER 25
Network Tools and Techniques

Introduction

Businesses and organizations rely on computer networks for information, applications, communication, and interchange, in the form of analysis, reporting, email, Web access, and personal productivity. It is common for the organization's computer network to be so integrated into its operations and culture that its availability is assumed. When a technical problem causes the network to be unavailable, network and system administrators have the responsibility to identify and resolve the problem and reassure the integrity of the network. All this has to be done in as little time as possible. This chapter identifies the **Network Operating System (NOS)** utilities and tools that are commonly a part of the troubleshooting process.

Structure

The chapter covers the following topics:

- Troubleshooting tools
- Troubleshooting commands

Objective

By the end of this chapter, you will be able to identify and describe the sub-objectives of the following Server+ examination objective: *Given a scenario, troubleshoot network connectivity issues*.

Troubleshooting tools

We have discussed the tools in this section at one point or another in this as well as the preceding chapters. However, we should also look at them in the context of how each is used when troubleshooting network problems. You should also expect to encounter these tools on the Server+ exam.

Check link lights

The LED lights, which can be green, orange, yellow, or red, on a NIC card, also called an Ethernet card, do have some meanings. Here are the basic versions:

- **Blinking light:** A blinking light (color not important) means that the port is actively transmitting data. In other words, it is operating normally.
- **Solid light:** A light (color not important) that is constantly on, simply means that a communication session is in progress between the device and another.
- **No light:** This means that there is no active connection or communication.

Some manufacturers give meaning to the colors of the lights for specific meanings beyond the abovementioned ones. Check with the manufacturer's documentation or website for that information.

Confirm power supply

A procedure that should be on any computer preventive maintenance checklist is the confirmation of the PSU. This procedure can be done in several ways, but the best way is to use a multimeter. Using a multimeter, you can test the connectivity and voltage of the 24 pins of the power connector to the motherboard. The steps of this procedure are as follows:

1. Disconnect the PSU from the AC power source.
2. Open the computer's system case to access the PSU.
3. Unplug the large 24-pin connector from the motherboard.
4. Use a jumper bridge tool or a 16-gauge piece of wire to bridge pin 16 to either pin 15 or pin 17, as shown in *Figure 25.1*, to shorten the Power On pin. If the fan turns and the LED lights come on, this test indicates that the PSU will power up.
5. Reconnect the PSU to the AC power source.

6. Connect a multimeter probe to a ground and then to each of the voltage pins. If the voltages are correct, the PSU is good.

Refer to the following figure:

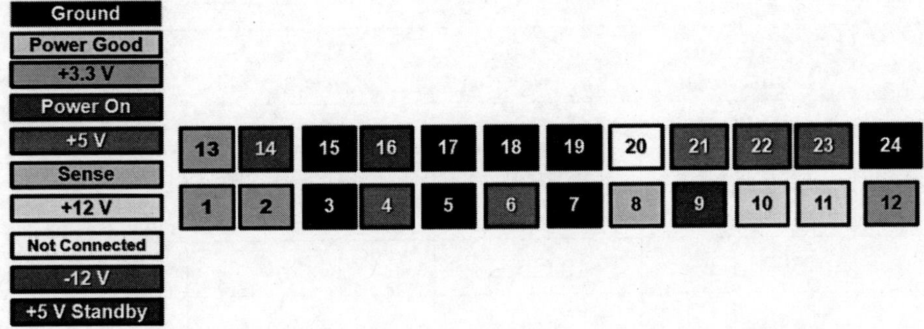

Figure 25.1: *The pin positions of an ATX 24-pin motherboard connector*

If the results of step 4 or step 6 are other than the expected good results, the PSU could be failing or parts of it have already failed.

Verify cable integrity

There are three levels of network cable testing to prove the integrity of the communication link. These are:

- **Verification:** Verification testing determines if the cable is connected properly. Verification testing is the first-level of cable troubleshooting. Verification testing checks for continuity functions, the distance from a test point to the end of the cable or to a trouble spot or flaw in the cable. A primary technology used for verification testing is **Time Domain Reflectometer** (**TDR**).
- **Qualification:** Qualification testing includes verification tests and adds tests to determine if the cabling can support specific standards or technologies, such as 100BASE-TX, VoIP, Gigabit Ethernet, etc.
- **Certification:** Certification testing determines if an installed cable meets established cabling standards, such as TIA-568-B, CAT 5e, CAT 6, and ISO 11801 Class D or E. This level of testing is normally performed by a commercial cable installer and or enterprise-level facility managers. Many cable manufacturers require certification testing for warranty validation.

Cable selection

Using the cable type best suited for an organization's network helps minimize problems and maximize performance. The right cable with the proper installation and maintenance is crucial for the successful operation of the network. However, choosing the right cable type to install can be daunting, given all the identification codes, types, terms, and capabilities.

There are many types of "Ethernet" cables, most of which are identified as one "Cat" or another. "Cat" refers to "category," which is a classification scheme that identifies the build of a cable and the capabilities it supports. *Table 25.1* lists the cable categories and their capabilities:

Category	Maximum Bandwidth	Maximum Throughput	Maximum Distance	Use / Standard
Cat 5e	100 MHz	1 Gbps	100 m	100BaseT Ethernet
Cat 6	250 MHz	10 Gbps	1 Gbps - 100 m 10Gbps- 37 m	Gigabit Ethernet
Cat 6a	500 MHz	10 Gbps	100 m	Gigabit Ethernet
Cat 7	600 MHz	10 Gbps	100 m	10 Gbps Core
Cat 7a	1 GHz	100 Gbps	10 Gbps - 100 m 100 Gbps - 15 m	10 Gbps Core
Cat 8.1	2 GHz	25 Gbps	30 m	25 Gbps Core
Cat 8.2	2 GHz	40 Gbps	30 m	40 Gbps Core

***Table 25.1:** Category cable characteristics*

Missing from *Table 25.1* are Categories 1 through 5, which are no longer active for network cabling. The entries in this table represent the current cabling categories available.

Choosing the right cabling for a network involves the following five factors:

1. **Maximum throughput:** This measurement represents the data speed of the cable. The speed of the cable should match the application or use for a workstation or the network on the whole. Multimedia production certainly needs more throughput than document preparation.

2. **Required segment length:** While throughput can be important, it has a limiting factor in distance. Essentially, the higher the data speed, the lower the effective distance. For example, a Cat 6a cable can run 1 gigabyte per second (Gbps) for 100 meters (about 328 feet). A Cat 7a cable can provide up to 100 Gbps of throughput, but for only 15 meters (about 50 feet). If speed is most important, then consider if the distance is a problem. If the distance is a problem, then consider if the speed will suffice.

3. **Internet speed:** It does not make sense, in the short run, to install cabling that is way faster than your Internet service. Installing Cat 7a cabling with a data rate of up to 100 Gbps is perhaps overkill for an Internet service that provides only 1 Gbps of throughput.

4. **Use:** Standard category cable for an indoor Ethernet network is not constructed for outdoor use. If a LAN must also include exterior workstations or nodes, cabling

with a **polyethylene** (**PE**) shielding or direct burial cable should be installed inside conduit to protect it from water and underground pressures.

Troubleshooting commands

Let us now go over some troubleshooting commands.

ipconfig/ifconfig

The Windows **`ipconfig`** command and its Linux and macOS version **`ifconfig`**, are used to display the network-oriented configuration of a host's interfaces. These commands are used to display and manage the details of the IP and DNS configurations for each of a computer's network interfaces.

Windows

The **Internet Protocol Configuration (ipconfig)** command is executed from a command prompt or PowerShell. *Figure 25.2* shows a sampling of the display from its **`/all`** option. *Table 25.2* lists the options for this command:

```
PS C:\> ipconfig /all

Windows IP Configuration

   Host Name . . . . . . . . . . . . : DESKTOP-5I0RQST
   Primary Dns Suffix  . . . . . . . :
   Node Type . . . . . . . . . . . . : Hybrid
   IP Routing Enabled. . . . . . . . : No
   WINS Proxy Enabled. . . . . . . . : No

Ethernet adapter Ethernet:

   Media State . . . . . . . . . . . : Media disconnected
   Connection-specific DNS Suffix  . :
   Description . . . . . . . . . . . : Intel(R) Ethernet Connection (11) I219-LM
   Physical Address. . . . . . . . . : 98-EE-CB-D3-DE-D5
   DHCP Enabled. . . . . . . . . . . : Yes
   Autoconfiguration Enabled . . . . : Yes

Ethernet adapter Ethernet 2:

   Connection-specific DNS Suffix  . :
   Description . . . . . . . . . . . : VirtualBox Host-Only Ethernet Adapter
   Physical Address. . . . . . . . . : 0A-00-27-00-00-06
   DHCP Enabled. . . . . . . . . . . : No
   Autoconfiguration Enabled . . . . : Yes
   Link-local IPv6 Address . . . . . : fe80::3ef0:e167:445:a2f7%6(Preferred)
   IPv4 Address. . . . . . . . . . . : 10.10.10.40(Preferred)
   Subnet Mask . . . . . . . . . . . : 255.255.255.0
   Default Gateway . . . . . . . . . :
   DHCPv6 IAID . . . . . . . . . . . : 285868071
   DHCPv6 Client DUID. . . . . . . . : 00-01-00-01-29-A4-43-35-44-AF-28-B3-D4-09
   NetBIOS over Tcpip. . . . . . . . : Enabled

Ethernet adapter Ethernet 3:

   Connection-specific DNS Suffix  . :
   Description . . . . . . . . . . . : VirtualBox Host-Only Ethernet Adapter #2
   Physical Address. . . . . . . . . : 0A-00-27-00-00-12
   DHCP Enabled. . . . . . . . . . . : No
```

***Figure 25.2:** The output of the ipconfig command*

Refer to the following table:

Option	Function
/all	Display the full TCP/IP configuration information for all network adapters.
/release	Release the IPv4 address for the specified adapter.
/release6	Release the IPv6 address for the specified adapter.
/renew	Renew the IPv4 address for the specified adapter.
/renew6	Renew the IPv6 address for the specified adapter.
/flushdns	Purges the DNS Resolver cache.
/registerdns	Refreshes all DHCP leases and re-registers DNS names.
/displaydns	Display the contents of the DNS Resolver Cache.
/showclassid	Displays all the DHCP class IDs allowed for adapter.
/setclassid	Modifies the DHCP class ID.
/showclassid6	Displays all the IPv6 DHCP class IDs allowed for adapter.
/setclassid6	Modifies the IPv6 DHCP class ID.
/?	Displays the help information for ipconfig.

Table 25.2: *The options for the ipconfig command*

Linux/macOS

The **Interface Configuration (ifconfig)** command has been largely deprecated on most Linux distros but is still available on macOS. On Linux, it has been replaced by the **ip** command, which is covered in the next section.

ip

The **Internet Protocol (ip)** command is a part of the Linux net-tool bundle for configuring and managing network interfaces. The **ip** command has largely replaced the **ifconfig** command on Linux systems.

The format of the **ip** command is:

```
ip [option] object {command | help}
```

The parameters of the ip command are:

- **Object:** The object parameter is required and represents the specific network component to be acted upon. The most commonly used objects are:

- **Address:** An IPv4 or IPv6 address. *Figure 25.3* shows an example of the information display by the **`ip address`** command:

```
bpbonline: $ip addr
1: lo: <LOOPBACK,UP,LOWER_UP> mtu 65536 qdisc noqueue state UNKNOWN group default qlen 1000
    link/loopback 00:00:00:00:00:00 brd 00:00:00:00:00:00
    inet 127.0.0.1/8 scope host lo
       valid_lft forever preferred_lft forever
    inet6 ::1/128 scope host
       valid_lft forever preferred_lft forever
2: eth0: <BROADCAST,MULTICAST,UP,LOWER_UP> mtu 1500 qdisc mq state UP group default qlen 1000
    link/ether 00:15:5d:fa:1a:e4 brd ff:ff:ff:ff:ff:ff
    inet 172.20.16.74/20 brd 172.20.31.255 scope global eth0
       valid_lft forever preferred_lft forever
    inet6 fe80::215:5dff:fefa:1ae4/64 scope link
       valid_lft forever preferred_lft forever
```

Figure 25.3: The output of an ip address command

- **Link:** A network interface, either physical or logical.
- **Neighbor:** A neighboring interface using ARP or IPv6 **Neighbor Discovery (NDISC)** protocol information.
- **Route:** An entry in a routing table.
- **Rule:** A policy rule for routing that sets route precedents.

- **Option:** The options of an ip command designate the action to be performed on the object in the command string. The most commonly used options are:
  - **`-version`:** Display the version of the ip command and exit.
  - **`-statistics`:** Display information.
  - **`-loops`:** The maximum number of loops the address flush option is to take before ending.
  - **`-family`:** The protocol family is identified with one of the following options: inet, inet6, bridge, ipx, dnet, or link.
  - **`-4`:** Shorthand for -family inet.
  - **`-6`:** Shorthand for -family inet6.
  - **`-0`:** Shorthand for -family link.
  - **`-resolve/-r`:** Display DNS names in place of host addresses.

- **Command:** The command specifies the action to be performed on the object identified in the command string. The primary commands are: **`add`**, **`delete`**, and **`show (list)`** objects, but not all objects allow all of these commands to be used. The **`help`** command is available to all objects. The default command, if no command is included, is list.

Ping

The **Packet Internet Groper** (**ping**) command is primarily used to verify a connection from a host and a destination address, which can be the localhost or a distant site. The ping command accepts an FQDN, host name, domain name, or IP address as its target. Ping works by sending out a 64-byte **Internet Command Message Protocol** (**ICMP**) echo request message to the target address. If the target is identified with anything other than an IP address, then the DNS or the local HOSTS file is used to resolve it to an IP address. If an echo response message is received back from the destination, the time measurements of this interchange are displayed. This action occurs three times to average the time required for the cycle. *Figure 25.4* shows a sample of the output of the ping command:

```
PS C:\> ping bpbonline.com

Pinging bpbonline.com [23.227.38.65] with 32 bytes of data:
Reply from 23.227.38.65: bytes=32 time=24ms TTL=57
Reply from 23.227.38.65: bytes=32 time=24ms TTL=57
Reply from 23.227.38.65: bytes=32 time=26ms TTL=57
Reply from 23.227.38.65: bytes=32 time=24ms TTL=57

Ping statistics for 23.227.38.65:
    Packets: Sent = 4, Received = 4, Lost = 0 (0% loss),
Approximate round trip times in milli-seconds:
    Minimum = 24ms, Maximum = 26ms, Average = 24ms
```

Figure 25.4: *The output of a successful ping command*

Tracert/traceroute

This command `tracert` on a Windows system and `traceroute` on a Linux or macOS system, tests the network route between a host and a destination address. Like the ping command, the destination can be an FQDN, host name, domain name, or IP address and everything besides the IP address is resolved through DNS.

The `traceroute/tracert` command tests the network path in an iterative incremental process. Initially, an ICMP echo requests with a **time-to-live (TTL)** of 1, meaning after reaching 1 router on the path the message is discarded, and only the first router (hop) sends back an echo response. In successive iterations, the TTL is increased by 1 and sent out and responded to by the router associated with the hop equal to the TTL, until the final destination address is reached and no response is received. *Figure 25.5* shows an example of the output of a Windows `tracert` command:

```
PS C:\> tracert bpbonline.com

Tracing route to bpbonline.com [23.227.38.65]
over a maximum of 30 hops:

  1     7 ms     7 ms     7 ms  192.168.0.1
  2    16 ms    16 ms    13 ms  10.131.0.1
  3    14 ms    14 ms    14 ms  24.144.1.101
  4    15 ms    15 ms    15 ms  208.180.33.89
  5    26 ms    26 ms    25 ms  173.219.239.49
  6    27 ms    25 ms    25 ms  173.219.201.112
  7    26 ms    24 ms    27 ms  173.219.152.193
  8    59 ms    60 ms    53 ms  111100.dal.equinix.com [206.223.118.145]
  9    56 ms    49 ms    55 ms  172.71.172.2
 10    53 ms    52 ms    53 ms  myshopify.com [23.227.38.65]

Trace complete.
```

Figure 25.5: *The output of a tracert command on a Windows system*

nslookup

The **nslookup** command looks up FQDNs, domains, and IP addresses in a DNS name server and displays the IP address and domain of a host on the network. *Figure 25.6* shows an example of **nslookup** on a Windows system, which provides two sets of information: the FQDN and IP address of the DNS server used, and the FQDN and IP address for the requested URL. The response of a "non-authoritative answer" means that this is the information on the referenced DNS server at the time of the request.

```
PS C:\> nslookup bpbonline.com
Server:  dns.opendns.com
Address:  208.67.222.222

Non-authoritative answer:
Name:    bpbonline.com
Address:  23.227.38.65
```

Figure 25.6: *The output of the nslookup command*

nbtstat

NetBIOS over TCP/IP status or **nbtstat** is a Windows system command that is used primarily for diagnosing or troubleshooting NetBIOS name issues. NetBIOS over TCP/IP resolves NetBIOS names to IP addresses using local cache, WINS server queries, broadcast messages, hosts file lookups, and DNS server queries. However, should a name resolution result in a wrong identity or not finding a matching entry, the **nbtstat** command can be used to view the NetBIOS namespace. It can also display the NetBIOS services running on another host or check if there is a logged-in user on a particular host. *Figure 25.7* shows an example of the output from the **nbtstat** command:

```
PS C:\> nbtstat -n

vEthernet (Default Switch):
Node IpAddress: [172.25.192.1] Scope Id: []

                NetBIOS Local Name Table

       Name               Type         Status
    ---------------------------------------------
    WORKGROUP       <00>  GROUP       Registered
    DESKTOP-5I0RQST<00>  UNIQUE      Registered
    DESKTOP-5I0RQST<20>  UNIQUE      Registered

Ethernet 2:
Node IpAddress: [10.10.10.40] Scope Id: []

                NetBIOS Local Name Table

       Name               Type         Status
    ---------------------------------------------
    WORKGROUP       <00>  GROUP       Registered
    DESKTOP-5I0RQST<00>  UNIQUE      Registered
    DESKTOP-5I0RQST<20>  UNIQUE      Registered

Ethernet 3:
Node IpAddress: [10.10.20.40] Scope Id: []

                NetBIOS Local Name Table

       Name               Type         Status
    ---------------------------------------------
    WORKGROUP       <00>  GROUP       Registered
    DESKTOP-5I0RQST<00>  UNIQUE      Registered
    DESKTOP-5I0RQST<20>  UNIQUE      Registered

Ethernet:
Node IpAddress: [0.0.0.0] Scope Id: []

    No names in cache
```

Figure 25.7: *An excerpt from the output of the nbtstat command on a Windows system*

There is no direct equivalent for the **nbtstat** command on a Linux system. However, two commands can display the same information in slightly different formats. These commands are the **nbtscan** and the **nmblookup**.

nbtscan

The **nbtscan** command looks for open NetBIOS nameservers on the local or remote TCP/IP networks. It operates essentially in the same way as the **nbtstat** command, but with a range of addresses instead of just one. *Figure 25.8* shows the results of a scan for all of the nodes on the 192.168.0.0 network (192.168.0.1/24):

```
bpbonline: $ sudo nbtscan -r 192.168.0.1/24
Doing NBT name scan for addresses from 192.168.0.1/24

IP address       NetBIOS Name     Server    User             MAC address
------------------------------------------------------------------------------
192.168.0.79     DESKTOP-5I0RQST  <server>  <unknown>        44:af:28:b3:d4:09
192.168.0.100    HYPERSYS         <server>  <unknown>        5c:e0:c5:b6:b3:9a
192.168.0.61     DESKTOP-9SPTV07  <server>  <unknown>        5c:e0:c5:b6:17:d7
192.168.0.101    EPSONB759B9      <server>  <unknown>        00:00:00:00:00:00
```

Figure 25.8: *An example of the output of the nbtscan command on a Linux system*

nmblookup

The **nmblookup** uses NetBIOS over TCP/IP queries to associate NetBIOS names and IP addresses. The name queries can be directed at a particular IP broadcast domain or a specific node. *Figure 25.9* shows a sample of the output of this command:

```
bpbonline: $ nmblookup -S DESKTOP-5I0RQST
172.20.16.1 DESKTOP-5I0RQST<00>
Looking up status of 172.20.16.1
        DESKTOP-5I0RQST <00> -          B <ACTIVE>
        WORKGROUP       <00> - <GROUP> B <ACTIVE>
        DESKTOP-5I0RQST <20> -          B <ACTIVE>

        MAC Address = 00-15-5D-34-0D-02

172.28.112.1 DESKTOP-5I0RQST<00>
Looking up status of 172.28.112.1
No reply from 172.28.112.1

192.168.0.79 DESKTOP-5I0RQST<00>
Looking up status of 192.168.0.79
        DESKTOP-5I0RQST <00> -          B <ACTIVE>
        WORKGROUP       <00> - <GROUP> B <ACTIVE>
        DESKTOP-5I0RQST <20> -          B <ACTIVE>

        MAC Address = 44-AF-28-B3-D4-09

name_query failed to find name DESKTOP-5I0RQST
```

Figure 25.9: *The output of the nmblookup command on a Linux system*

netstat

The Network Statistics (**netstat**) command displays information that details how a host is communicating with other nodes, local or remote. One of the few network utilities that runs on Windows, Linux, and macOS, the **netstat** command provides an overview of network activities and displays open ports and the ports with established connections. The information displayed by this command is used to troubleshoot a variety of networking issues. *Table 25.3* lists the most commonly used options for the **netstat** command:

Option	Action
-a	Lists the open sockets in addition to active connections
-b	Displays the executable file involved in creating a connection or listening port
-e	Ethernet statistics (bytes received and sent, data packets, etc.)
-f	Returns the FQDN or domain of remote addresses
-n	Displays addresses and port numbers numerically
-o	Presents connections with the associated process ID in each case
-q	Lists all connections: all listening/non-listening TCP sockets/ports
-r	Shows the contents of the routing table
-s	Shows stats on network protocols, including IP, IPv6,ICMP, TCP, and UDP

Table 25.3: *The options of the netstat command*

dig

The **Domain Information Groper (dig)** is a Linux command used as a network and DNS troubleshooting and display command. The **dig** command is not available on Windows systems by default and must be added by installing the **Berkeley Internet Name Domain (BIND)**, which is an implementation of DNS protocols and includes the **dig** command.

The basic syntax of the dig command is:

```
dig [server] [name] [type]
```

The parameters in the dig command are:

- **Server:** IP address or hostname of the DNS name server to query. If hostname is used, dig resolves it to an IP address before querying the name server. If the server parameter is not specified, the system default DNS server is used.
- **Name:** The domain name and TLD of the resource record queried.
- **Type:** The DNS record type of the query, such as A, MX, etc. The default is A.

Telnet

The **Teletype Network (telnet)** protocol allows a local computer to connect to another local computer and provides virtual terminal service. In the connection, the connecting computer is designated as the local computer and the target computer as the remote computer, even though both are physically local. Using the **telnet** connection, the user on the local computer can execute commands on the remote computer, with the results displayed on the local computer's monitor. **Telnet** is a client/server protocol with the local computer using a telnet client program and the remote computer running a telnet server program.

Netcat

Netcat (nc, ncat) is a command line utility that uses TCP and UDP connections to read and write on a network. Unfortunately, it can be used for attacking, but it is intended use is for security, debugging, investigating attacks, monitoring network connections, scanning for open ports, transferring data, and more.

Netcat runs on virtually all operating systems. As the **nc** utility, it is included in Linux distros and the macOS. It can be installed on a Windows system as a part of the **nmap** package. The syntax of the netcat utility is:

```
nc [<options>] <host><port>
```

The most commonly used options for the netcat utility are listed in *Table 25.4*:

Option	Description
-4	Use IPv4 only.
-6	Use IPv6 only.
-u	Use UDP connection. (Default is TCP connection.)
-p <port>	Sets the source port to <port>.
-s <host>	Sets the host to <host>.
-l	Listens for connections instead of using connect mode.
-k	Keeps a connection open.
-v	Verbosity level. Repeat to increase verbosity.
-z	Display connection status without connecting.

Table 25.4: *Netcat utility options*

The **`<host>`** is either a numeric IP address or a hostname. The **`<port>`** is either a numeric port or service name.

One of the more common uses for the netcat utility is port scanning. Netcat will scan a single port of a range of ports. For example, the command can be entered to scan port 80 or to scan ports 30 through 80 for a particular IP address. The command for the latter example is:

```
nc -z -v 10.10.8.8 30-80
```

The output of this command would be something like that shown in *Figure 25.10*:

```
nc: connect to 10.10.8.8 port 20 (tcp) failed: Connection refused
nc: connect to 10.10.8.8 port 21 (tcp) failed: Connection refused
Connection to 10.10.8.8 22 port [tcp/ssh] succeeded!
nc: connect to 10.10.8.8 port 23 (tcp) failed: Connection refused
...
nc: connect to 10.10.8.8 port 79 (tcp) failed: Connection refused
Connection to 10.10.8.8 80 port [tcp/http] succeeded!
```

Figure 25.10: *The output of an Netcat port scanning command*

route

The **`route`** command is used to view and modify the IP routing table on a Windows system. Its equivalent on a Linux system is the **`ip route`** command. On a computer with a single network interface connected to a LAN with a single edge or gateway router, the routing table is relatively simple and not usually a source of any network problems. If there is a problem connecting to or accessing other computers or networks, the **`route`** command can be used to investigate if there may be a bad entry in the routing table. However, if that same computer is configured as a router, its routing table can be a source of trouble. Setting up a routing table properly is crucial for the configuration of the routing function.

Routing table

Figure 25.11 shows the output of a routing table on a Windows system:

```
PS C:\> route print
===========================================================================
Interface List
 11...98 ee cb d3 de d5 ......Intel(R) Ethernet Connection (11) I219-LM
 63...0a 00 27 00 00 3f ......VirtualBox Host-Only Ethernet Adapter
 74...0a 00 27 00 00 4a ......VirtualBox Host-Only Ethernet Adapter #2
 21...46 af 28 b3 d4 09 ......Microsoft Wi-Fi Direct Virtual Adapter
 23...44 af 28 b3 d4 0a ......Microsoft Wi-Fi Direct Virtual Adapter #3
  6...44 af 28 b3 d4 09 ......Intel(R) Wi-Fi 6 AX201 160MHz
  1...........................Software Loopback Interface 1
 12...00 15 5d ee 18 c3 ......Hyper-V Virtual Ethernet Adapter
 58...00 15 5d 34 0d 02 ......Hyper-V Virtual Ethernet Adapter #2
===========================================================================

IPv4 Route Table
===========================================================================
Active Routes:
Network Destination        Netmask          Gateway       Interface  Metric
          0.0.0.0          0.0.0.0      192.168.0.1     192.168.0.79     30
        127.0.0.0        255.0.0.0         On-link         127.0.0.1    331
        127.0.0.1  255.255.255.255         On-link         127.0.0.1    331
  127.255.255.255  255.255.255.255         On-link         127.0.0.1    331
      172.20.16.0    255.255.240.0         On-link       172.20.16.1   5256
      172.20.16.1  255.255.255.255         On-link       172.20.16.1   5256
    172.20.31.255  255.255.255.255         On-link       172.20.16.1   5256
     172.28.112.0    255.255.240.0         On-link      172.28.112.1   5256
     172.28.112.1  255.255.255.255         On-link      172.28.112.1   5256
   172.28.127.255  255.255.255.255         On-link      172.28.112.1   5256
      192.168.0.0    255.255.255.0         On-link      192.168.0.79    286
     192.168.0.79  255.255.255.255         On-link      192.168.0.79    286
    192.168.0.255  255.255.255.255         On-link      192.168.0.79    286
     192.168.56.0    255.255.255.0         On-link      192.168.56.1    330
     192.168.56.1  255.255.255.255         On-link      192.168.56.1    330
   192.168.56.255  255.255.255.255         On-link      192.168.56.1    330
     192.168.98.0    255.255.255.0         On-link      192.168.98.1    330
     192.168.98.1  255.255.255.255         On-link      192.168.98.1    330
   192.168.98.255  255.255.255.255         On-link      192.168.98.1    330
        224.0.0.0        240.0.0.0         On-link         127.0.0.1    331
        224.0.0.0        240.0.0.0         On-link      192.168.0.79    286
        224.0.0.0        240.0.0.0         On-link      172.28.112.1   5256
        224.0.0.0        240.0.0.0         On-link       172.20.16.1   5256
        224.0.0.0        240.0.0.0         On-link      192.168.56.1    330
        224.0.0.0        240.0.0.0         On-link      192.168.98.1    330
  255.255.255.255  255.255.255.255         On-link         127.0.0.1    331
  255.255.255.255  255.255.255.255         On-link      192.168.0.79    286
  255.255.255.255  255.255.255.255         On-link      172.28.112.1   5256
  255.255.255.255  255.255.255.255         On-link       172.20.16.1   5256
  255.255.255.255  255.255.255.255         On-link      192.168.56.1    330
  255.255.255.255  255.255.255.255         On-link      192.168.98.1    330
===========================================================================
```

Figure 25.11: *The contents of a routing table display with the route print command on a Windows system*

As shown in *Figure 25.11*, each entry has the following five fields displayed for the IPv4 portion of the routing table:

- **Network Destination:** This IP address is actually the address of the destination subnet and matches the granularity of the subnet mask.
- **Netmask:** This is the subnet mask that is applied to a destination address in an outgoing message to identify the destination subnet.
- **Gateway:** The IP address of the default or assigned gateway router to which a message with the address of a particular destination subnet is to be forwarded. On-link indicates that no gateway router is needed.

- **Interface:** The IP address of the interface port on the gateway router through which a message with a particular destination subnet's address is forwarded.
- **Metric:** This number represents the number of routers (hops) between the source and the destination gateway routers.

In the IPv6 portion of the route print command, the fields are:

- **Interface List:** This list contains an interface number, the MAC address, and the name of each of the network interfaces on the host device.
- **Active Routes:** This table identifies the routing for destination addresses. Its fields are:
    - o **Interface number (If):** The number of the interface (from the Interface List) that a message with the Network Destination address is to be forwarded.
    - o **Metric:** The metric is a priority weighting used to differentiate different routes to the same destination address.
    - o **Network Destination:** This is the IPv6 address of a destination network. FE80 represents a local link address, and FF00 is a multicast address.
    - o **Gateway:** On-link addresses can be resolved without the need for a router.

The IPv6 portion of the route print command is shown in the following *Figure 25.12:*

```
PS C:\> route print -6
===========================================================================
Interface List
 11...98 ee cb d3 de d5 ......Intel(R) Ethernet Connection (11) I219-LM
 63...0a 00 27 00 00 3f ......VirtualBox Host-Only Ethernet Adapter
 74...0a 00 27 00 00 4a ......VirtualBox Host-Only Ethernet Adapter #2
 21...46 af 28 b3 d4 09 ......Microsoft Wi-Fi Direct Virtual Adapter
 23...44 af 28 b3 d4 0a ......Microsoft Wi-Fi Direct Virtual Adapter #3
  6...44 af 28 b3 d4 09 ......Intel(R) Wi-Fi 6 AX201 160MHz
  1...........................Software Loopback Interface 1
 12...00 15 5d ee 18 c3 ......Hyper-V Virtual Ethernet Adapter
 58...00 15 5d 34 0d 02 ......Hyper-V Virtual Ethernet Adapter #2
===========================================================================

IPv6 Route Table
===========================================================================
Active Routes:
 If Metric Network Destination      Gateway
  1    331 ::1/128                  On-link
  6    286 fe80::/64                On-link
 12   5256 fe80::/64                On-link
 58   5256 fe80::/64                On-link
 63    281 fe80::/64                On-link
 74    281 fe80::/64                On-link
 12   5256 fe80::7dfa:79a0:92a8:3fb9/128
                                    On-link
 63    281 fe80::a787:768b:28aa:3429/128
                                    On-link
 74    281 fe80::ac92:67e9:428b:d266/128
                                    On-link
  6    286 fe80::d0ad:4520:902c:3553/128
                                    On-link
 58   5256 fe80::d2bc:1492:1714:8d24/128
                                    On-link
  1    331 ff00::/8                 On-link
  6    286 ff00::/8                 On-link
 12   5256 ff00::/8                 On-link
 58   5256 ff00::/8                 On-link
```

Figure 25.12: *The output of the route print command for IPv6 addresses on a Windows system*

Add, change, or remove routes

The route command can also be used to modify the routing table by adding, changing, or deleting routing entries. The basic syntax for the command used to modify a routing table is:

```
route [-p] command dest [mask subnet] gateway [-if interface]
```

The parameters in this command are:

- **Persistence:** The **-p** parameter indicates that the routing entry being added is to be permanent. If this option is not included, the entry is removed the next time the system is restarted.
- **Command:** This indicates the action being taken, that is, add, delete, or change.
- **Destination (dest):** The IP address of the destination subnet.
- **Mask subnet:** This is the **subnet mask** that is to be applied to extract the network ID of a destination address. If no subnet mask is included in a command string, the default mask of 255.255.255.255 is used, resulting in only a single host being addressed and not a subnet. It is the best practice to include a subnet mask.
- **Gateway:** The IP address of the destination network's gateway router.
- **-if interface:** On a computer with only one network interface, this field is not needed. However, on a multihomed or a device with multiple interface ports, this IP address is needed.

Here is an example of a command to add a routing entry:

The network has two routers, with one serving as a link to a different private subnet with a subnet address of 192.168.2.0 that has a subnet mask 255.255.255.0. The local side interface port has an IP address of 192.168.1.200. If a routing entry is needed that adds a static route that forwards packets addressed to the 192.168.2.0 subnet to the second router, the command is:

```
route -p add 192.168.2.0 mask 255.255.255.0 192.168.1.200
```

To later change the IP address of the second router to 192.168.1.112, the command is:

```
route change 192.168.2.0 mask 255.255.255.0 192.168.1.222
```

And even later, it is decided the route is not needed any longer, the command is:

```
route delete 192.168.2.0
```

Conclusion

When a technical problem causes a network to be unavailable, network and system administrators have the responsibility to identify, isolate, and resolve the problem and reassure the integrity of the network. This chapter identified the NOS utilities and tools commonly used in the troubleshooting process. Each of these software utilities and tools has a specific purpose and use as a part of the identification, diagnostics, and resolution of a network server or host issue.

The next chapter wraps up the network-related common issues with a focus on the security settings, controls, and countermeasures used to protect a network.

Points to remember

- The LED lights on a NIC card indicate the state of the device through blinking lights, solid lights, or no lights.
- Any computer preventive maintenance checklist should include a PSU confirmation that tests the connectivity and voltage of each of the pins in connection to the motherboard.
- The three levels of cable testing are: verification, qualification, and certification.
- Choosing the right network cabling involves five factors: maximum throughput, segment length, speed, and use.
- Troubleshooting commands you will see on the Server+ exam are: ipconfig/ifconfig, ip, ping, tracert/traceroute, nslookup, nbtstat, nbtscan, nmblookup, netstat, dig, telnet, netcat, route.

Join our book's Discord space

Join the book's Discord Workspace for Latest updates, Offers, Tech happenings around the world, New Release and Sessions with the Authors:

https://discord.bpbonline.com

CHAPTER 26
Troubleshooting Security Issues

Introduction

Data security requires constant attention and scrutiny to ensure that stored data, data in transit, and data in use are protected by the guidelines of the **Confidential-Integrity-Availability (CIA)** model. This chapter identifies and describes the security issues and consequences of misapplied or missing controls and safeguards to protect an organization's data and information, software, and hardware resources on its computer networks. The problems, causes, and tools discussed in this chapter are the topics and concepts you should expect to see on the Server+ exam.

Structure

The chapter covers the following topics:

- Common data security concerns
- Commonly used security tools

Objective

By the end of this chapter, you will be able to identify and describe the sub-objectives of the following Server+ examination objective: *Given a scenario, troubleshoot security problems.*

Common data security concerns

Network servers, by the nature of their role in a network, are subject to a variety of security issues, both physical and logical, attacks by external threat actors as well as internal ones, and harm that can disrupt the organization's operations or finances. For the Server+ certification exam, the security issues and concerns you should know and understand are the following:

- **File integrity:** File integrity means that data, files, and system resources have not been the target of a successful attack and have not been modified in any way by an unauthorized user or malware or rogue software. The integrity of a file can be compromised by an attacker from either inside or outside an organization, maliciously, purposefully or accidentally. Monitoring the integrity of data and critical software should be an integral element of any security monitoring process. **File Integrity Monitor** (**FIM**) software, such as ManageEngine's **ADAudit Plus** and Samhain's open-source **File Integrity**, uses checksums and hashing to detect changes to a file. The most common hashing algorithm used is **Message Digest 5** (**MD5**).
- **Privilege escalation:** This is a type of cyberattack in which an attacker can gain unauthorized access to a system or network and take advantage of security flaws, weaknesses, and vulnerabilities in the system to gain higher user account rights and privileges. The attacker exploits program bugs, system flaws, human behaviors, misconfigurations, or weak or non-existent security access controls to increase the level of access and control of what is typically a standard user account. With escalated user privileges, an attacker gains access to deeper penetration of networks, assets, and sensitive information. As privilege escalation attacks can impact business reputation and continuity, strategic measures should be implemented for prevention, early detection, and mitigation. There are two types of privilege escalation:
    - **Vertical:** This type of privilege attack is also called **privilege elevation**. The objective is to elevate a compromised user account with low privileges to a level where an attacker or malware can access data, programs, or other content requiring higher privileges, rights, and permissions.
    - **Horizontal:** In this type of privilege escalation attack, also called "lateral movement," an attacker increases the permissions and access rights of the compromised user account to gain access to system or network resources reserved or assigned to another user or user group.
- **Applications will not load:** On virtually all **Operating Systems** (**OS**), the ownership of a data or software resource or its directory or folder can affect the performance or accessibility of data, an application, or a service. The ownership designation of a folder, directory, or file determines who or what has permission

to read, write, or execute it or its contents. The ownership of a disk drive can be altered by malware, which may have removed, renamed, or corrupted a disk, partition, or file.

To change the ownership of a resource on a Windows system, follow these steps:

1. On the **File Explorer**, right-click the icon of the disk drive on which the resource is located in the **File Explorer.**
2. On the pop-up menu, select **Properties** and then click on the **Advanced** button near the bottom right corner of the dialog box. This opens the **Advanced Security Settings** for the drive, as shown in *Figure 26.1*, on which the owner can be changed.

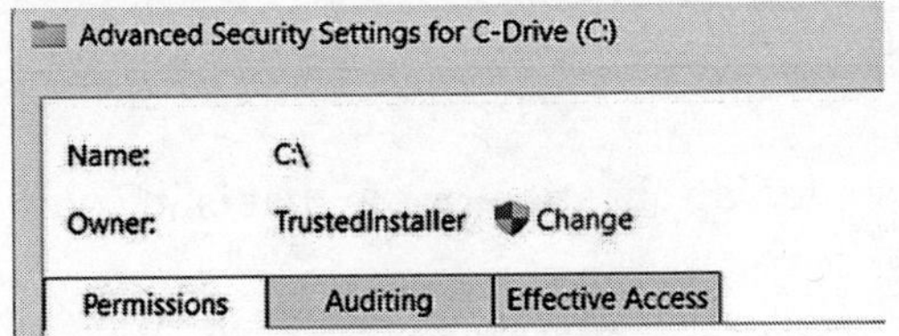

Figure 26.1: *Changing the ownership of a disk drive*

On a Linux system, the issue is likely the same as discussed above, with a similar remedy. However, on a Linux system, you can change the owner of a file or directory directly. To change the ownership of a directory or file (including programs) on a Linux system, use the following steps:

1. Move to the directory to be affected or containing the file on which the ownership is to be changed. Use the ls -l command to display the current ownership of the directory or file to be changed. *Figure 26.2* shows that "root" is the owner of the **`testdir`** folder:

```
drwxr-xr-x  2 root root        4096 Jun 24 16:53 testdir
```

Figure 26.2: *The permissions, owner, and group of Linux directory*

2. To change the owner of the folder or a file, use the chown command. Its syntax is:

```
chown <file or directory name><new owner name or ID>
```

Figure 26.3 shows the sequence of commands used to change the ownership of a file:

```
bpbonline: $ ls -l
total 0
-rw-r--r-- 1 root root 0 Jun 25 12:32 testfile
bpbonline: $ sudo chown ron testfile
bpbonline: $ ls -l
total 0
-rw-r--r-- 1 ron root 0 Jun 25 12:32 testfile
```

Figure 26.3: *An example of the chown command to change the owner of a file*

Some other data security concerns are as follows:

- **Cannot access network file/shares:** This error condition indicates that a shared resource is either unavailable or the share does not exist, for at least the user attempting to access it. Various things that could be causing this error include, network adapter on the computer, the permissions of the remote user, the permissions of the resource, and if the resource is configured for sharing.
- **Unable to open files:** This error and a couple of others like it are commonly the result of:
    - Problems with the file, application or service itself, as shown in *Figure 26.4*.
    - A third-party application that is not quite compatible with the operating system.
    - A newly installed application or file that is in conflict with the anti-malware software.
    - **User Account Control** (**UAC**) is not enabled.
    - Certain applications will not open for the **Built-in Administrator** (**BIA**) account, log off and change the logged in account.

Refer to the following figure:

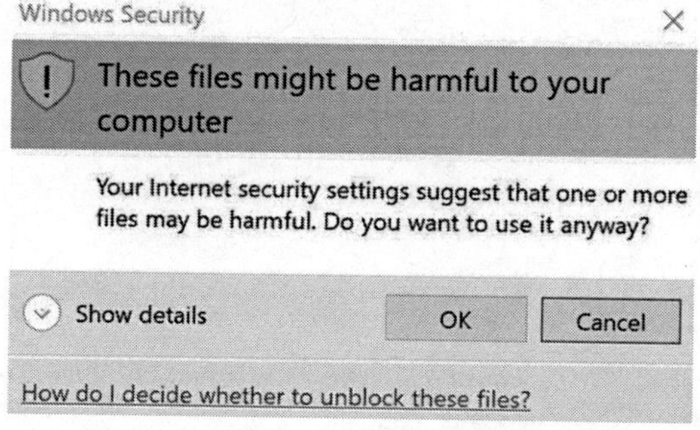

***Figure 26.4:** A warning message on a Windows system regarding a blocked file*

On a Linux or a Mac OS system, this error or warning is likely a conflict of installed services.

- **Excessive access:** As mentioned several times in this book, a core principle for data resource management and security is the **principle of least privilege**. This principle says that users should only have access and rights to those, and only those, resources that are absolutely required to perform their assigned tasks. User accounts should not have or, generally, do not need access to data resources beyond those related to that user's duties.
- **Excessive memory utilization:** Malware, unauthorized accessing and downloading of data files, excessive memory leaks in an application, etc., are just a few actions

that could cause high memory use on a network server or a host. Windows systems provide the **Windows Memory Diagnostic** utility that can advise on what is using so much memory. On Linux or macOS, the `syslog` log file may contain information on out of memory conditions, and the `free -m` command displays the current allocation of primary memory.

Common security issue causes

After discovering an attack on a server, host, or network-attached device, any action taken must be focused on identifying the exploited vulnerability and the nature of the attack. Many of the issues, vulnerabilities, or exploits discussed in the sections that follow are typically addressed in a hardening plan that has the aim of reducing the attack surface as much as possible and making it more difficult for attackers to exploit the system's weaknesses. Hardening should be a periodic and constant process to allow systems to keep up with the evolution of cyber threats. The causes of security issues, vulnerabilities, and exploits have some emphasis on the Server+ exam, so expect to see questions relating to the topics in the following sections.

Active services

Any OS starts a group of services when it boots up. These services may in turn, start up other services (dependencies). A server administrator should periodically audit the active services running on the network servers and hosts. This audit should also identify deprecated protocols, open TCP/UDP ports, and their associated applications, protocols, or services. Unnecessary services create vulnerabilities, which lead to threats. Knowing which required services are running on a server should help define a network's firewall and router rules. On a Windows system, the services running on a system can be listed with the command net start, as shown in *Figure 26.5*:

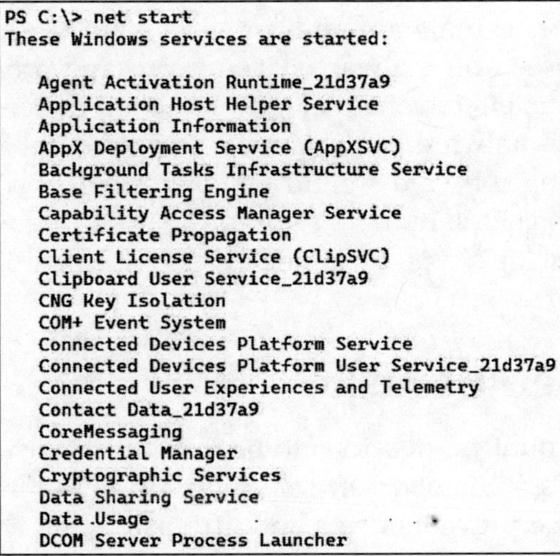

```
PS C:\> net start
These Windows services are started:

   Agent Activation Runtime_21d37a9
   Application Host Helper Service
   Application Information
   AppX Deployment Service (AppXSVC)
   Background Tasks Infrastructure Service
   Base Filtering Engine
   Capability Access Manager Service
   Certificate Propagation
   Client License Service (ClipSVC)
   Clipboard User Service_21d37a9
   CNG Key Isolation
   COM+ Event System
   Connected Devices Platform Service
   Connected Devices Platform User Service_21d37a9
   Connected User Experiences and Telemetry
   Contact Data_21d37a9
   CoreMessaging
   Credential Manager
   Cryptographic Services
   Data Sharing Service
   Data Usage
   DCOM Server Process Launcher
```

Figure 26.5: *A portion of a list of active services on a Windows system*

On a Linux system, the **`service -status-all`** command lists active services, as shown in *Figure 26.6*:

```
bpbonline: $ sudo service --status-all
 [ ? ]  alsa-utils
 [ - ]  anacron
 [ - ]  apache-htcacheclean
 [ - ]  apache2
 [ - ]  apparmor
 [ - ]  avahi-daemon
 [ - ]  bluetooth
 [ - ]  cron
 [ - ]  cups
 [ - ]  cups-browsed
 [ - ]  dbus
 [ - ]  exim4
 [ - ]  gdm3
 [ - ]  gdomap
 [ - ]  haveged
 [ - ]  hddtemp
 [ ? ]  hwclock.sh
 [ ? ]  kmod
```

Figure 26.6: *A portion of a list of active services on a Linux system*

Inactive accounts

An inactive account is not the same as a disabled account. An inactive account has not been logged in over a defined period of time. A disabled account cannot be used without being re-enabled. Inactive accounts should be monitored primarily because they are still usable and can represent a vulnerability.

Anti-malware configurations

The configuration of the anti-malware and antivirus software can be as important as firewall rules. A server-based anti-malware system scans and protects the network nodes automatically. However, the effectiveness of the protection depends on the configuration of that software. The anti-malware configuration and its database should be reviewed and updated regularly. The software should be configured to scan all network devices every day at a time when the least number of users are on the network. Review the results of each scan and log files for alerts, false negatives, false positives, and other possible configuration-related errors.

Misconfigured permissions

It is common for user account permissions to be in conflict with the permissions of any group the user account is a member of, especially on larger networks. Applying the **principle of least privilege** prevents users and groups having access to more than they need to perform their jobs.

Open ports

An open or enabled port is "listening" for incoming **sockets** (IP address and port number combinations) that contain its TCP or UDP port number. For example, a socket containing 172.101.10.115:80 is addressed to that particular IP address and the application associated with port 80 (HTTP). An open port can be a vulnerability that could be exploited. Hardening a server or host includes disabling all unnecessary ports. *Figure 26.7* shows a **`netstat -a`** listing of the active ports on a Windows system:

```
PS C:\> netstat -a

Active Connections      Port Numbers

  Proto  Local Address          Foreign Address        State
  TCP    0.0.0.0:80             DESKTOP-5I0RQST:0      LISTENING
  TCP    0.0.0.0:135            DESKTOP-5I0RQST:0      LISTENING
  TCP    0.0.0.0:445            DESKTOP-5I0RQST:0      LISTENING
  TCP    0.0.0.0:514            DESKTOP-5I0RQST:0      LISTENING
  TCP    0.0.0.0:623            DESKTOP-5I0RQST:0      LISTENING
  TCP    0.0.0.0:808            DESKTOP-5I0RQST:0      LISTENING
  TCP    0.0.0.0:2179           DESKTOP-5I0RQST:0      LISTENING
  TCP    0.0.0.0:3389           DESKTOP-5I0RQST:0      LISTENING
  TCP    0.0.0.0:5040           DESKTOP-5I0RQST:0      LISTENING
  TCP    0.0.0.0:7680           DESKTOP-5I0RQST:0      LISTENING
  TCP    0.0.0.0:9001           DESKTOP-5I0RQST:0      LISTENING
  TCP    0.0.0.0:16992          DESKTOP-5I0RQST:0      LISTENING
```

Figure 26.7: *A partial list of the active ports on a Windows system*

Rogue processes/services

Rogue processes or services are those running on a system that a user or administrator did not initiate. These processes and services consume resources and may cause harm. The immediate remedy is to stop (kill) them. In order to do so, you need to first get the **Process ID (PID)** of the rogue software. On a Windows system, use the **Task Manager's Details** tab and on a Linux or macOS system, the **`ps-eda`** command's output includes the PID. *Figure 26.8* and *Figure 26.9* shows where the PID number is found on the **Task Manager** window and an example of the output of a Linux **`ps`** command, respectively. With the PID, you can use the **`taskkill <PID>`** command in Windows (at a command line prompt) or the **`kill -9`** command in Linux/macOS.

Details — Run new task | End task | •••

Name	PID	Status	User name	CPU	Memory (ac...	Architec...	Description
WUDFHost.exe	2028	Running	LOCAL SER...	00	2,032 K	x64	Windows Driver Foundation
WUDFHost.exe	2768	Running	LOCAL SER...	00	912 K	x64	Windows Driver Foundation
WUDFHost.exe	6152	Running	LOCAL SER...	00	2,128 K	x64	Windows Driver Foundation
wslservice.exe	7952	Running	SYSTEM	00	1,928 K	x64	Windows Subsystem for Lin
wlanext.exe	6560	Running	SYSTEM	00	460 K	x64	Windows Wireless LAN 802
WINWORD.EXE	13372	Running	ronpr	00	139,528 K	x64	Microsoft Word
winlogon.exe	16076	Running	SYSTEM	00	1,088 K	x64	Windows Logon Applicatio
wininit.exe	1160	Running	SYSTEM	00	572 K	x64	Windows Start-Up Applicat
WidgetService.exe	12912	Running	ronpr	00	4,208 K	x64	WidgetService.exe

Figure 26.8: *The Details tab on the Windows Task Manager lists the PID of a process*

Refer to the following figure:

```
bpbonline: $ ps -eda
  PID TTY          TIME CMD
    1 ?        00:00:00 init(Debian)
    4 ?        00:00:00 init
   22 ?        00:00:00 SessionLeader
   23 ?        00:00:00 Relay(24)
   24 pts/0    00:00:00 bash
   26 pts/0    00:00:00 ps
```

***Figure 26.9:** The output of the Linux **ps -eda** command includes the PID of a process*

Zombie/orphan

On a UNIX/Linux system, there are two specific types of rogue processes: zombies and orphans. One by intent and the other by happenstance. A **zombie** process is started as a child process by a parent who has stopped running and issued a system call exit to its parent. However, the child process remains listed in the process table with a PID. A parent process executes a child process and then pauses itself. The child process performs its task and reports to the parent process that it is ending. At this point, the child process becomes a zombie (dead process) and cannot terminate itself. The parent process is reactivated to execute the command to terminate the zombie and remove it from the process table.

An **orphan** is a child process that continues to run after its parent process has ended or has been terminated without waiting for the child's execution to complete. In most cases, a child process becomes an orphan unintentionally, like when the parent is killed or crashes. Although called orphans, these processes are immediately re-parented by the OS and allowed to be completed. Orphan processes can continue processing and consume the system resources needed by other non-orphan processes. There are three ways to deal with an orphan process:

- **Termination:** The orphan is terminated with a **`kill`** command.
- **Reincarnation:** The parent is located and the orphan is terminated.
- **Expiration:** Processes are allotted a time period in which to complete its task. When the time expires, if the process has not asked for more time, it is terminated.

Intrusion detection configurations

Intrusion Detection Systems (**IDS**) and **Intrusion Prevention Systems** (**IPS**) are software that attempts to detect intrusions by unauthorized network traffic. The network traffic in question is not necessarily malware, which it could be, but it can be a network message whose content, addressing, or protocol violates the filtering rules configured into an organization's IDS device. The rules in an IDS should represent the organization's security policies, acceptable use policies, or standard security practices.

A detected event can be the result of a variety of incoming traffic, including an attacker attempting to gain unauthorized access to a network, an authorized user seeking to gain escalated or expanded privileges, and malware. While the intent is to detect intentional malicious events, an event can also be the result of a user error. Detecting and mitigating errors in the configuration of an IDS device can detect the causes of several types of security threats:

- **Input validation error:** This event occurs when an incoming message is not properly checked, which can result in a vulnerability that can be exploited with certain message and data sequences. The two primary results of an input validation errors are:
    - **Buffer overflow:** A buffer overflow event is caused when an input (message payload, injection attack, and so on) received by a system is larger that expected but is not checked. When the input data is placed in the input buffer of the processing software, it overflows its memory allocation.
    - **Boundary condition error:** An input received by a system causes a process to exceed its an assumed boundary, which could be a memory size limit, a disk address, bandwidth, or an erroneous variable value in the process.
- **Configuration error:** Errors, mistakes, and poor judgment, among other factors, cause configuration errors on IDS devices. These errors can create a vulnerability on the system.

Improperly configured local/group policies

The causes of local user or group errors or problems can come from various sources on a Windows system. These sources can include the errors in the permissions of an individual folder or file, misassigned rights and permissions of a user or group account, and errors made when using either of Windows' two policy editors:

- **The Local Group Policy Editor:** Used by systems administrators to change settings for computers and users of a network. This tool also manages and controls settings for a local computer and the local user accounts.
- **The Local Security Policy Editor:** This utility app, as shown in *Figure 26.10* allows an administrator to access the security settings of a standalone Windows system, which means it is not on an domain. The security settings accessible include:
    - Logging onto a system as a service, via a network, or interactively.
    - User account access rights and privileges.
    - Security measures to allow or deny software and app access.
    - Auditing policies for local computer security.

Refer to the following figure:

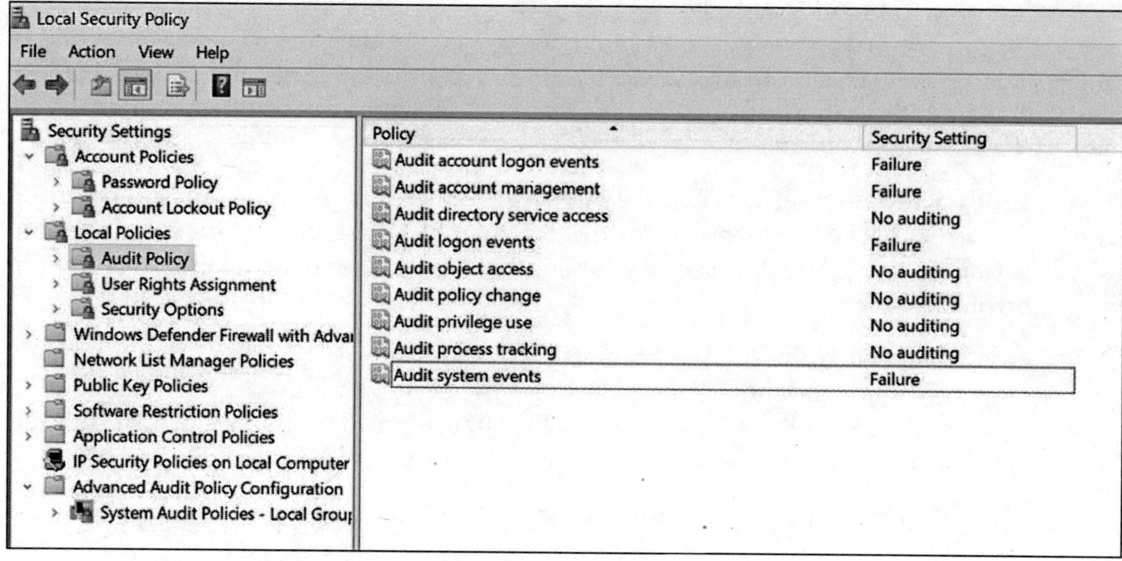

Figure 26.10: *The Windows Local Security Policy Editor*

Misconfigured firewall rules

An improperly configured firewall, either software or hardware, can leave an entire network vulnerable to attack. The following are some of the more common configuration errors or omissions on firewalls:

- **Access to firewall configuration:** Firewall(s) should be isolated on a dedicated network segment or VLAN, which prevents it being visible to the Internet. Access to the configuration management should use **Multi-Factor Authentication** (**MFA**), and access to commonly used network protocols, such as HTTPS, SSH, etc., should be restricted.

- **IPS enabled:** If the IPS or the combined **IDS/IPS** (**IDPS**) system is disabled, an important layer of a network's first line of defense is missing. With this feature disabled, the network could be vulnerable to **Denial of Service** (**DoS**) and malware attacks.

- **Secure Shells (SSH) port open:** SSH/TLS is a client/server protocol that requires a dedicated and open port to successfully protect encrypted or tunneled network traffic. Many firewalls have a dedicated SSH/TLS port by default.

- **Updates and patches:** The patches and updates for a firewall should be reviewed and applied when they are issued, to fix known vulnerabilities in its firmware and software.

Commonly used security tools

A server administrator typically has a set of tools that they use to perform their tasks. The utilities and apps you should know for the Server+ exam are:

- **Port scanners:** A port scanner or analyzer scans a server (or host) to identify open or closed TCP/UDP ports. This software allows an administrator to verify that the configuration of system aligns with an organization's security policies. Some port scanners scan for only the well-known TCP/UDP ports (ports 0 – 1024). Some scan for the ports most commonly exploited and others scan for the full range of port numbers (up to 65536). Ports are assigned a status, which are, Open (Accepted), Closed (Denied), or Filtered (Blocked). Open ports are the important ones to review, as these are the ones that can create security vulnerabilities. *Figure 26.11* shows an example of the **nmap** port scanner utility:

```
PS C:\> nmap -Pn 192.168.0.0/24
Starting Nmap 7.94 ( https://nmap.org )
Nmap scan report for 192.168.0.1
Host is up (0.0052s latency).
Not shown: 988 closed tcp ports (reset)
PORT      STATE    SERVICE
22/tcp    filtered ssh
23/tcp    filtered telnet
80/tcp    open     http
111/tcp   filtered rpcbind
443/tcp   filtered https
1026/tcp  filtered LSA-or-nterm
1027/tcp  filtered IIS
1028/tcp  filtered unknown
1029/tcp  filtered ms-lsa
2222/tcp  filtered EtherNetIP-1
9000/tcp  filtered cslistener
49152/tcp open     unknown
MAC Address: 02:10:18:CE:19:C3 (Unknown)
```

Figure 26.11: *The output of the nmap utility*

- **Sniffers:** Also called **packet sniffers**, a **sniffer** examines the payload of an incoming network packet looking for a variety of content, as specified by an administrator, such as passwords, usernames, account numbers, and other **Personally Identifiable Information** (**PII**). Sniffers can be hardware appliances or software programs. *Figure 26.12* shows an example of the Wireshark utility:

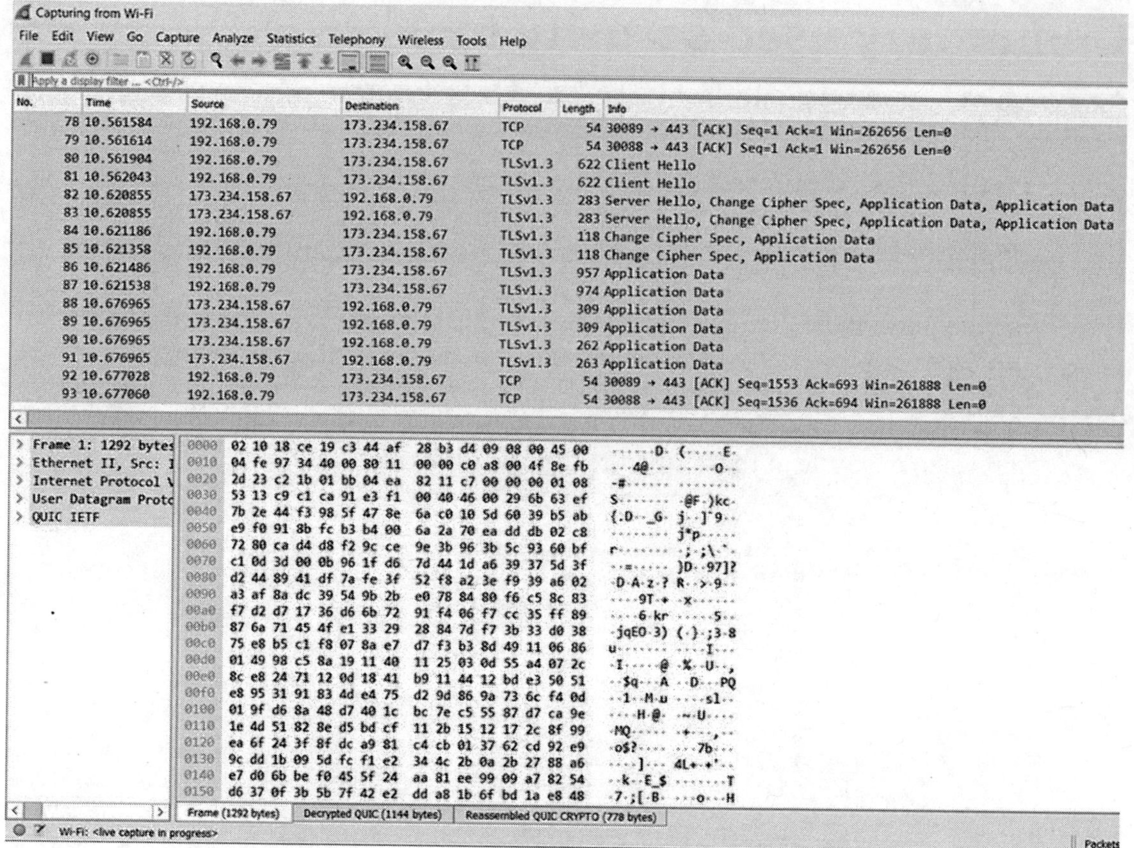

Figure 26.12: An example of the Wireshark packet sniffer

- **Checksums:** A **checksum** is a value generated by an algorithm that represents the contents of an original string. The checksum generated for a file, packet, string, or any digital object should be identical to a checksum generated for any copy of that object. The commonly used checksum algorithms **Message Digest 5 (MD5), Secure Hash Algorithm (SHA)-1, SHA-256,** and **SHA-512**. SHA-256 and SHA-512 represent the number of bits in the signature (hash value) they generate. *Table 26.1* shows an example of the generated signatures from the checksum algorithms mentioned:

Checksum Algorithm	Checksum
MD5	E4D909C290D0FB1CA068FFADDF22CBD0
SHA-1	22B759D30862CC7C7EB3CE9616A9D4E853B1E14D
SHA-256	EF537F25C895BFA782526529A9B63D97AA631564D5D789C2B-765448C8635FB6C

Checksum Algorithm	Checksum
SHA-512	91EA1245F20D46AE9A037A989F54F1F790F0A47607EEB8A14D-12890CEA77A1BB C6C7ED9CF205E67B7F2B8FD4C7DFD3A7A8617E45F3C463D481C7E-586C39AC1ED

***Table 26.1:** The checksum results for "The quick brown fox jumps over the lazy dog."*

- **Telnet:** Short for **teletype network**. **Telnet** is used to establish a command line interface on a remote device. A telnet client is available on most OSs and on some access points, routers, firewalls, and other networking devices. Telnet came out before most TCP/IP protocols and developments, and so, it does not support encryption, which means it communicates everything as text. Telnet is insecure and its use should be limited for connections within a LAN or intranet. Regardless, its use should be as limited as possible. Other tools that can be used in place of telnet are **PuTTy**, which adds SSH encryption, **Microsoft PowerShell**, and **netcat** for macOS.

Anti-malware and antivirus

Anti-malware is a software application for protecting networks, servers, and hosts from malicious software (**malware**). Ant-malware software runs in background to scan for, detect, and remove or quarantine any malware or viruses found.

Malware is designed to penetrate a computer's defenses, if any, to harvest or damage its data or operations. The different types of malware can disrupt a computer's operations, copy sensitive and personal information, or gain access to network resources and servers. Typically, malware gains a presence on a computer as a script or program that is hidden in downloaded or shared files, images, and other digital content, often unknowingly by users.

The most common malware types are:

- **Viruses:** A virus is software that can replicate itself and spread from one computer to another.
- **Worms:** A worm, which is similar to a virus, can spread itself independent of other programs.
- **Trojans:** A Trojan (or Trojan horse) typically has the appearance or is presented as something benign or desirable, like a computer game or a graphic image. However, like the horse in the Greek legend, it is something else altogether. A Trojan malware is actually hiding malicious code intended to cause harm to a computer or to provide access to an attacker.

Anti-malware systems provide protection by:

- Preventing users from visiting websites that have been identified as containing malware.
- Preventing the spread of malware from one computer to another.
- Providing statistics on the number and type of malware infections.
- Providing information on how malware may have compromised or harmed a device or network.

Malware and viruses are typically used interchangeably but are not technically the same. A virus is only one type of malware and not all types of malware are viruses. A virus is the most common malware type that gains access to a computer or network with the purpose of harm. Malware is not self-replicating and has a single focus, where a virus can replicate itself and may have multiple objectives.

Monitoring vs. detection

The basic difference between monitoring and detection is:

- **Monitoring:** Listening, watching, analyzing, and/or recording the functions and actions of a computer system or networking device to maintain and improve its operations.
- **Detecting:** Noticing, observing, or sensing an event or discovering a hidden or disguised action or event, to determine the correct or appropriate responsive action.

Monitoring

There are no official standards for computer system monitoring systems or procedures, but there is some general agreement on several types of monitoring. They are as follows:

- **System monitoring:** This form of monitoring tracks basic system performance metrics, such as uptime and resource utilization. Also referred to as **availability monitoring**, system monitoring is also used for server, infrastructure, and network monitoring and management.
- **Web performance monitoring:** This is a form of system monitoring used specifically to monitor web servers. Web performance monitoring tracks various performance metrics, including page and web element load times, errors, and their source. The information produced by this type of monitoring helps an organization ensure that its web servers and websites are up and available and meeting the needs of its customers and visitors.
- **Application performance management (APM):** APM tools track the performance of user-facing applications to identify any issues before they can become a problem

for their users. Modern APM tools include routines that troubleshoot performance issues without human intervention.

- **Security monitoring:** This is a specialized subset of system monitoring that detects breaches in security and any unusual network activity.

Detecting

Detecting is essentially diagnosing a problem and identifying its cause. A Windows system has three built-in performance and diagnostic tools: the **Performance Monitor**, the Task Manager's **Performance** tab, and the **Windows Memory Diagnostic**. These tools can be used to determine if there is a system problem or a performance issue, as discussed here:

- **Performance Monitor (perfmon):** The Performance Monitor, shown in *Figure 26.13*, is the most complete tool for locating, identifying, and diagnosing a hardware or system issue. To run the Performance Monitor, follow the given steps:
    1. Open the **Run** box (*Win+R*), enter **`perfmon`** in the **Open** box, and press **OK**.
    2. In the left-side navigation pane, expand **Repots**, expand **System**, expand **System Diagnostics**, and choose the computer name.

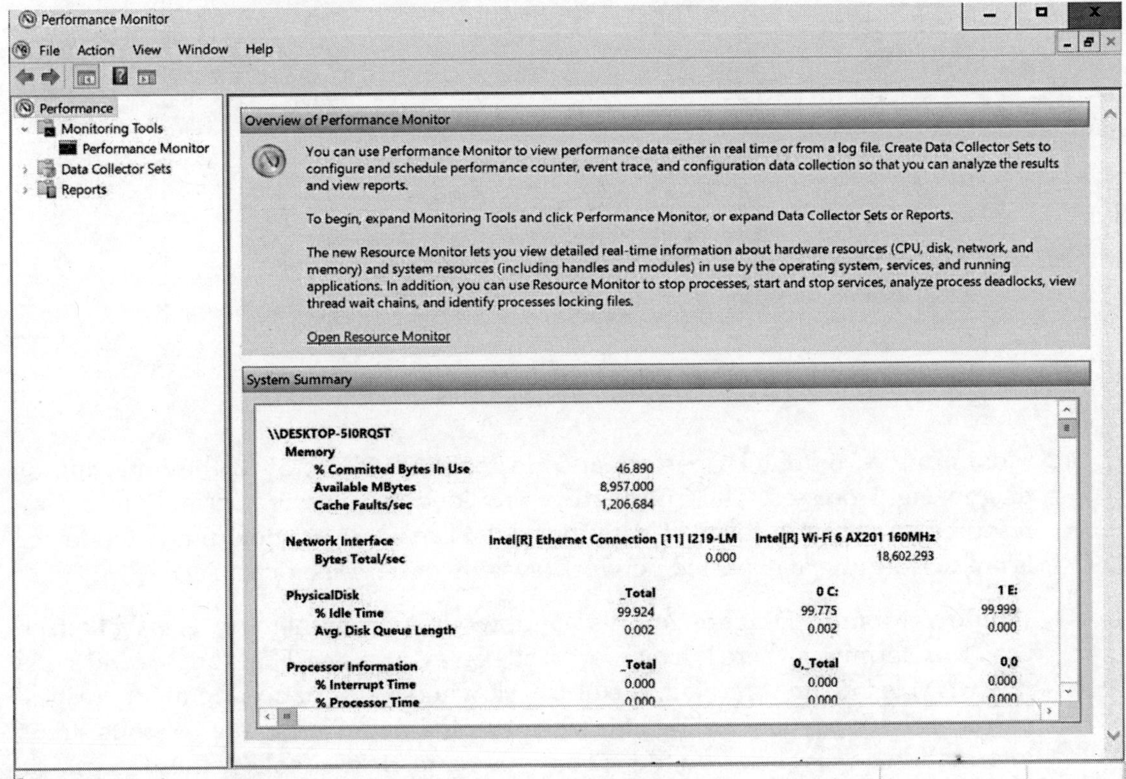

Figure 26.13: The Windows Performance Monitor's opening page

The report should include checks on the computer's hardware, software, CPU, network, data storage, memory, and other statistics. For statistics on specific devices, use the Monitoring Tools and Performance Monitor options or define a specific collector in the Data Collector Sets.

- **Task Manager Performance tab:** The Performance tab, shown in *Figure 26.14*, provides real-time data on the performance of a computer. Separate graphs depict the performance of the CPU, memory, data storage drives, network connections, and the graphics processor.

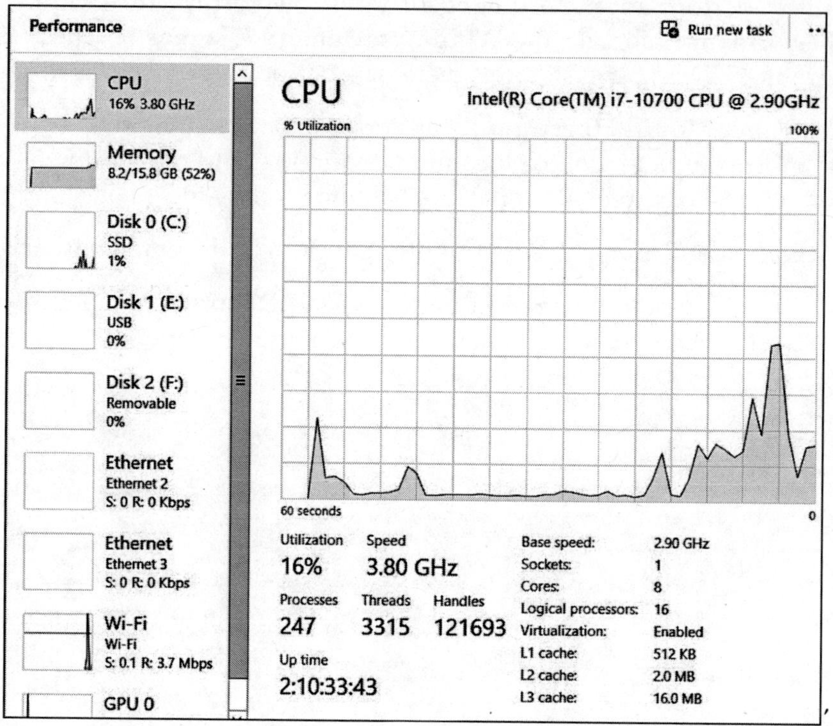

Figure 26.14: The Performance tab of the Windows Task Manager

Monitoring a computer's performance in real-time is a part of the detecting or diagnosing processes. The information provided can provide insights into how resources are being utilized. This information can also help determine if a device is not performing at expected network, system, or device efficiencies.

- **Windows Memory Diagnostic:** This Windows utility runs memory tests that can be used to determine if there is a memory issue on a computer. There are several signs that RAM is beginning to fail, including slowing performance, frequent crashes, video card drivers not loading at boot, corrupted data files, and erroneous status information on RAM. To run the **Memory Diagnostic** tool, follow these steps:

1. Open the **Run** box (*Win+R*) and enter `mdsched` in the **Open** box, and click **OK**.

2. The diagnostics are executed at startup. You will be asked if you wish to reboot Windows now to run the diagnostics or have the diagnostics run the next time the system is restarted by a message box, as shown in *Figure 26.15*:

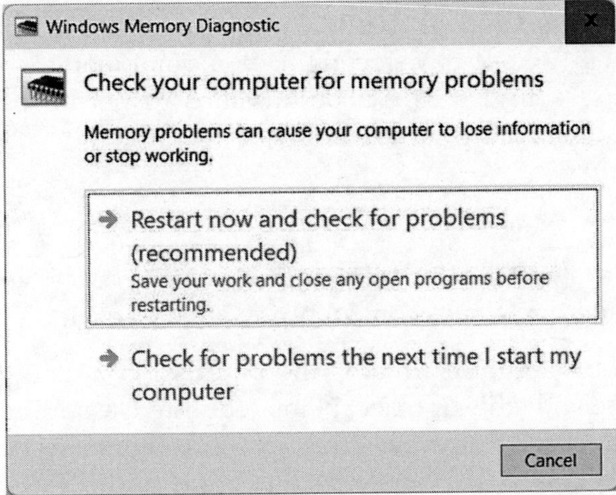

Figure 26.15: *The message box that appears when the Windows Memory Diagnostic is executed*

The diagnostics test takes a few minutes to run, and when it is complete, the computer will restart. When the restart is complete, the results of the diagnostics are displayed.

User access controls

Access control, in general, is an important part of any security policy and application. Access control sets the parameters of which users are allowed access to a system or network and its resources and, with access, what they are able to do. Access control is implemented in a variety of ways that range from the standard **Authentication, Authorization, and Accounting** (AAA) principles, to the control of access to specific devices, locations, roles, and uses. The primary objective of access control is security and specifically data confidentiality and integrity. Access control procedures prevent data and PII from being stolen or damaged.

Windows

On a Windows system, there are four primary types of access control:

- **Discretionary access control** (DAC): Every object has a specific owner, who can grant access to other users at their discretion.
- **Mandatory access control** (MAC): The access granted in a MAC access to a user is much like a security clearance. The access rights for any object are centrally administered to all users.

- **Role-Based Access Control** (**RBAC**): Access rights are based on the task or job of the individual, rather than the user's identity. RBAC implements the principle of least privilege.
- **Rule-Based Access Control** (**RuBAC**): Access rights are based on one or more factors, such as time-of-day, location, or a combination of identifying factors. RuBAC can use a user's RBAC permissions to permit or deny access from a particular location during certain hours of the day.

Linux/macOS

On a Linux or macOS system, the Linux kernel controls user access to directories and files. This is done by applying two access control types: DAC and MAC, in that order:

- **DAC:** The Linux kernel compares the permission and rights of the requesting process to those of the file or object being requested; assuming a user with the right permissions executed the requesting process. If tighter restrictions are needed, an **Access Control List** (**ACL**) can be used to apply additional permission controls.
- **MAC:** Also called policy-based access control. This type of control is applied through the **Linux Security Module** (**LSM**), based on policies that define the operations allowed on an object by a process.

User account control

The Windows feature that protects the OS from unauthorized changes is **User Account Control** (**UAC**). With UAC enabled, any change a user attempts that requires administrator-level rights and permissions, the user is notified and asked whether the change should be allowed or not, or that the elevated permissions are needed. One of the purposes of UAC is that it adds an additional layer of complexity to the access of data or programming to ward off malware. UAC is enabled by default and requires administrator privileges to be configured.

Security-enhanced Linux

Security-enhanced Linux (**SELinux**) provides additional security control over who is authorized to access a system than is available in standard Linux distro. SELinux provides a robust access control system built into the Linux kernel that enforces policies defining the level of access that users, programs, and services have on the system. SELinux, by default, denies and logs any unauthorized attempts to access system resources, using the principle of least privilege concept, which requires explicit access and use of privileges and rights for files, directories, sockets, and other Linux services.

Conclusion

The server and network security problems you need to know and understand are file integrity, privilege escalation, applications not loading, network file/share access, unable to open files, excessive access, and excessive memory use. The causes of common security problems include active services, inactive accounts, anti-malware configuration, misconfigured permissions, open ports, and rogue processes. In addition, the system utilities and apps used to identify, diagnose, and resolve system operational and security issues include port scanners, sniffers, checksums, and user account and access controls.

Points to remember

- File integrity means system resources have not been attacked or modified by an unauthorized user, malware, or rogue software.
- Privilege escalation is a cyberattack in which an attacker takes advantage of security flaws to gain higher user account rights and privileges. The two types of privilege escalation are vertical and horizontal.
- Ownership of a folder, directory, or file determines who has permission to read, write, or execute it or its contents.
- Under the principle of least privilege, users should only have access and rights to those resources absolutely required to perform their assigned tasks.
- A server administrator should perform a periodical audit of the active services running on the network servers and hosts.
- Inactive accounts should be monitored because they are still usable and can represent a vulnerability.
- The anti-malware configuration and its database should be reviewed and updated regularly.
- An open port may create a vulnerability. Hardening a server includes disabling all unnecessary ports.
- Rogue processes consume resources and may cause harm.
- The two types of rogue processes are zombies and orphans.
- An IDS attempts to detect intrusions into a system, such as malware, an attacker, or a malicious user. IDS detects security threats like an input validation error, buffer overflow, or boundary condition error.
- User or group account problem sources include, object permissions, user or group account rights, and errors in local group policies.

- An improperly configured firewall can leave an entire network vulnerable to attack.
- A port scanner identifies open and closed TCP/UDP ports.
- A sniffer examines incoming packets looking for specific content.
- A checksum is generated by an algorithm and represents the contents of an original object, such as a packet payload. Commonly used checksum algorithms include MD5, SHA-1, SHA-256, and SHA-512.
- Telnet is used to establish a command line interface on a remote device.
- Anti-malware is software that protects systems from malicious software. Common malware types are viruses, worms, and Trojans.
- A virus is a type of malware but not all malware are viruses.
- Monitoring is watching, analyzing, and/or recording the actions of a computer for maintenance and operation improvement. Detecting is observing or sensing an event to determine the correct response.
- Access control sets what users are allowed to access and what they are able to do. On Windows, the access control types are DAC, MAC, and RBAC. On Linux or macOS, the kernel applies DAC and MAC.
- UAC protects the Windows OS from unauthorized changes.
- SELinux provides access control that enforces policies defining access levels for users, programs, and services.

APPENDIX A

CompTIA Server+ Certification Exam: Practice Test 1

Choose the best answer available for each of the following multiple choice and match the following questions. The answers to these questions are in Appendix E.

1. **What is the software licensing model that is commonly used in virtualized environments for VM running on a host?**

   a. Per core

   b. Per instance

   c. Per subscriber

   d. Per socket

2. **What type of server hosts protocols like DNS, DHCP, VoIP, and NTP?**

   a. Proxy server

   b. File server

   c. Messaging server

   d. Network server

3. **True or False: A virtual server is any server that hosts virtual private networks.**

   a. True

   b. False

4. **What is the standard height dimension of a rack unit or "U"?**
   a. 1.75 inches
   b. 2.75 inches
   c. 3.50 inches
   d. 50 millimeters

5. **What are the voltages produced by an ATX PSU for the internal components of server hardware? Choose all that apply:**
   a. +3.3VDC
   b. 110VAC
   c. +5VDC
   d. +/- 12VDC
   e. -48VDC
   f. 230VDC

6. **Which of the following are performance or functional difference between an HDD and an SDD? Choose two:**
   a. Rotational delay
   b. Access time
   c. Storage capacity
   d. All of the above

7. **An SSD device uses one of which two of the following interfaces? Choose two:**
   a. PATA
   b. SATA
   c. SCSI
   d. SAS

8. **Which of the following storage technologies describes a number of independent disks not configured into an array?**
   a. RAID
   b. DAS
   c. SAN
   d. JBOD

9. **Which one of the following is a serious malfunction of an electronics or mechanical device in a computer that requires a repair or replacement?**

   a. Hard failure

   b. Soft failure

   c. Catastrophic failure

   d. Predictive failure

10. **Which two of the following identify the access to data resources in a SAN for servers and hosts?**

    a. File permissions

    b. LUN zoning

    c. LUN masking

    d. Filesystem

11. **What is the cloud structure model that is a completely proprietary computing network architecture specific to an organization and its users?**

    a. Community

    b. Public

    c. Private

    d. Hybrid

12. **Which two of the following features are used to restrict system changes to only authorized users on Windows and Linux systems, respectively?**

    a. UAC

    b. Windows Explorer

    c. chown

    d. sudo

13. **What are two redundancy methods applied in the different RAID levels? Choose two:**

    a. Mirroring

    b. Compression

    c. Encryption

    d. Striping

14. Which of the following is not a data redundancy level of RAID?

a. RAID 0

b. RAID 1

c. RAID 5

d. RAID 10

15. A system that is fully operational and accessible by users for a significant percentage of time is:

a. Fault tolerant

b. Fault averse

c. High availability

d. Extreme availability

16. Match the name on the left to the description on the right that best describes it:

a. Hot swap	1. requires the powering down of a system to affect replacements or repairs.
b. Cold swap	2. the immediate switchover or replacement of a failed component completed while a system remains fully operational
c. Warm swap	3. the suspension of operations, although still powered, to affect the replacement of a failed component

17. What is a basic function of a network server?

a. Communicating with the internet

b. Providing services to network clients

c. Intrusion detection and prevention

d. Providing proxy server functions

18. True or False: Backward compatibility is a condition or property of software and hardware technologies that provides a newer version of a product to be interoperable with one or more previous or legacy versions of that product.

a. True

b. False

19. Which of the following is not a system resource managed by an operating system?

a. IRQ

b. I/O address

c. Device driver

d. DMA address

20. On virtually all operating systems, what are the values defining the operating environment for apps and programs?

a. Environment variable

b. Global variable

c. Universal variable

d. Local variable

21. A computer operating system has three primary parts. Which of the following is not one of those parts?

a. Device drivers

b. Kernel

c. Shell

d. Filesystem

22. What are the two most common firmware system configuration systems? Choose two:

a. CMOS

b. BIOS

c. FAT32

d. UEFI

e. APFS

23. What identifies a server for the purposes of communication and access to network resources?

a. User account name

b. Hostname

c. Server name

d. Group account name

24. On a Windows Server network, the network administrator may grant a domain user what access level? Choose all that apply:

a. Local computer resources

b. Server-based resources

c. Network-attached resources

d. WAN resources

25. True or False: One of the basic scripting types is server-side.

a. True

b. False

26. Which of the following best describes an IPv4 address?

a. Classless

b. 5 classes of 32-bits in 4 octets

c. 128-bits in 8 sections of 16 bits.

d. Network identifier has fixed size.

27. Which IPv4 address class uses 16 bits to identify the network portion of an address?

a. Class A

b. Class B

c. Class C

d. Class D

e. IPv4 is classless.

28. What network service provides an alias public address to internal network nodes with private LAN addresses?

a. DHCP

b. DNS

c. WINS

d. NAT

29. Which of the following is an example of CIDR notation?

a. 2020::15AD:0:25FF

b. 201.110.25.16/24

c. 10.0.0.0

d. 198.168.32.10:80

30. What is the significance of a double-colon inserted in an IPv6 address?

a. It masks one or more sections not used for routing.

b. It masks one or more sections containing all zeroes.

c. It masks one or more sections containing $FFFF_{16}$.

d. It indicates a TCP/UDP port number.

31. Which of the following can be used to display the IPv4 and IPv6 addresses of a network workstation?

a. ping
b. traceroute/tracert
c. nslookup
d. ipconfig/ifconfig

32. What is the total number of TCP/UDP ports identified by the IANA?

a. 65535
b. 49151
c. 1024
d. There is no set number.

33. Which two of the following are the general types of twisted-pair cabling?

a. Coaxial
b. Fiber optic
c. UTP
d. STP
e. FDDI

34. What is the EIA/TIA 568 cabling standard for the maximum cable length between network stations?

a. 500 meters
b. 185 meters
c. 100 meters
d. 90 meters
e. 10 meters

35. What is the registered jack connector that is the standard for Ethernet networks?

a. RJ-11
b. RJ-31
c. RJ-45
d. RS-232

36. Which of the following copper cable categories is also known as "Gigabit Ethernet" cabling?

a. CAT 5

b. CAT 5e

c. CAT 6

d. CAT 7

37. Which one of the following is not considered a cable testing level?

a. Verification

b. Certification

c. Attenuation

d. Qualification

38. Which of the two transmission modes of fiber optic cabling has the longest attenuation rating?

a. Single-mode

b. Multi-mode

c. Subscriber connector

d. Local connector

39. What is the acronym used for the legal contracts between a software developer or publisher and an end-user who purchases a use license for a software package?

a. AUP

b. EULA

c. SOP

d. DRP

40. What device allows an administrator to use local input and output devices to control a remote system?

a. COM

b. ITAM

c. KVM

d. LCAM

41. KVM over IP is an example of what type of device or service?

a. Localhost

b. Network-based administration

c. GUI

d. SSH

42. A system administrator can use which of the following to manage the OS of a remote workstation?

a. RSAT

b. CLI over SSH

c. VNC

d. RDP

e. All of the above

f. None of the above

43. Which of the following best describes a metered software subscription?

a. Based on the number of accesses a user purchases in advance

b. Usage of the software is automatically recorded and charged against a pre-paid or billed amount

c. Facilitates the use of a software package by a project team or group

d. Sets a specific period during which a user can use the software

44. Which of the following is not a common form of system documentation?

a. Service manuals

b. Architecture diagrams

c. Recovery plans

d. Typing tutor

45. Effective documentation has four qualities: clear language, relative information, ______, and timeliness.

a. policies

b. completeness

c. appropriateness

d. lengthy

46. Which one of the following is not one of the basic construct types of a programming statement?

a. Sequence

b. Selection

c. Syntactical

d. Iteration

47. Which of the following is not a phase of a change control process?

a. Approval

b. Immediate application

c. Implement

d. Purpose

e. Scope

f. Test

48. One difference between a change management program and a patch management program is:

a. Patch management should be a priority.

b. Patches should use the same change management process as major OS updates.

c. Patch management requires no testing.

d. A software patch only affects the user interface.

49. Which one of the following is typically not the cause of a *partition inaccessible* error on a computer?

a. Corrupted disk sector

b. Corrupted user access permissions

c. CRC errors

d. Corrupted MFT or FAT

50. What is the more common reference to what is technically a stop error code message screen?

a. BSOD

b. RSOD

c. PSOD

d. System freeze

51. If the BIOS/UEFI startup process detects an error or possible error, it signals the code to identify the issue and its source. What are these audible signals commonly called?

a. Error indicators

b. Failure alarms

c. Beep codes

d. POST alerts

52. The objective of a preventive maintenance program is to:

a. Extend the service life of a server component

b. Avoid component failures

c. Maintain server uptime commitments

d. All of the above.

53. Which of the following provides that data, files, and system resources have not been the target of an attack or have not been modified by an unauthorized user or malware?

a. Integrity

b. Confidentiality

c. Availability

d. Immutable

54. The server cluster configuration in which a standby or failover server is available to replace a failed server, if required, is a(n):

a. Active/active

b. Active/passive

c. Passive/passive

d. Hot swappable

55. A failed server device or component that an administrator may replace while a system remains running and productive is a:

a. Cold swap

b. Warm swap

c. Hot swap

d. Just right swap

56. Which of the following is not a virtualization technology used in computer networks?

a. Virtual private network

b. Virtual reality

c. Virtual local area network

d. Virtual server

57. What is an intentional attack by an unauthorized threat actor to view or harvest confidential, sensitive, or private information?

a. Data leak

b. Data breach

c. MitM attack

d. Eavesdropping attack

58. Which of the following is not a type of disaster recovery site?

a. Cold

b. Warm

c. Hot

d. Real-time

59. What is an accidental exposure of confidential, sensitive, or private information?

a. Data breach

b. Keylogger attack

c. Data leak

d. Rootkit attack

60. Between a data backup and a data replication, which stores a duplication of data that is real-time or near-real-time?

a. Data backup

b. Data replication

c. Both

d. Neither

61. Which replication method can be impacted by latency?

a. Synchronous

b. Asynchronous

c. Near-synchronous

d. Near-asynchronous

62. Which of the following are replication methodologies? Choose all that apply:

a. Disk-to-disk

b. Cluster-to-cluster

c. Server-to-server

d. All of the above

e. None of the above

63. Which data backup method resets an archive bit that was turned on after the last full back up?

a. Full

b. Incremental

c. Snapshot

d. Differential

e. Copy

64. Which of the following is not a category of data backup media?

a. Linear access

b. Random access

c. Layered access

d. Removable media

65. What is the metric that is the desired completion time of a disaster recovery plan?

a. 3-2-1

b. RTO

c. RPO

d. R2D2

66. Which of the following is not one of the ways in which DHCP servers allocate network configurations to hosts?

a. Automatic

b. Dynamic

c. APIPA

d. Static

67. Which method uses multiple authentication factors to verify a supplicant?

a. SFA

b. CHAP

c. DHCP

d. MFA

68. Which of the following is not a type of factor used in authentication?

a. Something you know

b. Something you have

c. Someone you know

d. Something you do

69. Which one of the following is used to determine the process, service, or application that an incoming message is to be forwarded to for processing?

a. Sockets

b. Ports

c. I/O addresses

d. IRQs

70. Which of the following is not a general threat category to a physical area?

a. Cyber

b. Environmental

c. Technical

d. Man-made

71. A company has a large server room with several rows of rack-mounted servers, power units, and network attached storage. It has arranged the devices in rows so that the HVAC system provides the right amount of cooling to each row. What is the environmental control approach in use in its server room?

a. Zone conditioning

b. Compartmentalization

c. Cold aisle/Hot aisle

d. On row/Off row

72. Which of the following is not typically scanned or reported by an environmental monitoring system?

a. Temperature

b. Logical intrusion

c. Smoke and chemical fumes

d. Humidity

73. Which two of the following are the most commonly used backup strategies?

a. 3-2-1

b. Daily

c. Grandfather-father-son

d. Annual

74. What device provides electrical power distribution to rack-mounted devices through multiple AC outlets?

a. PDU

b. HVAC

c. UPS

d. PSU

75. This type of virtualization creates independent virtual servers that share the OS kernel of the host system:

a. Full virtualization

b. OS virtualization

c. Para-virtualization

d. Network virtualization

76. Which of the following is not a commonly used identification factor of access control?

a. Group

b. Role or assignment

c. Application type

d. Computer name

77. The permissions and rights assigned to a specific user or group is defined in what element?

a. ACL

b. ACX

c. ACE

d. ACR

78. The application of a cryptographic algorithm to data for the purpose of restricting access to its content is

a. Confidentiality

b. Authentication

c. Authorization

d. Encryption

79. Which of the following is a method for removing data from a disk drive:

a. Delete

b. Wipe

c. Erase

d. Shred

e. All the above

f. None of the above

80. Which of the following describes the status of any data on a disk drive after formatting:

a. Unrecoverable

b. Destroyed

c. Recoverable

d. Unreadable

81. What is the objective of hardening a system or device?

a. Extending service life

b. Strengthening its case

c. Reducing vulnerability

d. Taking it offline

82. True or False: Application hardening modifies the binary code of an application.

a. True

b. False

83. Setting a BIOS/UEFI password is an example of which of the following?

a. Application hardening

b. OS hardening

c. Network hardening

d. Hardware hardening

84. What is the unique ID number assigned to an HDD and used by an OS to identify the storage devices on a system?

a. Device ID

b. Disk signature

c. Hash code

d. MAC address

85. What diagnostic activity is a structured process used to identify and isolate a computer problem?

a. Maintenance

b. Analysis

c. Troubleshooting

d. System testing

86. What is the first step in the process to determine the source or cause of a computer performance issue?

a. Identify the problem

b. Reboot the computer

c. Shutdown the computer

d. Test a possible solution

87. Perhaps, the best way to verify that a reported problem exists is to do which of the following?

a. Determine whether the problem is hardware or software

b. Remove the suspected hardware or software

c. Recreate the problem

d. Reboot the system.

88. Before starting any work on a computer to isolate and identify a problem, what cautionary action should you take?

a. Open a command prompt window

b. Back up the entire hard disk

c. Remove the hard disk drive

d. Boot the computer from a floppy disk

89. Which one of the following is a collection of group policy settings defining the rights and privileges of a defined user group on a Windows system?

a. RTC

b. SCA

c. GPO

d. PID

90. What is the term used to describe a child process that continues to run after its parent process has ended or has been terminated without waiting for the child's execution to complete?

a. Zombie

b. Orphan

c. Step-child

d. Dead object

APPENDIX B

CompTIA Server+ Certification Exam: Practice Test 2

Choose the best answer available for each of the following multiple choice or matching questions. The answers to these questions are in Appendix F.

1. **Before starting any work on a computer to isolate and identify a problem, what cautionary action should you take?**
   a. Open a command prompt window
   b. Back up the entire hard disk
   c. Remove the hard disk drive
   d. Boot the computer from a floppy disk

2. **An SMA is an agreement that the software publisher commits to providing technical support, fixes, and updates for its product.**
   a. True
   b. False

3. **Which of the following are common software issues? (Choose all that apply).**
   a. Corrupted system files
   b. Improperly installed software
   c. Malware attacks
   d. All the above
   e. None of the above

4. **If you are able to access a folder and its files on a remote network server, but you are unable to delete out-of-date files. What folder permission are you lacking?**
    a. Execute
    b. Read
    c. Write
    d. Delete

5. **What notification display is caused by a variety of issues, including bad device drivers, faulty hardware, or components exceeding their operating limits?**
    a. BSOD
    b. POST beep codes
    c. Flashing console lights
    d. Desktop freeze

6. **The condition created when a program fails to release allocated memory when it's no longer in use is which of the following?**
    a. Memory overflow
    b. Memory parity error
    c. Memory crash
    d. Memory leak

7. **Which of the following can be used to identify corrupted files on a hard disk partition?**
    a. systemctl
    b. GRUB
    c. SFC
    d. UAC

8. **Of the following methods, which can be used to free up space on a hard disk drive?**
    a. Windows Disk Management
    b. Disk compression
    c. Virtual memory
    d. fdisk

9. **What is the feature that reserves a portion of the hard disk to extend the size and capacity of main memory?**
   a. Virtual machine
   b. Virtual memory
   c. Virtual disk
   d. Virtual LAN

10. **Operating systems create and maintain a record of events, actions, errors, and warnings of the applications and services executing on a system. These records are recorded in what type of a file?**
    a. Spool
    b. Queue
    c. Log
    d. Index
    e. Registry

11. **The Windows WinSxS folder contains a variety of vital software components for installing, updating, backing up, and customizing the OS.**
    a. True
    b. False

12. **A local network host cannot complete its startup process without a successful interaction with the DHCP server. True or False.**
    a. True
    b. False

13. **What is the type of threat actor who has the objective to cause as much harm and destruction as possible, typically related to a social or political cause.**
    a. Script kiddie
    b. Hacktivist
    c. Insider
    d. Cyberterrorist

14. **What is the formal name of a virtual structure that logically creates a broadcast domain through a switch port?**
    a. VPN
    b. VM
    c. VLAN
    d. ISL

15. Which of the following is the term for a communication link that interconnects two switch interface ports and runs an IEEE 802.1Q protocol?

a. Frame relay

b. Tagged port

c. Flapping port

d. Trunking port

16. A network technician installs a number of network hosts in a new branch office located in another state. What command line utilities could she use to verify that each of the new hosts is able to "see" the network server in the home office? (Choose two).

a. nslookup

b. ping

c. tracert/traceroute

d. ARP/RARP

17. What is the Linux command-line utility used for displaying and modifying network interface configuration settings?

a. ifconfig

b. ipconfig

c. net config

d. net setup

18. Which of the following data storage devices has no storage-related moving parts?

a. HDD

b. SDD

c. DVD

d. CD

19. The Red Flags rule is intended to prevent physical theft?

a. True

b. False

20. What type of recovery facility has the needed computing, network, and communication equipment pre-installed that is synchronized to a production system on a weekly or monthly basis?

a. Cold site

b. Warn site

c. Hot site

d. Off-site

21. The information needed by the boot process about a hard disk partition is found in what data block?

a. Registry

b. MBR

c. Filesystem

d. Disk buffer

22. On a Windows system,.what system utility can view the contents of the system log files?

a. Task Manager

b. Device Manager

c. Control Panel

d. Event Viewer

23. What is the action that increases security by reducing the vulnerability of a workstation, server, and network.

a. Anti-malware

b. Strengthening

c. Hardening

d. Port closure

24. True or False: A virtual server is any server that hosts virtual private networks.

a. True

b. False

25. What is the standard height dimension of a rack unit or "U"?

a. 1.75 inches

b. 2.75 inches

c. 3.50 inches

d. 50 millimeters

26. What are the voltages produced by an ATX PSU for the internal components of server hardware? Choose all that apply?

a. +3.3VDC

b. 110VAC

c. +5VDC

d. +/- 12VDC

e. -48VDC

f. 230VDC

27. Which two of the following are differences between an HDD and an SDD? (Choose two.)

a. Rotational delay

b. Access time

c. Storage capacity

d. Form factor

28. An SSD device uses which two of the following interfaces? (Choose two).

a. PATA

b. SATA

c. SCSI

d. SAS

29. Which of the following storage technologies describes a number of independent disks not configured into an array?

a. RAID

b. DAS

c. SAN

d. JBOD

30. Which of the following statements best describes a SAN?

a. One or more storage devices directly connected to a computer.

b. A cluster of data storage devices that appear to be direct-attached storage.

c. A self-contained storage device network and switches that provides high-speed access to data.

d. Zoning that identifies the access permissions of servers and hosts.

31. SAMBA is an implementation of which Application Layer protocols?

a. HTTP/FTP

b. IPSec/WPA

c. SBA/TCP

d. SMB/CIFS

32. What are the two redundancy methods applied in the different RAID levels? (Choose two).

a. Mirroring

b. Compression

c. Encryption

d. Striping

33. Which of the following is not a data redundancy level of RAID?

a. RAID 0

b. RAID 1

c. RAID 5

d. RAID 10

34. A system that is fully operational and accessible by users for a significant percentage of time is

a. Fault tolerant

b. Fault averse

c. High availability

d. Extreme availability

35. What is the type of authentication method that facilitates a user to sign into two or more applications or website through the entry of one set of credentials?

a. Federated user accounts

b. MFA

c. Single-sign-on

d. Anonymous

36. Which of the following is not a system resource managed by an operating system?

a. IRQ

b. I/O address

c. Device driver

d. DMA address

37. An operating has three primary parts. Which of the following is not one of those parts?

a. Device drivers

b. Kernel

c. Shell

d. Filesystem

38. What are the two most common firmware system configuration systems? (Choose two.)

a. CMOS

b. BIOS

c. FAT32

d. UEFI

e. APFS

39. What identification identifies a server for the purposes of communication and access to network resources?

a. User account name

b. Hostname

c. Server name

d. Group account name

40. A network administrator wishes to power up and boot a remote PC attached to an organization's network. Which of the following services will enable this action?

a. QoS

b. DMI

c. PXE

d. TFTP

41. Which of the following best describes an IPv4 address?

a. Classless

b. 5 classes of 32-bits in 4 octets

c. 128-bits in 8 sections of 16 bits.

d. Network identifier has fixed size.

42. Which IPv4 address class uses 16 bits to identify the network portion of an address?

a. Class A

b. Class B

c. Class C

d. Class D

e. IPv4 is classless.

43. What network service provides an alias public address to internal network nodes with private LAN addresses?

a. DHCP

b. DNS

c. WINS

d. NAT

44. Which of the following is an example of CIDR notation?

a. 2020::15AD:0:25FF

b. 201.110.25.16/24

c. 10.0.0.0

d. 198.168.32.10:80

45. What is the significance of a double-colon inserted in an IPv6 address?

a. It masks one or more sections not used for routing.

b. It masks one or more sections containing all zeroes.

c. It masks one or more sections containing FFFF16.

d. It indicates a TCP/UDP port number.

46. What is the EIA/TIA 568 cabling standard for the maximum cable length between network stations?

a. 500 meters

b. 185 meters

c. 100 meters

d. 90 meters

e. 10 meters

47. Which of the following is not a state in which data can exist?

a. Data-at-rest

b. Data-in-transit

c. Data-in-computation

d. Data-in-use

48. What device allows an administrator to use local input and output devices to control a remote system?

a. COM

b. ITAM

c. KVM

d. LCAM

49. KVM over IP is an example of what type of device or service?

a. Localhost

b. Network-based administration

c. GUI

d. SSH

50. A system administrator can use which of the following to manage the OS of a remote workstation?

a. RSAT

b. CLI over SSH

c. VNC

d. RDP

e. All of the above

f. None of the above

51. The management activities of information technology assets are known as:

a. LCAM

b. ITAM

c. RSAT

d. iDRAC

52. Which of the following is not a common form of system documentation?

a. Service manuals

b. Architecture diagrams

c. Recovery plans

d. Typing tutor

53. Effective documentation has four qualities: clear language, relative information, ______, and timeliness.

a. policies

b. completeness

c. appropriateness

d. lengthy

54. System documentation has four characteristics: purpose, effectiveness, __________, and completeness.

a. availability

b. integrity

c. intended audience

d. currency

55. Which of the following is not a phase of a change control process?

a. Approval

b. Immediate application

c. Implement

d. Purpose

e. Scope

f. Test

56. One difference between a change management program and a patch management program is

a. Patch management should be a priority.

b. Patches should use the same change management process as major OS updates.

c. Patch management requires no testing.

d. A software patch only affects the user interface.

57. What type of software provides scheduled device checks, including checks against pre-set thresholds, hard disk utilization, disk IOPS, and other system health metrics on a server?

a. Asset management systems

b. SNMP-MIBs

c. Server monitors

d. Packet sniffers

58. What is the significance of the IOPS metric?

a. It is an estimate of the maximum channel/bus bandwidth.

b. It represents the maximum number of reads and writes (input/output operations) to and from non-contiguous storage locations on secondary storage devices.

c. It reflects the number of independent operations a CPU performs in a second.

d. It measures the number of I/O operations per second made by the CPU.

59. A data security policy typically does not address which of the following elements?

a. Access control

b. Encryption

c. Backup and recovery

d. Employee contact information

60. The objective of a preventive maintenance program is to

a. Extend the service life of a server component

b. Avoid component failures

c. Maintain server uptime commitments

d. All of the above.

61. Improving process throughput and responsiveness by interconnecting two or more servers in a cluster to operate as a single device – describes what server configuration?

a. Active/active

b. Active/passive

c. Passive/passive

d. Hot swappable

62. As a best practice, in which of the following locations should antivirus software be installed? (Choose two)

a. Only on the administrator's workstation

b. Only on the domain controller

c. Only on the general manager's workstation

d. On all servers

e. On all workstations

63. Which of the following is the best description for an HCL?

a. Permissions for network access and routing

b. An approved hardware list

c. Permissions for file sharing

d. The method for attaching a server to a SAN

64. An administrator recently performed an upgrade of the NIC device drivers on several servers. The network is now experiencing lost packets and disconnected switches. Which of the following is the best action the administrator should take to resolve this issue?

a. Restart the server and see if the issue still remains. If the issue still exists open a case with the OEM of the NIC.

b. Call the OEM of the NIC and open a case with them to investigate the issue. Roll back the NIC driver to the previous working revision.

c. Call the OEM of the NIC and open a case with them to investigate the issue.

d. Go to the OEM's website and download another NIC driver to test.

65. When a server issue is being diagnosed by a technician, what should the technician do to ensure that should the problem reoccur in the future, the process the technician uses could be duplicated in the future?

a. Verify system functionality and implement preventive measures.

b. Document the findings, actions, and outcomes throughout the process.

c. Determine if there is a common element or symptom.

d. Notify the impacted users before implementing any changes.

66. What is the security control that validates one or more of a person's physical characteristics?

a. OTP

b. Biometrics

c. RFID

d. Security cameras

67. An administrator wishes to avoid users losing access to a file server in the event of a short power outage. What should the administrator do to ensure the server remains available during short power outages?

a. Connect the server to a KVM.

b. Use cable management.

c. Connect the server to a redundant network.

d. Connect the server to a UPS.

68. Which of the following access control policies assigns a user permission based on the duties or tasks of the user?

a. Scope-based

b. Role-based

c. Location-based

d. Rule-based

69. Before installing a server OS on an older computer, what should the technician do to ensure that the OS will operate properly?

a. Consult the HCL to ensure everything is supported.

b. Migrate the physical server to a virtual server.

c. Low-level format the hard drives to ensure there is no old data remaining.

d. Make sure the case and the fans are free from dust to ensure proper cooling.

70. When installing a new server with four network ports, the technician assigns two of the ports with the IP addresses of the replaced server. What should the technician do to complete the setup of the server and ensure that security best practices are followed?

a. Interconnect the unused ports to create an unusable loop.

b. Disable the unused network ports on the server side.

c. Connect the unused network ports to a network switch for future expansion.

d. Insert loopback adapters into the unused network ports.

71. Which of the following is typically the software licensing type for cloud computing services?

a. Per socket

b. Perpetual

c. Subscription-based

d. Site-based

72. You host an application on a web server for Internet users to access. What protocol should be used to communicate with the application that ensures the data transfer between clients and the server is reliable?

a. TCP

b. UDP

c. IP

d. ICMP

73. What is the action that mirrors a storage device to another system or distributes parts of a database to multiple storage units spread out geographically.

a. Data replication

b. Data duplication

c. Data deduplication

d. Backup

74. You wish to set filtering on an FTP server and configure it to filter port 20. All FTP traffic be filtered now.

a. True

b. False

75. Which of the following describes differential backup?

a. A differential backup backs up all the information on the disk to an offline device such as tape.

b. A differential backup backs up only the information that is added since previous differential backup.

c. A differential backup backs up only the information that is added since last full backup.

d. A differential backup backs up only the information that is added since last incremental backup.

76. It is completely sufficient to install antivirus only on network servers and those systems that are exposed to internet.

a. True

b. False

77. Which of the following RAID levels should not be used as a fault tolerant measure?

a. RAID 0

b. RAID 1

c. RAID 3

d. RAID 5

78. Which of the following tape backup methods reset the archive bit? (Choose two.)

a. Differential

b. Sequential

c. Full

d. Incremental

79. Which one of the following is not a basic construct type of programming statements?

a. Sequence

b. Selection

c. Computation

d. Iteration.

80. Recently, you installed server hardware at a client's place of business. The client contacts you to complain that the server is functioning erratically. After observing the server's symptoms, you suspect the problem is being caused by the RAM. What process will help you to isolate this problem?

a. Remove all the memory modules and restart the Server

b. Remove and replace one single RAM module at a time and observe the beeps

c. Just replace all the RAM modules and restart the server

d. None of the above

81. Match the name on the left to the description on the right that best describes it.

a. Hot swap	1.requires the powering down of a system to affect replacements or repairs.
b. Cold swap	2. The immediate switchover or replacement of a failed component completed while a system remains fully operational
c. Warm swap	3. The suspension of operations, although still powered, to affect the replacement of a failed component

82. Which of the following is a Linux system filesystem?

a. NTFS

b. VMFS

c. ReFS

d. ext4

e. None of the above

83. Which one of the following is not a phase in a data life-cycle management program?

a. Capture

b. Storage

c. Archival

d. Warehouse

84. Which of the following is best described by "a vulnerability that could be exploited by a threat actor, who has a specific motivation, to cause damage, destruction, or loss"?

a. Attack

b. Breach

c. Risk

d. Mitigation

85. All failovers are considered to be active-passive.

a. True

b. False

86. Which of the following describes the RF frequency concept of refraction?

a. The signal passes through the surface.

b. The is reflected, typically at an angle.

c. The surface absorbs the signal.

d. None of the above.

87. Which of the following is a condition that an environmental monitoring system is used to detect?

a. Temperature

b. Humidity

c. Voltage and Power

d. Smoke

e. All of the above

f. None of the above

88. **Which of the following best describes a privileged user account on a Windows system?**
    a. A standard user account with parental controls.
    b. Accounts with the highest rights and privileges.
    c. Uses an e-mail address for access to many Microsoft devices and services.
    d. A basic user account.

89. **Which one of the following is not one of the three levels of cable testing?**
    a. Verification
    b. Tensile
    c. Qualification
    d. Certification.

90. **Overprovisioning allocates more of a resource than is needed by a VM.**
    a. True
    b. False

Appendix C

CompTIA Server+®

Acronyms

The following are the acronyms you may encounter on the Server+ exam and their meanings or spelled out names. This list is from the CompTIA *Server+ Certification Exam Objectives Exam Number: SK0-005.*

Acronym	Meaning
ACL	Access Control List
AD	Active Directory
APIPA	Automatic Private IP Address
BCP	Business Continuity Plan
BIA	Business Impact Analysis
BIOS	Basic Input/Output System
BSOD	Blue Screen of Death
CIDR	Classless Inter-Domain Routing
CIFS	Common Internet File System
CIMC	Cisco Integrated Management Controller
CLI	Command Line Interface

CMOS	Complementary Metal-Oxide-Semiconductor
COOP	Continuity of Operations
CPU	Central Processing Unit
CRU	Customer Replaceable Unit
DAS	Direct Attached Storage
DC	Domain Controller
DDoS	Distributed Denial of Service
DHCP	Dynamic Host Configuration Protocol
DLP	Data Loss Prevention
DLT	Digital Linear Tape
DMZ	Demilitarized Zone
DNS	Domain Name Service
DR	Disaster Recovery
ECC	Error Checking and Correction
EFS	Encrypting File System
ESD	Electrostatic Discharge
FAT	File Allocation Table
FCoE	Fibre Channel over Ethernet
FQDN	Fully Qualified Domain Name
FRU	Field Replaceable Unit
FTP	File Transfer Protocol
FTPS	File Transfer Protocol over SSL
GFS	Grandfather Father Son
GPO	Group Policy Object
GPT	GUID Partition Table
GPU	Graphics Processing Unit
GUI	Graphical User Interface
HBA	Host Bus Adapter

HCL	Hardware Compatibility List
HID	Human Interface Device
HIDS	Host Intrusion Detection System
HIPS	Host Intrusion Prevention System
HTTP	Hyper Text Transport Protocol
HTTPS	Secure Hyper Text Transport Protocol
HVAC	Heating Ventilation and Air Conditioning
IDF	Intermediate Distribution Frame
iDRAC	Integrated Dell Remote Access Control
IDS	Intrusion Detection System
IIS	Internet Information Services
iLO	Integrated Lights Out
IMAP4	Internet Mail Access Protocol
Intel-VT	Intel Virtualization Technology
IOPS	Input Output Operations per Second
IP	Internet Protocol
IP KVM	Internet Protocol Keyboard-Video-Mouse
IPMI	Intelligent Platform Management Interface
IPS	Intrusion Prevention System
IPSec	Internet Protocol Security
IPv6	Internet Protocol version 6
iSCSI	Internetworking Small Computer System Interface
ISO	International Organization for Standardization
JBOD	Just a Bunch of Disks
KVM	Keyboard-Video-Mouse
LAN	Local Area Network
LC	Lucent Connector / Little Connector
LCD	Liquid Crystal Display

LDAP	Lightweight Directory Access Protocol
LED	Light Emitting Diode
LTO	Linear Tape-Open
LUN	Logical Unit Number
LVM	Logical Volume Management
MAC	Media Access Control
MBR	Master Boot Record
MDF	Main Distribution Frame
MFA	Multifactor Authentication
MIB	Management Information Base
MMC	Microsoft Management Console
MRU	Most Recently Used
MTBF	Mean Time Between Failure
MTTR	Mean Time to Recover
NAC	Network Access Control
NAS	Network Attached Storage
NAT	Network Address Translation
NetBIOS	Network Basic Input Output System
NFS	Network File System
NIC	Network Interface Card
NIDS	Network Intrusion Detection System
NIST	National Institute of Standards and Technology
NLB	Network Load Balancing
NOS	Network Operating System
NTFS	New Technology File System
NTP	Network Time Protocol
OEM	Original Equipment Manufacturer
OS	Operating System

OTP	One-Time Password
OU	Organizational Units
P2V	Physical to Virtual
PAT	Port Address Translation
PCI	Peripheral Component Interconnect
PCI DSS	Payment Card Industry Data Security Standard
PCIe	Peripheral Component Interconnect Express
PCI-X	Peripheral Component Interconnect Extended
PDU	Power Distribution Unit
PII	Personally Identifiable Information
PKI	Public Key Infrastructure
POST	Power on Self-Test
PSU	Power Supply Unit
PXE	Pre-boot Execution Environment
QSFP	Quad-Small Form Factor Pluggable
RADIUS	Remote Authentication Dial-in User Service
RAID	Redundant Array of Integrated Disks
RAM	Random Access Memory
RAS	Remote Access Server
RDP	Remote Desktop Protocol
ReFS	Resilient File System
RFC	Request for Comments
RFID	Radio Frequency Identification
RIS	Remote Installation Service
RJ45	Registered Jack 45
RPM	Rotations per Minute
RPO	Recovery Point Objective

RTO	Recovery Time Objective
SAN	Storage Area Network
SAS	Serial Attached SCSI
SATA	Serial ATA
SC	Standard Connector
SCCM	System Center Configuration Management
SCP	Secure Copy Protocol
SCSI	Small Computer System Interface
SD	Secure Digital
SELinux	Security Enhanced Linux
SFP	Small Form Factor Pluggable
SFTP	Secure File Transfer Protocol
SLA	Service Level Agreement
SMTP	Simple Mail Transport Protocol
SNMP	Simple Network Management Protocol
SQL	Structured Query Language
SSD	Solid State Drive
SSH	Secure Shell
SSL	Secure Sockets Layer
SSO	Single Sign-On
ST	Straight Tip
TACACS	Terminal Access Controller Access Control System
TCP	Transmission Control Protocol
TCP/IP	Transmission Control Protocol/Internet Protocol
TFTP	Trivial File Transfer Protocol
TLS	Transport Layer Security
UAC	User Account Control
UDP	User Datagram Protocol

UEFI	Unified Extensible Firmware Interface
UID	Unit Identification
UPS	Uninterruptible Power Supply
URL	Universal / Uniform Resource Locator
USB	Universal Serial Bus
UUID	Universal Unique Identifier
VBS	Visual Basic Script
VLAN	Virtual Local Area Network
VM	Virtual Machine
VMFS	VMWare File System
VNC	Virtual Network Computing
vNIC	Virtual Network Interface Card
VoIP	Voice over IP
VPN	Virtual Private Network
VSS	Volume Shadow Service
VT	Virtualization Technology
WDS	Windows Deployment Services
WINS	Windows Internet Naming Service
WMI	Windows Management Instrumentation
WOL	Wake on LAN
WSUS	Windows Software Update Services
WWNN	World Wide Node Name
WWPN	World Wide Port Name
XD	Execute Disable
ZFS	Z File System

Join our book's Discord space

Join the book's Discord Workspace for Latest updates, Offers, Tech happenings around the world, New Release and Sessions with the Authors:

https://discord.bpbonline.com

APPENDIX D
Key Terms/ Concepts

Term/concept	Description
1000BaseT	Gigabit Ethernet -- 1 gigabit per second (Gbps) on copper cables
10GigE (10 gigabit Ethernet)	Operates in full-duplex mode. Runs on CAT6, CAT6a, or CAT7 copper cabling.
3-2-1 backup strategy	Creates 3 copies of backup data: 2 copies stored locally, 1 stored off-site.
AAA	Authentication, authorization, and accounting.
Accelerated Graphics Port (AGP)	A graphics expansion card
Access control list (ACL)	Defines which users can access system resources.
Access time	The total time between a disk controller initiating an I/O action and the data being read or written to or from a disk.
Active Directory (AD)	A repository of the information about authorized users and devices and what each can do on a Windows system.

Term/concept	Description
Advanced RISC Machine (ARM)	A series of RISC architectures that require fewer resources than either x32 or x64 architectures.
Apple Filing Protocol (AFP)	A macOS file formatting protocol for Apple PCs.
Application programming interface (API)	Software that interfaces with and passes requests made to a file system.
Application server	Delivers web content and enables interactions between network users and server-side applications.
Application virtualization	Encapsulated by the host OS to include virtual support services that interact with host OS services and data storage as needed.
Asymmetric encryption	Encryption method that uses two keys: a public key, used to encrypt data, and a private key used to decrypt data.
Attack surface	An organization's vulnerabilities or attack vectors that an attacker could exploit.
Authentication	The process in which a supplicant must prove authorization for access to the secured space.
Automatic Private IP Addressing (APIPA)	An IPv4 address in the range of the range of 169.254.0.0 to 169.254.254.255 that is automatically assigned to a host that cannot connect to a DHCP server.
Backdoor	A malware type that allows an attacker to remotely access a computer.
Backplane	A printed circuit board with slots for expansion cards that allows for communication between the connected cards.
Backward compatibility	Software and hardware technologies that provides newer versions of a product to be interoperable with previous or legacy versions of that product.
Bare metal	A computer with no operating system, a type of virtualized server installation, or server hardware before an OS is installed.
Baseline	The performance measurements of a newly installed or modified system against which future measurements are compared.
Basic Input/Output System (BIOS)	A firmware-level utility that provides configuration data when a computer boots up.
Bit-serial interface	An interface type that requires a **host-bus adapter** (**HBA**) to connect a server to a network storage device.

Term/concept	Description
Blade chassis	An enclosure into which blade computers are inserted.
Blade computer	A scaled-down computer on a single circuit board.
Blue Screen of Death (BSOD)	A display message to inform a user that a critical error has occurred with a hardware device, a device driver, or with the Windows OS.
Bollard	A post embedded or installed on a pathway to mark a boundary, perimeter, or prevent entry.
Boolean algebra	A type of algebra in which values are true and false and are denoted as 1 and 0.
Buffer overflow	A system error that occurs when a process writes data into a buffer that is too large for the space available.
Business continuity plan (BCP)	A documented plan for how an organization will continue its operations in the event of a major disaster or security incident.
Business impact analysis (BIA)	A document that identifies the effects of accidents, emergencies, and disasters on a business.
CAT5e	Ethernet cables that support up to 1000Mbps.
CAT6/CAT6a	Cat 6 supports 10 Gigabit Ethernet up to 164 feet. Cat 6a enables 10 Gigabit Ethernet up to 328 feet.
CAT7	CAT7 is not an IEEE standard and is not approved by TIA/EIA.
CAT8	Supports **Power over Ethernet** (**PoE**) for power and data over a single cable with a maximum range of 98 ft. (30 m).
Centralized version control system (CVCS)	A type of version control system in which a server acts as a centralized repository where all versions of source code is stored.
Change management	Defines a process for the management and implementation of changes to systems to minimize disruptions of service.
Checksum	A value generated by an algorithm that represents the contents of an original string.
Chef	Chef, also known as, Progress Chef. A system configuration management tool for managing an infrastructure.
Children's Online Privacy Protection Act (COPPA)	Governs the online collection of personal information from children under 13.

Term/concept	Description
chown	A Linux command that is used to change the ownership of a directory or file.
CIA Triad	The security principles of confidentiality, integrity, and availability.
Cipher	A process or algorithm that changes plaintext into unreadable coding to hide the original message.
Cladding	Layers of material with low refraction in contact with core materials of higher refraction in a fiber optic cable.
Classless Inter-Domain Routing (CIDR)	CIDR is also known as supernetting. It addresses notation that indicates the number of high-order bits defining the network address in an IPv4 address.
Clock skew	Occurs on synchronous circuits when a clock signal is received at differing times due to latency caused by propagation on a wire.
Cloning	Copying the contents of one storage device to another to create an exact duplicate.
Cloud firewall	Cloud firewall, also known as, **Firewall-as-a-Service (FaaS)** is a cloud-based firewall service.
Cloud service provider (CSP)	An IT company that provides on-demand, scalable computing resources over the Internet.
Coaxial cable	A solid-core conductor encased in a conductive shield. Commonly used to transmit high-frequency signals in telephone, internet, cable television, and receiver to antenna connections.
Cold site	A type of recovery facility with minimum basic utilities and services, but typically without computing equipment.
Cold swap	A replacement method that requires a system to be powered off before upgrades, replacements, or repairs can be applied.
Command-line interface (CLI)	A means of interacting with a computer with commands in the form of text.
Common Gateway Interface (CGI)	A standard that defines how information is transferred between web servers, databases, and scripts.
Common Internet file system (CIFS)	A client-server programming model in which a client requests access to a file from a remote server. CIFS is now considered to be obsolete.
Community cloud	A cloud environment in which several organization or individuals share the benefits of a public cloud with the control and security of a private cloud.

Term/concept	Description
Complementary metal-oxide semiconductor (CMOS)	A semiconductor technology in most of **integrated circuits (ICs)** based on MOSFET technology.
Complex instruction set computer (CISC)	Computer architecture structured so that a single instruction can execute several low-level operations.
Configuration management	The procedures for establishing and maintaining preferred and constant operational and functional settings for software and hardware devices.
Console server	A service that provides a link over which a remote administrator can access server room devices over a network.
Containerization	The packaging of software code with necessary components so they can be isolated. An alternative form of implementing a virtual machine.
Conversational user interface	An interface type that allows a user to speak vocal commands that the system identifies through voice recognition capabilities.
CPU affinity	A configuration setting allowing a system to designate on which CPU or processor core(s) a process or application is executed.
CPU utilization	A series of metrics used to determine the current load on a CPU, including % of processor time, % of user time, % of interrupt time, and the processor queue length
Cybercriminal	A type of threat actor operating independently or in an organized group to steal sensitive data, PII, identities, and money.
Cyclic redundancy check (CRC)	An error-detecting code used to detect changes to digital data.
Cylinder-head-sector (CHS) addressing	The identification of a physical block of data on a disk by its read / write head, cylinder, and track numbers.
Data breach	An intentional attack by an unauthorized threat actor to view or harvest confidential, sensitive, or private information.
Data deduplication	A process to remove unwanted duplicated data.
Data exfiltration	The theft or unauthorized removal or movement of any data from a device.
Data infiltration	The introduction of unauthorized data from an external source into a system.
Data leak	The unintentional or accidental exposure of confidential, sensitive, or private information.

Term/concept	Description
Data life-cycle management (DLM)	The process of managing data from its creation to its disposal.
Data loss prevention (DLP)	A data security strategy focused on detecting and preventing data leaks, data breaches, and unauthorized use of stolen data.
Data migration	The process involving the conversion of data as it is moved from one location to another or from one system to another.
Data replication	Mirrors a storage device to another system or the distribution of a database to multiple storage units spread out geographically.
Data retention	The application of an organization's policies and governmental laws and regulations or the guidelines of trade and industry associations.
Data transfer	The process of collecting and duplicating datasets from one system to another.
Data transfer rate (DTR)	The time required to move data from the read/write head to memory or from memory to a read/write head.
Data-at-rest	Data stored on a secondary storage device.
Database management system (DBMS)	A software system that manages data manipulation, user authentication, and inserting or extracting data in a database.
Data-in-transit	Data in transmission between one station and another.
Data-in-use	Data in RAM, moving between a storage device and memory, or on the system bus structures.
Decision support system (DSS)	An application that collects, organizes, and analyzes data to enhance decision-making.
Decommissioning	The process of removing a server from an IT network.
Deep packet inspection (DPI)	A form of packet filtering that locates, identifies, classifies, and reroutes or blocks packets based on the data or code in their payloads.
Default gateway	The primary link, typically to a router, of an internal network for connecting and communicating with external networks.
Degaussing	Removes data from magnetic storage media by passing a high-powered magnet over the media, which scrambles the magnetic field of the stored data and effectively destroys it.

Term/concept	Description
Device driver	Software or firmware that enables a hardware device to communicate with an operating system.
Differential backup	A type of data backup that copies the data added or changed since the last full backup without resetting the archive bit.
Direct memory access (DMA)	A system feature that allows input/output devices to access RAM directly without going through the CPU.
Disaster recovery plan (DRP)	A formal document that provides detailed procedures for the recovery of computing services following a natural disaster or catastrophic event.
Discretionary access control (DAC)	A type of access control that grants or restricts object access through the access policy of an object's owner or group.
Disk cache	A reserved space on a disk drive that receives and holds data until the read/write operations are available.
Disk Cleanup	A deprecated Windows maintenance utility used to free up disk space on a computer's hard drive.
Disk quotas	An operating system setting that is used to limit the amount of disk storage space a user has available.
Distributed version control system (DVCS)	A type of version control system in which each developer has their own repository and working copy.
DNS zones	Designated areas of the DNS hierarchy assigned to a person, organization, or corporation for administration and maintenance.
DOCSIS 3.1	An international telecommunications standard that permits the addition of high-bandwidth data transfer to an existing cable system.
Domain Name System (DNS)	A TCP/IP service that provides a translation of Internet domain names into their corresponding **Internet Protocol (IP)** addresses.
Dot-decimal	A presentation format that inserts a dot (period) between the octets of an IPv4 address, such as in 10.0.0.1.
Dual inline memory module (DIMM)	A memory module containing several (RAM) chips on an expansion circuit board.
Dynamic disk	A Windows HDD configuration formatted in **Logical Disk Manager (LDM)** managed volumes.
Dynamic Host Configuration Protocol (DHCP)	A TCP/IP client/server protocol that provides a network host with its IP address and other related configuration settings.

Term/concept	Description
Electromagnetic interference (EMI)	The electrical noise disturbance generated by an external electrical source that affects an electrical circuit through electromagnetic induction, electrostatic coupling, or conduction.
Electrostatic discharge (ESD)	A momentary flow of an electric current between two electrically charged objects caused by contact, an electrical short or dielectric breakdown.
Embedded system	A computer system with a specified, limited, or dedicated purpose that is a part of a larger system.
Encryption key	A string of alphanumeric data applied by an encryption algorithm to encrypt plaintext into ciphertext or to decrypt ciphertext back to plaintext.
End of life (EOL)	A notification that an OEM will no longer be marketing, selling, or updating a device, product, or services as of a certain date.
End-user licensing agreement (EULA)	A legal contract between a software developer and an end-user purchasing a license for a software package that specifies how the software can be used, the number of times the software can be installed, the limitations for copying, modifying, or sharing the software, and any other restrictions the developer chooses to enforce.
eSATA USB Hybrid Port (EUHP)	EUHP is also called eSATAp. An interface that merges four USB pins with two 12-volt power pins to eliminate the need for an external power cable.
Exabyte	One million **gigabytes (GB)**
Extended file system – four (ext4)	A Linux-based journaling filesystem with a maximum file size of 16 TB that supports volume sizes up to 1 exabyte.
Extensible Messaging and Presence Protocol (XMPP)	An open communication protocol designed for instant messaging, presence information, and contact list maintenance.
Extent	On a Linux system: The smallest amount of storage space that can be allocated to a file.
External SATA (eSATA)	An interface technology that is used to connect external peripheral devices to a computer.
Failback	Technology used to return a system back to the primary system from a failover system.

Term/concept	Description
Failover	A mechanism used to provide continuous availability to a network in the event of a disruptive event or a planned maintenance activity that requires a replicated system be immediately available.
Fair and Accurate Credit Transaction Act (FACTA)	Establishes provisions that require financial institutions and creditors to implement identity theft prevention programs.
FAT 32-bit (FAT32)	A **file allocation table** (FAT) version for storage devices, including hard drives, SSDs, memory sticks, and microSD cards that uses 32 bits of data for identifying data clusters.
Fault tolerance	The capability for a system or component to continue its normal operations if a system or major component fails.
fdisk	A utility program that is used to create and format disk drive partitions.
Federal Information Security Management Act (FISMA)	Federal agencies must implement programs to secure their information and information systems.
Fiber Channel (FC)	A high-speed networking technology used for transmitting data among data centers, computer servers, switches, and storage devices at data transfer rates up to 128 Gbps.
Fibre Channel over Ethernet (FCoE)	A storage protocol that enables FC communications to run directly over Ethernet.
Fibre Channel Protocol (FCP)	A SCSI interface protocol that uses an underlying FC connection to provide high-speed data transfers between workstations, storage devices, and displays.
File Allocation Table (FAT)	A legacy file system developed for personal computers
File integrity monitor (FIM)	A crucial security measure for any organization that wants to ensure the integrity of files and detect any unauthorized modifications that could indicate a security breach.
Firewall	A hardware or software device that examines incoming or outgoing message traffic to allow only authorized traffic, based on defined rules, pass in or out.
Firmware	Software embedded on a electronic device that provides basic machine instructions that allow the hardware to function and communicate with other software running on a device.
Flashing	The process used to install or update firmware stored in flash memory and commonly used to update BIOS/UEFI.

Term/concept	Description
Form factor	A standard that describes the size, configuration, or physical arrangement of a computing device, including the arrangement of a device, case, chassis, or motherboard.
Freeware	Copyrighted software made available to anyone who wants it free of charge.
Full backup	A backup that copies all data on a storage media with an archive bit set to turn on and off.
Full packaged product (FPP)	The retail bundle that includes the packaging, documentation, and activation keys for a purchases software license.
Full virtualization	A virtualization type in which a server runs a hypervisor, which services **virtual machine (VM)** requests for data and CPU services and communicates them with the host physical computer's components.
Fully qualified domain name (FQDN)	A domain name that specifies its exact location in the hierarchy of the DNS.
General Data Protection Regulation (GDPR)	Requires businesses to protect the personal data and privacy of EU citizens for transactions that occur within EU member states.
Gigabit Ethernet	The general name for services that transmit Ethernet frames at one gigabit per second, such as 1000BaseT.
Globally Unique Identifier (GUID)	A 128-bit structure unlikely to ever repeat or create a collision.
GPT header	A data element that contains a hexadecimal signature that identifies the disk as a GPT disk and the GPT partition table.
Gramm-Leach-Bliley Act (GLBA)	A US federal law that protects consumer's personal information held by financial institutions.
Grandfather-father-son backup strategy	A backup media rotation scheme in which there are three or more backup cycles.
Graphics processing unit (GPU)	A specialized electronic device that accelerates computer graphics and image processing.
Group Policy Object (GPO)	A Windows OS snap-in with a collection of group policy settings that set the rights and privileges of a defined user group.
Guest system	An operating system installed on a VM or partitioned disk.
GUID partition table (GPT)	A standard for the partition tables on a physical computer storage device that uses GUIDs.

Term/concept	Description
Hacktivist	A blend of *hacker* and *activist*. Motivation is strictly to further a cause.
Hardening	The process to increase the security of a server, host, or device by reducing its vulnerability.
Hardware compatibility list (HCL)	The recommended hardware and processing capabilities necessary for software to operate properly. Specifies the internal and peripheral hardware and system software compatible with the system to be installed.
Health Information Technology for Economic and Clinical Health Act (HITECH)	Additional new requirements concerning privacy and security for patient health information to HIPAA.
Health Insurance Portability and Accountability Act (HIPAA)	Requires the adoption of standards for electronic health care transactions and code sets.
High availability (HA)	A strategy for server availability and failed component replacement.
Host system	The physical computer and perhaps its OS in a virtualized environment.
Host-bus adapter (HBA)	An interface that connects a computer system bus to other network and storage devices.
Hosts	An Windows OS file that maps hostnames to IP addresses.
Hot site	An active backup of an operational system that can be switched to in an emergency with minimum delay.
Hot swap	Immediate switchover or physical replacement while a system is running and operational.
Hybrid cloud	Combines an organization's private cloud with other services available on the public cloud.
Hypertext Markup Language (HTML)	The standard markup language for creating Web pages
I/O operations per second (IOps)	Measures the efficiency of a storage device using the number of input and output operations occurring in one second.
I/O port address	It is also called a port address. A memory space on a peripheral device controller that is used to pass control signals and data.

Term/concept	Description
ifconfig	Interface configuration. The Linux equivalent to the Windows `ipconfig` command used to display a network device's IP configuration.
Image file	A complete copy of a computer's software and settings. The file extension is .IMG.
Incremental backup	A data backup method that copies only the data added or changed since the last full or incremental backup. It also resets the archive bit off.
Information technology asset management (ITAM)	Involves the tracking, maintenance, monitoring, and disposal of the IT assets used in the processing and reporting of data and information.
Inode	Inode is the short for Index Node. A Linux data structure storing file information. The inode value is used to retrieve the metadata from the inode table.
Institute for Electrical and Electronics Engineers (IEEE)	A global association of professionals concerned with the development, implementation and maintenance of technology-centered products and services.
Intangible assets	Assets that are not physical, such as software, licenses, and electronically stored data.
International Electrotechnical Commission (IEC)	An organization focusing on the preparation and publication of international standards for all electrical, electronic, and related technologies.
Internet Command Message Protocol (ICMP)	A network layer protocol used by network devices to diagnose network communication issues.
Internet Corporation for Assigned Names and Numbers (ICANN)	An American nonprofit organization responsible for coordinating namespaces and numerical spaces of the Internet.
Internet Engineering Task Force (IETF)	The Internet standards organization responsible for the technical standards that make up the Internet protocol suite (TCP/IP).
Internet Printing Protocol (IPP)	A specialized protocol for communication between client devices and printers over the Internet.
Internet Protocol (IP)	Defines the methods used to navigate the Internet through the computing and routing devices of the unstructured network.
Internet protocol, version 4 (IPv4)	The widely used protocol in data communication over networks. IPv4 is a connectionless protocol used in packet-switched layer networks, such as Ethernet.

Term/concept	Description
Internet protocol, version 6 (IPv6).	A suite of standard protocols for Internet addressing. IPv6 is the replacement for IPv4.
Internet SCSI (iSCSI)	Defines how SCSI packets are transmitted over a TCP/IP network.
Interrupt requests (IRQ)	An indicator between an application and the OS that a service is required from the OS.
Intrusion detection system (IDS)	Hardware appliances or software that analyzes network traffic to detect possible intrusions to a network.
Intrusion protection system (IPS)	Hardware appliances or software that analyzes network traffic to prevent possible intrusions to a network.
ip addr	This Linux command is used to adjust IP addresses, NICs, and routing rules.
ipconfig	The primary tool for viewing, setting, or managing the IP configuration of any Windows network-connected device.
Journaling	A type of file system that logs file and directory changes made but not committed.
Kernel panic (KP)	An alert issued by the Linux OS kernel when a fatal system error is detected.
Key card	Security instruments used to gain entrance into a secured space.
Keyboard-video-mouse (KVM) switches	A switchable device that allows one set of keyboard, video, and mouse to be connected to multiple computers.
LC connector	A fiber optic cable connector that is common where there is a high-density of cables and connectors in smaller spaces.
Link Aggregation Control Protocol (LACP)	Provides load balancing and failover protection for incoming and outgoing network traffic.
Link Aggregation Group (LAG)	Used in static teaming where NICs and network switches are configured groups.
Load balancing	The process for distributing incoming client requests to a cluster of servers.
Load-reduced DIMM (LRDIMM)	Buffering is used to reduce the electrical load and provide the highest memory capacity on a server.
Local account	Windows default local accounts are administrator, guest, HelpAssistant, local service, network service, and system.
Local group	A group of user accounts with rights, permissions, and access to the local computer.

Term/concept	Description
Local version control systems (LVCS)	A type of version control that tracks file versions and (differences between files in a special format on a disk drive.
Localhost address	Also called the loopback address (lo). This is internal communication port with the address of 127.0.0.n.
Logical block addressing (LBA)	The relative addressing scheme used by MBRs and GPTs for data storage devices.
Logical configuration	The net effect of formatting or partitioning a storage device.
Logical Disk Manager (LDM)	Used by dynamic disks to manage volumes.
Logical disk units (LUNs)	The organization scheme used by a SAN and network clients, seen as a logical disk volume.
Logical volume management (LVM)	A data storage management method for Linux systems.
Lossless compression	This compression type can reproduce an original object without the loss of its original quality.
Lossy compression	This compression type selects needless or redundant data and omits it from the compressed file.
M.2	A form factor that supports smaller SSDs using either SATA or NMVe interfaces.
Mandatory access control (MAC)	Using this access control method, the access rights for an object is centrally administered.
Mantrap	An area between two entry doors that separates a secure area (inner door) from an exterior (outside) door.
Master boot code (MBC)	The first set of instructions in the MBR for booting a system.
Master boot record (MBR)	Located in the first sector of a hard disk volume; includes the number and sizes of the partitions on the volume and which partition contains the boot data.
Master File Table (MFT)	Contains an entry for each file on a volume, including size, time and date stamps, permissions, and data content.
Master partition table (MPT)	A component of the MBR that contains a description of the partitions on the hard disk drive, like their types and sizes.
Mean time between failures (MTBF)	A metric representing the average time between recoverable failures in a system, network, or component.

Term/concept	Description
Mean time to recover (MTTR)	This metric may represent one of four measurements: mean time to repair, recover, respond, or resolve. It is the average time required to put a failed component back in service.
Media access control (MAC)	A unique identifying number code in any networkable device that has two parts: an OUI and a serial number.
Memory address range	An allocated area in main memory used by a running process to pass or receive data from other processes.
Memory leak	A condition that exists when a process fails to release its allocated memory.
Memory virtualization	Occurs when an OS combines the memory of networked servers into a single memory pool.
Menu-driven interface	A list of options from which users can select the action they wish to take.
Message Digest 5 (MD5)	A one-way cryptographic algorithm that accepts a message of any length and produces a fixed-length value for use in authenticating a message.
Metal-oxide-semiconductor field-effect transistor (MOSFET)	A type of electronic transistor that controls electronic signals.
Microsoft Management Console (MMC)	A Windows utility used to create, save, and open administrative tools to manage the hardware, software, and network components.
Millions of transfers per second (MT/s)	The number of transfer cycles or operations a device can perform in one second.
Mirroring	The duplication of data to one or more storage devices.
Mitigation	The application of security policies and procedures to eliminate or reduce the risk or harm of a threat.
Most recently used (MRU)	In routing and switching, the last forwarding decision is best for a request.
Multifactor authentication (MFA)	The combination of two or more identification factors for user authentication.
Multimode	A type of optical fiber used for short distance communication.
Namespace	An abstract container or environment created to hold a logical grouping of unique identifiers or symbols.

Term/concept	Description
National Electrical Manufacturers Association (NEMA)	A trade association of electrical equipment manufacturers in the US.
nbtscan	A CLI command that looks for open NetBIOS nameservers on a local network or a remote TCP/IP network.
nbtstat	A CLI command used for diagnosing or troubleshooting NetBIOS name issues.
NetCat	It is also known as ncat or nc. It is a CLI utility that uses TCP and UDP connections to read and write on a network.
netstat	A CLI command that details how a host is communicating with other nodes, local or remote.
Network Address Translation (NAT)	A TCP/IP protocol that provides a means for private IPv4 addresses to be transmitted over the internet.
Network attached storage (NAS)	A centralized data storage system that provides network users and devices with data retrieval and storage services.
Network file system (NFS)	A file system method that allows a system to share directories and files with others over a network.
Network mask	A binary number series that is applied through a Boolean AND process to extract the network ID from an IP address.
Network time protocol (NTP)	A system protocol that provides clock synchronization in a computer system.
New Technology File System (NTFS).	A proprietary journaling file system developed by Microsoft.
Next-generation firewall (NGFW)	A security appliance that processes network traffic and applies rules to block potentially dangerous traffic using capabilities beyond a traditional firewall.
NIC bonding	On a Linux system, a procedure that groups physical NICs into one **virtual NIC (vNIC)**.
NIC teaming	A procedure that groups physical NICs into one vNIC.
nmblookup	A Windows CLI command that uses NetBIOS over TCP/IP queries to associate NetBIOS names and IP addresses.
Non-volatile memory express (NVMe)	A protocol for SSDs and flash drives with data transfer speeds of up to 2,600 MBps using the PCIe connection interface.

Term/concept	Description
nslookup	A CLI command that displays the information in the DNS PTR record for a domain.
Open-source	A type of freeware software that includes its source code, which a user is free to add to or modify without restriction.
Operating system (OS)	A collection of software that manages computer hardware resources and provides common services for computer programs.
Organizationally unique identifier (OUI)	A 24-bit hexadecimal number that uniquely identifies a vendor, manufacturer, or other organization.
Orphan process	A child process that continues to run after its parent process has ended without waiting for its child's execution to complete.
OS virtualization	The type of virtualization that creates independent virtual servers that share the OS kernel of the host system.
Out-of-band management (OOBM)	The system and server administration performed over a telecommunication link rather than a direct link or in-house.
Package management system	Software that can automate the installation, upgrade, configuration, and removal of computer programs and applications from a system.
Packet sniffer	A software utility that examines the payload of incoming network packets for specific content, such as passwords, usernames, account numbers, and other PII.
Parallel Advanced Technology Attachment (PATA)	Once known as IDE, a standard for connecting hard drives into computer systems using parallel signaling technology,
Parallel interface	A transmission method that transmits bits across multiple wires or channels simultaneously.
Paravirtualization	The OS running on a VM is recompiled specifically for its configuration.
Parity space	A RAID technique that stores a single copy of a file along with parity data that can be used to reconstruct the file should there be a hardware failure.
Partition table	A disk volume element that contains the location addressing the partitions on the disk.
Patch management	The process that controls the processes of identifying and deploying updates to OSs, system software, and applications.
Patch panel	A hardware device with multiple ports that helps organize network cables.

Term/concept	Description
Payment Card Industry Data Security Standard (PCI DSS)	A standard that defines the cybersecurity controls and business practices required of companies accepting credit card payments.
PCI Express (PCIe) interface	An interface standard that connects high-speed components to the motherboard.
Peripheral component interconnect (PCI)	A local computer bus for attaching hardware devices in a computer that is a part of the PCI Local Bus standard
Personally identifiable information (PII)	Any representation of information that permits the identity of an individual to whom the information applies to be reasonably inferred by either direct or indirect means.
Physical assets	An item of economic, commercial, or exchange value that has a material existence – a tangible asset.
Physical-to-virtual (P2V)	Also called hardware virtualization - the migration of physical machines to **virtual machines** (VMs)
ping	A CLI command used to verify a connection between a host and a destination address.
Pluggable Authentication Module (PAM)	Linux distros incorporate this feature for authenticating username and password credentials.
Port	The addressing method used by applications and services to communicate with one another over the internet.
Port Address Translation (PAT)	An extension to NAT that permits multiple private address devices on a LAN to be mapped to a single public IP address.
Port scanner	A software utility that scans a network server or host to identify open or closed TCP/UDP ports.
Power distribution unit (PDU)	A rack mounted device that provides multiple electrical outlets.
Power supply unit (PSU)	A computer component that converts AC power from an external outlet into the DC power required by internal components.
Power-on self-test (POST)	The process that runs immediately after a computer is powered on to verify if the physical devices configured in the BIOS or UEFI are attached, powered, and read for use.
PowerShell	A CLI scripting language for automating tasks on Windows systems.
Pre-boot execution environment (PXE)	A client-server interface used to boot host systems from a server

Term/concept	Description
Predictive Failure Analysis (PFA)	A software utility used to predict the failure of CPUs, memory, I/O devices, and data storage devices.
Preventive maintenance	Regular and routine maintenance on components and devices of a computer system to reduce the chance of failure and unplanned downtime.
Primary partition	The first sector of a GPT containing protective MBR, GPT header, and the partition table.
Principle of least privilege	The rights and permissions of a user should be only those, that are required for the user to perform assigned duties
Print server	A process in an OS, a software application, a network appliance, a cloud service, or a networked computer that accepts print requests, manages the print queue, and directs print jobs to the appropriate printing devices.
Private addresses	IP addresses reserved specifically for use on LANs that cannot be routed but can be used on any LAN without restriction.
Private cloud	An organization's internal cloud that is a completely proprietary computing network architecture specific to that organization.
Privilege escalation	A form of cyberattack that seeks to gain access to a system with elevated privileges.
Privileged account	A user account category that includes administrator accounts with high-level rights and privileges.
Process id (PID)	A number assigned by an OS kernel to uniquely identify an active process.
Protocol	A standardized set of rules or procedures for transmitting data between electronic devices.
Provisioning	Assessing and assigning storage capacity to host computers, servers, and other devices.
Proximity card	A type of key card that transmits credentials to a card reader using a RFID signals.
Proxy firewall	Also known as application gateways, this type of firewall uses **deep packet inspection** (**DPI**) or packet sniffing to examine all the data in a packet.
Public cloud	The type of cloud service delivery mode to which subscribers have access to software-based services via the Internet.
Puppet	A server configuration management tool that can configure and monitor multiple servers simultaneously.

Term/concept	Description
Quad SFP+ (QSFP+)	A type of compact fiber transceiver that can reach speeds of 10 Gbps per line.
Rack mount chassis	A mounting device that is built into a rackmount cabinet with a standard width of 19" or 24" and from 1U to 4U in height.
Rack unit (U)	The height of rackmount device is measured in U, which is standardized at 1.75 inches per U.
Racking systems	Racks and cabinetry that are designed to hold standard rack-mountable devices.
RAID 0	A RAID level that does not provide redundancy or data recovery and uses striping on two or more disk drives.
RAID 1	A RAID level that copies a mirror image of a data block to another disk drive.
RAID 10 (1+0)	A RAID level that combines striping and mirroring.
RAID 5	A RAID level that uses striping with parity.
RAID 6	A RAID level that uses striping for data and mirroring for parity.
RAID controller	A hardware device that provides the interface between the disk array and the user.
Rail kit	A rack mounting kit with horizontally mounted rails on which the device sits, and fasteners to secure the device to the vertical rails.
RAW partition	A disk partition that is not formatted or affected through malware or a failure during a formatting process.
Real Time clock (RTC)	A battery-powered integrated circuit on a computer motherboard that continues to keep the time when the main power is off.
Recovery point objective (RPO)	A relative point in time objective for when operations can resume after an interruption of service.
Recovery time objective (RTO)	The length of time goal for a recovery process to complete and restore the operations of a failed system or component.
Red Flags rule	An FTC regulation that businesses accepting card payments must have a formal identity theft prevention program.
Reduced instruction set computer (RISC)	A computer architecture designed to simplify the individual instructions given to the computer to accomplish tasks.

Term/concept	Description
Redundancy	The intentional duplication of critical components or functions of a system with the goal of increasing the reliability of the system.
Redundant Array of Independent Disks (RAID)	A data storage virtualization technology that combines multiple physical disk drive components into one or more logical units for the purposes of data redundancy, performance improvement, or both.
Registered DIMM (RDIMM)	A type of DIMM that inserts a register between the CPU and the memory chips to buffer data transmission.
Remote Desktop Protocol (RDP)	A Windows tool that provides remote access to network-connected systems.
Remote Server Administration Tools (RSAT)	A suite of administration and management tools that provide for remote management of a Windows Server OS.
Replication	The process of taking snapshots, backups, and data mirroring, redundancy, resilience, and reliability.
Representational state transfer (REST)	An architectural style for providing standards between computer systems on the web, making it easier for systems to communicate with each other.
Request for comments (RFC)	A formal document from the IETF containing specifications and organizational notes about topics related to the Internet and computer networking.
Resilient File System (ReFS)	A fault-tolerant storage technology that maximizes data availability, scalability, and data integrity.
Resource allocation	Resources are allocated to VMs based on resource shares, resource allocation reservations, and resource allocation limits.
Resource share	An indication of the relative importance of a VM for resource allocations, typically specified as High, Normal, or Low.
Risk assessment	A process used to discover any gaps or flaws in an organization's security measures and controls which identifies that the assets should be protected and measures the effectiveness of any security controls that are in place.
Risk management	A program for identifying and classifying assets, defining security measures, implementing the security measures, and regular reviews of effectiveness.
Rogue process	A process running on a system that a user or administrator did not initiate.

Term/concept	Description
Role-based access control (RBAC)	A user's access rights are based on the task or job of the individual.
Rootkit	Malware that can hide its actions from the OS and gain advanced security privileges and permissions
Rotational latency	The time required for disk platter to rotate the targeted data sector under the read / write head.
route	A Windows CLI command used to view and modify the IP routing table. Its Linux equivalent is the **ip route** command
Routing table	Contain rules, each of which is used to determine where data frames should be sent in order to reach their destination addresses.
Rule-based access control (RBAC)	A form of access control that allows or denies access to resources based on rules pre-defined by an administrator or resource owner.
RunAs command	Commonly used by administrators to execute commands requiring administrator privileges when logged in with a standard user account or to run a program as a different user.
Safe Mode	This OS operating mode loads only the essential elements of an OS and the device drivers for the display and data entry devices.
Sarbanes-Oxley Act (SOX)	A US federal act to improve auditing and public disclosure of publicly traded corporations.
SC connector	A standard-duplex fiber-optic connector that has a square body with push-pull locking.
Scratch space	A dedicated space on a disk drive or RAM set-aside for use as temporary storage.
Script kiddie	This threat actor is typically someone who is trying out someone else's attack software, primarily to see what it does.
Secure copy protocol (SCP)	A CLI command that is used to transfer data between computers securely using the SSH protocol.
Secure digital (SD)	A small memory card with large storage capacity, a high data transfer rate, and low-battery or power consumption.
Secure Hash Algorithm (SHA)	A hashing function that converts an input to hash value known as a message digest.
Secure Shell (SSH)	A software utility used to connect remote systems over an encrypted connection.

Term/concept	Description
Security event management (SEM)	Real-time monitoring, correlation of events, notifications, and console view.
Security information and event management (SIEM)	This is a combination of SEM and SIM that identifies potential vulnerabilities and threats before an attack can occur.
Security information management (SIM)	Software that automates the collection of event log data from security devices.
Security risk	The chance or probability that a vulnerability could be exploited to cause damage, destruction, or loss.
Security zones	Windows defines four security zones: Internet, Local Intranet, Trusted Sites, and Restricted Sites, which can be set independently.
Security-enhanced Linux (SELinux)	A distribution of Linux that provides additional security control over who is authorized to access a system.
Seek time	The time for the actuator arm to move the read/write head over the disk track that contains the targeted data sector.
Separation of duties	A security control recommending that certain duties be separated into discrete tasks, each performed by a different individual.
Serial ATA (SATA)	An interface type that communicates over a serial connection and is limited to one disk drive on a connection.
Serial interface	Data is transmitted as a single stream of bits from one digital system to another.
Serial-attached SCSI (SAS)	A point-to-point serial interface protocol that moves data to and from computer-storage devices.
Server cluster	Two or more interconnected servers operating as a single unit.
Server Message Block (SMB)	A client/server protocol that controls access to files and whole directories along with the information exchange between processes on a system.
Server monitor	Software that provides administrators with automated and on-demand reporting for devices nearing user-defined thresholds.
Server-side	Programming and services running on a server, instead of on the client.
Service level agreement (SLA)	A contract between a service provider and a customer that defines the types and standards of services offered.

Term/concept	Description
SFP+	An updated version of SFP that supports high speeds up to 10 Gbps.
Shared-disk file system	On a SAN, this file system provides direct access to the data blocks for multiple network clients.
Shareware	Copyrighted software shared by the copyright holder for demonstration or trial use at no cost or for a price.
Shielded twisted pair (STP)	A type of copper network wiring that adds an outer covering or shield. It also functions as a ground for ordinary TP wiring.
Shutdown script	A script file that can contain any number of actions that take place before a system shuts down.
Signal blocking	Materials or devices that keep RF signals within a defined space and keeps out externally-sourced signals.
Simple volume	Another term for a standard basic disk volume.
Single point of failure (SPOF)	A component, program, or device on a computer system that, if it fails, stops the entire system from working.
Single sign-on (SSO)	An authentication method that facilitates a user to sign into two or more applications or a website using one set of credentials.
Single-mode	This fiber optic cable type has one filament over which a single signal is transmitted with a maximum range of 30 miles.
Single-user mode	The Linux equivalent to the Windows Safe Mode in which an administrator can make corrections, do repairs or maintenance, and reset passwords.
Slipstreaming	A process that combines downloaded update files with the installation files onto a new installation medium.
Small Computer Serial Interface (SCSI)	A type of storage and device connection in a PC that refers to the cables and ports used to connect certain types of devices to a computer.
Snapshot	A backup type that captures the state of a system at a specific point of time.
Social engineering	A type of attack in which the objective is to obtain login credentials or other information from a targeted user.
Socket	An addressing method that combines a port number and an IP address.

Term/concept	Description
Soft failure	An error condition that indicates something is wrong somewhere in a system, but the system overall is still reliable.
Software as a service (SaaS)	A cloud-based software delivery model through which a CSP develops and maintains application software and makes it available to its customers via the internet.
Software clock	A clock function that is managed by an OS to synchronize the software and hardware components within a computer system.
Solid-state device (SSD)	A data storage device with no moving parts that is a random-access device on which data is accessed directly.
Spanned volume	A type of disk storage volume made up of merged unallocated spaces from multiple dynamic disks.
Split key	A two-person authentication approach in which an administrator and a user each have a part of the key.
Stateful firewall	A type of firewall system that monitors the status of active network connections and inspects message traffic for potential risks.
State-sponsored	A type of threat actor employed or sponsored by a foreign government with the purpose of obtaining sensitive information.
Static teaming	A technique in which NICs and network switches are manually configured into a LAG.
Storage area network (SAN)	A network data storage service that clients see as a single entity. It provides centralized data access and security for structured data in block form.
Storage Spaces	A Windows feature that allows for two or more physical disk drives to be combined into a storage pool.
Storage virtualization	A process that combines multiple storage devices into a single virtual device with a mapping between the logical and physical storage.
Striping	A RAID process that divides data into blocks that are stored across two or more disk drives.
Structured data	Data stored with uniform or standard formatting, such as, in a relational database.
Subnet mask	The binary mask applied through a Boolean ANDing operation to extract the network address.
sudo	A Linux command that provides user control elevation for one command.

Term/concept	Description
Swap file	A virtual memory system file used as temporary storage on a disk drive for memory pages swapped out of RAM when additional memory space is required.
Symmetric encryption	The encryption type that uses the same password or encryption key to both encrypt and decrypt data.
Symmetric multiprocessing (SMP)	On a SMP multicore processor, each core functions as a separate processor that process instructions independently, while sharing common system services.
Synchronous digital hierarchy (SDH)	A fiber optic transmission method that enables low-bit rate data streams to combine with high-rate data streams.
Synchronous optical network (SONET)	A communication protocol used to transmit large amounts of data over long distances using optical fiber.
Synthetic full backup	This backup type builds on the last full backup by applying all the incremental backups since that full backup to create a new full backup.
System Center Configuration Manager (SCCM)	A Windows tool that an administrator can use to manage, deploy, and secure system resources on an enterprise network.
System File Checker (SFC)	A Windows utility that scans the hard disk for corrupted system files and folders.
systeminfo	A CLI command used to benchmark the components of a system.
Tailgating attack	The action of an unauthorized person entering a secured entrance immediately following an authorized person.
telnet	Used to connect a local computer to another local computer over a virtual terminal service.
Thick provisioning	A virtualization technique that allocates the total amount of resource a VM requests.
Thin provisioning	A virtualization technique that allocates less resource than the total amount allocated to a VM.
Threat actors	The individuals or groups who are unauthorized to access and exploit computer or network vulnerabilities.
Tower chassis	The form factor of standalone computer contained in a rectangular or square system case.
Transceiver	An electronic device that combines a radio transmitter and receiver.

Term/concept	Description
Transmission Control Protocol (TCP)	A standard protocol that defines how to establish and maintain a network connection to exchange data.
Trojan	A type of malware that gives the appearance or is presented as something benign or desirable yet contains another malware component.
Troubleshooting	A systematic approach to problem solving often used to find and correct issues with computers and software systems.
Trunking	A technology that provides network access to multiple clients simultaneously by sharing a set of circuits, carriers, channels, or frequencies.
Twisted pair (TP)	Cabling that is made up of multiple pairs of copper wires with each pair twisted around each other. TP cables can be either **unshielded** (UTP) or **shielded** (STP).
Two-factor authentication (2FA)	An identity and access management security method that requires two forms of identification to access resources and data.
Unbuffered DIMM (UDIMM)	A type of DIMM that does not buffer data transmissions, which increases its performance by eliminating latency.
Unified Extensible Firmware Interface (UEFI)	A firmware process that defines the architecture used for booting a computer and interfacing with an operating system.
Uniform resource locator (URL)	A text reference to a web resource specifying its location on a network and the protocol or mechanism for retrieving it.
Uninterruptible power supplies (UPS)	An electrical device that provides emergency power to a computer or device when the main power source fails.
Universal serial bus (USB)	A standard plug-and-play connection type used for several types of devices.
Universally Unique Identifier (UUID)	A 128-bit value applied to uniquely identify an object or entity on the Internet.
Unshielded twisted pair (UTP)	Twisted-pair cabling with no internal shielding.
Unstructured data	A format for data storage that is non-relational and stored as flat files.
User Account Control (UAC)	A Windows feature that protects the OS from unauthorized changes.
User Datagram Protocol (UDP)	A core TCP/IP communication protocol used to send datagrams to other hosts without the reliability features of TCP.

Term/concept	Description
User identity number (UID)	Linux systems identify users with a value, which when combined with the GID determines the system resources a user can access.
User interface (UI)	This technology allows humans to interact with computers by enabling a human to issue commands and make selections and the computer to provide feedback and information to the user.
Very long instruction word (VLIW)	A CPU instruction set that specifies multiple numbers of operations that are grouped together.
Virtual CPU (vCPU)	A time allotment on a physical core of a processor.
Virtual local area network (VLAN)	A logical network configuration that organizes two or more network workstations and devices into logical network.
Virtual machine (VM)	A software created computing resource with its own operating system and functions that run separately from other VMs.
Virtual machine disk (VMDK)	A file format that describes containers for virtual hard disk drives used by virtual machines.
Virtual Machine File System (VMFS)	A cluster file system that runs on VMs for storing files on VMDKs.
Virtual memory	A small space on a hard disk set aside as a temporary storage space to hold idle pages of RAM when more space is needed.
Virtual Network Computing (VNC)	Utility software that provides a GUI desktop using the **Remote Frame Buffer** (**RFB**) protocol for the control and management of a remote system over a network.
Virtual NIC (vNIC)	Software that emulates the functions of a NIC for a VM.
Virtual private network (VPN)	An encrypted communication connection over the internet from a device to a network.
Virtualization	The process of emulating virtual devices to leverage hardware and software resources.
VLAN hopping	An attack method that sends packets to a port from within one VLAN to gain access to another VLAN on the same network
VLAN Member Policy Server (VMPS)	A network file that contains the list of nodes belonging to each VLAN.

Term/concept	Description
Volume Shadow Copy Service (VSS)	This is a set of COM APIs that allows volume backups to be performed while applications on a system continue to write to the volumes.
vSwitch	A software program that allows a VM to communicate with another VM or to a physical network.
Vulnerability	A weakness, flaw, error, or omission in the physical or logical security measures of an organization and its computing resources that can be exploited by an attacker.
Warm site	This type of facility has the needed computing, network, and communication equipment pre-installed.
Warm swap	This type of device requires a system or the failed component to be idle while the replacement is made.
Web server	A type of server that stores website content and fulfills authorized requests from client web browsers for the stored website files.
Windows Defender Firewall with Advanced Security	This is a management snap-in for the Windows Firewall in which detailed controls, including rules and exceptions are defined.
Windows Disk Management	This is a Windows utility that supports the creation, modification, removal, extension, and redesignation of disk volumes and partitions.
Windows Event Viewer	This Windows app is used to view, manage, archive, and customize the content and display of each log file.
Windows Memory Diagnostic	This Windows utility runs memory tests that can be used to determine if there is a memory issue on a computer.
Windows Registry	A hierarchical database of the low-level settings for the Windows OS and applications.
Windows Server Update Service (WSUS)	A Microsoft network service that enables administrators to manage the distribution of updates to computers in a corporate environment.
Windows Side by Side (WinSxS)	A folder on a Windows system that contains a variety of vital software components for installing, updating, backing up, and customizing the OS.
Windows Task Scheduler	A windows app that monitors the user-defined time or event criteria and executes a task when the criteria are met.
Word-serial interface	This type of interface transfers data in 8-bit, 16-bit, or 32-bit words. SCSI and PATA are word-serial interfaces.

Term/concept	Description
X64	This computer architecture supports 64-bit CPUs, which support more RAM and virtual memory.
X86	This computer architectures support 32-bit systems, except for the 8086, a 16-bit architecture.
YAML	This is a human-readable data-serialization language that is used for configuration files and applications in which data is stored or transmitted.
Yobibyte (YiB)	2^{80} bytes or 1,208,925,819,614,629,174,706,176 bytes
Z file system (ZFS)	An open-source 128-bit Linux file system capable of managing several ZB of data.
Zero-configuration networking (zeroconf)	This protocol provides automatic addressing and locating services for printer devices on a wireless network.
Zettabyte	1,000 exabytes or 1 billion terabytes.
Zombie process	This is a process that was started by a parent process that has stopped running but remains in the process table with a PID and cannot terminate itself.

Appendix E

Answers to Practice Test 1

This appendix contains the answers to CompTIA Server+ (SK0-005) Certification Exam Practice Test 1 (Appendix A):

Question	Answer(s)	Chapter(s)	Section title: To learn more
1	b	11	Subscriptions
2	d	5	IP configuration
3	b	8	Virtualized
4	a	1	Rack dimensions
5	a, c, & d	20 25	Power supply unit Confirm power supply
6	a & b	2	Hard disk drives Solid-state devices
7	b & c	2	Solid-state devices
8	d	2	Just a bunch of disks
9	a	20	Predictive failures
10	b & c	2	Storage area network

Question	Answer(s)	Chapter(s)	Section title: To learn more
11	c	8	Cloud models
12	a & d	22	User account controls
13	a & d	4	Striping and mirroring
14	a	4	RAID levels
15	c	7	High availability
16	a – 2; b – 1, c - 3	7	Swaps
17	b	6	Server roles and requirements
18	a	11	Version compatibility
19	c	24	System resources
20	a	9	Windows environment variables Linux environment variables
21	a	1	Software interfaces
22	b & d	1	BIOS/UEFI maintenance
23	b	9	Linux environment variables
24	a & c	14	User account logins
25	a	9	Scripting types
26	b	5	Internet Protocol addressing
27	b	5	IPv4 address
28	d	8	Network aAddress tTranslation
29	b	24	Unable to reach remote subnets
30	b	5	IPv6
31	d	25	Troubleshooting commands
32	a	5	Firewall ports
33	c & d	1	Copper cabling
34	c	25	Cable selection
35	c	21 1	Cable and connector problems Hot-swappable devices
36	c	25	Cable selection
37	c	25	Verify cable integrity
38	a	1	Fiber optic cabling

Question	Answer(s)	Chapter(s)	Section title: To learn more
39	b	11	Licensing agreements
40	c	3	Keyboard-Video-Mouse
41	b	3	Out-of-band management
42	e	3	Out-of-band management
43	b	11	Subscriptions
44	d	1	Documentation content
45	b	10	Documentation management
46	c	9	Basic scripting constructs
47	b	1	Internal documentation
48	a	1	Patch management
49	a	21	Common disk drive problems
50	a	22	Hardware-related software problems
51	c	20	POST errors
52	d	21	Visual and auditory inspections
53	a	12	Data encryption
54	b	7	Server clusters
55	c	7	Swaps
56	b	8	Virtualization types
57	b	15	Data theft
58	d	7	Swaps
59	c	15	Data theft
60	b	18	Replication
61	a	18	Replication
62	d	18	Replication
63	d	17	Backup types
64	c	3	Backup media
65	b	1	Policies and procedures
66	c	24	APIPA
67	d	14	Password policies
68	c	14	Password policies
69	b	5	Firewall ports
70	a	13	Environmental controls
71	c	13	Environmental controls

Question	Answer(s)	Chapter(s)	Section title: To learn more
72	b	13	Environmental monitoring
73	a & c	17	Backup strategies
74	a	1	Power distribution unit
75	b	8	Virtualization types
76	d	13	Access controls
77	c	26	User access controls
78	d	12	Encryption
79	e	1	Media destruction
80	c	16	Hardening
81	c	16	Hardening
82	a	16	Hardening
83	d	12	BIOS/UEFI passwords
84	b	4	Master boot record
85	c	19	Troubleshooting steps
86	a	19	Troubleshooting steps
87	c	19	Troubleshooting steps
88	b	19	Troubleshooting steps
89	c	3	Group policy object
90	b	26	Zombie/orphan

APPENDIX F
Answers to Practice Test 2

This appendix has the answers to CompTIA Server+ (SK0-005) Certification Exam practice test 2:

Question	Answer(s)	Chapter(s)	Section title - To learn more
1	b	21	Common disk drive problems
2	a	11	Software license and maintenance agreements
3	d	19	Software problems
4	c	22	User account controls
5	a	20	Blue Screen of Death
6	d	22	Common OS problems
7	c	22	Windows file recovery
8	a and b	6	Disk quotas
9	b	21	Virtual memory problems
10	c	22	Log files
11	b	17	Side by side
12	b	24	DHCP server
13	d	15	Threat actors
14	c	5	Virtual local area networks

Question	Answer(s)	Chapter(s)	Section title - To learn more
15	d	24	VLAN configuration errors
16	b and c	25	Ping and Tracert and traceroute
17	a	5	The Linux ifconfig command
18	b	2	Solid-State devices
19	b	15	The Red Flags rule
20	b	18	Recovery sites
21	b	4	Master Boot Record
22	d	20	Windows event logs
23	c	3	Hardening
24	b	8	Direct access
25	a	1	Rack dimensions
26	a, c and d	25	Confirm power supply
27	a and b	2	Hard disk drive specifications
28	b and c	2	Solid-State devices
29	d	2	Just a bunch of disks
30	c	2	Storage area network
31	d	2	Shared storage
32	a and d	2	Striping and mirroring
33	a	2	RAID levels and types
34	c	1	Hot-swappable hardware
35	c	14	Single sign-on
36	c	22	Common OS problems
37	a	12	Bootloader password
38	b and d	1	BIOS/UEFI maintenance
39	b	24	Cannot reach server
40	c	4	Scripted installations
41	b	5	Internet Protocol addressing
42	b	5	Classful IP addressing
43	d	8	Network address translation
44	b	24	Unable to reach remote subnets
45	b	5	IPv6
46	c	1	Small form-factor pluggable
47	c	12	Data security

Question	Answer(s)	Chapter(s)	Section title - To learn more
48	c	1	Keyboard-video-mouse
49	b	3	Out-of-band management
50	e	4	Remote server administration
51	b	1	Asset management
52	d	1	Documentation management
53	b	1	Documentation updates
54	c	1	Documentation management
55	b	3	Change management
56	a	3	Change management
57	a	1	Asset management
58	b	2	Hard disk specifications
59	d	12	Data security
60	d	19	Implementing preventive measures
61	a	7	Server clusters
62	d and e	26	Anti-malware and antivirus
63	b	4	Hardware compatibility list
64	b	22	Common OS problems
65	b	1	Documentation content
66	b	13	Authentication factors
67	d	1	Uninterrupted power supply
68	b	14	Permissions
69	a	4	Hardware compatibility list
70	b	3	Adding or removing ports
71	c	11	Subscriptions
72	a and b	3	Adding or removing ports
73	a	18	Replication
74	b	5	Firewall methods and Firewall ports
75	c	17	Backup types
76	b	26	Anti-malware configurations
77	a	2	RAID levels
78	c and d	17	Backup types
79	c	9	Scripting terminology
80	b	20	Memory troubleshooting

Question	Answer(s)	Chapter(s)	Section title - To learn more
81	a – 2; b – 1, c - 3	7	Swaps
82	d	21	Common disk drive problems
83	d	12	Data life-cycle management
84	c	15	Security risks
85	b	18	Failover
86	a	13	Signal blocking
87	e	13	Environmental controls
88	b	14	Local user account types
89	b	25	Verify cable integrity
90	a	8	Overprovisioning

Index

D

N

O

P

Q

R

S